Get Instant Access
to thousands of editors and agents @

D1303027

—TEAR ALONG PERFORATION

2008 POET'S MARKET
KEY TO SYMBOLS

this market is recently established and appearing for the first time in *Poet's Market*

this market did not appear in the previous edition of *Poet's Market*

this market is located in Canada

this market is located outside the U.S. and Canada

this market publishes primarily online

$ this market pays a monetary amount

this market welcomes submissions from beginning poets

this market prefers submissions from skilled, experienced poets; will consider work from beginning poets

this market prefers submissions from poets with a high degree of skill and experience

this market has a specialized focus

this market does not consider unsolicited submissions

this market is currently closed to *all* submissions

● indicates market information of special note

(For words and expressions relating specifically to writing and publishing, see the Glossary in the back of this book.)

TEAR ALONG PERFORATION

WritersMarket.com
WHERE & HOW TO SELL WHAT YOU WRITE

Here's what you'll find at WritersMarket.com:

More than 6,000 listings — At WritersMarket.com, you'll find thousands of listings that couldn't fit in the book! It's the most comprehensive database of verified markets available.

Easy-to-use searchable database — Looking for a specific magazine or book publisher? Just type in the title or keyword for broad category results.

Listings updated daily — It doesn't look good to address your query letter to the wrong editor or agent...and with WritersMarket.com, that will never happen. You'll be on top of all the industry developments...as soon as they happen!

Personalized for you — Customized **Favorites Folders** keep your best-bet markets, manuscript submissions and more just a click away; and your personalized **Dashboard** provides updated market listings, query reminders and recommended resources at-a-glance, every time you log in.

And so much more!

Exclusive 30-day free trial.
Visit WritersMarket.com to sign up today!

updated DAILY

Tear out your handy bookmark
for fast reference to symbols and abbreviations used in this book

PM08

2008
Poet's Market®

Nancy Breen, Editor

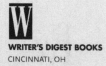
WRITER'S DIGEST BOOKS
CINCINNATI, OH

Editorial Director, Writer's Digest Books: Jane Friedman
Managing Editor, Writer's Digest Market Books: Alice Pope

Poet's Market Web page: wwww.poetsmarket.com
Writer's Market Web site: www.writersmarket.com
Writer's Digest Web site: www.writersdigest.com
F + W Publications Bookstore: http://fwbookstore.com

Distributed in Canada by Fraser Direct
100 Armstrong Ave.
Georgetown, ON, Canada L7G 5S4
Tel: (905) 877-4411

Distributed in the U.K. and Europe by David & Charles
Brunel House, Newton Abbot, Devon, TQ12 4PU, England
Tel: (+44) 1626 323200, Fax: (+44) 1626 323319
E-mail: postmaster@davidandcharles.co.uk

Distributed in Australia by Capricorn Link
P.O. Box 704, Windsor, NSW 2756, Australia
Tel: (02) 4577-3555

Distributed in New Zealand by David Bateman Ltd.
P.O. Box 100-242, N.S.M.C., Auckland 1330, New Zealand
Tel: (09) 415-7664, Fax: (09) 415-8892

Distributed in South Africa by Real Books
P.O. Box 1040, Auckland Park 2006, Johannesburg, South Africa
Tel: (011) 837-0643, Fax: (011) 837-0645
E-mail: realbook@global.co.za

ISSN: 0883-5470
ISBN-13: 978-1-58297-499-6
ISBN-10: 1-58297-499-3

Cover design and illustration by Josh Roflow
Interior design by Clare Finney
Production coordinated by Kristen Heller and Greg Nock
Photographs on selected pages © Frédéric Cirou/PhotoAlto

Attention Booksellers: This is an annual directory of F + W Publications. Return deadline for this edition is December 31, 2008.

Contents

From the Editor

In these Internet-dominated times, the word "portal" usually refers to a site that serves as a point of admission to other sites—a destination that leads to other destinations. According to my dusty old Webster's, "portal" in its traditional sense means "door, entrance, especially a grand or imposing one; the approach or entrance to a bridge or tunnel."

What does this have to do with *Poet's Market*? So often I read and hear comments that the book is "big and unwieldy," "overwhelming," packed with so much information "it's hard to know where to begin." I completely understand the reaction. However, *Poet's Market* is meant to be a user-friendly tool that readers of any skill level can utilize to help them publish their work.

I realized that *Poet's Market* is best regarded as a "portal." Sure, it might be a bit "grand and imposing" with all these market listings, all these dos and don'ts from editors, all these *opportunities* waiting to be explored. Yet, if all readers see before them is a brick wall or a confounding labyrinth, they may just turn and walk away. And that would be a shame.

So, please—come on in. It's not such a scary place. New to the world of poetry publishing? There are articles covering the basics: how to format a manuscript, how to prepare a submission, how to relate to editors (they're not so scary, either). Still feeling overwhelmed? Take the magazines, publishers and contests one by one. Meander through the pages; you can learn a lot simply by perusing the listings. If you feel lost, just shut the book. It will be easier next time, I promise.

The features and Insider Reports in this edition can help. Whether you don't know what a "blog" (Web log) is or are already a blogger yourself, you'll find Anne Bowling's roundtable discussion with **poets-who-blog** intriguing. F.J. Bergmann offers her perspectives on what should constitute **"industry standards" for poetry publishing and contests**. You'll meet poets **Anne Marie Macarie, Hank Hudepohl,** and **Christine Swanberg**; explore what **online poetry communities** have to offer; pick up some tips on **revising your "second-rate" poems**; find out **how poetry empowers a group of prison inmates**; and learn about **bilingual poetry and translations** from **Stanley Barkan**, founder and head of Cross-Cultural Communications (CCC).

Don't be cowed by this big, complicated-looking book. Step right in! It's your portal to discoveries, information—and, I hope, publishing success.

Nancy Breen

Nancy Breen
poetsmarket@fwpubs.com

What's New in 2008

The 2008 edition of *Poet's Market* has undergone some big changes from previous editions. If you're already familiar with the format and content of *Poet's Market*, keep reading to discover what's new and different. If you're a new reader, you may find the following points helpful as you learn to use this book.

SECTIONS HAVE CHANGED

In the past, all magazines, journals, publishers and presses were grouped alphabetically under the section title "Publishers of Poetry." With the 2008 edition, here is how listings are now organized:

- **Magazines/Journals**—All literary magazines, poetry journals, zines and online poetry publications are listed in this section.
- **Book/Chapbook Publishers**—This new section breaks out presses that publish books and chapbooks of poetry. **NOTE:** Because so many book and chapbook manuscripts are selected for publication through contests, be sure to check the Contests & Awards section for many additional opportunities to have your collection considered for publication.

There are significant changes in these sections as well:

- **Contests & Awards**—In most instances, separate listings have been created for contests previously contained in listings for magazines and book/chapbook publishers. However, since some magazines and publishers still include contest information in their regular listings, be sure to check the Additional Contests & Awards index at the back of this section for cross-references to opportunities you might otherwise overlook.
- **Conferences, Workshops & Festivals**—The title of this section has been updated to reflect the increasing number of poetry and literary festivals being held across the U.S. and worldwide. In addition, this section now has its own Additional Conferences, Workshops & Festivals list, a cross-reference to listings in the other sections that include information about a workshop, conference or similar activity, large or small.

The **Organizations** and **Additional Resources** sections are unchanged; however, don't forget they also have their own "additional" cross-reference lists at the end of each section.

CLEANER TITLE LINES

In previous editions of *Poet's Market*, the title line of each listing often included several items. For example, in the 2007 edition, ***The Comstock Review*, Comstock Writer's Group, Inc., Muriel Craft Bailey Memorial Award**, and the **Jesse Bryce Niles Memorial Chapbook**

Award were all crowded into the title line of *The Comstock Review* listing. Now, only *The Comstock Review* appears in the title line in the Magazines/Journal listing; the Muriel Craft Bailey Memorial Award and the Jesse Bryce Niles Memorial Chapbook Award each have separate listings in the Contests & Awards section; and Comstock Writer's Group, Inc. appears in the General Index, cross-referenced back to *The Comstock Review*. Although it sounds a little confusing in explanation, this improvement provides less visual clutter, and a clearer indication of what each listing contains.

NEW ICONS

Two new listing icons have been added for 2008:

- The "computer terminal" icon (■) means "this market publishes primarily online"; in other words, most of the publishing activity takes place on a Web site, although the magazine or press may also produce print anthologies or "best of" volumes. This "on-line market" icon will let you know at a glance if a market is Web-oriented. (This icon is *not* used to indicate if a market has a Web site—most do.)
- The "stop sign" icon (⊘) means "this market does not consider unsolicited submissions." Consequently, the "slashed circle" icon (⊘) means *only* "this market is currently closed to all submission." This change is intended to avoid the confusion that resulted when the "slashed circle" represented both "no simultaneous submissions" and "closed to all submissions."

For a key to all listing icons used in this book, see the inside covers, page 6, or the convenient tear-out bookmark just inside the front cover.

IMPROVED INDEXES

The specialty indexes at the back of the book have been tweaked to make them more efficient:

- **Chapbook Publishers Index** and **Book Publishers Index**—In the past, entries for these indexes were pulled only from the Publishers of Poetry section. With the new organization of the book, entries are now pulled from Magazines/Journals, Book/Chapbook Publishers and Contests & Awards to make these lists more complete.
- **Geographical Index**—In previous editions, the geographical index was limited to subheads for Publishers of Poetry and Conferences & Workshops. For 2008, a new subhead was created for Book/Chapbook Publishers, expanding the geographical breakdown of the book's listings according to U.S. states, Canadian territories and countries outside the U.S. and Canada.
- **Subject Index**—All subject categories were reviewed, with several new categories created to make this index more effective. In addition, more parenthetical descriptions appear after market titles in certain subject categories to further clarify that market's specialization.

For additional information on using *Poet's Market* to best advantage, see "Getting Started (and Using This Book)" on page 4 and Frequently Asked Questions on page 9.

Getting Started

(and Using This Book)

Delving into the pages of *Poet's Market* indicates a commitment—you've decided to take that big step and begin submitting your poems for publication. How do you *really* begin, though? Here are eight quick tips to help make sense of the marketing/submission process:

1. Be an avid reader. The best way to hone your writing skills (besides writing) is to immerse yourself in poetry of all kinds. It's essential to study the masters; however, from a marketing standpoint, it's equally vital to read what your contemporaries are writing and publishing. Read journals and magazines, chapbooks and collections, anthologies for a variety of voices; scope out the many poetry sites on the Internet. Develop an eye for quality, and then use that eye to assess your own work. Don't rush to publish until you know you're writing the best poetry you're capable of producing.

2. Know what you like to write—and what you write best. Ideally, you should be experimenting with all kinds of poetic forms, from free verse to villanelles. However, there's sure to be a certain style with which you feel most comfortable, that conveys your true "voice." Whether you favor more formal, traditional verse or avant-garde poetry that breaks all the rules, you should identify which markets publish work similar to yours. Those are the magazines and presses you should target to give your submissions the best chance of being read favorably—and accepted. (See the Subject Index beginning on page 517 to observe how some magazines and presses specify their needs.)

3. Learn the "business" of poetry publishing. Poetry may not be a high-paying writing market, but there's still a right way to go about the "business" of submitting and publishing poems. Learn all you can by reading writing-related books and magazines. Read the articles and interviews in this book for plenty of helpful advice. Surf the Internet for a wealth of sites filled with writing advice, market news and informative links. (See Additional Resources on page 463 for some leads.)

4. Research the markets. Study the listings in *Poet's Market* thoroughly; these present submission guidelines, editorial preferences and editors' comments as well as contact information (names, postal and e-mail addresses, Web site URLs). The Magazines/Journals section begins on page 41, the Book/Chapbook Publishers section on page 322, with the Contests & Awards section following on page 356. In addition, the indexes in the back of this book provide insights into what an editor or publisher may be looking for.

However, studying market listings alone won't cut it. The best way to gauge the kinds of poetry a market publishes is to read several issues of a magazine/journal or several of a press's books to get a feel for the style and content of each. If the market has a Web site, log on and take a look. Web sites may include poetry samples, reviews, archives of past issues,

Submission Tracker

Poem Title	Publication/ Contest	Editor/Contact	Date Sent	Date Returned	Date Accepted	Date Published	Pay Received	Comments

2008 POET'S MARKET KEY TO SYMBOLS

N this market is recently established and appearing for the first time in *Poet's Market*

✪ this market did not appear in the previous edition of *Poet's Market*

✪ this market is located in Canada

🌐 this market is located outside the U.S. and Canada

◼ this market publishes primarily online

$ this market pays a monetary amount

◯ this market welcomes submissions from beginning poets

◑ this market prefers submissions from skilled, experienced poets; will consider work from beginning poets

◐ this market prefers submissions from poets with a high degree of skill and experience

◎ this market has a specialized focus

⊘ this market does not consider unsolicited submissions

⊘ this market is currently closed to *all* submissions

● indicates market information of special note

ms, mss manuscript(s)

b&w black & white (art/photo)

SASE self-addressed, stamped envelope

IRC International Reply Coupon (replaces return postage when mailing to countries other than your own)

(For words and expressions relating specifically to poetry and submissions, see the Glossaries in the back of this book.)

Find a handy pull-out bookmark, a quick reference to the icons used in this book, right inside the front cover.

---

exclusive content, and especially submission guidelines. (If the market is an online publication, the current issue will be available in its entirety.) If the market has no online presence, send for guidelines and sample copies (include a SASE—self-addressed stamped envelope—for guidelines; include appropriate cost for sample copy).

Submission guidelines are pure gold for the specific information they provide. However you acquire them—by SASE or e-mail, online, or in a magazine itself—make them an integral part of your market research.

5. Start slowly. It may be tempting to send your work directly to *The New Yorker* or *Poetry*, but try to adopt a more modest approach if you're just starting out. Most listings in this book display symbols that reflect the level of writing a magazine or publisher prefers to receive. The (**◯**) symbol indicates a market that welcomes submissions from beginning or unpublished poets. As you gain confidence and experience (and increased skill in your writing), you can move on to markets coded with the (**◐**) symbol. Later, when you've built a publication history, submit to the more prestigious magazines and presses (the **◎** markets). Although it may tax your patience, slow and steady progress is a proven route to success.

6. Be professional. Professionalism is not something you should "work up to." Make it show in your first submission, from the way you prepare your manuscript to the attitude you project in your communications with editors.

Follow those guidelines. Submit a polished manuscript. (See "Frequently Asked Questions" on page 9 for details on manuscript formatting and preparation.) Choose poems carefully with the editor's needs in mind. *Always* include a SASE with any submission or inquiry. Such practices show respect for the editor, the publication and the process; and they reflect *your* self-respect and the fact that you take your work seriously. Editors love that; and even if your work is rejected, you've made a good first impression that could help your chances with your next submission.

7. Keep track of your submissions. First, do *not* send out the only copies of your work. There are no guarantees your submission won't get lost in the mail, misplaced in a busy editorial office, or vanish into a black hole if the publication or press closes down. Create a special file folder for poems you're submitting. Even if you use a word processing program and store your manuscripts on disk, keep a hard copy file as well (and be sure to back up your electronic files).

Second, establish a tracking system so you always know which poems are where. This can be extremely simple: index cards, a chart created with word processing or database software, or even a simple notebook used as a log. (You can enlarge and photocopy the Submission Tracker on page 5 or use it as a model to design your own version.) Note the titles of the poems submitted (or the title of the collection if you're submitting a book/chapbook manuscript); the name of the publication, press, or contest; date sent; estimated response time; and date returned *or* date accepted. Additional information you may want to log: the name of the editor/contact, date the accepted piece is published and/or issue number of the magazine, type/amount of pay received, rights acquired by the publication or press, and any pertinent comments.

Without a tracking system, you risk forgetting where and when manuscripts were submitted. This is even more problematic if you simultaneously send the same manuscripts to different magazines, presses or contests. And if you learn of an acceptance by one magazine or publisher, you *must* notify the others that the poem or collection you sent them is no longer available. You run a bigger chance of overlooking someone without an organized approach. This causes hard feelings among editors you may have inconvenienced, hurting your chances with these markets in the future.

8. Don't fear rejection. Learn from it. No one enjoys rejection, but every writer faces it. The best way to turn a negative into a positive is to learn as much as you can from your rejections. Don't let them get you down. A rejection slip isn't a permission slip to doubt yourself, condemn your poetry or give up.

Look over the rejection. Did the editor provide any comments about your work or reasons why your poems were rejected? Probably he or she didn't. Editors are extremely busy and don't necessarily have time to comment on rejections. If that's the case, move on to the next magazine or publisher you've targeted and send your work out again.

If, however, the editor *has* commented on your work, pay attention. It counts for something that the editor took the time and trouble to say anything, however brief, good or bad. And consider any remark or suggestion with an open mind. You don't have to agree, but you shouldn't automatically disregard the feedback, either. Tell your ego to sit down and be quiet, then use the editor's comments to review your work from a new perspective. You might be surprised by how much you'll learn from a single scribbled word in the margin; or how encouraged you'll feel from a simple "Try again!" written on the rejection slip.

Keep these eight tips in mind as you prepare your poetry submissions, and keep *Poet's Market* at hand to help you along. Believe in yourself and don't give up! As the number of listings in this book shows, there are many opportunities for beginning poets to become published poets.

GUIDE TO LISTING FEATURES

On page 8 is an example of a Magazines/Journal listing (Book/Chapbook Publishers listings follow a similar format). Note the callouts that identify various format features of the listing. A key to the symbols displayed at the beginning of each listing is located on page 6, on the inside covers of this book and on a pull-out bookmark just inside the front cover.

EASY-TO-USE
REFERENCE
ICONS

TYPES OF
POETRY
CONSIDERED

SUBMISSION
DETAILS

E-MAIL/
WEB SITE
INFORMATION

SPECIFIC
CONTACT
NAMES

EDITOR'S
COMMENTS

SLANT: A Journal of Poetry
Box 5063, University of Central Arkansas, 201 Donaghey Ave., Conway AR 72035-5000. (501)450-5107. Web site: www.uca.edu/english/Slant/. Established 1987. **Contact:** James Fowler, editor.

Magazine Needs *Slant: A Journal of Poetry*, published annually in May, aims "to publish a journal of fine poetry from all regions of the United States and beyond." Wants "traditional and 'modern' poetry, even experimental; moderate length, any subject on approval of Board of Readers." Doesn't want "haiku, translations." Has published poetry by Susan H. Case, Philip Dacey, Elizabeth Howrd, Timothy Martin, Gilbert Wesley Purdy, and Nancy Scott. *Slant* is 120 pages, professionally printed on quality stock, flat-spined, with matte card cover. Receives about 1,400 poems/year, accepts 70-80. Press run is 175 (70-100 subscribers). Sample: $10.

How to Submit Submit up to 5 poems at a time. Lines/poem: poems should be of moderate length. No previously published poems or simultaneous submissions. Submissions should be typed; include SASE. "Put name, address (including e-mail if available), and phone number at the top of each page." Reads submissions September 1-November 15. Comments on rejected poems "on occasion." Guidelines available in magazine, for SASE, or on Web site. Responds in 3-4 months from November 15 deadline. Pays one contributor's copy. Poet retains rights.

Advice "We tend to publish those poems whose execution, line by line, does full justice to their conception. Often the decision to accept comes down to the matter of craft, language."

Frequently Asked Questions

The following FAQ (Frequently Asked Questions) section provides the expert knowledge you need to submit your poetry in a professional manner. Answers to most basic questions, such as "How many poems should I send?", "How long should I wait for a reply?" and "Are simultaneous submissions okay?" can be found by simply reading the listings in the Magazines/Journals and Book/Chapbook Publishers sections. See the introduction to each section for an explanation of the information contained in the listings. Also, see the Glossary of Listing terms on page 474.

Is it okay to submit handwritten poems?

Usually, no. Now and then a publisher or editor makes an exception and accepts handwritten manuscripts. However, check the preferences stated in each listing. If no mention is made of handwritten submissions, assume your poetry should be typed or computer-generated.

How should I format my poems for submission to magazines and journals?

If you're submitting poems by regular mail (also referred to as *land mail*, *postal mail* or *snail mail*), follow this format (also see sample on page 10):

Poems should be typed or computer-printed on white 8½×11 paper of at least 20 lb. weight. Left, right and bottom margins should be at least one inch. Starting ½ inch from the top of the page, type your name, address, telephone number, e-mail address (if you have one) and number of lines in the poem in the *upper right* corner, in individual lines, single-spaced. Space down about six lines and type the poem title, either centered or flush left. The title may appear in all caps or in upper and lower case. Space down another two lines (at least) and begin to type your poem. Poems are usually single-spaced, although some magazines may request double-spaced submissions. (Be alert to each market's preferences.) Double-space between stanzas. Type one poem to a page. For poems longer than one page, type your name in the *upper left* corner; on the next line type a key word from the title of your poem, the page number, and indicate whether the stanza begins or is continued on the new page (i.e., MOTHMAN, Page 2, continue stanza *or* begin new stanza).

If you're submitting poems by e-mail (also see sample on page 11):

First, make sure the publication accepts e-mail submissions. This information, when available, is included in all *Poet's Market* listings. In most cases, editors will request that poems be pasted within the body of your e-mail, *not* sent as attachments. Many editors prefer this format because of the danger of viruses, the possibility of software incompatibility, and other concerns associated with e-mail attachments. Editors who consider e-mail attachments taboo may even delete the message without opening the attachment.

(handwritten margin notes): ½" / name / address / tel / email / # of lines / } 6 lines / Title or center

Mailed Submission Format

DO leave ¹/₂" margin on top, at least 1" on sides and bottom.

DO list contact information and number of lines in upper right corner.

DO space down about 6 lines.

DO type title in all caps or upper/lower case. Center it or type flush with left margin.

DON'T type a byline but **DO** space down at least 2 lines.

DO double-space between stanzas.

DO type poems single-spaced unless guidelines specify double spacing.

For multi-page poems, **DO** show your name, key word(s) from title, page number, and "continue stanza" or "new stanza."

DO space down at least 3 lines before resuming poem.

S. T. Coleridge
1796 Ancient Way
Mariner Heights, OH 45007
(852)555-5555
albatross@strophe.vv.cy
54 lines

KUBLA KHAN

In Xanadu did Kubla Khan
a stately pleasure dome decree:
where Alph, the sacred river, ran
through caverns measureless to man
down to a sunless sea.
So twice five miles of fertile ground
with walls and towers were girdled round:
and there were gardens bright with sinuous rills,
where blossomed many an incense-bearing tree;
and here were forests ancient as the hills,
enfolding sunny spots of greenery.

But oh! that deep romantic chasm which slanted
down the green hill athwart a cedarn cover!
A savage place! as holy and enchanted
as e'er beneath a waning moon was haunted
by woman wailing for her demon lover!
And from this chasm, with ceaseless turmoil seething,
as if this earth in fast thick pants were breathing,
a mighty fountain momently was forced:
amid whose swift half-intermitted burst
huge fragments vaulted like rebounding hail,
or chaffy grain beneath the thresher's flail:
And 'mid these dancing rocks at once and ever
it flung up momently the sacred river.

S. T. Coleridge
KUBLA KAHN, Page 2, continue stanza

Five miles meandering with a mazy motion
through wood and dale the sacred river ran,
then reached the caverns measureless to man,
and sank in tumult to a lifeless ocean:
and 'mid this tumult Kubla heard from afar
ancestral voices prophesying war!

The shadow of the dome of pleasure
floated midway on the waves;
where was heard the mingled measure
from the fountain and the caves.
It was a miracle of rare device,
a sunny pleasure dome with caves of ice!

A damsel with a dulcimer
in a vision once I saw:
It was an Abyssinian maid,

E-mail Submission Format

DO use a basic typeface and point size.

DO use the appropriate e-mail address.

DO consult guidelines for special instructions about formatting the subject line.

DO follow basic guidelines for a good cover letter.

DO provide contact information, including regular mail address.

DO be aware that formatting can become lost in an electronic submission. Keep it simple.

DO paste all poems within one message, one after the other, unless guidelines specify otherwise.

DON'T send submissions by e-mail unless editor says it's okay (in market listing or guidelines).

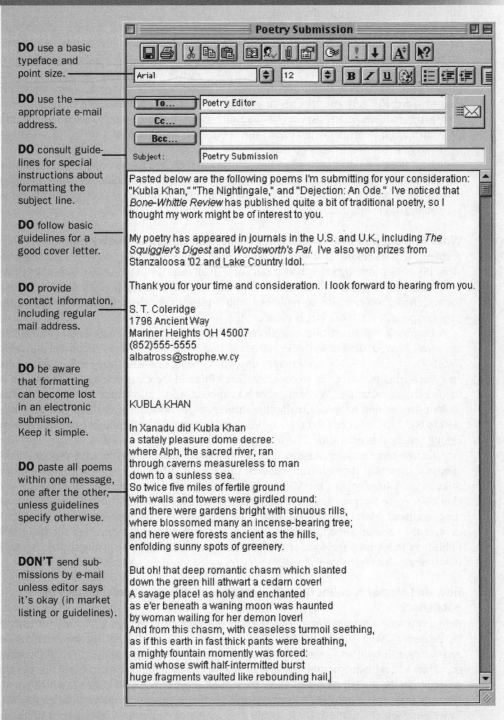

Poetry Submission

Arial   12   **B** *I* <u>U</u>

To...   Poetry Editor
Cc...
Bcc...
Subject: Poetry Submission

Pasted below are the following poems I'm submitting for your consideration: "Kubla Khan," "The Nightingale," and "Dejection: An Ode." I've noticed that *Bone-Whittle Review* has published quite a bit of traditional poetry, so I thought my work might be of interest to you.

My poetry has appeared in journals in the U.S. and U.K., including *The Squiggler's Digest* and *Wordsworth's Pal*. I've also won prizes from Stanzaloosa '02 and Lake Country Idol.

Thank you for your time and consideration. I look forward to hearing from you.

S. T. Coleridge
1796 Ancient Way
Mariner Heights OH 45007
(852)555-5555
albatross@strophe.w.cy

KUBLA KHAN

In Xanadu did Kubla Khan
a stately pleasure dome decree:
where Alph, the sacred river, ran
through caverns measureless to man
down to a sunless sea.
So twice five miles of fertile ground
with walls and towers were girdled round:
and there were gardens bright with sinuous rills,
where blossomed many an incense-bearing tree;
and here were forests ancient as the hills,
enfolding sunny spots of greenery.

But oh! that deep romantic chasm which slanted
down the green hill athwart a cedarn cover!
A savage place! as holy and enchanted
as e'er beneath a waning moon was haunted
by woman wailing for her demon lover!
And from this chasm, with ceaseless turmoil seething,
as if this earth in fast thick pants were breathing,
a mighty fountain momently was forced:
amid whose swift half-intermitted burst
huge fragments vaulted like rebounding hail,

Of course, other editors do accept, and even prefer e-mail submissions as attachments. This information should be clearly stated in the market listing. If it's not, you're probably safer submitting your poems in the body of the e-mail. (All the more reason to pay close attention to details given in the listings.)

Note, too, the number of poems the editor recommends including in the e-mail submission. If no quantity is given specifically for e-mails, go with the number of poems an editor recommends submitting in general. Identify your submission with a notation in the subject line. While some editors simply want the words "Poetry Submission," others want poem titles. Check the market listing for preferences. **Note:** Because of spam, filters and other concerns, some editors are strict about what must be printed in the subject line and how. If you're uncertain about any aspect of e-mail submission formats, double-check the Web site (if available) for information or contact the publication for directions.

If you're submitting poems on disk:

Submit poems on disk *only* when the publication indicates this is acceptable. Even then, if no formatting preferences are given, contact the publisher for specifics before sending the disk. Make sure your disk is virus-free. Always include a hard copy (i.e., printed copy) of your submission with the disk.

What is a chapbook? How is it different from a regular poetry book?

A chapbook is a booklet, averaging 24-50 pages in length (some are shorter), usually digest-sized (5½×8½, although chapbooks can come in all sizes, even published within the pages of a magazine). Typically, a chapbook is saddle-stapled with a soft cover (card or special paper); chapbooks can also be produced with a plain paper cover the same weight as the pages, especially if the booklet is photocopied.

A chapbook is a much smaller collection of poetry than a full-length book (which runs anywhere from 50 pages to well over 100 pages, longer for "best of" collections and retrospectives). There are probably more poetry chapbooks being published than full-length books, and that's an important point to consider. Don't think of the chapbook as a poor relation to the full-length collection. While it's true a chapbook won't attract big reviews, qualify for major prizes or find national distribution through chain bookstores, it's a terrific way for a poet to build an audience (and reputation) in increments, while developing the kind of publishing history that may attract the attention of a book publisher one day.

Although some presses consider chapbooks through a regular submission process, many choose manuscripts through competitions. Check each publisher's listing for requirements, send for guidelines or visit the Web site (absolutely vital if a competition is involved), and check out some sample chapbooks the press has already produced (usually available from the press itself). Most chapbook publishers are as choosy as book publishers about the quality of work they accept. Submit your best poems in a professional manner. (See the Chapbook Publishers Index on page 480 for markets that consider chapbook manuscripts; the Book Publishers Index begins on page 483.)

How do I format a collection of poems to submit to a book/chapbook publisher?

Before you send a manuscript to a book/chapbook publisher, request guidelines (or consult the publisher's Web site, if available). Requirements vary regarding formatting, query letters and samples, length, and other considerations. Usually you will use 8½×11, 20 lb. white paper; set left, right and bottom margins of at least one inch; put your name and title of your collection in the top left corner of every page; limit poems to one per page (although poems certainly may run longer than one page); and number pages consecutively. Individual publisher requirements might include a title page, table of contents, credits page (indicating where previously published poems originally appeared) and biographical note.

If you're submitting your poetry book or chapbook manuscript to a competition, you *must* read and follow the guidelines. Failure to do so could disqualify your manuscript. Guidelines for a competition might call for an official entry form to accompany the submission, a special title page, a minimum and maximum number of pages, and specific formatting instructions (such as paginating the manuscript and not putting the poet's name on any of the manuscript pages).

What is a cover letter? Do I have to send one? What should it say?

A cover letter is your introduction to the editor, telling him a little about yourself and your work. Most editors indicate their cover letter preferences in their listings. If an editor states a cover letter is "required," absolutely send one! It's also better to send one if a cover letter is "preferred." Experts disagree on the necessity and appropriateness of cover letters, so use your own judgment when preferences aren't clear in the listing.

A cover letter should be professional but also allow you to present your work in a personal manner. (See the fictional cover letter on page 14 as an example.) Keep your letter brief, no more than one page. Address your letter to the correct contact person. (Use "Poetry Editor" if no contact name appears in the listing.) Include your name, address, phone number and e-mail address (if available). If a biographical note is requested, include 2-3 lines about your background, interests, why you write poetry, etc. Avoid praising yourself or your poems in your letter (your submission should speak for itself). Include titles (or first lines) of the poems you're submitting. You may list a few of your most recent publishing credits, but no more than five; and keep in mind that some editors find publishing credits tiresome—they're more interested in the quality of the work you're submitting to *them*.

Show your familiarity with the magazine to which you're submitting: comment on a poem the magazine published, tell the editor why you chose to submit to her magazine, mention poets the magazine has published. Use a business-style format for a professional appearance, and proofread carefully; typos, misspellings and other errors make a poor first impression. Remember that editors are people, too. Respect, professionalism and kindness go a long way in poet/editor relationships.

What is a SASE? An IRC (with SAE)?

A SASE is a self-addressed, stamped envelope—and you should never send a submission by regular mail without one. Also include a SASE if you send an inquiry to an editor. If your submission is too large for an envelope (for instance, a bulky book-length collection of poems), use a box and include a self-addressed mailing label with adequate return postage paper-clipped to it.

An IRC is an International Reply Coupon, enclosed with a self-addressed envelope for manuscripts submitted to foreign markets. Each coupon is equivalent in value to the minimum postage rate for an unregistered airmail letter. IRCs may be exchanged for postage stamps at post offices in all foreign countries that are members of the Universal Postal Union (UPU). When you provide the adequate number of IRCs and a self-addressed envelope (SAE), you give a foreign editor financial means to return your submission (U.S. postage stamps cannot be used to send mail *to* the United States from outside the country). Purchase price is $2 per coupon. Call your local post office to check for availability (sometimes only larger post offices sell them).

Important note about IRCs: Foreign editors sometimes find the IRCs have been stamped incorrectly by the U.S. post office when purchased. This voids the IRCs and makes it impossible for the foreign editor to exchange the coupons for return postage for your manuscript. When buying IRCs, make sure yours have been stamped correctly before you leave the

Important

Preparing Your Cover Letter

DO type on one side of 8½ x 11 20 lb. paper.

DO proofread carefully.

DO use a standard 12-point typeface (like Times New Roman).

DO list the poems you're submitting for consideration.

DO mention something about the magazine and about yourself.

DO be brief!

Perry Lineskanner
1954 Eastern Blvd.
Pentameter, OH 45007
(852) 555-5555
soneteer@trochee.vv.cy

April 24, 2008

Spack Saddlestaple, Editor
The Squiggler's Digest
Double-Toe Press
P.O. Box 54X
Submission Junction, AZ 85009

Dear Mr. Saddlestaple:

Enclosed are three poems for your consideration for *The Squiggler's Digest*: "The Diamond Queen," "The Boy Who Was Gromit," and "The Maker of Everything."

Although this is my first submission to your journal, I'm a long-time reader of *The Squiggler's Digest* and enjoy the scope of narrative poetry you feature. I especially enjoyed Sydney Dogwood's poetry cycle in Issue 4.

My own poetry has appeared recently in *The Bone-Whittle Review*, *Bumper-Car Reverie*, and *Stock Still*.

Thank you for considering my manuscript. I look forward to hearing from you.

Sincerely,

Perry Lineskanner

Note: The names used in this letter are intended to be fictional; any resemblance to real people, publications or presses is purely coincidental.

counter. (The Postal Service clerk must place a postmark in the block with the heading *control stamp of the country of origin*.) More information about International Reply Coupons is available on the USPS Web site (www.usps.com).

To save time and money, poets sometimes send disposable manuscripts to foreign markets and inform the editor to discard the manuscript after it's been read. Some enclose an IRC and SAE for reply only; others establish a deadline after which they will withdraw the manuscript from consideration and market it elsewhere.

How much postage does my submission need?

As much as it takes—you do *not* want your manuscript to arrive postage due. Purchase a postage scale or take your manuscript to the post office for weighing. Remember, you'll need postage on two envelopes: the one containing your submission and SASE, and the return envelope itself. Submissions without SASEs usually will not be returned (and possibly may not even be read).

Note: New postage rates went into effect on May 14, 2007. There is now a new fee structure for First-Class Postage. For letters and cards (including business-size envelopes), the First-Class rate is 41 cents for the first ounce, and 17 cents per additional ounce up to and including 3.5 ounces. **Letter-sized mail that weighs more than 3.5 ounces is charged the "flats" rate** ("flats" include any envelope large enough to mail an $8\frac{1}{2} \times 11$ manuscript page unfolded) of 80 cents for the first ounce, and 17 cents for each additional ounce up to and including 13 ounces. This means if you send a large envelope that weighs only one ounce, it costs 80 cents at the First-Class flats rate instead of the 41 cents charged for First-Class letters and cards. (See the charts on page 16 for First-Class rates for letters and flats, or go to www.usps.com for complete information on all rates questions.)

Mail over 13 ounces can still be sent Priority Mail (in the envelope provided by the USPS) at the new cost of $4.60, regardless of weight or destination. Priority Mail Flat Rate using the box provided by the USPS now costs $9.15, regardless of weight (up to a 70 lb. maximum) or destination. Envelopes and boxes are available at the post office or can be ordered online at www.usps.com. If sending a bulky parcel (a full-length book manuscript, for instance), check with the post office for correct rates and packaging.

The USPS also offers its Click-N-Ship® program, which allows a customer to print domestic and international shipping labels with postage, buy insurance and pay for postage by credit card. See the USPS Web site for a one-time software download, to check system requirements and to register for an account.

The Web site is also your source for ordering supplies (such as postage scale and labels), reviewing postal regulations, calculating postage and more. Canada Post information and services are available at www.canadapost.com.

What does it mean when an editor says "no previously published" poems? Does this include poems that have appeared in anthologies? What if one of my poems appeared online through a group or forum?

If your poem appears *anywhere* in print for a public audience, it's considered "previously" published. That includes magazines, anthologies, Web sites and online journals, and even printed programs (say for a church service, wedding, etc.). See the explanation for rights below, especially *second serial (reprint) rights* and *all rights* for additional concerns about previously published material.

One exception to the above guidelines is if your poem appears online in a *private* poetry forum, critique group, etc. As long as the site is private (i.e., a password is required to view and participate), your poem isn't considered "published." However, if your poem is printed

Articles & Information

Postage Information

First-Class Mail Rates: Letters & Cards

1 ounce	$0.41	3 ounces	0.75
2 ounces	$0.58	3.5 ounces	0.92

First-Class Mail Rates: Flats

Weight not over (ounces)	Rate	Weight not over (ounces)	Rate
1	$0.80	8	1.99
2	0.97	9	2.16
3	1.14	10	2.33
4	1.31	11	2.50
5	1.48	12	2.67
6	1.65	13	2.84
7	1.82		

Source: Web site of the United States Postal Service (www.usps.com)

U.S. and Canadian Postal Codes

AL	Alabama	MN	Minnesota	VA	Virginia
AK	Alaska	MS	Mississippi	WA	Washington
AZ	Arizona	MO	Missouri	WV	West Virginia
AR	Arkansas	MT	Montana	WI	Wisconsin
CA	California	NE	Nebraska	WY	Wyoming
CO	Colorado	NV	Nevada		
CT	Connecticut	NH	New Hampsire	**Canada**	
DE	Delaware	NJ	New Jersey	AB	Alberta
DC	District of	NM	New Mexico	BC	British Columbia
	Columbia	NY	New York	MB	Manitoba
FL	Florida	NC	North Carolina	NB	New Brunswick
GA	Georgia	ND	North Dakota	NL	Newfoundland &
GU	Guam	OH	Ohio		Labrador
HI	Hawaii	OK	Oklahoma	NS	Nova Scotia
ID	Idaho	OR	Oregon	NT	Northwest
IL	Illinois	PA	Pennsylvania		Territories
IN	Indiana	PR	Puerto Rico	NU	Nunavut
IA	Iowa	RI	Rhode Island	ON	Ontario
KS	Kansas	SC	South Carolina	PE	Prince Edward
KY	Kentucky	SD	South Dakota		Island
LA	Louisiana	TN	Tennessee	QC	Quebec
ME	Maine	TX	Texas	SK	Saskatchewan
MD	Maryland	UT	Utah	YT	Yukon
MA	Massachusetts	VT	Vermont		
MI	Michigan	VI	Virgin Islands		

on a online forum or bulletin board that's available for public viewing, even if you must use a password to post the poem or to comment, then your poem is considered "published" as far as rights are concerned.

What rights should I offer for my poems? What do these different rights mean?

Editors usually indicate in their listings what rights they acquire. Most journals and magazines license *first rights* (a.k.a. *first serial rights*), which means the poet offers the right to publish the poem for the first time in any periodical. All other rights to the material remain with the poet. (Note that some editors state that rights to poems "revert to poets upon publication" when first rights are acquired.) When poems are excerpted from a book prior to publication and printed in a magazine/journal, this is also called *first serial rights*. The addition of *North American* indicates the editor is the first to publish a poem in a U.S. or Canadian periodical. The poem may still be submitted to editors outside of North America or to those who acquire reprint rights.

When a magazine/journal licenses *one-time rights* to a poem (also known as *simultaneous rights*), the editor has *nonexclusive* rights to publish the poem once. The poet may submit that same poem to other publications at the same time (usually markets that don't have overlapping audiences).

Editors/publishers open to submission of work already published elsewhere seek *second serial (reprint) rights*. The poet is obliged to inform them where and when the poem previously appeared so they can give proper credit to the original publication. In essence, chapbook or book collections license reprint rights, listing the magazines in which poems previously appeared somewhere in the book (usually on the copyright page or separate credits page).

If a publisher or editor requires you to <u>relinquish *all rights*</u>, be aware that you're giving up ownership of that poem or group of poems. You cannot resubmit the work elsewhere, nor can you include it in a poetry collection without permission or by negotiating for reprint rights to be returned to you. Before you agree to this type of arrangement, ask the editor first if he or she is willing to acquire first rights instead of all rights. If you receive a refusal and you don't want to relinquish all rights, simply write a letter withdrawing your work from consideration. Some editors will reassign rights to a writer after a given amount of time, such as one year.

With the growth in Internet publishing opportunities, *electronic rights* have become very important. These cover a broad range of electronic media, including online magazines, CD recordings of poetry readings and CD-ROM editions of magazines. When submitting to an electronic market of any kind, find out what rights the market acquires upfront (many online magazines also stipulate the right to archive poetry they've published so it's continually available on their Web sites).

What is a copyright? Should I have my poems copyrighted before I submit them for publication?

Copyright is a proprietary right that gives you the power to control your work's reproduction, distribution and public display or performance, as well as its adaptation to other forms. In other words, you have legal right to the exclusive publication, sale or distribution of your poetry. What's more, your "original works of authorship" are protected as soon as they are "fixed in a tangible form of expression," i.e., written down or recorded. Since March 1989, copyright notices are no longer required to secure protection, so it's not necessary to include them on your poetry manuscript. Also, in many editors' minds, copyright notices signal the work of amateurs who are distrustful and paranoid about having work stolen.

If you still want to indicate copyright, use the © symbol or the word *copyright*, your name and the year. If you wish, you can register your copyright with the Copyright Office for a $45 fee, using Form TX (directions and form available for download from www.copyright.gov). Since paying $45 per poem is costly and impractical, you may prefer to copyright a group of unpublished poems for that single fee. Further information is available from the U.S. Copyright Office, Library of Congress, 101 Independence Ave. S.E., Washington DC 20559-6000; by download from www.copyright.gov; or by calling (202)707-3000 between 8:30 a.m. and 5:00 p.m. (EST) weekdays.

Special note regarding Copyright Office mail delivery: The "effective date of registration" for copyright applications is usually the day the Copyright Office actually receives all elements of an application (application form, fee and copies of work being registered). Because of security concerns, all USPS and private-carrier mail is screened off-site prior to arrival at the Copyright Office. This can add 3-5 days to delivery time and could, therefore, impact the effective date of registration. See the Web site for details about proper packaging, special handling and other related information.

Roundtable:
Poets and Blogs

by Anne Bowling

There isn't much the Internet hasn't touched—and to varying degrees, transformed. The poetry community is no exception. The last 10 years have seen a dramatic rise in poetry blogs, and they're as varied and colorful as the poets who maintain them.

For the uninitiated, a blog ("Web log") is basically a Web site where entries are written in a journal style and displayed in reverse chronological order. The content of poetry blogs includes the expected: news, book reviews, publication and reading announcements and, in some cases, poetry.

But readers also find the unexpected: scanned art incorporating poetry; photo caption contests; and personal musings on everything from marriage to Michael Caine's acting ability. And readers find links, hundreds and hundreds of them, creating an international network of poets and poetry lovers who communicate online sometimes as frequently as every day.

While the Internet has made changes to form possible (as with Flarf or Google-sculpting— i.e., creating and shaping poems based on the results of specific kinds of Google searches), blogs have helped the introduction of new forms spread at an unprecedented pace. Last year, an L.A. screenwriter invited readers of his blog to submit "Fibs," or six-line poems based on a mathematical progression known as the Fibonacci sequence, sparking what he estimated at some 1,000 Fibs created online in a matter of weeks.

But maybe the most important contribution of blogs to the poetry community is, well, community. Says Janet Holmes, poet, blogger and director of Ahsahta Press, "The main thing the blog world offers is the feeling of being in the midst of like minds, among people who care about the same things. I have that to a limited extent where I live and teach, in Boise, Idaho, but blogs broaden that community and make it more representative."

In this roundtable, we talk with five poet-bloggers about what they post, why they post and how blogging may (or may not) have an impact on the path to publication.

Amanda Johnston serves on the board of directors for the National Women's Alliance and the African-American Arts Technical Resource of Austin. The recipient of many honors and awards for her poetry, Johnston is also a member of the Austin Project, co-founder of The Gibbous Moon Collective, and founding editor of *Torch, poetry, prose, and short stories by African American Women*. Find her blog at http://amandajohnston.blogspot.com.

Janet Holmes is author of several volumes of poetry, and her work has twice been included in the annual *The Best American Poetry* anthology. She is director of Ahsahta Press,

ANNE BOWLING is a freelance writer living in Cincinnati, Ohio. She's the former editor of *Novel & Short Story Writer's Market* (F+W Publications/Writer's Digest Books).

an all-poetry publishing house at Boise State University, where she has taught in the MFA program since 1999. Find her blog, "Humanophone," at www.humanophone.com.

Jilly Dybka is a poet whose work has seen publication in numerous anthologies and literary journals, from *storySouth* to *Harpur Palate*. She is also a Windows network administrator, and has maintained her poetry blog for more than 10 years. Find her blog, "Poetry Hut Blog," at www.poetryhut.com/wordpress/.

Reb Livingston is author of *Your Ten Favorite Words* (Coconut Books, forthcoming) and two chapbooks. Her work appears in literary magazines, has been nominated for two Pushcart prizes, and was included in *The Best American Poetry 2006*. She writes a monthly poetry column called "Crucial Rooster" at The Happy Booker. Find her blog, "Home-Schooled by a Cackling Jackal," at http://cacklingjackal.blogspot.com.

C. Dale Young practices medicine full-time, and teaches in the Warren Wilson MFA program. He also serves as poetry editor of the *New England Review*, and has published two volumes of poetry. Find his blog, "Avoiding the Muse," at http://avoidmuse.blogspot.com.

Why a blog? What was your intent?

Johnston: I created a personal blog as an act of public writing, or getting over my hang-ups around writing under the public eye. As someone who entered writing in a very nontraditional way, I've always been very insecure about my work. Not the tone or the subject matter, but the way it looked and moved on the page. I worried so much about my writing being technically right that I wouldn't let anyone look at my work. Starting a blog was a wonderful way for me to stay detached enough from my work to feel protected, yet still vulnerable enough to begin the work of releasing my writings to public scrutiny.

Holmes: I don't keep a journal, and I thought having a public space to talk about my reading (mostly) would cause me to write thoughtfully about it and invite some feedback. I was also interested in having a centralized place where people could find out about my work.

Dybka: I had become seriously interested in writing poetry about a year prior to starting the blog, while I was recovering from a serious illness. I have an M.S. in Information Sciences (and an MFA in poetry from the University of Charlotte), and I've been working with the Web since 1997; and then I developed an interest in poetry. So I've had Web sites since 1995, and I was doing Web searches for daily poetry news anyway, just out of my own curiosity. So I decided to start posting the poetry news daily on a blog.

Livingston: I have a number of intents for my blog. My primary goals: build community among poets, hone my own voice as a writer through practice, develop readers that will hopefully translate to my other work, develop creative projects, and pick up the slack where print publications are floundering (for example, book reviews).

Young: It started as a New Year's resolution to do something different and to do something others might not expect me to do.

What do blogs offer that general Web sites do not?

Johnston: Blogs are economical. Most blog spaces are available for free, whereas Web sites require a hosting fee. I like that blogs make the author more accessible to the reader. When posts are uploaded, readers can comment and build a dialogue around the work. You also get a better sense of who the author is. I post more than just poetry: pictures of events, family outings, and random audio, videos, etc., that inspire and entertain. It's fun and, in my opinion, builds a closer connection between my readers and me.

Holmes: The content of blogs changes regularly, and readers get to know the personalities of the bloggers. If I'm reading someone who posts nearly every day (like [Ron] Silliman), I know so much about his preferences and peeves that it's much like an ongoing (if one-sided) conversation. I love Kate Greenstreet's "Every Other Day" blog because it's just the opposite:

I never know what she's going to be doing there. When you finally meet someone whose blog you've been reading, it's the strangest phenomenon. You actually know quite a lot about that person's opinions, life details, and whatever has been said over time in the blog, but you don't really know the person.

Livingston: Personality, depth, an evolution. Most general Web sites are stagnant or updated only at intervals. They're good for general information; for instance, if someone is looking for information on an author, a site may have a bio, her publishing credits, links to her books, a schedule of her readings. That can be a useful place to start for a writer one already has an interest in, but that's not going to generate interest or dialogue or an exchange of ideas. A general author Web site is more like a press kit. A blog's possibilities are numerous.

Young: They are an odd mix of journal and conversation. Readers can post comments, so a community develops. Many of the people who comment have their own blogs; some do not. It is fascinating to see the discussions take place at times.

How do you decide what content to post?

Johnston: It's a personal blog, so I post whatever I want! I upload poems, videos, links to articles, etc. It really is the potpourri of my mind on display.

Holmes: I like to talk about what I'm reading or teaching, the painting I've been doing, movies I've seen. When I travel for poetry reasons, I like to post about those events and the people I've met. I've made a conscious decision not to write about the work I do at Ahsahta Press in terms of manuscript selection, though I do announce the books we publish as they become available.

Dybka: An arbitrary sense of what I think is interesting or notable, even if I don't agree with it, or think it is ridiculous. I usually don't comment on the news links—people are smart enough to decide what they agree with or don't. I just put it out there because it has caught my eye in some way.

Livingston: I write about things I care about. Whether it's about a new book I'm editing or a poet I really like or my own writing—or often it doesn't have a direct literary connection at all. Often I write about whatever is on my mind at the moment.

Young: I have never planned what my content would be. I talk about poetry, medicine (at times), publishing, my life, what I am reading, what I admire. I write a fair bit about pop culture and gay culture. It is a hodgepodge of things, really. The blog is titled ''Avoiding the Muse.'' And its entire purpose, for me and my readers, seems to be about distraction. My blog hit an all-time high for visitors in April of 2006. I got married that month, and my mind was very much absorbed in the whole thing. I suspect the reality-TV aspect was interesting and addictive to readers. During that time, I had over 600 visitors per day. Now it has leveled back off to its usual number of stalwart visitors.

Has blogging created a new poetry community? Or, rather, has it broadened and reshaped the existing community?

Johnston: Both. Blogging has created its own community of folks writing online who peruse each other's work; but mainstream journals and established writers have added blogs to their Web sites. The familiarity blogs offer is bringing the edges of our separate spheres closer together. I think this strengthens our communities collectively.

Holmes: The latter. It can make someone in Boise aware of what's going on in New York, and vice versa. That's valuable on both ends. It also offers a voice to poets who aren't yet well known, or who may or may not be publishing yet, but who have interesting perspectives.

Dybka: I live in a small town . . . near Nashville. Nashville has a pretty good poetry slam-type scene, but I'm more of a page poet. So I am not really part of the local poetry scene.

Through blogs, I've found out about publications and poets that I might not have learned about otherwise.

Livingston: Blogging has introduced me to hundreds of poets I probably never would have met or had any interaction with. There is definitely a poetry blogging scene and many smaller communities within the larger, based on aesthetics, interests, backgrounds and location. When I say community, it's not all love-fests. These connections include disagreements that range from civilized to heated to occasionally out-of-control. It's often the out-of-control blow-ups that get the attention, because let's face it, many stop to watch the fist fight. But one can also walk right past it and keep on going, if one wants. Although that's not always easy.

Young: I don't think it has created a new community, but it has given many a chance to connect to folks very far away from them in ways that were not very easy previously.

Has blogging affected the form of poetry?

Johnston: If it has affected the form in any way, it is that the delivery is open to more mediums. Posting text, audio, video and even scanned art that incorporates poetry is easier than ever. With a click of a button you can upload work in varied formats and allow your readers to experience the work in multiple ways.

Holmes: I don't think so. It may have facilitated some collaborations, though I think Listservs have also been influential in introducing poets to each other. The "Flarf Collective" formed, I believe, from poets who knew each other through blogs and Listservs, and began to share and promote their work derived from Google searches.

Dybka: There are two forms of poetry that I know got some publicity on blogs—Hay(na)ku* and Fibonacci poems. *[a three-line form, with one word in line one, two words in line two, and three words in line three]

Livingston: Possibly. I would broaden that to the Internet as a whole. Via blogs a couple of years ago I first became aware of Flarf and Google-sculpting.

Young: I am not, to be honest, sure it has. It hasn't really affected my own poems.

What opportunities do blogs offer in addition to self-promotion?

Johnston: As a reader of blogs, I appreciate the grassroots social commentary, the contemporary writing and other unfiltered information being shared.

Holmes: Practically speaking, there aren't frequently announcements of readings, contests and calls for submissions on blogs. But a more important role, I think, is that blogs can begin and propagate the kinds of discussions that often occur at, say, literary conferences, but in a time frame that is much less restrictive.

Dybka: I've found out about publication opportunities and new journals reading blogs.

Livingston: Participating in a literary community, practicing writing (with a readership) on a daily basis, learning what my contemporaries are doing, discovering new (to me) poets.

Young: I suppose it gives people access to you in a different way. But it comes down to the style and content of the blog. If people aren't interested, they won't read you, and this isn't necessarily good for "promotion." I like to think of the blog and my poems as separate things. They require very different modes of inhabiting them. Blogs offer different things to readers: information, entertainment, challenges, discussion, prompts, etc. What they offer the writer of the blog is less easy to define.

How does blogging change your audience? Or does it?

Johnston: The random Web surfer not looking for poetry could stumble onto your blog. I love it! I get visitors all the time who come to my blog through search engines looking for something completely different and decide to stay and check it out. Completely random and much appreciated. It's like reading in a coffee shop or bookstore, but better. You get a bigger variety of walk-ins. Some unassuming Web surfer could start out shopping for a new MP3 player online and end up reading my poetry.

Holmes: Aside from extending that audience, I'm not sure that it does.

Livingston: I wouldn't say change, but there are possibilities for expansion.

Young: I suppose it can. I know I have gotten e-mails from folks who discovered my blog (primarily folks living in different countries) who then became curious about my poetry. Some of them have even bought books. I guess it has broadened my readership, but again I think this is mostly outside the U.S. I don't have any real way of tracking this, but this is my best guess.

Is blogging a helpful tool toward publication?

Johnston: As far as people being aware of your work and opportunities to submit for publication coming your way, yes. But this still does not replace the act of following submission guidelines, sending your work out and having an anonymous body of reviewers decide if your work will be published in their journal or not. If anything, it's a great way to get eyes on your work and some good feedback to help you decide if your work is ready for submission.

Holmes: That's difficult to say. My own blogging hasn't helped me towards publication at all, but I wouldn't want to extrapolate my own experience to a general statement.

Livingston: With a popular blog, there's an opportunity to create some name recognition. This doesn't get anyone publication, but it's kind of like an introduction, and introductions help. If an editor recognizes a name, she might give your work a little extra attention. Sometimes I get invitations from editors to send work; some of those editors first became aware of my work and me through my blog.

Young: The best tool toward publication is to write good poems. That might sound snarky, but having a blog isn't necessarily going to change your chances of publication in magazines and journals. It might alert an editor or press to your existence, but the work you produce still has to demand publication when it is sitting in front of an editor.

What would you warn a potential poet-blogger against?

Johnston: A blog is a public space—always remember that. Know that thousands of people could potentially read and respond to your work. This really is no different than publishing work in books or anthologies, but publishing work to a personal blog makes you more vulnerable; it's more of a risk.

Holmes: Excessive self-exposure. I've seen a few young poets make some very foolish statements on their blogs that will likely haunt them for some time.

Dybka: I would caution them against some of the same things that one should be aware of on the Internet in general. Be careful what kind of information you share. Also, have some decorum.

Livingston: Nobody wants to read a blog if it's just a list of publications, accomplishments and upcoming appearances. If that's the only goal, a general Web site is the way to go. Yes, there's a lot of opportunity to direct people to one's work, but if one doesn't have something to contribute, ideas or commentary, a reason for why readers would want to read your blog, there's no purpose in blogging.

Young: No warnings. I am always telling people to write what they want to write. If there is an audience for it, they will find you. I tell folks the same thing about writing poems.

What would you call your greatest satisfaction in maintaining your blog?

Johnston: Having a voice in the online community and offering a space to celebrate others.

Holmes: The fact that it's out there means that people sometimes contact me, either people I've lost touch with through the years or people I've never met before who have been affected by things I've written.

Dybka: It's nice when people say they enjoy reading the news each day.

Young: I like the fact that I have a record of my mind's ramblings over time. I can read one of my old posts and instantly know what was going on in my life at that time, whether or not I wrote about it on the blog. So, my satisfaction is purely selfish and self-involved. In many ways, my poems are similar. Every poem I have conjures for me a time in my life. The blogs, my poems, my paintings, they are all like pieces of string tied to branches in a very large and dark forest. They help me find my way back.

Related Blogs

Amanda Johnston: http://amandajohnston.blogspot.com
Avoiding the Muse (C. Dale Young): http://avoidmuse.blogspot.com
Every Other Day (Kate Greenstreet): www.kickingwind.com
FLARF: http://mainstreampoetry.blogspot.com/
GottaBook (originator of the Fib): http://gottabook.blogspot.com/
Humanophone (Janet Holmes): www.humanophone.com
Home-Schooled by a Cackling Jackal (Reb Livingston): http://cacklingjackal.
   blogspot.com
More Goods on the Chatelaine (Eileen R. Tabios/hay(na)ku): http://goodchat
   ty.blogspot.com/
Poetry Hut Blog (Jilly Dybka): www.poetryhut.com/wordpress
Silliman's Blog (Ron Silliman): http://ronsilliman.blogspot.com/

Professional Opinion:

Setting Industry Standards

by F.J. Bergmann

In 2005 I sent the work of a client of my poetry submission service, PoemFactotum.com, to the *Wayne Literary Review*. The journal's most recent *Poet's Market* listing had given a three-month response time, which had passed. They were no longer listed in the 2006 *Poet's Market* and had no Web site or posted guidelines. A polite letter of inquiry accompanied by a SASE and e-mail address (as was the original submission) went unanswered.

Through the university English department, I finally was able to reach the editor by phone. He informed me that he habitually did not respond to submissions, and that it was "standard operating procedure in the industry" for rejection to be implied if no response was received from a publication within 30 days!

In sending out hundreds of submissions per year, I have never encountered that policy—few journals respond in less than two months, and no journal I know of expects poets to infer rejection without so stating in their guidelines.

However, this incident provoked my speculation about what poetry "industry standards" are. The CLMP (Council of Literary Magazines and Presses) Code of Ethics states:

> We encourage publishers to adopt and abide by the following Code, and we recommend that the Code itself be included along with contest guidelines and a conflict-of-interest statement:
>
> CLMP's community of independent literary publishers believe that ethical contests serve our shared goal: to connect writers and readers by publishing exceptional writing. Intent to act ethically, clarity of guidelines, and transparency of process form the foundation of an ethical contest. To that end, we agree (1) to conduct our contests as ethically as possible and to address any unethical behavior on the part of our readers, judges, or editors; (2) to provide clear and specific contest guidelines—defining conflict of interest for all parties involved; and (3) to make the mechanics of our selection process available to the public. This Code recognizes that different contest models produce different results, but that each model can be run ethically. We have adopted this Code to reinforce our integrity and dedication as a publishing community and to ensure that our contests contribute to a vibrant literary heritage.

F.J. BERGMANN (www.fibitz.com) teaches workshops on poetic devices and is the author of two chapbooks, *Sauce Robert* (Pavement Saw Press, 2003) and *Aqua Regia* (Parallell Press, 2007). She is the co-editor of the 2008 *Wisconsin Poets' Calendar*, the Webmaster of madpoetry.org and the Wisconsin Fellowship of Poets Web site (www.wfop.org), and runs PoemFactotum.com, a poetry submission service. She has no literary academic qualifications, but is kind to those so encumbered.

While this is a step in the right direction, note that this code does not deal with standardizing mechanics; it merely encourages individual contests to reveal their practices and does not address journal policies at all.

While journal guidelines are as inconsistent as those of contests, some practices appear to be more functional than others, and can be structured to benefit both poets and editors.

INDUSTRY STANDARDS FOR JOURNALS
Accessible, current guidelines

Poet's Market listings are free to journals, magazines, presses, contests, conferences and organizations. Where possible, the following information should be provided:

Reading period. This may follow the academic calendar—or be arbitrary.

Submission frequency. Should state how often submissions may be sent, e.g., once per year or reading period, number of months to wait after last rejection, etc.

Simultaneous submissions. Some editors request that simultaneous submissions be identified. It would appear that identifying all submissions as simultaneous, where requested, may at best speed response time, and at worst have no adverse consequences. To clarify two terms that are increasingly confused: *simultaneous* means sending the *same* poem to more than one publication; *multiple submissions* means sending more than one, different manuscript to the *same place* (generally only applicable to contests).

Previously published poems. Unless stated otherwise, assume that poems submitted for consideration must be *un*published.

Number of poems to submit; page or line limit per submission or per individual poem.

Style of poetry. Not always stated, even though strong editorial preferences may exist at a given publication. Poets *do* have an obligation to investigate what sort of poetry the journal prints.

Snail-mail vs. e-mail. If e-mail submissions are accepted, additional considerations would include whether submissions should be sent as attachments or pasted into the body of the message; and specific wording of the subject line.

Special formatting constraints. Under the heading of extreme idiosyncrasies would be requirements for unusual formatting (double-spaced poems, use of a specific font, etc.), whether disk submissions are accepted, or whether to submit multiple copies.

Response time. Sometimes this is a specific date, if the publication has a yearly or seasonal deadline.

Rights acquired. Be suspicious if asked for more than first North American rights and online rights. All rights should revert to the poet following publication.

Pay (if any). Most journals do not pay in cash. Poets should receive at least one contributor's copy from a print publication.

Time between acceptance and publication. If it's more than one year, this should be mentioned in the guidelines. Contributors should be notified if complications arise.

The new online submission manager CLMP is marketing to journals and contests (see www.clmp.org/about/sub_mgr_form.html), which is already getting glowing reports by users like the journal *jubilat*, appears to be a godsend for poets in terms of ease of submission and being able to track the fate of a specific submission. (Several times a year I send out inquiries regarding unanswered submissions, only to be told that no one at the publications in question has any recollection of those poems ever being received).

Guidelines online

While a Web site (or at least a Web page with posted guidelines) makes it easier for poets to feel confident that they're accessing current information, some journals choose not to have an online presence, or are unable to muster staff with the necessary skills. On the other hand, leaving out-of-date information posted online may be worse than having no Web site at all.

Two of the most exasperating practices are to have an active Web site that displays information from Year One that has never been updated; or (why? why?) to put each successive year's information on a new Web page while leaving the outdated information on the site. Guess which URL returning submitters have bookmarked?

At the very least, old pages should be altered to indicate that they are archives, with a link provided to the current page. Webmasters: This problem is avoided by giving your pages names like "guidelines.html" or "contest.html" and keeping them updated, not adding a new page like "contest07spring.html" for each year that passes.

Lack of guidelines: some basic assumptions

In the absence of clear guidelines, any guidelines or instructions to the contrary, I assume these "standards" when submitting to journals:

The journal . . .

- reads submissions year-round.
- considers simultaneous submissions, but not previously published poems.
- accepts snail mail with SASE, or e-mail with poems pasted into body of message.
- wants poems single-spaced, with name, address, telephone number, e-mail in upper-right corner.
- acquires first North American rights for accepted work.
- pays one contributor's copy for accepted work (print publications).
- publishes work within a year of acceptance.

Poets . . .

- may send five poems, any length.
- may send inquiry after six months if no response.
- should wait for response before submitting again.

A timely response

A few journals have a don't-call-us-we'll-call-you policy; I've even seen it stated that this process may take as long as two years, which is outrageous. A response time should always be specified. Poets should avoid submitting to any journal, press or competition that does not give a response time, or whose response time is longer than 6 months; plenty of markets have more congenial practices. Many journals are able to respond in less than a month; some in less than a week!

E-mail submissions and queries continue to be problematic. Spam filters block messages they shouldn't at both ends of the process. In the past, a distressingly large percentage of my e-mail submissions, or responses to my submissions, have not been received due to overenthusiastic spam filters and the vagaries of cyberspace. E-mail submissions appear to be becoming more reliable, but I still try to always request an immediate reply that my e-mail has been received. A number of sites have software that acknowledges receipt of submissions automatically; a few even specify when a response will be forthcoming.

A journal overwhelmed with submissions, and lacking sufficient staff, should take immediate steps to rectify the situation: close submissions temporarily; limit the submission period (David Baratier, the editor of *Pavement Saw*, says that his short submission window ensures that most submissions are sent at the proper time and are appropriate to the journal—as the guidelines are available *only* in the journal itself); or develop a more rapid triage method. As a means of saving trouble for both editors and poets, it seems perfectly appropriate to inform submitters that rejection can be inferred if no response is received within a stated time, *as long as this is clearly posted in the guidelines*. This solves some of those tedious lost-in-the-mail issues as well.

The simultaneous submission question

The whole simultaneous submission thing is puzzling. Many journals that consider simultaneous submissions require that these be identified, yet assure the poet that this affects neither the likelihood of acceptance nor the speed of the process—in which case, what's the point?

To reiterate, it's incumbent upon the poet to notify an editor *immediately* of an acceptance, if the same poem was submitted to more than one journal. What if another suitable opportunity arises *after* a poem is under consideration at a journal that allows simultaneous-submissions-if-identified? A sensible editorial policy is to assume that all submissions are simultaneous and expedite the selection process.

I feel that *not* allowing simultaneous submissions benefits journals with sluggish consideration practices. Journals with larger staffs, or who are able to devote more time to reading manuscripts, have an advantage here. Poets don't want to disappoint editors who are devoting their limited time to producing a good literary magazine. However, simultaneous submissions allow the journals with rapid turnaround to reap the benefit of quick decision-making, which is good for poets as well. Poets may want to consider submitting to journals that forbid simultaneous submissions *only* if their response time is extremely short—say two months or less.

When standards are ignored

When you encounter difficulties with editorial practices that cannot be resolved through courteous correspondence, posting the information on a blog or Listserv—and notifying *Poet's Market*—will benefit your fellow poets and may improve that editor's practices. (For more on poet-editor relationships, see "Mistakes Poets Make" on page 31 and "Dealing With Problem Editors" on page 33.)

INDUSTRY STANDARDS FOR CONTESTS

In the wake of Foetry.com, accusations of unethical behavior have been levied against both competitions and judges. While these charges appear to be justified in a number of cases, judges cannot necessarily recognize work they've previously seen, much less its context. (Nor can editors always do so. I once accidentally resubmitted some poems, unrevised, to a publication that had rejected them only a few months before—and one was accepted the second time around!)

Contest administrators may not be aware of inappropriate relationships between judges and entrants. Judges should be protected from inappropriate submissions, which they can't be expected to recognize reliably, by placing defined contractual obligations on entrants instead. This should include wording that obliges those who violate rules to pay legal expenses for the recovery of the prizes or their value in case of publication (and one hopes infractions would be nipped in the bud long before it came to that).

While industrious older judges may not remember every student they've ever taught, students certainly remember their instructors. The task of identifying a relationship with the judge that would preclude entering a competition ought to be placed on the entrant. That mandates naming the judge before the contest opens. At a level of competition where it would be disingenuous to pretend that blind judging could occur because of mutual familiarity, judging by a panel or jury becomes appropriate.

Other fields of endeavor strictly regulate allowable judge-competitor relationships. Why should poetry be different? In equestrian competitions, judges are named, and competitors are expected to determine their own eligibility. The governing entities police violations within their membership through internal fines, suspensions and expulsions; and they have no compunction about taking issues to civil or criminal court where legal transgressions are involved. Even nonmember competitions use the same schematic to enforce adherence. Rules forbid entering a competition under a judge with whom there has been any financial or tutelary relationship within a stated time period. Similar, concrete rules should be formulated for poetry contests.

Many contests already require entry forms and signed agreements. Although the latter generally are meant to deal with plagiarism and copyright rather than eligibility factors, there is no reason why contests can't demand affirmation from an entrant that there is no improper relationship with the judge. This facilitates enforcement; obtaining goods and services by fraud is illegal, whereas it may be difficult to prove direct material benefit to the judge involved.

Perhaps there are judges who are capable of considering, absolutely objectively, a manuscript by a poet with whom they have a relationship. However, suppose that manuscript is really the best, and wins. What happens is this: Most poets, despite assurances, will no longer believe in the integrity of the judge, the winning poet or the contest administration. As the CLMP monograph *Publishing Contests* points out, *". . . the appearance of unethical behavior often produces as many problems as actual breaches of ethics."*

Evaluating contests

The following standards can be used to evaluate the integrity of a contest a poet wishes to enter:

Named judge. As I discuss above, naming a judge before a contest opens enables entrants to determine previous relationships that might preclude entering a competition.

I think, however, that concern about preliminary readers is overkill. Assurance that any recognized manuscript at this level will be passed on to another reader should be sufficient. This is a triage stage, where obviously noncompetitive manuscripts can be weeded out. Where the total number of manuscripts is not excessive, having each reader pick their top 10%, and then sending those selections to the final judge, ensures a more diverse group of finalists.

Blind judging. This should go without saying. Note that *blind* judging means no poets' names appear on manuscripts; *anonymous* judging means the judge is not identified by name.

Appropriate entry fee. A consistent ratio of prize money-to-entry fee exists among reputable competitions. Contests with entry fees of more than 2% of the prize money are suspect, unless the fee entitles the entrant to a significant benefit (such as a copy of the winning book, a journal subscription, a really cool T-shirt or other premium, etc.) Given how little remuneration is available to poets where their art is concerned, charities ought to be seeking out more lucrative prey for fund-raising. No journal or press should charge a reading fee solely to consider a manuscript for publication.

Entrant limitations. Specify who may not enter a given contest: e.g., students or friends of the judge; faculty; publication staff; or family members of the preceding. The Academy of American Poets, for its prestigious Walt Whitman Award, puts it this way: *"Poets are not eligible to apply if they are close friends or colleagues, were mentored by the judge, or have studied with the judge in full-time accredited courses within the last five years."*

Consistent, appropriate standards for eligibility and time limitations should be drafted; e.g., workshop/conference student, okay; undergrad student, one year; graduate student, five years, degree advisee, 10 years. Constraints like these are reasonable, in terms of both records accessibility and the vagaries of human memory.

Format. Normally, one print copy of manuscript, single-spaced, name on cover sheet only.

Response time. As with journal submissions, there is no reason not to give a projected response date. Surely no contest would hire a judge without imposing a deadline. Naming a date by which results will be available reassures competitors as to the competence of the contest administration and encourages entries. Allow an extra month when announcing response times; competitors will be impressed when they receive results early!

Entrant responsibilities

Do not enter contests where your manuscript's eligibility, your eligibility or your relationship with the judge can be questioned—it's not fair to embarrass the judge with an unwelcome discovery after the results have been announced. Bear in mind that the more insignificant the contest, the more likelihood that petty quarrels will arise over its adjudication.

Do not enter work that has already won a contest, or placed and won a monetary prize. While generally an unspoken rule, it is universally agreed that, unless specifically mentioned, prize-winning work cannot be submitted to other contests.

Never inquire about the status of your submission before the stated response time has elapsed. Failure to respect notification dates is one reason many contests and journals are reluctant to provide access by other than snail mail.

Judge responsibilities

Judge entries promptly and meet deadlines as agreed upon. Immediately notify the contest administrator regarding any violation of contest regulations; e.g., identified manuscripts, recognition of a student's or friend's work, contact by a competitor, etc.

Administrative responsibilities

Hire judges and announce their names well before the contest opens. Clearly state entrant eligibility constraints. Ensure that sufficient staff is available to deal with submissions, and that the judge will furnish a decision on time. Announce results promptly.

As mentioned earlier, keep online guidelines up-to-date and remove older announcements and rules from the site. Most contests prefer not to receive the bulk of their entries right at the deadline; posting guidelines well in advance will encourage early entries.

It should always be possible to make inquiries—and get rapid answers, preferably via a current, working e-mail address or phone number. It's also in the contest's best interests for entrants to be able to contact them immediately—and get confirmation back—in case of a manuscript being accepted elsewhere.

Contests that cash entry-fee checks promptly should be equally well organized in sending out results. Sadly, this is not the norm. When I received results within less than two weeks from *Compass Rose*'s Pat Parnell Poetry Contest, the turnaround was so rapid as to make me question the process (especially since the rejection slip did not mention the contest). Professor Jean Monroe, the contest administrator, was kind enough to set me straight: a week after the deadline, the journal's staff spent three hours narrowing one hundred entries to five for the consideration of the final judge. Another team considered entries for publication in the journal. All entries not selected as finalists or for publication were promptly sent rejection slips.

Professor Monroe stated, "We believe it is important to send notification as quickly as we can. This way those who aren't accepted for the upcoming issue can continue to send those pieces out." This is both courteous and commendably efficient; I will certainly enter that competition again. *Never* assume that your poems were not given due consideration because of a quick response.

HAVING AN IMPACT

The CLMP Code of Ethics is important. However, CLMP is an organization of presses and publishers, not writers. Perhaps the time has come to form an organization of poets—or to pressure existing organizations to exert themselves—to agitate for specific journal submission and contest standards. Editors impose standards by making policies for their journals; poets are in a position to create standards as well, by refusing to submit to shoddily run or unethical journals or competitions.

Mistakes Poets Make

In putting together listings for *Poet's Market*, we ask editors for any words of advice they want to share with our readers. Often the editors' responses include comments about what poets should and shouldn't do when submitting work—the same comments, over and over. That means a lot of poets are repeating similar mistakes when they send out their poems for consideration.

The following list includes the most common of those mistakes—the ones poets should work hardest to avoid.

Not reading a publication before submitting work

Researching a publication is essential before submitting your poetry. Try to buy a sample copy of a magazine (by mail, if necessary) or at least see if an issue is available at the library. It may not be economically feasible for poets to purchase a copy of every magazine they target, especially if they send out a lot of poems. However, there are additional ways to familiarize youself with a publication.

Read the market listing thoroughly. If guidelines are available, send for them by e-mail or regular mail, or check for them online. A publication's Web site often presents valuable information, including sample poems, magazine covers—and guidelines.

Submitting inappropriate work

Make good use of your research so you're sure you understand what a magazine publishes. Don't rationalize that a journal favoring free verse might jump at the chance to consider your long epic poem in heroic couplets. Don't convince yourself your experimental style will be a good fit for the traditional journal filled with rhyming poetry. Don't go into denial about whether a certain journal and your poetry are made for each other. It's counterproductive and ultimately wastes postage (not to mention time—yours and the editor's).

Submitting an unreasonable number of poems

If an editor recommends sending three to five poems (a typical range), don't send six. Don't send a dozen poems and tell the editor to pick the five she wants to consider. If the editor doesn't specify a number (or the listing says "no limit"), don't take that as an invitation to mail off 20 poems. The editors and staff of literary magazines are busy enough as it is, and they may decide they don't have time to cope with you. (When submitting book or chapbook manuscripts to publishers, make sure your page count falls within the range they state.)

Don't go to the other extreme and send only *one* poem, unless an editor says it's okay (which is rare). One poem doesn't give an editor much of a perspective on your work, and it doesn't give you very good odds on getting the piece accepted.

Ignoring the editor's preferences regarding formats

If an editor makes a point of describing a preferred manuscript format, follow it, even if that format seems to contradict the standard. (Standard format includes using $8\frac{1}{2} \times 11$ white paper and conventional typeface and point size; avoid special graphics, colors or type flourishes; put your name and address on every page.) Don't devise your own format to make your submission stand out. Keep everything clean, crisp and easy to read (and professional).

Be alert to e-mail submission formats. Follow directions regarding what the editor wants printed in the subject line, how many poems to include in a single e-mail, whether to use attachments or paste work in the body of the message, and other elements. Editors have good reasons for outlining their preferences; ignoring them could mean having your e-mail deleted before your poems are even read.

Omitting a self-addressed stamped envelope (SASE)

Why do editors continuously say "include a SASE with your submission"? Because so many poets don't do it. Here's a simple rule: Unless the editor gives alternate instructions, include a #10 SASE, whether submitting poems or sending an inquiry.

Writing bad cover letters (or omitting them completely)

Cover letters have become an established part of the submission process. There are editors who remain indifferent about the necessity of a cover letter, but many consider it rude to be sent a submission without any other communication from the poet.

Unless the editor says otherwise, send a cover letter. Keep it short and direct, a polite introduction of you and your work. (See pages 13-14 in "Frequently Asked Questions" for more tips on cover letters, and an example.) Here are a few important Don'ts:

- **Don't** list all the magazines where your work has appeared; limit yourself to five magazine titles. The work you're submitting has to stand on its own.
- **Don't** tell the editor what a good poet you are—or how good someone else thinks you are.
- **Don't** tell the editor how to edit, lay out or print your poem. Some of those decisions are up to the editor, assuming she decides to accept your poem in the first place.
- **Don't** point out the poem is copyrighted in your name or include the copyright symbol. All poems are automatically copyrighted in the poet's name as soon as they're "fixed" (i.e., written down), and editors know this.

Not maintaining good editor/poet relations

Most editors are hard-working poetry lovers dedicated to finding and promoting good work. They aspire to turn submissions around as quickly as possible and to treat all poets with respect. They don't want to steal your work. Often they aren't paid for their labor and may even have to dip into their own pockets just to keep their magazines going.

Poets should finesse their communications with editors regarding problems, especially in initial letters and e-mail. Editors (and their magazines and presses) aren't service-oriented businesses, like the phone company. Getting huffy with an editor as if arguing with your cable provider about an overcharge is inappropriate. Attitude isn't going to get you anywhere; in fact, it could create additional obstacles.

That's not to say poets shouldn't feel exasperated when they're inconvenienced or ill treated. None of us likes to see our creations vanish, or to pay good money for something we're never going to receive (like a subscription or sample copy). However, exasperated is one thing; outraged is another. Too often poets go on the offensive with editors and make matters worse. Experts on how to complain effectively recommend you keep your cool and stay professional, no matter what kind of problem you're trying to work out.

For additional advice on editor/poet relations, see "Dealing With Problem Editors" on page 33.

Dealing With Problem Editors

There *are* problem editors out there, and we've all encountered them at one time or another. Some rip people off, prey on poets' desires to be published, or treat poets and their work with flagrant disregard. Fortunately, such editors are very much in the minority.

Now and then you may discover the disorganized editor or the overwhelmed editor; these two cause heartache (and heartburn) by closing up shop without returning manuscripts, or failing to honor paid requests for subscriptions and sample copies. More often than not, their transgressions are rooted in chaos and irresponsibility, not malicious intent. Frustrating as such editors are, they're not out to get you.

There are many instances, too, where larger circumstances are beyond an editor's control. For example, a college-oriented journal may be student-staffed, with editors changing each academic year. Funds for the journal may be cut unexpectedly by administration belt-tightening, or a grant could be cancelled. The editorial office may be moved to another part of the university. An exam schedule could impact a publishing schedule. All of these things cause problems and delays.

Then again, a literary journal may be a one-person, home-based operation. The editor may get sick or have an illness in the family. Her regular job may suddenly demand lots of overtime. There may be divorce or death with which the editor has to cope. A computer could crash. Or the editor may need to scramble for money before the magazine can go to the printer. Emergencies happen, and they take their toll on deadlines. The last thing the editor wants is to inconvenience poets and readers, but sometimes life gets in the way.

Usually, difficulties with these kinds of "problem" editors can be resolved satisfactorily through communication and patience. There are always exceptions, though. Here are a few typical situations with problem editors and how to handle them:

An editor is rude. If it's a matter of bad attitude, take it with a grain of salt. Maybe he's having a rotten day. If there's abusive language and excessive profanity involved, let us know about it. (See the complaint procedure on page 34.)

An editor harshly criticizes your poem. If an editor takes time to comment on your poetry, even if the feedback seems overly critical, consider the suggestions with an open mind and try to find something valid and useful in them. If, after you've given the matter fair consideration, you think the editor was out of line, don't rush to defend your poetry or wave your bruised ego in the editor's face. Allow that the editor has a right to her opinion (which you're not obligated to take as the final word on the quality of your work), forget about it and move on.

An editor is slow to respond to a submission. As explained above, there may be many

Articles & Information

reasons why an editor's response takes longer than the time stated in the market listing or guidelines. Allow a few more weeks to pass beyond the deadline, then write a polite inquiry to the editor about the status of your manuscript. (Include a SASE if sending by regular mail.) Understand an editor may not be able to read your letter right away if deadlines are pressing or if he's embroiled in a personal crisis. Try to be patient. If you haven't received a reply to your inquiry after a month or so, however, it's time for further action.

An editor won't return your manuscript. Decide whether you want to invest any more time in this journal or publisher. If you conclude you've been patient long enough, write a firm but professional letter to the editor withdrawing your manuscript from consideration. Request that the manuscript be returned; but know, too, a truly indifferent editor probably won't bother to send it back or reply in any way. Keep a copy of your withdrawal letter for your files, make a new copy of your manuscript and look for a better market.

Also, contact *Poet's Market* by letter or e-mail with details of your experience. We always look into problems with editors, although we don't withdraw a listing on the basis of a single complaint unless we discover further evidence of consistent misbehavior. We do, however, keep complaints on file and watch for patterns of unacceptable behavior from any specific market.

An editor takes your money. If you sent a check for a subscription or sample copy and you haven't received anything, review your bank statement to see if the check has been cashed. If it has, send the editor a query. Politely point out the editor has cashed your check, but you haven't yet received the material you were expecting. Give the editor the benefit of the doubt: An upcoming issue of a magazine could be running late, your subscription vould have been overlooked by mistake, or your copy could have been lost in transit or sent in error to the wrong address.

If your check has *not* been cashed, query the editor to see if your order was ever received. It may have been lost (in the mail or on the editor's desk), the editor may be holding several checks to cash at one time, or the editor may be waiting to cash checks until a tardy issue is finally published.

If you get an unsatisfactory response from the editor (or no response at all), wait a few weeks and try again. If the matter still isn't resolved, let us know about it. We're especially

Complaint Procedure

Important

If you feel you have not been treated fairly by a market listed in *Poet's Market*, we advise you to take the following steps:

- First, try to contact the market. Sometimes one phone call or letter can quickly clear up the matter. Document all your communications with the market.

- When you contact us with a complaint, provide the details of your submission, the date of your first contact with the market and the nature of your subsequent communication.

- We will file a record of your complaint and further investigate the market.

- The number and severity of complaints will be considered when deciding whether or not to delete a market from the next edition of *Poet's Market*.

interested in publishers who take money from poets but don't deliver the goods. Be sure to send us all the details of the transaction, plus copies of any correspondence (yours and the editor's). We can't pursue your situation in any legal way or act as mediator, but we can ban an unscrupulous publisher from *Poet's Market* and keep the information as a resource in case we get later complaints.

Should you continue trying to get your money back from such editors? That's your decision. If your loss is under $10 (say, for a subscription or sample copy), it might cost you less in the long run to let the matter go. And the fee for a ''stop payment'' order on a check can be hefty—possibly more than the amount you sent the editor in the first place. Yes, it's infuriating to be cheated, but sometimes fighting on principle costs more than it's worth.

If your monetary loss is significant (for instance, you shelled out a couple hundred dollars in a subsidy publishing agreement), consider contacting your state attorney general's office for advice about small claims court, filing a complaint and other actions you can take.

Is It a 'Con'?

Think Before You Trust

What is a "con"? Con is short for "confidence," an adjective defined by Webster's as "of, relating to, or adept at swindling by false promise," as in "confidence man" or "confidence game." While the publishing world is full of legitimate opportunities for poets to gain honor and exposure for their work, there are also plenty of "cons." How can you tell the difference? The following are some of the most common situations that cost poets disappointment, frustration—and cash. Learn to spot them before submitting your work, and don't let your vanity be your guide.

ANTHOLOGIES

Has this happened to you? You see an ad in a perfectly respectable publication announcing a poetry contest with big cash prizes. You enter, and later you receive a glowing letter congratulating you on your exceptional poem, which the contest sponsor wants to include in his deluxe hardbound anthology of the best poetry submitted to the contest. The anthology costs only, say, $65. You don't have to buy it—they'll still publish your poem—but wouldn't you be proud to own one? And wouldn't it be nice to buy additional copies to give to family and friends? And for an extra charge you can include a biographical note. And so on . . .

Of course, when the anthology arrives, the quality of the poetry may not be what you were expecting, with several poems crammed unattractively onto a page. Apparently everyone who entered the contest was invited to be published; you basically paid cash to see your poem appear in a phone book-like volume with no literary merit whatsoever.

Were you conned? Depends on how you look at it. If you bought into the flattery and believed you were being published in an exclusive, high-quality publication, no doubt you feel duped. On the other hand, if all you were after was seeing your poem in print, even knowing you'd have to pay for the privilege, then you got what you wanted. (Unless you've deceived yourself into believing you've truly won an honor and now have a worthy publishing credit; you don't).

If you don't want to add insult to injury, resist additional spiels, like having your poem printed on coffee mugs and t-shirts (you can do this yourself through print shops or online services like www.cafepress.com) or spending large sums on awards banquets and conferences. And, before you submit a single line of poetry, find out what rights the contest sponsor acquires. You may be relinquishing all rights to your poem simply by mailing it in or submitting it through a Web site. If the poem no longer belongs to you, the publisher can do whatever he wishes with it. Don't let your vanity propel you into a situation you'll always regret.

READING AND CONTEST FEES

Suppose you notice a promising market for your poetry, but the editor requires a set fee just to consider your work. Or you see a contest that interests you, but you have to pay the sponsor a fee just to enter. Are you being conned?

In the case of reading fees, keep these points in mind: Is the market so exceptional that you feel it's worth risking the cost of the reading fee to have your work considered? What makes it so much better than markets that do *not* charge fees? Has the market been around awhile, with an established publishing schedule? What are you paid if your work is accepted? Are reasonably priced samples available so you can judge the production values and quality of the writing?

Reading fees don't necessarily signal a suspicious market. In fact, they're increasingly popular as editors struggle with the costs of publishing books and magazines, including the man-hours required to read loads of (often bad) submissions. However, fees represent an additional financial burden on poets, who often don't receive any monetary reward for their poems to begin with. It's really up to individual poets to decide whether paying a fee is beneficial to their publishing efforts. Think long and hard about fee-charging markets that are new and untried, don't pay poets for their work (at the very least a print publication should offer a contributor's copy), charge high prices for sample copies or set fees that seem unreasonable.

Entry fees for contests often fund prizes, judges' fees, honorariums and expenses of running and promoting the contest (including publishing a "prize" collection or issue of a magazine). Other kinds of contests charge entry fees, from Irish dancing competitions to bake-offs at a county fair. Why not poetry contests?

That's not to say you shouldn't be cautious. Watch out for contests that charge higher-than-average fees, especially if the fees are out of proportion to the amount of prize money being given. (Look through the Contests & Awards section beginning on page 356 to get a sense of what most competitions charge; you'll also find contests in other sections of this book by consulting the Additional Contests & Awards index on page 415.) Find out how long the contest has been around, and verify whether prizes have been awarded each year and to whom. In the case of book and chapbook contests, send for one of the winning publications to confirm that the publisher puts out a quality product. Regard with skepticism any contest that tells you you've won something, then demands payment for an anthology, trophy or other item. (It's okay if a group offers an anthology for a modest price without providing winners with free copies. Most state poetry societies have to do this; but they also present cash awards in each category of the contest, and their entry fees are low.)

SUBSIDY PUBLISHERS, PRINT-ON-DEMAND

Poetry books are a hard sell to the book-buying public. Few of the big publishers handle these books, and those that do feature the "name" poets (i.e., the major prize winners and contemporary masters with breathtaking reputations). Even the small presses publish only so many books per year—far less than the number of poets writing.

No wonder so many poets decide to pay to have their poetry collections published. While some may self-publish (i.e., take full control of their book, working directly with a printer), others turn to subsidy publishers (also called "vanity publishers") and print-on-demand (POD) publishers.

There are many differences between subsidy publishing and POD publishing, as well as similarities (having to pay to get published is a big one). Whether or not you get conned is entirely up to you. *You* have to take responsibility for asking questions, doing research on presses, and reading the fine print on the contract to make sure you know exactly what you're paying for. There are landmines in dealing with subsidy and POD publishers, and you have to investigate thoroughly and intelligently to avoid damage.

Some questions to keep in mind: Are fees inflated compared to the product and services you'll be receiving? Will you still own the rights to your book? Does the publisher put out a quality product that's attractive and cleanly printed? (Get a sample copy and find out.) How many copies of the book will you receive? How much will you have to pay for additional copies? How will your book be sold and distributed? (Don't count on seeing your volume in bookstores.)

Will you receive royalties? How much? Does the publisher offer any kind of promotional assistance or is it all up to you? Will those promotion efforts be realistic and results-oriented? (Sometimes "promotion" means sending out review copies, which is a waste—such volumes are rarely reviewed.) Don't wait until *after* you've signed a contract (and a check) to raise these issues. Do your homework first.

Obviously, poets who don't stay on their toes may find themselves preyed upon. And a questionable publishing opportunity doesn't have to be an out-and-out rip-off for you to feel cheated. In every situation, you have a choice *not* to participate. Exercise that choice, or at least develop a healthy sense of skepticism before you fling yourself and your poetry at the first smooth talker who compliments your work. Poets get burned because they're much too impatient to see their work in print. Calm your ego, slow down and devote that time, energy and money toward reading other poets and improving your own writing. You'll find that getting published will eventually take care of itself.

Helpful Web sites

For More Info

The following Web sites include specific information about questionable poetry publishers and awards. For more Web sites of value to poets, see Additional Resources on page 463.

- An Incomplete Guide to Print On Demand Publishers offers articles on POD publishing, comparisons of POD publishers (contracts, distribution, fees, etc.) and an online forum: *http://booksandtales.com/pod/index.php*

- Answers to frequently asked questions about poetry awards from the Academy of American Poets: *www.poets.org/page.php/prmID/116*

- Poets will find warnings and other valuable publishing information on the Preditors & Editors Web site: *www.anotherealm.com/prededitors/*

- Writer Beware tracks contests, publishers and literary agents: *www.sfwa.org/beware*

- "Literary Contest Caution" at *http://windpub.com/literary.scams*

Promote Your Work

Attracting Readers Is Up to You

These days, all writers have to promote themselves and their work in order to attract readers. This is especially true for poets. Does the idea of "putting yourself out there" make you uncomfortable? Think of self-promotion as a means of sharing poetry as well as promoting it. Here are a few suggestions to get you started:

Meet the public.

Do poetry readings and book signings. Get in touch with bookstores and coffeehouses: call, send postcards (see below) or press releases, let them know you're available. Find out when and where open mic readings are scheduled. Sign up, read your poems. If you've published a book or chapbook, be creative about handselling your collection. It's hard to break into the big chain bookstores, but independent stores may be happy to stock your publication (especially if you're a local author) and arrange a book signing.

Widen your scope: Would the local historical society be interested in an appearance? Is there a community group who might enjoy having you read and sign books as part of their meeting program? Would a friend be willing to sponsor a "poetry night" house party with you as the featured reader?

Create poetry postcards.

Think specially designed postcards, not the plain ones you buy at the post office. You can create postcards on your computer, or paste up a master design from typewritten copy and clip art. (You could even use rubber stamps to dress up a plain printed card.) If you design the postcards on your computer, you can print them out yourself as well. (Special perforated postcard stock for home printers is available in various sizes at your local office supply store.) Or you can take your master design to a quick print shop and have the postcards printed there. (If you're printing a lot of postcards, this might be the less expensive option.)

Postcards can be informational (i.e., used to announce a reading or new publication), but they can also be used to share your poetry. Simply type one of your poems on one side of the card, using an attractive, readable font. Leave the other side blank; or, if the poem is from a book or chapbook you want to promote, indicate the title of the collection and include ordering information. Keep all text and design elements on the far left side of the postcard back so they don't interfere with the addressee portion of the card.

Postcard mailings get results, but remember that postcards don't have to be mailed to be effective. Don't be shy about giving out postcards at readings, especially your poem postcards. Offer to sign them. Your audience will enjoy having a personalized souvenir of your reading, and they may decide later to order your book or chapbook.

Use poetry postcards for personal communications, too. Turn a simple note into a chance to enhance someone's day with poetry.

Step into the media spotlight.

It doesn't have to be a *big* spotlight. Your community newspaper probably prints "news-maker" tidbits like award and publication announcements, and it may even be interested in doing a feature on a "local poet." (Regional magazines are another possibility.) Newspapers usually have calendar sections where you can list a reading or bookstore appearance. (Be sure to provide all the necessary details.) TV and radio stations may also broadcast arts and entertainments calendars, and locally produced programs may be very happy to schedule a poet for an interview segment or to promote a reading. You never know until you ask. (Be polite, never pushy.)

Create a Web site. Start a blog.

It's helpful to have a URL to list on press releases, business cards and postcards. A Web site or blog is a shortcut for anyone who wants to know more about you, from biographical information to samples of your poetry. Your "place on the Web" can be as complicated or as simple as you wish. There are plenty of books and software programs available to help, even if you're a first-timer with few computer skills. There's also a lot of free information on the Web, including free blog-hosting sites that make it easy to become a "poet-blogger." (For more information and perspectives on blogging, see "Roundtable: Poets and Blogs" on page 19.)

Whether you try these approaches or come up with some new, creative techniques of your own, don't hesitate to promote yourself and your work. Every reading, book signing, interview, and Web site is an opportunity to attract new readers to poetry.

Important Market Listing Information

Important

- Listings are based on questionnaires completed by editors, and on subsequent verified copy. Listings are not advertisements, *nor* are markets necessarily endorsed by the editors of this book.

- Information in the listings comes directly from the publishers and is as accurate as possible. However, publications and editors come and go, and poetry needs fluctuate between the publication date of this directory and the date of purchase.

- If you are a poetry publisher and would like to be considered for a listing in the next edition, e-mail us at poetsmarket@fwpubs.com or send a SASE (or SAE and IRC) to *Poet's Market*—QR, 4700 East Galbraith Road, Cincinnati OH 45236. Questionnaires and questionnaire requests received after February 7, 2008, will be held for the 2010 edition.

- *Poet's Market* reserves the right to exclude any listing that does not meet its requirements.

Magazines/ Journals

Literary magazines and journals usually provide a poet's first publishing success. In fact, you shouldn't be thinking about book/chapbook publication until your poems have appeared in a variety of magazines, journals and zines (both print and online). This is the preferred way to develop an audience, build publishing credits and learn the ins and outs of the publishing process.

In this section you'll find hundreds of magazines and journals that publish poetry. They range from small black-and-white booklets produced on home computers to major periodicals with high production values and important reputations. To help you sort through these markets and direct your submissions most effectively, we've organized information in each listing according to a basic format.

HOW LISTINGS ARE FORMATTED

Content of each market listing was provided or verified by a representative of the publication (editor, poetry editor, managing editor, etc.). Here is how that content is arranged within the listing:

Symbols. Icons at the beginning of each listing offer visual signposts to specific information about the publication: (ⓝ) this market is recently established and new to *Poet's Market*; (★) this market did not appear in the 2007 edition; (▣) this market publishes primarily online (although it may also produce an annual print version or a "best of" anthology); (⛁) this market is located in Canada or (⊕) outside the U.S. and Canada; ($) this market pays a monetary amount (as opposed to contributor's copies); (○) this market welcomes submissions from beginning poets; (◨) this market prefers submissions from skilled, experienced poets, will consider work from beginning poets; (◐) this market prefers submissions from poets with a high degree of skill and experience; (◎) this market has a specialized focus (listed in parentheses after magazine/journal title); (⊘) this market does not consider unsolicited submissions; and (⊘) this market is closed to *all* submissions. (Keys to these symbols are listed on the inside covers of this book and on page 6.)

Contact information. Depending on what was provided by each editor, contact information includes: magazine/journal title (in bold) with areas of specialization noted in parentheses where appropriate; regular mail address; telephone number; fax number; e-mail address; Web site address; year the publication was established; the name of the person to contact (or an editorial title); and membership in small press/publishing organizations. (**Note:** If a magazine/journal publishes only online and/or wants submissions by e-mail exclusively, no street address may be given.)

Magazine Needs. It's important to study this section as you research potential markets.

Here you'll find such helpful information as the editor's overview of the publication, with individual poetry needs and preferences; a list of recently published poets; production information (number of pages, printing/binding details, type of cover); the number of poetry submissions the publication receives vs. the number accepted; and press run, distribution and price information.

How to Submit. This section focuses on the specific details of submitting work: how many poems to send; minimum/maximum number of lines per poem; whether previously published poems or simultaneous submissions are considered; submission format preferences (including whether to submit by e-mail, and how); response times; payment; rights acquired and more.

Additional Information. Editors may use this section to explain other publishing activities, elaborate on some aspect of the magazine/journal, suggest future plans—anything beyond the basic details that readers may find of interest.

Contest/Award Offerings. This section discusses prizes and competitions associated with the publication, with either brief guidelines or a cross-reference to a separate listing in the Contests & Awards section.

Also Offers. Describes additional offerings associated with this publication (i.e., sponsored readings, Web site activities such as blogs and forums, related poetry groups, etc.).

Advice. Provides direct quotes from editors about everything from pet peeves to tips on writing to perspectives on the state of poetry today.

GETTING STARTED, FINDING MARKETS

If you don't have a certain magazine or journal in mind, read randomly through the listings, making notes as you go. (Don't hesitate to write in the margins, underline, use highlighters; it also helps to flag markets that interest you with Post-It Notes). Browsing the listings is an effective way to familiarize yourself with the kind of information presented and the publishing opportunities that are available at various skill levels.

If you have a specific market in mind, however, begin with the General Index. Here all the book's listings are alphabetized along with additional references that may be buried within a listing (such as an press name or competition title). Also, markets from the 2007 edition that don't appear in this book are included in the General Index, accompanied by a two-letter code explaining the market's absence (a key to these codes appears at the beginning of the General Index). Furthermore, publications that have changed names since the 2007 edition are listed in the General Index, cross-referenced to the new titles.

REFINE YOUR SEARCH

To supplement the General Index, we provide the following indexes to help you refine your marketing plan for submitting your poems to publications. Not every listing appears in one of these indexes, so use them only to reinforce your other research efforts:

Openness to Submissions Index categorizes markets according to the icons (☐ ◐ ◑ ◉) that appear at the beginning of each listing—signposts that indicate the level of writing an editor prefers to see. (For an explanation of these symbols, see page 6, the inside covers of this book or the handy tear-out bookmark just inside the front cover.)

Geographical Index sorts magazines and journals by state or by countries outside the U.S. Some markets are more open to poets from their respective regions, so this index is helpful when pinpointing local opportunities.

Subject Index groups markets according to areas of special focus. These include all specialized markets (appearing with the ◉ symbol) as well as broader categories such as online markets, poetry for children, markets that consider translations and others. When you want to submit a poem that features a certain topic or theme, is written in a specific form or style or addresses a unique audience, check this index first.

THE NEXT STEP

Once you know how to interpret the listings in this section and identify markets for your work, the next step is to start submitting your poems. See "Getting Started (and Using This Book)" on page 4 and "Frequently Asked Questions" on page 9 for advice, guidelines for preparing your manuscript and proper submissions procedures.

ADDITIONAL FEATURES

The Magazines/Journals section includes six Insider Reports that cover a wide range of artists and topics: Amy Ratto Parks interviews poet **Anne Marie Macari** about the relationship of motherhood and myth to her work; poet **Jane K. Kretschmann** offers advice on how to make your "second rate" poems first rate; **Brian Daldorph** discusses how poetry empowers a group of prison inmates; **Donya Dickerson** conducts a roundtable discussion of online poetry communities with poets who oversee and participate in those communities; **Christine Swanberg** offers perspectives on how to live the well-imagined life; and Erika O'Connell talks to poet **Hank Hudepohl** about poetry and connections.

This section also includes the covers of 10 literary magazines that reflect the range of print publications being produced today. Such images tell a lot about a publication's style and content, as do the comments by editors regarding the cover images and why they were selected. (When evaluating a potential market for your work, consider everything about the magazine or journal: the style and quality of content, the kinds of poets the magazine favors, submissions guidelines, editorial comments, cover art and even ads.)

☑ ⓞ **THE AARDVARK ADVENTURER (Specialized: light verse; humor; subscribers given preference)**

Pickle Gas Press, 31 Rolling Meadows Way, Penfield NY 14526. (585)388-6968. E-mail: bypaul@net acc.net. Established 1996. **Contact:** Paul Agosto, editor.

Magazine Needs *The Aardvark Adventurer*, published 3 times/year, is "a family-fun digest-style zine of humor, thought, and verse. Very short stories (less than 500 words) are sometimes included." Wants "light, brief humorous verse; any style; any 'family-acceptable' subject matter." Does not want anything "obscene, overly forboding; no graphic gore or violence." Has published poetry by Paul Humphrey, Ray Gallucci, and Max Gutmann. *The Aardvark Adventurer* is 12 pages, digest-sized, photocopied, saddle-stapled. Receives about 500 poems/year, accepts about 40%. Press run is 150 (100 subscribers). Single copy: $4; subscription: $8. Make checks payable to Paul Agosto. **"Subscription not required, but subscribers given preference."**

How to Submit Lines/poem: 16 maximum. Considers previously published poems and simultaneous submissions, if indicated. Accepts e-mail submissions (pasted into body of message). Cover letter is preferred. Time between acceptance and publication is up to 9 months. Seldom comments on rejected poems. Occasionally publishes theme issues. Guidelines available for SASE. Responds in 2 months. Pays one contributor's copy. Acquires one-time rights.

Advice "*The Aardvark Adventurer*, a digest-style publication with a very playful format, is a perfect opportunity for the aspiring poet."

☐ ☑ **ABBEY**

5360 Fallriver Row Court, Columbia MD 21044. E-mail: greisman@aol.com. Established 1970. **Contact:** David Greisman, editor.

Magazine Needs *Abbey*, published quarterly online, is "a more-or-less informalzine looking for poetry that does for the mind what the first sip of Molson Ale does for the palate." Does not want "pornography or politics." Has published poetry by Richard Peabody, Ruth Moon Kempher, Carol Hamilton, Harry Calhoun, Wayne Hogan, and Edmund Conti. *Abbey* is usually 20-26 pages, magazine-sized, photocopied, and held together with one low-alloy metal staple in the top left corner. Receives about 1,000 poems/year, accepts about 150. Press run is 200. Subscription: $2. Sample: 50¢.

How to Submit Responds in one month "except during baseball season." Pays 1-2 contributor's copies.

Additional Information Abbey Cheapochapbooks come out once or twice every 5 years, averaging 10-15 pages. For chapbook consideration, query with 4-6 sample poems, bio, and list of publications. Responds in 2 months "including baseball season." Pays 25-50 author's copies.

Advice "I'm definitely seeing poetry from two schools—the nit'n'grit school and the textured/reflective school. I much prefer the latter."

☒ ☐ ☑ **ABRAMELIN, THE JOURNAL OF POETRY AND MAGICK**

P.O. Box 337, Brookhaven NY 11719. E-mail: nessaralindaran@aol.com. Web site: www.abramelin .net. Established 2006. **Contact:** Vanessa Kittle, editor.

Magazine Needs *Abramelin, the Journal of Poetry and Magick*, published quarterly online, offers "literary poetry and essays concerning the western esoteric traditions." Wants "poetry that shows rather than tells. Poems that make me jealous of the writer. Poems that are inspired with wonderful language and imagery. In short—literature. Poetry submissions needn't be about magick at all. I feel that real poetry is magick. In fact, poetry that is literally magickal in theme has to be twice as good." Does not want "rhyming poems. Very short fiction. But beware, I learned from the best." Considers poetry by teens. Has published poetry by Simon Perchik, Rich Kostelanetz, and Lyn Lifshin. *Abramelin* receives about 1,000 poems/year, accepts about 5%. Distributed free online. Number of unique visitors: 3,000/issue.

How to Submit Submit 1-5 poems at a time. Lines/poem: no minimum/maximum. Considers previously published poems and simultaneous submissions (with notification). Accepts e-mail (pasted into body of message) and disk submissions. Cover letter is preferred. Reads submissions year round. Submit seasonal poems 2 months in advance. Time between acceptance and publication is 1-3 months. Often comments on rejected poems. Sometimes publishes theme issues. Upcoming themes available in magazine or on Web site. Guidelines available by e-mail or on Web site. Responds in one month. Pays one contributor's copy. Acquires one-time rights, with option to include in a yearly print anthology. Rights revert to poets upon publication.

Additional Information Publishes an annual print anthology—40 pages, digest-sized, professionally printed, perfect-bound, with glossy full color cover. Single copy: $9.50. Make checks payable to Vanessa Kittle.

Contest/Award Offerings "Beginning in 2007, we will publish one chapbook per year through our annual contest." Prize is 20 author copies. Submit between 20 and 30 pages of poetry. **Entry fee:** $15. **Deadline:** December 1. Winner announced December 31.

Advice "Bring the reader into the moment. Be as specific as possible."

☐ ◎ THE ACORN (Specialized: young authors)

1530 Seventh St., Rock Island IL 61201. (309)788-3980. Established 1988. **Contact:** Betty Mowery, poetry editor.

Magazine Needs *The Acorn*, published quarterly, is a "publication for young authors, as well as teachers or anyone else interested in our young authors." Considers poetry and fiction from children and teens in grades K-12. "Young authors submitting to *The Acorn* should put either age or grade on manuscripts." Accepts well over half of submitted mss. Press run is 100 (6 libraries). Subscription: $10. Sample: $3. Make all checks payable to *The Oak*.

How to Submit Submit 5 poems at a time. Lines/poem: 35 maximum. Considers previously published poems and simultaneous submissions. Include SASE with all submissions. Responds in one week. "*The Acorn* does not pay in dollars or copies, but you need not purchase to be published." Acquires first or second rights. All rights revert to poet upon publication.

Contest/Award Offerings Sponsors numerous poetry contests. Guidelines available for SASE.

▣ ◪ THE ADIRONDACK REVIEW

521 56th St., 2F, Brooklyn NY 11220. E-mail: diane@blacklawrencepress.com. (inquiries); tarpoetry @blacklawrencepress.com. (submissions). Web site: www.adirondackreview.homestead.com. Established 2000. **Contact:** Diane Goettel, editor.

Magazine Needs *The Adirondack Review*, published quarterly online, is a literary journal dedicated to quality free verse poetry and short fiction as well as book and film reviews, art, photography, and interviews. "We are open to both new and established writers. Our only requirement is excellence. We would like to publish more French and German poetry translations as well as original poems in these languages. We publish an eclectic mix of voices and styles, but all poems should show attention to craft. We are open to beginners who demonstrate talent, as well as established voices. The work should speak for itself." Wants "well-crafted, thoughtful writing full of imagery." Does not want "religious, overly sentimental, horror/gothic, rhyming, greeting card, pet-related, humor, or science fiction poetry." Has published poetry by Bob Hicok, Timothy Liu, Lola Haskins, D.C. Berry, David Rigsbee, and Paul Guest. Accepts about 3-5% of poems submitted.

How to Submit Submit 2-7 poems at a time. Considers simultaneous submissions (with notification); no previously published poems. Accepts e-mail submissions only. "All submissions should be pasted into the body of an e-mail (no attached files, please). We no longer accept postal submissions. All postal submissions will be discarded unread." Cover letter is preferred. Reads submissions year round. Submit seasonal poems 3 months in advance. Time between acceptance and publication is 1-3 months. Seldom comments on rejected poems. Guidelines available on Web site.

Responds in one week to 4 months. Acquires first or one-time rights. Rights revert to poet upon publication. "We reserve the right to reprint the work in the event of a print-based anthology at a later date." Reviews books of poetry. Send materials for review consideration.

Contest/Award Offerings With Black Lawrence Press, offers The Fiddlehead Poetry Prize, to be awarded once each year for a previously unpublished poem. Winner receives $300 and publication in *The Adirondack Review*. Honorable Mention poems will also be published and receive an honorarium of $30. Accepts simultaneous submissions if notified immediately of acceptance elsewhere. Submit up to 3 original poems, unpublished in either print or on-line publications. **Submissions should be sent to fiddleheadprize@blacklawrencepress.com.** with poet's name, address, phone number, and e-mail address included. E-mail should be titled FIDDLEHEAD PRIZE SUBMISSION in subject line; poems must be pasted into body of message. Guidelines available by e-mail (from diane@blacklawrencepress.com) or on Web site. **Entry fee:** $5 for one poem, $8 for 2 poems, $10 for 3 poems. Make payment through Web site via PayPal. **Deadline:** May 1. Judges: *The Adirondack Review* editors. Winners announced during the summer.

Advice "Get your hands on all the good writing you can, including international, past, contemporary, Web-based, and print. Read much, write well, and send us what you love."

○ ADVOCATE, PKA'S PUBLICATION

1881 Little West Kill Rd., Prattsville NY 12468. (518)299-3103. Established 1987.

Magazine Needs *Advocate, PKA's Publication*, published bimonthly, is an advertiser-supported tabloid using "original, previously unpublished works, such as feature stories, essays, 'think' pieces, letters to the editor, profiles, humor, fiction, poetry, puzzles, cartoons, or line drawings." Wants "nearly any kind of poetry, any length. Poetry ought to speak to people and not be so oblique as to have meaning only to the poet. If I had to be there to understand the poem, don't send it. Also looking for horse-related poems, stories, drawings, and photos." Does not want "religious or pornographic poetry." Considers poetry by children and teens (when included with release form signed by adult). Accepts about 25% of poems received. Circulation is 10,000; all distributed free. Subscription: $16.50 (6 issues). Sample: $4 (includes guidelines).

How to Submit Submit any number of poems at a time. Lines/poem: open. No previously published poems or simultaneous submissions. "Please, no work that has appeared on the Internet." Submissions may be typed or legibly handwritten. "Send a SASE with your submission; no postcards, please." Time between acceptance and publication is up to 6 months. Occasionally comments on rejected poems. Responds in 2 months. Guidelines available with sample copy ($4). Pays 2 contributor's copies. Acquires first rights only.

Advice "Always looking for horse/equine-oriented works."

$☺ AGNI

Boston University, 236 Bay State Rd., Boston MA 02215. (617)353-7135. Fax: (617)353-7134. E-mail: agni@bu.edu. Web site: www.agnimagazine.org. Established 1972. **Contact:** Sven Birkerts, editor.

- Work published in *AGNI* has been included regularly in *The Best American Poetry* and *The Pushcart Prize*.

Magazine Needs *AGNI*, published semiannually, prints poetry, fiction, and essays "by both emerging and established writers. We publish quite a bit of poetry in forms as well as 'language' poetry, but we don't begin to try and place parameters on the 'kind of work' that *AGNI* selects." Wants readable, intelligent poetry—mostly lyric free verse (with some narrative and dramatic)—that somehow communicates tension or risk. Has published poetry by Adrienne Rich, Seamus Heaney, Maxine Scates, Rosanna Warren, Chinua Achebe, and Ha Jin. *AGNI* is typeset, offset-printed, perfect-bound. Circulation is 3,000 for subscriptions, mail orders, and bookstore sales. Subscription: $17. Sample: $10 ($12 for *30th Anniversary Poetry Anthology*).

How to Submit Submit no more than 5 poems at a time. Considers simultaneous submissions; no previously published poems. No e-mail submissions. Cover letter is required ("brief, sincere"). "No fancy fonts, gimmicks. Include SASE or e-mail address; no preformatted reply cards." Reads submissions September 1-May 31. Pays $10/page ($150 maximum), 2 contributor's copies, a one-year subscription, and 4 gift copies. Acquires first serial rights.

▣ ☑ AGNIESZKA'S DOWRY (AGD)

A Small Garlic Press (ASGP), 5445 N. Sheridan Rd., #3003, Chicago IL 60640. E-mail: marek@entera ct.com. and ketzle@ketzle.net. (send submissions to both e-mail addresses simultaneously). Web site: http://asgp.org. Established 1995. **Contact:** Marek Lugowski and katrina grace craig, co-editors.

Magazine Needs *Agnieszka's Dowry (AgD)* is "a magazine published both in print and as a permanent Internet installation of poems and graphics, letters to Agnieszka. The print version consists of professionally crafted chapbooks. The online version comprises fast-loading pages employing an intuitive, if uncanny, navigation in an interesting space, all conducive to fast and comfortable reading. No restrictions on form or type. We use contextual and juxtapositional tie-ins with other material in making choices, so **visiting the online** *AgD* or reading a chapbook of an *AgD* issue is required of anyone making a submission." Single copy: $2 plus $2 shipping, if ordered from Web site by an individual. Make checks payable to A Small Garlic Press.

How to Submit Submit 5-10 poems at a time. Accepts e-mail submissions **only** (**NOTE:** pasted into body of message in plain text, sent to both editors simultaneously; no attachments). "Prisoners may make submissions by regular mail, and we will waive the requirement that they read a print issue." Sometimes comments on rejected poems. Guidelines and annotated catalog available on Web site only. Responds by e-mail or SASE, usually within 2 months. Pays one contributor's copy. Acquires one-time rights where applicable.

Additional Information A Small Garlic Press (ASGP) publishes up to 3 chapbooks of poetry/year. Query with a full online ms, ASCII (plain text) only.

▢ THE AGUILAR EXPRESSION

1329 Gilmore Ave., Donora PA 15033. (724)379-8019. E-mail: xyz0@access995.com. (inquiries only). Web site: www.wordrunner.com/xfaguilar. Established 1986. **Contact:** Xavier F. Aguilar, editor/publisher.

Magazine Needs *The Aguilar Expression*, published semiannually in summer and winter, encourages "poetics that deal with now, which our readers can relate to. In publishing poetry, I try to exhibit the unique reality that we too often take for granted and acquaint as mediocre." Has published poetry by Martin Kich and Gail Ghai. *The Aguilar Expression* is 4-20 pages, 5×7, typeset, printed on 20 lb. paper. Receives about 10-15 poems/month, accepts about 10-15/year. Circulation is 200. Sample: $8. Make checks payable to Xavier Aguilar.

How to Submit Submit up to 3 poems at a time. Lines/poem: 30 maximum. No e-mail submissions. Cover letter is required (include writing background). SASE (for contact purposes) is required. Manuscripts should be submitted in clear, camera-ready copy. Submit copies, not originals; manuscripts will not be returned. "**We encourage all writers to send a SASE for writer's guidelines before submitting.**" Responds in 2 months. Pays 2 contributor's copies.

$ ▨ ◎ AIM MAGAZINE (Specialized: racial harmony & peace)

P.O. Box 390, Milton WA 90354-0390. E-mail: apiladoone@aol.com. Web site: www.aimmagazine. org. Established 1974. **Contact:** Ruth Apilado, poetry editor.

Magazine Needs *Aim Magazine*, published quarterly, is "dedicated to racial harmony and peace." Uses 3-4 poems ("poetry with social significance mainly") in each issue. Considers poetry by high school students. Has published poetry by J. Douglas Studer, Wayne Dowdy, Ned Pendergast, and

Maria DeGuzman. *Aim* is magazine-sized with glossy cover. Receives about 30 submissions/year, accepts about half. Press run is 10,000 (2,000 subscribers including the libraries of K-12 schools, colleges, and universities). Single copy: $5; subscription: $20.

How to Submit Considers simultaneous submissions. Lines/poem: 32 average. Publishes theme issues. Upcoming themes available for SASE. Guidelines available on Web site. Responds in 6 weeks. Pays $10/poem and one contributor's copy. Does not send an acceptance notice: "We simply send payment and magazine copy."

Advice "Read the work of published poets."

☑ ALASKA QUARTERLY REVIEW

University of Alaska Anchorage, 3211 Providence Dr., Anchorage AK 99508. Phone/fax: (907)786-6916. E-mail: ayaqr@uaa.alaska.edu. Web site: www.uaa.alaska.edu/aqr. Established 1981. **Contact:** Ronald Spatz, executive editor.

  • Poetry published in *Alaska Quarterly Review* has been selected for inclusion in *The Best American Poetry*, *Pushcart Prize*, and *Beacon's Best* anthologies.

Magazine Needs *Alaska Quarterly Review*, published in 2 double issues/year, is "devoted to contemporary literary art. We publish both traditional and experimental fiction, poetry, literary nonfiction, and short plays." Wants all styles and forms of poetry, "with the most emphasis perhaps on voice and content that displays 'risk,' or intriguing ideas or situations." Has published poetry by Maxine Kumin, Jane Hirshfield, David Lehman, Pattiann Rogers, Albert Goldbarth, and Billy Collins. *Alaska Quarterly Review* is 224-300 pages, digest-sized, professionally printed, perfect-bound, with card cover with color or b&w photo. Receives up to 5,000 submissions/year, accepts 40-90. Press run is 4,000 (500 subscribers, 32 libraries). Subscription: $10. Sample: $6.

How to Submit No fax or e-mail submissions. Reads submissions mid-August to mid-May; manuscripts are *not* read May 15-August 15. Responds in up to 4 months, "sometimes longer during peak periods in late winter." Pay depends on funding. Acquires first North American serial rights.

Additional Information Guest poetry editors have included Stuart Dybek, Jane Hirshfield, Stuart Dischell, Maxine Kumin, Pattiann Rogers, Dorianne Laux, Peggy Shumaker, Nancy Eimers, Michael Ryan, and Billy Collins.

☑ ◎ ALBATROSS (Specialized: environmental & nature poetry)

The Anabiosis Press, 2 S. New St., Bradford MA 01835. (978)469-7085. E-mail: rsmyth@anabiosispress.org. Web site: www.anabiosispress.org. **Contact:** Richard Smyth, editor.

Magazine Needs *Albatross*, published "as soon as we have accepted enough quality poems to publish an issue—about one per year," considers the albatross "to be a metaphor for the environment. The journal's title is drawn from Coleridge's *The Rime of the Ancient Mariner* and is intended to invoke the allegorical implications of that poem. This is not to say that we publish only environmental or nature poetry, but that we are biased toward such subject matter. We publish mostly free verse, and we prefer a narrative style." Wants "poetry written in a strong, mature voice that conveys a deeply felt experience or makes a powerful statement." Does not want "rhyming poetry, prose poetry, or haiku." Has published poetry by Mitchell LesCarbeau, Joan Colby, Simon Perchik, Jackie White, and Fredrick Zydek. *Albatross* is 28 pages, digest-sized, laser-typeset, with linen cover. Subscription: $8/2 issues. Sample: $5.

How to Submit Submit 3-5 poems at a time. Lines/poem: 200 maximum. No simultaneous submissions. Accepts e-mail submissions if included in body of message (but is "often quicker at returning mailed submissions"). Name and address must accompany e-mail submissions. Cover letter is not required. "We do, however, need bio notes and SASE for return or response. Poems should be typed single-spaced, with name, address, and phone number in upper left corner." Time between acceptance and publication is up to 6 months to a year. Guidelines available for SASE or on Web site. Responds in 1-2 months. Pays one contributor's copy. Acquires all rights. Returns rights provided that "previous publication in *Albatross* is mentioned in all subsequent reprintings."

Contest/Award Offerings The Anabiosis Press Chapbook Contest (see separate listing Contests & Awards).

Advice "We expect a poet to read as much contemporary poetry as possible. We want to be moved. When you read our poetry, we hope that it moves you in the same way that it moves us. We try to publish the kind of poetry that you would want to read again and again."

Cover art by Lynn De Turk; cover design by Richard Smyth.

Richard Smyth, editor and publisher of *Albatross*, also designed the cover of issue #17, using the tree frog watercolor by Lynn DeTurk. "I chose this image because our journal focuses upon environmental poetry . . . The painting has a zen-like serenity and simplicity about it which is soothing to behold."

N ⊘ ◎ ALIMENTUM, THE LITERATURE OF FOOD (Specialized: poems about/referencing food; menupoems; recipe poems)

P.O. Box 776, New York NY 10163. E-mail: submissions@alimentumjournal.com. (inquiries only). Web site: www.alimentumjournal.com. Established 2005. **Contact:** Cortney Davis, poetry editor.

Magazine Needs *Alimentum, The Literature of Food*, published semiannually in winter and summer, is "the only literary journal all about food." Wants "fiction, creative nonfiction, and poetry all around the subject of food." Has published poetry by Carly Sachs, Dick Allen, Gaylord Brewer, Jen Karetnick, and Leslie McGrath. *Alimentum* is 128 pages, 6 × 7½, perfect-bound, with matte coated cover with 4-color art, interior b&w illustration includes ads. Receives about 1,000 poems/year, accepts about 30-40. Press run is 2,000. Single copy: $10 ($14 Canada/foreign); subscription: $18 for one year ($24 Canada/foreign). Make checks payable to *Alimentum* (payment available online through credit card or PayPal).

How to Submit Submit no more than 5 poems at a time. Lines/poem: no minimum or maximum. Considers simultaneous submissions; no previously published poems. No e-mail submissions; postal submissions only. Include SASE. Reads submissions year round. Guidelines available on Web site. Responds 1-3 months. Pays contributor's copy. Acquires First North American Serial rights. Rights revert to poets upon publication.

Also Offers Publishes an annual broadside of "menupoems" for restaurants during National Poetry Month in April.

Advice "While food is our subject, we like poems to be about more than just the food. As in the stories we publish, the poems should also carry a personal element, even a story, not just a list of ingredients. Some special poem categories that we look for are menupoems and recipe poems."

✦ ⊘ AMARYLLIS

P.O. Box 6330, Montgomery AL 36106-0330. Fax: (334)244-3740. E-mail: amaryllis.journal@gmail.com. Established 1985. **Contact:** Nancy Anderson, Lynn Jinks, Donald Nobles, editors.

Magazine Needs *Amaryllis*, published annually in December ("more often depending on submissions"), is a national magazine of high-quality poetry, fiction, essays, and reviews. Open to all forms and styles, including experimental forms, with no restriction on subject. Does not want trite verse or inspirational work. *Amaryllis* is 75-150 pages, digest-sized, professionally offset-printed, perfect-bound, with heavy matte cardstock cover with line illustration. Accepts about 5% of poems submitted. Press run is 500. Single copy: $5. Sample: $3. Make checks payable to *Amaryllis*.

How to Submit Submit 7 poems at a time. Lines/poem: any length will be considered. No previously published poems or simultaneous submissions. No fax, e-mail, or disk submissions. Cover letter is required. "Please submit in triplicate and include SASE for response." Reads submissions year round. Time between acceptance and publication varies. Poems are circulated to an editorial board. "All submissions are discussed by three editors; works are reviewed in a roundtable discussion." Seldom comments on rejected poems. Guidelines available in magazine, for SASE, or by fax or e-mail. Responds in 2 months. Sometimes sends prepublication galleys. Pays 5 contributor's copies. Acquires one-time rights. Reviews books of poetry in 1,000 words, single- and multi-book format.

THE AMERICAN DISSIDENT (Specialized: engaged writing; poetry in English, French, Spanish)

1837 Main St., Concord MA 01742. E-mail: todslone@yahoo.com. Web site: www.TheAmericanDissident.org. Established 1998. **Contact:** G. Tod Slone, editor.

Magazine Needs *The American Dissident*, published 2 times/year, provides "a forum for examining the dark side of the academic/literary industrial complex." Wants "poetry and short (250-750 words) essays in English, French, or Spanish, written on the edge with a dash of personal risk and stemming from personal experience, conflict with power, and/or involvement." Submissions should be "iconoclastic and parrhesiastic in nature." *The American Dissident* is 56-64 pages, digest-sized, offset-printed, perfect-bound, with card cover. Press run is 200. Single copy: $8; subscription: $16.

How to Submit Submit 3 poems at a time. Considers simultaneous submissions; no previously published poems. No e-mail submissions. "Include SASE and cover letter containing not credits, but rather personal dissident information and specific events that may have pushed you to reject indoctrination and 'go upright and vital, and speak the rude truth in all ways' (Emerson)." Time between acceptance and publication is up to 2 months. Almost always comments on rejected poems. Guidelines available for SASE. Responds in one month. Pays one contributor's copy. Acquires first North American serial rights. Reviews books/chapbooks of poetry and other magazines in 250 words, single-book format. Send materials for review consideration.

Advice "For the sake of democracy, poetry needs to be much more than safe, comfortable, diversionary intellectual entertainment, and poets much more than public court jesters. If only the latter endeavored to be more than just working the poem and filling out applications for grants, fellowships, and contests. If only they questioned and challenged, rather than accepted. If only they heeded Villon ('*Estoit-il lors temps de moy taire*'), Thoreau ('Let your life be a counter friction to stop the machine'), Wole Soyinka ('Criticism, like charity, starts at home'), Solzhenitsyn ('Poetry under a tombstone, truth under a stone'), Parra ('*La poesía morirá si no se la ofende, hay que poseerla y humillarla en público*'), and James Baldwin ('The peculiar nature of this [the writer's] responsibility is that he must never cease warring with it [society], for its sake and for his own'). Do not be afraid to name names!"

AMERICAN LITERARY REVIEW

University of North Texas, P.O. Box 311307, Denton TX 76203-1307. (940)565-2755. E-mail: americanliteraryreview@yahoo.com. Web site: www.engl.unt.edu/alr. **Contact:** Bruce Bond and Corey Marks, poetry editors.

Magazine Needs *American Literary Review*, published semiannually, considers all forms and modes of poetry, nonfiction, and fiction. "We are especially interested in originality, substance, imaginative power, and lyric intensity." Has published poetry by Kathleen Pierce, Mark Irwin, Nance Van Winkle, William Olsen, Eric Pankey, and Nancy Eimers. *American Literary Review* is about 120 pages, digest-sized, attractively printed, perfect-bound, with color card cover with photo. Subscription: $10/year, $18 for 2 years. Sample: $6.

How to Submit Submit up to 5 typewritten poems at a time. Considers simultaneous submissions. No fax or e-mail submissions. Cover letter is required. Include author's name, address, phone number, and poem titles. Reads mss September 1-May 1. Guidelines available on Web site. Responds in up to 3 months. Pays 2 contributor's copies.

Contest/Award Offerings Send SASE for details.

THE AMERICAN POETRY JOURNAL

P.O. Box 2080 Aptos CA 95001-2080. E-mail: editor@americanpoetryjournal.com. Web site: www.a mericanpoetryjournal.com. Established 2004. **Contact:** J.P. Dancing Bear, editor.

Magazine Needs *The American Poetry Journal*, published semiannually (January and July), seeks "to publish work using poetic device, favoring image, metaphor, and good sound. We like alliteration, extended metaphors, image, movement, and poems that can pass the 'so what' test. *The American Poetry Journal* has in mind the reader who delights in discovering what a poem can do to the tongue and what the poem paints on the cave of the mind." Wants poems "that exhibit strong, fresh imagery, metaphor, and good sound." Does not want "narratives about family, simplistic verse, annoying word hodge-podges." Has published poetry by C.J. Sage, Nicole Cuddeback, Margot Schilpp, Kelle Groom, and Steven Schroeder. *The American Poetry Journal* is 50 pages, digest-sized. Accepts about 1% of poems submitted. Single copy: $6; subscription: $10. Make checks payable to J.P. Dancing Bear.

How to Submit Submit 3-5 poems at a time. Considers simultaneous submissions; no previously published poems. No e-mail or disk submissions. Cover letter is preferred. Considers unsolicited submissions September 1-April 30 (poets may submit no more than twice during the reading period). "We consider submissions from subscribers year round." Time between acceptance and publication is 6 months. "Poems are read first for clarity and technique, then read aloud for sound quality." Seldom comments on rejected poems. Guidelines available on Web site. Responds in 2 months. Pays one contributor's copy. Acquires first rights.

Contest/Award Offerings The American Poet Prize awards $300 and publication in *The American Poetry Journal*. All entries will be considered for publication, and all entrants receive a year's subscription. Send 3 original, unpublished poems without identifiers on any page, a cover letter with poem titles, author's name, contact information, optional stamped postcard for delivery confirmation, and SASE. **Entry fee:** $15. Make checks payable to J.P. Dancing Bear. **Deadline:** June 30. Also offers *The American Poetry Journal* Book Prize (see separate listing in Contests & Awards).

Advice "Know your target before submitting. It's not that difficult, but it helps your odds when the editor can tell that you get what the magazine is about. Reading an issue is the easiest way to do this."

AMERICAN TANKA (Specialized: English-language tanka)

P.O. Box 120-024, Staten Island NY 10312. E-mail: editorsdesk@americantanka.com. Web site: www.americantanka.com. Established 1996. **Contact:** Laura Maffei, editor. Executive Director: Tim Younce.

Magazine Needs *American Tanka*, published annually, is devoted to single English-language tanka. Wants "concise and vivid language, good crafting, and echo of the original Japanese form, but with unique and contemporary content." Does not want anything that's not tanka. Considers poetry by children and teens. Has published poetry by Sanford Goldstein, Marianne Bluger, Michael McClintock, Michael Dylan Welch, Jane Reichhold, and George Swede. *American Tanka* is 95-120 pages, digest-sized, perfect-bound, with glossy cover. Single copy: $12; subscription: $20 for 2 issues, $28 for 3 issues. Make checks/money orders payable to *American Tanka* and send to Tim Younce, 4906 W. State Route 55, Troy OH 45373.

Magazines/Journals

How to Submit Submit up to 5 poems at a time (one submission/reading period). No previously published poems or simultaneous submissions. Accepts submissions by e-mail (pasted into body of message). Guidelines available for SASE, by e-mail, or on Web site. Responds in up to 4 months. Acquires first North American serial rights.

Advice "Become familiar with the tanka form by reading both translations and English-language tanka. In your own tanka, be natural and concrete and vivid. Avoid clichés, overcrowded imagery, or attempting to imitate Japanese poems."

$⬙ ◎ ANCIENT PATHS (Specialized: Christian)

P.O. Box 7505, Fairfax Station VA 22039. E-mail: SSBurris@msn.com. Web site: www.editorskylar. com. Established 1998. **Contact:** Skylar H. Burris, editor.

Magazine Needs *Ancient Paths*, published biennially in odd-numbered years, provides "a forum for quality Christian literature and contains poetry, short stories, art, and chapbook reviews." Wants "traditional rhymed/metrical forms and free verse; subtle Christian themes. I seek poetry that makes the reader both think and feel." Does not want " 'preachy' poetry, inconsistent meter, or forced rhyme; no stream of conscious or avant-garde work; no esoteric academic poetry." Has published poetry by Giovanni Malito, Ida Fasel, Diane Glancy, Walt McDonald, and Donna Farley. *Ancient Paths* is 80+ pages, digest-sized, photocopied, perfect-bound, with cardstock cover. Receives about 600 poems/year, accepts about 7%. Press run is 200 (55 paid subscribers, 55 individual copy sales); 80 distributed free to churches, libraries, and authors. Single copy: $12. Make checks payable to Skylar Burris.

How to Submit Submit up to 5 poems at a time. Lines/poem: 60 maximum. Considers previously published poems and simultaneous submissions. Accepts e-mail submissions "only if you reside outside the U.S.; submissions should be pasted directly into the message, single-spaced, one poem per message, using a small or normal font size, with name and address at the top of each submission. Use subject heading: ANCIENT PATHS SUBMISSION, followed by your title." For postal submissions, poems should be single-spaced; "always include name, address, and line count on first page of all submissions, and note if the poem is previously published and what rights (if any) were purchased." Check Web site for reading period for Issue 15. Time between acceptance and publication is up to one year. Often comments on rejected poems. Guidelines available for SASE or on Web site. Responds in 3-4 weeks "if rejected, longer if being seriously considered." Pays $2/poem and one contributor's copy; offers contributors discount off cover price for pre-ordered copies. Acquires one-time or reprint rights. Reviews religious poetry chapbooks in 100 words.

Advice "Read the great religious poets: John Donne, George Herbert, T.S. Eliot, Lord Tennyson. Remember not to preach. This is a literary magazine, not a pulpit. This does not mean you do not communicate morals or celebrate God. It means you are not overbearing or simplistic when you do so."

⬙ ◎ ANGEL FACE (Specialized: poems arranged according to Mysteries of the Rosary)

℅ MaryAnka Press, P.O. Box 102, Huffman TX 77336. Web site: www.maryanka.com. Established 2004. **Contact:** Mary Agnes Dalrymple, editor.

Magazine Needs *Angel Face*, appearing annually in the spring, publishes poems "arranged according to the pattern of the Rosary (according to the Rosary Mysteries), but submitting poets need not be Catholic or Christian. I am open to many different viewpoints and have published poetry by Jewish and other non-Christian poets, as well as Catholic and Protestant poets. My goal is to bring the Rosary 'into life.' " Wants "poetry written from the life of the poet, but I am also open to poems written from the Biblical and traditional source material of the Rosary Mysteries. Some themes of the Rosary are birth, rebirth, joy, light, sorrow, abandonment, death, epiphany, redemption, resurrection, hope, transformation, forgiveness, the seasons of nature, the cycle of life, and the search for God in everyday life. Additional Rosary information can be found through the links page of my Web site." Does not want "rhyming or didactic poems. Also nothing negative or derogatory." *Angel Face* is 50 pages, digest-sized, desktop-published, hand-bound by the editor with waxed Irish linen thread, with cardstock cover with color artwork. Receives about 300 submissions/year, accepts about 40 poems. Press run is 100. Single copy: $7; subscription: $14 (2 copies). Make checks payable to Mary Agnes Dalrymple.

How to Submit Submit up to 5 poems at a time. Lines/poem: about 60 maximum. Considers previously published poems and simultaneous submissions. Accepts submissions by postal mail only. "For information on why I do not accept e-mailed submissions, go to guidelines page of Web site and click on the Editor's Notes." Cover letter is preferred. Reads submissions year round. Time between acceptance and publication is 4 months to one year. Sometimes comments on rejected poems. "If I see something I like but think it still needs work, I will comment." Guidelines available for SASE or on Web site. Responds in about 3 months ("longer when I am putting an issue together"). Pays one contributor's copy. Acquires one-time rights. Rights revert to poet upon publication.

Advice "Write it, and then rewrite it. Consider each poem to be a child. No responsible person would send a child out half-naked on an empty stomach with no way to get back home. Poetry shouldn't be sent out that way, either. Provide the right size SASE with proper postage. Most of the poems published in *Angel Face* were not written with the Rosary in mind. Send your best poems, even if you are not sure they will fit the Rosary prayer pattern."

$☑ THE ANTIOCH REVIEW

P.O. Box 148, Yellow Springs OH 45387. (937)769-1365. Web site: www.review.antioch.edu. Established 1941. **Contact:** Judith Hall, poetry editor.

- Work published in *The Antioch Review* has been included frequently in *The Best American Poetry* and *The Pushcart Prize*.

Magazine Needs *The Antioch Review* "is an independent quarterly of critical and creative thought. For well over 50 years, creative authors, poets, and thinkers have found a friendly reception—regardless of formal reputation. We get far more poetry than we can possibly accept, and the competition is keen. Here, where form and content are so inseparable and reaction is so personal, it is difficult to state requirements or limitations. Studying recent issues of *The Antioch Review* should be helpful." Does not want " 'light' or inspirational verse." Has published poetry by Edward Hirsch, David Lehman, W.S. Merwin, and Harryette Mullen. Receives about 3,000 submissions/year. Circulation is 5,000 (large percentage of subscribers are libraries); 70% distributed through bookstores and newsstands. Subscription: $40. Sample: $7.

How to Submit Submit 3-6 poems at a time. No previously published poems or simultaneous submissions. Include SASE with all submissions. Reads submissions September 1-May 1 only. Guidelines available on Web site. Responds in 4-6 months. Pays $15/published page plus 2 contributor's copies; additional copies available at 40% discount.

$▣ ☐ ◎ AOIFE'S KISS (Specialized: fantasy; science fiction)

P.O. Box 782, Cedar Rapids IA 52406-0782. E-mail: aoife@samsdotpublishing.com. Web site: www. samsdotpublishing.com. Established 2002. **Contact:** Tyree Campbell, managing editor. Member: The Speculative Literature Foundation (http://SpeculativeLiterature.org).

Magazine Needs *Aoife's Kiss*, published quarterly in print and online (the 2 versions are different), prints "fantasy, science fiction, sword and sorcery, alternate history, horror short stories, poems, illustrations, and movie and book reviews." Wants "fantasy, science fiction, spooky horror, and speculative poetry with minimal angst." Does not want "horror with excessive blood and gore." Considers poetry by children and teens. Has published poetry by Bruce Boston, Karen A. Romanko, Mike Allen, Corrine De Winter, Julie Shiel, and Marge B. Simon. *Aoife's Kiss* (print version) is 32 pages, magazine-sized, offset-printed, saddle-stapled, with color paper cover, includes ads. Receives about 300 poems/year, accepts about 50 (17%). Press run is 140 (50 subscribers, 50 shelf sales); 5 distributed free to reviewers. Single copy: $7; subscription: $18/year, $34/2 years. Make checks payable to Tyree Campbell/Sam's Dot Publishing.

How to Submit Submit up to 5 poems at a time. Lines/poem: prefers less than 100. Considers previously published poems; no simultaneous submissions. Accepts e-mail submissions (pasted into body of message); no disk submissions. "Submission should include snail mail address and a short (1-2 lines) bio." Reads submissions year round. Submit seasonal poems 6 months in advance. Time between acceptance and publication is 2-5 months. Often comments on rejected poems. Guidelines available on Web site. Responds in 4-6 weeks. Pays $5/poem, $3/reprint, $1 for scifaiku and related forms, and one contributor's copy. Acquires first North American serial rights. Reviews books/chapbooks of poetry. Send materials for review consideration to Tyree Campbell.

Advice "It's up to the writer to take the first step and submit work. Some of our best poems have come from poets who weren't sure if they were good enough. Horror poetry is a difficult sell with us."

▧ ▨ ▣ ◪ APPLE VALLEY REVIEW: A JOURNAL OF CONTEMPORARY LITERATURE

E-mail: editor@leahbrowning.net. Web site: www.applevalleyreview.com. Established 2005. **Contact:** Leah Browning, editor. Member: Council of Literary Magazines and Presses (CLMP).

Magazine Needs *Apple Valley Review: A Journal of Contemporary Literature*, published semiannually online, features "beautifully crafted poetry, short fiction, and essays." Wants "work that has both mainstream and literary appeal. All work must be original, previously unpublished, and in English. Translations are welcome if permission has been granted. Preference is given to short (under two pages), non-rhyming poetry." Does not want "erotica, work containing explicit language or violence, or work that is scholarly, critical, inspirational, or intended for children." Considers poetry by children and teens; "all work is considered regardless of the author's age." Has published poetry by Anna Evans, Lyn Lifshin, Sid Miller, Rochelle Ratner, Hal Sirowitz, and Janet Zupan. Receives about 5,000+ poems/year, accepts less than 1%.

How to Submit Submit 2-6 poems at a time. Lines/poem: "no limit, though we prefer short poems (under two pages). No previously published poems or simultaneous submissions. Accepts e-mail submissions (pasted into body of message, with "poetry" in subject line); no disk submissions. Cover letter is preferred. "Include name, address, phone number, e-mail address, and a short biography (maximum 150 words)." Reads submissions year round. Submit seasonal poems 6 months in advance, "though our interest in seasonal poems is very limited." Time between acceptance and publication is 1-6 months. Sometimes comments on rejected poems. Guidelines available by e-mail or on Web site. Responds in 1 week to 3 months. Sometimes sends prepublication galleys. "This is not a paying market. However, all work published in the *Apple Valley Review* during a given calendar year will be considered for the annual *Apple Valley Review* Editor's Prize [see below]." Acquires first rights and first serial rights and retains the right to archive the work online for an indefinite period of time. "As appropriate, we may also choose to nominate published work for awards or recognition. Author retains all other rights."

Contest/Award Offerings Offers the annual *Apple Valley Review* Editor's Prize. Award varies. "In 2006, the prize was $100 and a book of poetry." Submit 2-6 poems. **Entry fee:** none. **Deadline:** rolling; all submissions to the *Apple Valley Review*, and all work published during a given calendar year will be considered for the prize.

Advice "Try to read as much as possible, and submit to markets that are publishing work that you enjoy. They are more likely to be a good fit."

▨ $◪ ARC POETRY MAGAZINE

P.O. Box 81060, Ottawa ON K1P 1B1 Canada. E-mail: arc@arcpoetry.ca. Web site: www.arcpoetry.ca. Established 1978. **Contact:** Anita Lahey, editor.

Magazine Needs *Arc Poetry Magazine*, published semiannually, prints poetry, poetry-related articles, interviews, and book reviews. "Tastes are eclectic. International submissions are welcome and encouraged." Has published poetry by Evelyn Lau, Michael Crummey, Erin Mouré, Patricia Young, and Joelene Heathcote. *Arc Poetry Magazine* is 130-160 pages, perfect-bound, printed on matte white stock "with a crisp, engaging design and a striking visual art portfolio in each issue." Receives about 1,000 submissions/year, accepts about 40-50 poems. Press run is 1,500 (1,000 subscribers). Single copy: $12.50 CAD, $18 CAD (U.S.), $20 CAD (overseas); subscription: 2 issues/one year—$17.95 CAD (in Canada); 4 issues/2 years—$34.95 CAD (in Canada), $42.95 USD, $45.95 USD (overseas). Online ordering available for subscriptions and single copies (with occasional promotions).
How to Submit Submit 4-8 poems at a time. No previously published poems or simultaneous submissions. No e-mail submissions. Cover letter is required. Submissions should be single-spaced, with name and address on each page. Publishes theme issues. Upcoming themes available in magazine or on Web site. Guidelines available for SAE and IRC or on Web site. Responds in 4-6 months. Pays $40 CAD/page plus 2 contributor's copies. Acquires first Canadian serial rights.
Contest/Award Offerings The Confederation Poets Prize is an annual award of $200 for the best poem published in *Arc* that year. *Arc* also sponsors an international Poem of the Year Contest: 1st Prize: $1,500 CAD; 2nd Prize: $1,000 CAD; 3rd Prize: $750 CAD. **Entry fee:** $23 CAD/4 poems. **Deadline:** June 30. Other awards include the Lampman Award for Poetry, Critic's Desk Award, and the Diana Brebner Prize for Poetry. Guidelines available on Web site.

⬭ ◎ ARCH AND QUIVER (Specialized: erotica)

P.O. Box 99595, Seattle WA 98199-0595. E-mail: archandquiver@yahoo.com. Web site: www.archandquiver.com. Established 2005. **Contact:** Tanisha Jackland, editor.
Magazine Needs *Arch and Quiver*, published annually in November/December, is "an erotic poetry journal specializing in romantic, dark eroticism and sensual poems." Wants "any style of verse; looking for highly crafted work." Does not want "anything outlandish or lengthy, long-winded poetry." *Arch and Quiver* is digest-sized, includes ads. Subscription: $9. Make checks payable to Tanisha Jackland.
How to Submit Submit 5 poems at a time. Lines/poem: 30 maximum, "but will make exceptions for highly crafted work." Considers previously published poems. Accepts e-mail submissions (as attachment); no disk submissions. "Include three- to five-sentence bio with SASE." Reads submissions year round. Time between acceptance and publication is 7-8 months. Poems are circulated to an editorial board. Sometimes comments on rejected poems. Sometimes publishes theme issues. Guidelines available on Web site. Responds in 2 weeks. No payment. Rights revert to poet upon publication.
Advice "Concise poems exposing sensual revelations are always considered."

⬭ ◩ ARIES: A JOURNAL OF CREATIVE EXPRESSION

Dept. of Languages and Literature, Texas Wesleyan University, 1201 Wesleyan St., Fort Worth TX 76105-1536. (817)531-4907. Fax: (817)531-6503. E-mail: sneeley@txwes.edu. (inquiries only; no submissions). Web site: www.ariesjournal.com. Established 1985. **Contact:** Stacia Dunn Neeley, general editor.
Magazine Needs *Aries: A Journal of Creative Expression*, published annually in August, prints quality poetry, b&w art, fiction, essays, and one-act plays. Wants poetry in all forms up to 50 lines. "Special needs: original Spanish language poetry and translation thereof (send both versions)." Does not want erotica. Has published poetry by Virgil Suárez, Richard Robbins, Susan Smith Nash, Gerald Zipper, and Lynn Veach Sadler. *Aries* is 60 pages, digest-sized, offset-printed, perfect-bound, with heavy cardstock cover and b&w art (1,500 dpi scans). Receives about 800 poems/year, accepts about 10%. Press run is 300 (100 subscribers, 3 libraries, 125 shelf sales). Single copy: $7; subscription: $7. Make checks payable to Stacia Neeley.
How to Submit Submit 5 poems maximum at a time. Lines/poem: 3 minimum, 50 maximum.

Considers simultaneous submissions; no previously published poems. No fax, e-mail, or disk submissions. Cover letter is required. "Blind submissions only—cover letter with titles; no identifying marks on submissions." Accepts submissions September 1-January 31 only. Time between acceptance and publication is 3 months. "At least four editors read every submission blindly. Personal response to every submission accompanied by a SASE or functioning e-mail address." Always comments on rejected poems. Guidelines available in magazine, for SASE, by e-mail, or on Web site. Responds in up to 6 months (notification of acceptance in April). Offers 50% off 2 contributor's copies. Acquires first rights.

Advice "Write in the voice that speaks from your unique position in the world. Our editors tend to choose works where 'there's something at stake.'"

$ ▣ ☑ ◎ ARKANSAS LITERARY FORUM (Specialized: AR resident writers only)

Henderson State University, Box 7601, Arkadelphia AR 71999-0001. (870)230-5272. E-mail: beggsm @hsu.edu. Web site: www.hsu.edu/alf. Established 1999. **Contact:** Marck L. Beggs, editor.

Magazine Needs *Arkansas Literary Forum*, published annually online in October, brings "the best of Arkansas to the world." Wants "well-written, image-rich poetry that surprises the reader" **from Arkansas residents only**. Does not want "message-oriented or sentimental poetry." Has published poetry by Miller Williams, Michael Heffernan, Andrea Hollander Budy, Jo McDougall, Terry Wright, and Jennifer Horne. Receives about 200 poems/year, accepts about 20-30.

How to Submit Submit 2-4 poems at a time. Lines/poem: no limit. No previously published poems or simultaneous submissions. Accepts e-mail submissions (pasted into body of message or as attachment in Word or WordPerfect); no disk submissions. Cover letter is preferred. "The cover letter should clarify the poet's connection to Arkansas." Reads submissions during January and February only. Time between acceptance and publication is 6-8 months. Poems are circulated to an editorial board. Never comments on rejected poems. Guidelines available in magazine or on Web site. Responds in 1-2 months. Always sends prepublications galleys. Pays $25/poem upon publication. Acquires first rights. Rights revert to poet upon publication.

Advice "Read everything you can get your hands on; however, don't read about how to write poems, read *poems*."

☐ ◎ ARKANSAS REVIEW: A JOURNAL OF DELTA STUDIES (Specialized: work that evokes 7-state Mississippi River Delta region)

P.O. Box 1890, State University AR 72467-1890. (870)972-3043. Fax: (870)972-3045. E-mail: tswillia @astate.edu. Web site: www.clt.astate.edu/arkreview. Established 1968 (as *Kansas Quarterly*). **Contact:** Tom Williams, general editor & creative materials editor.

Magazine Needs *Arkansas Review: A Journal of Delta Studies*, published 3 times/year, is "a regional studies journal devoted to the seven-state Mississippi River Delta. Interdisciplinary in scope, we publish academic articles, relevant creative material, interviews, and reviews. Material must respond to or evoke the experiences and landscapes of the seven-state Mississippi River Delta (St. Louis to New Orleans)." Has published poetry by Greg Fraser, Jo McDougall, and Catherine Savage Brosman. *Arkansas Review* is 92 pages, magazine-sized, photo offset-printed, saddle-stapled, with 4-color cover. Receives about 500 poems/year, accepts about 5%. Press run is 600 (400 subscribers, 300 libraries, 20 shelf sales); 50 distributed free to contributors. Subscription: $20. Sample: $7.50. Make checks payable to ASU Foundation.

How to Submit Submit any number of poems at a time. No previously published poems or simultaneous submissions. Accepts e-mail and disk submissions. Cover letter is preferred. Include SASE. Time between acceptance and publication is about 6 months. "The Creative Materials Editor makes the final decision based, in part, on recommendations from other readers." Often comments on rejected poems. Occasionally publishes theme issues. Guidelines available for SASE or by e-mail. Responds in 4 months. Pays 3 contributor's copies. Acquires first rights. Staff reviews books/

chapbooks of poetry "that are relevant to the Delta" in 500 words, single- and multi-book format. Send materials for review consideration to Tom Williams ("inquire in advance").

THE ARMCHAIR AESTHETE

Pickle Gas Press, 31 Rolling Meadows Way, Penfield NY 14526. (585)388-6968. E-mail: bypaul@net acc.net. Established 1996. **Contact:** Paul Agosto, editor.

Magazine Needs *The Armchair Aesthete*, published 3 times/year, is a zine of "thoughtful, well-crafted, concise fiction and poetry. Interested in both fiction and poetry." *The Armchair Aesthete* is 60-80 pages, digest-sized, desktop-published, photocopied, with card cover. Receives about 300 poems/year, accepts about 25-30%. Subscription: $15/year. Sample: $5 postpaid. Make checks payable to Paul Agosto.

How to Submit Lines/poem: 60 maximum. Considers previously published poems and simultaneous submissions, if indicated. Accepts e-mail submissions (pasted into body of message). Cover letter is preferred. Time between acceptance and publication is up to 9 months. Seldom comments on rejected poems. Guidelines available for SASE. Responds in 2 months. Pays one contributor's copy. Acquires one-time rights.

ARS PULCHRIS, THE MAGAZINE OF THE TRUTH IN ART MOVEMENT (Specialized: traditional lyric verse; subscribers only)

P.O. Box 8401, Albuquerque NM 87198. (505)573-5995. E-mail: cathinst@comcast.net. Web site: www.cathinst.com. Established 2005. **Contact:** Joseph Charles McKenzie.

Magazine Needs *Ars Pulchris, The Magazine of the Truth in Art Movement*, published semiannually, is the official publication of the Catholic Institute of Arts and Letters. Wants "works reflecting loftiest, noblest standards of traditional poetry." Considers poetry by teens. *Ars Pulchris* is 24-34 pages, magazine-sized, laser/digitally-printed, saddle-stapled, with paper cover, includes ads. Single copy: $25; subscription: $50. Make checks payable to Catholic Institute of Arts and Letters.

How to Submit Submit 4 poems at a time. Lines/poem: no restrictions. Considers previously published poems and simultaneous submissions. Accepts e-mail submissions (as attachment). Cover letter is preferred. "All submissions become the property of the Catholic Institute of Arts and Letters and shall not be returned. Do not send original or unique manuscripts." Reads submissions year round. Time between acceptance and publication is 1-6 months. Poems are circulated to an editorial board. Never comments on rejected poems. **Contributors must subscribe.** Guidelines available by e-mail. Responds in 6 months. Pays one contributor's copy. Acquires first North American serial rights. Rights do not revert to poets upon publication.

Contest/Award Offerings The annual Catholic Academy of Letters Prize in Poetry (see separate listing in Contests & Awards).

ART TIMES: A LITERARY JOURNAL AND RESOURCE FOR ALL THE ARTS

P.O. Box 730, Mt. Marion NY 12456. Phone/fax: (845)246-6944. E-mail: info@arttimesjournal.com. (inquiries only). Web site: www.arttimesjournal.com. Established 1984. **Contact:** Raymond J. Steiner, poetry editor.

Magazine Needs *Art Times*, published monthly, is a tabloid newspaper devoted to the fine and performing arts. Focuses on cultural and creative articles and essays, but also publishes some poetry and fiction. Wants "poetry that strives to express genuine observation in unique language. All topics, all forms." *Art Times* is 20-26 pages, newsprint, includes ads. Receives 300-500 poems/month, accepts about 40-50/year. Circulation is 27,000, of which 5,000 are subscriptions; most distribution is free through galleries, theatres, etc., in the Northeast Corridor of the US. Subscription: $15/year. Sample: $1 with 9×12 SAE and 3 first-class stamps.

How to Submit Submit 4-5 typed poems at a time. Lines/poem: up to 20. No e-mail submissions.

Include SASE with all submissions. Has an 18-month backlog. Guidelines available for SASE. Responds in 6 months. Pays 6 contributor's copies plus one-year subscription.

⚃ ◌ ART WITH WORDS POETRY QUARTERLY

1050A McGhee St., Milton WV 25541. (304)743-9913 (daytime); (304)417-0139 (evenings). E-mail: artwithwords@hotmail.com. Web site: www.freewebs.com/artwithwords/index.htm. Established 2004. **Contact:** Debra J. Harmes Kurth, owner/editor.

Magazine Needs *Art With Words Poetry Quarterly* publishes "a variety of poetry, prose, and the occasional short story. I hope that anyone who picks up this quarterly will find a poem that speaks to their soul." Wants "poetry that is alive, that breathes, shouts, or whispers to the reader; poetry that makes you stop and think, tells a story, or makes a statement. Poetry that is a picture of your thoughts cleverly crafted into a web of words. I do accept religious poetry; by that I mean all kinds of religious poetry, from any religious faction that wishes to express their thoughts through the written word. In the same vein, I accept political, headline news, and controversial topics, if presented well in the form of a poem." Considers poetry by children and teens. "Once submission is received, a letter and release will be sent to the child's home for both child (under 19) and parent to sign." Has published poetry by Laurence Thomas, Juanita Torrence Thompson, Laura Stamps, Mary Sue Kessell Rosen, Paul Prose, and Virginia Artrip Snyder. *Art With Words* is about 100 pages, magazine-sized, professionally photocopied, stapled, with paper cover with artwork. Receives about 1,000 poems/year, accepts about 60%. Press run is 200-300 (15 libraries, 5 shelf sales); distributed free to schools ("five at the present time"). Single copy: $6; subscription: $20. Make checks payable to *Art With Words*.

How to Submit Submit 5 poems at a time. Lines/poem: no more than one printed page. Considers previously published poems and simultaneous submissions. Accepts e-mail (pasted into body of message) and disk submissions. Cover letter is preferred. "Always include a brief bio and contact information. We do not accept poetry that appears to be prejudicial or intentionally hostile." Reads submissions year round. Submit seasonal poems 3 months in advance. Time between acceptance and publication is up to 6 months. Often comments on rejected poems. Guidelines available for SASE. Responds in 3-4 weeks. No payment. "We do not send out free copies." Acquires one-time rights. Rights revert to poets upon publication. Reviews books/chapbooks of poetry and other magazines/journals in 150-200 words.

Contest/Award Offerings Sponsors quarterly contest, offering half of collected entry fees as prize. Submit unlimited number of poems, no more than one printed page. Guidelines available for SASE. **Entry fee:** $2 for first entry, $1 for additional entries. **Deadline:** one month before publication deadline; see Web site for current dates.

Also Offers *Art With Words* offers "several interactive columns where we love to hear from our readers/writers about the questions or comments presented. We also have several pages dedicated to comments on the poetry printed in the issue from our readers, A Word To Our Poets. We also have Exercises in Creativity and a column dedicated to the critique of one piece of poetry per quarter, which was submitted for that purpose."

Advice "You'll never see your work in print if you do not submit it. Never believe you can't get any better at your art than you are now. As long as we are breathing, we can learn."

⚄ ARTISAN, A JOURNAL OF CRAFT

P.O. Box 157, Wilmette IL 60091. E-mail: editor@artisanjournal.com. Web site: www.artisanjourna l.com. Established 1995. **Contact:** Joan Daugherty, editor.

Magazine Needs *artisan, a journal of craft,* published tri-quarterly, is based on the idea that "anyone who strives to express themselves with skill is an artist, and artists of all kinds can learn from each other." Wants "poetry with its head in the clouds but its feet on the ground—simple and elegant, but not snobby or pompous." Considers poetry by children and teens. Has published poetry by Adrian Robert Ford, Kathleen Gunton, and Joanna Rose. *artisan* is about 40 pages (including cover), $7 \times 8\frac{1}{2}$. Receives about 300 poems/year, accepts about 20%. Press run is 200 (100 subscribers); 100 distributed free to coffeehouses and local libraries. Subscription: $18. Sample: $6. Make checks payable to "artisan, ink."

How to Submit Submit 3-5 poems at a time. Lines/poem: 70 maximum. Considers simultaneous submissions "if noted in cover letter or on submission"; no previously published poems. Accepts e-mail submissions (as attachment, ASCII text format). Cover letter is not necessary; however, "if you send a cover letter, make it personal. We don't need to see any writing credentials; poems should stand on their own merit." Guidelines available for SASE or on Web site. Responds in up to 6 months. Pays 2 contributor's copies. Acquires first rights.

$\blacksquare$ \$$\square$ ARTS & LETTERS JOURNAL OF CONTEMPORARY CULTURE

Campus Box 89, Georgia College & State University, Milledgeville GA 31061. (478)445-1289. E-mail: al@gcsu.edu. Web site: http://al.gcsu.edu. Established 1999. **Contact:** Laura Newbern, poetry editor. Editor: Martin Lammon.

● Work published in *Arts & Letters Journal* has received the Pushcart Prize.

Magazine Needs *Arts & Letters Journal of Contemporary Culture*, published semiannually, is devoted to contemporary arts and literature, featuring ongoing series such as The World Poetry Translation Series and The Mentors Interview Series. Wants work that is of the highest literary and artistic quality. Does not want genre fiction, light verse. Has published poetry by Margaret Gibson, Marilyn Nelson, Stuart Lishan, R.T. Smith, Laurie Lamon, and Miller Williams. *Arts & Letters Journal of Contemporary Culture* is 180 pages, offset-printed, perfect-bound, with glossy cover with varied artwork, includes ads. Receives about 4,000 poems/year, accepts about .5%. Press run is 1,500 (1,000 subscribers, 20 libraries). Single copy: $8 plus $1 postage for current issue; subscription: $15 for 2 issues (one year). Sample: $5 plus $1 postage for back issue. Make checks payable to Georgia College & State University.

How to Submit Submit 5 poems at a time. Considers simultaneous submissions "if notified immediately of publication elsewhere"; no previously published poems. No fax, e-mail, or disk submissions. Cover letter is preferred. Include SASE. Reads submissions September 1-March 1. "Poems are screened, discussed by group of readers, then if approved, submitted to poetry editor for final approval." Seldom comments on rejected poems. Guidelines available in magazine, for SASE, by e-mail, or on Web site. Responds in 1-2 months. Always sends prepublication galleys. Pays $10/published page ($50 minimum) plus 2 contributor's copies and one-year subscription. Acquires one-time rights. Reviews books of poetry in 500 words, single-book format. Query first to Martin Lammon.

Contest/Award Offerings Annual *Arts & Letters*/Rumi Prize for Poets offers $1,000, publication in *Arts & Letters Journal*, and a visit to campus for awards program. Guidelines available on Web site. **Entry fee:** $15 USD; includes one-year subscription. Make checks/money orders payable to "GCSU" (note "Arts & Letters" in memo section). **Deadline:** January 1-March 15 (postmark). 2006 winner was Margaret Rabb. 2007 judge: A. Van Jordan; entries screened by editorial staff.

Also Offers Annual Arts & Letters Workshops (May of each year, one-week residential workshops in several genres, including poetry).

$\blacksquare$ $\square$ $\oslash$ ASCENT ASPIRATIONS MAGAZINE

1560 Arbutus Dr., Nanoose Bay BC V9P 9C8 Canada. (250)468-7313. E-mail: ascentaspirations@shaw.ca. Web site: www.ascentaspirations.ca. Established 1997. **Contact:** David Fraser, editor.

Magazine Needs *Ascent Aspirations Magazine*, published quarterly online (February, May, August, November) and semiannually in print (late fall and late spring), specializes in poetry, short fiction, essays, and visual art. "A quality electronic and print publication, *Ascent* is dedicated to encouraging aspiring poets and fiction writers. We accept all forms of poetry on any theme. Poetry needs to be unique and touch the reader emotionally with relevant human, social, and philosophical

Anne Marie Macari

Christian myth and motherhood

Magazines/Journals

A nne Marie Macari's poems first came to me as a gift: four poems photocopied and left with a short note on my desk. But what a gift! What I read there gave me the immediate sense that I was witnessing something huge in the poetry world: the new realm of real—raw—poems about pregnancy, birth and motherhood. Macari's writing has been praised for its originality, its sensuality and its reexamination of Christian myth; but her poems about Mary have generated an underground following of writers fascinated by this exploration of a new frontier.

Of course, lots of other people were already infatuated with Macari by the time I read her work. Her first book of poems, *The Ivory Cradle,* was selected by Robert Creeley for the 2000 *American Poetry Review*/Honickman First Book Prize. Her second collection, *Gloryland,* was published by Alice James Books. Macari is on the core faculty of the New England College low-residency MFA Program, on the poetry faculty of the Prague Summer Workshops and on the Board of Directors of Alice James Books.

Many of the poems in *Gloryland* are about pregnancy and birth, so I know you have children. How old are they? How long did these poems percolate? They feel as if they took years to crystallize.

Oh, yes. I have three sons: two in college (22 and 18) and one who's 15 and still at home—so I've been doing this for awhile, and I've had time to grow into, to expand my own feelings and notions of motherhood. In the "Mary" poems I wanted to find a way to get at the subject of birth without just telling my particular story. The "Mary" poems opened me up and gave me a way of talking about it. Of course, my own experiences are in there, but I was able to direct it in other ways.

It seems that working with Christian myths is a way of making the personal-universal become universal again.

Yes, there are times you just don't want to be saying, "I." And that's where I was. Christianity, or my reexamination of Christian myth, has been one of my subjects, so it made sense. I was drawn to write about these things that haven't been written about before. In *Gloryland* there are poems about birth, about being inside a woman's body, that are much more personal; but my jumping off place was the "Mary" poems. In many ways they are all "Mary" poems.

Your poems have gained attention for the way they describe women's bodies. So I'm wondering if your sons have read your poems?

They've come to readings, but I don't know if they've ever sat down and read the books. It's always funny, you sit down to write and think, "Oh, they're going to read the poem," but they don't want to know! They've heard the poems, and they're very sweet and supportive. My eldest son came to a reading recently, and he said, "That was hard for me to listen to, but I was really proud of you."

How did your process change and continue to mutate as your kids got older?

When the kids were little, I worked best late at night. I'd get snatches of time in here and there. Now, I have a lot more time, and I can't stay up late at night anymore—I don't have the energy! Having more time has allowed me to really get inside the work much more deeply and realize how hard those years were when I couldn't get a couple of hours at a time. It took me years to get it all together; but in some ways that's fine, because I feel like the work that finally did come out was mature work.

But, you know, part of me was saying, "You lost a lot of time." I guess women just go through this, whatever careers they're in. It was a real dilemma. I was a single parent, and that was another issue—a single and basically only parent, so it took a lot of will to keep writing. You have to have a strong will to pursue, to persevere, to believe that "one day I'm going to write the poem I want to write and someone's going to want to publish it." You just have to keep going.

During that time, was there anyone you looked to for faith that, if you kept at this, you would at least find some kind of personal redemption?

Well, for a lot of years I was just lost, I'd say. I was just writing and not getting very far. My kids were still pretty young when I got an MFA, and then I had tons of support.

You hear a lot of complaining about MFA programs and poetry, but there are so many voices that can come out of MFA programs that wouldn't have appeared without that support. The marginalized voices—that's happening a lot now. I'm not sure I could have gotten it all together if I hadn't had that support and that place to be with other writers. There were people, my mentors especially, who said, "Yes, you're on the right track." And that's all I needed. I just needed one person to say "yes." I got that in spades when I was getting my MFA at Sarah Lawrence. I had wonderful teachers.

I love the last poem in your book, "What Will You Feed Them," because it integrates the realm of literal food and literal sustenance to the figurative sustenance you have to offer as a mother.

Yes, that poem asks, "How do we feed each other? In what ways do we feed ourselves?" And it's full of conflict, but it's the communion and the passing on of the deepest kind of nourishment to each other and ourselves; and when we can do that, it's an achievement. Even if you're not successful in the eyes of the world, that ability to nourish, to feed family, friends and oneself, that's important, essential. That's what I was trying to write about: what it means to be doing this invisible work. When I think about my life with my family, I guess that's what I think about—coming together, nourishing each other.

What Will You Feed Them?

Scraping corn till its milk covers
my hands. Silky pile of husks. Tomato,
rosemary, chives from the garden.
Dreaming back far into the flesh of the plant.
How we are plants grown awkward and strange.

We saw the tail hanging from the hawk's
beak as it flew off, an apple protruding
from the mouth of the deer.

I whisked and pounded, sifted
and sliced. It was mortar
for their bones. It was what
we found in the woods.
The egg that fit so well in my palm
and what came out of it.

Fire. Blood. Fungus.
Muscle. Marrow. Greens.
Nuts and garlic, wild carrot.

It's the food inside the food,
the invisible heart of the berry,
how it goes on beating
in the hallways of the body.

When the Complete comes to find me
the one question will be, What did
you feed them? *As if I could*
remember the colors arranged

just so, the balance, a lifetime
of salt thrown into the pot
and whirling there. As if each
bite was language broken
down in the mouth, each word

tasting of its sour its bitter
its sweet, to stem the craving.
What we swallowed all those years—

platter of distress, bowl
of hope. What I chewed—my own
fingers and lip. What did you feed them?

I fed them love. What did you feed them?
Love and bones, gristle,
sermons, air, mercy,
rain, ice, terror and soup, anger and dandelion
and love. What did

you feed them? *Go to sleep*

in the straw and when you wake up
I will give you something warm in a cup,
I will mix it myself, and when the Complete
finally comes for me I'll have water
hot on the stove, the tea

just right, I'll say I've sucked
the bread of this life
but I'm never full, I'll go
with my mouth open—

(from *Gloryland* [Alice James Books, ©2005]; reprinted with permission)

Tell me a little bit about your writing process. How do you know when a poem is "finished"?

I have to be surprised. I don't want to write from an idea, I want to write from a passionate and surprised place, where I'm discovering things.

Someone asked me recently if I thought of my books as projects. I really don't like that word, because even though there's a lot of thinking and reading behind the poems, the poems themselves have to come from a different place. Otherwise I could be writing essays. So, yes, I like the idea of extended inquiries or quests. I like to think about subjects in a big way, and still turn that into poetry and have it be intimate and personal at the same time. It's challenging; it's what I like to do. And really, I need to be surprised in my own poems. A poem isn't finished for me until I've felt that moment of awakening, till I think, "Oh, that's what I'm trying to get at, that's what this poem is about."

—Amy Ratto Parks

Amy Ratto Parks teaches English at the University of Montana. Her chapbook, *Bread and Water Body*, was the winner of the Merriam Frontier Chapbook Prize.

imagery." Does not want poetry "that focuses on mainstream overtly religious verse." Considers poetry by children and teens. Has published poetry by Janet Buck and Taylor Graham. Work is considered for the print editions of *Ascent* through contests (see below). Receives about 1,500 poems/year, accepts about 15%.

How to Submit Submit 1-5 poems at a time. Considers previously published poems and simultaneous submissions. Prefers e-mail submissions (pasted into body of message or as attachment in Word); no disk submissions. "If you must submit by postal mail because it is your only avenue, provide a SASE with IRCs or Canadian stamps." Reads submissions on a quarterly basis year round. Time between acceptance and publication is 3 months. Editor makes decisions on all poems. Seldom comments on rejected poems. Occasionally publishes theme issues. Upcoming themes available on Web site. Responds in 3 months. Acquires one-time rights.

Contest/Award Offerings To fund the printing of the 2 semiannual anthologies, *Ascent* offers a contest for poetry and fiction. 1st Prize: $100 CAD; 2nd Prize: $75 CAD; 3rd Prize: $50 CAD; 4th Prize: $25 CAD; 5 Honorable Mentions: $10 CAD each. All winners and honorable mentions receive 2 copies of anthology; all other entrants published in anthology receive one free copy. Guidelines available for SASE, by e-mail, or on Web site. **Entry fee:** $5 CAD/poem or $10 CAD/3 poems. **Deadlines:** "these vary for each contest." **NOTE: "Fee, awards, and the number of copies for winners of contests can change. Refer always to the Web site for the most up-to-date information."**

Advice "Write with passion for your material. In terms of editing, always proofread to the point where what you submit is the best it can possibly be. Never be discouraged if your work is not accepted; it may be just not the right fit for the current publication.''

⊘ ASHEVILLE POETRY REVIEW

P.O. Box 7086, Asheville NC 28802. (828)649-0217. E-mail: editor@ashevillereview.com. Web site: www.ashevillereview.com. Established 1994. **Contact:** Keith Flynn, founder/managing editor.

Magazine Needs *Asheville Poetry Review*, published ''every 200 days,'' prints ''the best regional, national, and international poems we can find. We publish translations, interviews, essays, historical perspectives, and book reviews as well.'' Wants ''quality work with well-crafted ideas married to a dynamic style. Any subject matter is fit to be considered so long as the language is vivid with a clear sense of rhythm. We subscribe to the Borges dictum that great poetry is a combination of 'algebra and fire.' '' Has published poetry by Sherman Alexie, Eavan Boland, Gary Snyder, Colette Inez, Robert Bly, and Fred Chappell. *Asheville Poetry Review* is 160-200 pages, digest-sized, perfect-bound, laminated, with full-color cover. Receives about 8,000 submissions/year, accepts about 5%. Press run is 1,000. Subscription: $22.50/2 years, $43.50/4 years. Sample: $13. **''We prefer poets purchase a sample copy prior to submitting.''**

How to Submit Submit 3-5 poems at a time. No previously published poems or simultaneous submissions. No e-mail submissions. Cover letter is required. Include comprehensive bio, recent publishing credits, and SASE. Reads submissions January 15-July 15. Time between acceptance and publication is up to one year. Poems are circulated to an editorial board. Seldom comments on rejected poems. Occasionally publishes theme issues. Guidelines available for SASE. Responds in up to 7 months. Pays one contributor's copy. Rights revert back to author upon publication. Reviews books and chapbooks of poetry. Send materials for review consideration.

▣ ⊘ ◎ ASININE POETRY (Specialized: humor, satire)

Mongrel Publications, P.O. Box 1349, New York NY 10276. E-mail: editor@asininepoetry.com. Web site: www.asininepoetry.com. Established 1998 (print), 2001 (online). **Contact:** R. Narvaez, editor.

• Voted Cool Site of the Month, February 2003.

Magazine Needs *asinine poetry*, published monthly online, ''features 10-12 new poems each month. We specialize in poetry that does not take itself too seriously.'' Wants ''any form of poetry, but for us the poetry must be in a humorous, parodic, or satirical style. Many submissions to our site are slapdash, too broad, or funny on just one snickering level. We prefer well-crafted poems that may contain serious elements or cover serious subjects—but which are also amusing, absurd, or hilarious. We also love topical and occasional poems.'' Does not want serious, straightforward poems. Has published poetry by Hal Sirowitz, William Trowbridge, Allan Planz, Graham Everett, and Colonel Drunky Bob. Receives about 800 poems/year, accepts about 10%.

How to Submit Submit 3-4 poems at a time. Lines/poem: 50 maximum. Considers previously published poems and simultaneous submissions. Accepts e-mail (pasted into body of message) and disk submissions. Reviews books/chapbooks of poetry. Send materials for review consideration.

Contest/Award Offerings Sponsors 2 contests/year. Guidelines available on Web site.

◖ ATLANTA REVIEW

P.O. Box 8248, Atlanta GA 31106. E-mail: dan@atlantareview.com. (inquiries only). Web site: www.atlantareview.com. Established 1994. **Contact:** Dan Veach, editor/publisher.

• Work published in *Atlanta Review* has been included in *The Best American Poetry* and *The Pushcart Prize*.

Magazine Needs *Atlanta Review*, published semiannually, is devoted primarily to poetry, but occasionally features interviews and b&w artwork. Wants ''quality poetry of genuine human appeal.'' Has published poetry by Seamus Heaney, Billy Collins, Derek Walcott, Maxine Kumin, Alicia Stallings, and Thomas Lux. *Atlanta Review* is 128 pages, digest-sized, professionally printed on acid-free paper, flat-spined, with glossy color cover. Receives about 10,000 poems/year, accepts about 1%. Press run is 2,500 (1,000 subscribers, 50 libraries, 1,000 shelf sales). Single copy: $6; subscription: $10. Sample: $5.

How to Submit Submit no more than 5 poems at a time. No previously published poems. No e-mail submissions from within the U.S.; postal submissions only. Include SASE for reply. "Authors living outside the United States and Canada may submit work via e-mail." Cover letter is preferred. Include brief bio. Put name and address on each poem. Reads submissions according to the following deadlines: June 1 for Fall; December 1 for Spring. "While we do read year round, response time may be slower during summer and the winter holidays." Time between acceptance and publication is 6 months. Seldom comments on rejected poems. Guidelines available for SASE, by e-mail, or on Web site. Responds in 2 weeks. Pays 2 contributor's copies, author's discounts on additional copies. Acquires first North American serial rights.

Contest/Award Offerings *Atlanta Review* sponsors the Poetry 2008 International Poetry Competition (see separate listing in Contests & Awards).

$ THE ATLANTIC MONTHLY

P.O. Box 130149, Boston MA 02113. Web site: www.theatlantic.com. Established 1857. **Contact:** David Barber, poetry editor.

Magazine Needs *The Atlantic Monthly* publishes some of the most distinguished poetry in American literature. "We read with interest and attention every poem submitted to the magazine and, quite simply, we publish those that seem to us to be the best." Wants "the broadest possible range of work: traditional forms and free verse, the meditative lyric and the 'light' or comic poem, the work of the famous and the work of the unknown." Has published poetry by Maxine Kumin, Stanley Plumly, Linda Gregerson, Philip Levine, Ellen Bryant Voigt, and W.S. Merwin. Has a circulation of 500,000 (5,800 libraries). Receives about 60,000 poems/year, accepts about 30-35. Subscription: $24.50 for 10 issues. Sample: $7.50 (back issue).

How to Submit Submit 2-6 poems at a time. No previously published poems or simultaneous submissions. No e-mail or disk submissions; postal submissions only. SASE required. Responds in 2-6 weeks. Always sends prepublication galleys. Pays about $4/line. Acquires first North American serial rights only.

Advice "We have long been committed to the discovery of new poets. Our one limitation is length; we are unable to publish very long poems, and authors should consult back issues of the magazine for precedents."

THE AUROREAN (Specialized: seasonal focus)

Encircle Publications, P.O. Box 187, Farmington ME 04938. (207)778-0467. E-mail: aurorean@encirclepub.com. (inqueries only). Web site: www.encirclepub.com. Established 1992 (Encircle Publications); 1995 (*The Aurorean*). **Contact:** Cynthia Brackett-Vincent, editor.

Magazine Needs *The Aurorean*, published semiannually (spring/summer, fall/winter), uses "well crafted poetry that is inspirational (not overly religious), meditational, or reflective of the Northeast. Seasonal focus." Wants short poems, haiku, and well-done humor. "We use mostly free verse, occasional rhyme, and welcome the beginner and the well published." Does not want "ranting, swearing for shock value. Nothing hateful." Considers poetry by children and teens (will publish "if it works"). Has published poetry by Jerome L. McElroy, A.D. Winans, Lynn Parrish Sutton, and Carol Smallwood. *The Aurorean* is digest-sized, professionally printed, perfect-bound, with seasonal design. Press run is 500-550. Single copy: $11 U.S., $12 international; subscription: $21 U.S. (2 issues), $25 international. Sample: back issues from previous quarterly format, $3 each; back issues of current semiannual format, $7 each. Make checks payable to *The Aurorean*.

How to Submit Submit 1-5 poems at a time. Lines/poem: 40 maximum. Considers previously published poems and simultaneous submissions if notified at time of submission. "If they are simultaneous, be aware that none can be withdrawn once we have gone to press." Cover letter is preferred. "Fold cover letter separately and fold poems together. Poems folded individually are a nightmare for editors, and we are unable to review them. Include SASE with sufficient postage for return/reply. Manuscripts are acknowledged with a postcard or by e-mail upon receipt. Poets will be asked to return a 50-word bio upon acceptance. Poets may send a 50-word bio with their submission if they choose. (We cannot edit a long bio and will not use information from a cover letter for a bio.)" Reads submissions according to the following deadlines: February 15 for late April publication; August 15 for late October publication. Responds in 3 months maximum. Always sends prepublication galleys. Pays 2 contributor's copies per poem published (maximum 4 copies/issue). Acquires one-time rights. Appreciates credit if later published elsewhere.

Contest/Award Offerings 1) Awards Featured Poet in each issue (a body of work that best captures the season of that issue); awards publication of up to 3 poems with a 100-word bio, 10 copies of magazine, and a one-year subscription. 2) In each issue, an independent judge picks Best Poem; winner receives $20. 3) Anyone may send entries for Poetic Seasonal Quote: Send 4 seasonal lines maximum from a not-too-obscure poet; source MUST be cited to verify quote, which cannot be acknowledged or returned. Winner receives 2 free issues; same deadlines as above. "Query via e-mail for more information about these opportunities for recognition."

Additional Information Editor recommends one chapbook/issue ("small blurb and ordering information; we do not publish reviews"). Chapbook must have been published within the last 6 months; cannot be acknowledged or returned. Query via e-mail for more information.

Also Offers *The Unrorean*, a broadsheet, appears twice/year, publishing poems too long, experimental, or dark for the magazine. "Still, nothing hateful." Broadsheet is 2-4 pages, 11×17, laser-printed. Sample: $2 postpaid. Include SASE for return/reply. No proofs, acknowledgments, or bios; open submission dates. Pays one contributor's copy/poem. "Poets may submit for the magazine or broadsheet individually. Work sent to the magazine will also be considered for the broadsheet, unless otherwise requested in cover letter."

Advice "Be familiar with your markets; don't submit blindly. Keep writing. Support the markets that support poets. *Poet's Market* is your best friend."

▣ ◖ ◎ AUTUMN LEAVES (Specialized: poems from Native Americans)

E-mail: sjball@mindspring.com. Web site: www.sondra.net/al. Established 1996. **Contact:** Sondra Ball, publisher.

Magazine Needs *Autumn Leaves*, published bimonthly online, is a "magazine of original poetry, mostly by Native American authors, although I accept and publish poems by other people also." Wants "poetry of all styles." Does not want "anti-Indian poetry; seldom publish pro-war poetry." Considers poetry written by children "under 14 for my 'kids' section. I WANT to be told the age of the child." Has published poetry by Johnny Rustywire, Larry Kibby, Harvest McCampbell, Richard Vallance, Shigeki Matsumura, and John Christina Hopkins. Receives about 7,000 poems/year, accepts about 15%.

How to Submit Submit 1-4 poems at a time. Lines/poem: no limit, "although I probably would not publish a book-length poem." Considers previously published poems and simultaneous submissions. Accepts e-mail submissions (pasted into body of message); no disk submissions. Cover letter is preferred. "If a person is a Native American (or First Nations) person, I would like to be told that, and also told what nation they are affiliated with." Reads submissions year round. Submit seasonal poems 2 months in advance. Time between acceptance and publication "anywhere from 2 months to a year." Sometimes comments on rejected poems. Sometimes publishes theme issues. "I publish theme issues on unexpected current events (such as Katrina) if I receive enough submissions on that issue; but I don't usually plan it beforehand." Guidelines available by e-mail. Responds in 2-3 months. No payment, "but I do send the author the URL of the individual poems." Acquires one-time rights. Rights revert to poet upon publication.

✏ ◎ AVOCET, A JOURNAL OF NATURE POEMS (Specialized: nature; spirituality)

P.O. Box 8041, Calabasas CA 91372-8041. Web site: www.csun.edu/~pjs44945/avocet.html. Established 1997. **Contact:** Patricia Swenson, editor.

Magazine Needs *Avocet, A Journal of Nature Poems*, published quarterly, is "devoted to poets seeking to understand the beauty of nature." Wants "poetry that shows man's interconnectedness with nature; discovering the Divine in nature." Does not want "poems that have rhyme or metrical schemes, cliché, abstraction, or sexual overtones." Has published poetry by Peter Leverich, Barbara Bennett, Gary Every, Greg Gregory, John Grey, and Lorraine Vail. *Avocet* is 30 pages, $4\frac{1}{4} \times 5\frac{1}{2}$, professionally printed, saddle-stapled, with card cover. Single copy: $6; subscription: $24. Make checks payable to Patricia Swenson.

How to Submit Submit 3-5 poems at a time. Considers previously published poems, if acknowledged; no simultaneous submissions. Cover letter is required. Include SASE for reply only; mss will not be returned. Time between acceptance and publication is up to 6 months. Responds in up to 3 months. Pays one contributor's copy.

◎ THE AWAKENINGS REVIEW (Specialized: people living with mental illness)

5 Forest Hill Dr., Suite 201, Glen Ellyn IL 60137. E-mail: awakeningsreview@aol.com. Web site: www.theawakeningsproject.org. Established 1999. **Contact:** Robert Lundin, editor.

Magazine Needs *The Awakenings Review*, published annually, prints works by people living with mental illness. Poet "must live with mental illness: consumer, survivor, family member, ex-patient." Wants "meaningful work, good use of the language. Need not be *about* mental illness." Has published poetry by Joan Rizzo, Wanda Washko, Ben Beyerlein, and Trish Evers. *The Awakenings Review* is 150 pages, digest-sized, perfect-bound, with glossy b&w cover. Receives about 800 poems/year, accepts about 20%. Press run is 1,000 (100 subscribers, 2 libraries, 600 shelf sales); 300 distributed free to contributors, friends. Single copy $16; subscription: $32. Sample: $12 (includes postage). Make checks payable to *The Awakenings Review*.

How to Submit Submit 5 poems at a time. No previously published poems or simultaneous submissions. No e-mail submissions. Cover letter is preferred. Include SASE and short bio. Submit seasonal poems 6 months in advance. Time between acceptance and publication is 8 months. Poems are read by a board of editors. Often comments on rejected poems. Occasionally publishes theme issues. Guidelines available in magazine, for SASE, by e-mail, or on Web site. Responds in one month. Pays one contributor's copy, plus discount on additional copies. Acquires first rights. Send materials for review consideration.

Advice "Write a cover letter outlining your relationship to mental illness: consumer, survivor, ex-patient, family member, therapist."

✏ AXE FACTORY REVIEW

Cynic Press, P.O. Box 40691, Philadelphia PA 19107. E-mail: cynicpress@yahoo.com. Established 1986 (*Axe Factory Review*), 2996 (Cynic Press). **Contact:** Joseph Farley, editor/publisher.

Magazine Needs *Axe Factory Review*, published 1-4 times/year, spreads "the disease known as literature. The content is mostly poetry and essays, but we use short stories, too." Wants "eclectic work. Will look at anything but suggest potential contributors purchase a copy of the magazine first to see what we're like." Does not want "greeting card verse." Has published poetry by Taylor Graham, A.D. Winans, Normal, and John Sweet. *Axe Factory Review* is 20-40 pages, magazine-sized, neatly printed, saddle-stapled, with light card cover. Press run is 200. Single copy: $9 (current issue); subscription: $24/4 issues. Sample: $8 (back issue). Make checks payable to Cynic Press or Joseph Farley.

How to Submit Submit up to 10 poems at a time. Considers previously published poems ("sometimes, but let me know up front") and simultaneous submissions. Cover letter is preferred, "but not a form letter; tell me about yourself." Often comments on rejected poems. Pays 1-2 contributor's copies; " 'featured poet' receives more." Reserves right to anthologize poems under Cynic Press; all other rights returned. Reviews books of poetry in 10-1,000 words. Send materials for review consideration.

Additional Information Cynic Press occasionally publishes chapbooks. Has published *Childhood* by B.Z. Niditch, *Rule of Thumb* by Kelley Jean White, M.D., *Yellow Flower Girl* by Xu Juan, *Under the Dogwoods* by Joseph Banford, *Ceiling of Mirrors* by Shane Allison, and *13 Ways of Looking at Godzilla* by Michael Hafer. **Reading fee:** $20. Make checks payable to Cynic Press. **No guarantee of publication.** Several anthologies planned; upcoming themes available in magazine, for SASE, or by e-mail.

Contest/Award Offerings Contest information available by e-mail.

Advice "Writing is a form of mental illness, spread by books, teachers, and the desire to communicate."

★ 🖿 ◑ ◎ BABEL: THE MULTILINGUAL, MULTICULTURAL ONLINE JOURNAL AND COMMUNITY OF ARTS AND IDEAS (Specialized: bilingual/foreign language)

E-mail: submissions@towerofbabel.com. Web site: www.towerofbabel.com. Established 1995. **Contact:** Jennifer Low, submissions editor.

Magazine Needs "*Babel* is an electronic zine that publishes regional reports from international stringers all over the planet, as well as features, round table discussions, fiction, columns, poetry, erotica, travelogues, and reviews of all the arts and editorials. We want to see poetry from all over the world, including multicultural or multilingual work, as well as poetry that has been translated from or into another language, as long as it is also in English. We also appreciate gay/lesbian and bisexual poetry. Writers whose work discriminates against the opposite sex, different cultures, or belief systems will not be considered."

How to Submit Submit no more than 10 poems at a time. Considers previously published poems and simultaneous submissions. Accepts e-mail submissions only. Cover letter is required. "Please send submissions with a résumé or bio as a Microsoft Word or RTF document attached to e-mail." Time between acceptance and publication varies; "usually no more than a month or two depending on how busy we are." Seldom comments on rejected poems. Guidelines available on Web site. Responds in 2-4 weeks. Reviews books/chapbooks of poetry and other magazines, single- and multi-book format. Open to unsolicited reviews. Send materials for review consideration.

Advice "Try stepping into someone elses's shoes and writing from their point of view, even if it's writing in the voice of someone of the opposite sex. Don't try to capture the style of a well known poet, though. Instead, find your own style and express yourself and most importantly, write passionately."

🖿 ◑ BABY CLAM PRESS

E-mail: BabyClamPress@yahoo.com. Web site: www.BabyClamPress.com. Established 2004. **Contact:** AJ Martin, chief editor.

Magazine Needs *Baby Clam Press*, published 2-3 times/year online, is "a journal for the unconventional poet, publishing fresh, creative poetry." Wants "any style, genre, or form that is creatively and skillfully crafted with crisp sonics and fresh imagery." Does not want "greeting card verse, pornography, teenage angst, or sermons." Considers poetry by children and teens. Has published poetry by Bruce Niedt, Dan Maguire, Andrea Jazwiecki, Rachel Bunting, Anna Evans, and Patricia Wellingham-Jones. Receives about 200-250 poems/year, accepts about 10-15%. Sample: free on Web site.

How to Submit Submit 4-6 poems at a time. Lines/poem: less than 40. Considers previously published poems ("author must indicate where and when published") and simultaneous submissions ("author must inform which poems are simultaneous subs and immediately notify editors if a piece is selected for publication elsewhere"). Accepts e-mail submissions (pasted into body of message); no disk submissions. Cover letter is preferred. "Include full name, e-mail address, and phone number. Please keep introductory letter, bio, and previous publishing credits short and concise. Check Web site for reading times." Submit seasonal poems 3 months in advance. Time between acceptance and publication is 4-5 months. Poems are circulated to an editorial board. Sometimes comments on rejected poems. **"At author's request, we will critique poems for a fee of $5 per poem.** See Web site for more details." Sometimes publishes theme issues. Guidelines available on Web site. Responds in 8-10 weeks. Sometimes sends prepublication galleys. "Will publish work on Web site once and archive it. Author allows use of work again in 'best of' issues." Rights revert to poet upon publication.

Contest/Award Offerings Sponsors the *Baby Clam Press* Poetry Contest at varied times during the year. Offers "a percentage of total entry fees or other prizes as listed on Web site." See Web site for entry fees, deadlines, and guidelines.

Advice "Poets seeking publication for the first time should read previous issues of the journal/ magazine to which they're submitting in order to determine if their poetry would be a good fit with that publication. Beginning poets should read good poetry every day, write something every day, and join a critique group to help them improve their writing."

$☐ ◎ BABYBUG MAGAZINE (Specialized: children ages 6 months-2 years)

Carus Publishing, 70 E. Lake St., Suite 300, Chicago IL 60601. Web site: www.cricketmag.com. Established 1994. **Contact:** Submissions Editor.

Magazine Needs *BABYBUG Magazine*, published 10 times/year, is a read-aloud magazine for ages 6 months to 2 years. Wants "rhythmic, rhyming" short poems. *BABYBUG* is 24 pages, $6\frac{1}{4} \times 7$, printed on cardstock with nontoxic glued spine. Receives more than 1,200 submissions/month, accepts 25-30. Circulation is 48,000. Subscription: $35.97/year (10 issues). Sample: $5; sample pages available on Web site.

How to Submit Submit no more than 5 poems at a time. Lines/poem: 8 lines maximum. Considers previously published poems. Include SASE. Guidelines available for SASE or on Web site. Responds in 6 months. Pays $25 minimum on publication. Acquires North American publication rights for previously published poems; rights vary for unpublished poems.

Advice "Before attempting to write for *BABYBUG*, be sure to familiarize yourself with this age child and with the magazine itself."

☐ BABYSUE®

P.O. Box 15749, Chattanooga, TN 37415. Web site: www.babysue.com. and www.LMNOP.com. **Contact:** Don W. Seven, editor/publisher.

Magazine Needs *babysue®*, published twice/year, offers obtuse humor for the extremely open-minded. "We are open to all styles, but prefer short poems." No restrictions. Has published poetry by Edward Mycue, Susan Andrews, and Barry Bishop. *babysue®* is 32 pages, offset-printed. "We print prose, poems, and cartoons. We usually accept about 5% of what we receive." Subscription: $16 for 4 issues. Sample: $5.

How to Submit Considers previously published poems and simultaneous submissions. Deadlines are March 30 and September 30 of each year. Seldom comments on rejected poems. Responds "immediately, if we are interested." Pays one contributor's copy. "We do occasionally review other magazines."

◖ BACKSTREET (formerly *Backstreet Quarterly*)

P.O. Box 1377, Berthoud CO 80513. E-mail: backstreetqtrly@earthlink.net. Established 2004. **Contact:** Ray Foreman, editor.

Magazine Needs *Backstreet*, published 6 times/year, wants "strong, clear narrative poems relevant to the times and the human condition, and appropriate for a readership of experienced poets. We are a 'poet's magazine for poets' whose purpose is keeping them writing by providing an easy and regular publishing outlet. We are privately subsidized, never run contests, and offer subscriptions at minimal cost to poets who read other poets' work." Does not want "poems that are obscure in any way or poems that have meaning only to the writer." Has published poetry by A.D. Winans, Anselm Brocki, Charles Ries, Laurel Speer, Arthur Gotlieb, and Steven Levi. *Backstreet* "has a special layout that has the equivalent content of a 36-page magazine," laser-printed, stapled, with paper cover. Receives about 600 poems/year, accepts about 200. Press run is 150 (110 subscribers). Single copy: $2; subscription: $4/year (4 issues), $10 for 10 issues. Make checks payable to R. Foreman.

How to Submit Submit 3 poems at a time. Lines/poem: 15 minimum, 50 maximum. "Maximum width is 65 characters per line." Considers previously published poems and simultaneous submissions. No e-mail or disk submissions. "SASE for first submission only. No cover letter, bio, or credits list. No graphic layout. Flush left, preferably in Times Roman or Garamond. No long skinnys. Disposable sharp hard copies. Your work speaks for you." Reads submissions year round. Time between acceptance and publication is 3 months. Sometimes comments on rejected poems. Responds in one week to one month. Acquires one-time rights. Rights revert to poet upon publication.

Advice "To write better poems, read poems in current anthologies to get a feel for what is good. It almost never happens at most poetry readings. Poetry is essentially an abbreviated short story literary art on the page."

☐ BACKWARDS CITY REVIEW

Backwards City Publications, P.O. Box 41317, Greensboro NC 27404-1317. E-mail: editors@backwardscity.net. Web site: www.backwardscity.net. Established 2004. **Contact:** Tom Christopher, editor. Member: CLMP.

• One of *Library Journal*'s Top Ten New Magazines for 2004.

Magazine Needs *Backwards City Review*, published biannually, gathers "strong diverse voices from different genres in order to create a journal that caters to the world above, beyond, below, around, near, within-sight-of, and slightly out of tune with conventional literary outlets." Does not want "light verse, seasonal verse." Has published poetry by Gabriel Gudding, Johannes Goransson, Joyelle McSweeney, John Latta, and Denise Duhamel. *Backwards City Review* is 128 pages, digest-sized, offset-printed (50# offset 512 PPI), perfect-bound, with 10 pt. color cover, includes ads. Receives about 500 poems/year, accepts about 30. Press run is 750 (300 subscribers, 25 libraries, 50 shelf sales); 100 distributed free to writing programs, reviewers, previous contributors, etc. Single copy: $5; subscription: $12. Make checks payable to Backwards City Publications.

How to Submit Submit 5 poems at a time. Lines/poem: no requirements. Considers simultaneous submissions; no previously published poems. Accepts e-mail submissions (pasted into body of message); no disk submissions. Cover letter is preferred. "Please include short, three-line bio with submission and SASE." Reads submissions year round. Time between acceptance and publication is 6 months. Poems are circulated to an editorial board. Sometimes comments on rejected poems. Sometimes publishes theme issues. Upcoming themes available on Web site. Guidelines available in magazine, for SASE, or on Web site. Responds in 3 months. Sometimes sends prepublication galleys. Pays 3 contributor's copies. Acquires first North American serial rights as well as electronic rights for Web site, and anthology rights. Rights revert to poet upon publication.

Additional Information Backwards City Publications publishes one chapbook/year. Manuscripts are selected through the *Backwards City Review* Poetry Chapbook Contest. "Manuscripts selected for the Backwards City Chapbook Series are on a **solicitation basis only**, except for contest entries, all of which are considered for the series." Chapbooks are 26-60 pages, laser-set, saddle-stapled, with digital-output covers, sometimes include art/graphics. Chapbook mss may include previously published poems. Order sample chapbooks by sending $5 to Backwards City Publications

Contest/Award Offerings The *Backwards City Review* Literary Contest offers $400 and publication. Submit 4 poems maximum; poems may be of any length. Guidelines available in magazine, for SASE, or on Web site. **Entry fee:** $15. **Deadline:** March 15. Also offers the *Backwards City Review* Poetry Chapbook Contest (see separate listing in Contests & Awards).

Advice "Check out our Web site and a previous issue to get a sense of what we like. Don't get frustrated."

◌ BARBARIC YAWP

Boneworld Publishing, 3700 County Rt. 24, Russell NY 13684. (315)347-2609. Established 1996. **Contact:** John and Nancy Berbrich, editors.

Magazine Needs *Barbaric Yawp*, published quarterly, prints "the best fiction, poetry, and essays available." Encourages beginning writers. "We are not preachers of any particular poetic or literary school. We publish any type of quality material appropriate for our intelligent and wide-awake audience; all types considered: blank, free, found, concrete, traditional rhymed and metered forms." Does not want "any pornography, gratuitous violence, or any whining, pissing, or moaning." Considers poetry by teens. Has published poetry by Nancy Henry, Mark Spitzer, and Jeff Grimshaw. *Barbaric Yawp* is a 60-page booklet, stapled, with 67 lb. cover. Receives 1,000 poems/year, accepts about 5%. Press run is 120 (50 subscribers, 4 libraries). Single copy: $4; subscription: $15/year (4 issues). Make checks payable to John Berbrich.

How to Submit Submit up to 5 poems at a time. Lines/poem: 50 maximum. Considers previously published poems and simultaneous submissions. Cover letter is preferred (one page). Include a short publication history (if available) and a brief bio. Include SASE. Reads submissions year round. Time between acceptance and publication is up to 6 months. Often comments on rejected poems. Guidelines available for SASE. Responds in up to 2 months. Pays one contributor's copy. Acquires one-time rights.

Advice "Read a lot—Dead White Males and Living Black Females—and everyone in-between. Write often, summon the Muse, and don't fear rejection!"

▣ ⬙ ◎ THE BAREFOOT MUSE (Specialized: formal/metrical verse only)

P.O. Box 115, Hainesport NJ 08036. E-mail: submissions@barefootmuse.com. Web site: www.barefootmuse.com. Established 2005. **Contact:** Anna Evans, editor.

Magazine Needs *The Barefoot Muse*, published semiannually online, prints "only formal/metrical poetry (rhyme is optional). Poems in formal structures are most welcome. These include (but are not limited to) sonnets, villanelles, sestinas, triolets, pantuns, and rondeaus." Does not want "free verse; also, please do not send me rhyming poetry without first finding out what meter is." Has published poetry by Denise Duhamel, Jared Carter, Gail White, and Leo Yankevich. Receives about 800 poems/year, accepts about 5%.

How to Submit Submit up to 5 poems at a time. Lines/poem: less than 40 preferred. Considers previously published poems ("by invitation only") and simultaneous submissions ("with notification"). Accepts e-mail submissions (pasted into body of message). Reads submissions year round. Time between acceptance and publication is up to 6 months. Sometimes comments on rejected poems. Guidelines available on Web site. Responds in 2 months. Always sends prepublications galleys. Acquires one-time rights. Rights revert to poet upon publication.

▣ $⬙ BARNWOOD

4604 47th Ave. S., Seattle WA 98118-1824. (206)225-6887. E-mail: barnwoodpress@earthlink.net. (inquiries only). Web site: www.barnwoodpress.org. Established 1975. **Contact:** Tom Koontz, editor.

Magazine Needs *Barnwood*, published online, "serves poets and readers by publishing excellent poems." Does not want "expressions of prejudice such as racism, sexism." Has published poetry by Bly, Goedicke, Friman, and Stafford. Receives about 3,000 poems/year, accepts about 1%.

How to Submit Submit 1-3 poems at a time. Considers simultaneous submissions; no previously published poems. No e-mail submissions; postal submissions only. "Include SASE or no response." Reads submissions September 1-May 31 only. Time between acceptance and publication is one day. Seldom comments on rejected poems. Responds in one month. Pays $25/poem. Acquires one-time rights.

Advice "Emphasize imagination, passion, engagement, artistry."

◙ BARROW STREET

P.O. Box 1831, New York NY 10156. E-mail: info@barrowstreet.org. Web site: www.barrowstreet.org. Established 1998. **Contact:** Lorna Blake, Patricia Carlin, Peter Covino, and Sarah Hannah, editors.

- Poetry published in *Barrow Street* is often selected for *The Best American Poetry*.

Magazine Needs *Barrow Street*, published semiannually, "is dedicated to publishing new and established poets." Wants "poetry of the highest quality; open to all styles and forms." Has published poetry by Molly Peacock, Lyn Hejinian, Carl Phillips, Marie Ponsot, Charles Bernstein, and Stephen Burt. *Barrow Street* is 96-120 pages, digest-sized, professionally printed, perfect-bound, with glossy cardstock cover with color or b&w photography. Receives about 3,000 poems/year, accepts about 3%. Press run is 1,000. Subscription: $15/year, $28 for 2 years, $42 for 3 years. Sample: $8.

How to Submit Submit up to 5 poems at a time. Considers simultaneous submissions (when notified); no previously published poems. Cover letter is preferred. Include brief bio. Reads submissions year round. Poems are circulated to an editorial board. Sometimes comments on rejected poems. Occasionally publishes theme issues. Guidelines available for SASE or on Web site. Responds in up to 6 months. Always sends prepublication galleys. Pays 2 contributor's copies. Acquires first rights.

Contest/Award Offerings The Barrow Street Press Book Contest (see separate listing in Contests & Awards).

Advice "Submit your strongest work."

◘ BATHTUB GIN

Pathwise Press, P.O. Box 1164, Champaign IL 61824. E-mail: pathwisepress@hotmail.com. Web site: www.pathwisepress.com. Established 1997. **Contact:** Christopher Harter, editor.

- **PLEASE NOTE:** "*Bathtub Gin*/Pathwise Press may be going on temporary hiatus after spring 2007; interested parties should contact the magazine to check on status."

Magazine Needs *Bathtub Gin*, published semiannually in April and October, has "an eclectic aesthetic—we want to keep you guessing what is on the next page." Wants poetry that "takes a chance with language or paints a vivid picture with its imagery, has the kick of bathtub gin, which can be experimental or a sonnet." Does not want "trite rhymes, Bukowski wannabes (let the man rest), or confessionals." Has published poetry by Kell Robertson, Tom Kryss, Mike James, and Richard Krech. *Bathtub Gin* is about 60 pages, digest-sized, laser-printed, saddle-stapled, with 80 lb. coverstock cover. Receives about 1,200 poems/year, accepts about 5%. Press run is 300-350 (70 subscribers, 30 shelf sales); 10 distributed free to reviewers, other editors, and libraries. Single copy: $5; subscription: $8. Sample (back issue): $3.50. Foreign orders add $2. Make checks payable to Christopher Harter.

How to Submit Submit 4-6 poems at a time. Considers previously published poems and simultaneous submissions. Accepts e-mail submissions (pasted into body of message). Cover letter is required. "Three- to five-line bio required if you are accepted for publication; if none provided, we make one up." Include SASE. Reads submissions June 1-September 15 only, but accepts contributions for 2 issues. Time between acceptance and publication is up to 8 months. Sometimes comments on rejected poems. Guidelines available in magazine, for SASE, by e-mail, or on Web site. Responds in up to 2 months. Pays 2 contributor's copies. "We also sell extra copies to contributors at a discount, which they can give away or sell at full price."

Additional Information Pathwise Press's goal is to publish chapbooks, broadsides, and "whatever else tickles us." Has published *The Levelling Wind* by Kell Robertson, *Nothing But Love* by Mike James, *The United Colors of Death* by Mark Terrill, and *Living Room, Earth* by Carmen Germain. Guidelines available for SASE or on Web site.

Also Offers "We feature a 'News' section where people can list their books, presses, events, etc."

⭐ ◨ ◎ BEAR CREEK HAIKU (Specialized: haiku/senryu; poems under 15 lines)

P.O. Box 3787, Boulder CO 80307. Established 1991. **Contact:** Ayaz Daryl Nielsen, editor.

Magazine Needs *bear creek haiku* prints haiku/senryu and any form/style less than 15 lines. Has published poetry by Quinn Rennerfeldt, Carl Mayfield, Heyoka, and Sean Perkins. *bear creek haiku* is 24 pages, photocopied on legal-sized blue paper cut in thirds lengthwise, stacked 3-high, folded, and stapled. Receives about 6,000 poems/year, accepts about 5%. Press run is about 200/issue (153 subscribers). Single copy: free for SASE; subscription: $5. Make checks payable to Daryl Nielsen.

How to Submit Submit 5-20 poems at a time. Considers previously published poems and simultaneous submissions. "Include name, address, and several poems on each page. Keep your postage expenses at two First-Class stamps, one of which is on the SASE." Reads submissions year round. Time between acceptance and publication varies. Response time varies. Pays 2 contributor's copies. Acquires first rights.

Advice "We appreciate receiving your own personal favorites, be they simultaneously submitted or published elsewhere or never seen before. Write, create your poems—the heart, spirit, shadow, ancestors, readers, other poets, an occasional editor, etc., will benefit deeply."

$ ◎ THE BEAR DELUXE (Specialized: nature/ecology)

P.O. Box 10342, Portland OR 97296-0342. (503)242-1047. E-mail: bear@orlo.org. Web site: www.or lo.org. Established 1993. **Contact:** Casey Bush, poetry editor. Editor: Tom Webb.

- *The Bear Deluxe* is published by Orlo, a nonprofit organization exploring environmental issues through the creative arts.

Magazine Needs *The Bear Deluxe*, published quarterly, provides "a fresh voice amid often strident and polarized environmental discourse. Street-level, non-dogmatic, and solution-oriented, *The Bear Deluxe* presents lively creative discussion to a diverse readership." Wants poetry "with innovative environmental perspectives." Does not want "rants." Has published poetry by Judith Barrington, Robert Michael Pyle, Mary Winters, Stephen Babcock, Carl Hanni, and Derek Sheffield. *The Bear Deluxe* is 48 pages, 9×12, newsprint, saddle-stapled, with brown Kraft paper cover. Receives about 1,200 poems/year, accepts about 20-30. Press run is 20,000 (750 subscribers, 20 libraries); 18,000 distributed free on the streets of the western U.S. and beyond. Subscription: $16. Sample: $3. Make checks payable to Orlo.

How to Submit Submit 3-5 poems at a time. Lines/poem: 50 maximum. Considers previously published poems and simultaneous submissions "so long as noted." Accepts e-mail submissions (pasted into body of message). "We can't respond to e-mail submissions but do look at them." Poems are reviewed by a committee of 3-5 people. Publishes one theme issue/year. Guidelines available for SASE. Responds in 6 months. Pays $20/poem, one contributor's copy (more if willing to distribute), and subscription. Acquires first or one-time rights.

⭐ 🌐 ◨ ◎ THE BEATNIK COWBOY (Specialized: Beat-influenced poetry)

Ruamchoke Condoview 2, 37/447 Moo 2, Khao Pratumnak Rd., Nongprue, Banglamung, Chonburi 20150 Thailand. E-mail: beatnik_cowboy@yahoo.com.au. Established 2004. **Contact:** Mr. David Solomon.

Magazine Needs *The Beatnik Cowboy*, published quarterly, wants "Beat-influenced poetry from all poets. We are a young and vibrant magazine, seeking to publish poems from poets all around the world." Has published poetry by Steve Dalchinsky, Herschell Silverman, Randall Rogers, and Joe Speer. *The Beatnik Cowboy* is 32 pages, magazine-sized, computer-generated, side-stapled (will be bound in the future), includes ads. Receives about 200 poems/year. Press run is 30 (5 subscribers, 2 libraries, 5 shelf sales); 15 distributed free. Single copy: $6 USD. Make checks payable to Randall Rogers.

How to Submit Submit 5 poems at a time. Lines/poem: short poems preferred. Considers previously published poems and simultaneous submissions. Accepts e-mail (as attachment) and disk submissions. Cover letter is preferred. SAE with IRCs required for return of poems. Reads submissions year round. Submit seasonal poems 2 months in advance. Time between acceptance and publication is 3 months. Never comments on rejected poems. Guidelines available in magazine, for SASE, or by e-mail. Responds in 2 months. Acquires one-time rights.

◻ ◎ BELLEVUE LITERARY REVIEW (Specialized: humanity, health, and healing)

New York University School of Medicine, OBV-A612, 550 First Ave., New York NY 10016. (212)263-3973. E-mail: info@BLReview.org. Web site: www.BLReview.org. Established 2001. **Contact:** Stacy Bodziak, managing editor. Member: CLMP.

• Work published in *Bellevue Literary Review* has appeared in *The Pushcart Prize*.

Magazine Needs *Bellevue Literary Review*, published semiannually, prints "works of fiction, nonfiction, and poetry that touch upon relationships to the human body, illness, health, and healing." Has published poetry by Rafael Campo, Sharon Olds, James Tate, Rick Moody, John Stone, and Floyd Skloot. *Bellevue Literary Review* is 160 pages, digest-sized, perfect-bound, includes ads. Receives about 1,100 poems/year, accepts about 3%. Press run is 5,000 (2,000 subscribers, 30 libraries); distributed free to lit mag conferences, promotions, and other contacts. Single copy: $7; subscription: $12/year, $30 for 3 years (plus $5/year postage to Canada, $8/year postage foreign). Make checks payable to *Bellevue Literary Review*.

How to Submit Submit up to 3 poems at a time. Lines/poem: prefers poems of one page or less. Considers simultaneous submissions; no previously published poems. No e-mail or disk submissions. "We accept poems via regular mail and through our Web site; when submitting via regular mail, please include SASE." Cover letter is preferred. Reads submissions year round. Time between acceptance and publication is about 6-7 months. "Poems are reviewed by two independent readers, then sent to an editor." Sometimes comments on rejected poems. Sometimes publishes theme issues. Upcoming themes available on Web site. Guidelines available for SASE or on Web site. Responds in 3-5 months. Always sends prepublication galleys. Pays 2 contributor's copies and one-year subscription for author, plus one-year gift subscription for friend. Acquires first North American serial rights. Rights revert to poet upon publication.

Contest/Award Offerings Sponsors the Magliocco Prize for Poetry, offering an annual award of $1,000 and publication in *Bellevue Literary Review*. Submit up to 3 poems (5 pages maximum). **Entry fee:** $15 ($20 includes one-year subscription). **Deadline:** see Web site. Guidelines available for SASE or on Web site.

◪ BELLINGHAM REVIEW

Western Washington University, Mail Stop 9053, Bellingham WA 98225. (360)650-4863. E-mail: bhreview@cc.wwu.edu. Web site: www.wwu.edu/~bhreview. Established 1975. **Contact:** Poetry Editor. Editor-in-Chief: Brenda Miller.

Magazine Needs *Bellingham Review*, published twice/year, has no specific preferences as to form. Wants "well-crafted poetry, but are open to all styles." Has published poetry by David Shields, Tess Gallagher, Gary Soto, Jane Hirshfield, Albert Goldbarth, and Rebecca McClanahan. *Bellingham Review* is digest-sized, perfect-bound, with matte cover. Circulation is 1,500. Subscription: $14/year, $27 for 2 years, $40 for 3 years; $20/year for libraries and institutions. Sample: $7. Make checks payable to *Bellingham Review*.

How to Submit Submit 3-5 poems at a time. Considers simultaneous submissions with notification. No e-mail submissions; accepts submissions by postal mail only. Include SASE. Reads submissions

September 15-February 1 only (submissions must be postmarked within this reading period). Guidelines available for SASE or on Web site. Responds in 2 months. Pays 2 contributor's copies, a year's subscription, plus monetary payment (if funding allows). Acquires first North American serial rights. **Contest/Award Offerings** The 49th Parallel Poetry Award (see separate listing in Contests & Awards).

BELL'S LETTERS POET (Specialized: subscribers preferred)

P.O. Box 2187, Gulfport MS 39505-2187. E-mail: jimbelpoet@aol.com. Established 1956. **Contact:** Jim Bell, editor/publisher.

Magazine Needs *Bell's Letters Poet*, published quarterly, **must be purchased by contributors before they can be published.**" Many say they stop everything the day [the magazine] arrives." Wants "clean writing in good taste; no vulgarity, no artsy vulgarity." Has published poetry by Betty Wallace, Paul Pross, Carrie Quick, and Kalman Gayler. *Bell's Letters Poet* is about 60 pages, digest-sized, photocopied on plain bond paper (including cover), saddle-stapled. Single copy: $6; subscription: $24. Sample: $5. "Send a poem (20 lines or under, in good taste) with your sample order, and we will publish it in our next issue."

How to Submit Submit 4 poems at a time. Lines/poem: 4-20. Considers previously published poems "if cleared by author with prior publisher"; no simultaneous submissions. No e-mail submissions; accepts submissions by postal mail only. Submission deadline is 2 months prior to publication. Accepted poems by subscribers are published immediately in the next issue. Guidelines available in magazine or for SASE. No payment for accepted poetry, but "many patrons send cash awards to the poets whose work they especially like." Reviews books of poetry by subscribers.

Contest/Award Offerings "The Ratings" is a competition in each issue. Readers are asked to vote on their favorite poems, and the "Top 40" are announced in the next issue, along with awards sent to the poets by patrons. News releases are then sent to subscriber's hometown newspaper.

Also Offers *Bell's Letters Poet* also features a telephone and e-mail exchange among poets, a birthdate listing, and a profile of its poets.

Advice "Tired of seeing no bylines this year? Subscription guarantees a byline in each issue."

BELOIT POETRY JOURNAL

P.O. Box 151, Farmington ME 04938. (207)778-0020. E-mail: sharkey@maine.edu. (inquiries only). Web site: www.bpj.org. Established 1950. **Contact:** John Rosenwald and Lee Sharkey, editors.

● Poetry published in the *Beloit Poetry Journal* has been included in *The Best American Poetry, Best New Poets*, and *The Pushcart Prize*.

Magazine Needs *Beloit Poetry Journal*, published quarterly, prints "the most outstanding poems we receive, without bias as to length, school, subject, or form. For more than 58 years of continuous publication, we have been distinguished for the extraordinary range of our poetry and our discov-

The Vol. 57, No. 1 cover of *The Beloit Poetry Journal* features editor Lee Sharkey's photograph of a webworm net cloth, a visual image which, says Sharkey, "fascinates and appals. The image reflects in the brilliance of its webbing a quality we're looking for in poems."

Cover photography by Lee Sharkey; cover design by Mary Greene.

ery of strong new poets." Wants "visions broader than the merely personal; language that makes us laugh and weep, recoil, resist—and pay attention. We're drawn to poetry that grabs hold of the whole body, not just the head." Has published poetry by Lucille Clifton, Albert Goldbarth, Patricia Goedicke, Karl Elder, John Haines, and Peter Streckfus. *Beloit Poetry Journal* is about 48 pages, digest-sized, saddle-stapled, attractively printed, with 4-color cover with tasteful art. Circulation is 1,250 (700 subscribers, 235 libraries). Subscription: $18/year, $48 for 3 years (individuals); $23/year, $65 for 3 years (institutions). Sample: $5 (includes guidelines).

How to Submit No previously published poems or simultaneous submissions. No e-mail submissions. "Submit any time, without query, in any legible form; no bio necessary. Unless it's a long poem, send what will go in a business envelope for one stamp. Don't send your life's work. We respond to most submissions within two weeks. Manuscripts under active consideration we keep for up to 4 months, circulating them among our readers, and continuing to winnow. At the quarterly meetings of the Editorial Board, we read aloud all the surviving poems and put together an issue of the best we have." Guidelines without sample copy available for SASE or on Web site. Pays 3 contributor's copies. Acquires first serial rights. Editor for Reviews and Exchanges reviews books by and about poets. Send materials for review consideration to Marion Stocking, 24 Berry Cove Rd., Lamoine ME 04605.

Additional Information "To diversify our offerings, we occasionally publish chapbooks; these are almost never the work of a single poet."

Contest/Award Offerings Awards the Chad Walsh Poetry Prize ($3,000) to a poem or group of poems published in the calendar year. "Every poem we publish in 2008 will be considered for the 2008 prize."

Advice "We are always watching for fresh music, live forms and language."

$🖳 ◎ BELTWAY POETRY QUARTERLY (Specialized: Washington, D.C.-area poets)

E-mail: beltway.poetry@juno.com. Web site: www.beltwaypoetry.com. Established 2000. **Contact:** Kim Roberts, editor.

Magazine Needs *Beltway Poetry Quarterly*, published online, "features poets who live or work in the greater Washington, D.C., metro region. *Beltway* showcases the richness and diversity of Washington, D.C., authors, with poets from different backgrounds, races, ethnicities, ages, and sexual orientations represented. We have included Pulitzer Prize winners and those who have never previously published. We publish academic, spoken word, and experimental authors—and those whose work defies categorization." Takes unsolicited submissions only for special themed issues. Themes change annually; check Web site for details. Has published poetry by Cornelius Eady, Anthony Hecht, E. Ethelbert Miller, Jane Shore, Sharan Strange, and Hilary Tham.

How to Submit *Other than annual themed issue, we consider poems by invitation only.* Theme issues have included poetic responses to Walt Whitman, the war in Iraq, and D.C. Places. Two issues per year feature five poets from the greater-D.C. region, and these issues are open only by invitation. One issue per year is guest-edited." Never comments on rejected poems. Guidelines available on Web site.

Also Offers "Monthly Poetry News section has information on new publications, calls for entries, workshops, readings, and performances. Extensive links also include the most complete listing anywhere of artist residency programs in the U.S."

$🖳 ◯ ◎ BETWEEN KISSES NEWSLETTER (Specialized: fantasy; science fiction; horror)

P.O. Box 782, Cedar Rapids IA 52406-0782. E-mail: betweenkisses@samsdotpublishing.com. Web site: www.samsdotpublishing.com. Established 2002. **Contact:** Tyree Campbell, editor. Member: The Speculative Literature Foundation.

Magazine Needs *Between Kisses Newsletter*, published bimonthly online, presents fantasy, science fiction, sword and sorcery, alternate history, horror short stories, poems, illustrations, and movie and book reviews. Wants fantasy, science fiction, spooky horror, and speculative poetry. Does not want "horror with excessive blood and gore." Considers poetry by children and teens. Has published poetry by Bruce Boston, Karen A. Romanko, Erin Donahoe, Cythera, Kristine Ong Muslim, and Aurelio Rico Lopez III. Receives about 150 poems/year, accepts about 35 (23%).

How to Submit Submit up to 5 poems at a time. Lines/poem: prefers less than 100. Considers previously published poems; no simultaneous submissions. Accepts e-mail submissions (pasted into body of message); no disk submissions. "Submission should include snail mail address and a short (1-2 lines) bio." Reads submissions year round. Submit seasonal poems 6 months in advance. Time between acceptance and publication is 1-2 months. Often comments on rejected poems. Guidelines available on Web site. Responds in 4-6 weeks. Pays $2/poem, $1/reprint. Acquires first North American serial rights. Reviews books/chapbooks of poetry. Send materials for review consideration to Tyree Campbell.

Advice "*Between Kisses* is a good place for beginning writers to submit their work."

$□ ◎ BEYOND CENTAURI (Specialized: fantasy, science fiction, & mild horror for older children and teens)

P.O. Box 782, Cedar Rapids IA 52406-0782. E-mail: beyondcentauri@samsdotpublishing.com. Web site: www.samsdotpublishing.com. Established 2003. **Contact:** Tyree Campbell, managing editor. Member: The Speculative Literature Foundation.

Magazine Needs *Beyond Centauri*, published quarterly, contains "fantasy, science fiction, sword and sorcery, very mild horror short stories, poetry, and illustrations for readers ages 9-18." Wants "fantasy, science fiction, spooky horror, and speculative poetry for younger readers." Does not want "horror with excessive blood and gore." Considers poetry by children and teens. Has published poetry by Bruce Boston, Bobbi Sinha-Morey, Andy Miller, Dorothy Imm, Cythera, and Terrie Leigh Relf. *Beyond Centauri* is 32 pages, magazine-sized, offset-printed, saddle-stapled, with paper cover with color art, includes ads. Receives about 200 poems/year, accepts about 50 (25%). Press run is 100 (20 subscribers, 50 shelf sales); 5 distributed free to reviewers. Single copy: $6; subscription: $17/year, $33/2 years. Make checks payable to Tyree Campbell/Sam's Dot Publishing.

How to Submit Submit up to 5 poems at a time. Lines/poem: prefers less than 100. Considers previously published poems; no simultaneous submissions. Accepts e-mail submissions (pasted into body of message); no disk submissions. "Submission should include snail mail address and a short (1-2 lines) bio." Reads submissions year round. Submit seasonal poems 6 months in advance. Time between acceptance and publication is 1-2 months. Often comments on rejected poems. Guidelines available on Web site. Responds in 4-6 weeks. Pays $2/original poem, plus one contributor's copy. Acquires first North American serial rights. Reviews books/chapbooks of poetry. Send materials for review consideration to Tyree Campbell.

Advice "We like to see submissions from younger writers."

✖ $◩ ◎ BIBLE ADVOCATE (Specialized: Christian)

P.O. Box 33677, Denver CO 80233. E-mail: bibleadvocate@cog7.org. Web site: www.cog7.org/BA. Established 1863. **Contact:** Sherri Langton, associate editor.

Magazine Needs *Bible Advocate*, published 8 times/year, features "Christian content—to be a voice for the Bible and for the church." Wants "free verse, some traditional, with Christian/Bible themes." Does not want "avant-garde poetry." *Bible Advocate* is 32 pages, magazine-sized. Receives about 30-50 poems/year, accepts about 10-20. Press run varies (13,500 subscribers); all distributed free.

How to Submit Submit no more than 5 poems at a time. Lines/poem: 5 minimum, 20 maximum. Considers previously published poems (with notification) and simultaneous submissions. Accepts e-mail submissions (pasted into body of message; no attachments). Cover letter is preferred. "No handwritten submissions, please." Time between acceptance and publication is up to one year. "I

read them first and reject those that won't work for us. I send good ones to editor for approval.''
Seldom comments on rejected poems. Publishes theme issues. Guidelines available for SASE or on
Web site. Responds in 2 months. Pays $20 and 2 contributor's copies. Acquires first, reprint, electronic, and one-time rights.

Advice ''Avoid trite or forced rhyming. Be aware of the magazine's doctrinal views (send for doctrinal beliefs booklet).''

✪ ☻ ◎ ⊘ BIBLIOPHILOS (Specialized: bilingual/foreign language; ethnic/nationality; nature/ecology; social issues)

200 Security Building, Fairmont WV 26554. Established 1981. **Contact:** Gerald J. Bobango, editor.

Magazine Needs ''*Bibliophilos* is an academic journal for the literati, illuminati, amantes artium,
and those who love animals; scholastically oriented, for the liberal arts. Topics include fiction
and nonfiction, literature and criticism, history, art, music, theology, philosophy, natural history,
educational theory, contemporary issues and politics, sociology, and economics. Published in English, French, German, and Romanian.'' Also publishes one all-poetry issue per year, containing
the winners of an annual poetry contest (see below). Wants ''traditional forms, formalism, structure, rhyme; also blank verse. Aim for concrete visual imagery, either in words or on the page.''
Does not want ''inspirational verse, or anything that Ann Landers or Erma Bombeck would publish.'' Considers poetry written by children ages 10 and up. Has published poetry by Anselm Brocki,
Esther Cameron, Paul Bray, Jack C. Wolf, Eugene C. Flinn, and Bernie Bernstein. *Bibliophilos* is 72
pages, digest-sized, laser-photography-printed, saddle-stapled, with light card cover, includes ads.
Receives about 200 poems/year, accepts about 30%. Press run is 300 (200 subscribers). Subscription: $18/year, $35/2 years. Sample: $5.25. Make checks payable to The Bibliophile. West Virginia
residents, please add 6% sales tax.

How to Submit *Closed to unsolicited submissions.* Query first with SASE and $5.25 for sample and
guidelines. Then, if invited, submit 3-5 poems at a time, with name and address on each page.
Considers previously published poems and simultaneous submissions. Cover letter with brief bio
is preferred. Time between acceptance and publication is up to one year. Often comments on
rejected poems. Guidelines available for SASE. Responds in 2 weeks. Pays 2 contributor's copies.
Acquires first North American serial rights. Staff reviews books and chapbooks of poetry in 750-
1,000 words, single-book format. Send materials for review consideration.

Contest/Award Offerings Sponsors an annual poetry contest. 1st Prize: $25 plus publication. Guidelines available for SASE.

Advice ''Do not send impressionistic, 'Why did he/she leave me, I can't live without him/her'
poems about 'relationships,' which have no meaning beyond the author's psyche. Send poetry
lamenting the loss of millions of acres of farmland to miserable Wal-Marts, or the lives lost by
industrial rape and pollution.''

▣ ☑ ◎ THE BIG UGLY REVIEW (Specialized: theme-driven issues)

490 Second St., Suite 200, San Fransisco CA 94107. E-mail: info@biguglyreview.com. (inquiries);
poetry@biguglyreview.com. (submissions). Web site: www.biguglyreview.com. Established 2004.
Contact: Miriam Pirone, poetry editor.

Magazine Needs *The Big Ugly Review*, published 2 times/year online, showcases ''emerging and
established writers, photographers, filmmakers, and musicians. Each issue includes fiction (short
stories and flash fiction), creative nonfiction, poetry, photo-essays, short films of five minutes or
less, and downloadable songs, all related to that issue's theme.'' Wants ''vivid and accurate poetry
of any style, form, or length.'' Has published poetry by Edward Smallfield, Jennifer C. Chapis,
Valerie Coulton, Stephen Hemenway, Diana Der-Hovanessian, and James Cihlar. Receives about
750-1,000 poems/year, accepts about 20.

How to Submit Submit no more than 6 poems at a time. Considers previously published poems and simultaneous submissions. Accepts e-mail submissions (pasted into body of message and as attachment); no disk submissions. "Send documents in Word or Word-readable attachments. Also paste the poems into the body of the e-mail text. Include your name, address, phone number, and e-mail on the first page." Cover letter is preferred. Reads submissions year round. Time between acceptance and publication is 1-2 months. Sometimes comments on rejected poems. Regularly publishes theme issues. Guidelines available on Web site. Responds "approximately one month after close of the issue's submission deadline." No payment. Author retains all rights.

THE BITTER OLEANDER

4983 Tall Oaks Dr., Fayetteville NY 13066-9776. (315)637-3047. Fax: (315)637-5056. E-mail: info@bitteroleander.com. Web site: www.bitteroleander.com. Established 1974. **Contact:** Paul B. Roth, editor/publisher.

• Poetry published in *The Bitter Oleander* has been included in *The Best American Poetry*; recognized by Public Radio's *Excellence In Print* award for best literary journal of 2005.

Magazine Needs *The Bitter Oleander*, published semiannually in April and October, seeks "highly imaginative poetry whose language is serious. Particularly interested in translations." Has published poetry by Alan Britt, George Kalamaras, Duane Locke, Silvia Scheibli, Shawn Fawson, Anthony Seidman, and Christine Boyka Kluge. *The Bitter Oleander* is 128 pages, digest-sized, offset-printed, perfect-bound, with glossy 4-color cover with art, includes ads. Receives about 12,000 poems/year, accepts less than 1%. Press run is 1,500 (1,000 shelf sales). Single copy: $8; subscription: $15. Make checks payable to Bitter Oleander Press.

How to Submit Submit up to 8 poems at a time. Lines/poem: 30 maximum. No previously published poems or simultaneous submissions. No e-mail submissions unless outside U.S. Cover letter is preferred. Include name and address on each page of ms. Does not read mss during July. Time between acceptance and publication is 6 months. "All poems are read by the editor only, and all decisions are made by this editor." Often comments on rejected poems. Guidelines available for SASE or on Web site. Responds within one month. Pays one contributor's copy.

Contest/Award Offerings Sponsors the Frances Locke Memorial Poetry Award, offering $1,000 and publication in *The Bitter Oleander*. Submit any number of poems. **Entry fee:** $10 for 5 poems, $2 each additional poem. **Deadline:** submit March 15-June 15 (postmark).

Advice "We simply want poetry that is imaginative and serious in its delivery of language. So much flat-line poetry is written today that anyone reading one magazine after another cannot tell the difference."

BLACK BOOK PRESS

1608 Wilmette Ave., Wilmette IL 60091. (847)302-9547. E-mail: blackbookpress1984@yahoo.com. (inquiries only). Web site: myspace.com/blackbookpress. Established 2004. **Contact:** Kyle Van Heck, founder/editor.

Magazine Needs *Black Book Press*, published monthly, "is an independent poetry zine, aiming to give small and unpublished authors and artists a place to call home." Wants "non-rhyming free verse poetry, anything daring, out of the ordinary, or offbeat." Does not want "anything sounding like Robert Frost; no nature poetry, no greeting card verse. Do not prefer rhyming poetry." *Black Book Press* is about 22 pages, magazine-sized, photocopied, center stapled, with colored paper cover with b&w artwork. Receives about 500 submissions/year, accepts about 80%. Press run is 60 (30 subscribers, 10 shelf sales); 20 distributed free to possible contributors and interested writers. Single copy: $2; subscription: $10 ("pays for stamps and paper only!"). Sample: $2 plus 6×9 SASE with 63¢ postage. Make any and all checks payable to Kyle Van Heck.

How to Submit Submit up to 5 poems at a time. Lines/poem: 4 minimum, up to 1-5 pages maximum. Considers previously published poems and simultaneous submissions. No e-mail submissions; postal submissions only. Cover letter is required. "Always include short (3 lines) bio and SASE.

Please type poems and include name, address, phone number, and e-mail on each page." Reads submissions year round. Submit seasonal poems 2 months in advance. Time between acceptance and publication is 1-2 months. "I am the editor (and a struggling writer). If the work is good and/ or if I like it, I'll publish it. If it's interesting, strange, original, or different, I'll publish it." Often comments on rejected poems. **Prefers (but doesn't require) that contributors purchase a copy for $2 or a subscription for $10.** Guidelines available in magazine, for SASE, by e-mail, or on Web site. Responds "once a month by sending copy with published work (if accepted) or a reason for not publishing." Pays one contributor's copy; additional copies may be purchased for $2 each. Acquires one-time rights.

Additional Information Promotional stickers are available, 2/$1; pins, $1.50 (large) and $1 (small). Make any and all checks payable to Kyle Van Heck.

Advice "Getting published can be tough and frustrating, but it will never happen if you don't try. Just send your work!"

$⬛ BLACK WARRIOR REVIEW

P.O. Box 862936, Tuscaloosa AL 35486-0027. (205)348-4518. E-mail: bwr@ua.edu. Web site: http://webdelsol.com/bwr. Established 1974. **Contact:** Dave Welch, poetry editor.

- Poetry published in *Black Warrior Review* has been included in *The Best American Poetry* and *The Pushcart Prize*.

Magazine Needs *Black Warrior Review*, published semiannually in March and October, prints poetry, fiction, and nonfiction by up-and-coming as well as accomplished writers. Has published poetry by Aimee Nezhukumatathil, Bob Hicok, Rachel Zucker, Tony Tost, Joshua Beckman, and Carol Guess. *Black Warrior Review* is 180 pages, digest-sized. Press run is 2,000. Subscription: $16/ year, $28/2 years, $40/3 years. Sample: $10. Make checks payable to the University of Alabama.

How to Submit Submit up to 7 poems at a time. Considers simultaneous submissions if noted. No e-mail or disk submissions. Responds in up to 5 months. Pays up to $75 and one-year subscription. Acquires first rights. Reviews books of poetry in single- or multi-book format. Send materials for review consideration.

Advice "Subscribe or purchase a sample copy to see what we're after. For 33 years, we've published new voices alongside Pulitzer Prize winners. Freshness and attention to craft, rather than credits, impress us most."

⬛ BLACKWIDOWS WEB OF POETRY

87788 Blek Dr., Veneta OR 97487. E-mail: sunris2set@aol.com. Web site: www.geocities.com/ blackwidowswebofpoetry1/BlackWidowsMagazine.index.html. Established 2001. **Contact:** J. Margiotta, chief editor.

Magazine Needs *Blackwidows Web of Poetry*, published 3 times/year, is "a growing magazine striving to open the door to beginning poets, dedicated to publishing great poetry. We now also accept short stories (less than 2 pages)." Wants well-crafted poetry, all styles and forms. "We love unique, strong imagery and have a soft spot for nature, humor, narrative, etc. Rhyming less likely. We encourage all subject matters." Does not want overly religious, sexual, political poems; no racist/violent poetry. Has published poetry by Cleo Griffith, Debra J. Harmes-Kurth, Robert Demaree, and Gary Miron. *Blackwidows Web of Poetry* is 40-60 pages, digest-sized, laser-printed, photocopied, saddle-stapled, with color cover on 65 lb. cardstock with smooth finish. Receives about 1,00 poems/year, accepts about 40%. Press run is 200; 25 distributed free to coffeehouses, local areas of interest. Single copy: $7; subscription: $17. Make checks payable to J. Margiotta.

How to Submit Submit 5 poems at a time; haikus 10 to a page. Lines/poem: 3 minimum, 30 maximum ("very long line length not encouraged"). Considers previously published poems; no simultaneous submissions. No e-mail or disk submissions. Cover letter is required. "Include a brief bio, name, address, and phone number. SASE is required. Overseas poets will receive an e-mail response only; no SASE is needed.'' Reads submissions all year. Submit seasonal poems 3 months in advance. Time between acceptance and publication is 4 months. ''Do not send unfinished work for critique. Read the guidelines carefully! We do not accept careless submissions. Poems are in review for opinion, style, content, originality, punctuation, etc.'' Often comments on rejected poems (''I like personal contact with each poet''). ''We recommend you invest in a copy to see what we're all about, but it's not required. We appreciate all your support now and in the future.'' Guidelines available on Web site only. Responds in one month or less. Sometimes sends prepublication galleys. Pays one contributor's copy. ''No payment is able to be made to overseas contributors due to funds, though copies are available for purchase—and we appreciate those who have.'' Acquires one-time rights with future credit to *Blackwidow's Web of Poetry*. Reviews other magazines/journals.

Advice ''Trust yourself, write what you know, keep your pen alive, and revise, revise!''

THE BLIND MAN'S RAINBOW: A JOURNAL OF POETRY AND ART

The Blind Press, P.O. Box 1190, Troy MT 59935. E-mail: editor@theblindpress.com. (inquiries only). Web site: www.theblindpress.com. Established 1993. **Contact:** Melody Sherosky, editor.

Magazine Needs *The Blind Man's Rainbow: A Journal of Poetry and Art*, published quarterly, offers ''a diverse collection of art and poetry from around the world.'' Wants ''all forms of poetry (Beat, rhyme, free verse, haiku, etc.). All subject matter accepted.'' Considers poetry by children and teens. Has published poetry by B.Z. Niditch, Alessio Zanelli, A.D. Winans, Ed Galing, Donald Everett Axinn, and R. Kimm. *The Blind Man's Rainbow* is 32 pages, magazine-sized, laser-printed, saddle-stitched, with 60 lb. coverstock cover with art. Receives about 500 submissions/month. Subscription: $14 U.S., $18 foreign. Sample: $4 U.S., $5 foreign. Make checks payable to The Blind Press; subscriptions and samples are also available through PayPal on Web site.

How to Submit Submit 2-10 poems at a time. Considers previously published poems and simultaneous submissions, ''but it is nice to let us know.'' No e-mail submissions; postal submissions only. Cover letter is preferred. Put name and address on each poem. Include SASE. ''Submissions returned only if requested and with adequate postage.'' Time between acceptance and publication is up to one year. Often comments on rejected poems. Guidelines available for SASE, by e-mail, or on Web site. Responds in up to 6 months. Pays one contributor's copy. Acquires one-time rights.

Contest/Award Offerings The Blind Press Biannual Poetry Contest awards 3 cash prizes (1st Prize of at least $100). Winners and honorable mentions will be printed in *The Blind Man's Rainbow*. ''Submit up to 10 poems. No line limit. Anonymous judging. Contest submissions must include a short poet bio. Mark contest submissions clearly so they are not confused with regular submissions by including 'Poetry Contest' in the address on the envelope.'' Include SASE for results only; mss will not be returned. Guidelines available on Web site. **Entry fee:** $4 for first poem, $2 for each additional poem. **Deadlines:** May 15 and November 15. Entries postmarked after the contest deadline will be held for the next contest. Winners will be contacted directly and announced in the magazine and on the Web site.

Also Offers Additional services offered include designing and distributing advertising and promotional materials for artists and writers. ''We design, produce, and distribute chapbooks, postcards, bookmarks, and flyers. Interested parties should contact us with project ideas for a price quote.''

BLUE COLLAR REVIEW (Specialized: social, political, & working class issues)

Partisan Press, P.O. Box 11417, Norfolk VA 23517. E-mail: red-ink@earthlink.net. (inquiries only). Web site: www.partisanpress.org. Established 1997 (*Blue Collar Review*); 1993 (Partisan Press). **Contact:** A. Markowitz, editor. Co-Editor: Mary Franke.

Magazine Needs *Blue Collar Review (Journal of Progressive Working Class Literature)*, published quarterly, contains poetry, short stories, and illustrations ''reflecting the working class experience— a broad range from the personal to the societal. Our purpose is to promote and expand working class literature and an awareness of the connections between workers of all occupations and the social context in which we live. Also to inspire the creativity and latent talent in 'common' working people.'' Wants "writing of high quality that reflects the working class experience from delicate internal awareness to the militant. We accept a broad range of style and focus—but are generally progressive, political/social." Does not want anything "racist, sexist-misogynist, right wing, or overly religious. No 'bubba' poetry, nothing overly introspective or confessional, no academic/abstract or 'Vogon' poetry. No simple beginners rhyme or verse." Has published poetry by Simon Perchik, Joya Lonsdale, Kathryn Kirkpatrick, Marge Piercy, Alan Catlin, and Rob Whitbeck. *Blue Collar Review* is 60 pages, digest-sized, offset-printed, saddle-stapled, with colored card cover, includes ads. Receives hundreds of poems/year, accepts about 30%. Press run is 500 (350 subscribers, 8 libraries). Subscription: $15/year, $25/2 years. Sample: $5. Make checks payable to Partisan Press.

How to Submit Submit up to 4 poems at a time; "no complete manuscripts, please." Considers previously published poems; no simultaneous submissions. No e-mail submissions; postal submissions only. Cover letter is preferred. Include full-size SASE for response. "Poems should be typed as they are to appear upon publication. Author's name and address should appear on every page. Overly long lines reduce chances of acceptance as line may have to be broken to fit the page size and format of the journal." Time between acceptance and publication is 3 months to a year. Poems are reviewed by editor and co-editor. Seldom comments on rejected poems. Guidelines available on Web site. Responds in 3 months. Sends prepublication galleys only upon request. Pays 1-3 contributor's copies. Reviews of chapbooks and journals accepted.

Additional Information Partisan Press looks for "poetry of power that reflects a working class consciousness and moves us forward as a society. Must be good writing reflecting social/political issues." Publishes about 3 chapbooks/year; not presently open to unsolicited submissions. "Submissions are requested from among the poets published in the *Blue Collar Review*." Has published *Explanation* by Peggy Safire and *American Sounds* by Robert Edwards. Chapbooks are usually 20-60 pages, digest-sized, offset-printed, saddle-stapled or flat-spined, with card or glossy covers. Sample chapbooks are $5 and listed on Web site.

Contest/Award Offerings Sponsors the annual Working People's Poetry Competition (see separate listing in Contests & Awards).

Advice "Don't be afraid to try. Read a variety of poetry and find your own voice. Write about reality, your own experience, and what moves you."

☑ BOGG: A JOURNAL OF CONTEMPORARY WRITING

Bogg Publications, 422 N. Cleveland St., Arlington VA 22201-1424. Established 1968. **Contact:** John Elsberg (USA), Wilga Rose (Australia: 13 Urara Rd., Avalon Beach, NSW 2107 Australia), and Sheila Martindale (Canada: 36114 Talbot Line, Shedden ON N0L 2E0 Canada), poetry editors.

Magazine Needs *Bogg: A Journal of Contemporary Writing*, published twice/year, combines "innovative American work with a range of writing from England and the Commonwealth. It features poetry (including haiku and tanka, prose poems, and experimental/visual poems), very short experimental or satirical/wry fiction, interviews, essays on the small press scenes (both in America and in England/the Commonwealth), reviews, review essays, and line art. We also publish occasional free-for-postage pamphlets." Uses a great deal of poetry in each issue (with featured poets). Wants "poetry in all styles, with a healthy leavening of shorts (under 10 lines). *Bogg* seeks original voices." Considers all subject matter. "Some have even found the magazine's sense of play offensive. Overt religious and political poems have to have strong poetical merits—statement alone is not sufficient." *Bogg* started in England and in 1975 began including a supplement of American work; it is now published in the U.S. and mixes U.S., Canadian, Australian, and UK work with reviews of small press publications from all of those areas. Has published poetry by Richard Peabody, Ann Menebroker, LeRoy Gorman, Marcia Arrieta, Kathy Ernst, and Steve Sneyd. *Bogg* is 56 pages, digest-sized, typeset, saddle-stapled, in a format "that leaves enough white space to let each poem stand and breathe alone." Receives more than 10,000 American poems/year, accepts about 100-150. Press run is 800 (400 subscribers, 20 libraries). Single copy: $6; subscription: $15 for 3 issues. Sample: $4.

How to Submit Submit 6 poems at a time. Considers previously published poems "occasionally, but with a credit line to a previous publisher"; no simultaneous submissions. Cover letter is preferred ("it can help us get a 'feel' for the writer's intentions/slant"). SASE required or material will be discarded ("no exceptions"). Prefers typewritten mss, with author's name and address on each sheet. Guidelines available for SASE. Responds in one week. Pays 2 contributor's copies. Acquires one-time rights. Reviews books/chapbooks of poetry and other magazines/journals in 250 words. Send materials to relevant editor (by region) for review consideration.

Additional Information Occasionally publishes pamphlets and chapbooks **by invitation only**, with the author receiving 25% of the print run. Recent chapbooks include *Cleft Brow Totem* by Dave Wright, *South Jersey Shore* by David Check and John Elsberg, and *78 RPM* by John Yamrus. Obtain free chapbook samples by sending digest-sized SASE with 2 ounces worth of postage.

Advice "Become familiar with a magazine before submitting to it. Long lists of previous credits irritate us. Short notes about how the writer has heard about *Bogg* or what he or she finds interesting or annoying in the magazine are welcome."

⬤ BOMBAY GIN

Writing and Poetics Dept., Naropa University, 2130 Arapahoe Ave., Boulder CO 80302. (303)546-3540. Fax: (303)546-5297. E-mail: bgin@naropa.edu. Web site: www.naropa.edu/writingandpoetics/bombaygin.html. Established 1974. **Contact:** Amy Catanzano.

Magazine Needs *Bombay Gin*, published annually in June, is the literary journal of the Jack Kerouac School of Disembodied Poetics at Naropa University. "Produced and edited by MFA students, *Bombay Gin* publishes established writers alongside unpublished and emerging writers. It has a special interest in works that push conventional literary boundaries. Submissions of poetry, prose, visual art, translation, and works involving hybrid forms and cross-genre exploration are encouraged. Translations are also considered. Guidelines are the same as for original work. Translators are responsible for obtaining any necessary permissions." Has published poetry by Amiri Baraka, Joanne Kyger, Jerome Rothenberg, Lawrence Ferlinghetti, Edwin Torres, and Edward Sanders. *Bombay Gin* is 150-200 pages, digest-sized, professionally printed, perfect-bound, with color card cover. Receives about 300 poems/year, accepts about 5%. Press run is 500 (400 shelf sales); 100 distributed free to contributors. Single copy: $12.

How to Submit Submit up to 3 pages of poetry at a time. No previously published poems or simultaneous submissions. Accepts e-mail (as attachment) and disk (PC format) submissions. Cover letter is preferred. **Contact info should not appear anywhere on the ms (only on cover letter).** Poems should be typed/computer-generated in 12-pt. Times New Roman. SASE required for reply. Submissions are accepted September 1-December 1 only. Notification of acceptance/rejection: February 15. Guidelines available for SASE, by e-mail, or on Web site. Pays 2 contributor's copies. Acquires one-time rights.

✖ ▣ ⬤ BORN MAGAZINE

E-mail: editors@bornmagazine.org. Web site: www.bornmagazine.org. Established 1996. **Contact:** Anmarie Trimble, editor. Contributing Editors: David J. Daniels, Tenaya Darlington, Jennifer Grotz, Michael Robins, Bruce Smith.

Magazine Needs *Born Magazine*, published quarterly online, is "an experimental venue that marries literary arts and interactive media. We publish four to eight multimedia 'interpretations' of poetry and prose in each issue, created by interactive artists in collaboration with poets and writers." Wants poems suited to "interpretation into a visual or interactive form. Due to the unusual, collaborative nature of our publication, we represent a variety of styles and forms of poetry." Has published poetry by Edward Hirsch, Marvin Bell, Michele Glazer, Crystal Williams, Major Jackson, and Joyelle McSweeney.

How to Submit Submit 2-5 poems at a time. Considers previously published poems; no simultaneous submissions. Accepts e-mail submissions only (as Word documents or .txt files). Reads submissions year round. Submit seasonal poems 6 months in advance. Time between acceptance and publication is 3-6 months. "Poems must be accepted by the editor and one contributing editor. Selected works are forwarded to our art department, which chooses an artist partner to work with the writer. Artist and writer collaborate on a concept, to be realized by the artist. We also accept proposals for collaborating with an artist to create a piece from scratch." Never comments on rejected poems. Guidelines available on Web site. Responds in 3 weeks to e-mail queries. Always sends prepublication galleys. No payment. "We can offer only the experience of participating in a collaborative community, as well as a broad audience (we average 40,000 readers to our site per month)." Acquires one-time rights.

Advice "We accept new and previously published work. *Born*'s mission is to nurture creativity and co-development of new literary art forms on the Web."

$\star$ $\$\square$ $\circledcirc$ BRAVE HEARTS (Specialized: inspiring, upbeat, humorous poetry)

Ogden Publications, 1503 SW 42nd St., Topeka KS 66609-1265. (785)274-4300. Fax: (785)274-4305. Web site: www.braveheartsmagazine.com. Established 1879. **Contact:** K.C. Compton, editor-in-chief.

Magazine Needs *Brave Hearts*, published quarterly in February, May, August, and November, is an inspirational magazine featuring themes and humorous or inspiring poems. "Poems should be short." Sample: $4.95.

How to Submit Lines/poem: 16 or less. Upcoming themes available in magazine or for SASE. Guidelines available for SASE or on Web site. Pays $5-12/poem; additional payment of $2 if poem is used on Web site.

Advice "Poems chosen are upbeat, sometimes humorous, always easily understood. Short poems of this type fit our format best."

$\square$ $\circledcirc$ THE BRIAR CLIFF REVIEW (Specialized: focus on Siouxland writers/subjects)

Briar Cliff College, 3303 Rebecca St., Sioux City IA 51104-2340. E-mail: jeanne.emmons@briarcliff.edu. (inquiries only). Web site: www.briarcliff.edu/bcreview. Established 1989. **Contact:** Jeanne Emmons, poetry editor. Managing Editor: Tricia Currans-Sheehan. Member: CLMP; American Humanities Index; EBSCO/Humanities International Complete.

Magazine Needs *The Briar Cliff Review*, published annually in April, is "an attractive, eclectic literary and cultural magazine focusing on (but not limited to) Siouxland writers and subjects." Wants "quality poetry with strong imagery; especially interested in regional, Midwestern content with tight, direct, well-wrought language." Has published poetry by Sharon Schmielarz, Julie Sheehan, and David Evans. *The Briar Cliff Review* is 100 pages, magazine-sized, professionally printed on 100# Altima Satin text paper, perfect-bound, with 4-color cover on dull stock. Receives about 1,000 poems/year, accepts about 30. Press run is 1,000. Sample: $12.

How to Submit Considers simultaneous submissions, but expects prompt notification of acceptance elsewhere; no previously published poems. No e-mail submissions; postal submissions only. Cover letter is required. "Include short bio. Submissions should be typewritten or letter quality, with author's name and address on each page. No manuscripts returned without SASE." Reads submissions August 1-November 1 only. Time between acceptance and publication is up to 6 months. Seldom comments on rejected poems. Guidelines available on Web site. Responds in 6-8 months. Pays 2 contributor's copies. Acquires first serial rights.

Contest/Award Offerings The Briar Cliff Review Annual Fiction, Poetry and Creative Nonfiction Contest (see separate listing in Contests & Awards).

✅ ◎ BRILLIANT CORNERS: A JOURNAL OF JAZZ & LITERATURE (Specialized: jazz-related literature)

Lycoming College, Williamsport PA 17701. (570)321-4279. Fax: (570)321-4090. E-mail: feinstein@lycoming.edu. Web site: www.lycoming.edu/BrilliantCorners. Established 1996. **Contact:** Sascha Feinstein, editor.

Magazine Needs *Brilliant Corners*, published biannually, features jazz-related poetry, fiction, and nonfiction. "We are open as to length and form." Wants "work that is both passionate and well crafted—work worthy of our recent contributors." Does not want "sloppy hipster jargon or improvisatory nonsense." Has published poetry by Amiri Baraka, Jayne Cortez, Yusef Komunyakaa, Philip Levine, Sonia Sanchez, and Al Young. *Brilliant Corners* is 100 pages, digest-sized, commercially printed, perfect-bound, with color card cover with original artwork, includes ads. Accepts about 5% of work received. Press run is 800 (200 subscribers). Subscription: $12. Sample: $7.

How to Submit Submit 3-5 poems at a time. No previously published poems or simultaneous submissions. No e-mail or fax submissions. Cover letter is preferred. Reads submissions September 1-May 15 only. Seldom comments on rejected poems. Responds in 2 months. Pays 2 contributor's copies. Acquires first North American serial rights. Staff reviews books of poetry. Send materials for review consideration.

✅ ◎ BROKEN BRIDGE REVIEW (Specialized: emerging adult writers)

398 Pomfret St., Pomfret CT 06258-0128. (860)963-5220. E-mail: eds@brokenbridge.us. Web site: www.brokenbridge.us. Established 2005. **Contact:** Brad Davis, editor.

Magazine Needs *Broken Bridge Review*, published annually in August/September, presents "the best new work by emerging adult writers (poems, stories, interviews, reviews of first books of poetry). Beautifully designed." Also welcomes college/graduate student submissions (indicate in cover letter); interested in writers with private school connections (indicate in cover letter). Wants poetry "of all kinds." Does not want "anything sloppy or handwritten." *Broken Bridge Review* is 200 pages, digest-sized, perfect-bound, with matte coverstock cover with full-color art on front, includes ads. Press run is 500. Single copy: $12. Order from Web site or make check payable to Pomfret School, Inc.

How to Submit Submit up to 5 poems at a time. Lines/poem: no limit. No previously published poems or simultaneous submissions. No e-mail or disk submissions. Cover letter is preferred. "Mention private school connection, if any, in cover letter. No SASE necessary; we respond by e-mail." Reads submissions September-November. Time between acceptance and publication is up to one year. Never comments on rejected poems. Guidelines available by e-mail or on Web site. Responds in less than 2 months. Always sends prepublications galleys. Pays 2 contributor's copies. Rights revert to poet upon publication. Prints reviews of first books of poetry in 1,000 words, single-book format. "Author must submit review, reviewer's name with contact info, and a copy of book reviewed." Send materials for review consideration to Brad Davis.

Contest/Award Offerings The Broken Bridge Poetry Prize (see separate listing in Contests & Awards).

Advice "The editor takes 'emerging' to refer to a writer with a few good publications, perhaps a chapbook or first book, possibly a first prize or near miss in the contest department, or to any writer who knows s/he is not on the po-biz A-list."

✴ ✅ BRYANT LITERARY REVIEW

Faculty Suite F, Bryant University, Smithfield RI 02917. Web site: http://web.bryant.edu/~blr. Established 2000. **Contact:** Tom Chandler, editor. Member: CLMP.

Magazine Needs *Bryant Literary Review*, published annually in May, features poetry, fiction, photography, and art. "Our only standard is quality." Has published poetry by Michael S. Harper, Mary Crow, Denise Duhamel, and Baron Wormser. *Bryant Literary Review* is 125 pages, digest-sized, offset-printed, perfect-bound, with 4-color cover with art or photo. Receives about 3,000 poems/year, accepts about 1%. Press run is 2,500. Single copy: $8; subscription: $8.

How to Submit Submit 3-5 poems at a time. Cover letter is required. "Include SASE; please submit only once each reading period." Reads submissions September 1-December 31. Time between acceptance and publication is 5 months. Seldom comments on rejected poems. Guidelines available in magazine or on Web site. Responds in 3 months. Pays 2 contributor's copies. Acquires one-time rights.

Advice "No abstract expressionist poems, please. We prefer accessible work of depth and quality."

BUFFALO CARP

1715 Second Ave., Rock Island IL 61201. (309)793-1213. Fax: (309)793-1265. E-mail: info@quadcit yarts.com. Web site: www.quadcityarts.com. Established 1998. **Contact:** Managing Editor.

Magazine Needs *Buffalo Carp* is "a national literary journal featuring the best unpublished writing in the genres of poetry, fiction, and narrative nonfiction." Wants "any style of poetry as long as it is well crafted, vivid, and accessible." Has published poetry by John E. Smelcer, Jack R. Ridl, Carolyn Brook Morrell, Terry Savoie, and Matt Schumacher. *Buffalo Carp* is 50 pages, digest-sized, offset-printed, perfect-bound, with coated, full-color cover with jury-selected, original artwork. Press run is 500; distributed free to selected libraries and schools. Single copy: $10. Sample: $4. Make checks payable to Quad City Arts.

How to Submit Submit up to 5 poems at a time per annual reading period. Lines/poem: 1-2 pages; "longer if excellent work." Considers simultaneous submissions "if notified immediately of other acceptance"; no previously published poems. Accepts e-mail submissions; no fax or disk submissions. Cover letter is preferred. Include SASE for acknowledgment only; "we do not return work." Reads submissions September-March. "We respond in July/August with acceptance or rejection." Time between acceptance and publication is about 6 months. Poems are circulated to an editorial board. Sometimes comments on rejected poems. "Although we can't comment on all submissions, we do offer advice to writers whose work shows promise." Sometimes publishes theme issues. Guidelines available in magazine. Pays 2 contributor's copies. Acquires first North American serial rights.

Advice "Good writing contains the same qualities found in a breeze-blown Midwestern lake; the surface exudes a sparkle and liveliness which compels deeper examination. Soon many details, movements, and meanings are discovered, and a clarity surprising for the depth."

BURNSIDE REVIEW

P.O. Box 1782, Portland OR 97207. E-mail: sid@burnsidereview.org. Web site: www.burnsiderevie w.org. Established 2004. **Contact:** Sid Miller, editor.

Magazine Needs *Burnside Review*, published every 9 months, prints "the best poetry we can get our hands on." Each issue includes a featured poet from the Northwest, with interview and poems. "We tend to publish poetry that finds beauty in truly unexpected places; that combines urban and natural imagery; that breaks the heart." Open to all forms. Translations are encouraged. "Would like to see more lyric poetry." Has published poetry by Linda Bierds, Dorianne Laux, Christopher Howell, Kim Addonizio, Paul Guest, and Joshua Marie Wilkinson. *Burnside Review* is 64 pages, 6×6, professionally printed, perfect-bound. Receives about 2,500 poems/year, accepts about 50. Press run is 500 (25 subscribers, 50 shelf sales). Single copy: $8; subscription: $13. Make checks payable to *Burnside Review* or order online.

How to Submit Submit 3-5 poems at a time. Considers simultaneous submissions; no previously published poems. Accepts e-mail (preferred; as attachment) and postal submissions. "E-mailed submissions should include all poems and cover letter in one Word or RTF file sent as an attachment. The subject line should read 'Poetry Submission.' Send to submissions@burnsidereview.org. Check Web site for complete details. If sending by postal mail, cover letter and SASE are required. Please put name and address on each poem." Reads submissions year round. Submit seasonal poems 3-6 months in advance. Time between acceptance and publication is up to 9 months. "Editors read all poems.'' Seldom comments on rejected poems. Guidelines available on Web site. Responds in 2-4 months. Pays one contributor's copy. Acquires first rights.

Contest/Award Offerings The *Burnside Review* Chapbook Competition (see separate listing in Contests & Awards).

$⬛ BUTTON MAGAZINE

P.O. Box 77, Westminster MA 01473. E-mail: sally@moonsigns.net. Web site: http://moonsigns.net. Established 1993. **Contact:** Maude Piper, poetry editor.

Magazine Needs *Button*, published annually, is ''New England's tiniest magazine of fiction, poetry, and gracious living.'' Wants ''poetry that incises a perfect figure eight on the ice, but also cuts beneath that mirrored surface. Minimal use of vertical pronoun.'' Does not want ''sentiment; no 'musing' on who or what done ya wrong.'' Has published poetry by Amanda Powell, Brendan Galvin, Jean Monahan, Mary Campbell, Kevin McGrath, and Ed Conti. *Button* is 30 pages, $4^1/_4 \times 5^1/_2$, saddle-stapled, with cardstock offset cover with illustrations that incorporate one or more buttons. Press run is 1,200 (more than 500 subscribers, 750 shelf sales). Subscription: $5/4 issues, $25/lifetime. Sample: $2 and one first-class stamp.

How to Submit Submit no more than 2 poems at a time. ''Do not submit more than twice in one year.'' No previously published poems. Cover letter is required. Time between acceptance and publication is up to 6 months. Poems are circulated to an editorial board. Often comments on rejected poems. Guidelines available by e-mail. Responds in 4 months. Pays honorarium, subscription, and at least 5 contributor's copies. Acquires first North American serial rights.

Advice ''Writing as therapy is fine. Publishing as therapy is not. Take the vertical pronoun (I) and write your poem without it. Still got something to say? Also, *Button* tries to reflect a world one would want to live in—this does not mean we make the space for various uncatalogued human vices (self-pity, navel gazing). If you can be really amusing about those, that's another story. Finally, writers who need to say they've published 1,200 poems in various magazines and then name all of the magazines—well, we don't really need to know. Aim high, write often, but refine, refine, refine.''

$⬛ ◎ BYLINE MAGAZINE (Specialized: writers & writing)

P.O. Box 111, Albion NY 14411. (585)355-3290. E-mail: dmarbach@rochester.rr.com. Web site: www.bylinemag.com. Established 1981. **Contact:** Donna M. Marbach, poetry editor.

Magazine Needs *ByLine*, published monthly, is a magazine for the encouragement of writers and poets. Uses 8-10 poems/issue. Wants ''any subject, any style; must be well-crafted.'' Has published poetry by Judith Tate O'Brien, Katharyn Howd Machan, and Harvey Stanbrough. *ByLine* is magazine-sized, professionally printed, includes ads. Receives about 2,500 poetry submissions/year, accepts about 100. Subscription: $24. Sample: $5.

How to Submit Submit up to 3 poems at a time. Lines/poem: less than 30 preferred. No previously published poems. Accepts e-mail submissions (preferred). Guidelines available for SASE or on Web site. Pays $10/poem. Acquires first North American serial rights. Reviews books of poetry in 250-500 words. Pays $25/review.

Additional Information Also seeking poetry-related how-to articles. Pays $35/article (500-700 words) and $100/article (1,500-1,800 words).

Contest/Award Offerings Sponsors up to 20 poetry contests. Guidelines available for #10 SASE or on Web site.

Advice ''Because our primary goal is to assist writers in improving and growing their craft, we are looking for poetry that is top-quality and shows skillful knowledge of poetic devices, techniques, and forms. Articles and book reviews should focus on poetic craft and the submission process. While we encourage new writers and are happy to work with them, we are seeking poetry that is concise, original, and a positive model for other poets.''

◙ CALIFORNIA QUARTERLY

P.O. Box 7126, Orange CA 92863-7126. (949)854-8024. E-mail: jipalley@aol.com. (inquiries only). Web site: www.californiaquarterly.blogspot.com. Established 1972. **Contact:** The Editors.

Magazine Needs *California Quarterly*, the official publication of the California State Poetry Society (an affiliate of the National Federation of State Poetry Societies), is designed "to encourage the writing and dissemination of poetry." Wants poetry on any subject. "No geographical limitations. Quality is all that matters." Has published poetry by Michael L. Johnson, Lyn Lifshin, and Joanna C. Scott. *California Quarterly* is 64 pages, digest-sized, offset-printed, perfect-bound, with heavy paper cover with art. Receives 3,000-4,000 poems/year, accepts about 5%. Press run is 500 (300 subscribers, 24 libraries, 20-30 shelf sales). Membership in CSPS is $25/year and includes a subscription to *California Quarterly*. Sample: $6 (includes guidelines).

How to Submit Submit up to 6 poems at a time. Lines/poem: 60 maximum. No previously published poems. Accepts submissions by postal mail only; no e-mail submissions. Put name and address on each sheet, include SASE. Seldom comments on rejected poems. Guidelines available for SASE. Responds in up to 8 months. Pays one contributor's copy. Acquires first rights. Rights revert to poet after publication.

Advice "Since our editor changes with each issue, we encourage poets to resubmit."

⚞ ◎ CALLIOPE MAGAZINE (Specialized: world history; children/teens ages 8-14)

Editorial Dept., Cobblestone Publishing, 30 Grove Street, Suite C, Peterborough NH 03458. Web site: www.cricketmag.com. **Contact:** Rosalie Baker.

Magazine Needs *CALLIOPE Magazine*, published 9 times/year, looks for "lively, original approaches" to world history (East/West) for readers ages 8-14. "All material must relate to the theme of a specific upcoming issue in order to be considered." Wants "clear, objective imagery. Serious and light verse considered. Must relate to theme." Subscription: $29.95/year (9 issues). Sample: $5.95 plus $2.00 s&h (include 10×13 SASE); sample pages available on Web site.

How to Submit Query first. Lines/poem: up to 100. No e-mail submissions or queries. Include SASE. Reads submissions according to deadlines for queries (see Web site for schedule and details). Always publishes theme issue. Themes and guidelines available on Web site. Pays varied rates. Acquires all rights.

Advice "Writers are encouraged to study recent back issues for content and style."

◯ ◎ CALYX, A JOURNAL OF ART AND LITERATURE BY WOMEN (Specialized: poetry by & about women; multicultural)

Calyx Books, P.O. Box B, Corvallis OR 97339-0539. (541)753-9384. Fax: (541)753-0515. E-mail: calyx@proaxis.com. Web site: www.calyxpress.org. Established 1976. **Contact:** Beverly McFarland, senior editor.

Magazine Needs *CALYX, A Journal of Art and Literature by Women*, published 3 times every 18 months, contains poetry, prose, art, book reviews, essays, and interviews by and about women. Wants "excellently crafted poetry that also has excellent content." Has published poetry by Maurya Simon, Diane Averill, Carole Boston Weatherford, and Eleanor Wilner. *CALYX* is 6×8, handsomely printed on heavy paper, flat-spined, with glossy color cover. Single copy: $9.50 plus shipping; subscription: $21/volume (3 issues), $39/2 volumes (6 issues). Sample: $12.50. See Web site for foreign and institutional rates.

How to Submit Send up to 6 poems at a time. Considers previously published poems "occasionally" and simultaneous submissions "if kept up-to-date on publication." No fax or e-mail submissions. Include SASE and short bio. "We accept copies in good condition and clearly readable." *CALYX* is edited by a collective editorial board." Reads submissions postmarked October 1-December 31 only. **Manuscripts received outside of reading period will be returned unread.** Guidelines available for

SASE, by e-mail, or on Web site. Responds in 9 months. Pays one contributor's copy/poem, plus subscription. Send materials for review consideration.

Additional Information CALYX Books publishes one book of poetry/year. All work published is by women. Has published *Storytelling in Cambodia* by Willa Schneberg and *Black Candle: Poems about Women from India, Pakistan, and Bangladesh* by Chitra Banerjee Divakaruni. **Closed to submissions until further notice.**

Contest/Award Offerings The annual Lois Cranston Memorial Poetry Prize (see separate listing in Contests & Awards).

Advice "Read the publication and be familiar with what we have published."

$⬛ $☑ ◎ CANADIAN WRITER'S JOURNAL (Specialized: poetry writing)

White Mountain Publications, Box 1178, New Liskeard ON P0J 1P0 Canada. (705)647-5424. Fax: (705)647-8366. E-mail: cwj@cwj.ca. Web site: www.cwj.ca. **Contact:** Deborah Ranchuk, editor.

Magazine Needs *Canadian Writer's Journal*, published bimonthly, uses a few "short poems or portions thereof as part of 'how-to' articles relating to the writing of poetry, and occasional short poems with tie-in to the writing theme. We try for 90% Canadian content but prefer good material over country of origin or how well you're known." *Canadian Writer's Journal* is digest-sized. Subscription: $35/year, $67.50/2 years (add 7% GST in Canada). Sample: $9.

How to Submit Submit up to 5 poems at a time. No previously published poems. Accepts e-mail submissions (pasted into body of message, with 'Submission' in the subject line). Include SASE with postal submissions. "U.S. postage accepted; do not affix to envelope. Poems should be titled. Hard copy and SASE required if accepted." Responds in 3-6 months. Pays $2-5/poem and one contributor's copy.

⬛ $☑ THE CAPILANO REVIEW (Specialized: avant-garde, experimental)

2055 Purcell Way, North Vancouver BC V7J 3H5 Canada. (604)984-1712. E-mail: tcr@capcollege.bc.ca. Web site: www.thecapilanoreview.ca. Established 1972. **Contact:** Submissions.

Magazine Needs *The Capilano Review*, published 3 times/year, is a literary and visual arts review. Wants "avant-garde, experimental, previously unpublished poetry of sustained intelligence and imagination. We are interested in poetry that is new in concept and in execution." Has published poetry by bill bissett, Phyllis Webb, and Michael Ondaatje. *The Capilano Review* is 90-100 pages, digest-sized, finely printed, perfect-bound, with glossy full-color card cover. Circulation is 800. Sample: $10 CAD prepaid.

How to Submit Submit 5-6 poems minimum. No simultaneous submissions. No e-mail or disk submissions. Cover letter is required. Include SAE with IRCs; "submissions with U.S. postage will not be considered." Responds in up to 3 months. Pays $50-200 CAD, subscription, and 2 contributor's copies. Acquires first North American serial rights.

Advice "Read the magazine before you submit. *The Capilano Review* receives several manuscripts each week; unfortunately, the majority of them are simply inappropriate for the magazine."

⬛ $☐ ◎ CAPPER'S (Specialized: everyday situations; upbeat, humorous)

Ogden Publications, 1503 SW 42nd St., Topeka KS 66609-1265. (785)274-4300. Fax: (785)274-4305. Web site: www.cappers.com. Established 1879. **Contact:** K.C. Compton, editor-in-chief.

Magazine Needs *Capper's*, published monthly, is a tabloid (newsprint) going to 240,000 mail subscribers, mostly small-town and rural families. Wants short poems (4-16 lines preferred, lines of one-column width) "relating to everyday situations, nature, inspirational, humorous. Most poems used in *Capper's* are upbeat in tone and offer the reader a bit of humor, joy, enthusiasm, or encouragement." Considers poetry by children ages 12 and under. Has published poetry by Elizabeth Searle Lamb, Robert Brimm, Margaret Wiedyke, Helena K. Stefanski, Sheryl L. Nelms, and Claire Puneky. Sample: $1.95. Not available on newsstand.

Second-Rate Poems

They rate a second chance

Jane K. Kretschmann   ©Edison Community College

I have many of them, and I'll bet you too have them, too—poems you like but that aren't ready to be published. The quality of the work is uneven or the language isn't as effective as it could be. The poem doesn't grab you right from the start or leave you satisfied. The piece does too much or too little.

Short of saving these poems in a shoebox until you're famous (at which point *someone* will publish them), what are your options? I propose four methods for giving your work a second chance. They've worked for me, and they may work for you as well.

1. Put the poem away, don't look at it for awhile, then write it again.

You'll hear the work afresh, perhaps in a new form. Certainly you'll change some of the language or line breaks, providing an alternative to your original poem.

When I used this approach with my poem "Not Another One," which calls for a "moratorium on poems / about Emily Dickinson," I gained three improvements to the original. The first version decried the way too many writers treat Dickinson's poems as if they're "ornamental" origami. I substituted "literary" for "ornamental," an adjective fitting the context and avoiding redundancy, since works of origami are usually considered decorative.

In another passage, I toned down some of the language and took myself out of the picture. "I don't care if you are an Amy Lowell" became "Even if you are an Amy Lowell," wording I preferred.

I improved the ending, too, adding richness through repetition of sounds. Here is the original followed by the revision (in italics):

And please, Mr. Collins,
stop undressing her—
from tippet to corset—
in public. Let her rest.

And please, Mr. Collins,
stop undressing her—
from tippet to corset—
in public. Leave her
in Amherst. Let her rest.

Overall, the rewritten poem was not satisfactory, but I was able to pull out these three changes to revise my original.

2. Cut out any weak parts of the poem.

If your creative process is to let the words flow, then revise by cutting. A poem needs a strong beginning, so take out anything that lessens its immediate impact.

For example, I dropped the following first stanza from "Beeswax and Honey," a poem I'd written praising my favorite college professor, because those lines dealt with academics but not with Dr. Wade himself.

> *Philip Wade, 1960s literature professor*
> *par excellence, would not fit in today*
> *with the academic worship of small*
> *group work and the three-part syllabus.*

Besides, that beginning wasn't as interesting as what now begins the poem:

> *Dr. Philip Wade lectured faster than we*
> *could scribble and gave pop vocabulary*
> *quizzes, insisting we could not read*
> *Milton if we didn't know his language.*

(from *Imagining a Life* [FootHills Publishing, ©November 2006]; reprinted with permission)

On the other hand, my narrative poem "Crazy Quilt" needed to be cut at the end. It tells the story of the day my pregnant grandmother was taken to an asylum after threatening to kill her husband, and begins with a description of the quilt the sheriff wrapped her in. I thought I needed to "explain" how I came to possess the quilt, so I originally ended the poem with two stanzas telling how the ward nurse had sent the quilt to my grandfather after Grandma Clara died. I decided readers would logically infer that her belongings were returned to her family, so I cut those stanzas and ended with the most poignant lines in the piece:

> *There Clara delivered her child, stillborn.*
> *For three more years her moans*
> *were lullaby to her empty arms.*

(from *Muscadine Lines: A Southern Anthology*, Kathy Hardy Rhodes, editor [Cold Tree Press, ©July 2006]; reprinted with permission)

How many of us have the courage to ask what is truly worth keeping? What if the answer is "only one stanza"? Better to start over with that one stanza than to waste it in a second-rate poem. What if the answer is "only one line or phrase"—and that one line or phrase is the original impetus for the poem? Put the piece away for awhile, giving your mind a chance to cleanse itself of the poem that didn't work; then, start over.

3. Incorporate the poem into a larger one.

Integrating little poems into longer works can result in one first-rate poem instead of two or three second-rate ones.

For instance, I realized that two small poems I'd written, "Going to Alabama for Mama's Funeral" and "Will," could be parts of the same longer poem because the theme of each was an unwanted inheritance from which I cannot escape: I live with the realization that I might develop a form of dementia, as my mother did before her death. In another little poem, "Mama's Memory," I presented early evidence that my mother possibly had some type of mental problem.

Dropping the original titles but making few other changes, I created a three-part poem titled "Legacy," which begins with these early glimpses of Mama's mental instability ("Mama's Memory"), moves to my recognition of its impact on me ("Going to Alabama"), and concludes with the reading of the will ("Will"). It is there that my sister and I inherit

> . . . the house, seven acres,
> and enough stories to keep us going
> until our own minds wander off course.

(from *Artistry of Life: An Online Literary Magazine*, Issue #5 (July 2005); reprinted with permission)

Integrating poems can work in a different way. While rereading a draft of my poem "More," about my need to take walks in order to create, I realized I was telling, not showing, and wondered how I could demonstrate my creative process. At first I thought I might have to write some new lines for the poem to make that process clear.

Then I recalled a small work I'd written about my husband's response to my writing habits. I incorporated it into my walking poem as illustration, weaving in lines so they worked in their new context.

Here's an excerpt from the middle of "More"; the non-italicized words were incorporated from the poem originally titled "My Husband Laments":

My husband laments
that since I've taken up writing
poetry
I ask the strangest questions
        Moving around
the house, putting away laundry,
I taste tidbits of lines,
        and smile for no reason
licking them like mixing spoons.
        He cannot imagine
        that the sheer joy
        of writing a poem
        is like having your breast
        touched—
Filling a notebook
I go from room to room . . .

(from *Imagining a Life* [FootHills Publishing, ©November 2006]; reprinted with permission)

4. Have the poem critiqued by a trusted reader or readers.

Feeling a bit of frustration at how I could do almost everything in my life more easily than I could write, I tried to capture that frustration in "If Only." The figurative half of each one-line simile came from writing; each literal half from other elements of my life. Impressed with my own cleverness, I submitted the poem to three journals that ask for short poems. I got back three rejections to this second-rate poem:

If Only

writing were comfortable as walking my dog
metaphors close at hand as a dust cloth
images clear as rinsed glasses in a porcelain rack
rhythm natural as balancing a checkbook
word-smithing simple as serving guests
stories instinctive as a cat's purring

dialog real as my childhood memories
meaning solid as my own study door

Then I wised up and took the work to some writer friends. They responded that, while some of the individual images were strong, the poem didn't move anywhere. Even though there were only eight lines, some found the listing a bit tedious. They didn't know what I meant by "a porcelain rack" and didn't think balancing a checkbook is natural or rhythmic.

Grateful for their honest criticism, I gave the poem a new title, putting it into a context, and kept the focus on writing poetry, rather than mixing in fiction. I used the similes in clauses that led to a conclusion, rather than leaving the suppositions up in the air. I made it clear that the glasses were "on a porcelain shelf" and substituted "word choice" for "word-smithing," an unusual term for the context.

I replaced "balancing a checkbook" with "singing / my grandson to sleep" because the latter is a rhythmic activity, and the alliteration resonates with language in the previous line. I gained more effective line endings by employing some enjambment and changed the form to suit the new line count. This improved version soon found publication:

After Trying to Write at Home

If only writing were as comfortable
as walking my dog, metaphors close

as a dust cloth, images clear as rinsed
glasses on a porcelain shelf. If word

choice were as simple as serving guests
and rhythm were as natural as singing

my grandson to sleep, I could create
poems as instinctively as a cat purrs,

with a voice real as childhood memories
and meaning as solid as my study door.

(from *ByLine Magazine*, July/August 2006; reprinted with permission)

Certainly I have used other approaches to revision—trying a different point of view, writing in a different form, creating a companion poem. Still the methods illustrated above are the ones I depend on the most to give my second-rate poems a second chance.

—*Jane K. Kretschmann*

Jane K. Kretschmann teaches at a community college in Ohio. Her poems have been broadcast on NPR and WKCR in New York and published in journals such as *Ibbetson Street* and *The Ledge Poetry & Fiction Magazine*. Her chapbook, *Imagining a Life* (FootHills Publishing), was released in November 2006.

How to Submit Submit 5-6 poems at a time. Lines/poem: 14-16. No simultaneous submissions. No e-mail or fax submissions. Returns mss with SASE. Publishes seasonal theme issues. Guidelines available for SASE or on Web site. Responds in 3 months. Pays $10-15/poem; additional payment of $5 if poem is used on Web site. Acquires one-time rights.

Advice "Poems chosen are upbeat, sometimes humorous, always easily understood. Short poems of this type fit our format best."

◪ CAVEAT LECTOR

400 Hyde St., Apt. 606, San Francisco CA 94109-7445. Phone/fax: (415)928-7431. E-mail: editors@c aveat-lector.org. Web site: www.caveat-lector.org. Established 1989. **Contact:** Christopher Bernard, Ho Lin, and Anna Sears, principals.

Magazine Needs *Caveat Lector*, published 2 times/year, "is devoted to the arts and cultural and philosophical commentary. We publish visual art and music as well as literary and theoretical texts. Our Web site includes an art gallery and a multimedia section offering video and audio." Wants poems "on any subject, in any style, as long as the work is authentic in feeling and appropriately crafted. We are looking for accomplished poems, something that resonates in the mind long after the reader has laid the poem aside. We want work that has authenticity of emotion and high craft; poems that, whether raw or polished, ring true—and if humorous, are actually funny, or at least witty. Classical to experimental." Has published poetry by Joanne Lowery, Simon Perchik, Les Murray, Alfred Robinson, and Ernest Hilbert. *Caveat Lector* is 24-32 pages, $11 \times 4^{1}/_{4}$, photocopied, saddle-stapled, with b&w cover. Receives 200-600 poems/year, accepts about 2%. Press run is 250 (20 subscribers, 230 freely distributed). Single copy: $3.50; subscription: $15/4 issues. Sample: $3.

How to Submit Submit up to 6 short poems, 3 medium-length poems, or one long poem at a time. Lines/poem: short, up to 50 each; medium, 51-100; long, up to 500. Considers simultaneous submissions, "but please inform us." Cover letter is required. "Place name, address, and (optional) telephone number on each page. Include SASE and brief bio (100 words or less)." Reads submissions January-June. Time between acceptance and publication is one year. Sometimes comments on rejected poems. Guidelines available for SASE. Responds in one month. Pays 2 contributor's copies. Acquires first publication rights.

Advice "The two rules of writing are: 1) Revise it again. 2) Revise it again. The writing level of most of our submissions is pleasingly high. A rejection by us is not always a criticism of the work, and we try to provide comments to our more promising submitters."

◻ CC&D/CHILDREN, CHURCHES AND DADDIES (formerly *Children, Churches and Daddies*)

Scars Publications, 829 Brian Court, Gurnee IL 60031. E-mail: ccandd96@scars.tv. Web site: http://scars.tv. Established 1993. **Contact:** Janet Kuypers, editor/publisher.

Magazine Needs *CC&D/Children, Churches and Daddies (The Unreligious, Non-Family-Oriented Literary Magazine)*, published monthly, contains poetry, prose, art, and essays. "We also run electronic issues and collection books. We accept poetry of almost any genre, but we're not keen on rhyme, and we're not keen on religious poems (look at our current issue for a better idea of what we're like). We are okay with gay/lesbian/bisexual, nature/rural/ecology, political/social issues, women/feminism." Does not want "racist, sexist (therefore we're not into pornography, either), or homophobic stuff." Has published poetry by Rochelle Holt, Angeline Hawkes-Craig, Cheryl Townsend, Kurt Nimmo, Kenneth DiMaggio, and Janine Canan. *CC&D/Children, Churches and Daddies* (print) has ranged from 30 to 100 pages, been both digest-sized and standard-sized, photocopied, saddle-stapled. Receives hundreds of poems/year, accepts about 40%. Sample: $6 (print); free electronic sample online. Make checks payable to Janet Kuypers.

How to Submit Lines/poem: accepts longer works, "within two pages for an individual poem is appreciated." Considers previously published poems and simultaneous submissions. Accepts e-mail submissions (preferred, pasted into body of message or as attachment in Microsoft Word .doc file) or disk submissions. "When submitting via e-mail in body of message, explain in preceding paragraph that it is a submission; for disk submissions, mail floppy disk with ASCII text, or Macintosh disk." Comments on rejected poems "if asked." Guidelines available for SASE, by e-mail, or on Web site. Responds in 2 weeks.

Contest/Award Offerings Scars Publications sometimes sponsors a contest "where writing appears in an annual book." Write or e-mail (editor@scars.tv) for information.

Also Offers Also able to publish electronic chapbooks. Additional information available by e-mail or on Web site.

Advice "The Web site is a more comprehensive view of what *CC&D/Children, Churches and Daddies* does. All the information is there."

☐ CEREMONY, A JOURNAL OF POETRY AND OTHER ARTS

Dance of My Hands Publishing, 120 Vista Dr., Warminster PA 18974. E-mail: danceofmyhands@aol .com. Web site: www.danceofmyhands.com. **Contact:** Melanie M. Eyth, editor.

Magazine Needs *Ceremony, a journal of poetry and other arts*, published semiannually, encourages "all expression and articism. We do not judge or criticize submissions, but publish most work offered. Beginning poets are especially encouraged." Wants poetry, short pieces of prose, photography, drawings, and other printable arts. Considers poetry by children and teens. *Ceremony* is digest-sized, home computer-printed on 20 lb. standard white paper, stapled. Receives about 100 submissions/year, accepts "nearly as many." Single copy: $2.50.

How to Submit Submit up to 6 poems at a time. Considers previously published poems and simultaneous submissions. Accepts e-mail submissions only. Reads submissions year round. Time between acceptance and publication is 4-6 months. Sometimes comments on rejected poems. Sometimes publishes theme issues. Guidelines available in magazine. Pays one contributor's copy. Rights revert to poet upon publication.

☑ THE CHAFFIN JOURNAL

Dept. of English, Case Annex 467, Eastern Kentucky University, Richmond KY 40475-3102. (859)622-3080. Web site: www.english.eku.edu/chaffin_journal. Established 1998. **Contact:** Robert W. Witt, editor.

Magazine Needs *The Chaffin Journal*, published annually in December, prints quality short fiction and poetry by new and established writers/poets. Wants any form, subject matter, or style. Does not want "poor quality." Has published poetry by Taylor Graham, Diane Glancy, Judith Montgomery, Simon Perchik, Philip St. Clair, and Virgil Suárez. *The Chaffin Journal* is 120 pages, digest-sized, offset-printed, perfect-bound, with plain cover with title only. Receives about 500 poems/year, accepts about 10%. Press run is 300 (65 subscribers, 4 libraries, 180 shelf sales); 40-50 distributed free to contributors. Single copy: $6; subscription: $6/year. Sample (back issue): $5. Make checks payable to *The Chaffin Journal*.

How to Submit Submit 5 poems at a time. Considers simultaneous submissions (although not preferred); no previously published poems. No e-mail or disk submissions. Cover letter is preferred. "Submit typed pages with only one poem per page. Enclose SASE." Reads submissions June 1-October 1. Time between acceptance and publication is 6 months. Poems are reviewed by the general editor and 2 poetry editors. Never comments on rejected poems. Guidelines available in magazine or on Web site. Responds in 3 months. Pays one contributor's copy. Acquires one-time rights.

Advice "Submit quality work during our reading period; include cover letter and SASE."

🗭 ☐ ◎ CHALLENGER INTERNATIONAL (Specialized: poetry for/by teens)

(250)991-5567. E-mail: danlukiv@sd28.bc.ca. Web site: http://challengerinternational.20m.com/index.html. Established 1978. **Contact:** Dan Lukiv, editor.

Magazine Needs *Challenger international*, published annually, contains "poetry and (on occasion) short fiction." Wants "any type of work, especially by teenagers (our mandate: to encourage young writers, and to publish their work alongside established writers), providing it is not pornographic, profane, or overly abstract." Has published poetry from Canada, the continental U.S., Hawaii, Switzerland, Russia, Malta, Italy, Slovenia, Ireland, England, Korea, Pakistan, Australia, Zimbabwe, Argentina, and Columbia. *Challenger international* is generally 20-50 pages, magazine-sized, laser-printed, side-stapled. Press run is 50. *Challenger international* is distributed free to McNaughton Centre Secondary Alternate School sudents.

How to Submit Considers previously published poems and simultaneous submissions. Cover letter is required. Include list of credits, if any. Accepts e-mail submissions only; no postal submissions. ''Sometimes we edit to save the poet rejection.'' Responds in 4 months. Payment is one e-copy (sent as an e-mail attachment) of the issue in which the author's work appears. Poet retains rights.

Additional Information Island Scholastic Press publishes chapbooks by authors featured in *Challenger international*. Pays 3 author's copies. Copyright remains with author. Distribution of free copies through McNaughton Centre.

Advice ''We like imagistic poetry that makes sense.''

$ ⬛ ◎ CHAMPAGNE SHIVERS (Specialized: horror poetry only)

E-mail: ChampagneShivers@hotmail.com. (accepts submissions by e-mail only). Web site: http://samsdotpublishing.com/vineyard/Champagne%20Shivers.htm. Established 2002. **Contact:** Cathy Buburuz, editor.

Magazine Needs *Champagne Shivers* is ''a classy horror magazine. This is not the place to submit offensive language. We prefer poetic, well-written horror.'' Wants ''horror poetry only. We prefer poems that do not rhyme, but all verse will be considered. Long poems stand the best chance for acceptance, especially if they're scary and entertaining.'' Does not want ''anything that isn't horror related, and always proof and edit before you send your submission. If your work does not have high entertainment or high impact, do not send it here.'' Has published poetry by Lee Clark Zumpe, Nancy Bennett, Steve Vernon, Kurt Newton, W.B. Vogel III, and Keith W. Sikora. *Champagne Shivers* is 40-60 pages, magazine-sized, professionally printed, saddle-stapled, with b&w cover with scary art. Receives about 1,000 poems/year, accepts 7 poems/issue. Press run and subscriber base vary; the only free copies go to reviewers and contributors. Single copy: $12 U.S. and Canada. Sample: $10 U.S. and Canada. (''Foreign countries, please inquire about costs.'') Make checks payable to Tyree Campbell, Sam's Dot Publishing, P.O. Box 782, Cedar Rapids IA 52406-0782 (for subscriptions and sample copies only; DO NOT SEND SUBMISSIONS TO THIS ADDRESS).

How to Submit Submit one poem at a time. Lines/poem: 20-30. Considers previously published poems; no simultaneous submissions. Accepts e-mail submissions only (pasted into body of message; DO NOT SEND ATTACHMENTS). Cover letter is preferred. ''Submit one poem with a bio written in the third person, your mailing address, and your e-mail address.'' Reads submissions year round. Submit seasonal poems 4 months in advance. Time between acceptance and publication is less than 6 months. Always comments on rejected poems. Guidelines available by e-mail or on Web site. Pays 10¢/line for unpublished poems; 5¢/line for previously published poems (let the editor know where and when the poem appeared), plus one contributor's copy. Acquires first North American serial rights to unpublished poems, one-time rights to previously published poems. All rights revert back to the writer upon publication.

Contest/Award Offerings Sam's Dot Publishing offers The James Award (Trophy) annually. ''Submit one poem per e-mail, but submit as often as you like.'' **Entry fee:** ''None—it's free.'' **Deadline:** December 31. Guidelines available on Web site. ''Never send snail mail submissions; always submit in the body of an e-mail after reading the information under How to Submit above.''

Also Offers *Expressions (A Newsletter for Creative People Worldwide)*, edited by Cathy Buburuz (visit the Web site at www.samsdotpublishing.com/expressions.htm).

Advice ''Submit horror poems only. I love psychological horror poetry, horror poetry about the Old West, horror poems about asylums, or anything that's just plain scary. I do not want poems about werewolves, vampires, ghosts, or traditional monsters. I want to read poetry that's fresh and exciting. Most of all, send me something that's high in entertainment, that's never been done before. Send poems that will give me and my audience the shivers.''

◼ ◖ CHANTARELLE'S NOTEBOOK

E-mail: chantarellesnotebook@yahoo.com. Web site: www.chantarellesnotebook.com. Established 2005. **Contact:** Kendall A. Bell and Christinia Bell, editors.

Magazine Needs *Chantarelle's Notebook*, published quarterly online, seeks "quality work from undiscovered poets. We enjoy poems that speak to us—poems with great sonics and visuals." Wants "all styles of poetry, as long as it's quality work." Does not want "infantile rants, juvenile confessionals, greeting card-styled verse, political posturing, or religious outpourings." Considers poetry by children and teens. "There are no age restrictions, but submissions from younger people will be held to the same guidelines and standards as those from adults." Has published poetry by Patrick Carrington, Kristina Marie Darling, Jeanpual Ferro, Taylor Graham, Corey Mesler, and Simon Perchik. Receives about 500 poems/year, accepts about 24%. Sample: see Web site for latest issue.

How to Submit Submit 3-5 poems at a time. Lines/poem: "shorter poems have a better chance, but long poems are fine." Considers previously published poems; no simultaneous submissions. Accepts e-mail submissions (pasted into body of message; "we will not open any attachments—they will be deleted"). Cover letter is required. "Please include a short bio of no more than 75 words, should we decide to accept your work." Reads submissions year round. Submit seasonal poems 2-3 months in advance. "The editors will review all submissions and make a decision within a week's time." Never comments on rejected poems. Guidelines available on Web site. "Please follow the guidelines—all the information is there!" Responds in one week. Acquires one-time rights. Rights revert to poets upon publication.

Also Offers "*Chantarelle's Notebook* will publish a 'best of' print journal that will cull poems from each of the previous four quarterly issues in the past year. The authors of the poems chosen will receive one contributor's copy and can buy additional copies at $5 each."

Advice "Read as much poetry as you can. Immerse yourself in work other than your own. Turn off your television. Write from the pit of your stomach. Revise. Edit. Rewrite. Do not let rejections keep you off your path. The only way to become a great poet is to learn from all experiences, good and bad."

◈ ◖ ◎ CHAPMAN (Specialized: Scottish culture)

Chapman Publishing, 4 Broughton Place, Edinburgh EH1 3RX Scotland. (44)(131)557-2207. E-mail: chapman-pub@blueyonder.co.uk. Web site: www.chapman-pub.co.uk. Established 1970. **Contact:** Joy Hendry, editor.

Magazine Needs *Chapman*, published 3 times/year, "is controversial, influential, outspoken, and intelligent. Established in 1970, it has become a dynamic force in Scottish culture covering theatre, politics, language, and the arts. Our highly respected forum for poetry, fiction, criticism, review, and debate makes it essential reading for anyone interested in contemporary Scotland. *Chapman* publishes the best in Scottish writing—new work by well-known Scottish writers in the context of lucid critical discussion. It also, increasingly, publishes international writing. With our strong commitment to the future, we energetically promote new writers, new ideas, and new approaches." Also interested in receiving poetry dealing with women's issues and feminism. Has published poetry by Liz Lochhead, Sorley MacLean, Edwin Morgan, Willa Muir, Tom Scott, and Una Flett. *Chapman* is 144 pages, digest-sized, professionally printed in small type on matte stock, perfect-bound, with glossy card cover. Press run is 2,000 (1,500 subscribers, 300 libraries). Receives "thousands" of poetry submissions/year, accepts about 200. Single copy: £6.50; subscription: £20. Sample: £5 (overseas). "Please enquire about prices in U.S. dollars and euros."

How to Submit Submit 4-10 poems at a time. No simultaneous submissions. Cover letter is required. "Submissions must be accompanied by a SASE/IRC. Please send sufficient postage to cover the return of your manuscript. Do not send foreign stamps. Limit one poem/page. We do not usually publish single poems." Responds "as soon as possible." Always sends prepublication galleys. Pays in contributor's copies. Staff reviews books of poetry. Send materials for review consideration.

Additional Information *Chapman Publishing is currently not accepting submissions of books or chapbooks.*

Advice "Poets should not try to court approval by writing poems especially to suit what they perceive as the nature of the magazine. They usually get it wrong and write badly."

$⬛ THE CHARITON REVIEW (Specialized: subscribers preferred)

821 Camino de Jemez, Santa Fe NM 87501. Established 1975. **Contact:** Jim Barnes, editor.

Magazine Needs *The Chariton Review*, published semiannually, prints "open and closed forms—traditional, experimental, mainstream. We do not consider verse, only poetry in its highest sense, whatever that may be." Does not want "the sentimental and the inspirational. Also, no more 'relativism' (short stories and poetry centered around relatives)." Has published poetry by Michael Spence, Kim Bridgford, Sam Maio, Kenneth Lincoln, Wayne Dodd, and Lynne McMahon. *The Chariton Review* is 100+ pages, digest-sized, professionally printed, flat-spined, with glossy cover with photographs. Receives 8,000-10,000 submissions/year, accepts about 35-50. Press run is about 600 (400 subscribers, 100 libraries). Subscription: $10/year, $18/2 years.

How to Submit Submit 3-5 poems at a time. No simultaneous submissions. Poems should be typed single-spaced. Do not write for guidelines. Responds "quickly"; accepted poems often appear within a few issues of notification. Always sends prepublication galleys. Pays $5/printed page when funds are available. Acquires first North American serial rights. **Contributors are expected to subscribe or pay $5 reading fee for each submission.**

⬛ CHAUTAUQUA LITERARY JOURNAL

P.O. Box 613, Chautauqua NY 14722. E-mail: CLJEditor@aol.com. Web site: http://writers.ciweb.org. Established 2003. **Contact:** Richard Foerster, editor.

- Poetry published in *Chautauqua Literary Journal* has been included in *The Pushcart Prize* anthology.

Magazine Needs *Chautauqua Literary Journal*, published annually in June, prints poetry, short fiction, creative nonfiction, and book reviews. "We welcome poems that exhibit the writer's craft and attention to language, employ striking images and metaphors, engage the mind as well as the emotions, and reveal insights into the larger world of human concerns. The editor invites traditional as well as experimental work." Does not want "hackneyed inspirational versifying; poems typed in all capitals or on pastel paper." Has published poetry by Patricia Smith, Karl Shapiro, Douglas Goetsch, William Heyen, Robert Cording, and Randall Watson. *Chautauqua Literary Journal* is 178 pages, digest-sized, offset-printed, with notch adhesive binding and glossy cover with original artwork, includes ads. Receives about 4,000 poems/year, accepts about 40. Press run is 2,000 (1,200 subscribers, 500 shelf sales); 300 distributed free to contributors and others. Single copy: $10; subscription: $18. Make checks payable to *Chautauqua Literary Journal*.

How to Submit Submit 4 poems maximum at a time. Considers simultaneous submissions (if notified); no previously published poems. No e-mail or disk submissions. Cover letter is preferred. "We prefer single-spaced manuscripts in 12-pt. font. Cover letters should be brief and mention recent publications (if any). SASE is mandatory." Reads submissions year round. Time between acceptance and publication is up to one year. "The editor is the sole arbiter, but we do have advisory editors who periodically make recommendations." Sometimes comments on rejected poems. Guidelines available on Web site. Responds in 3 months or less. Always sends prepublication galleys. Pays 2 contributor's copies. Acquires first rights "plus one-time non-exclusive rights to reprint accepted work in an anniversary issue." Reviews books/chapbooks of poetry in 750-1,000 words, single- and multi-book format. Send materials for review consideration to *Chautauqua Literary Journal*/Reviews, P.O. Box 2039, York Beach ME 03910.

Contest/Award Offerings Annual contest awards two $1,500 prizes (payable upon publication), one for best poem or group of poems, one for best prose work. Winners are selected in anonymous competitions by the magazine's editor and advisory staff. Winning entries are published in *Chautauqua Literary Journal*, and all work entered is considered for publication. "Submit up to 6 poems or a maximum of 500 lines. Each entry will be judged for overall artistic excellence; the poems do not have to be related by theme. Only original, previously unpublished work is eligible. See guidelines (available for SASE or on Web site) for formatting instructions." **Entry fee:** $15 U.S. Make checks payable to *Chautauqua Literary Journal*. Each entrant will receive a copy of the *Journal* containing the prize-winning entries. **Deadline:** September 30 (postmark). Winners will be announced in early January. Mail to: *Chautauqua Literary Journal* Annual Contests, P.O. Box 2039, York Beach ME 03910 **(do not send entries to Chautauqua, NY address)**.

Advice "Poets who are not avid readers of contemporary poetry will most likely not be writing anything of interest to us."

$ ◎ CHILD LIFE (Specialized: children ages 9-11; health-related themes)

Children's Better Health Institute, 1100 Waterway Blvd., Indianapolis IN 46202. Web site: www.cbhi.org or www.childlifemag.org.

Magazine Needs *Child Life*, published by The Children's Better Health Institute, is a magazine for ages 9-11. Has a "nostalgic and whimsical style." Wants poetry appropriate for the age group with health-related themes. " 'Health' is a broad topic that includes exercise, sports, safety, nutrition, hygiene, and drug education." **Does not encourage writing submissions from children.** Reviews submissions for possible use in all Children's Better Health Institute publications. Subscription: $15.95/year each ($23.95 outside U.S.). Sample: $2.95.

How to Submit No simultaneous submissions. Manuscripts must be typewritten with poet's contact information in upper right-hand corner of each poem's page. SASE required. Submit seasonal material at least 8 months in advance. Guidelines available for SASE or on Web site. Responds in about 3 months. Pays $25 minimum for poetry. Acquires all rights.

Advice "We receive too many poetry submissions that are about kids, not for kids. Or, the subject matter is one that adults think children would or should like. Reading our guidelines is not enough. Careful study of current issues will acquaint writers with each title's 'personality.' "

$ ◎ CHILDREN'S DIGEST (Specialized: children ages 10-12; health-related themes)

Children's Better Health Institute, 1100 Waterway Blvd., Indianapolis IN 46202. Web site: www.cbhi.org. or www.childrensdigestmag.org.

Magazine Needs *Children's Digest*, published bimonthly for The Children's Better Health Institute, is a magazine for ages 10-12. "Prepares kids for the teen years." Wants poetry appropriate for the age group with health-related themes. " 'Health' is a broad topic that includes exercise, sports, safety, nutrition, hygiene, and drug education." **Does not encourage writing submissions from children.** Reviews submissions for possible use in all Children's Better Health Institute publications. Subscription: $15.95/year each ($23.95 outside U.S.). Sample: $2.95.

How to Submit No simultaneous submissions. Manuscripts must be typewritten with poet's contact information in upper right-hand corner of each poem's page. SASE required. Submit seasonal material at least 8 months in advance. Guidelines available for SASE or on Web site. Responds in about 3 months. Pays $25 minimum for poetry. Acquires all rights.

Advice "We receive too many poetry submissions that are about kids, not for kids. Or, the subject matter is one that adults think children would or should like. Reading our guidelines is not enough. Careful study of current issues will acquaint writers with each title's 'personality.' "

$ ◎ CHILDREN'S PLAYMATE (Specialized: children ages 6-8; health-related themes)

Children's Better Health Institute, 1100 Waterway Blvd., Indianapolis IN 46202. Web site: www.cbhi.org. or www.childrensplaymatemag.org.

Magazine Needs *Children's Playmate*, published bimonthly by The Children's Better Health Institute, is a magazine for ages 6-8. "Strives to make learning fun." Wants poetry appropriate for the age group with health-related themes. " 'Health' is a broad topic that includes exercise, sports, safety, nutrition, hygiene, and drug education." **Does not encourage writing submissions from children.** Reviews submissions for possible use in all Children's Better Health Institute publications. Subscription: $15.95/year each ($23.95 outside U.S.). Sample: $2.95.

How to Submit No simultaneous submissions. Manuscripts must be typewritten with poet's contact information in upper right-hand corner of each poem's page. SASE required. Submit seasonal material at least 8 months in advance. Guidelines available for SASE or on Web site. Responds in about 3 months. Pays $25 minimum for poetry. Acquires all rights.

Advice "We receive too many poetry submissions that are about kids, not for kids. Or, the subject matter is one that adults think children would or should like. Reading our guidelines is not enough. Careful study of current issues will acquaint writers with each title's 'personality.' "

🗂 ⊚ THE CHRISTIAN GUIDE (Specialized: Christian)

P.O. Box 14622, Knoxville TN 37914. Established 1989. **Contact:** J. Brian Long, poetry editor.

Magazine Needs *The Christian Guide*, a regional quarterly publication, features articles, announcements, advertisements, photographs, and poetry. Wants "positive, accessible poetry that concerns itself with the interaction between God and the nature of (and surrounding) mankind in micro- or macrocosm. All poems themed to the gentler tenets of the devotion reciprocated between Heaven and Earth are welcomed, but only the most well-crafted will be accepted." Does not want forced, trite rhyme. Has published poetry by Jill Alexander Essbaum, C.E. Chaffin, Teresa White, and Charles Semones. *The Christian Guide* is magazine-sized, with full-color cover with photographs and/or artwork, includes ads. Press run is 25,000.

How to Submit Submit 1-5 poems at a time. Lines/poem: 200 maximum. Considers previously published poems and simultaneous submissions. No e-mail or disk submissions. Cover letter is required. "Include brief bio, list of publishing credits, and a SASE." Reads submissions year round. Submit seasonal poems 6 months in advance. Seldom comments on rejected poems. Responds in 3 months. Pays 2 contributor's copies. Acquires one-time rights.

Advice "Subtlety. Subtlety. Subtlety. We are seeking poems that inspire awe, but do so by speaking to (and through) the reader with that 'small, still voice.' "

$ 🗂 THE CHRISTIAN SCIENCE MONITOR

The Home Forum Page, One Norway St., Boston MA 02115. E-mail: homeforum@csmonitor.com. Web site: www.csmonitor.com. Established 1908. **Contact:** Judy Lowe, Home Forum editor.

Magazine Needs *The Christian Science Monitor*, an international daily newspaper, regularly features poetry in The Home Forum section. Wants "finely crafted poems that explore and celebrate daily life; that provide a respite from daily news and from the bleakness that appears in so much contemporary verse." Does not want "work that presents people in helpless or hopeless states; poetry about death, aging, or illness; or dark, violent, sensual poems. No poems that are overtly religious or falsely sweet." Considers free verse and fixed forms. Has published poetry by Diana Der-Hovanessian, Marilyn Krysl, and Michael Glaser. Publishes 1-4 poems/week.

How to Submit Submit up to 5 poems at a time. Lines/poem: "For us, 20 lines is a long poem." No previously published poems or simultaneous submissions. Accepts e-mail submissions only (by attachment in MS Word, one poem/e-mail). Responds within 3 weeks. Pays $20/haiku; $40/poem.

🗂 ⊚ CHRISTIANITY AND LITERATURE (Specialized: Christian; spirituality/ inspirational)

Humanities Division, Pepperdine University, 24255 Pacific Coast Highway, Malibu CA 90263. Web site: www.pepperdine.edu/sponsored/ccl/journal. **Contact:** Maire Mullins, poetry editor.

Magazine Needs *Christianity and Literature*, a quarterly scholarly journal, publishes about 4-6 poems/issue. Press run is 1,350 (1,125 subscribers, 525 libraries). Single copy: $10; subscription: $25/year, $45/2 years. Make checks payable to CCL.

How to Submit Submit 1-6 poems at a time. No previously published poems or simultaneous submissions. Accepts submissions by surface mail only. Cover letter is required. Submissions must be accompanied by SASE. Time between acceptance and publication is 1-2 years. "Poems are chosen by our poetry editor." Guidelines available on Web site. Responds within 4 months. Pays 2 contributor's copies "and a dozen offprints to poets whose work we publish." Rights revert to poets upon written request. Reviews collections of literary, Christian poetry occasionally in some issues (no chapbooks).

Advice "We look for poems that are clear and surprising. They should have a compelling sense of voice, formal sophistication (though not necessarily rhyme and meter), and the ability to reveal the spiritual through concrete images. We cannot return submissions that are not accompanied by SASE."

⭐ $☑ ◎ CHRYSALIS READER (Specialized: spirituality; themes)

1745 Gravel Hill Rd., Dillwyn VA 23936. Fax: (434)983-1074. E-mail: chrysalis@hovac.com. Web site: www.swedenborg.com/chrysalis. Established 1985. **Contact:** Robert F. Lawson, poetry editor. Editor: Carol S. Lawson.

Magazine Needs *Chrysalis Reader*, published annually in September by the Swedenborg Foundation, is a "contribution to the search for spiritual wisdom, a book series that challenges inquiring minds through the use of literate and scholarly fiction, essays, and poetry." Wants "poetry that surprises, that pushes the language, gets our attention." Does not want anything "overly religious or sophomoric." Has published work by Robert Bly, Linda Pastan, Wesley McNair, Wyn Cooper, William Kloefkorn, and Virgil Suárez. *Chrysalis Reader* is 208 pages, 7 × 10, professionally printed on archival paper, perfect-bound, with coated coverstock. Receives about 1,000 submissions/year, accepts about 16 poems. Press run is 3,500. Sample: $10. (Sample poems available on Web site.)

How to Submit Submit no more than 5-6 poems at a time. Considers simultaneous submissions "if notified immediately when work is accepted elsewhere"; no previously published poems. Include SASE. Reads submissions year round. Time between acceptance and publication is typically 18 months. Regularly publishes theme issues (the 2008 issue theme is "Renewal"). Themes and guidelines available for SASE or on Web site. Responds in 3 months. Always sends prepublication galleys. Pays $25 and 3 contributor's copies. Acquires first-time rights. "We expect to be credited for reprints after permission is given."

Contest/Award Offerings The Bailey Prize (see separate listing in Contests & Awards).

Advice "Purchase a back issue or request your favorite bookstore to order a reading copy so that you can better gauge what to submit."

$☐ ◎ CICADA MAGAZINE (Specialized: teens, ages 14 and up)

Carus Publishing, 70 E. Lake St., Suite 300, Chicago IL 60601. Web site: www.cricketmag.com. Established 1998. **Contact:** Submissions Editor.

Magazine Needs *CICADA Magazine*, published semimonthly, is "the groundbreaking teen literary magazine that raises the issues that today's young adults find most important; a high-quality literary magazine for ages 14 and up." Wants "serious or humorous poetry; rhymed or free verse." Considers poetry by teens. *CICADA* is 128 pages, digest-sized, perfect-bound, with full-color cover. Receives more than 1,200 submissions/month, accept 25-30. Circulation is 17,000. Subscription: $35.97/year (6 issues). Sample: $8.50; sample pages available online.

How to Submit Submit no more than 5 poems at a time. Lines/poem: up to 25. Considers previously published poems. Show line count on each poem submitted. Include SASE. Guidelines available for SASE or on Web site. Responds in 6 months. Pays up to $3/line on publication. Acquires North American publication rights for previously published poems; rights vary for unpublished poems.

Also Offers "The Slam," an online writing forum "for young writers who want the world to see what they can do with words."

Advice "Our standards are very high, and we will accept only top-quality material. Please familiarize yourself with *CICADA* before submitting."

☑ CIDER PRESS REVIEW

777 Braddock Lane, Halifax PA 17032. E-mail: editor@ciderpressreview.com. (inquiries only). Web site: http://ciderpressreview.com. Established 1999. **Contact:** Caron Andregg and Robert Wynne, co-editors.

Magazine Needs *Cider Press Review*, published annually, features "the best new work from contemporary poets." Wants "thoughtful, well-crafted poems with vivid language and strong images. We prefer poems that have something to say. We would like to see more well-written humor. We also encourage translations." Does not want "didactic, inspirational, greeting card verse, empty word play, therapy, or religious doggerel." Has published poetry by Robert Arroyo, Jr., Virgil Suárez, Linda Pastan, Naomi Shihab Nye, Tim Seibles, and Mark Cox. *Cider Press Review* is 120 pages, digest-sized, offset-printed, perfect-bound, with 4-color coated card cover. Receives about 1,500 poems/year, accepts about 5%. Press run is 750. Single copy: $12; subscription: $20 for 2 issues (one journal, one book from the *Cider Press Review* Book Award). Sample: $10 (journal).

How to Submit Submit up to 5 poems at a time. No previously published poems or simultaneous submissions. Submit by postal mail or through online submission form. "International authors or special needs, please query via e-mail. Do not send unsolicited disk or e-mail submissions." Cover letter is preferred. Include short bio (50 words maximum). SASE required for reply. Reads submissions April 1-August 31 only. Time between acceptance and publication is 6-9 months. Poems are circulated to an editorial board. Guidelines available for SASE or on Web site. Responds in 1-4 months. Always sends prepublication galleys. Pays one contributor's copy. Acquires first North American serial rights.

Contest/Award Offerings *The Cider Press Review* Book Award (see separate listing in Contests & Awards).

☑ CIMARRON REVIEW

205 Morrill Hall, Oklahoma State University, Stillwater OK 74078-0135. E-mail: cimarronreview@yahoo.com. Web site: http://cimarronreview.okstate.edu. Established 1967. **Contact:** Lisa Lewis, Alfred Corn, and Ai, poetry editors.

Magazine Needs *Cimarron Review*, published quarterly, is a literary journal that takes "pride in our eclecticism. We like evocative poetry (lyric or narrative) controlled by a strong voice. No restrictions as to subject matter." Wants "poems whose surfaces and structures risk uncertainty and which display energy, texture, intelligence, and intense investment." Does not want "sing-song verse." Has published poetry by William Stafford, Gerry LaFemina, Phillip Dacey, Holly Prado, Mark Halliday, and Kim Addonizio. *Cimarron Review* is 100-150 pages, digest-sized, perfect-bound, with color cover. Press run is 600 (one-third of subscribers are libraries). Single copy: $7; subscription: $24/year ($28 Canada), $42/2 years ($48 Canada), $65/3 years ($72 Canada).

How to Submit Submit 3-5 poems at a time. Put name and address on each poem, which may be typed single- or double-spaced. Considers simultaneous submissions, "but please note in cover letter." No e-mail submissions; accepts postal submissions only. "Writers outside North America may query by e-mail." No response without SASE. Guidelines available on Web site. Responds in up to 6 months. Pays 2 contributor's copies. Acquires first North American serial rights only. Reviews books of poetry in 500-900 words, single-book format, occasionally multi-book.

$☑ THE CINCINNATI REVIEW

P.O. Box 210069, Cincinnati OH 45221-0069. (513)556-3954. E-mail: editors@cincinnatireview.com. Web site: www.cincinnatireview.com. Established 2003. **Contact:** Don Bogen, poetry editor.

Magazine Needs *The Cincinnati Review*, published semiannually, is devoted "to publishing the best new poetry and literary fiction, as well as book reviews, essays, and interviews. Open to any schools, styles, forms—as long as the poem is well made and sophisticated in its language use and subject matter." *The Cincinnati Review* is 180-200 pages, digest-sized, perfect-bound, with matte paperback cover with full-color art, includes ads. Press run is 1,000. Single copy: $9 (current issue); subscription: $15. Sample: $7 (back issue).

How to Submit Submit up to 10 pages of poetry at a time. Considers simultaneous submissions with notification; no previously published poems. No e-mail or disk submissions. Cover letter is preferred. SASE required. Reads submissions September 1-May 31. Time between acceptance and publication is 6 months. "First-round reading by small, trained staff. Final decisions made by genre editors." Seldom comments on rejected poems. Guidelines available for SASE or on Web site. Responds in 6 weeks. Always sends prepublication galleys. Pays $30/page and 2 contributor's copies. Acquires first North American serial rights. Reviews books of poetry in 1,500 words, single-book format.

CLARK STREET REVIEW (Specialized: narrative and prose poetry)

P.O. Box 1377, Berthoud CO 80513. E-mail: clarkreview@earthlink.net. Established 1998. **Contact:** Ray Foreman, editor.

Magazine Needs *Clark Street Review*, published 8 times/year, uses narrative poetry and short shorts. Tries "to give writers and poets cause to keep writing by publishing their best work." Wants "narrative poetry under 100 lines that reaches readers who are mostly published poets and writers. Subjects are open." Does not want "obscure or formalist work." Has published poetry by Charles Ries, Anselm Brocki, Ed Galling, Ellaraine Lockie, and J. Glenn Evans. *Clark Street Review* is 20 pages, digest-sized, photocopied, saddle-stapled, with paper cover. Receives about 1,000 poems/year, accepts about 10%. Press run is 200 (150 subscribers). Single copy: $2; subscription: $10 for 10 issues postpaid for writers only. Make checks payable to R. Foreman.

How to Submit Submit 1-5 poems at a time. Lines/poem: 20 minimum, 75 maximum. Considers previously published poems and simultaneous submissions. Send "disposable sharp copies. Maximum width—65 characters. Include SASE for reply. No cover letter." Time between acceptance and publication is 4 months. "Editor reads everything with a critical eye of 30 years of experience in writing and publishing small press work." Often comments on rejected poems. Guidelines available for SASE or by e-mail. Responds in 3 weeks. Acquires one-time rights.

Advice "*Clark Street Review* is geared to the more experienced poet and writer deeply involved in the writer's life. There are tips and quotes throughout each issue that writers appreciate. As always, the work we print speaks for the writer and the magazine. We encourage communication between our poets by listing their e-mail addresses. Publishing excellence and giving writers a reason to write is our only aim. Well-crafted, interesting, and accessible human narrative poems will see ink in *CSR*."

COAL CITY REVIEW

English Dept., University of Kansas, Lawrence KS 66045. E-mail: briandal@ku.edu. Established 1989. **Contact:** Brian Daldorph, editor.

Magazine Needs *Coal City Review*, published annually in the fall, prints poetry, short stories, reviews, and interviews—"the best material I can find. As Pound said, 'Make it new.'" Does not want "experimental poetry, doggerel, five-finger exercises, or beginner's verse." Has published poetry by Gary Lechliter, Phil Miller, Cheela Chilala, Maggie Sawkins, and Denise Low. *Coal City Review* is 100 pages, digest-sized, professionally printed on recycled paper, perfect-bound, with colored card cover. Accepts about 5% of material received. Press run is 200 (50 subscribers, 5 libraries). Subscription: $10. Sample: $6.

How to Submit Submit 6 poems at a time. Considers previously published poems "occasionally"; no simultaneous submissions. No e-mail submissions. "Please do not send list of prior publications." Include name and address on each page. Seldom comments on rejected poems. Guidelines available for SASE. Responds in up to 3 months. Pays one contributor's copy. Reviews books of poetry in 300-1,000 words, mostly single-book format. Send materials for review consideration.

Additional Information *Coal City Review* also publishes occasional books and chapbooks as issues of the magazine, but **does not accept unsolicited book/chapbook submissions**. Most recent book is *voyeur poems* by Matt Porubsky.

Advice "Care more (much more) about writing than publication. If you're good enough, you'll publish."

⚡ $ ◎ COBBLESTONE MAGAZINE (Specialized: American history; children/teens ages 9-14)

Editorial Dept., Cobblestone Publishing, 30 Grove Street, Suite C, Peterborough NH 03458. Web site: www.cricketmag.com. **Contact:** Meg Chorlian.

Magazine Needs *COBBLESTONE Magazine*, published 9 times/year, is a magazine of American history for children ages 9-14. "All material must relate to the theme of a specific upcoming issue in order to be considered." Wants "clear, objective imagery. Serious and light verse considered. Must relate to theme." Subscription: $29.95/year (9 issues). Sample: $5.95 plus $2.00 s&h (include 10×13 SASE); sample pages available on Web site.

How to Submit Query first. Lines/poem: up to 100. No e-mail submissions or queries. Include SASE. Reads submissions according to deadlines for queries (see Web site for schedule and details). Always publishes theme issue. Themes and guidelines available on Web site. Pays varied rates. Acquires all rights.

Advice "Writers are encouraged to study recent back issues for content and style."

◎ COLD MOUNTAIN REVIEW

English Dept., Appalachian State University, Boone NC 28608. (828)262-7108. Fax: (828)262-2133. E-mail: coldmountain@appstate.edu. (inquiries only). Web site: www.coldmountain.appstate.edu. **Contact:** Betty Miller Conway, managing editor; Joseph Bathanti, editor.

Magazine Needs *Cold Mountain Review*, published twice/year (January and July), features poetry, interviews with poets, poetry book reviews, and b&w graphic art. "We're open to diverse perspectives and styles." Especially interested in translations, politically engaged poetry, and poetry that emphasizes form—either traditional or experimental. Does not want light verse or wry or self-indulgent free verse. Has published poetry by Sarah Kennedy, Robert Morgan, Susan Ludvigson, Aleida Rodríguez, R.T. Smith, and Virgil Suárez. *Cold Mountain Review* is about 72 pages, digest-sized, neatly printed with one poem/page (or 2-page spread), perfect-bound, with light cardstock cover. Publishes only 10-12 poems/issue; "hence, we are extremely competitive: send only your best." Sample: send SASE or make donation to *Cold Mountain Review*.

How to Submit Submit 3-5 poems at a time. No previously published poems or simultaneous submissions. No e-mail submissions; postal submissions only. Cover letter is required. Include short bio and SASE. "Please include name, address, phone number, and (if available) e-mail address on each poem." Reads submissions August-May. Guidelines available for SASE. Responds in up to 3 months. Pays 2 contributor's copies.

$◙ COLORADO REVIEW

Center for Literary Publishing, Dept. of English, Colorado State University, Fort Collins CO 80523. (970)491-5449. E-mail: creview@colostate.edu. Web site: http://coloradoreview.colostate.edu. Established 1956 (as *Colorado Review*), 1966 (resurrected as *Colorado State Review*), 1985 (renamed *Colorado Review*). **Contact:** Donald Revell, editor. General Editor; Stephanie G'Schwind.

• Poetry published in *Colorado Review* has been included in *The Best American Poetry*.

Magazine Needs *Colorado Review*, published 3 times/year, prints short fiction, poetry, and personal essays. Has published poetry by Robert Creeley, Kazim Ali, Rusty Morrison, Lucie Brock-Broido, Cynthia Cruz, and Fanny Howe. *Colorado Review* is about 224 pages, digest-sized, professionally printed, notch-bound, with glossy card cover. Press run is 1,300 (1,000 subscribers, 100 libraries). Receives about 10,000 submissions/year, accepts about 2%. Subscription: $24/year. Sample: $10.

How to Submit Submit about 5 poems at a time. Considers simultaneous submissions, "but you must notify *Colorado Review* immediately if accepted elsewhere"; no previously published poems. No e-mail submissions. SASE required for response. Reads submissions September 1-May 1 only. Responds in 2 months, "often sooner." Pays $5/printed page. Acquires first North American serial rights. Reviews books of poetry, fiction, and nonfiction. "Most book reviews are solicited, but feel free to query." Send materials for review consideration.

Contest/Award Offerings Colorado Prize for Poetry (see separate listing in Contests & Awards).

COMMON GROUND REVIEW

21 Primrose St., West Springfield MA 01089. Web site: www.cgreview.org. Established 1999. **Contact:** Larry O'Brien, editor.

• *Common Ground Review* is affiliated with Western New England College.

Magazine Needs *Common Ground Review*, published biannually, prints poetry and original artwork. Wants poetry with strong imagery; well-written free or traditional forms. Does not want greeting card verse, overly sentimental or political poetry. Has published poetry by James Doyle, Martin Galvin, Lyn Lifshin, Virgil Suárez, and Rennie McQuilken. *Common Ground Review* is 40-58 pages, digest-sized, perfect-bound, with 4-color cover. Receives about 1,000 poems/year, accepts less than 10%. Press run is 125-150. Single copy: $12.50. Orders: Make checks payable to *Common Ground Review* and send to 43 Winton Rd., East Windsor CT 06088.

How to Submit Submit 1-5 poems at a time. Lines/poem: 60 maximum. No previously published poems or simultaneous submissions. No disk submissions. Cover letter is required, as is biography. "Poems should be single-spaced; include name, address, phone number, e-mail address, brief biography, and SASE (submissions without SASE will be discarded)." Reads submissions year round, but deadline for non-contest submissions is August 31. Submit seasonal poems 6 months in advance. Time between acceptance and publication is 4-6 months. "Editor reads and culls submissions. Final decisions made by editorial board." Seldom comments on rejected poems. Guidelines available in magazine or on Web site. Responds in 2 months. Pays one contributor's copy. Acquires one-time rights.

Contest/Award Offerings Sponsors an annual poetry contest. Offers 1st Prize: $150; 2nd Prize: $75; 3rd Prize: $50; Honorable Mentions. **Entry fee:** $10 for 1-3 unpublished poems. **Deadline:** February 28 for contest submissions only. All contest submissions are considered for publication in *Common Ground Review*.

Advice "Read journal before submitting. Beginning poets need to read what's out there, get into workshops, and work on revising. Attend writers' conferences. Listen and learn."

COMMON THREADS (Specialized: submissions by members only)

3520 State Route 56, Mechanicsburg OH 43044. (937)834-2666. Established 1928. **Contact:** Amy Jo Zook, editor.

Magazine Needs *Common Threads*, published biannually in April and October, is the Ohio Poetry Association's member poetry magazine. **Only members of OPA may submit poems.**" We use beginners' poetry, but would like it to be good, tight, revised. In short, not first drafts. We'd like poems to make us think as well as feel something." Does not want to see poetry that is highly sentimental, overly morbid, religiously coercive, or pornograpic. Considers poetry by teens "if members or high school contest winners." Has published poetry by Bill Reyer, Michael Bugeja,

Timothy Russell, Yvonne Hardenbrook, and Dalene Stull. *Common Threads* is 52 pages, digest-sized, computer-typeset, with matte card cover. *"Common Threads* is a forum for our members, and we do use reprints so new members can get a look at what is going well in more general magazines." Annual dues, including 2 issues of *Common Threads*: $15; $12 for seniors (over age 65). Single copy: $2; $5 for students (through college).

How to Submit Lines/poem: "nothing over 40 (unless exceptional)." Considers previously published poems, if "author is upfront about them." Accepts submissions by postal mail only. Reads submissions year round. Frequently publishes seasonal poems. Guidelines available for SASE. All rights revert to poet after publication.

Advice "Read a lot to see what is being done by good poets nationally. Write what you know and love. Revise!!"

⬡ $⬡ ◎ COMMONWEAL (Specialized: Catholic)

475 Riverside Dr., Room 405, New York NY 10115. E-mail: editors@commonwealmagazine.org. Web site: www.commonwealmagazine.org. **Contact:** Rosemary Deen, poetry editor.

Magazine Needs *Commonweal*, published every 2 weeks, is a Catholic general interest magazine for college-educated readers. Wants serious, witty, well-written poems. Does not publish inspirational poems. Circulation is 20,000. Subscription: $47. Sample: $7.

How to Submit Lines/poem: 75 maximum. No simultaneous submissions. Accepts e-mail submissions (as MS Word attachments). Reads submissions September 1-June 30 only. Pays 50¢/line plus 2 contributor's copies. Acquires all rights. Returns rights when requested by the author. Reviews books of poetry in 750-1,000 words, single- or multi-book format.

◖ THE COMSTOCK REVIEW

4956 St. John Dr., Syracuse NY 13215. (315)488-8077. E-mail: poetry@comstockreview.org. (inquiries only). Web site: www.comstockreview.org. Established 1987 (as *Poetpourri*). **Contact:** John M. Bellinger, managing editor.

Magazine Needs *The Comstock Review*, published semiannually (Volume I in summer, Volume II in winter) by the Comstock Writers' Group, Inc., seeks "well-written free and traditional verse." Wants "metaphor and fresh, vivid imagery." Does not want "obscene, obscure, patently religious, or greeting card verse. Few Haiku." Has published poetry by Melanie Almeder, Robert Cooperman, Barbara Crooker, Elton Glaser, Richard Jones, and Enid Shomer. *The Comstock Review* is about 100 pages, digest-sized, professionally printed, perfect-bound. Press run is 600. Single copy: $9; subscription: $16/year, $28/2 years. Sample: through year 2004, $6 each.

How to Submit Submit 3-6 poems at a time. Lines/poem:up to 40. No previously published poems or simultaneous submissions. No e-mail submissions; postal submissions only. Cover letter is preferred. Include short bio. Put name, address, and phone number or e-mail address on each page. Reads submissions January 1-March 15 only (at present; check Web site). Acceptances mailed out 6-8 weeks after close of reading period. "Rejections may receive editorial commentary and may take slightly longer." Guidelines available in magazine, for SASE, or on Web site. Pays one contributor's copy. Acquires first North American serial rights.

Contest/Award Offerings The annual Muriel Craft Bailey Memorial Award and the Jesse Bryce Niles Memorial Chapbook Award (see separate listings in Contests & Awards).

◖ CONCHO RIVER REVIEW

P.O. Box 10894, Angelo State University, San Angelo TX 76909. (915)942-2273. Fax: (915)942-2155. E-mail: jerry.bradley@lamar.edu. Web site: www.angelo.edu/dept/english/publications/concho_river_review.htm. Established 1984. **Contact:** Jerry Bradley, poetry editor. Editor: Mary Ellen Hartje.

Magazine Needs *Concho River Review*, published twice/year, is a literary journal "particularly looking for poems with distinctive imagery and imaginative forms and rhythms. The first test of a poem will be its imagery. We prefer shorter poems; few long poems accepted." Has published poetry by Walt McDonald, Robert Cooperman, Mary Winters, William Wenthe, and William Jolliff. *Concho River Review* is 120-138 pages, digest-sized, professionally printed, flat-spined, with matte card cover. Receives 1,000 poems/year, accepts 60. Press run is 300 (200 subscribers, 10 libraries). Subscription: $14. Sample: $5.

How to Submit Submit 3-5 poems at a time. No simultaneous submissions. Accepts e-mail submissions (as attachment in Word). "No reply without SASE or e-mail address. No handwritten manuscripts accepted." Responds in 2-3 months. Pays one contributor's copy. Acquires first rights.

Advice "We're always looking for good, strong work—from well-known poets and those who have never been published before."

$⬛ CONFRONTATION MAGAZINE

English Dept., C.W. Post Campus, Long Island University, 720 Northern Blvd., Brookville NY 11548-1300. (516)299-2720. Fax: (516)299-2735. E-mail: martin.tucker@liu.edu. (inquiries only). Web site: www.liu.edu/confrontation. Established 1968. **Contact:** Isaac Cates, poetry editor. Editor-in-Chief: Martin Tucker.

Magazine Needs *Confrontation Magazine*, published semiannually, is interested "in all forms. Our only criterion is high literary merit. We think of our audience as an educated, lay group of intelligent readers. We prefer lyric poems." Does not want "sentimental verse." Considers poetry by children and teens. Has published poetry by David Ray, T. Alan Broughton, David Ignatow, Philip Appleman, Jane Mayhall, and Joseph Brodsky. *Confrontation* is about 300 pages, digest-sized, professionally printed, flat-spined. Receives about 1,200 submissions/year, accepts about 150. Circulation is 2,000. Subscription: $10/year. Sample: $3.

How to Submit Submit no more than 10 pages of poetry at a time. Lines/poem: "length generally should be kept to two pages." No previously published poems. "Prefer single submissions. Clear copy." No e-mail submissions; postal submissions only. Reads submissions September-May. "Do not submit mss June through August." Publishes theme issues. Upcoming themes available for SASE. Guidelines available on Web site. Responds in 2 months. Sometimes sends prepublication galleys. Pays $5-50 and one contributor's copy with discount available on additional copies. Staff reviews books of poetry. Send materials for review consideration.

Additional Information Occasionally publishes "book" issues or "anthologies." Most recent "occasional" book is *Life as a novice* by Jeffrey Kane, a poetic sequence on the transcendence of guilt.

Advice "We want serious poetry, which may be humorous and light-hearted on the surface."

$⬛ THE CONNECTICUT POETRY REVIEW

P.O. Box 392, Stonington CT 06378. Established 1981. **Contact:** J. Claire White and Harley More, poetry editors.

Magazine Needs *The Connecticut Poetry Review*, published annually, looks for "poetry of quality that is both genuine and original in content. No specifications except length: 10-40 lines." Has published poetry by John Updike, Robert Peters, Diane Wakoski, and Marge Piercy. *The Connecticut Poetry Review* is 45-60 pages, digest-sized, flat-spined, "printed letterpress by hand on a Hacker Hand Press from Monotype Bembo." Receives more than 2,500 submissions/year, accepts about 20. Press run is 400 (80 subscribers, 35 libraries). Sample: $5.

How to Submit Lines/poem: 10 minimum, 40 maximum. Reads submissions April-June and September-December only. Responds in 3 months. Pays $5/poem plus one contributor's copy.

Advice "Study traditional and modern styles. Study poets of the past. Attend poetry readings and write. Practice on your own."

◪ CONNECTICUT REVIEW

Southern Connecticut State University, 501 Crescent St., New Haven CT 06515. (203)392-6737. Fax: (203)392-5748. E-mail: ctreview@southernct.edu. (inquiries only). Web site: www.southernct .edu/projects/ctreview. Established 1968. **Contact:** Vivian Shipley, editor.

- Poetry published in *Connecticut Review* has been included in *The Best American Poetry* and *The Pushcart Prize* anthologies; has received special recognition for Literary Excellence from Public Radio's series *The Poet and the Poem*; and has won the Phoenix Award for Significant Editorial Achievement from the Council of Editors of Learned Journals (CELJ).

Magazine Needs *Connecticut Review*, published biannually, contains essays, poetry, articles, fiction, b&w photographs, and color artwork. Has published poetry by Jack Bedell, Colette Inez, Maxine Kumin, Tony Fusco, Dana Gioia, and Marilyn Nelson. *Connecticut Review* is 208 pages, digest-sized, offset-printed, perfect-bound, with glossy 4-color cover. Receives about 2,500 poems/year, accepts about 5%. Press run is 3,000 (400 libraries); 1,000 distributed free to Connecticut State libraries and high schools. Sample: $8. Make checks payable to Connecticut State University.

How to Submit Submit 3-5 typed poems at a time. Accepts submissions by postal mail only. Name, address, and phone number in the upper left corner of each page. Include SASE for reply only. Guidelines available for SASE. Pays 2 contributor's copies. Acquires first or one-time rights.

$ ◪ ◎ CONTEMPORARY HAIBUN (Specialized: haibun, haiga)

P.O. Box 2461, Winchester VA 22604-1661. (540)722-2156. E-mail: jim.kacian@redmoonpress.c om. (inquires only). Web site: www.redmoonpress.com. Established 1999 (as *American Haibun & Haiga*). **Contact:** Jim Kacian, editor/publisher.

Magazine Needs *contemporary haibun*, published annually in April, is the first Western journal dedicated to haibun and haiga. Considers poetry by children and teens. Has published poetry by Marlene Mountain, Dru Philippou, John W. Sexton, and Jason Sanford Brown. *contemporary haibun* is 128 pages, digest-sized, offset-printed on quality paper, with 4-color heavy-stock cover. Receives several hundred submissions/year, accepts about 5%. Print run is 1,000 for subscribers and commercial distribution. Subscription: $16.95 plus $4 p&h. Sample available for SASE or by e-mail.

How to Submit Submit up to 3 haibun or haiga at a time. Considers previously published poems. Accepts submissions online at www.poetrylives.com/cho/ as well as disk and postal submissions. Include SASE for postal submissions. Time between acceptance and publication varies according to time of submission. Poems are circulated to an editorial board. "Only haibun and haiga will be considered. If you are unfamiliar with the form, consult *Journey to the Interior*, edited by Bruce Ross, *contemporary haibun online* (at www.redmoonpress.com), or previous issues of *contemporary haibun*, for samples and some discussion." Guidelines available in magazine, for SASE, by e-mail, or on Web site. Pays $1/page. Acquires first North American serial rights.

Also Offers Publishes *The Red Moon Anthology*, "an annual volume of the finest English-language haiku and related work published anywhere in the world." (See separate listing in this section.)

Advice "It is best if you familiarize yourself with what is happening in the genre (and its close relatives) today before submitting. We strive to give all the work we publish plenty of space in which to resonate, and to provide a forum where the best of today's practitioners can be published with dignity and prestige."

◪ COTTONWOOD (Specialized: Midwest emphasis)

Cottonwood Magazine and Press, 1301 Jayhawk Blvd., Room 400, Kansas Union, University of Kansas, Lawrence KS 66045. (7850)864-3777. E-mail: pwedge@ku.edu. Established 1965. **Contact:** Philip Wedge, poetry editor.

Magazine Needs *Cottonwood*, published semiannually, emphasizes the Midwest "but publishes the best poetry received regardless of region." Wants poems "on daily experience, perception; strong narrative or sensory impact, non-derivative." Does not want " 'literary,' not 'academic.' "

Has published poetry by Rita Dove, Virgil Suárez, Walt McDonald, and Luci Tapahonso. *Cottonwood* is 112 pages, digest-sized, printed from computer offset, flat-spined. Receives about 3,000 submissions/year, accepts about 20. Press run is 500-600 (150 subscribers, 75 libraries). Single copy: $8.00. Sample: $5.

How to Submit Submit up to 5 pages of poetry at a time. Lines/poem: 60 maximum. No simultaneous submissions. Sometimes comments on rejected poems. Responds in up to 5 months. Pays one contributor's copy.

Additional Information Cottonwood Press "is auxiliary to *Cottonwood Magazine* and publishes material by authors in the region. **Material is usually solicited.**" Has published *Violence and Grace* by Michael L. Johnson and *Midwestern Buildings* by Victor Contoski.

Advice "Read the little magazines and send to ones you like."

$☑ CRAB ORCHARD REVIEW

Dept. of English, Mail Code 4503, Faner Hall 2380, Southern Illinois University Carbondale, 1000 Faner Dr., Carbondale IL 62901. Web site: www.siu.edu/~crborchd. Established 1995. **Contact:** Allison Joseph, editor and poetry editor.

- *Crab Orchard Review* received a 2004 Literary Award and a 2005 Operating Grant from the Illinois Arts Council; poetry published in *Crab Orchard Review* has appeared in *The Best American Poetry* and *Beacon's Best of 1999* and *2000*.

Magazine Needs *Crab Orchard Review*, published semiannually in February and August, prints poetry, fiction, creative nonfiction, interviews, book reviews, and novel excerpts. Wants all styles and forms from traditional to experimental. Does not want greeting card verse; literary poetry only. Has published poetry by Luisa A. Igloria, Betsy Sholl, Cathy Song, and Bro. Yao (Hoke S. Glover III). *Crab Orchard Review* is 280-300 pages, digest-sized, professionally printed, perfect-bound, with (usually) glossy card cover with color photos. Receives about 12,000 poems/year, accepts about 1%. Press run is 2,500 (2,000 subscribers, 400 libraries); 100 exchanged with other journals; remainder in shelf sales. Subscription: $15. Sample: $10.

How to Submit Submit up to 5 poems at a time. Considers simultaneous submissions with notification; no previously published poems. Postal submissions only. Cover letter is preferred. "Indicate stanza breaks on poems of more than one page." Reads submissions April-November for Summer/Fall special theme issue, February-April for regular, non-thematic Winter/Spring issue. Time between acceptance and publication is 6 months to a year. "Poems that are under serious consideration are discussed and decided on by the managing editor and poetry editor." Seldom comments on rejected poems. Publishes theme issues. Upcoming themes available in magazine, for SASE, or on Web site. Guidelines available for SASE or on Web site. Responds in up to 9 months. Pays $20/page ($100 minimum), 2 contributor's copies, and one year's subscription. Acquires first North American serial rights. Staff reviews books of poetry in 500-700 words, single-book format. Send materials for review consideration to Jon C. Tribble, Managing Editor.

Contest/Award Offerings The Crab Orchard Series in Poetry Open Competition Awards, The Crab Orchard Series in Poetry First Book Award, and The Richard Peterson Poetry Prize (see separate listings in Contests & Awards).

Advice "Do not send any submissions via e-mail! Include SASE (#10 or larger) with all submissions and all queries—no postcards or small envelopes. Before you send work, check the Web site to see what issue we are currently reading submissions for. Being familiar with our reading schedule will help you submit appropriate work at the right time."

$☑ CRAZYHORSE

Dept. of English, College of Charleston, 66 George St., Charleston SC 29424. (843)953-7740. E-mail: crazyhorse@cofc.edu. Web site: http://crazyhorse.cofc.edu. Established 1960. **Contact:** Garrett Doherty and Carol Ann Davis, poetry editors.

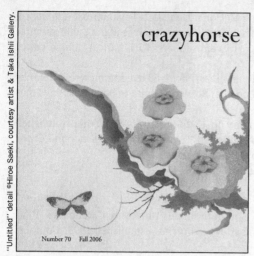

"Untitled" detail ©Hiroe Saeki, courtesy artist & Taka Ishii Gallery.

Number 70   Fall 2006

The cover of *Crazyhorse* No. 70 features the artwork of Hiroe Saeki. "The *Crazyhorse* editors enjoyed how the art took off from traditional Japanese painting and the work's level of detail," says editor Garrett Doherty. "It's a meticulous pencil drawing!"

• Poetry published in *Crazyhorse* has appeared in *The Best American Poetry* and *The Pushcart Prize*.

Magazine Needs *Crazyhorse*, published semiannually, prints fine fiction, poetry, and essays. "Send your best words our way. We like to print a mix of writing regardless of its form, genre, school, or politics. We're especially on the lookout for writing that doesn't fit the categories. Before sending, ask 'What's reckoned with that's important for other people to read?'" Has published poetry by David Wojahn, Mary Ruefle, Nance Van Winkle, Dean Young, Marvin Bell, and A.V. Christie. *Crazyhorse* is 160 pages, $8^3/_4 \times 8^1/_2$, perfect-bound, with 4-color glossy cover. Receives about 15,000 poems/year. Circulation is 2,000. Single copy: $9; subscription: $16/year, $26.50 for 2 years, $38 for 3 years. Sample: $6. Make checks payable to *Crazyhorse*.

How to Submit Submit 3-5 poems at a time. Considers simultaneous submissions; no previously published poems. No fax, e-mail, or disk submissions. Cover letter is preferred. Reads submissions year round. "We read slower in summer." Time between acceptance and publication is 6 months. Seldom comments on rejected poems. Guidelines available in magazine, for SASE, by e-mail, or on Web site. Responds in 3 months. Sometimes sends prepublication galleys. Pays $20/page, 2 contributor's copies, and one-year subscription (2 issues). Acquires first North American serial rights.

Contest/Award Offerings Sponsors the annual Lynda Hull Memorial Poetry Prize, awarding $2,000 and publication in *Crazyhorse*. All entries will be considered for publication. Submit up to 3 poems (no more than 10 pages) with cover letter and SASE. **Entry fee:** $15 (includes one-year subscription). Guidelines available for SASE or on Web site.

Advice "Feel strongly; then write."

◙ THE CREAM CITY REVIEW

Dept. of English, University of Wisconsin—Milwaukee, P.O. Box 413, Milwaukee WI 53201. (414)229-4708. E-mail: creamcity@uwm.edu. (inquiries only). Web site: www.uwm.edu/Dept/English/ccr. **Contact:** Jen Collins and Dawn Tefft, poetry editors.

• Poetry published in *The Cream City Review* has been included in *The Best American Poetry*.

Magazine Needs *The Cream City Review*, published twice/year, seeks "all forms of writing, from traditional to experimental. We strive to produce issues that are challenging, diverse, and of lasting quality." Does not want "sexist, homophobic, racist, or formulaic writings." Has published poetry by Elizabeth Bradfield, Annie Finch, Timothy Liu, Thylias Moss, Lee Ann Roripaugh, and Larissa Szporluk. *The Cream City Review* is about 200 pages, digest-sized, perfect-bound, with full-color cover on 70 lb. paper. Press run is 1,000 (500 subscribers, 50 libraries). Single copy: $12; subscription: $22/year, $41 for 2 years ($35/year for institutions). Sample: $8.

How to Submit Submit no more than 5 poems at a time. Considers simultaneous submissions when notified. No e-mail submissions; postal submissions only. Include SASE. Cover letter is preferred. "Please include a few lines about your publication history and other information you think of interest." Reads submissions August 1-April 1 only. Sometimes comments on rejected poems. Publishes theme issues; "inquire regularly." Guidelines available for SASE or on Web site. Responds in 6-8 months. Payment includes one-year subscription. Acquires first rights. Reviews books of

poetry in 1-2 pages. Send materials for review consideration to the book review editor.
Contest/Award Offerings Sponsors an annual poetry contest. Awards $500 plus publication. **Entry fee:** $15 for 3-5 poems. All entries are considered for publication. Guidelines available on Web site.

$☐ ⊚ CRICKET MAGAZINE (Specialized: for young readers ages 9-14)

Carus Publishing, 70 E. Lake St., Suite 300, Chicago IL 60601. Web site: www.cricketmag.com. Established 1973. **Contact:** Submissions Editor.
Magazine Needs *CRICKET Magazine*, published monthly, is a literary magazine for young readers ages 9-14. Wants ''serious and humorous poetry, nonsense rhymes.'' Does not want ''forced or trite rhyming or imagery that doesn't hang together to create a unified whole.'' *CRICKET* is 64 pages, 8×10, saddle-stapled, with color cover. Circulation is 73,000. Subscription: $35.97/year (12 issues). Sample: $5; sample pages available on Web site.
How to Submit Submit no more than 5 poems at a time. Lines/poem: 50 (2 pages) maximum. Considers previously published poems. Put line count on each poem submitted. Include SASE. Guidelines available for SASE or on Web site. Responds in 6 months. Payment is up to $3/line on publication. Acquires North American publication rights for previously published poems; rights vary for unpublished poems.
Contest/Award Offerings Sponsors poetry contests for readers.
Advice ''Our standards are very high, and we will accept only top-quality material. Before attempting to write for *CRICKET*, be sure to familiarize yourself with this age child and with the magazine itself.''

☑ CRUCIBLE

Barton College, College Station, Wilson NC 27893. (252)399-6344. E-mail: tgrimes@barton.edu. Established 1964. **Contact:** Terrence L. Grimes, editor.
Magazine Needs *Crucible*, published annually in November, uses ''poetry that demonstrates originality and integrity of craftsmanship as well as thought. Traditional metrical and rhyming poems are difficult to bring off in modern poetry. The best poetry is written out of deeply felt experience which has been crafted into pleasing form.'' Wants ''free verse with attention paid particularly to image, line, stanza, and voice.'' Does not want ''very long narratives, poetry that is forced.'' Has published poetry by Robert Grey, R.T. Smith, and Anthony S. Abbott. *Crucible* is 100 pages, digest-sized, professionally printed on high-quality paper, with matte card cover. Press run is 500 (300 subscribers, 100 libraries, 200 shelf sales). Sample: $7.
How to Submit Submit 5 poems at a time. No previously published poems or simultaneous submissions. ''We require three unsigned copies of the manuscript and a short biography including a list of publications, in case we decide to publish the work.'' Reads submissions between Christmas and mid-April only. Responds in up to 4 months. Pays in contributor's copies.
Contest/Award Offerings The Sam Ragan Prize ($150), in honor of the former Poet Laureate of North Carolina, and other contests (prizes of $150 and $100). Guidelines available for SASE.

⊛ ☑ CURRENT ACCOUNTS

16-18 Mill Lane, Horwich, Bolton BL6 6AT England. Phone/fax: (44)(120 4)669858. E-mail: bswscribe@aol.com. Web site: http://hometown.aol.co.uk/bswscribe/myhomepage/newsletter.html. Established 1994. **Contact:** Rod Riesco, editor.
Magazine Needs *Current Accounts*, published semiannually, prints poetry, fiction, and nonfiction by members of Bank Street Writers, and other contributors. Open to all types of poetry. ''No requirements, although some space is reserved for members.'' Considers poetry by children and teens. Has published poetry by Pat Winslow, M.R. Peacocke, and Gerald England. *Current Accounts* is 52 pages, A5, photocopied, saddle-stapled, with card cover with b&w or color photo or artwork. Receives about 300 poems/year, accepts about 5%. Press run is 80 (6 subscribers, 40 shelf sales); 8

distributed free to competition winners. Subscription: £6. Sample: £3. Make checks payable to Bank Street Writers (sterling checks only).

How to Submit Submit up to 6 poems at a time. Lines/poem: 100 maximum. No previously published poems (unpublished poems preferred) or simultaneous submissions. Accepts e-mail submissions (pasted into body of message). Cover letter is required. SAE or IRC essential for postal submissions. Time between acceptance and publication is 6 months. Seldom comments on rejected poems. Guidelines available for SASE, by fax, e-mail, or on Web site. Responds in 3 months. Pays one contributor's copy. Acquires first rights.

Also Offers Bank Street Writers meets once/month and offers workshops, guest speakers, and other activities. Write for details.

Advice "We like originality of ideas, images, and use of language. No inspirational or religious verse unless it's also good in poetic terms."

DANDELION ARTS MAGAZINE (Specialized: member-subscribers only)

Fern Publications, 24 Frosty Hollow, East Hunsbury, Northants NN4 OSY England. Fax: (44)(160)470-1730. Established 1978. **Contact:** Mrs. Jacqueline Gonzalez-Marina, M.A, editor/publisher.

Magazine Needs *Dandelion Arts Magazine*, published semiannually in May and December, is "a platform for new and established poets and prose writers to be read throughout the world." **Poets must become member-subscribers of *Dandelion Arts Magazine* and poetry club in order to be published.** Wants poetry that is "modern but not wild." Does not want "bad language poetry, religious or political, nor offensive to any group of people in the world." Has published poetry by Andrew Duncan, Donald Ward, Andrew Pye, John Brander, and Gerald Denley. *Dandelion Arts* is about 25 pages, A4, thermal-bound, with original cover design, includes ads. Receives about 200-300 poems/year, accepts about 40%. Press run is up to 1,000 (about 100 subscribers, 10% are universities and libraries); some distributed free to chosen organizations. Subscription: £16 UK, £30 Europe, £70 U.S. Sample: half price of subscription. Make checks payable to Fern Publications.

How to Submit Submit 4-6 poems at a time. Lines/poem: 40-80 maximum. Considers simultaneous submissions; no previously published poems. No fax submissions. Cover letter is required. "Submissions must be typed out clearly and ready for publication, if possible, accompanied by a SAE or postal order to cover the cost of postage for the reply." Reads submissions year round. Time between acceptance and publication is 2-6 months. "The material sent to Fern Publications is read by the editor when it arrives, and a decision is made straight away." Sometimes offers "constructive" comments on rejected poems. Guidelines available for SASE (or SAE and IRC) or by fax. Responds within 3 weeks. Reviews books of poetry. Send materials for review consideration.

Additional Information Fern Publications is a press for artistic, poetic, and historical books. Books are usually 50-80 pages, A5 or A4, thermal-bound or hand-finished. Query first with 6-10 poems. **Requires authors to subscribe to *Dandelion Arts Magazine*.** Responds to queries and mss in 3 weeks. Subsidizes costs for books, paying no royalties. "**All books are published at a cost agreed on beforehand and paid in advance.**"

Also Offers *Dandelion Arts* includes information on poetry competitions and art events.

Advice "Consider you are submitting material for an international magazine where subjects such as war or religious issues or bad language are not accepted."

DARKLING MAGAZINE (Specialized: poetry of a dark nature)

Darkling Publications, RR 3, Box 67, Colome SD 57528. (605)842-1402. E-mail: darkling@mitchelltelecom.net. (inquiries only). Established 2005. **Contact:** James C. Van Oort, editor-in-chief.

Magazine Needs *Darkling Magazine*, published annually in June, is "primarily interested in poetry. All submissions should be dark in nature. Horror poetry is acceptable but not a requisite. All poetry submissions should help expose the darker side of man. Poetry of any form, style, etc., that is either dark or depressing will be strongly considered." Does not want "poetry aimed at making one feel good or experience the warm fuzzies. Such submissions will be trash-canned and will merit no response. 'Dark nature' does not mean whiny or overly murderous, and certainly being depressed does not make an artist's work dark. We do not publish pornography or excessive profanity.'' Has published poems by Robert Cooperman and Simon Perchik, among others. Subscription: $15 with s&h. Make checks payable to Darkling Publications.

How to Submit Submit up to 8 poems at a time. Lines/poem: any length is acceptable, but ''epic poems must be of exceptional quality.'' Considers previously published poems and simultaneous submissions. No e-mail or disk submissions. Cover letter is required. Reads submissions year round. Time between acceptance and publication is 2 months. Poems are circulated to an editorial board. Sometimes comments on rejected poems. Sometimes publishes theme issues. Guidelines available in magazine. Responds in 5-8 months, announcing rejections and acceptance in April or May. Pays one contributor's copy. All rights revert to author upon publication.

Advice ''Find your own voice and develop it. If your voice is a dark one and we like it, we will publish it. We are always looking for new poets who have a voice we feel needs to be heard. Do not be afraid to ask questions. Our editorial staff will be very happy to communicate with you.''

✪ THE DERONDA REVIEW (formerly *The Neovictorian/Cochlea*)

P.O. Box 55164, Madison WI 53705. E-mail: eacam@execpc.com. Web site: www.pointandcircumf erence.com. Established 1995. **Contact:** Esther Cameron, editor. Co-Editor for Israel: Mindy Aber Barad, P.O.B. 7731, Jerusalem 91077.

Magazine Needs *The Deronda Review*, published semiannually, seeks to ''promote poetry of introspection, dialogue, and social concern.'' Wants ''poetry of beauty and integrity with emotional and intellectual depth, commitment to subject matter as well as language, and the courage to ignore fashion. Welcome: well-crafted formal verse, social comment (including satire), love poems, philosophical/religious poems. *The Deronda Review* has a standing interest in work that sees Judaism as a source of values and/or reflects on the current situation of Israel and of Western civilization. Open, in principle, to writers of all ages.'' Has published poetry by Yakov Azriel, Ruth Blumert, Ida Fasel, Constance Rowell Mastores, Richard Vallance, and Marc Widershien. *The Deronda Review* is 28-32 pages, magazine-sized, photocopied, saddle-stapled, with cardstock cover. Press run is 275 (60 subscribers). Single copy: $6; subscription: $10.

How to Submit Submit 3-5 poems at a time. Considers simultaneous submissions and previously published poems ''on rare occasions.'' Cover letter is unnecessary. ''Do include SASE with sufficient postage to return all manuscripts or with 'Reply Only' clearly indicated. First-time contributors in the U.S. are requested to submit by surface mail. Poets whose work is accepted will be asked for titles of books available, to be published in the magazine.'' Time between acceptance and publication is up to one year. Often comments on rejected poems. Does not offer guidelines because ''the tradition is the only 'guideline.' We do encourage contributors to write for a sample.'' Responds in up to 4 months. Pays 2 contributor's copies. Acquires first rights.

Additional Information *The Deronda Review* publishes the addresses of poets who would welcome correspondence. ''Poets can also submit longer selections of work for publication on the 'Point and Circumference' Web site.''

Advice ''The poem should speak to the ear and to the understanding, and it should be understood that understanding has social consequences. Like all our social functioning, poetry today suffers from a loss of community, which translates into a lack of real intimacy with the reader. Poets can work against this trend by remaining in touch with the poetry of past generations, by forming relationships in which poetry can be employed as the language of friendship, and by at least contemplating the concept of covenant. Publication should be an afterthought.''

☑ DESCANT: FORT WORTH'S JOURNAL OF POETRY AND FICTION

English Dept., Texas Christian University, Box 297270, Fort Worth TX 76129. Fax: (817)257-6239. E-mail: descant@tcu.edu. Web site: www.descant.tcu.edu. Established 1956. **Contact:** Dave Kuhne, editor.

Magazine Needs *descant: Fort Worth's Journal of Poetry and Fiction*, published annually during the summer, seeks "well-crafted poems of interest. No restrictions as to subject matter or form." *descant* is 100+ pages, digest-sized, professionally printed and bound, with matte card cover. Receives about 3,000 poems/year. Press run is 500 (350 subscribers). Single copy: $12 ($18 outside U.S.). Sample: $10.

How to Submit Lines/poem: 60 or fewer, "but sometimes longer." No simultaneous submissions. No fax or e-mail submissions. Reads submissions September-March only. Responds in 6 weeks. Pays 2 contributor's copies.

Contest/Award Offerings Sponsors the annual Betsy Colquitt Award for Poetry, offering $500 to the best poem or series of poems by a single author in a volume. *descant* also offers a $250 award for an outstanding poem in an issue. No application process or reading fee; all published submissions are eligible for consideration.

☑ ☑ DEVIL BLOSSOMS

Asterius Press, P.O. Box 5122, Seabrook NJ 08302-3511. E-mail: theeditor@asteriuspress.com. Web site: www.asteriuspress.com. Established 1997. **Contact:** John C. Erianne, editor.

• **Devil Blossoms is closed to new submissions until further notice.**

Magazine Needs *Devil Blossoms*, published irregularly 1-2 times/year, seeks "poetry in which the words show the scars of real life. Sensual poetry that's occasionally ugly. I'd rather read a poem that makes me sick than a poem without meaning." Wants poetry that is "darkly comical, ironic, visceral, horrific; or any tidbit of human experience that moves me." Does not want "religious greetings, 'I'm-so-happy-to-be-alive' tree poetry." Has published poetry by Marie Kazalia, Stephanie Savage, Mitchell Metz, Normal, John Sweet, and Alison Daniel. *Devil Blossoms* is 32 pages, $7\frac{1}{2} \times 10$, saddle-stapled, with matte card cover with ink drawings. Receives about 10,000 poems/year, accepts about 1%. Press run is 750 (200 shelf sales). Single copy: $5; subscription: $14. Make checks payable to John C. Erianne.

How to Submit Submit 3-5 poems at a time. Considers simultaneous submissions "if so informed." Accepts e-mail submissions (pasted into body of message; no attachments). Cover letter is preferred. Time between acceptance and publication is up to one year. "I promptly read submissions, divide them into a 'no' and a 'maybe' pile. Then I read the 'maybes' again." Seldom comments on rejected poems. Guidelines available on Web site. Responds in up to 2 months. Pays one contributor's copy. Acquires first rights.

Advice "Write from love; don't expect love in return, don't take rejection personally, and don't let anyone stop you."

☑ ☑ DIAGRAM

648 Crescent NE, Grand Rapids MI 49503. E-mail: poems@thediagram.com. Web site: www.thediagram.com. Established 2000. **Contact:** Ander Monson, editor. Member: CLMP.

• Work appearing in *DIAGRAM* has been reprinted on the Poetry Daily and Verse Daily Web sites.

Magazine Needs *DIAGRAM*, published semimonthly online, prints "poetry, prose, and schematic (found or created), plus nonfiction, art, and sound. We're especially interested in unusual forms and structures, and work that blurs genre boundaries." Does not want light verse. Has published poetry by Arielle Greenberg, Anne Boyer, Jason Bredle, GC Waldrep, Simone Muench, and Medbh McGuckian. Receives about 1,000 poems/year, accepts about 10%. Number of unique visitors: receives about 150,000+ hits/month.

How to Submit Submit 3-6 poems at a time. Lines/poem: no limit. Considers simultaneous submissions; no previously published poems. Accepts e-mail submissions (as attachment); no disk submissions. "E-mail submissions MUCH preferred; print submissions must include SASE." Cover letter is preferred. Reads submissions year round. Time between acceptance and publication is 1-10 months. Poems are circulated to an editorial board. Sometimes comments on rejected poems. Sometimes publishes theme issues. Guidelines available on Web site. Responds in 1-3 months. Always sends prepublication galleys. Acquires first rights and first North American serial rights. Rights revert to poet upon publication. Reviews books/chapbooks of poetry in 500-1,500 words, single- or multi-book format. Send materials for review consideration to Aaron Welborn, reviews editor.

Additional Information *DIAGRAM* also publishes periodic perfect-bound print anthologies.

Contest/Award Offerings Sponsors the annual *DIAGRAM*/Michigan Press Chapbook Contest (see separate listing in Contests & Awards).

◖ ◎ DIAL BOOKS FOR YOUNG READERS (Specialized: poetry for children/teens)

345 Hudson St., New York NY 10014. Web site: www.penguin.com. **Contact:** Submissions.

Book/Chapbook Needs Dial publishes some illustrated books of poetry for children. Has published poetry by J. Patrick Lewis and Nikki Grimes.

How to Submit "Submit entire picture book manuscripts, or the first three chapters of longer works. Please include a cover letter with brief bio and publication credits." Considers simultaneous submissions; no previously published poems. "Please note that, **unless interested in publishing them, Dial will not respond to unsolicited submissions.** Please do not include a self-addressed, stamped envelope with your submission. If Dial is interested, you can expect a reply from us within four months." Payment varies.

▣ ◯ ◎ DIAMOND DUST E-ZINE (Specialized: poetry for/by teens; Christian; inspirational)

E-mail: DiamondEditor@yahoo.com. Web site: www.freewebs.com/diamonddustmagazine. Established 2005. **Contact:** Laura and Stephanie Rutlind, co-editors.

Magazine Needs *Diamond Dust E-zine*, published monthly online, is "a magazine and e-newsletter for teens and adults. Our goal is to inspire our readers in their Christian walk." Wants "poetry, short fiction, articles, book and music reviews, and fillers. Poetry of all types and all topics is considered. Submissions are not required to be religious, but we ask that they include good morals and clean content. 'Inspirational' is key." Does not want "to see anything that does not have clean content or high morals, or anything that is not inspirational." Considers poetry by teens. "Teens are encouraged to submit their work, but they must include their age and name or pen name." Accepts 24-36 poems/year. Available for free online.

How to Submit Submit 3 poems at a time. Lines/poem: less than 30. Considers previously published poems. Accepts e-mail submissions (pasted into body of e-mail); no disk submissions. Cover letter is required. "Tell us who you are and what you write. Include bio. If you're a teen, please include your age." Reads submissions year round. Submit seasonal poems 2 months in advance. Time between acceptance and publication is approximately 1-3 months ("unless held for a future seasonal or theme issue"). Always comments on rejected poems. Sometimes publishes theme issues. Guidelines available by e-mail or on Web site. Responds within 3 weeks. No payment, but will include an author bio and contact links on Web site. "We acquire one-time electronic rights. All rights are given back to the author after publication. All pieces remain on our Web site for two months and then they are deleted." Send materials for review consideration to Laura and Stephanie Rutlind.

Advice "We love to work with beginning writers, so take a look at our current issue online. If you follow our guidelines, your submission has a good chance of achieving publication."

⊠ $⊚ **DIG MAGAZINE (Specialized: archeology & exploration; theme-specific; children/teens ages 9-14)**

Editorial Dept., Cobblestone Publishing, 30 Grove Street, Suite C, Peterborough NH 03458. Web site: www.cricketmag.com. **Contact:** Rosalie Baker.

Magazine Needs *DIG Magazine*, published 9 times/year in partnership with *Archeology* magazine, features archeology and exploration for children ages 9-14. "All material must relate to the theme of a specific upcoming issue in order to be considered." Wants "clear, objective imagery. Serious and light verse considered. Must relate to theme." Subscription: $32.97/year (9 issues). Sample: $5.95 plus $2.00 s&h (include 10×13 SASE); sample pages available on Web site.

How to Submit Query first. Lines/poem: up to 100. No e-mail submissions or queries. Include SASE. Reads submissions according to deadlines for queries (see Web site for schedule and details). Always publishes theme issue. Themes and guidelines available on Web site. Pays varied rates. Acquires all rights.

Advice "Writers are encouraged to study recent back issues for content and style."

▣ ☺ **DMQ REVIEW**

E-mail: editors@dmqreview.com. Web site: www.dmqreview.com. **Contact:** Sally Ashton, editor-in-chief.

Magazine Needs *DMQ Review*, published quarterly online, is "a quality magazine of poetry presented with visual art." Wants "finely crafted poetry that represents the diversity of contemporary poetry." Has published poetry by Amy Gerstler, Bob Hicok, Ilya Kaminsky, and Jane Hirshfield. Receives about 3,000-5,000 poems/year, accepts about 1%.

How to Submit Submit up to 3 poems at a time ("no more than once per quarter"). Considers simultaneous submissions (with notifications only); no previously published poems. Accepts e-mail submissions (pasted into body of message; no attachments will be read) only. "Please read and follow complete submission guidelines on our Web site." Reads submissions year round. Time between acceptance and publication is 1-3 months. Poems are circulated to an editorial board. Never comments on rejected poems. Responds within 3 months. Acquires first rights.

Additional Information Nominates for the Pushcart Prize. "We also consider submissions of visual art, which we publish with the poems in the magazine, with links to the artists' Web sites."

Advice "Read recent issues of *DMQ Review* before submitting, and send your best work."

⊠ ▣ $⊚ **DOVETAIL: A JOURNAL BY AND FOR JEWISH/CHRISTIAN FAMILIES (Specialized: Jewish/Christian interfaith marriage)**

775 Simon Greenwell Lane, Boston KY 40107. (800)530-1596. E-mail: DI-IFR@bardstown.com. Web site: www.dovetailinstitute.org. Established 1991. **Contact:** Mary Rosenbaum, editor.

Magazine Needs *Dovetail: A Journal by and for Jewish/Christian Families*, published quarterly online, provides "strategies and resources for interfaith couples, their families, and friends." Wants poetry related to Jewish/Christian marriage issues; uses some material related to other sorts of interfaith marriage, especially Muslim/Christian and Muslim/Jewish. Does not want poetry on general religious themes. Has published work by Janet Landman, Donald R. Stoltz, and Eric Wolk Fried. Receives about 10 poems/year, accepts about 1%. Press run is 1,000 (700 subscribers). Single copy: $5.50; subscription: $39.95. Sample: available to download free online. Make checks payable to DI-IFR.

How to Submit Submit one poem at a time. Considers previously published poems and simultaneous submissions. Accepts e-mail (pasted into body of message) submissions. Time between acceptance and publication is up to one year. Poems are circulated to an editorial board. "Clergy and other interfaith professionals review draft issues." Seldom comments on rejected poems. Publishes theme issues. Guidelines available for SASE or by e-mail or fax. Responds in one month. Pays $10-

20. Acquires first North American serial rights. Reviews other magazines in 500 words, single- and multi-book format.

Advice "We get 20 inappropriately denomination-oriented poems for every one that actually relates to interfaith marriage. Don't waste your time or ours with general Christian or 'inspirational' themes."

🖥 〇 DOWN IN THE DIRT

Scars Publications, 829 Brian Court, Gurnee IL 60031. E-mail: alexrand@scars.tv. Web site: http://scars.tv. Established 2000. **Contact:** Alexandria Rand, editor.

Magazine Needs *Down in the Dirt*, published monthly online, prints "good work that makes you think, that makes you feel like you've lived through a scene instead of merely read it." Also can consider poems. Does not want smut, rhyming poetry, or religious writing. Has published work by I.B. Rad, Jennifer Rowan, Cheryl A. Townsend, Tom Racine, David-Matthew Barnes, and Michael Estabrook. *Down in the Dirt* is published "electronically as well as in print, either on the Web or in e-book form (PDF file)." Sample: available on Web site.

How to Submit Lines/poem: any length is appreciated. Considers previously published poems and simultaneous submissions. Accepts e-mail submissions (vastly preferred to snail mail; pasted into body of message or as Microsoft Word .doc file attachment) and disk submissions (formatted for Macintosh). Guidelines available for SASE, by e-mail, or on Web site. No payment. "Currently, accepted writings get their own Web page in the 'writings' section at http://scars.tv, and samples of accepted writings are placed into an annual collection book Scars Publications produces."

Contest/Award Offerings Scars Publications sponsors a contest "where accepted writing appears in a collection book. Write or e-mail (editor@scars.tv) for information."

Additional Information Also able to publish electronic chapbooks. Write for more information.

Advice "The Web site is a more comprehensive view of what *Down in the Dirt* does. All the information is there."

🔁 〇 THE ECLECTIC MUSE (Specialized: rhyme; neo-classicist revival)

Suite 307, 6311 Gilbert Rd., Richmond BC V7C 3V7 Canada. (604)277-3864. E-mail: jrmbooks@hotmail.com. Web site: www.thehypertexts.com. Established 1985. **Contact:** Joe M. Ruggier, publisher.

Magazine Needs *The Eclectic Muse*, published annually at Christmas, is devoted "to publishing all kinds of poetry (eclectic in style and taste) but specializing in rhyme- and neo-classicist revival." Does not want "bad work (stylistically bad or thematically offensive)." Has published poetry by Mary Keelan Meisel, John Laycock, Philip Higson, Roy Harrison, Michael Burch, and Ralph O. Cunningham. *The Eclectic Muse* is magazine-sized, digitally copied, saddle-stapled, with paper cover. The number of pages varies from year to year (32 minimum to 56 maximum). Receives about 300 poems/year, accepts about 15%. Press run is 200 (90 subscribers, 5 libraries); distributed free to all contributing authors plus selected gift subscription recipients. Single copy: $8; subscription: $25. Make checks payable to Joe M. Ruggier.

How to Submit Submit no more than 5 poems at a time. Lines/poem: 60 maximum; "please consult if longer." Considers previously published poems and simultaneous submissions. Accepts e-mail submissions (preferred, as a single .doc or .rtf attachment containing all 5 poems) and disk submissions. "Send your submission by regular mail only if you have no access to a computer or you are computer illiterature. Typeset everything in Times New Roman 12 point. If your poetry features indents and special line spacing, please make sure you reproduce these features yourself in your data entry since it will not be possible for the editor to determine your intentions." Cover letter is preferred. "Include brief bio (100 words maximum) with your name, credentials (degrees, etc.), occupation and marital status, your most major publication credits only, and any hobbies or interests." Provide SASE plus clear e-mail and postal addresses for communication and for sending contributor's copy. Reads submissions year round. Time between acceptance and publication is one year. Poems are circulated to an editorial board. Sometimes comments on rejected poems. **"If authors wish to have a manuscript carefully assessed and edited, the fee is $250 USD; will respond within 8 weeks."** Guidelines available in magazine or on Web site. Responds in 2 months. Pays 2 contributor's copies. Reviews books/chapbooks of poetry and other magazines/journals in 900 words. Send materials for review consideration to Joe M. Ruggier, managing editor.

Also Offers "Look us up on www.thehypertexts.com, where myself and my services are listed (featured) permanently. The host of this splendid poetry Web site is my U.S. associate, Mr. Michael Burch. He features, on this site, most of the leading names in contemporary North America."

Advice "An author's style is really the only thing which belongs to him as an artist to manipulate for his own purposes as he pleases. Truths and feelings do not belong to him exclusively and may not be bent or manipulated for his own purposes as he pleases. We do not want bad work where the poet feels that the message matters but the style is bad (not good workmanship), nor do we wish to publish work which seems to us to distort and bend truths and human feelings far too much."

☑ EDGZ

Edge Publications, P.O. Box 799, Ocean Park WA 98640. Established 2000. **Contact:** Blaine R. Hammond, editor/publisher.

Magazine Needs *Edgz*, published semiannually in (or around) May and November, prints "poetry of all sorts of styles and schools. Our purpose is to present poetry with transpersonal intentions or applications, and to put poets on a page next to other poets they are not used to appearing next to." Wants "a broad variety of styles with a transpersonal intent. *Edgz* has two main reasons for existence: Our weariness with the attitude that whatever kind of poetry someone likes is the only legitimate poetry; and our desire to present poetry addressing large issues of life. Must be engaged; intensity helps." Does not want "anything with a solely personal purpose; dense language poetry; poetry that does not take care with the basics of language, or displays an ignorance of modern poetry. No clichés, gushing, sentimentalism, or lists of emotions. Nothing vague or abstract. No light verse or doggerel, but humor is fine." Has published poetry by Barry Ballard, Joseph Barker, Leonard Cirino, Joan Payne Kincaid, and R. Yurman. *Edgz* is digest-sized, laser-printed on recycled paper, saddle-stapled, with 80 lb. cardstock cover with art/graphics. Single copy: $7; subscription: $13 for 2 issues. Sample: $4. Make checks payable to Edge Publications.

How to Submit Submit 3-5 poems at a time ("a longer poem may be submitted by itself"). Lines/ poem: no length restrictions. Considers simultaneous submissions; no previously published poems. Cover letter is "not required, but if we find something interesting in yours, it may appear in the magazine. We don't mind more than one poem to a page or well-traveled submissions; these are ecologically sound practices. We like recycled paper. Submissions without SASE will be gratefully used as note paper. No postcards in place of SASE. Please do not fold poems separately. Handwritten poems OK if poet is poor or incarcerated." Reads submissions by February 1 and August 1 deadlines. Time between acceptance and publication is 1-6 months. Comments on rejected poems "as we feel like it. We don't provide criticism services." Guidelines available for SASE. Responds in up to 6 months. Pays one contributor's copy/published poem, with discounts on additional copies. Acquires first rights plus anthology rights ("just in case").

Advice "It's one thing to require subscriptions in order to be published. It's something else to charge reading fees. In a world that considers poetry valueless, reading fees say it is less than valueless—that editors should be compensated for being exposed to it. I beg such editors to cease the practice. I advise everyone else not to submit to them, or the practice will spread. My most common rejection note is 'too personal for my thematic focus.' "

☑ ◎ EKPHRASIS (Specialized: ekphrastic verse)

Frith Press, P.O. Box 161236, Sacramento CA 95816-1236. E-mail: frithpress@aol.com. (inquiries only). Web site: www.hometown.aol.com/ekphrasis1. Established 1995 (Frith Press) and 1997 (*Ekphrasis*). **Contact:** Laverne Frith and Carol Frith, editors.

• Poems from *Ekphrasis* have been featured on *Poetry Daily*.

Magazine Needs *Ekphrasis*, published semiannually in March and September, is an "outlet for the growing body of poetry focusing on individual works from any artistic genre." Wants "poetry whose main content is based on individual works from any artistic genre. Poetry should transcend mere description. Open to all forms." Does not want "poetry without ekphrastic focus. No poorly crafted work. No archaic language." Has published poetry by Jeffrey Levine, Peter Meinke, David Hamilton, Barbara Lefcowitz, Molly McQuade, and Annie Boutelle. *Ekphrasis* is 40-50 pages, digest-sized, photocopied, saddle-stapled. Subscription: $12/year. Sample: $6. Make checks payable, in U.S. funds, to Laverne Frith.

How to Submit Submit 3-7 poems at a time. Considers previously published poems "infrequently, must be credited"; no simultaneous submissions. Accepts submissions by postal mail only. Cover letter is required, including short bio with representative credits and phone number. Include SASE. Time between acceptance and publication is up to one year. Seldom comments on rejected poems. Guidelines available for SASE or on Web site. Responds in 4 months. Pays one contributor's copy. Nominates for Pushcart Prize. Acquires first North American serial or one-time rights.

Additional Information Until further notice, Frith Press will publish **occasional chapbooks by invitation only**.

Contest/Award Offerings The Ekphrasis Prize, which awards $500 and publication for a single poem, is sponsored and judged by the editors of *Ekphrasis*. Guidelines available for SASE or on Web site. 2006 winner was Angela Ball ("The Bath").

Advice "With the focus on ekphrastic verse, we are bringing attention to the interconnections between various artistic genres and dramatizing the importance and universality of language. Study in the humanities is essential background preparation for the understanding of these interrelations."

◪ THE ELEVENTH MUSE

Poetry West, P.O. Box 2413, Colorado Springs CO 80901. E-mail: poetrywest@yahoo.com. Web site: www.poetrywest.org/muse.htm. Established 1982. **Contact:** Steven D. Schroeder, editor.

Magazine Needs *The Eleventh Muse*, published annually in March, is open to "any high-quality poetry: metrical or free verse, narrative or lyric, traditional or cutting-edge. Be sure you know contemporary poetry and craft." Has published poetry by Ted Kooser, Mark Irwin, Larissa Szporluk, Joel Brouwer, H.L. Hix, and Sarah Lindsay. *The Eleventh Muse* is 50-100 pages, digest-sized, perfect-bound. Receives about 1,000 poems/year, accepts about 5%. Press run is 500. Single copy: $8. Sample: $5. Make checks payable to Poetry West, or purchse via PayPal on Web site.

How to Submit Submit 3-5 poems at a time. Lines/poem: 100 maximum. Considers simultaneous submissions; no previously published poems. Accepts e-mail submissions only; no postal submissions. Cover letter is preferred. Reads submissions year round, "but the deadline for each issue is December 1." Time between acceptance and publication is up to a year. Poems are circulated to an editorial board. Sometimes comments on rejected poems. Guidelines available in magazine or on Web site. Responds in 1-3 months. Pays one contributor's copy. Reviews books/chapbooks of poetry and other magazines/journals. Send materials for review consideration.

Contest/Award Offerings Offers annual *The Eleventh Muse* Poetry Contest. 1st Prize: $200; winning and Honorable Mention poems will be published in *The Eleventh Muse*. Submit 1-6 previously unpublished poems, 100 lines maximum each. Guidelines available in magazine or on Web site. **Entry fee:** $5 for one poem, $10 for 3 poems, $15 for 6 poems ($15 entries entitle poet to a copy of *The Eleventh Muse* with the winning poems). **Deadline:** December 1.

Also Offers "Poetry West hosts monthly workshops, critique sessions designed to improve writing skills, and occasional poetry readings. Our goal is to provide a forum where people who enjoy writing, reading, and listening to poetry can come together to share this common interest. Our workshops are open to the public, as are our poetry salons. And, since we are a nonprofit organization, membership is tax deductible." Levels of membership/dues: $25/year, $250/life-time. See Web site for more details.

$⬚ ELLIPSIS

Westminster College of Salt Lake City, 1840 South 1300 East, Salt Lake City UT 84105. (801)832-2321. E-mail: ellipsis@westminstercollege.edu. (inquiries only). Web site: www.westminstercollege.edu/ellipsis. Established 1967. **Contact:** Poetry Editor (rotating editors). Faculty Advisor: Natasha Sajé.

Magazine Needs *Ellipsis*, published annually in April, needs "good literary poetry, fiction, essays, plays, and visual art." Has published poetry by Allison Joseph, Molly McQuade, Virgil Suárez, Maurice Kilwein-Guevara, Richard Cecil, and Ron Carlson. *Ellipsis* is 120 pages, digest-sized, perfect-bound, with color cover. Accepts about 5% of submissions received. Press run is 2,000; most distributed free through college. Sample: $7.

How to Submit Submit 3-5 poems at a time. Considers simultaneous submissions if notified of acceptance elsewhere; no previously published poems. No fax or e-mail submissions; postal submissions only. One poem per page, with name and contact information on every page. Include SASE and brief bio. Reads submissions August 1-November 1. Responds in up to 8 months. Pays $10/poem, plus two contributor's copies.

Contest/Award Offerings All accepted poems are eligible for the Ellipsis Award, which includes a $100 prize. Past judges have included Jorie Graham, Sandra Cisneros, Phillip Levine, and Stanley Plumly.

✪ ⬚ EMPLOI PLUS

DGR Publication, 1256, Rue L'Annonciation Nord, #203, Riviere-Rouge QC J0T 1T0 Canada. Phone/fax: (819)275-3293. Established 1988 (DGR Publication), 1990 (*Emploi Plus*). **Contact:** Daniel G. Reid, publisher.

- The most recent issue of *Emploi Plus* appeared in June 1997; **further publication postponed for now.**

Magazine Needs *Emploi Plus*, published irregularly, features poems and articles in French or English. Has published *Alexiville, Planet Earth* by D.G. Reid as well as poetry by Robert Ott. *Emploi Plus* is 100 pages, 7 × 8½, photocopied, stapled. Press run is 500; all distributed free. Sample: free.

How to Submit *Does not accept unsolicited submissions.*

⬚ ⬚ EMRYS JOURNAL

P.O. Box 8813, Greenville SC 29604. E-mail: ldishman@charter.net. Web site: www.emrys.org. Established 1982. **Contact:** Poetry Editor. Editor: L.B. Dishman.

- Not accepting work; will begin reading submissions again August 1, 2008.

Magazine Needs *Emrys Journal*, published annually in May, prints "literary or narrative poetry of less than 36 lines. Rhyming needs to be oustanding to be considered." Has published poetry by Kristin Berkey-Abbott, Adriano Scopino, John Popielaski, J. Morris, and Terri McCord. *Emrys Journal* is up to 120 pages, digest-sized, handsomely printed, flat-spined. Press run is 400 (250 subscribers, 10 libraries). Sample: $12 and 7 × 10 SASE with 4 first-class stamps.

How to Submit *No mss will be read until August 1, 2008.* Submit up to 5 poems at a time (per author). No previously published poems or simultaneous submissions. Accepts e-mail submissions (as attachment). Include SASE. Reads submissions August 1-November 1 only; no mss will be read outside the reading period. Time between acceptance and publication is up to 8 months. Guidelines available for SASE or on Web site. Responds "by the end of the reading period." Pays 5 contributor's copies.

Contest/Award Offerings Sponsors the annual Nancy Dew Taylor Award for excellence in the art of poetry. Offers $250 prize to the author of the best poem published in *Emrys Journal* that year.

☑ ENGLISH JOURNAL

Dept. of Teacher Education, Columbus State University, Columbus GA 31907-5645. (706)565-3682. Fax: (796)569-3134. E-mail: brewpoem@hotmail.com. (inquiries only). Web site: www.englishjournal.colostate.edu. Established 1912. **Contact:** James Brewbaker, poetry editor.

Magazine Needs *English Journal*, published 6 times annually by The National Council of Teachers of English, is a professional education journal that encourages poets and teachers "to submit their best work—on any subject and in any form or style—for our consideration. Submissions need not be on a topic related to teaching, learning, or the discipline of English itself. Circulation is better than 20,000 copies to a national and international readership." *English Journal* accepts fewer than 10% of submissions.

How to Submit Submit up to 5 poems at a time (2 copies of each). Lines/poem: 40 maximum. Consider simultaneous submissions with notification in cover letter; no previously published poems or simultaneous submissions. No fax or e-mail submissions. Cover letter is required. Include phone number, e-mail address, and brief biographical information. "Include your name, address, and e-mail address on each poem. Notification regarding acceptances and rejections is sent by e-mail. Enclose a SASE for return of manuscripts only; otherwise we will recycle." Seldom comments on rejected poems. Responds in 3-4 months. Pays 2 contributor's copies.

☑ EPICENTER: A LITERARY MAGAZINE

P.O. Box 367, Riverside CA 92502. E-mail: poetry@epicentermagazine.org. Web site: www.epicentermagazine.org. Established 1994. **Contact:** Rowena Silver.

Magazine Needs *Epicenter: A Literary Magazine,* published biannually, is open to all styles. *"Epicenter* is looking for poetry, essays, short stories, creative nonfiction, and artwork. We publish new and established writers." Considers translations. Does not want "angst-ridden, sentimental, or earthquake poetry. We are not adverse to graphic images as long as the work contains literary merit." Has published poetry by Virgil Suárez, Alba Cruz-Hacher, B.Z. Niditch, Egon Lass, and Zdravka Evtimova. *Epicenter* is 100 pages, perfect-bound. Receives about 2,000 submissions/year, accepts about 5%. Press run is 800 (250 shelf sales). Single copy: $7. Make checks payable to *Epicenter: A Literary Magazine.*

How to Submit Submit up to 5 poems at a time. Considers previously published poems and simultaneous submissions. Accepts e-mail submissions. Include SASE with sufficient postage for return of materials. Seldom comments on rejected poems. Guidelines available in magazine, for SASE, by e-mail, or on Web site. Pays one contributor's copy. Acquires one-time and electronic rights.

☑ ◎ EPITOME (Specialized: northeastern OH women writers only)

Implosion Press, 4975 Comanche Trail, Stow OH 44224-1217. (330)836-7808. E-mail: epitomepoetry @aol.com. Web site: http://epitomemag.com. Established 1984. **Contact:** Cheryl Townsend, poetry editor.

Magazine Needs *epitome* is a regional publication for and by northeastern OH women. Wants "poetry that addresses the power of women to overcome social obstacles and injustices; poetry that is not subserviant to anyone. Poetry that celebrates being a woman. Material should be straight from the gut, uncensored and real. Any length as long as it works. All subjects OK, providing there are no 'isms.' We publish **ONLY** northeastern Ohio women in our Poetry and Featured Artist sections." Does not want rhymed verse. Sample: $5. Make checks payable to Implosion Press.

How to Submit Submit 3-8 poems at a time. Lines/poem: prefers "shorter, to-the-point work." Considers previously published poems if noted as such (include when and where each poem was originally published). Accepts e-mail submissions (pasted into body of message). Appreciates "a cover letter that tells how the poet found out about our magazine." Include name and address on each page; SASE for reply/return. Time between acceptance and publication is generally 5 months.

Guidelines available for SASE, by e-mail, or on Web site. Responds within 4 months. Acquires one-time rights. Reviews books of poetry. Send materials for review consideration.

Additional Information In addition to *epitome*, Implosion Press publishes chapbooks by northeastern OH women writers.

Advice "Know your market. Request guidelines and/or a sample copy."

$☑ EPOCH

251 Goldwin Smith Hall, Cornell University, Ithaca NY 14853. (607)255-3385. Web site: www.arts.cornell.edu/english/epoch.html. Established 1947. **Contact:** Nancy Vieira Couto, poetry editor.

Magazine Needs *Epoch*, published 3 times/year, has a distinguished and long record of publishing exceptionally fine poetry and fiction. Has published poetry by Kevin Prufer, Peter Dale Scott, Martin Walls, Maxine Kumin, Heather McHugh, and D. James Smith. *Epoch* is 128 pages, digest-sized, professionally printed, perfect-bound, with glossy color cover. Accepts less than 1% of the many submissions received each year. Has 1,000 subscribers. Subscription: $11/year domestic, $15/year foreign. Sample: $5.

How to Submit No simultaneous submissions. Manuscripts not accompanied by SASE will be discarded unread. Reads submissions September 15-April 15. Responds in up to 10 weeks. Occasionally provides criticism on mss. Pays 3 contributor's copies and $5-10/page. "We pay more when we have more!" Acquires first serial rights.

Advice "Read the magazine."

✪ $☑ ◎ EVANGEL (Specialized: Christian)

Light and Life Communications, P.O. Box 535002, Indianapolis IN 46253-5002. Established 1897. **Contact:** J. Innes, editor.

Magazine Needs *Evangel*, published weekly, is an adult Sunday school paper. "Devotional in nature, it lifts up Christ as the source of salvation and hope. The mission of *Evangel* is to increase the reader's understanding of the nature and character of God and the nature of a life lived for Christ. Material that fits this mission and isn't longer than one page will be considered." Does not want rhyming work. *Evangel* is 8 pages, digest-sized (two $8^{1}/_{2} \times 11$ sheets folded), printed in 4-color, unbound. Accepts about 5% of poetry received. Press run is about 10,000. Subscription: $2.25/quarter (13 weeks). Sample: free for #10 SASE.

How to Submit Submit no more than 5 poems at a time. Considers simultaneous submissions. Cover letter is preferred. "Poetry must be typed on $8^{1}/_{2} \times 11$ white paper. In the upper left-hand corner of each page, include your name, address, phone number, and social security number. In the upper right-hand corner of cover page, specify what rights you are offering. One-eighth of the way down the page, give the title. All subsequent material must be double-spaced, with one-inch margins." Submit seasonal poems one year in advance. Seldom comments on rejected poems. Guidelines available for #10 SASE. "Write 'guidelines request' on your envelope so we can sort it from the submissions." Responds in up to 2 months. Pays $10 plus 2 contributor's copies. Acquires one-time rights.

Advice "Poetry is used primarily as filler. Send for sample and guidelines to better understand what and who the audience is."

☑ THE EVANSVILLE REVIEW

1800 Lincoln Ave., Evansville IN 47722. Phone/fax: (812)488-1042. E-mail: evansvillereview@evansville.edu. Web site: http://english.evansville.edu/EvansvilleReview.htm. Established 1989. **Contact:** Corinna McClanahan, poetry editor.

- Poetry published in *The Evansville Review* has been included in *The Best American Poetry* and *The Pushcart Prize*.

Magazine Needs *The Evansville Review*, published annually in April, prints "prose, poems, and drama of literary merit." Wants "anything of quality." No excessively experimental work; no erotica. Has published poetry by Joseph Brodsky, J.L. Borges, John Updike, Willis Barnstone, Rita Dove, and Vivian Shipley. *The Evansville Review* is 140-200 pages, digest-sized, perfect-bound, with art on cover. Receives about 2,000 poems/year, accepts about 2%. Press run is 1,500. Sample: $5.

How to Submit Submit 3-5 poems at a time. Considers previously published poems and simultaneous submissions. No fax or e-mail submissions; postal submissions only. Cover letter is required. Include brief bio. Manuscripts not returned without SASE. Reads submissions September 1-December 1 only. Time between acceptance and publication is 3 months. Poems are circulated to an editorial board. Seldom comments on rejected poems. Guidelines available for SASE or on Web site. Responds within 3 months of the deadline. Pays 2 contributor's copies. Rights remain with poet.

Contest/Award Offerings The Willis Barnstone Translation Prize (see separate listing in Contests & Awards).

◎ EXIT 13 (Specialized: geography/travel)

P.O. Box 423, Fanwood NJ 07023-1162. (908)889-5298. E-mail: exit13magazine@yahoo.com. Established 1987. **Contact:** Tom Plante, editor.

Magazine Needs *Exit 13*, published annually, uses poetry that is "short, to the point, with a sense of geography." Has published poetry by A.D. Winans, Adele Kenny, Edwin Romond, Penny Harter, Brent Fisk, and Charles Rammelkamp. *Exit 13* is about 76 pages. Press run is 300. Sample: $7.

How to Submit Considers simultaneous submissions and previously published poems. Accepts e-mail submissions (no attachments). Guidelines available in magazine or for SASE. Responds in 4 months. Pays one contributor's copy. Acquires one-time and possible anthology rights.

Advice "*Exit 13* looks for adventure, a living record of places we've experienced. Every state, region, country, and ecosystem is welcome. Write about what you know and have seen. Send a snapshot of an 'Exit 13' road sign and receive a free copy of the issue in which it appears."

◑ ◎ EYE (Specialized: poetry by editors & publishers)

P.O. Box 235, Waterville ME 04903. E-mail: pupil@watchtheeye.com. Web site: www.watchtheeye .com. Established 2004. **Contact:** Peter Schwartz, editor.

Magazine Needs *eye*, "released whenever 30 or so great voices can be found," seeks "poems by poets who can breathe in their own dimensions." Has published poetry by Patricia Wellingham-Jones, CL Bledsoe, Arlene Ang, and Juliet Cook. *eye* is published on high-quality paper, with a full-color cover. Subscription: $19.95/4 issues. Sample: $5.95.

How to Submit Submit 5-7 poems at a time. Lines/poem: unlimited. Considers previously published poems ("if really well written") and simultaneous submissions. Accepts e-mail submissions (ONLY if pasted into body of message); no disk submissions. Cover letter is preferred. "No need to send SASE if you provide a working e-mail address." Reads submissions year round. Sometimes comments on rejected poems. Guidelines available on Web site. Responds ASAP. Pays one contributor's copy. Acquires first rights only.

Advice "Send me poems that transform your reality and eclipse the known world."

✖ $◎ FACES MAGAZINE (Specialized: theme-specific; world cultures; children/teens ages 9-14)

Editorial Dept., Cobblestone Publishing, 30 Grove Street, Suite C, Peterborough NH 03458. E-mail: facesmag@yahoo.com. Web site: www.cricketmag.com. **Contact:** Elizabeth Crooker Carpentiere.

Magazine Needs *FACES Magazine*, published 9 times/year, features cultures from around the globe for children ages 9-14. "Readers learn how other kids live around the world and about the important inventions and ideas that a particular culture has given to the world. All material must relate to the theme of a specific upcoming issue in order to be considered." Wants "clear, objective imagery. Serious and light verse considered. Must relate to theme." Subscription: $29.95/year (9 issues).

Sample: $5.95 plus $2.00 s&h (include 10×13 SASE); sample pages available on Web site.

How to Submit Query first. Lines/poem: up to 100. Accepts e-mail queries. Include SASE for postal submissions and queries. Reads submissions according to deadlines for queries (see Web site for schedule and details). Always publishes theme issue. Themes and guidelines available on Web site. Pays varied rates. Acquires all rights.

Advice ''Writers are encouraged to study recent back issues for content and style.''

FAILBETTER.COM

2022 Grove Ave., Richmond VA 23220. E-mail: submissions@failbetter.com. Web site: www.failbetter.com. Established 2000. **Contact:** Mary Donnelly and Ben Gantcher, poetry editors. Publisher: Thom Didato. Member: CLMP.

- *failbetter.com* was the only online literary magazine to be included in *Best American Poetry 2006*; additional works have received recognition in various award anthologies including *The Pushcart Prize* and *Best of the Net*.

Magazine Needs *failbetter.com*, published online, seeks ''that which is at once original and personal. When choosing work to submit, be certain that what you have created could only have come from you.'' Publishes translations and interviews with such poets as Paul Muldoon, Marie Ponsot, Mary Jo Salter, and Billy Collins. Has published poetry by J. Allyn Rosser, Terrance Hayes, Mary Donnely, and Thaddeus Rutkowski. Receives about 2,000 poetry submissions/year, accepts about 9-12. Publishes 3-4 poets/issue.

How to Submit Submit 4-6 poems at a time. Lines/poem: ''we're not concerned with length—one good sentence may find a home here, as the bulk of mediocrity will not.'' Considers simultaneous submissions; no previously published poems. Encourages e-mail submissions (pasted into body of message). ''Send to submissions@failbetter.com only! Please read and follow submission guidelines posted on Web site. All e-mail submissions should include title in header. All poetry submissions must be included in the body of your e-mail. Please do not send attached files.'' Also accepts postal submissions; ''please note, however, any materials accepted for publication must ultimately be submitted in electronic format in order to appear on our site.'' Cover letter is preferred. Reads submissions year round. Time between acceptance and publication is 4 months minimum and upward. Poems are circulated to an editorial board. Often comments on rejected poems. ''It's not unusual to ask poets to re-submit, and their subsequent submissions have been accepted.'' Guidelines available on Web site. Responds in up to 4 months to e-mail submissions; up to 6 months by regular mail. ''We will not respond to any e-mail inquiry regarding receipt confirmation or status of any work under consideration.'' No payment. Acquires exclusive first-time Internet rights; works will also be archived online. All other rights, including opportunity to publish in traditional print form, revert to the poet.

Advice ''With a readership of more than 60,000 per issue, *failbetter* is one of the Web's widely read literary magazines, offering exposure of poets' works to a much broader, worldwide audience than the typical print journal. For both established and emerging poets our advice remains the same: We strongly recommend that you not only read the previous issue, but also sign up on our e-mail list (subscribe@failbetter.com) to be notified of future publications.''

THE FAIRFIELD REVIEW

544 Silver Spring Rd., Fairfield CT 06824-1947. (203)256-1960. E-mail: fairfieldreview@hpmd.com. Web site: www.fairfieldreview.org. Established 1997. **Contact:** Janet and Edward Granger-Happ and Pamela Pollak, editors.

Magazine Needs *The Fairfield Review*, published twice/year online, features poetry, short stories, and essays from new and established authors. ''Wants ''free style poems, approachable on first reading, but with the promise of a rich vein of meaning coursing along under the consonants and vowels.'' Does not want ''something better suited for a Hallmark card.'' Considers poetry written by children and teens; requires parents' permission/release for children under 18. Has published poetry by Taylor Graham, Lyn Lifshin, and John Jeffrey. Receives about 630 poems/year, accepts about 6%.

How to Submit Submit 3 poems at a time. Lines/poem: 75 maximum. Considers previously published poems with permission; no simultaneous submissions. Accepts e-mail submissions (**strongly preferred**; as attachment). "Notifications are sent exclusively via e-mail. An e-mail address is required with all submissions." Cover letter is preferred. Reads submissions continually. Time between acceptance and publication is "usually less than two months." Poems are circulated to an editorial board. Sometimes comments on rejected poems, if requested and submitted via e-mail. Guidelines available on Web site. Responds in up to one year. Always sends prepublication galleys (online only). Acquires first rights, right to retain publication in online archive issues, and the right to use in "Best of *The Fairfield Review*" anthologies. Occasionally reviews books of poetry. "We consider reviews of books from authors we have published or who are referred to us."

Contest/Award Offerings "We select poems from each issue for 'Editor's Choice' awards, plus 'Reader's Choice' awards based on readership frequency."

Advice "Read our article 'Writing Qualities to Keep in Mind."

⬛ FAT TUESDAY

560 Manada Gap Rd., Grantville PA 17028. (717)469-7159. E-mail: lionelstevroid@yahoo.com. Web site: http://groups.yahoo.com/group/FatTuesday. Established 1981. **Contact:** Lionel Stevroid, editor.

Magazine Needs *Fat Tuesday*, published irregularly, is "a Mardi Gras of literary, visual, and audio treats featuring voices, singing, shouting, sighing, and shining, expressing the relevant to irreverent." Wants "prose poems, poems of irreverence, gems from the gut. Particularly interested in hard-hitting 'autofiction.'" Considers poetry by children and teens. Has published poetry by Chuck Taylor, Charles Bukowski, Mark Cramer, and Cotolo Patrick Kelly. *Fat Tuesday* is up to 60 pages, typeset (large type, heavy paper), saddle-stapled, usually chapbook-style (sometimes magazine-sized, unbound), with card cover, includes ads. Receives hundreds of submissions/year, accepts about 3-5%. Sample: $5, postage paid (all editions).

How to Submit Accepts e-mail submissions (pasted into body of message). Cover letter is "fine, the more amusing the better." Publishes theme issues. Responds in up to 3 months. Pays 2 contributor's copies if audio. Rights revert to author after publication. "Please join our Web group (see Web site above) and submit all the material you want. Get read by other writers, non-writers, and wannabes."

Also Offers "In 1998, *Fat Tuesday* was presented in a different format with the production of a stereo audio cassette edition. *FatTuesday*'s Cool Noise features readings, music, collage, and songs, all in the spirit of *Fat*'s printed versions. *Fat Tuesday* has released other audio projects. In-print magazines will still be produced as planned when funds are available."

Advice "Support the magazine that publishes your work!"

⬛ FAULTLINE

Dept. of English & Comparative Literature, University of California, Irvine, Irvine CA 92697-2650. (949)824-1573. E-mail: faultline@uci.edu. Web site: www.humanities.uci.edu/faultline. Established 1991. **Contact:** Devin Becker, poetry editor.

● Poetry published by *Faultline* has been included in *The Pushcart Prize*.

Magazine Needs *Faultline*, published annually each spring, features new poetry, fiction, and translation. Has published poetry by C.K. Williams, Larissa Szporluk, Yusef Komunyakaa, Amy Gerstler, and Killarney Clary. *Faultline* is about 200 pages, digest-sized, professionally printed on 60 lb. paper, perfect-bound, with 80 lb. coverstock. Receives about 5,000 poems/year, accepts less than 1%. Press run is 1,000. Single copy: $10. Sample: $5.

How to Submit Submit up to 5 poems at a time. Considers simultaneous submissions, "but please note in cover letter that the manuscript is being considered elsewhere." No fax or e-mail submissions. Cover letter is required. Include name, postal and e-mail addresses, and titles of work submitted; do not put name and address on ms pages themselves. SASE required. Reads submissions September 15-February 15 only. Poems are selected by a board of up to 6 readers. Seldom comments on rejected poems. Guidelines available for SASE or on Web site. Responds in 3 months. Pays 2 contributor's copies. Acquires first or one-time serial rights.

✪ ◪ FEELINGS OF THE HEART

3317 SE Emerson St., Topeka KS 66605. (785)969-0321. E-mail: apoetesswitch28@aol.com or allypo etesswitch@yahoo.com. Web site: www.freewebs.com/feelingsoftheheartliteraryjournal. Established 1999. **Contact:** Alice M. Harnisch, editor/publisher/founder/poetess.

Magazine Needs *Feelings of the Heart*, published 2 times/year, seeks "poetry from the heart." Considers poetry by children and teens. Has published poetry by Mark Hurley, Jerry S. Reynolds, and Sharon Kroenlein. *Feelings of the Heart* is 50 pages, newsletter format, magazine-sized, computer-printed, stapled, includes ads. Receives about 100 poems/year, accepts about 95%. Press run is 100+. Single copy: $6; subscription: $18/year, $36 for 2 years (2-year subscribers receive free gift with order). Make checks payable to Alice M. Harnisch.

How to Submit Submit 5 poems at a time. Lines/poem: 20-40. Considers previously published poems and simultaneous submissions. Accepts e-mail (pasted into body of message or as attachment in Word) and disk submissions. Cover letter is "important." Include name and address on every poem submitted. "Please enclose SASE or IRC with all postal correspondence. No SASE or IRC, no reply!" Submit seasonal poems 2 months in advance. Time between acceptance and publication is less than 2 weeks with SASE or e-mail. Poems "are read by me, the editor, and decided by the poetic intent of poetry submitted." Often comments on rejected poems. "If asked why rejected, you will receive an answer." Guidelines available for SASE, by e-mail, or on Web site. Sometimes sends prepublication galleys. Acquires first rights. Reviews books/chapbooks of poetry and other magazines/journals in 200 words or less, single-book format. Send materials for review consideration.

Contest/Award Offerings Holds annual contests for cash prizes. Guidelines available on Web site.

Also Offers Prints poetry chapbooks for those interested **in being self-published**. Write for details.

Advice "Write poetry for yourself; publish for everyone else!"

◪ ◎ FEMINIST STUDIES (Specialized: feminism)

0103 Taliaferro Hall, University of Maryland, College Park MD 207427726. (301)405-7415. Fax: (301)405-8395. E-mail: creative@feministstudies.org. Web site: www.feministstudies.org. Established 1969. **Contact:** Minnie Bruce Pratt, creative writing editor.

Magazine Needs *Feminist Studies*, published 3 times/year, welcomes "all forms of written creative expression, which may include but is not limited to poetry and short fiction." Has published poetry by Dawn McDuffie, Liz Robbins, Maria Mazziotti Gillan, Mary Ann Wehler, Barbara Wiedemann, and Paola Corso. *Feminist Studies* is 250 pages, elegantly printed, flat-spined, paperback. Press run is 8,000 (7,000 subscribers, 1,500 libraries). Sample: $17.

How to Submit No previously published poems ("we only consider original work that is not under review elsewhere") or simultaneous submissions. No fax submissions. Send one hard copy of submission as well as an electronic version (disk, CD, or e-mail). "We will not process creative submissions until we receive both a hard copy and electronic version." Retain a copy; work will not be returned. Reads submissions twice/year according to May 1 and December 1 deadlines. Responds by July 15 and February 15 with notice of board's decision. Regularly publishes theme issues. Guidelines available on Web site. Always sends prepublication galleys. Pays 2 contributor's copies.

▣ ▣ ▨ ◎ FICKLE MUSES (Specialized: myth and legend)

E-mail: editor@ficklemuses.com. Web site: www.ficklemuses.com. Established 2006. **Contact:** Sari Krosinsky, editor.

Magazine Needs *Fickle Muses*, published weekly online, is a journal of myth and legend printing poetry, fiction, reviews, essays, and art. Open to all styles and forms. Has published poetry by Jeannine Hall Gailey, Robert Arthur Reeves, Carol L. MacKay, and Margarita Engle. Accepts about 10% of poems received. Number of unique visitors: 125/week.

How to Submit Submit up to 5 poems at a time. Lines/poem: no limits on length. Considers previously published poems and simultaneous submissions. Accepts e-mail submissions (pasted into body of message preferred, unless special formatting requires an attachment); no disk submissions. Cover letter is preferred. Reads submissions year round. Time between acceptance and publication is 3 months. Never comments on rejected poems. Guidelines available by e-mail or on Web site. Responds in up to 3 months. Acquires one-time rights. Rights revert to poets upon publication. Reviews books/chapbooks of poetry and other magazines/journals in 500 words, single-book format. For review consideration, query editor@ficklemuses.com.

$▨ FIELD: CONTEMPORARY POETRY AND POETICS

Oberlin College, 50 N. Professor St., Oberlin OH 44074. (440)775-8408. E-mail: oc.press@oberlin.edu. (inquiries only). Web site: www.oberlin.edu/ocpress. Established 1969. **Contact:** David Young.

• Work published in *FIELD* has been included frequently in *The Best American Poetry*.

Magazine Needs *FIELD: Contemporary Poetry and Poetics*, published semiannually in April and October, is a literary journal with "emphasis on poetry, translations, and essays by poets." Wants the "best possible" poetry. Has published poetry by Marianne Boruch, Miroslav Holub, Charles Wright, Franz Wright, Charles Simic, and Jean Valentine. *FIELD* is 100 pages, digest-sized, printed on rag stock, flat-spined, with glossy color card cover. Subscription: $14/year, $24 for 2 years. Sample: $7 postpaid.

How to Submit Submit up to 5 poems at a time. No previously published poems or simultaneous submissions. No e-mail submissions. Include cover letter and SASE. Reads submissions year round. Seldom comments on rejected poems. Guidelines available for SASE, by e-mail, or on Web site. Responds in 4-6 weeks. Always sends prepublication galleys. Pays $15/page and 2 contributor's copies. Staff reviews books of poetry. Send materials for review consideration.

Additional Information Oberlin College Press publishes books of translations in the FIELD Translation Series. Books are usually flat-spined paperbacks averaging 150 pages. Query regarding translations. Also publishes books of poetry in the FIELD Poetry Series, **by invitation only**. Has published *Lie Awake Lake* by Beckian Fritz Goldberg, *Chez Nous* by Angie Estes, *Stubborn* by Jean Gallagher, and *Red Studio* by Mary Cornish. Write for catalog or visit Web site to buy sample books.

Contest/Award Offerings Sponsors the annual FIELD Poetry Prize for a book-length collection of poems (see separate listing in Contests & Awards).

Advice "A sampling of 3-5 poems is desirable. Be sure to include enough postage on SASE if you want poems returned. We try to read promptly; please wait to submit poems elsewhere."

▣ ▣ $▢ ◎ THE FIFTH DI . . . (Specialized: fantasy; science fiction)

E-mail: fifth@samsdotpublishing.com. Web site: www.samsdotpublishing.com. Established 1994. **Contact:** J. Alan Erwine, editor.

• Honored by Preditors & Editors as Best Fiction Zine.

Magazine Needs *The Fifth Di . . .*, published quarterly online, features fiction and poetry from the science fiction and fantasy genres. Open to most forms, but all poems must be science fiction or fantasy. Does not want horror, or anything that is not science fiction or fantasy. Considers poetry by children and teens. Has published poetry by Bruce Boston, Cathy Buburuz, Marge Simon, Aurelio Rico Lopez III, Terrie Relf, and John Bushore. Receives about 200 poems/year, accepts about 20.

How to Submit Submit one poem at a time. Lines/poem: no limit. No previously published poems or simultaneous submissions. Accepts e-mail submissions only (as attachment); no disk submissions. Cover letter is preferred. Reads submissions year round. Time between acceptance and publication is one month. Sometimes comments on rejected poems. Guidelines available on Web site. Responds in 1-3 months. Pays $5. Acquires first rights.

⬛ FIGHT THESE BASTARDS

Platonic 3Way Press, P.O. Box 844, Warsaw IN 46581. (317)457-3505. E-mail: evilgenius@platonic3 waypress.com. Web site: www.Platonic3WayPress.com. Established 2005. **Contact:** Oren Wagner, Steve Henn, and Don Winter, co-editors.

Magazine Needs *Fight These Bastards*, published biannually, seeks "poetry of revolt, against the Academy, against the poetic mainstream." Wants "poetry accessible beyond the ivory towers of academia and outside the bounds of religious or politically correct restrictions. We enjoy poetry that celebrates honesty and humor. We enjoy poetry with some bite to it. We enjoy poetry that claims to represent the interests, views, or tastes of the common person, particularly as distinct from those of the rich and powerful." Does not want "cute bunny poems; no overtly political poems, no knee-jerk, poorly executed anti-(fill-in-the-blank) poems." Has published poetry by Linda McCarriston, Lyn Lifshin, Fred Voss, Gerald Locklin, Mike Kriesel, and Robert L. Penick. *Fight These Bastards* is about 35-40 pages, magazine-sized, photocopied in high resolution, side-stapled, with artwork on cover, includes ads. Accepts about 2% of poems submitted. Press run is 250. Single copy: $4; subscription: $10 (3 issues). Make checks payable to Platonic 3Way Press.

How to Submit Submit 3-5 poems at a time. Considers previously published poems ("if given the name of the journal where poem was published") and simultaneous submissions ("if so noted"). No e-mail or disk submissions. Cover letter is required. Reads submissions year round. Time between acceptance and publication is up to one year. Poems are circulated to an editorial board. Sometimes comments on rejected poems. Guidelines available in magazine or on Web site. Responds in 2 weeks to 4 months. Sometimes sends prepublication galleys. Pays one contributor's copy. Acquires one-time rights. Rights revert to poet upon publication. Reviews books/chapbooks of poetry and other magazines/journals in 250 words or less, single- and/or multi-book format.

Contest/Award Offerings Sponsors the annual Evil Genius Chapbook Contest (see separate listing in Contests & Awards).

Advice "Make it new; trust your gut. We like poetry that is wedded to the street, not the classroom. We like poetry without foreign phrases, myriad obscure allusions, and cross-references."

⬜ ⬛ FIGHTING CHANCE MAGAZINE (Specialized: horror; science fiction/fantasy)

Suzerain Enterprises, P.O. Box 60336, Worcester MA 01606. Established 1994. **Contact:** Milton Kerr, editor/publisher.

Magazine Needs *Fighting Chance Magazine*, published 3 times/year, gives "unpublished writers a chance to be published and to be paid for their efforts." Wants dark fiction, horror, and science fiction. Does not want "porn, ageism, sexism, racism, children in sexual situations." Has published poetry by A.H. Ferguson, Wayne Adams, Gary McGhee, Robert Donald Spector, Cecil Boyce, and Ellaraine Lockie. *Fighting Chance Magazine* is 15-30 pages, magazine-sized, photocopied, side-stapled, with computer-designed paper cover. Receives about 500 poems/year, accepts about 10%. Press run is 100 (70-80 subscribers). Subscription: $12/year. Sample: $4. Make checks payable to Suzerain Enterprises.

How to Submit Submit 3 poems at a time. Lines/poem: 20 maximum. Considers previously published poems and simultaneous submissions. Cover letter is preferred. "Proofread for spelling errors, neatness; must be typewritten in standard manuscript form. No handwritten manuscripts." Time between acceptance and publication is 3 months. Often comments on rejected poems. Guidelines available for SASE. Responds in 6 weeks. Acquires first or one-time rights.

Advice "Proofread your work. Edit carefully. Always include business-sized SASE with correct postage. Don't let rejection slips get you down. Keep submitting and don't give up. Don't be afraid to write something different."

◪ FIRST CLASS

Four-Sep Publications, P.O. Box 86, Friendship IN 47021. E-mail: christopherm@four-sep.com. Web site: www.four-sep.com. Established 1994. **Contact:** Christopher M., editor.

Magazine Needs *First Class*, published in February and August, prints "excellent/odd writing for intelligent/creative readers." Wants "short postmodern poems." Does not want "traditional work." Has published poetry by Bennett, Locklin, Roden, Splake, Catlin, and Huffstickler. *First Class* is 48-56 pages, $4\frac{1}{4} \times 11$, printed, saddle-stapled, with colored cover. Receives about 1,500 poems/year, accepts about 30. Press run is 300-400. Sample: $6 (includes guidelines), or mini version $1. Make checks payable to Christopher M.

How to Submit Submit 5 poems at a time. Considers previously published poems and simultaneous submissions. No fax or e-mail submissions. Cover letter is preferred. "Manuscripts will not be returned." Time between acceptance and publication is 2-4 months. Often comments on rejected poems. Guidelines available in magazine, for SASE, or on Web site. Responds in 3 weeks. Pays one contributor's copy. Acquires one-time rights. Reviews books of poetry and fiction. Send materials for review consideration.

Additional Information Chapbook production available.

Advice "Belt out a good, short, thought-provoking, graphic, uncommon piece."

◪ 5 AM

P.O. Box 205, Spring Church PA 15686. Web site: www.5ampoetry.com. Established 1987. **Contact:** Ed Ochester and Judith Vollmer, editors.

Magazine Needs *5 AM*, published twice/year, is a poetry publication open in regard to form, length, subject matter, and style. Does not want religious poetry or "naive rhymers." Has published poetry by Virgil Suárez, Nin Andrews, Alicia Ostriker, Edward Field, Billy Collins, and Denise Duhamel. *5 AM* is 24-pages, tabloid size, offset-printed. Receives about 5,000 poems/year, accepts about 2%. Press run is 1,200 (650 subscribers, 25 libraries, about 300 shelf sales). Subscription: $15 for 4 issues. Sample: $5.

How to Submit No previously published poems or simultaneous submissions. Seldom comments on rejected poems. Responds within 6 weeks. Pays 2 contributor's copies. Acquires first rights.

Advice "Read the magazine before submitting."

⊠ ◪ FIVE FINGERS REVIEW

P.O. Box 4, San Leandro CA 94577. Phone/fax: (510)632-5769. E-mail: jrobles@aaahawk.com. Web site: www.fivefingersreview.org. Established 1987. **Contact:** Jaime Robles, editor.

Magazine Needs *Five Fingers Review*, published annually in September, is "interested in quality work from a wide spectrum of ideas and styles; committed to publishing innovative work by emerging and established writers." Wants "all styles and forms; must be excellent and original work in the chosen form." Considers poetry by children and teens. Has published poetry by Gillian Conoley, Jackson Mac Low, Carl Phillips, Brenda Hillman, Elizabeth Robinson, and Peter Gizzi. *Five Fingers Review* is digest-sized, offset-printed, perfect-bound, with 4-color cover (usually work by contributing artist), includes ads. Press run is 1,000. Single copy: $13; subscription: $23 for 2 issues. Make checks payable to *Five Fingers Review*.

How to Submit Submit 3-5 poems at a time. Considers simultaneous submissions; no previously published poems. No e-mail or disk submissions. Cover letter is preferred. "Don't forget the SASE." Accepts submissions June 1-August 31. "Most poems are solicited by contributing editors. At least two people read unsolicited submissions." Seldom comments on rejected poems. Regularly publishes theme issues. Guidelines available for SASE or on Web site. Responds in up to 6 months. Always sends prepublication galleys. Pays 2 contributor's copies plus discount on additional copies. Acquires one-time rights. Reviews books/chapbooks of poetry and other magazines/journals. Send materials for review consideration to J. Robles.

Contest/Award Offerings Offers contest in poetry and fiction. **Deadline:** June 1. Guidelines available on Web site.

Also Offers Runs local reading series in San Francisco Bay area. Posts some work on Web site and publishes additional chapbook series under the imprint of Woodland Editions.

✪ ☑ FLINT HILLS REVIEW

Dept. of English, Box 4019, Emporia State University, 1200 Commercial St., Emporia KS 66801. Fax: (620)341-5547. E-mail: krabas@emporia.edu. Web site: www.emporia.edu/fhr/index.htm. Established 1995. **Contact:** The Editors.

Magazine Needs *Flint Hills Review*, published annually in late summer, is "a regionally focused journal presenting writers of national distinction alongside new authors." Wants all forms of poetry except rhyming. Does not want sentimental or gratuitous verse. Has published poetry by E. Ethelbert Miller, Elizabeth Dodd, Walt McDonald, and Gwendolyn Brooks. *Flint Hills Review* is about 100 pages, digest-sized, offset-printed, perfect-bound, with glossy card cover with b&w photo. Receives about 2,000 poems/year, accepts about 5%. Single copy: $7.

How to Submit Submit 3-5 poems at a time. Considers simultaneous submissions; no previously published poems. Accepts submissions by fax or e-mail (pasted into body of message). Cover letter is required. Include SASE. Reads submissions January-March only. Time between acceptance and publication is about one year. Seldom comments on rejected poems. Occasionally publishes theme issues. Guidelines available for SASE or on Web site. Pays one contributor's copy. Acquires first rights.

Advice "Send writing with evidence of a strong sense of place."

☑ FLYWAY, A LITERARY REVIEW

206 Ross Hall, Iowa State University, Ames IA 50011-1201. Fax: (515)294-6814. E-mail: flyway@iastate.edu. Web site: www.flyway.org. Established 1961. **Contact:** Stephen Pett, editor-in-chief.

Magazine Needs *Flyway, A Literary Review*, published 3 times/year, "is one of the best literary magazines for the money. It's packed with some of the most readable poems being published today—all styles, forms, lengths, and subjects." Does not want "elite-sounding free verse with obscure meanings, and pretty-sounding formal verse with obvious meanings." *Flyway* is 112 pages, digest-sized, professionally printed, perfect-bound, with matte card cover with color. Press run is 600 (400 subscribers, 100 libraries). Subscription: $18. Sample: $7.

How to Submit Submit 4-6 poems at a time. Cover letter is preferred. "We do not read manuscripts between the first of May and the end of August." Publishes theme issues (Native American, Latino, Arab American). Responds in 6 weeks (often sooner). Pays 2 contributor's copies. Acquires first rights.

Contest/Award Offerings Sponsors an annual award for poetry, fiction, and nonfiction. Details available for SASE or on Web site.

▣ ☻ FORPOETRY.COM

E-mail: submissions@forpoetry.com. Web site: www.forpoetry.com. Established 1999. **Contact:** Jackie Marcus, editor.

Magazine Needs *ForPoetry.Com*, published online with daily updates, seeks "to promote new and emerging poets, with or without MFAs. We will be publishing established poets, but our primary interest is in publishing excellent poetry, prose, and reviews." Wants "lyric poetry, vivid imagery, open form, natural landscape, philosophical themes—but not at the expense of honesty and passion." Does not want "city punk, corny sentimental fluff, or academic workshop imitations." Has published poetry by Sherod Santos, John Koethe, Jane Hirshfield, Erin Believ, and Kathy Fagan.

How to Submit Submit no more than 2 poems at a time. Considers simultaneous submissions; no previously published poems. Accepts e-mail submissions only (pasted into body of message; no attachments). Cover letter is preferred. Reads submissions September-May only. Time between acceptance and publication is 2-3 weeks. "We'll read all submissions and then decide together on the poems we'll publish." Comments on rejected poems "as often as possible. We receive lots of submissions and are very selective about acceptances, but we will always try to send a note back on rejections." Guidelines available on Web site. Responds in 2 weeks. Reviews books/chapbooks of poetry and other magazines in 800 words.

Advice "As my friend Kevin Hull said, 'Get used to solitude and rejection.' Sit on your poems for several months or more. Time is your best critic."

4AM POETRY REVIEW

(See Web site for mailing address.) E-mail: fourampoetryreview@gmail.com. Web site: www.foura mpoetryreview.i8.com. Established 2004. **Contact:** Maria Thibodeau, editor.

Magazine Needs *4AM Poetry Review*, published annually in August, "exists as an antidote to the usual, publishing poetry of meticulous craft written by word-addicts." Wants "imagery and a skillful interplay of sound and meaning. Narrative and free verse." Does not want "obtrusive rhyming, first drafts, prose with line breaks." *4AM* is up to 40 pages, digest-sized, laser-printed, thermal-bound, with cardstock cover with photo. Accepts about 40-60 poems/year. Press run is 200. Single copy: $5; subscription: $5. Make checks payable to Maria Thibodeau.

How to Submit Submit 3-5 poems at a time. Considers simultaneous submissions (with notice); no previously published poems. Accepts e-mail submissions (pasted into body of message); no disk submissions. "For e-mail submissions: one poem per e-mail; include notes regarding any special formatting. We accept e-mail submissions as sympathizers to the postage burden but expect poets to exhibit the same care as with postal submissions. For postal submissions: include name and e-mail on each page. (See Web site for mailing address.)" Reads submissions at specific times; "please check Web site for submission date openings before sending poems." Time between acceptance and publication is up to one year. Sometimes comments on rejected poems. Guidelines available in magazine, for SASE, by e-mail, or on Web site. Responds within 6 months after each deadline. Pays 2 contributor's copies. Acquires first rights.

Also Offers Chapbooks **by invitation only**.

Advice "Read more than you write."

FOURTEEN HILLS: THE SFSU REVIEW

Creative Writing Dept., San Francisco State University, 1600 Holloway Ave., San Francisco CA 94132. (415)338-3083. Fax: (415)338-7030. E-mail: hills@sfsu.edu. Web site: www.14hills.net. Established 1994. **Contact:** Poetry Editor.

Magazine Needs *Fourteen Hills: The SFSU Review*, published semiannually, is a journal of contemporary literary art. Wants "high-quality, innovative work." Has published poetry by Lawrence Ferlinghetti, Kim Addonizio, Marilyn Hacker, Robert Creeley, Naomi Shihab Nye, and Fanny Howe. *Fourteen Hills* is 170 pages, digest-sized, professionally printed, perfect-bound, with glossy card cover. Receives about 900 poems/year, accepts about 5-10%. Press run is 600 (125 subscribers, 25 libraries). Single copy: $9; subscription: $17/year, $32 for 2 years. Sample: $5 or $7 for back issue, depending on publication date.

How to Submit Submit up to 5 poems at a time. Considers simultaneous submissions if indicated; no previously published poems. No e-mail or fax submissions; postal submissions only. Cover letter is preferred. Reads submissions year round, although issue deadlines are September 1 (Winter/Spring) and February 1 (Summer/Fall). "The editorial staff is composed entirely of graduate students from the Creative Writing Program at SFSU." Seldom comments on rejected poems. Guidelines available in magazine or on Web site. Responds in 6 months. Always sends prepublication galleys. Pays 2 contributor's copies.

Advice "Please read an issue of *Fourteen Hills* before submitting."

◖ THE FOURTH RIVER

Chatham College, Woodland Rd., Pittsburgh PA 15232. E-mail: 4thriver@gmail.com. Web site: http://fourthriver.chatham.edu. Established 2005. **Contact:** Toni Jensen, editor.

Magazine Needs *The Fourth River*, published annually, features "literature that engages and explores the relationship between humans and their environments." Wants "writing that's thoughtful and daring, and richly situated at the confluence of place, space, and identity." *The Fourth River* is digest-sized, perfect-bound, with full-color cover by various artists. Accepts about 20-30 poems/year. Press run is 500. Single copy: $10; subscription: $18 for 2 years. Make checks payable to *The Fourth River*.

How to Submit Submit 3 poems at a time. Lines/poem: submit 10 pages maximum. No previously published poems. No e-mail or disk submissions. Cover letter is preferred. "SASE is required for response." Reads submissions August 1-February 15. Time between acceptance and publication is 5-8 months. Poems are circulated to an editorial board. Sometimes comments on rejected poems. Sometimes publishes theme issues. Guidelines available on Web site. Responds in 3-5 months. Acquires first North American serial rights.

◖ FREE LUNCH

P.O. Box 717, Glenview IL 60025-0717. Web site: www.poetsfreelunch.org. Established 1988. **Contact:** Ron Offen, editor.

Magazine Needs *Free Lunch*, published 2 times/year, is "interested in publishing the whole spectrum of what is currently being produced by American poets. Features a 'Mentor Series,' in which an established poet introduces a new, unestablished poet. Mentor poets are selected by the editor and have included Maxine Kumin, Denise Duhamel, Billy Collins, Lucille Clifton, Donald Hall, Carolyn Forché, Wanda Coleman, Lyn Lifshin, Stephen Dunn, and Edward Hirsch. *Free Lunch* is especially interested in experimental work and work by unestablished poets." Wants "metaphors, similes, arresting images, and a sensitive and original use of language. We are interested in all genres—experimental poetry, protest poetry, formal poetry, etc. No restriction on form (except no haikus, please), length, style, purpose. No aversion to form, rhyme." Has published poetry by Jared Carter, Donald Hall, James Reiss, Stephen Dunn, Lisel Mueller, and Cathy Song. *Free Lunch* is 32-40 pages, digest-sized, attractively printed and designed, saddle-stapled. Press run is 1,200 (1,000 free subscriptions, 200 paid subscriptions, 15 libraries). Subscription: $12 ($15 foreign). Sample: $5 ($6 foreign). "*Free Lunch* seeks to provide all serious poets living in the U.S. with a free subscription. For details on free subscription, send SASE."

How to Submit Submit no more than 3 poems at a time. Considers simultaneous submissions; no previously published poems. Cover letter is preferred. "Although a cover letter is not mandatory, I like them. I especially want to know if a poet is previously unpublished, as I like to work with new poets." Reads submissions September 1-May 31. "Submissions sent at other times will be returned unread." Always comments on rejected poems. Responds in 3 months. Guidelines available for SASE or on Web site. Pays one contributor's copy plus subscription.

Contest/Award Offerings The Rosine Offen Memorial Award, a prize of $200, is awarded to one poem in each issue of *Free Lunch*. Winners are selected solely by the Board of Directors of Free Lunch Arts Alliance, and are announced in the following issue.

Advice "Archibald MacLeish said, 'A poem should not mean/But be.' I have become increasingly leery of the ego-centered lyric that revels in some past wrong, good-old-boy nostalgia, or unfocused ecstatic experience. Not receptive to art- or literature-referenced poems or poems about writing poems, other poems, poetry reading, etc. Poetry is concerned primarily with language, rhythm, and sound; fashions and trends are transitory and to be eschewed. Perfecting one's work is often more important than publishing it.''

⦿ FREEFALL

Undead Poets Press, 15735 Kerstyn St., Taylor MI 48180. (734)941-8123. E-mail: mauruspoet@yaho o.com; **for Canada**, carson@rideau.net. Established 1999. **Contact:** Marc Maurus, editor/publisher; **for Canada**, T. Anders Carson, editor/publisher, R.R. #2, Portland ON K0G 1V0 Canada.

Magazine Needs *freefall*, published 3 times/year in April, July, and October, prints the quality work of beginners as well as established poets. ''Free verse or formal poetry is okay, and our acceptance policy is broad.'' Does not want ''concrete, shape, or greeting card verse; no gratuitous language or sex; no fuzzy animals or syrupy nature poems.'' Has published poetry by B.Z. Niditch, Lyn Lifshin, David Lawrence, Michael Estabrook, and Joe Speer. *freefall* is 40 pages, digest-sized, laser-printed, saddle-stapled, with cardstock cover with photographs. Receives about 200 poems/year, accepts about 50%. Press run is 250 (50 subscribers, 10 libraries, 25 shelf sales); 25 distributed free to small press reviewers. Single copy: $7.50; subscription: $15. Make checks payable to Marc Maurus.

How to Submit Submit 5-10 poems at a time. Lines/poem: 3 minimum, 80 maximum. Considers previously published poems with notification; no simultaneous submissions. Accepts e-mail submissions (pasted into body of message, no attachments); no fax or disk submissions. ''Snail mail preferred; please send SASE.'' Cover letter is preferred. Reads submissions all year. Submit seasonal poems 6 months in advance. Time between acceptance and publication is 6 months. ''If a poem is high quality, I accept it right away; poor work is rejected immediately; those on the fence are circulated to as many as three other guest editors.'' Often comments on rejected poems. Poems may be sent **for critique only for $2 each** plus SASE. Guidelines available for SASE. Responds in 2 weeks. Pays one contributor's copy. Acquires first rights. Rights revert to author on publication. Reviews chapbooks of poetry and other magazines/journals in 500 words, single-book format. Send materials for review consideration to Marc Maurus.

Advice ''We prefer to see crafted work, not unedited one-offs. We welcome as much formal verse as we can because we feel there is a place for it.''

⊞ ⦿ FREEFALL MAGAZINE

Alexandra Writers' Centre Society, 922 Ninth Ave. SE, Calgary AB T2G 0S4 Canada. (403)264-4730. E-mail: awcs@telusplanet.net. Web site: www.alexandrawriters.org. Established 1990. **Contact:** Micheline Maylor, editor. Managing Editor: Lynn Fraser. Member: AMPA.

Magazine Needs *FreeFall Magazine*, published in April and October, contains fiction, nonfiction, poetry, and interviews related to writers/writing, and artwork and photographs suitable for b&w reproduction. ''*FreeFall*'s mandate is to encourage the voices of new, emerging, and experienced writers and provide an outlet for their work.'' Wants ''poems in a variety of forms with a strong voice, effective language, and fresh images.'' Has published poetry by Christopher Wiseman, Sharon Drummond, Edna Alford, Joan Clarke, and Barry Butson. *FreeFall* is 100-120 pages, digest-sized, perfect-bound, glossy, with 60 lb. paper cover. Receives about 100 poems/year, accepts about 15%. Press run is 350 (270 subscribers, 20 libraries, 80 shelf sales); 30 distributed free to contributors, promotion. Single copy: $12.50 USD, $10 CAD; subscription: $25 USD, $20 CAD. Sample: $10 USD, $10 CAD.

How to Submit Submit up to 5 poems at a time. No previously published poems or simultaneous submissions. Accepts postal and disk submissions (ASCII, text format, must include hard copy); no e-mail submissions. Cover letter is required. Include 2-line bio and SASE. Reads submissions in January and July only. Time between acceptance and publication is 3 months. ''All submissions are read by eight editors.'' Seldom comments on rejected poems. Occasionally publishes theme issues. Guidelines available in magazine, for SAE and IRC, by e-mail, or on Web site. Responds in 3 months. Pays one contributor's copy. Acquires first North American serial rights.

Additional Information See Web site for information about the Alexandra Writers' Centre Society activities and services, and for additional information about *FreeFall Magazine*.

Contest/Award Offerings Hosts an annual fiction and poetry contest. **Deadline:** December 31. Guidelines available by e-mail or on Web site.

⊞ ☑ THE FROGMORE PAPERS

18 Nevill Rd., Lewes, East Sussex BN7 1PF England. Web site: www.frogmorepress.co.uk. Established 1983. **Contact:** Jeremy Page, poetry editor.

Magazine Needs *The Frogmore Papers*, published biannually, is a literary magazine with emphasis on new poetry and short stories. "Quality is generally the only criterion, although pressure of space means very long work (over 100 lines) is unlikely to be published." Has published poetry by Marita Over, Brian Aldiss, Carole Satyamurti, John Mole, Linda France, and Tobias Hill. *The Frogmore Papers* is 46 pages, photocopied in photo-reduced typescript, saddle-stapled, with matte card cover. Accepts 3% of poetry received. Press run is 300 (120 subscribers). Subscription: £7 ($20). Sample: £2 ($5). U.S. payments should be made in cash, not check.

How to Submit Submit 5-6 poems at a time. Lines/poem: rarely accepts poems over 100 lines. Considers simultaneous submissions. Rarely comments on rejected poems. Responds in 6 months. Pays one contributor's copy. Staff reviews books of poetry in 2-3 sentences, single-book format. Send materials for review consideration to Catherine Smith, 24 South Way, Lewes, East Sussex BN7 1LU England.

Contest/Award Offerings Sponsors the annual Frogmore Poetry Prize. Write for information.

Advice "My advice to people starting to write poetry is: Read as many recognized modern poets as you can, and don't be afraid to experiment."

$ ◎ FROGPOND: JOURNAL OF THE HAIKU SOCIETY OF AMERICA (Specialized: haiku and related forms; translations)

Haiku Society of America, P.O. Box 122, Nassau NY 12123. E-mail: ithacan@earthlink.net. Web site: www.hsa-haiku.org. Established 1978. **Contact:** John Stevenson, editor.

Magazine Needs *Frogpond*, published triannually (February, June, October), is the international journal of the Haiku Society of America. Wants "contemporary English-language haiku, ranging from 1-4 lines or in a visual arrangement, focusing on a moment keenly perceived and crisply conveyed, using clear images and non-poetic language." Also considers "related forms: senryu, sequences, linked poems, and haibun. We welcome translations of any of these forms." Considers poetry by children and teens. Has published poetry by Cor van den Heuvel, Michael McClintock, Peggy Willis Lyles, and Fay Aoyagi. *Frogpond* is 96 pages, digest-sized, perfect-bound. Receives about 20,000 submissions/year, accepts about 500. *Frogpond* goes to 800 subscribers (of which 15 are libraries) as well as to over a dozen foreign countries. Sample: $7 U.S. (back issue), $9 ROW. Make checks payable to Haiku Society of America.

How to Submit Submit 5-10 poems, with 5 poems per 8½ × 11 sheet. No simultaneous submissions. Accepts e-mail and disk submissions. Include SASE with postal submissions. Guidelines available for SASE or on Web site. Responds "usually" in 3 weeks or less. Pays $1/accepted item. Reviews books of poetry, usually in 1,000 words or less.

Contest/Award Offerings A "best of issue" prize is awarded to a poem from each issue of *Frogpond* through a gift from the Museum of Haiku Literature, located in Tokyo. The Haiku Society of America also sponsors The Harold G. Henderson Haiku Award Contest, the Gerald Brady Senryu Award Contest, the Bernard Lionel Einbond Memorial Renku Contest, the Nicholas A. Virgilio Memorial Haiku Competition for High School Students, the Mildred Kanterman Merit Book Awards for outstanding books in the haiku field. Guidelines available on Web site.

Advice "Submissions to *Frogpond* are accepted from both members and nonmembers, although familiarity with the journal will aid writers in discovering what it publishes."

$ ☑ FUGUE

200 Brink Hall, University of Idaho, P.O. Box 441102, Moscow ID 83844. E-mail: fugue@uidaho.edu. Web site: www.uidaho.edu/fugue. Established 1990. **Contact:** Rachel Berry, poetry editor.

Magazine Needs *Fugue*, published biannually in summer and winter, is a literary magazine of the University of Idaho. "There are no limits on type of poetry; however, we are not interested in trite or quaint verse." Has published poetry by Sonia Sanchez, Simon Perchik, Denise Duhamel, Dean Young, and W.S. Merwin. *Fugue* is up to 200 pages, perfect-bound. Receives about 400 poems/semester, accepts only 15-20 poems/issue. Press run is 250. There is also an online version. Sample: $8.

How to Submit Submit 3-5 poems at a time (10 pages maximum). No previously published poems. Considers simultaneous submissions "with the explicit provision that the writer inform us immediately if the work is accepted for publication elsewhere." No e-mail submissions. Cover letter is required. "Include name, address, e-mail, phone number, poem titles, and a brief bio citing any awards/publications. Submissions without a #10 SASE will not be considered." Reads submissions September 1-May 1 only. Time between acceptance and publication is up to one year. "Submissions are reviewed by staff members and chosen with consensus by the editorial board. No major changes are made to a manuscript without authorial approval." Publishes theme issues. Guidelines available for SASE or on Web site. Responds in up to 5 months. Pays at least one contributor's copy plus an honorarium (up to $25 as funds allow). Acquires first North American serial rights.

Contest/Award Offerings "For information regarding our spring poetry contest, please visit our Web site."

Advice "We are looking for poetry that takes risks while demonstrating powerful voice and careful attention to language and craft. Proper manuscript format and submission etiquette are expected; submissions without proper SASE will not be read or held on file."

⊠ ☑ FULCRUM: AN ANNUAL OF POETRY AND AESTHETICS

421 Huron Ave., Cambridge MA 02138. (617)864-7874. E-mail: editor@fulcrumpoetry.com. Web site: www.fulcrumpoetry.com. Established 2002. **Contact:** Philip Nikolayev, Katia Kapovich, editors. Member: CLMP.

Magazine Needs *Fulcrum: an annual of poetry and aesthetics* is "a one-of-a-kind international serial anthology of poetry and criticism, with a philosophical bent." Wants "poetry that exhibits a strong aesthetic compulsion and comes from a deep place. All forms and styles; no 'schools.' " Does not want "gibberish, 'metapoetry' (pensive poems about poems) or 'based-on' poetry." Has published poetry by Ben Mazer, Stephen Sturgeon, Jeet Thayil, Joe Green, and Vivek Narayanan. *Fulcrum* is 500 pages, digest-sized, professionally printed, flat-spined, with glossy cover with b&w art. Accepts about .5% of poems submitted. Press run is 2,000. Single copy: (postpaid domestic) $17 for individuals, $42 for libraries. Make checks payable to *Fulcrum* or subscribe through Web site.

How to Submit No e-mail or disk submissions. Cover letter is preferred. Include SASE (SAE with IRCs for international submissions). Reads submissions June-August only. Time between acceptance and publication is 6-8 months. "All poems and essays are accepted or rejected by the editors. Read *Fulcrum* before submitting!" Seldom comments on rejected poems. Guidelines available on Web site. Responds in 1-6 months. Always sends prepublication galleys. Pays one contributor's copy. Acquires first world rights.

Advice "There are no 'schools'—life is a vacation!"

▣ ☑ FULLOSIA PRESS

The Rockaway Park Philosophical Society, P.O. Box 280, Ronkonkoma NY 11779. E-mail: deanofRPPS @aol.com. Web site: http:/rpps_fullosia_press.tripod.com. Established 1971. **Contact:** jd collins.

Magazine Needs *Fullosia Press*, published monthly online, presents news, information, satire, and right/conservative perspective. Wants any style of poetry. "If you have something to say, say it. We consider many different points of view." Does not want "anti-American, anti-Christian." Considers poetry by children with parental consent. Has published poetry by Awesome David Lawrence, Peter Vetrano, Michael Levy, Dr. Kelley White, and Taylor Graham. Receives about 50 poems/year, accepts about 40%. Single copy: $15 and SASE (free online); subscription: $25/year (free online). Make checks payable to RPPS-Fullosia Press.

How to Submit Accepts e-mail (pasted into body of message) and disk submissions. "E-mail preferred. Final submission by disk or e-mail only." Cover letter is required. Reads submissions when received. Submit seasonal poems one month in advance. Time between acceptance and publication varies. "I review all poems: 1) Do they say something?; 2) Is there some thought behind it?; 3) Is it more than words strung together?" Always comments on rejected poems. Publishes theme issues. Guidelines available for SASE, by e-mail, or on Web site. Responds in one month. Acquires one-time rights. Reviews books/chapbooks of poetry and other magazines/journals. Send materials for review consideration to RPPS-Fullosia Press.

Advice "Say what you have in mind without tripping over your own symbolism. We like poems that are clear, concise, to the point; American traditional heroes; Arthurian legend; American states. Everybody sings about Texas; has anyone written a poem to New Jersey?"

$□ ◎ THE FUNNY PAPER (Specialized: light verse, humor)

F/J Writers Service, 615 NW Jacob Dr. #206, Lee's Summit MO 64081. E-mail: felixkcmo@aol.com. Web site: www.funnypaper.info. Established 1985. **Contact:** Felix Fellhauer, editor.

Magazine Needs *The Funny Paper*, published 4 times/year, provides "readership, help, and the opportunity to write for money to budding authors/poets/humorists of all ages." Wants "light verse; humor always welcome." Does not want "heavy, dismal, trite work. No pornography." Considers poetry by children and teens. *The Funny Paper* is 10 pages, magazine-sized, photocopied on colored paper, unbound. Receives about 300 poems/year, accepts about 10%. Single copy: $3; subscription: $10/year. Make checks payable to F/J Writers Service.

How to Submit Submit no more than 3 poems at a time. Lines/poem: 16 maximum. Accepts e-mail submissions (pasted into body of message). "We encourage beginners; handwritten poems OK. Include SASE for acknowledgment only; submissions will not be returned." Seldom comments on rejected poems. Guidelines available in magazine, for SASE, by e-mail, or on Web site. Pays $5-25.

Contest/Award Offerings Each issue offers a different contest, awarding $100. See Web site for details.

Advice "Get guidelines first."

▣ ○ THE FURNACE REVIEW

E-mail: submissions@thefurnacereview.com. Web site: www.thefurnacereview.com. Established 2004. **Contact:** Ciara LaVelle, editor.

Magazine Needs *The Furnace Review*, published quarterly online, is "dedicated to new writers and unique or groundbreaking work." Wants "all forms, from haiku to sonnets to free verse to totally experimental. Just make it interesting." Has published poetry by Sarah Lynn Knowles, David Gruber, Curtis Evans, and Richard Matthes. Receives about 500 pieces/year, accepts about 30.

How to Submit Submit up to 5 poems at a time. Lines/poem: 75 maximum. Considers simultaneous submissions; no previously published poems. Accepts e-mail submissions; no disk submissions. Cover letter is preferred. "Include a short biography with all submissions." Reads submissions year round. Time between acceptance and publication is 3 months. Poems are circulated to an editorial board. Sometimes comments on rejected poems. Guidelines available on Web site. Responds in 4 months. Acquires first North American serial rights.

▣ $○ GAMBARA MAGAZINE

P.O. Box 3887, Santa Cruz CA 95063. E-mail: editor@gambara.org. Web site: www.gambara.org. Established 2006. **Contact:** Scott Johnson, general editor.

Magazine Needs *Gambara Magazine*, published 6 times/year online (with an annual print edition in March), offers "general literary content. Many, but not all, pieces are published first on our Web site. Some pieces are reserved for the print edition." Wants "well-written poetry in any style." Considers poetry written by children and teens. Has published poetry by Joshua Pastor, Debra Brenegan, Charles Schubert, David Trame, Debra Wierenga, and Jennifer Armentrout. *Gambara* (print edition) is 192 pages, digest-sized, perfect-bound. Accepts about 1% of poems submitted. Press run is about 1,200 (shelf sales unknown); about 150 distributed free to contributors and reviewers. Single copy: $12 (in store); subscription: $12 for one issue, $20 for 2 issues. "See Web site for samples or to pre-order the print edition." Make checks payable to *Gambara*.

How to Submit Submit 3-5 poems at a time. Lines/poem: "keep it to a page." Considers previously published poems and simultaneous submissions. Accepts e-mail submissions (pasted into body of message or as attachment); no disk submissions. Cover letter is preferred, but not necessary. "If submitting by mail, you must provide a SASE for reply. Let me know if you also want the manuscript returned." Reads submissions year round. Submit seasonal poems 2 months in advance. Time between acceptance and publication is 2-3 months ("in most cases"). Poems are circulated to an editorial board. "If I like a poem, I pass it around to the others who work on this magazine, and to certain former and current contributors whose judgment I respect. Their input has some influence." Sometimes comments on rejected poems. Sometimes publishes theme issues. Guidelines available on Web site. Responds in 10 weeks or less. Sends prepublication galleys by e-mail. Pays $50/poem maximum and 2 contributor's copies. Acquires one-time rights plus non-exclusive right to publish poem(s) on Web site. Rights revert to poet upon publication.

◖ GARGOYLE MAGAZINE

Paycock Press, 3819 N. 13th St., Arlington VA 22201. (202)234-3287. E-mail: gargoyle@gargoyl emagazine.com. Web site: www.gargoylemagazi ne.com. Established 1976. **Contact:** Richard Peabody and Lucinda Ebersole, co-editors.

Magazine Needs *Gargoyle Magazine*, published annually, aims to produce "the best literary magazine we can. We generally run short, one-page poems. We like wit, imagery, killer lines." Has published poetry by Kate Braverman, Laura Chester, Thylias Moss, Eileen Myles, Toby Olson, Elizabeth Swados, and Paul West. *Gargoyle* is about 500 pages, digest-sized, offset-printed, perfect-bound, with color cover, includes ads. Accepts about 10% of the poems received each year. Press run is 2,000. Subscription: $20/2 issues (individuals); $25 (institutions). Sample: $10. Make checks payable to Richard Peabody.

How to Submit Submit 5 poems at a time. Considers simultaneous submissions. Accepts e-mail submissions (preferred; pasted into body of message). Reads submissions "all summer—June, July, and August." Time between acceptance and publication is 6-12 months. "The two editors make some concessions but generally concur." Often comments on rejected poems. Responds in

The out-of-this-world cover of *Gargoyle* #51 is a play "on the whole Roswell thing with 'Area 51.' Hence the spaceship beaming up all those interesting things," explains artist Patricia Storms. Editor Richard Peabody adds, "We gave Patricia free rein and she hit it out of the ballpark."

Cover art by Patricia Storms.

2 months. Always sends prepublication galleys. Pays one contributor's copy and offers 50% discount on additional copies. Acquires first rights.

Additional Information Paycock Press has published 14 books since 1976 and is **not currently seeking mss.**

☑ GECKO

P.O. Box 6492, Destin FL 32550. E-mail: geckogalpoet@hotmail.com. Established 1998. **Contact:** Rebecca Lu Kiernan, editor.

- **"Due to the overwhelming response of *Poet's Market* readers and personal projects of the editor, we are currenly closed to unsolicited manuscripts. We hope to change this in the future when an assistant will assume some of the editor's duties."**

☑ ◎ GENIE (Specialized: humorous poetry)

1753 Fisher Ridge, Horse Cave KY 42749. Established 2005. **Contact:** David Rogers, editor.

Magazine Needs *Genie*, published annually in August, features humorous poetry, "although good poems that are not funny are considered as well." Wants "poems that are humorous, satirical, or erotic. Short (200-300 words) political/social commentary. The editor has a bias toward liberal causes but will seriously consider any well-written satirical piece as long as it is genuinely funny. Feel free to blur the distinction between poetry and prose." Does not want "pornography (but erotica is good—know the difference) or anything that encourages violence or hate." Considers poetry by children and teens. "Don't care much about the age of the writer, as long as it's good." Has published poetry by Merlin Freehand, George Held, Alan Catlin, and Dave Church. *Genie* is 15 or more pages ("depending on the number of good submissions that come in"), $4^{1}/_{4} \times 5^{1}/_{2}$, laser-printed, saddle-stapled or perfect-bound, with cardstock cover with color printing. Receives about 150 poems/year, accepts about 10%. Press run is 100 (10 subscribers, 10 shelf sales); 50 distributed free to contributors/" anyone who's interested." Single copy: $2; subscription: $6. Make checks payable to David Rogers.

How to Submit Submit up to 5 poems at a time. Lines/poem: 100. Considers previously published poems and simultaneous submissions ("but PLEASE do not withdraw submitted poems"). No disk submissions. Cover letter is required. Reads submissions year round. Time between acceptance and publication is up to one year. Never comments on rejected poems. Guidelines available in magazine. Responds in up to 6 months. Pays one or more contributor's copies. Acquires one-time rights. Reviews books/chapbooks of poetry in 100 words. Send materials for review consideration to David Rogers.

Advice "Be funny. Watch Comedy Central and read Hal Sirowitz and Billy Collins (see his 'Another Reason Why I Don't Keep a Gun in the House')—not to imitate, but for inspiration. A good humorous poem often resembles a bit from a stand-up comedy act in surprising ways."

☑ GEORGETOWN REVIEW

Box 227, 400 E. College St., Georgetown KY 40324. (502)863-8308. Fax: (502)868-8888. E-mail: gtownreview@georgetowncollege.edu. Web site: http://georgetownreview.georgetowncollege.edu. Established 1993. **Contact:** Steven Carter, editor. Member: CLMP.

Magazine Needs *Georgetown Review*, published annually in May, is a literary journal of poetry, fiction, and creative nonfiction. "We have no specific guidelines concerning form or content of poetry, but are always eager to see poetry that is insightful, rooted in reality, and human." Does not want "work that is merely sentimental, political, or inspirational." Considers poetry by children and teens. Has published poetry by Denise Duhamel, X.J. Kennedy, William Greenway, Fred Chappell, John Tagliabue, and Frederick Smock. *Georgetown Review* is 192 pages, digest-sized, offset-printed, perfect-bound, with 60 lb. glossy 4-color cover with art/graphics, includes ads. Receives about 1,000 poems/year, accepts about 50-60. Press run is 1,000. Single copy: $5; subscription: $5. Make checks payable to *Georgetown Review.*

How to Submit Submit 1-10 poems at a time. Lines/poem: open. Considers simultaneous submissions; no previously published poems. No fax, e-mail, or disk submissions. Cover letter is preferred. "In cover letter, please include short bio and a list of publications. Also, must include SASE for reply." Reads submissions September 1-March 15. Submit seasonal poems one year in advance. Time between acceptance and publication is 1-2 months. Poems are circulated to an editorial board. "The first reader passes the poem along to the poetry editor, and then a final decision is made by the poetry editor and the head editor." Seldom comments on rejected poems. Guidelines available for SASE, by e-mail, or on Web site. Responds in 1-3 months. Pays 2 contributor's copies. Acquires first North American serial rights. Reviews books/chapbooks of poetry in 1,000 words, multi-book format.

Contest/Award Offerings Sponsors annual contest, offering $1,000 prize and publication; runners-up also receive publication. Guidelines available for SASE, by e-mail, or on Web site. **Entry fee:** $10/poem, $5 for each additional poem.

✪ $✍ THE GEORGIA REVIEW

The University of Georgia, 012 Gilbert Hall, Athens GA 30602-9009. (706)542-3481. E-mail: garev@uga.edu. Web site: www.uga.edu/garev. Established 1947. **Contact:** The Editors.

Magazine Needs *The Georgia Review*, published quarterly, seeks "the very best work we can find, whether by Nobel laureates and Pulitzer Prize-winners or by little-known (or even previously unpublished) writers. All manuscripts receive serious, careful attention. We have featured first-ever publications by many new voices over the years, but encourage all potential contributors to become familiar with past offerings before submitting." Has published poetry by Andrea Hollander Budy, Stephen Dunn, John Kinsella, and Pattiann Rogers. *The Georgia Review* is 200-232 pages, 7×10, professionally printed, flat-spined, with glossy card cover. Publishes 60-70 poems/year, less than .5% of those received. Press run is 4,500. Subscription: $30/year. Sample: $8.

How to Submit Submit 3-5 poems at a time. No simultaneous submissions. Reads year-round, but submissions postmarked May 15-August 15 will be returned unread. Guidelines available for SASE or on Web site. Responds in 2-4 months. Always sends prepublication galleys. Pays $3/line, one-year subscription, and one contributor's copy. Acquires first North American serial rights. Reviews books of poetry. "Our poetry reviews range from 500-word 'Book Briefs' on single volumes to 5,000-word essay reviews on multiple volumes."

Advice "Needless to say, competition is extremely tough. All styles and forms are welcome, but response times can be slower during peak periods in the fall and late spring."

✪ ✍ ◎ GERTRUDE (Specialized: gay, lesbian, bisexual, transgendered, queer-identified & allied)

P.O. Box 83948, Portland OR 97283. E-mail: poetry@gertrudepress.org. Web site: www.gertrudepress.org. Established 1998. **Contact:** Steve Rydman, poetry editor. Founding Editor: Eric Delehoy.

Magazine Needs *Gertrude*, published semiannually, is the literary publication of Gertrude Press (see separate listing in Books/Chapbooks), "a nonprofit 501(c)(3) organization showcasing and developing the creative talents of lesbian, gay, bisexual, trans, queer-identified, and allied individuals." Considers poetry by teens. Has published poetry by Judith Barrington, Deanna Kern Ludwin, Casey Charles, Michael Montlack, Megan Kruse, and Noah Tysick. *Gertrude* is 64-112 pages, digest-sized, offset-printed, perfect-bound, with glossy 4-color cardstock cover with art. Receives about 500 poems/year, accepts about 6-8%. Press run is 300 (100 subscribers, 15 libraries, 50 shelf sales); 50 distributed free. Single copy: $8.25; subscription: $15/year, $27 for 2 years. Sample: $6.25. Make checks payable to Gertrude Press.

How to Submit Submit 6 poems at a time. Lines/poem: open. Considers simultaneous submissions;

no previously published poems. Accepts e-mail submissions (as attachment); no disk submissions. Cover letter is preferred. Include short bio and SASE. Reads submissions year round. Time between acceptance and publication is 3-6 months. Poems are circulated to an editorial board. Sometimes comments on rejected poems. Guidelines available in magazine, by e-mail, or on Web site. Responds in 3 months. Sometimes sends prepublication galleys. Pays 2 contributor's copies plus discount on additional copies/subscriptions. Acquires one-time rights. Rights revert to poets upon publication.

Contest/Award Offerings The Gertrude Press Poetry Chapbook Contest (see separate listing in Contests & Awards).

Advice "*Gertrude* publishes the best poetry that is received. While we are a queer publication, poetry need not be lesbigay-specific, and publication is open to all poets regardless of background."

$✍ THE GETTYSBURG REVIEW

Gettysburg College, Gettysburg PA 17325. (717)337-6770. Fax: (717)337-6775. E-mail: mdrew@gett ysburg.edu. Web site: www.gettysburgreview.com. Established 1988. **Contact:** Peter Stitt, editor.

- Work appearing in *The Gettysburg Review* has been included frequently in *The Best American Poetry* and Pushcart Prize anthologies. Editor Peter Stitt won the first PEN/Nora Magid Award for Editorial Excellence.

Magazine Needs *The Gettysburg Review*, published quarterly, considers "well-written poems of all kinds." Has published poetry by Rita Dove, Beckian Fritz Goldberg, Charles Wright, Michelle Boisseau, Mark Doty, and Charles Simic. Accepts 1-2% of submissions received. Press run is 4,500 (2,700 subscribers). Subscription: $24/year. Sample: $7.

How to Submit Submit 3-5 poems at a time. Considers simultaneous submissions; no previously published poems. Cover letter is preferred. Include SASE. Reads submissions September-May only. Occasionally publishes theme issues. "Response time can be slow during heavy submission periods, especially in the late fall." Pays $2.50/line, one-year subscription, and one contributor's copy. Essay-reviews are featured in most issues. Send materials for review consideration.

▣ ✍ GHOTI MAGAZINE

E-mail: editors@ghotimag.com. Web site: www.ghotimag.com. Established 2005. **Contact:** CL Bledsoe, Donna Epler, and Jillian Meyer, editors.

Magazine Needs *Ghoti Magazine*, published quarterly online, prints "fiction, nonfiction, poetry, book reviews, and interviews with up-and-coming writers or those who have been ignored by the mainstream. *Ghoti Magazine* also publishes recipes by writers." Wants "fiction, poetry, nonfiction, and reviews of recent books. We are open to experimental and traditional styles, but our main criterion is quality. Is this piece of writing going to stay with a reader? In five years, will it be worth reading again? If so, *Ghoti Magazine* wants it." Does not want "self-absorbed work. If it's boring to you, it's boring to us." Has published poetry by Simon Perchik, Lyn Lifshin, Arlene Ang, Jo McDougall, Ace Boggess, and Barry Ballard. Receives about 1,000 poems/year, accepts about 40-50.

How to Submit Submit 3-5 poems at a time. Lines/poem: "there is no line limit, but longer poems must be able to sustain their length." Considers simultaneous submissions; no previously published poems. Accepts e-mail submissions only (pasted into body of message; "if the poems have complicated formatting, please paste them into the body of the e-mail and attach them to the e-mail as well"). Cover letter is preferred. Reads submissions year round. Submit seasonal poems 3 months in advance. Time between acceptance and publication is 3-6 months. "We have three editors. Generally at least two editors read each submission." Often comments on rejected poems. Guidelines available on Web site. Responds in 2 months. Acquires electronic rights. Rights revert to poet upon publication. Reviews books/chapbooks of poetry in 250-500 words, single-book format. "For review materials, contact the editors."

Advice "We are open to the prosaic, performance-oriented poetry that seems to mainly be written today, but we would much prefer to see poetry that experiments with language and sound, instead of just stating a case. Prosody is not a bad thing. We rarely publish political rants or anything that seems to be beating us over the heads with meaning. We judge each submission based on quality of the work, regardless of how many credits the author has."

THE GIHON RIVER REVIEW

Johnson State College, 337 College Hill, Johnson VT 05656. Established 2001. **Contact:** Poetry Editor for submissions; Editor-in-Chief for inquiries (editors are students; contact names change on a yearly basis).

Magazine Needs *The Gihon River Review*, published biannually, prints poetry, fiction, and creative nonfiction with a small compliment of art, usually photographs. Has published poetry by Stuart Friebert, Mark Borax, John David Christensen, Julia Shipley, Thomas Dorsett, and William Doreski. *The Gihon River Review* is 80 pages, digest-sized, offset-printed, perfect-bound, with full-color cover on glossy coverstock. Receives about 1,000 poems/year, accepts about 3%. Press run is 650 (10 subscribers, 2 libraries); 400 distributed free to U.S. colleges and universities with writing programs. Single copy: $5; subscription: $8/2 issues. Make checks payable to *The Gihon River Review*.

How to Submit Submit 5 poems at a time. No previously published poems or simultaneous submissions. No disk submissions. Cover letter is required ("brief cover letter, with SASE"). Reads submissions year round except summer months; submissions received in late spring are read in fall. Time between acceptance and publication is one month. "All *GRR* staff read poetry. Editorial process is a group effort." Never comments on rejected poems. Occasionally publishes theme issues. List of upcoming themes available for SASE. Guidelines available in magazine. Pays 2 contributor's copies plus one year's subscription (2 issues). Acquires one-time rights.

GNOME: THE ONLINE JOURNAL OF UNDERGROUND WRITING (Specialized: alternative, avant-garde, experimental)

Asterius Press, P.O. Box 5122, Seabrook NJ 08302-3511. E-mail: theeditor@asteriuspress.com. Web site: www.asteriuspress.com. Established 1997. **Contact:** John C. Erianne, editor.

Magazine Needs *Gnome: the online journal of underground writing*, published irregularly, seeks "non-traditional poetry and an occasional piece of experimental prose." Wants "Neo-populist, neo-beat, street, experimental, alternative, free-verse, performance, avant-garde, anti-academic rants and bloodlettings." Does not want "mainstream, teen angst, sainted granny inspirational garbage. Unoriginal riffs off of Bukowski, Ginsburg, Kerouac, Burroughs, Gil Scott Heron, Amiri Baraka, or any other poet who riffs off of any of these writers. Anything you'd find in *The New Yorker*, *Poetry*, or any other *Poetry*-wannabe publication." Has published poetry by Stephanie Savage, Mitchell Metz, John Sweet, Alison Daniel, B.Z Niditch, and Corey Ginsberg.

How to Submit Submit no more than 5 poems at a time. Considers simultaneous submissions, but they're "not encouraged"; no previously published poems. Accepts e-mail submissions (encouraged; pasted as text into body of message—no attachments). "Use 'submission' as the subject header. Any submission that comes as a file attachment will be deleted without reply." Cover letter is preferred; "should be brief and to the point." Include SASE for postal submissions. Time between acceptance and publication is up to one year. Seldom comments on rejected poems. Guidelines available on Web site. Responds in up to 2 months. Pays one contributor's copy. Acquires first rights, first electronic rights, and non-exclusive anthology rights.

Advice "Write from love; don't expect love in return, don't take rejection personally, and don't let anyone stop you."

THE GREAT AMERICAN POETRY SHOW

The Muse Media, P.O. Box 69506, West Hollywood CA 90069. (323)969-4905. E-mail: info@tgaps.net. Web site: www.tgaps.net. Established 2002. **Contact:** Larry Ziman, editor/publisher.

Magazine Needs *The Great American Poetry Show*, published about every 2 years, is an 8½×11 hardcover serial poetry anthology. Wants poems on any subject, in any style, of any length. Has published poetry by Sara Berkeley, Alan Britt, Hector E. Estrada, Heidi Nye, Tom Smith, and Sarah Brown Weitzman. *The Great American Poetry Show* is 150 pages, sheet-fed offset-printed, perfect-bound, with cloth cover with art/graphics. "For our first volume, we read about 8,000 poems from about 1,400 poets and accepted only 113 poems from 83 poets." Press run is 1,000. Single copy: $35 (print), $7.50 (e-book, download only).

How to Submit Submit any number of poems at a time. Considers previously published poems and simultaneous submissions. Accepts e-mail submissions (as attachment). Cover letter is optional. Include SASE. "If we reject a submission of your work, please send us another group to go through. We have four editors who can handle a lot of submissions." Responds in 1-3 months ("depends on how busy we are"). Pays one contributor's copy.

Also Offers "Please use our message boards where anyone can have us post poetry news, reviews, essays, articles, and recommended books."

Advice "We are very hard to please. But we are very easy to submit to. Do not get discouraged by rejections from us. Just keep sending us more poems to consider. Hopefully, we will find something we want to publish in your submissions. If we reject everything you send us, still do not get discouraged. Send your poems to other publishers until you find one who wants to publish your poetry."

▣ ◪ GREEN HILLS LITERARY LANTERN

McClain Hall, Truman State University, Kirksville MO 63501. (660)785-4513. E-mail: jbeneven@truman.edu. Web site: http://ll.truman.edu/ghllweb/. **Contact:** Joe Benevento, poetry editor.

Magazine Needs *Green Hills Literary Lantern*, published annually online in June, is "an open-access journal of short fiction and poetry of exceptional quality." Wants "the best poetry, in any style, preferably understandable. There are no restrictions on subject matter. Both free and formal verse forms are fine, though we publish more free verse overall." Does not want "haiku, limericks, or anything over two pages. Pornography and gratuitous violence will not be accepted. Obscurity for its own sake is also frowned upon." Has published poetry by Jim Thomas, Phillip Dacey, Susan Terris, Louis Philips, Francine Tolf, and Julie Lechevsky. Sample (back issue): $7.

How to Submit Submit 3-7 poems at a time. Considers simultaneous submissions, "but not preferred"; no previously published poems. No e-mail submissions. Cover letter is preferred. Include list of publication credits. Type poems one/page. Often comments on rejected poems. Guidelines available for SASE, by e-mail, or on Web site. Responds within 4 months. Always sends prepublication galleys. Pays 2 contributor's copies. Acquires one-time rights.

Advice "Read the best poetry and be willing to learn from what you encounter. A genuine attempt is made to publish the best poems available, no matter who the writer. First-time poets, well-established poets, and those in between, all can and have found a place in the *Green Hills Literary Lantern*. We try to supply feedback, particularly to those we seek to encourage."

◪ GREEN MOUNTAINS REVIEW

Johnson State College, Johnson VT 05656. (802)635-1350. Fax: (802)635-1210. E-mail: gmr@jsc.vsc.edu. Web site: http://greenmountainsreview.jsc.vsc.edu. Established 1975. **Contact:** Neil Shepard, poetry editor.

- Poetry published in *Green Mountains Review* has been included in *The Best American Poetry* and *The Pushcart Prize* anthologies.

Magazine Needs *Green Mountains Review*, published twice/year, includes poetry (and other writing) by well-known authors and promising newcomers. Has published poetry by Carol Frost, Sharon Olds, Carl Phillips, David St. John, and David Wojahn. *Green Mountains Review* is 150-200 pages, digest-sized, flat-spined. Receives about 3,000 submissions/year, publishes 30 authors. Press run is 1,800

(200 subscribers, 30 libraries). Single copy: $9.50; subscription: $15/year. Sample: $7 (back issue). **How to Submit** Submit no more than 5 poems at a time. Considers simultaneous submissions. No e-mail submissions. Reads submissions September 1-March 1 only. Sometimes comments rejected poems. Publishes theme issues. Guidelines available for SASE. Responds in up to 6 months. Pays 2 contributor's copies plus one-year subscription. Acquires first North American serial rights. Send materials for review consideration.

▧ ▣ ◖ THE GREEN MUSE (formerly *SaucyVox(Dot)Com*)

E-mail: thegreenmuse@gmail.com. Web site: http://thegreenmuse.net. Established 2001. **Contact:** Feithline Stuart.

Magazine Needs *The Green Muse*, published every 3 months online, is "primarily a literary maga-zine of poetry, prose, personal essays, articles, and photography. We offer print editions; check Web site for details." Wants "free verse by skilled and beginner poets, including tasteful erotic poetry. No themes, no taboos, though we tend not to publish erotica unless it is of the highest quality." Does not want "rhyming poetry." Has published poetry by John Sweet, Laine Perry, Robert Levin, and J. Fischer.

How to Submit Submit 5 poems minimum at a time; 10 to be considered as "featured poet." Accepts e-mail submissions only (pasted into body of message, no attachments); no disk submissions. "Once accepted, a bio and photograph will be requested." Reads submissions year round. Submit seasonal poems 3 months in advance. Publication months are November, February, May, and August. "We pay only featured poets, who receive a $10 honorarium. No print contributor's copies are offered, but PDF versions of the print edition are."

▨ THE GREENSBORO REVIEW

MFA Writing Program, 3302 Hall for Humanities and Research Administration, University of North Carolina at Greensboro, P.O. Box 26170, Greensboro NC 27402. (336)334-5459. E-mail: jlclark@unc g.edu. Web site: www.greensbororeview.org. Established 1966. **Contact:** Jim Clark, editor.

- Work published in *The Greensboro Review* has been consistently anthologized or cited in *Best American Short Stories*, *New Stories from the South*, *The Pushcart Prize*, and *Prize Stories: The O. Henry Awards*.

Magazine Needs *The Greensboro Review*, published twice/year, showcases well-made verse in all styles and forms, though shorter poems (under 50 lines) are preferred. Has published poetry by Stephen Dobyns, Natasha Trethewey, Claudia Emerson, Thomas Lux, Stanley Plumly, and Alan Shapiro. *The Greensboro Review* is 144 pages, digest-sized, professionally printed, flat-spined, with colored matte cover. Subscription: $10/year, $25/3 years. Sample: $5.

How to Submit Submit no more than 5 poems at a time. Lines/poem: under 50 lines preferred. No previously published poems or simultaneous submissions. No fax or e-mail submissions. Cover letter is preferred. Include number of poems submitted. Provide SASE for reply; sufficient postage for return. Reads submissions according to the following deadlines: mss must arrive by September 15 to be considered for the Spring issue (acceptances in December), or February 15 to be considered for the Fall issue (acceptances in May). "Manuscripts arriving after those dates will be held for consideration for the next issue." Guidelines available in magazine, for SASE, or on Web site. Responds in 4 months. Always sends prepublication galleys. Pays 3 contributor's copies. Acquires first North American serial rights.

Contest/Award Offerings The Robert Watson Literary Prizes offer publication (in Spring issue) and two $500 prizes (one for poetry, one for fiction). Guidelines available in magazine, for SASE, or on Web site. **Deadline:** September 15 annually.

Advice "We want to see the best being written regardless of theme, subject, or style."

$⧉ GULF COAST: A JOURNAL OF LITERATURE AND FINE ARTS

Dept. of English, University of Houston, Houston TX 77204-3013. (713)743-3223. Web site: www.gulfcoastmag.org. Established 1986. **Contact:** Darin Ciccotelli, managing editor; Nicole Zaza, associate editor; Jericho Brown, Paul Otremba, Kent Shaw, poetry editors.

Magazine Needs *Gulf Coast: A Journal of Literature and Fine Arts*, published twice/year in April and October, includes poetry, fiction, essays, interviews, and color reproductions of work by artists from across the nation. While the journal features work by a number of established poets, editors are also interested in "providing a forum for new and emerging writers who are producing well-crafted work that takes risks." Has published poetry by Anne Carson, Terrance Hayes, Srikanth Reddy, Karen Volkman, Susan Wheeler, and Dean Young. *Gulf Coast* is 230 pages, 7×9, offset-printed, perfect-bound. Single copy: $8; subscription: $14/year, $26/2 years. Sample: $7.

How to Submit Submit up to 5 poems at a time. Considers simultaneous submissions with notification; no previously published poems. Cover letter is required. List previous publications "if any" and include a brief bio. Reads submissions September-April. Guidelines available for SASE or on Web site. Responds within 6 months. Pays $50/poem and 2 contributor's copies. Returns all rights (except electronic) upon publication.

Contest/Award Offerings Sponsors an annual poetry contest, awarding $1,000 and publication. **Entry fee:** $15 (includes one-year subscription). Make checks payable to *Gulf Coast*. Guidelines available on Web site.

✪ ⧉ GULF STREAM MAGAZINE

English Dept., Florida International University, 3000 NE 151 St., North Miami Campus, North Miami FL 33181. (305)919-5599. E-mail: gulfstreamfiu@yahoo.com. (inquiries only). Web site: w3.fiu.edu/gulfstrm. Established 1989. **Contact:** Denise Sebesta Lanier, executive editor.

Magazine Needs *Gulf Stream*, published semiannually, is associated with the creative writing program at Florida International University. Wants "poetry of any style and subject matter as long as it's of high literary quality." Has published poetry by Gerald Costanzo, Naomi Shihab Nye, Jill Bialosky, and Catherine Bowman. *Gulf Stream* is 124 pages, digest-sized, flat-spined, printed on quality stock, with matte card cover. Accepts less than 10% of poetry received. Press run is 1,000. Subscription: $15. Sample: $5.

How to Submit Submit no more than 5 poems at a time. Considers simultaneous submissions with notification. Accepts electronic online submissions only; no snail mail/hard copy or e-mail submissions. "See Web site for details." Cover letter is required. Reads submissions September 1-March 1 only. Publishes theme issue every other issue. Guidelines available in magazine or on Web site. Responds in 3 weeks to 3 months. Pays 2 contributor's copies and 2 subscriptions. Acquires first North American serial rights.

⧉ HAIGHT ASHBURY LITERARY JOURNAL (Specialized: thematic issues)

558 Joost Ave., San Francisco CA 94127. (415)584-8264. E-mail: indigo@haightashbury.zzn.com. (inquiries only). Established 1979-1980. **Contact:** Indigo Hotchkiss, Alice Rogoff, Gail Mitchell, and Cesar Love, editors.

Magazine Needs *Haight Ashbury Literary Journal*, published 1-3 times/year, is a newsprint tabloid that uses "all forms [of poetry]. Subject matter sometimes political, but open to all subjects. Poems of background—prison, minority experience—often published, as well as poems of protest. Few rhymes." Has published poetry by Dan O'Connell, Diane Frank, Dancing Bear, Lee Herrick, Al Young, and Laura Beausoleil. *Haight Ashbury* is 16 pages, includes ads. Press run is 2,500. Subscription: $16 for 4 issues; $40 for a lifetime subscription (all future and 9 back issues). Sample: $3.

How to Submit Submit up to 6 poems at a time. No e-mail submissions; postal submissions only. "Please type one poem to a page, put name and address on every page, and include SASE. No bio." Always publishes theme issues (each issue changes its theme and emphasis). Guidelines available for SASE. Responds in 4 months. Pays 3 contributor's copies, plus small monetary amount to featured writers. Rights revert to author.

Additional Information An anthology of past issues, *This Far Together*, is available for $15.

Advice "Do not send work that is longer than our magazine!"

HANDSHAKE (Specialized: science fiction; fantasy; horror)

5 Cross Farm, Station Rd. N., Fearnhead, Warrington, Cheshire WA2 0QG England. Established 1992. **Contact:** J.F. Haines.

Magazine Needs *Handshake*, published irregularly, "is a newsletter for science fiction poets." Wants "science fiction/fantasy poetry of all styles. Prefer short poems." Does not want "epics or foul language." Has published poetry by Cardinal Cox, Neil K. Henderson, K.V. Bailey, John Light, and Joanne Tolson. *Handshake* is one sheet of A4 paper, photocopied, includes ads. "It has evolved into being one side of news and information and one side of poetry." Receives about 50 poems/year, accepts up to 50%. Press run is 60 (30 subscribers, 5 libraries). Subscription: SAE with IRC. Sample: SAE with IRC.

How to Submit Submit 2-3 poems. No previously published poems or simultaneous submissions. Cover letter is preferred. Poems must be typed and camera-ready. Time between acceptance and publication varies. Editor selects "whatever takes my fancy and is of suitable length." Seldom comments on rejected poems. Occasionally publishes theme issues. Responds ASAP. Pays one contributor's copy. Acquires first rights. Reviews books/chapbooks of poetry or other magazines/journals of very short length. Send material for review consideration.

Also Offers *Handshake* is also the newsletter for The Eight Hand Gang, an organization for British science fiction poets established in 1991. Currently has 60 members. Information about the organization available in *Handshake*.

HARP-STRINGS POETRY JOURNAL (Specialized: traditional forms of poetry)

Verdure Publications, P.O. Box 640387, Beverly Hills FL 34464-0387. E-mail: verdure@tampabay.rr .com. Established 1989. **Contact:** Madelyn Eastlund, editor.

Magazine Needs *Harp-Strings Poetry Journal*, published quarterly, features traditional forms of poetry. Wants "narratives, lyrics, prose poems, haibun, ballads, sestinas, and other traditional forms." Does not want "anything 'dashed off' or trite; no broken prose masquerading as poetry." Has published poetry by Ruth Harrison, Daniel Blackston, Jennifer Pearson, Robert Cooperman, and Barry Ballard. *Harp-Strings* is 20-24 pages, digest-sized, professionally printed on quality colored matte stock, saddle-stapled, with matte card cover. Accepts about 1% of poems received. Press run is 200 (105 subscribers). Subscription: $14. Sample: $4.00.

How to Submit Submit 3-5 poems at a time. Lines/poem: 14 minimum, 80 maximum ("more often find 40- to 60-line poems have best chance"). Considers previously published poems **by invitation only**; no simultaneous submissions. Accepts e-mail submissions (pasted into body of message or as Word attachment); no disk submissions. Cover letter is "not necessary, but if enclosed should contain information on poet or poems. *Harp-Strings* does use brief contributor notes. Always include a SASE—lately poets seem to forget." Reads submissions in February, May, August, and November only. Responds at the end of each reading period. Accepted poems will appear in the next issue being planned following each reading period. Seldom comments on rejected poems. "A poem might not be right for us, but right for another publication. Rejection does not necessarily imply poem needs revisions." Pays one contributor's copy. Acquires one-time rights.

Contest/Award Offerings Sponsors the annual Edna St. Vincent Millay "Ballad of the Harp Weaver" Award (see separate listing in Contests & Awards). "We may also sponsor a special contest during each quarter." Contest guidelines available for SASE.

Advice "Some things I've noticed in the past year or two are the number of submissions with no SASE, submissions stuffed into very small envelopes, failure to put the poet's name on each poem

Things Start Happening

Poetry as power for inmates

Brian Daldorph

He says, "Who's got one more? Who's got one more?"

It's almost 3 o'clock at Douglas County Jail in Lawrence, Kansas, when writing class ends; but inmate Jackson is keen for one more poem, one more, one more. That's the way class is here—once it gets going, it's hard to stop.

I've been teaching the writing class at Douglas County Jail for five years now. I teach *every* week, including Christmas week and New Year's week. That's when many inmates are missing their families and the routine of class is especially needed. Class starts with a read-through of inmate poems (which I typed up and copied into packets) from the previous class. Next, we free write for 20 minutes or so. In the third part of class, we take turns to read our just-written poems, or poems we've written during the week and brought in.

The population at the jail and in the writing class is transient: Guys go to trial, move on to a state correctional facility or get released. Though we usually have about 20 inmates in the weekly class, there's a big turnover of faces in the circle. Some inmates attend the class for many months. Others appear once, then we never see them again.

We have certain rules that Mike Caron, Douglas County Jail's program director, spells out at the beginning of class: no writing about inmate cases; no porn; no gangsta rap; no complaints about guards and the prison administration; nothing written to get under anyone else's skin. Some profanity is tolerated if it's an essential element of the poem. We have occasional problems with inmates going too far in their writing and violating ground rules, but these transgressions are rare. We most often deal with them by reminding the inmate of the rules.

Week after week I'm amazed by the talent and enthusiasm of the inmate writers. If only my university classes had this raw energy, this desire to express, this urgency to convey in words who they are in this world. If poetry is all about getting down to essential matters, as I would say it is, then that's what jail inmates often do. Many of them have lost so much that they're pretty much down to the essentials anyway. You want to know how it feels to be looking at ten years inside? You want to know about life in a tiny cell? About friends dropping away, about wives and lovers leaving? About dealing with guilt and shame? About all you have to do inside to keep your head above water? It's all here, similar themes recurring but with as many variations as there are inmates in the jail.

It's common enough for an incarcerated person to feel a sense of powerlessness. He often has to accept the names he's given (felon, criminal, danger to society, etc.) and someone else's way of telling his story. However, when he starts to write, he can find his own words to describe himself and say, "No matter what you call me, *this* is who I am." I often see the exhilaration that this new power can bring. As Ryan McCarty, English graduate student and long-term jail class assistant, puts it, "It's amazing to see someone discover that writing can be a source of power. It gives them a sense of importance that being an inmate, by definition, tends to take away."

During the free writing session, we sometimes use prompts (often song or poem titles or phrases) written on the board: *merciful dark, free wheeling, it's over, no limits, my full life ahead of me.* I encourage inmates to write, write, write, not to use the time to catch up on jail gossip. If I forget to put on music, an inmate reminds me—it's a vital part of the class. The Native American flute music of R. Carlos Nakai is a regular. One week we tried the radio instead and wrote to the accompaniment of R. Kelly and Stevie Wonder.

My training and interests are in literature. I am not a therapist, although I know from my own experience the therapeutic qualities of written expression. And I see it happen week after week: Guys who've lived fast lives on the outside slowing down because they have to when they get inside. Finally they must face up to some of their demons and some of the practical difficulties of their lives. How could they do it better than in poetry? I have seen lives transformed by inmates seizing the opportunity to tell their stories, to express what's most important to them. Though long-term good might come from the class, my basic goal is to help inmates through a hard time by holding a class that many of them look forward to. As Mike Caron says, "How many times have I heard inmates proclaim that it is the writing that has kept them from going crazy."

Some inmates first join the class as an opportunity to get out of their cells early in the afternoon; then they begin writing feverishly, bringing fat folders to class and wanting to read 10 poems when it's their turn in the circle. According to Caron, inmates often earn respect for the poetry they write and read in class. "Real respect and appreciation is a totally new experience for so many in here," he explains. "It's not enough to set anyone on a new road, but it is an essential step in changing the sense of utter despair and self doubt that permeates the vast majority of those who find themselves locked up again and again."

I'd started out thinking I'd run the class as a workshop, focusing on critiquing inmate poems, and tried to do it that way. But the class turned itself into what it needed to be, a forum for the 20 or so inmates who join the writers' circle each week to share, write and listen. So there's little discussion of poems—in class, at least. There's only just enough time to get around to everyone's work. Inmates in the circle listen carefully to what's read. They relish the opportunity to hear what that guy over there is *really* thinking.

One week in class there was a skinny elderly guy, bald but for a pony tail, who told us he didn't expect to be in jail—just some old offense he'd thought he was done with. He took his turn in the circle to say thanks, that the class was the *real deal*, all these guys telling the truth as they know it. Then he read his own poem about finding God. One long-term inmate and regular class participant told him, "Feels good, don't it, when you got all that stuff out of your system and you can think clearly again."

W.H. Auden contended that poetry makes nothing happen, but Jackson and I disagree. It's almost three o'clock and we want one more poem, one more attempt to make us laugh, or squirm or whatever it makes us do. One more honest expression.

Nick says, "Well, I do have one more song." He sorts a sheet from a thick stack; clears his throat, snaps his fingers, taps the desk, and raps about his hard-hearted lover.

You're wrong, Mr. Auden. Thursday at one o'clock at Douglas County Jail, things start happening—due to poetry.

—*Brian Daldorph*

Brian Daldorph teaches at the University of Kansas, Lawrence, and at Douglas County Jail. His three full-length poetry books are *The Holocaust and Hiroshima: Poems* (Mid-America Press), *Outcasts* (Mid-America Press) and *Senegal Blues* (219 Press). Daldorph also has taught in Japan, England, Senegal and Zambia. He edits *Coal City Review*. Contact him at briandal@ku.edu.

submitted. . . and, evidently, attention not paid to what the magazine lists as 'needs,' because we get haiku, tanka, and other short verse. We also get 8-12 poems submitted with a note that 'this is from my book,' or worse—we get entire manuscripts, especially by e-mail, which we must return because we are not a press. It looks like many poets 'gun shot' their submissions.''

HARTWORKS (Specialized: poetry for teens; African American issues)

D.C. Creative Writing Workshop, 601 Mississippi Ave. SE, Washington DC 20032. (202)445-4280. E-mail: info@dccww.org. Web site: www.dccww.org. Established 2000. **Contact:** Nancy Schwalb, artistic director.

● **Although this journal doesn't accept submissions from the general public, it's included here as an outstanding example of what a literary journal can be (for anyone of any age).**

Magazine Needs *hArtworks* appears 3 times/year. ''We publish the poetry of Hart Middle School students (as far as we know, Hart may be the only public middle school in the U.S. with its own poetry magazine) and the writing of guest writers such as Nikki Giovanni, Alan Cheuse, Arnost Lustig, Henry Taylor, Mark Craver, and Cornelius Eady, along with interviews between the kids and the grown-up pros. We also publish work by our writers-in-residence, who teach workshops at Hart, and provide trips to readings, slams, museums, and plays.'' Wants ''vivid, precise, imaginative language that communicates from the heart as well as the head.'' Does not want ''poetry that only 'sounds' good; it also needs to say something meaningful.'' Has published poetry by Luqman Abdullah, Reginald Conway, Nichell Kee, James Saunders, Monae Smith, and Renita Williams. *hArtworks* is 60 pages, magazine-sized, professionally printed, saddle-stapled, with card cover. Receives about 1,000 poems/year, accepts about 20%. Press run is 500 (150 subscribers, 2 libraries, 100 shelf sales); 100 distributed free to writers, teachers. Single copy: $10; subscription: $25. Make checks payable to D.C. Creative Writing Workshop.

How to Submit ''Writers-in-residence solicit most submissions from their classes, and then a committee of student editors makes the final selections. Each year, our second issue is devoted to responses to the Holocaust.''

Advice ''Read a lot; know something about how other writers approach their craft. Write a lot; build an understanding of yourself as a writer. Don't be so stubborn you settle into the same old poem you perfected in the past. Writing is not some static machine, but a kind of experience, a kind of growing.''

HAWAI'I PACIFIC REVIEW

1060 Bishop St., Honolulu HI 96813. (808)544-1108. Fax: (808)544-0862. E-mail: pwilson@hpu.edu. Web site: www.hpu.edu. Established 1986. **Contact:** Patrice M. Wilson, editor.

Magazine Needs *Hawai'i Pacific Review*, published annually in August or September by Hawai'i Pacific University, prints ''quality poetry, short fiction, and personal essays from writers worldwide. Our journal seeks to promote a world view that celebrates a variety of cultural themes, beliefs, values, and viewpoints. We wish to further the growth of artistic vision and talent by encouraging sophisticated and innovative poetic and narrative techniques.'' Has published poetry by Wendy Bishop, Rick Bursky, Virgil Suárez, Bob Hikok, Daniel Gutstein, and Linda Bierds. *Hawai'i Pacific Review* is 80-120 pages, digest-sized, professionally printed on quality paper, perfect-bound, with coated card cover. Receives 800-1,000 poems/year, accepts up to 30-40. Press run is about 500 (100 shelf sales). Single copy: $8.95. Sample: $5.

How to Submit Submit up to 5 poems at a time. Lines/poem: 100 maximum. No previously published poems or simultaneous submissions. No fax or e-mail submissions. Cover letter is required. Include 5-line professional bio including prior publications. SASE required. ''One submission per issue. No handwritten manuscripts. Include name on all pages.'' Reads submissions September 1-December 31 annually. Seldom comments on rejected poems. Guidelines available for SASE, by e-mail, or on Web site. Responds within 3 months. Pays 2 contributor's copies. Acquires first North

American serial rights. Rights revert to poet upon publication. "Must acknowledge *Hawai'i Pacific Review* as first publisher."

Advice "We'd like to receive more experimental verse. Good poetry is eye-opening; it investigates the unfamiliar or reveals the spectacular in the ordinary. Good poetry does more than simply express the poet's feelings; it provides both insight and unexpected beauty. Send us your best work!"

☑ HAZMAT REVIEW

Clevis Hook Press, P.O. Box 30507, Rochester NY 14603-0507. Web site: www.hazmatlitreview.org. Established 1996. **Contact:** Norm Davis, editor.

Magazine Needs *HazMat Review*, published semiannually, is "about 70% poetry, 25% short story, 5% miscellaneous (essays, reviews, etc.). *HazMat* stands for 'hazardous material,' which we believe poetry most definitely may be!" Wants "your best material; take chances. Political pieces welcome; also experimental and/or alternative; especially welcome pieces that show things are not what they appear to be. We think poetry and fiction of the highest quality always have a chance. New Age, witches, ghosts and goblins, vampires—probably not." Has published poetry by Eileen Myles, Marc Olmstead, Steve Hirsch, Thom Ward, Lawrence Ferlinghetti, and Anne Waldman. *HazMat Review* is 96 pages, digest-sized, professionally printed, perfect-bound, with glossy color or b&w cover. Receives about 700 poems/year, accepts up to 20%. Press run is 500 (60 subscribers, 5 libraries, 100 shelf sales); 100 distributed free to coffeehouses for publicity. Single copy: $14; subscription: $25/year. Sample: $7.

How to Submit Submit 3 poems at a time. Considers previously published poems; no simultaneous submissions. Accepts submissions on disk. "All submissions should come in an envelope marked 'Editor.'" Cover letter is preferred. SASE required for return. Time between acceptance and publication is up to 2 years. "Editors pass promising material to staff readers for second opinion and suggestions, then back to editors for final decision." Often comments on rejected poems. Guidelines available on Web site. Responds in 3 months. Pays 1-2 contributor's copies. Acquires one-time rights. Staff reviews chapbooks of poetry.

Advice "We are encouraged by the renewed interest in poetry in recent years. If at all possible, read the magazine first before submitting to get a feel for the publication."

$ ☑ ◎ HEARTLANDS: A MAGAZINE OF MIDWEST LIFE & ART (Specialized: work by Midwestern writers set in the Midwest)

Firelands Writing Center, BGSU Firelands, One University Rd., Huron OH 44839. (419)433-5560. Fax: (419)433-9696. E-mail: Lsmithdog@aol.com. (queries only). Web site: www.theheartlandstoday.net. Established 1990. **Contact:** David Shevin and Lin Ryan-Thompson, poetry editors. Member: CLMP.

Magazine Needs *Heartlands: A Magazine of Midwest Life & Art*, published annually by the Firelands Writing Center at Firelands College, contains "work by Midwestern writers about the Midwest Heartlands." Wants writing and photography "that is set in the Midwest today and deals revealingly and creatively with the issues we face—good writing and art that document our lives." Has published poetry by Alberta Turner, Chris Llewellyn, Jeff Gundy, and Lawrence Ferlinghetti. *Heartlands* is 96 pages, $8^{1}/_{2} \times 11$, perfect-bound. Accepts 20% of the poetry received. Press run is 800. Single copy: $7. Sample: $5.

How to Submit Submit up to 5 poems at a time. Considers simultaneous submissions. No e-mail submissions. Cover letter is required. Include brief bio. Reads submissions January 1-May 15 only. Often comments on rejected poems. Responds in 2 months "once reading period begins." Pays $10 and 2 contributor's copies. Acquires first or second rights.

☑ HIDDEN OAK

402 S. 25th St., Philadelphia PA 19146. E-mail: hidoak@att.net. Established 1999. **Contact:** Louise Larkins, editor.

Magazine Needs *Hidden Oak*, published 2 or 3 times/year, seeks "well-crafted poems that make imaginative use of imagery to reach levels deeper than the immediate and personal. Both traditional forms and free verse are accepted. Especially welcome are poems which include time-honored poetic devices and reveal an ear for the music of language." *Hidden Oak* is 68-72 pages, digest-sized, photocopied, stapled, with original art/photograph on cover. Receives about 600 poems/year, accepts up to 40%. Press run is 100+. Single copy: $5; subscription: $12. Sample: $4. Make checks payable to Louise Larkins.

How to Submit Submit 3-6 poems at a time. Lines/poem: 30 maximum. Considers previously published poems (occasionally); no simultaneous submissions. Accepts e-mail submissions; no disk submissions. Cover letter is preferred. Include SASE. Submit seasonal poems 2-3 months in advance. Time between acceptance and publication is up to 3 months. Seldom comments on rejected poems. Might publish theme issues in the future. Guidelines available for SASE or by e-mail. Responds in 3 weeks. Pays one contributor's copy. Does not review books or chapbooks.

☑ HIRAM POETRY REVIEW

P.O. Box 162, Hiram OH 44234. (330)569-7512. Fax: (330)569-5166. E-mail: greenwoodwp@hiram. edu. Established 1966. **Contact:** Willard Greenwood, poetry editor.

Magazine Needs *Hiram Poetry Review*, published annually in spring, features "distinctive, beautiful, and heroic poetry." Wants "works of high and low art. We tend to favor poems that are pockets of resistance in the undeclared war against 'plain speech,' but we're interested in any work of high quality." Press run is 400 (300 subscribers, 150 libraries). Subscription: $9/year; $23/3 years.

How to Submit Send 3-5 poems at a time. Lines/poem: under 50 (3 single-spaced pages or less). Considers simultaneous submissions. No e-mail submissions. Cover letter is required. Include brief bio. Reads submissions year round. Responds in up to 6 months. Pays 2 contributor's copies. Acquires first North American serial rights. Rights return to poets upon publication. Reviews books of poetry in single- or multi-book format, no set length. Send materials for review consideration.

$☑ THE HOLLINS CRITIC

P.O. Box 9538, Hollins University, Roanoke VA 24020-1538. (540)362-6275. Web site: www.hollins. edu/grad/eng_writing/critic/critic.htm. Established 1964. **Contact:** Cathryn Hankla, poetry editor.

Magazine Needs *The Hollins Critic*, published 5 times/year, prints critical essays, poetry, and book reviews. Uses a few short poems in each issue, interesting in form, content, or both. Has published poetry by William Miller, R.T. Smith, David Huddle, Margaret Gibson, and Julia Johnson. *The Hollins Critic* is 24 pages, magazine-sized. Press run is 500. Subscription: $8/year ($9.50 outside U.S.). Sample: $2.

How to Submit Submit up to 5 poems at a time. "Must be typewritten, with SASE." Reads submissions September 1-December 15. Submissions received at other times will be returned unread. Responds in 6 weeks. Pays $25/poem plus 5 contributor's copies.

☑ HOME PLANET NEWS

P.O. Box 455, High Falls NY 12440. Web site: www.homeplanetnews.org. Established 1979. **Contact:** Donald Lev, editor.

Magazine Needs *Home Planet News*, published 3 times/year, aims "to publish lively and eclectic poetry, from a wide range of sensibilities, and to provide news of the small press and poetry scenes, thereby fostering a sense of community among contributors and readers." Wants "honest, well-crafted poems, open or closed form, on any subject." Does not want "any work which seems to us to be racist, sexist, ageist, anti-Semitic, or imposes limitations on the human spirit." Considers poetry by children and teens. Has published poetry by Enid Dame, Antler, Lyn Lifshin, Gerald Locklin, Hal Sirowitz, and Janine Pommy Vega. *Home Planet News* is 24 pages, tabloid, web offset-printed, includes ads. Receives about 1,000 poems/year, accepts up to 3%. Press run is 1,000 (300 subscribers). Single copy: $4; subscription: $10/3 issues, $18/6 issues.

How to Submit Submit 3-6 poems at a time. Lines/poem: no limit on length, "but shorter poems (under 30 lines) stand a better chance." No previously published poems or simultaneous submissions. Cover letter is preferred. "SASE is a must." Time between acceptance and publication is one year. Seldom comments on rejected poems. Occasionally publishes theme issues. Upcoming themes available in magazine. Guidelines available for SASE or on Web site; "however, it is usually best to simply send work." Responds in 4 months. Pays one-year gift subscription plus 3 contributor's copies. Acquires first rights. Rights revert to poet upon publication. Reviews books/chapbooks of poetry and other magazines in 1,200 words, single- and multi-book format. Send materials for review consideration to Donald Lev. "Note: we do have guidelines for book reviewers; please write for them or check Web site. Magazines are reviewed by a staff member."

Advice "Read many publications, attend readings, feel yourself part of a writing community, learn from others."

◕ HOMESTEAD REVIEW

Box A-5, 156 Homestead Ave., Hartnell College, Salinas CA 93901. (831)755-6943. Fax: (831)755-6751. E-mail: homesteadreview@gmail.com. Web site: www.hartnell.cc.ca.us/homestead_review. Established 1985. **Contact:** Maria Garcia Teutsch, editor.

Magazine Needs *Homestead Review*, published semiannually in December and May, seeks "avant-garde poetry as well as fixed form styles of remarkable quality and originality." Does not want "Hallmark-style writing or first drafts." Considers poetry written by children and teens. Has published poetry by Ray Gonzalez, Kathryn Kirkpatrick, Dana Garrett, Virgil Suárez, Daphne Gottlieb, and Hal Sirowitz. Receives about 1,000 poems/year, accepts about 15%. Press run is 500 (300 subscribers/libraries); 200 are distributed free to poets, writers, bookstores. Single copy: $10; subscription: $20/year. Make checks payable to *Homestead Review*.

How to Submit Submit 3 poems at a time. No previously published poems or simultaneous submissions. No fax, e-mail, or disk submissions. Cover letter is required. "A brief bio should be included in the cover letter." Reads submissions year round. Submit seasonal poems 3 months in advance. Time between acceptance and publication is up to 5 months. "Manuscripts are read by the staff and discussed. Poems/fiction accepted by majority consensus." Often comments on rejected poems. Guidelines available for SASE. Responds in 5 months. Pays one contributor's copy. Acquires one-time rights.

Contest/Award Offerings Contest with categories for poetry and fiction. Offers 1st Prize: $150 plus publication in *Homestead Review*; 2nd Prize: $100; 3rd Prize: $50. All entries will be considered for publication in *Homestead Review*. Guidelines available on Web site. **Entry fee:** $15 for 3 poems. **Deadline:** see Web site for current dates.

Advice "Poetry is language distilled; do not send unpolished work. Join a workshop group if at all possible."

⊕ ◕ HQ POETRY MAGAZINE (THE HAIKU QUARTERLY)

The Day Dream Press, 39 Exmouth St., Kingshill, Swindon, Wiltshire SN1 3PU England. (44)(179)352-3927. Web site: www.noggs.dsl.pipex.com/hq/. Established 1990. **Contact:** Kevin Bailey, editor.

Magazine Needs *HQ Poetry Magazine*, published quarterly, is "a platform from which new and established poets can speak and have the opportunity to experiment with new forms and ideas." Wants "any poetry of good quality." Considers poetry by children and teens. Has published poetry by Al Alvarez, D.M. Thomas, James Kirkup, Cid Corman, Brian Patten, and Penelope Shuttle. *HQ*

Poetry Magazine is 48-64 pages, A5, perfect-bound, includes ads. Accepts about 5% of poetry received. Press run is 500-600 (500 subscribers, 30 libraries). Subscription (4 issues): £10 UK, £13 foreign. Sample: £2.80.

How to Submit No previously published poems or simultaneous submissions. Cover letter is required. Must include SASE (or SAE and IRCs). Time between acceptance and publication is 3-6 months. Often comments on rejected poems. Responds "as time allows." Pays one contributor's copy. Reviews books of poetry in about 1,000 words, single-book format. Send materials for review consideration.

Also Offers Sponsors "Piccadilly Poets" in London, and "Live Poet's Society" based in Bath, Somerset, England. Also acts as "advisor to Poetry on the Lake Annual Poetry Festival in Orta, Italy."

⚒ ◑ HUBBUB

5344 SE 38th Ave., Portland OR 97202. Established 1983. **Contact:** L. Steinman and J. Shugrue, editors.

Magazine Needs *Hubbub*, published once/year in the spring, is designed "to feature a multitude of voices from interesting contemporary American poets." Wants "poems that are well-crafted, with something to say. We have no single style, subject, or length requirement and, in particular, will consider long poems." Does not want light verse. Has published poetry by Madeline DeFrees, Cecil Giscombe, Carolyn Kizer, Primus St. John, Shara McCallum, and Alice Fulton. *Hubbub* is 50-70 pages, digest-sized, offset-printed, perfect-bound, with cover art. Receives about 1,200 submissions/year, accepts up to 2%. Press run is 350 (100 subscribers, 12 libraries, about 150 shelf sales). Subscription: $7/year. Sample: $3.35 (back issues), $7 (current issue).

How to Submit Submit 3-6 typed poems at a time. No previously published poems or simultaneous submissions. Include SASE. Guidelines available for SASE. Responds in 4 months. Pays 2 contributor's copies. Acquires first North American serial rights. "We review 2-4 poetry books/year in short (3-page) reviews; all reviews are solicited. We do, however, list books received/recommended." Send materials for review consideration.

Contest/Award Offerings Outside judges choose poems from each volume for 3 awards: Vi Gale Award ($100), Stout Award ($25), and Kenneth O. Hanson Award ($75). There are no special submission procedures or entry fees involved.

$◑ THE HUDSON REVIEW

684 Park Ave., New York NY 10021. Web site: www.hudsonreview.com. **Contact:** Candi Deschamps, editorial assistant.

● Work published in *The Hudson Review* has been included in *The Best American Poetry*.

Magazine Needs *The Hudson Review*, published quarterly, is considered one of the most prestigious and influential journals in the nation. Editors welcome all styles and forms; however, competition is extraordinarily keen. Has published poetry by Marilyn Nelson, Hayden Carruth, Louis Simpson, and Dana Gioia. *The Hudson Review* is 176 pages, flat-spined. Subscription: $32/year ($36 foreign), institutions $38/year ($42 foreign). Sample: $9.

How to Submit Submit no more than 10 poems at a time. No previously published poems or simultaneous submissions. **Nonsubscribers may submit poems April 1-June 30 only.** "Manuscripts submitted by subscribers who so identify themselves will be read throughout the year." Guidelines available in magazine, for SASE, or on Web site. Responds in 3 months. Always sends prepublication galleys. Pays 50¢/line and 2 contributor's copies.

Advice "Read the magazine to ascertain our style/sensibility."

$▣ HUMPTY DUMPTY'S MAGAZINE (Specialized: children ages 4-6; health-related themes)

Children's Better Health Institute, 1100 Waterway Blvd., Indianapolis IN 46202. Web site: www.cbh i.org orwww.humptydumptymag.org.

Magazine Needs *Humpty Dumpty's Magazine,* published bimonthly by The Better Health Institute, is for ages 4-6. "Designed to keep young minds growing and active bodies healthy and fit." Wants poetry appropriate for the age group with health-related themes. " 'Health' is a broad topic that includes exercise, sports, safety, nutrition, hygiene, and drug education." **Does not encourage writing submissions from children.** Reviews submissions for possible use in all Children's Better Health Institute publications. Subscription: $15.95/year each ($23.95 outside U.S.). Sample: $2.95.

How to Submit No simultaneous submissions. Manuscripts must be typewritten with poet's contact information in upper right-hand corner of each poem's page. SASE required. Submit seasonal material at least 8 months in advance. Guidelines available for SASE or on Web site. Responds in about 3 months. Pays $25 minimum for poetry. Acquires all rights.

Advice "We receive too many poetry submissions that are about kids, not for kids. Or, the subject matter is one that adults think children would or should like. Reading our guidelines is not enough. Careful study of current issues will acquaint writers with each title's 'personality.' "

$☑ HUNGER MOUNTAIN, The Vermont College Journal of Arts & Letters

Vermont College, 36 College St., Montpelier VT 05602. (802)828-8633. Fax: (802)828-8649. E-mail: hungermtn@tui.edu. Web site: www.hungermtn.org. Established 2002. **Contact:** Caroline Mercurio, managing editor. Member: CLMP.

Magazine Needs *Hunger Mountain, The Vermont College Journal of Arts & Letters,* published semi-annually, prints "high-quality poetry, prose, and artwork selected by guest editors from the Vermont College MFA in Writing Program." Wants poems "ready for publication." Does not want entire mss, or children's or young adult poetry. Has published poetry by Hayden Carruth, Mark Doty, Carol Muske-Dukes, Maxine Kumin, Charles Simic, and Ruth Stone. *Hunger Mountain* is about 200 pages, 7×10, professionally printed, perfect-bound, with full-bleed color artwork on cover, includes ads (only in back). Receives about 600 poems/year, accepts about 5%. Press run is 1,500 (700 subscribers, 50 libraries, 200 shelf sales); 100 distributed free to writing centers, book fairs, and other journals. Single copy: $10; subscription: $17/year, $32 for 2 years, $60 for 4 years. Make checks payable to *Hunger Mountain.*

How to Submit Submit 3-10 poems at a time. Considers simultaneous submissions; no previously published poems. No fax, e-mail, or disk submissions. Cover letter is preferred. "**Include double copies of everything**, including cover letter." Reads submissions year round. Time between acceptance and publication is 6 months. Poems are circulated to an editorial board. Occasionally comments on rejected poems. Guidelines available for SASE, by fax, e-mail, or on Web site. Responds in 4 months. Always sends prepublication galleys. Pays $5/page (minimum $30) and 2 contributor's copies. Acquires first North American serial rights.

Contest/Award Offerings The annual Ruth Stone Prize in Poetry (see separate listing in Contests & Awards).

Advice "Always read submission guidelines and make sure your poems are appropriate for the magazine or journal!"

☑ THE HURRICANE REVIEW: A NATIONAL JOURNAL OF POETRY AND SHORT FICTION

English/Communications Dept., Pensacola Junior College, 1000 College Blvd., Pensacola FL 32504. (850)484-1424. Fax: (850)484-1149. E-mail: mwernicke@pjc.edu. Web site: www.pjc.edu/academics/departments/english/hurricane.html. Established 1986. **Contact:** Marian Wernicke, faculty editor.

Magazine Needs *The Hurricane Review, A National Journal of Poetry and Short Fiction,* published annually in the fall, features poetry and short fiction. Wants poetry of "any style, any length. No biases other than quality." Does not want "inspirational or greeting card verse." Has published poetry by R.T. Smith, Sue Walker, Larry Rubin, and Simon Perchik. *The Hurricane Review* is 100 pages, digest-sized, professionally printed, perfect-bound, with matte card cover. Receives about 1,000 poems/year, accepts about 50-60. Press run is 500. Subscription: $4. Sample: $4.

How to Submit Submit 3-5 poems at a time. No previously published poems or simultaneous submissions. Cover letter is preferred. Include bio and/or publication history. SASE required. Reads submissions August 1-May 15 only. Responds in 3 months, faster when possible. Pays 3 contributor's copies. Acquires first rights.

Advice ''As David Kirby says, a poem should be well punctuated and give evidence of careful proofreading. It should be understandable to a reader who is not the poet.''

☑ ◎ IAMBS & TROCHEES (Specialized: metrical verse only)

6801 19th Ave. 5H, Brooklyn NY 11204. Web site: www.iambsandtrochees.com. Established 2001. **Contact:** William F. Carlson, editor/publisher.

Magazine Needs *Iambs & Trochees*, published semiannually in April and October, welcomes ''poetry written in the great tradition of English and American literature.'' Wants ''rhymed verse, blank verse, and metrically regular verse of any type, along with poems written in the various fixed forms. These include (but are not limited to) the sonnet, the villanelle, the ballade, the triolet, and the ottava rima. We are open to all genres: lyric, elegiac, satiric, narrative, or anything else. We have no restrictions on subject matter, nor do we demand that our writers follow any specific approach or ideology when handling their material. Our concern is strictly with the intrinsic aesthetic merit of a poem.'' Does not want free verse, syllabic verse. Has published poetry by Alfred Dorn, Jennifer Reeser, Bruce Bennett, and X.J. Kennedy. *Iambs & Trochees* is 64-124 pages, 7×9, digitally printed, perfect-bound, with paper cover. Single copy: $8; subscription: $15/year (2 issues). Make checks payable to Iambs & Trochees Publishing.

How to Submit Submit no more than 5 poems at a time. No previously published poems or simultaneous submissions. Accepts submissions by postal mail only. Include SASE for return of poems not accepted. Time between acceptance and publication is 2 months. Reads submissions by December 30 for Spring issue, June 30 for Fall issue. Poems are circulated to an editorial board. ''We select poems on how well they are crafted.'' Seldom comments on rejected poems. Guidelines available in magazine or for SASE. Responds in 2 months. Pays one contributor's copy. Acquires first North American serial rights. Reviews books of poetry only in 1,500 words.

Additional Information *Iambs & Trochees* may print winners of contests sponsored by the World Order of Narrative & Formalist Poets.

Advice ''Send metrical poems only, and only five per submission.''

☑ IBBETSON ST. PRESS

25 School St., Somerville MA 02143-1721. (617)628-2313. E-mail: dougholder@post.harvard.edu. Web site: http://homepage.mac.com/rconte. Established 1999. **Contact:** Doug Holder, editor. Submissions Editor: Robert K. Johnson.

Magazine Needs *Ibbetson St. Press*, published semiannually in June and November, prints '' 'down to earth' poetry that is well-written; has clean, crisp images; with a sense of irony and humor.'' Wants ''mostly free verse, but are open to rhyme.'' Does not want ''maudlin, trite, overly political, vulgar for vulgar's sake work.'' Has published poetry by Afaa Michael Weaver, Sarah Hannah, Gloria Mindock, Harris Gardner, and Deb Priestly. *Ibbetson St. Press* is 50 pages, magazine-sized, desktop-published, with glossy white cover, includes ads. Receives about 1,000 poems/year, accepts up to 30%. Press run is 200 (30 subscribers). Also archived at Harvard, Brown, University of Wisconsin, Poets House-NYC, and Buffalo University Libraries. Single copy: $7; subscription: $13. Make checks payable to *Ibbetson St. Press*.

How to Submit Submit 3-5 poems at a time. Considers previously published poems; no simultaneous submissions. No e-mail submissions; postal submissions only. Cover letter is required. Time between acceptance and publication is up to 5 months. ''Three editors comment on submissions.'' Guidelines available for SASE. Responds in 2 months or more. Pays one contributor's copy. Acquires one-time rights. Reviews books/chapbooks of poetry and other magazines in 250-500 words. Send materials for review consideration.

Additional Information *Does not accept unsolicited chapbook mss.* Has published *Way, Way Off the Road* by Hugh Fox, *Louisa Solano: The Grolier Poetry Book Shop* by Doug Holder/Steve Glines, and *American Wives Club* by Patricia Brodie. Responds to queries in one month.

Advice ''Please buy a copy of the magazine you submit to—support the small press. In your work, be honest.''

$◩ THE ICONOCLAST

1675 Amazon Rd., Mohegan Lake NY 10547-1804. Established 1992. **Contact:** Phil Wagner, editor/publisher.

Magazine Needs *The Iconoclast*, published 6 times/year, is a general interest literary journal. Wants ''poems that have something to say—the more levels the better. Try for originality; if not in thought, then expression. Look for the unusual in the usual, parallels in opposites, the capturing of what is unique or often unnoticed in an ordinary, or extraordinary, moment; what makes us human—and the resultant glories and agonies. Our poetry is accessible to a thoughtful reading public.'' Does not want ''greeting card verse or noble religious sentiments. Nothing sentimental, obscure, or self-absorbed.'' *The Iconoclast* is 64-96 pages, magazine-sized, photo offset-printed on 50 lb. white paper, includes ads. Receives about 2,000 poems/year, accepts up to 3%. Press run is 1,000-3,000 (700 subscribers). Subscription: $17 for 8 issues. Sample: $5.

How to Submit Submit 3-4 poems at a time. Time between acceptance and publication is 4 months to one year. Sometimes comments on rejected poems. Guidelines available for SASE. Responds in one month. Pays $2-5/poem for first North American rights (on publication), one contributor's copy per published page or poem, offers 40% discount on extras. Reviews books of poetry in 250 words, single-book format.

Advice ''If you're spending more time and money on TV, PDAs, and the Internet than on literature, perhaps you're not a small press person and should be sending your work to Time Warner or News Corp.''

▦ ▢ ◎ IDIOM 23 (Specialized: Central Queensland region of Australia)

Regional Centre of the Arts, Central Queensland University, Rockhampton 4702 Australia. E-mail: m.murfin@cqu.edu.au. Established 1988. **Contact:** Michelle Murfin, administrator/coordinator.

Magazine Needs *Idiom 23*, published annually, is ''named for the Tropic of Capricorn and is dedicated to developing the literary arts throughout the Central Queensland region. Submissions of original short stories, poems, articles, and black-and-white drawings and photographs are welcomed by the editorial collective. *Idiom 23* is not limited to a particular viewpoint but, on the contrary, hopes to encourage and publish a broad spectrum of writing. The collective seeks out creative work from community groups with as varied backgrounds as possible. The magazine hopes to reflect and contest idiomatic fictional representations of marginalized or non-privileged positions and values.'' Considers poetry written by children and teens (10 years of age and older). *Idiom 23* is about 140 pages, 7¾×10, professionally printed, perfect-bound, with 4-color cover, includes ads. Single copy: $15.

How to Submit Considers previously published poems. Cover letter is required. Poems are circulated to an editorial board. Reviews books of poetry in single-book format. Send materials for review consideration to Michelle Murfin.

Contest/Award Offerings Sponsors the Bauhinia Literary Awards for short stories and poetry in 3 categories: Open, Regional, and Student. Submit up to 3 poems, 50 lines maximum each. ''Where possible, please e-mail entries or send on a CD.'' Send SAE and IRC for complete details. **Entry fee:** $6. **Deadline:** June 30 (postmark). Winning entries will be announced at the CQ Multicultural Fair and CQU Open Day in August. Outstanding entries will be published in *Idiom 23*.

■ ☑ ◎ **THE IDIOT (Specialized: humor)**

E-mail: idiotsubmission@yahoo.com. Web site: www.theidiotmagazine.com. Established 1993. **Contact:** Sam Hayes, editor-in-chief (''President for Life''); Brian Campbell, co-conspirator (''Mussolini to my Hitler'').

Magazine Needs *The Idiot*, published monthly online with a print ''Best of'' issue every other year, is a humor magazine of ''mostly fiction, articles, and cartoons, but will use anything funny, including poetry. Nothing pretentious. We are a magazine of dark comedy. Death, dismemberment, and religion are all subjects of comedy. Nothing is sacred. But it needs to be funny, which brings us to—laughs! I mean belly laughs, laughing out loud, fall-on-the-floor funny. Bizarre, obscure, and/ or literary references are often appreciated but not necessary.'' Does not want ''whimsical; I don't want amusing, I don't want some fanciful anecdote about childhood. If it's cute, give it to your sweetheart or your puppy dog.'' Has published poetry by Freud Pachenko, Douglas O'Bee, and Larfus Markus. *The Idiot* (biennial print version) is 48 pages, digest-sized, professionally printed, staple-bound, with glossy cover. Receives about 250 submissions/year, accepts about 4-10. Press run is 1,000+. Subscription: $12. Sample: $7.

How to Submit Lines/poem: ''Length doesn't matter, but most comedy is like soup: It's an appetizer, not a meal. Short is often better.'' Considers previously published poems and simultaneous submissions. Accepts e-mail submissions (pasted into body of message) only. Seldom comments on rejected poems. Responds within one year. Pays one contributor's copy. Acquires one-time rights.

Advice ''Gather 'round, my children. Oh, come closer. Closer, don't be shy. Okay, scoot back, that's too close. Now listen carefully as there's something Uncle Sammy wants to tell you. Billy, get those fingers out of your ears and listen. I'd like to give you a little advice about submissions. You see, kids, most people send me poems that just aren't funny. We're a comedy magazine— emphasis on the word 'comedy.' We're looking for things that make people laugh. Anything less than that demeans us both (but mostly you). So please make sure that whatever you send isn't just amusing or cute, but really, really, really hilarious. Please note that we only publish a print copy every other year; but we need lots of material for the online magazine.''

■ ◯ **ILLOGICAL MUSE (Specialized: experimental & avant-garde preferred)**

P.O. Box 63, Buchanan MI 49107. E-mail: illogicalmuse@yahoo.com. Web site: www.geocities. com/illogicalmuse. Established 2004. **Contact:** Amber Rothrock, editor.

Magazine Needs *Illogical Muse*, published irregularly online, welcomes ''all poetry and fiction. To really understand what *Illogical Muse* is all about, visit the site. Prefer experimental and avant-garde.'' Does not want ''anything overly graphic or explicit in content.'' Considers poetry written by children and teens. ''Anyone under 18 should get their parents' permission before submitting.''

How to Submit Submit up to 6 poems at a time. Lines/poem: no more than 100. Considers previously published poems (''if poet owns rights'') and simultaneous submissions (''if alerted when accepted elsewhere''). Accepts e-mail submissions (pasted into body of message); no disk submissions. Cover letter is unnecessary. ''Please include a few short sentences about yourself. When submitting by postal mail, include SASE (or IRC) for response or include a valid e-mail address. Work can be returned if proper postage is supplied.'' Reads submissions year round. Submit seasonal poems 2-3 months in advance. Time between acceptance and publication ''could be three to four days or three to four months.'' Sometimes comments on rejected poems. ''Haven't published a theme issue, but may in the future.'' Guidelines available for SASE, by e-mail, or on Web site. Responds ''as soon as possible.'' No payment.

Also Offers Presents ''a monthly feature where I showcase a writer or artist. Please refer to the Web site for more information. I also post short fiction (up to 15,000 words) and artwork.''

Advice ''Rejections are a cold, hard fact of nature. I originally created *Illogical Muse* as a place where poets could have their work posted without fear of rejection. But, of course, as more submissions pour in, rejections will have to be made. Response time varies greatly as I run the Web site by myself. Rules and guidelines often change; it is wise to visit the site before submitting. I will not accept handwritten material. If I can't read it, I can't post it. I wish you luck!''

$⊙ ◎ IMAGE: ART, FAITH, MYSTERY (Specialized: religious faith; Judeo-Christian)

3307 3rd Ave. W., Seattle WA 98119. E-mail: image@imagejournal.org. Web site: www.imagejourn al.org. Established 1989. **Contact:** Gregory Wolfe, publisher.

Magazine Needs *Image: Art, Faith, Mystery*, published quarterly, ''explores and illustrates the relationship between faith and art through world-class fiction, poetry, essays, visual art, and other arts.'' Wants ''poems that grapple with religious faith, usually Judeo-Christian.'' Has published poetry by Philip Levine, Scott Cairns, Annie Dillard, Mary Oliver, Mark Jarman, and Kathleen Norris. *Image* is 136 pages, 10×7, printed on acid-free paper, perfect-bound, with glossy 4-color cover, includes ads. Receives about 800 poems/year, accepts up to 2%. Has 4,200 subscribers (100 are libraries). Subscription: $39.95. Sample: $16 postpaid.

How to Submit Submit up to 4 poems at a time. No previously published poems. No e-mail submissions. Cover letter is preferred. Time between acceptance and publication is one year. Guidelines available on Web site. Responds in 3 months. Always sends prepublication galleys. Pays 4 contributor's copies plus $2/line ($150 maximum). Acquires first North American serial rights. Reviews books of poetry in 2,000 words, single- or multi-book format. Send materials for review consideration.

⊠ ▣ ☑ IN OUR OWN WORDS

Burning Bush Publications, P.O. Box 4658, Santa Rosa CA 95402. Web site: www.bbbooks.com. **Contact:** Abby Bogomolny, editor.

Magazine Needs *In Our Own Words*, published two times/year online, seeks poetry and prose poems for its literary e-zine. Wants ''thought-provoking, creative, alternative writing. We choose work that inspires compassion, peace, and respect for diversity in original and unexpected ways.'' Does not want ''manuscripts of full-length books.'' Considers poetry from teens. Sample: past issues available on Web site.

How to Submit Cover letter is required. ''Send submissions to us by U.S. mail only. Include SASE. If you want us to reply via e-mail, include your e-mail address! We will ask you for a digital file via e-mail, if we want to publish your submission.'' Reads submissions according to the following deadlines: May 30 for Fall edition, December 22 for Spring edition. Guidelines available on Web site. Rights revert to poet upon publication.

Contest/Award Offerings The Burning Bush Poetry Prize (see separate listing in Contests & Awards).

Advice ''Our readers are interested in love, social and economic justice, investigative journalism, and improving the quality of life in all communities.''

☑ ◎ INDEFINITE SPACE (Specialized: experimental, visual, minimalistic)

P.O. Box 40101, Pasadena CA 91114. Established 1992. Web site: www.indefinitespace.net. **Contact:** Marcia Arrieta, editor/publisher.

Magazine Needs *Indefinite Space*, published annually, prints experimental, visual, and minimalistic poetry. Does not want rhyming poetry. Has published poetry by Martha Reed, Anne Blonstein, Kevin Magee, Petra Backonja, Peter Layton, and Jill Magi. *Indefinite Space* is 48 pages, digest-sized. Single copy: $7; subscription: $12/2 issues. Make checks payable to Marcia Arrieta.

How to Submit Considers simultaneous submissions; no previously published poems. Seldom comments on rejected poems. Guidelines available on Web site. Responds in up to 3 months. Poet retains copyright.

☑ ◎ THE INDENTED PILLOW (Specialized: Tantra, sacred sexuality)

P.O. Box 3502, Camarillo CA 93011. E-mail: rjones@mymailstation.com. Established 2003. **Contact:** Ronald K. Jones, editor/publisher.

Magazine Needs *The Indented Pillow*, published annually in January, prints poems relating to the Tantric Experience. Wants "poems reflecting sexuality and sex practices of the Eastern philosophical tenets of Tantra, i.e., sex and spirit as one." *The Indented Pillow* is one or more pages ($8\frac{1}{2} \times 11$ single sheets), photocopied on 67 lb. paper, folded. Receives about 20 poems/year, accepts about 50%. Press run is 200 (30 subscribers); 170 distributed free to bookstores and relevant organizations. "Since *The Indented Pillow* is a free publication, circulation is often more than stated." Single copy: one First-Class stamp; subscription: one First-Class stamp.

How to Submit Submit 6 poems at a time. Lines/poem: 20 maximum. Considers previously published poems and simultaneous submissions. Accepts e-mail submissions (pasted into body of message). Reads submissions year round. Time between acceptance and publication is one year. Often comments on rejected poems. Guidelines available for SASE. Responds in one month. Pays 2 contributor's copies. Acquires one-time rights.

Advice "If you've had a spiritual experience in a sexual encounter, then you already know the meaning of Tantra."

INTERPRETER'S HOUSE

19 The Paddox, Oxford OX2 7PN England. Web site: www.interpretershouse.org.uk. Established 1996. **Contact:** Merryn Williams.

● Business correspondence (including subscriptions) should go to Matt Bright, Upper Flat, 251 Abingdon Rd., Oxford OX1 4TH England.

Magazine Needs *Interpreter's House*, published 3 times/year in February, June, and October, prints short stories and poetry. Wants "good poetry, not too long." Does not want "Christmas-card verse or incomprehensible poetry." Has published poetry by Dannie Abse, Tony Curtis, Pauline Stainer, Alan Brownjohn, Peter Redgrove, and R.S. Thomas. *Interpreter's House* is 74 pages, A5, with attractive cover design. Receives about 1,000 poems/year, accepts up to 5%. Press run is 300 (200 subscribers). Single copy: £3 plus 55p. postage; subscription: £12 for 3 issues. Sample: £3.50.

How to Submit Submit 5 poems at a time. No previously published poems or simultaneous submissions. Cover letter is preferred. Time between acceptance and publication is 2 weeks to 3 months. Often comments on rejected poems. Guidelines available for SASE (or SAE and IRC). Responds "fast." Pays one contributor's copy.

Contest/Award Offerings Sponsors the Bedford Open Poetry Competition. Send SAE and IRC for details.

INVERTED-A HORN (Specialized: traditional poetry with meter and rhyme)

Inverted-A, Inc., P.O. Box 267, Licking MO 65542. E-mail: amnfn@well.com. Established 1977. **Contact:** Nets Katz and Aya Katz, editors.

Magazine Needs *Inverted-A Horn*, published irregularly, welcomes political topics, social issues, and science fiction. Wants traditional poetry with meter and rhyme. Does not want to see anything "modern, formless, existentialist." *Inverted-A Horn* is usually 9 pages, magazine-sized, offset-printed. Press run is 300. Sample: SASE with postage for 2 ounces (subject to availability).

How to Submit Considers simultaneous submissions. Accepts e-mail submissions (as attachment, ASCII). Responds in 4 months. Pays one contributor's copy; offers 40% discount on additional copies.

Additional Information Inverted-A, Inc. is a very small press that evolved from publishing technical manuals for other products. "Our interests center on freedom, justice, and honor." Publishes one chapbook/year.

Advice "I strongly recommend that would-be contributors avail themselves of this opportunity to explore what we are looking for. Most of the submissions we receive do not come close."

⬛ IODINE POETRY JOURNAL

P.O. Box 18548, Charlotte NC 28218-0548. (704)595-9526. E-mail: iodineopencut@aol.com. Web site: www.iodinepoetryjournal.com. Established 2000. **Contact:** Jonathan K. Rice, editor/publisher.
- Poetry published in *Iodine Poetry Journal* has been selected for inclusion in *The Best American Poetry*.

Magazine Needs *Iodine Poetry Journal*, published biannually, provides "a venue for both emerging and established poets." Wants "good poetry of almost any style, including form (e.g., pantoum and sestina) and experimental." Does not want rhyme, religion, or pornography. Has published poetry by Fred Chappell, David Chorlton, Robert Cooperman, Colette Inez, and R.T. Smith. *Iodine Poetry Journal* is 64 pages, digest-sized, perfect-bound, with full-color laminated cover, includes ads. Receives about 2,000 poems/year, accepts about 60 poems/issue. Press run is 350 (60 subscribers, 6 libraries). Single copy: $6; subscription: $10/year (2 issues). Sample: "Some back issues are $4 and $5. See Web site." Make checks payable to *Iodine Poetry Journal*.

How to Submit Submit 3-5 poems at a time. Lines/poem: 40 or less preferred, "but not totally averse to longer poems." No previously published poems or simultaneous submissions. Accepts e-mail submissions from international poets only; no disk submissions. Cover letter is preferred. "Always include SASE, and specify if SASE is for return of manuscript or reply only. I like a brief introduction of yourself in the cover letter." Reads submissions year round. Submit seasonal poems 6 months in advance. Time between acceptance and publication is 6 months to one year. Poems are circulated to an editorial board. "I occasionally have other readers assist in the selection process, but editor makes the final decision." Sometimes comments on rejected poems. Guidelines available in magazine, for SASE, or on Web site. Responds in 1-2 months. Sometimes sends prepublication galleys. Pays one contributor's copy and discounts extra copies of the issue in which work appears. Acquires first North American serial rights.

Also Offers "Shorter work is published in *Open Cut*, the summer broadside. Payment is three copies of the broadside. The broadside is 11×17 folded to pamphlet size, which will fit into a #10 envelope. It's a free publication that appears between the Spring and Fall issues of *Iodine* and is distributed to subscribers and at poetry readings hosted by the editor. Sample copies can be obtained by sending a #10 SASE. *Open Cut* is archived in the Special Collections of some university libraries."

$⬛ THE IOWA REVIEW

308 EPB, University of Iowa, Iowa City IA 52242. (319)335-0462. E-mail: iowa-review@uiowa.edu. Web site: www.iowareview.org. Established 1970. **Contact:** David Hamilton, editor.
- Poetry published in *The Iowa Review* has appeared often in *The Best American Poetry* and *The Pushcart Prize*.

Magazine Needs *The Iowa Review*, published 3 times/year, prints fiction, poetry, essays, reviews, and, occasionally, interviews. "We simply look for poems that, at the time we read and choose, we find we admire. No specifications as to form, length, style, subject matter, or purpose. Though we print work from established writers, we're always delighted when we discover new talent." *The Iowa Review* is 192 pages, professionally printed, flat-spined. Receives about 5,000 submissions/year, accepts up to 100. Press run is 2,900 (1,000 subscribers, about 500 libraries); 1,500 distributed to stores. Subscription: $24. Sample: $8.

How to Submit Submit 3-6 poems at a time. No e-mail submissions. Cover letter (with title of work and genre) is encouraged. SASE required. Reads submissions "only during the Fall semester, September through November, and then contest entries in the spring." Time between acceptance and publication is "around a year." Occasionally comments on rejected poems or offers suggestions on accepted poems. Responds in up to 4 months. Pays $25 for the first page and $15 for each subsequent page, 2 contributor's copies, and a one-year subscription. Acquires first North American serial rights, non-exclusive anthology rights, and non-exclusive electronic rights.

Contest/Award Offerings *The Iowa Review* Awards in Poetry, Fiction, and Essay offer $1,000 and publication to each genre winner. All submissions will be considered for publication in *The Iowa Review*. Guidelines available on Web site. **Entry Fee:** $15. **Deadline:** submit in January. Outside judges select winners from finalists.

IRIS: A JOURNAL ABOUT WOMEN (Specialized: women's issues, feminism)

UVA Women's Center, P.O. Box 800588, University of Virginia, Charlottesville VA 22908. (434)924-4500. Fax: (434)982-2901. E-mail: iris@virginia.edu. Web site: http://iris.virginia.edu. Established 1980. **Contact:** Lauren Russo, editor; Katy Shively, submissions.

Magazine Needs *iris: a journal about women*, published semiannually in April and November, focuses "on issues concerning women worldwide." Features quality poetry, prose, and artwork—mainly by women, but will also accept work by men "if it illuminates some aspect of a woman's reality." Also publishes translations. Wants "new and original language and diverse perspectives in well-crafted poems." Has published poetry by Sharon Olds, Mary Oliver, Charlotte Matthews, Rebecca B. Rank, Lisa Russ Spaar, and Gregory Orr. *iris* is 78 pages, magazine-sized, professionally printed on heavy glossy stock, saddle-stapled, with full-color glossy card cover. Press run is 2,000+ (about 40 library subscriptions, 1,000 shelf sales). Single copy: $5; subscription: $9/year, $17/2 years. Sample: $6.50.

How to Submit Submit no more than 5 poems at a time. Considers simultaneous submissions if notified immediately of acceptance elsewhere. Accepts e-mail submissions (pasted into body of message; no attachments); no fax submissions. For E-mail submissions, include "Submission Poetry" in subject line; for postal submissions, include SASE. Cover letter is required. "Include list of poems submitted and a brief bio. Name, address, and phone number should be listed on every poem." Publishes theme issues. Upcoming themes available in magazine, for SASE, or on Web site. Guidelines available for SASE or on Web site. Responds in 6 months. Pays 5 contributor's copies. Acquires first rights.

Advice "The poetry staff at *iris* is interested in pieces exploring all aspects of women's lives—especially the lives of younger women. Because many poems are on similar topics, freshness of imagery and style are even more important."

$ ISOTOPE: A JOURNAL OF LITERARY NATURE AND SCIENCE WRITING

Dept. of English, Utah State University, 3200 Old Main Hill, Logan UT 84322-3200. (435)797-3697. Fax: (435)797-3797. E-mail: lbrown@cc.usu.edu. Web site: http://isotope.usu.edu. Established 2003. **Contact:** Leslie Brown, managing editor. Member: CLMP.

Magazine Needs *Isotope*, published semianually, features literary nature and science writing. Has published poetry by Pattiann Rogers, Susan Maurer, Joanne Lowery, John Gilgun, Jim Fisher, and Thomas Joswick. *Isotope* is 52 pages, magazine-sized, offset-printed, saddle-stapled, with coverstock cover with color artwork. Receives about 1,200 poems/year, accepts about 20. Press run is 1,400 (1,000 subscribers, 12 libraries, 100 shelf sales); 300 distributed free to contributors, funders, and reviewers. Single copy: $5; subscription: $10. Make checks payable to *Isotope*.

How to Submit Submit 5 poems at a time. Considers simultaneous submissions; no previously published poems. No fax, e-mail, or disk submissions. Cover letter is preferred. "Include SASE, brief bio in cover letter." Reads submissions September 1-November 30. Time between acceptance and publication is 6-18 months. "Decisions are made by Poetry Editor and Magazine Editor." Rarely comments on rejected poems. Sometimes publishes theme issues. Guidelines available for SASE or on Web site. Responds in 6-9 months. Sends prepublication galleys. Pays $50/poem, 4 contributor's copies, and one-year subscription. Acquires first North American serial rights. Rights revert to poet upon publication.

Contest/Award Offerings *Isotope* sponsors an Editors' Prize in poetry. Offers annual award of $300 and publication. Submit up to 5 poems totaling no more than 10 pages. All entries are considered for publication. Guidelines available for SASE or on Web site. **Entry fee:** $15 (includes magazine subscription). **Deadline:** submit September 1-November 30 (postmark).

$ ⊚ JACK AND JILL (Specialized: children ages 7-10; health-related themes)

Children's Better Health Institute, 1100 Waterway Blvd., Indianapolis IN 46202. Web site: www.cb hi.org or www.jackandjillmag.org. Established 1938.

Magazine Needs *Jack and Jill*, published bimonthly by The Children's Better Health Institute, is a magazine for ages 7-10. Wants poetry appropriate for the age group with health-related themes. " 'Health' is a broad topic that includes exercise, sports, safety, nutrition, hygiene, and drug education." **Does not encourage writing submissions from children.** Reviews submissions for possible use in all Children's Better Health Institute publications. Subscription: $15.95/year each ($23.95 outside U.S.). Sample: $2.95.

How to Submit No simultaneous submissions. Manuscripts must be typewritten with poet's contact information in upper right-hand corner of each poem's page. SASE required. Submit seasonal material at least 8 months in advance. Guidelines available for SASE or on Web site. Responds in about 3 months. Pays $25 minimum for poetry.

Advice "We receive too many poetry submissions that are about kids, not for kids. Or, the subject matter is one that adults think children would or should like. Reading our guidelines is not enough. Careful study of current issues will acquaint writers with each title's 'personality.' "

⊘ ALICE JAMES BOOKS

University of Maine at Farmington, 238 Main St., Farmington ME 04938. Phone/fax: (207)778-7071. E-mail: ajb@umf.maine.edu. Web site: www.alicejamesbooks.org. Established 1973. **Contact:** Contest Coordinator.

Book/Chapbook Needs "The mission of Alice James Books, a cooperative poetry press, is to seek out and publish the best contemporary poetry by both established and beginning poets, with particular emphasis on involving poets in the publishing process." Has published poetry by Jane Kenyon, Jean Valentine, B.H. Fairchild, and Matthea Harvey. Publishes flat-spined paperbacks of high quality, both in production and contents. Does not want children's poetry or light verse. Publishes 6 paperback books/year, 80 pages each, in editions of 1,500.

How to Submit Manuscripts are selected through competitions (see below).

Contest/Award Offerings The Kinereth Gensler Award and The Beatrice Hawley Award (see separate listings in Contests & Awards).

$ ▤ ⊘ ⊚ JERRY JAZZ MUSICIAN (Specialized: mid-20th century America)

2207 NE Broadway, Portland OR 97232. (503)287-5570. Fax: (801)749-9896. E-mail: jm@jerryjazz.c om. Web site: www.jerryjazz.com.

Magazine Needs *Jerry Jazz Musician*, published monthly online, "celebrates mid-20th century America, with an emphasis on jazz, film, literature, art, civil rights history, and politics of the era. Open to all topics and poetic forms." Considers poetry by children and teens. Has published poetry by Pablo Neruda, Jim Harrison, Kenneth Rexroth, Golda Soloman, and Bunny M. Receives about 100 poems/year, accepts about 20. Has 4,000 subscribers; distributed free to 150,000 unique Internet visitors/month.

How to Submit Submit 1-2 poems at a time. Lines/poem: 6-100. Considers previously published poems and simultaneous submissions. Accepts fax, e-mail, and disk submissions. "Would prefer e-mail submissions pasted into message; however, if font and style are essential to the poem's success, will accept a Microsoft Word attachment." Cover letter is preferred. Reads submissions year round. Submit seasonal poems 4 months in advance. Time between acceptance and publication is one month. "Editor consults with a variety of readers, or may make choice on his own." Often comments on rejected poems. Guidelines available on Web site. Responds in one month. Pays $20.

Acquires electronic rights ("would require permission for other Web sites to publish"). Rights revert to poet upon publication, except Web publication rights.

Advice "We value creative writing and wish to encourage writers of short fiction and poetry to pursue their dream of being published. *Jerry Jazz Musician* would like to provide another step in the career of an aspiring writer."

$ ⬛ ◎ JEWISH WOMEN'S LITERARY ANNUAL (Specialized: poetry by Jewish women only)

820 Second Ave., New York NY 10017. (212)751-9223. Established 1994. **Contact:** Dr. Henny Wenkart, editor.

Magazine Needs *Jewish Women's Literary Annual*, published in April, prints poetry and fiction by Jewish women. Wants "poems by Jewish women on any topic, but of the highest literary quality." Has published poetry by Linda Zisquit, Merle Feld, Helen Papell, Enid Dame, Marge Piercy, and Lesléa Newman. *Jewish Women's Literary Annual* is 230 pages, digest-sized, perfect-bound, with laminated card cover. Receives about 1,500 poems/year, accepts about 10%. Press run is 1,500 (650 subscribers). Subscription: $18 for 3 issues. Sample: $7.50.

How to Submit No previously published poems. Poems are circulated to an editorial board. Often comments on rejected poems. Guidelines available for SASE. Responds in up to 5 months. Pays one contributor's copy plus a small honorarium. Rights remain with the poet.

Advice "Send only your very best. We are looking for humor, as well as other things, but nothing cutesy or smart-aleck. We do no politics; prefer topics other than 'Holocaust'."

⬛ ⬛ JONES AV.

OEL Press, 88 Dagmar Ave., Toronto ON M4M 1W1 Canada. (416)461-8739. E-mail: oel@interlog.com. Web site: www.interlog.com/~oel. Established 1994. **Contact:** Paul Schwartz, editor/publisher.

Magazine Needs *Jones Av.,* published quarterly, contains "poems from the lyric to the ash can; starting poets and award winners." Wants poems "concise in thought and image. Prose poems sometimes. Rhymed poetry is very difficult to do well these days; it better be good." Has published poetry by Bert Almon, Michael Estabrook, John Grey, Bernice Lever, B.Z. Niditch, and Elana Wolff. *Jones Av.* is 24 pages, digest-sized, photocopied, saddle-stapled, with card cover. Receives about 300 poems/year, accepts 30-40%. Press run is 100 (40 subscribers). Subscription: $12. Sample: $3. Make checks payable to Paul Schwartz.

How to Submit Submit 3-5 poems at a time. Lines/poem: up to 30. No previously published poems or simultaneous submissions. Accepts e-mail submissions (pasted into body of message). Cover letter is required. Include bio and SASE (or SAE with IRCs). "Remember, U.S. stamps cannot be used in Canada." Time between acceptance and publication is up to one year. Often comments on rejected poems. Occasionally publishes theme issues. Upcoming themes available in magazine. Guidelines available for SASE or on Web site. Responds in 3 months. Pays one contributor's copy. Acquires first rights. Staff reviews books/chapbooks of poetry and other magazines/journals in 50-75 words, multi-book format. Send materials for review consideration.

Advice "Request and study a sample issue of the publication if you are not familiar with the editor's taste."

⬛ ⬛ ◎ THE DAVID JONES JOURNAL (Specialized: David Jones; the Great War; mythology; visual arts)

The David Jones Society, 22 Gower Rd., Sketty, Swansea, W. Glam SA2 9BY Wales. (44)(179)220-6144. Fax: (44)(179)247-5037. E-mail: anne.price-owen@sihe.ac.uk. Established 1997. **Contact:** Anne Price-Owen, editor.

Magazine Needs *The David Jones Journal*, published annually, features "material related to David Jones, the Great War, mythology, and the visual arts." Wants "poetry that evokes or recalls themes and/or images related to the painter/poet David Jones (1895-1974)." Has published poetry by John Mole, R.S. Thomas, Seamus Heaney, and John Montague. *The David Jones Journal* is about 160 pages, digest-sized, camera ready-printed, perfect-bound, with full-color card cover. Receives about 12 poems/year, accepts about 8%. Press run is 400 (300 subscribers). Single copy: $12; subscription: $35. Sample: $10. Make checks payable to The David Jones Society.

How to Submit Submit one poem at a time. Considers simultaneous submissions; no previously published poems. Accepts e-mail and disk submissions. Cover letter is preferred. Time between acceptance and publication is 6 months. "Two editors agree on publication." Occasionally publishes theme issues. Guidelines available by e-mail. Responds in 6 weeks. Sometimes sends prepublication galleys. Pays 2 contributor's copies. Acquires first rights. Reviews books/chapbooks of poetry and other magazines in 750 words, single-book format. Open to unsolicited reviews. Send materials for review consideration.

THE JOURNAL

17 High St., Maryport, Cumbria CA15 6BQ England. E-mail: smithsssj@aol.com. Web site: http://members.aol.com/smithsssj/index.html. Established 1994. **Contact:** Sam Smith.

Magazine Needs *The Journal*, published annually, features English poetry/translations, reviews, and articles. Wants "new poetry howsoever it comes; translations and original English-language poems." Does not want "staid, generalized, all form/no content." Has published poetry by David H. Grubb, Gary Allen, and Ozdemir Asaf. *The Journal* is 40 pages, A4, offset-printed, stapled. Receives about 1,000 poems/year, accepts about 5%. Press run is 100-150 (80 subscribers, 12 libraries). Single copy: £2.50; subscription: £7 for 3 issues. Sample: £2 or £3 (sterling). Make checks payable to Sam Smith.

How to Submit Submit up to 6 poems at a time. Considers previously published poems and simultaneous submissions. Accepts e-mail submissions. Cover letter is preferred. "Please send 2 IRCs with hard-copy submissions." Time between acceptance and publication is up to one year. Often comments on rejected poems. Guidelines available for SASE (or SAE and IRC). Responds in one month. Always sends prepublication galleys. Pays one contributor's copy.

Additional Information In 1997, Original Plus Press began publishing collections of poetry. Has published books by Richard Wonnacott, James Turner, Don Ammons, Idris Caffrey, and RG Bishop. Send SASE (or SAE and IRC) or e-mail for details.

Advice "I prefer poetry that has been written with thought—both to what it is saying and how it is being said."

JOURNAL OF NEW JERSEY POETS
(Specialized: of, by, for NJ poets)

English Dept., County College of Morris, 214 Center Grove Rd., Randolph NJ 07869-2086. (973)328-5471. Fax: (973)328-5425. E-mail: szula

The Issue 43 cover of *Journal of New Jersey Poets* features "Heavenly Blue Morning Glories" by Madeline Zulauf. "This stunning photograph captures the fleeting beauty of flowers that open only for one summer morning . . . each one a natural symbol of *carpe diem*," says editor Sander Zulauf.

Photograph by Madeline Zulauf; cover layout by Ellen Bastante.

uf@ccm.edu. Established 1976. **Contact:** Sander Zulauf, editor. Associate Editors: North Peterson, Debra DeMattio, and Gina Serafin.

Magazine Needs *Journal of New Jersey Poets*, published annually in April, is "not necessarily about New Jersey—but of, by, and for poets from New Jersey." Wants "serious work that is regional in origin but universal in scope." Has published poetry by Joe Weil, X.J. Kennedy, Tina Kelley, Gerald Stern, Kenneth Burke, and Catherine Doty. *Journal of New Jersey Poets* is about 90 pages, perfect-bound, offset-printed on recycled stock. Press run is 600. Single copy: $10; subscription: $16 for 2 issues ($16/issue for institutions). Sample: $5.

How to Submit Submit up to 3 poems at a time. Accepts fax and e-mail submissions, "but they will not be acknowledged nor returned. Include SASE with sufficient postage for return of manuscript, or provide instructions to recycle." Annual deadline for submissions: September 1. Time between acceptance and publication is within one year. Guidelines available for SASE or by e-mail. Responds in up to one year. Pays 2 contributor's copies and a one-year subscription. Acquires first North American serial rights. All reviews are solicited. Send materials for review consideration.

Advice "Read the *Journal* before submitting. Realize we vote on everything submitted, and rejection is mostly an indication of the quantity of submissions received and the enormous number of poets submitting quality work."

⬤ ◎ JOURNAL OF REGIONAL CRITICISM (Specialized: surrealism; science fiction/fantasy; spirituality; symbols)

Arjuna Library Press, 1025 Garner St., D, Space 18, Colorado Springs CO 80905-1774. E-mail: pfuphoff@earthlink.net. Web site: http://home.earthlink.net/~pfuphoff/. Established 1963 (library), 1979 (press). **Contact:** Ct. Pf. Joseph A. Uphoff, Jr., executive director.

Magazine Needs *Journal of Regional Criticism*, published frequently in varied format, features "surrealist prose poetry, visual poetry, dreamlike, short and long works; no obscene, profane (will criticize but not publish), unpolished work." Has published work by Dr. Shari O'Brien, David Lawrence, Holly Day, Pearl Keve, John Grey, and Woodrow G. Moore, II. *Journal of Regional Criticism* is published in JPG files (on CD-ROM) of collage, writing, mathematical, fine art theory, and criticism.

How to Submit Send one or two short poems at a time. "Upon request will treat material as submitted for reprint, one-time rights." Accepts submissions by postal mail only. Cover letter is required. Include SASE. Guidelines (on sample CD) available for SASE. Reviews books of poetry "occasionally." Send materials for review consideration.

Additional Information "The Arjuna Library Press is avant-garde, designed to endure the transient quarters and marginal funding of the literary phenomenon (as a tradition) while presenting a context for the development of current mathematical ideas in regard to theories of art, literature, and performance; publication is now by CD-ROM, JPG, and ASF files. Each disk is unique. The poet is sent a color Xerox hard copy, poems illustrated by photogrpahic and artistic experiments in an irregular format. Photocopy printing allows for very limited editions and irregular format. Quality is maintained as an artistic materialist practice." Publishes 6-12 disks/year, averaging 600 MB (50 pages) each. Sample: $10.

Also Offers "The Arjuna Library Digital Visual Dream Laboratory and Acoustic Studio is extending publication beyond photocopy printing while maintaining respect for artistic relics such as manuscript copies and original photographs or papers. The format will remain varied and irregular (poetic, stream of consciousness production). Poetry is published in writing and with video of poets reading their works. Austerity is due to limited resources and expense of equipment and supplies. Works are now illustrated in color. Development work is continuing of the publication of poetry by the writers listed (O'Brien, Day, et. al.)."

Advice "Web site exhibition of visual poetics and literature has proceeded through the Mail Art phenomenon. This is an excellent means of contacting the public in an impersonal way; it remains true that there are other venues to develop the commercial profile. As a general rule, we should use principles of scientific observation (minimum interference) such that the proferred dimensions are not strained or reconfigured. If the membership grows too large, rather than excluding contributors by pyramidal elitism, more organization can be founded. In this way, an accurate assessment can be maintained as to how many individuals are requesting service. Instead of redesigned organization, the pyramidal elitism can be established by supplemental organization. It follows that acceptance then rises to the level of competency of the artist or writer within a system that provides continuing adequate support for newcomers and advancing practitioners. Thus, we do not need a surrender by vulgar insults: irony can be separated from the other reputable constructs. The audience can gravitate to protected interests."

◨ ◎ JOURNAL OF THE AMERICAN MEDICAL ASSOCIATION (JAMA) (Specialized: poetry related to a medical experience)

515 N. State St., Chicago IL 60610. (312)464-444. Fax: (312)464-5824. E-mail: jamams@jama-archives.org. Web site: www.jama.com. Established 1883. **Contact:** Charlene Breedlove, associate editor.

Magazine Needs *Journal of the American Medical Association (JAMA)*, published weekly, includes a poetry and medicine column and publishes poetry "in some way related to a medical experience, whether from the point of view of a health care worker or patient, or simply an observer. No unskilled poetry." Has published poetry by Jack Coulehan, Floyd Skloot, and Walt McDonald. *JAMA* is magazine-sized, flat-spined, with glossy paper cover. Receives about 750 poems/year, accepts about 7%. Has 360,000 subscribers (369 libraries). Subscription: $66. Sample: free, "no SASE needed."

How to Submit No previously published poems or simultaneous submissions. Accepts submissions by fax or through *JAMA*'s Web-based submissions and review system at http://manuscripts.jama.com. (or click the "Information for Authors/Reviewers" button on thewww.jama.com. home page). "I always appreciate inclusion of a brief cover letter. Mention of other publications and special biographical notes are always of interest." Publishes theme issues (i.e., in 2007: access to care; malaria; chronic diseases of children; violence/human rights; medical education; poverty and human development). "However, we would rather that poems relate obliquely to the theme." Guidelines available on Web site. Pays one contributor's copy, more by request. "We ask for a signed copyright release, but publication elsewhere is always granted."

◑ ◎ KAIMANA: LITERARY ARTS HAWAI'I (Specialized: HI, Pacific references)

Hawai'i Literary Arts Council, P.O. Box 11213, Honolulu HI 96828. Web site: www.hawaii.edu/hlac. Established 1974. **Contact:** Tony Quagliano, editor.

● Poets published in *Kaimana* have received the Pushcart Prize, the Hawaii Award for Literature, the Stefan Baciu Award, the Cades Award, and the John Unterecker Award.

Magazine Needs *Kaimana: Literary Arts Hawai'i*, published annually, is the magazine of the Hawai'i Literary Arts Council. Wants poems with "some Pacific reference—Asia, Polynesia, Hawai'i—but not exclusively." Has published poetry by Kathryn Takara, Howard Nemerov, Anne Waldman, Reuel Denney, Haunani-Kay Trask, and Simon Perchik. *Kaimana* is 64-76 pages, $7\frac{1}{2} \times 10$, saddle-stapled, with high-quality printing. Press run is 1,000 (600 subscribers, 200 libraries). Subscription: $15, includes membership in HLAC. Sample: $10.

How to Submit Cover letter is preferred. Sometimes comments on rejected poems. Guidelines available in magazine or on Web site. Responds with "reasonable dispatch." Pays 2 contributor's copies.

Advice "Hawai'i gets a lot of 'travelling regionalists,' visiting writers with inevitably superficial observations. We also get superb visiting observers who are careful craftsmen anywhere. *Kaimana* is interested in the latter, to complement our own best Hawai'i writers."

$ ◎ KALEIDOSCOPE: EXPLORING THE EXPERIENCE OF DISABILITY THROUGH LITERATURE AND THE FINE ARTS (Specialized: disability themes)

701 S. Main St., Akron OH 44311-1019. (330)762-9755. Fax: (330)762-0912. E-mail: mshiplett@uds akron.org. Web site: www.udsakron.org/kaleidoscope.htm. Established 1979. **Contact:** Gail Willmott, editor-in-chief.

Magazine Needs *Kaleidoscope: Exploring the Experience of Disability through Literature and the Fine Arts*, published twice/year in January and July, is based at United Disability Services, a not-for-profit agency. Poetry should deal with the experience of disability, but is not limited to that experience when the writer has a disability. Wants "high-quality poetry with vivid, believable images and evocative language." Does not want "stereotyping, patronizing, or offending language about disability." Has published poetry by Jeanne Bryner, Jeff Worley, Barbara Crooker, and Sandra J. Lindow. *Kaleidoscope* is 64 pages, magazine-sized, professionally printed, saddle-stapled, with 4-color semigloss card cover. Press run is 1,500 (for libraries, social service agencies, health care professionals, universities, and individual subscribers). Single copy: $6; subscription: $10 individual, $15 agency.

How to Submit Submit up to 6 poems at a time. Considers previously published poems and simultaneous submissions "as long as we are notified in both instances." Accepts fax and e-mail submissions. Cover letter is required. Send photocopies with SASE for return of work. "All submissions must be accompanied by an autobiographical sketch and should be double-spaced, with pages numbered and author's name on each page." Reads submissions by March 1 and August 1 deadlines. Publishes theme issues. Upcoming themes available in magazine, for SASE, by fax, e-mail, or on Web site. Guidelines available for SASE, by fax, e-mail, and on Web site. Responds within 3 weeks; acceptance or rejection may take 6 months. Pays $10-25 plus 2 contributor's copies. Rights revert to author upon publication. Staff reviews books of poetry. Send materials for review consideration.

◙ KARAMU

Dept. of English, Eastern Illinois University, Charleston IL 61920. Web site: www.eiu.edu/~kara mu. Established 1966. **Contact:** Olga Abella, editor.

 • *Karamu* has received grants from the Illinois Arts Council, and has won recognition and money awards in the IAC Literary Awards competition.

Magazine Needs *Karamu*, published annually in May or June, aims to "provide a forum for the best contemporary poetry and fiction that comes our way. We especially like to print the works of new writers. We like to see poetry that shows a good sense of what's being done with poetry currently." Wants "poetry that builds around real experiences, real images, and real characters, and that avoids abstraction, overt philosophizing, and fuzzy pontifications. We prefer well-structured free verse, poetry with an inner, sub-surface structure as opposed to, let's say, the surface structure of rhymed quatrains. We have definite preferences in terms of style and form, but no such preferences in terms of length or subject matter." Does not want "the openly didactic poem. We don't want poems that preach against or for some political or religious viewpoint. The poem should first be a poem." Has published poetry by Glen Sheldon, Julie Perry Price, William Jolliff, Christopher Burawa, LL Harper, and Tracy Ahrens. *Karamu* is 120 pages, digest-sized, handsomely printed (narrow margins), with matte cover. Receives submissions from about 300 poets each year, accepts 40-50 poems. Press run is 500 (300 subscribers, 15 libraries). Single copy: $8. Sample: $6 for 2 back issues.

How to Submit Submit no more than 5 poems at a time. No previously published poems or simultaneous submissions. "Always include a SASE for reply and return of material. Sufficient postage is necessary for return of work." Reads submissions September 1-February 15 only; "for fastest decision, submit January through February 15." Critiques "a few of the better poems. We want the poet to consider our comments and then submit new work." Time between acceptance and publication is up to one year. Occasionally publishes theme issues. Guidelines available for SASE. Pays one contributor's copy. Acquires first serial rights.

Advice "Follow the standard advice: Know your market. Read contemporary poetry and the magazines you want to be published in. Be patient."

☐ ◎ KELSEY REVIEW (Specialized: Mercer County, NJ writers only)

Liberal Arts Division, Mercer County Community College, P.O. Box B, Trenton NJ 08690. E-mail: kelsey.review@mccc.edu. Web site: www.mccc.edu/community_kelsey-review.shtml. Established 1988. **Contact:** Ed Carmien or Holly-Katharine Johnson, editors.

Magazine Needs *Kelsey Review*, published annually in September by Mercer County Community College, serves as "an outlet for literary talent of people living and working in Mercer County, New Jersey only." Has no specifications as to form, length, subject matter, or style. Does not want to see poetry "about kittens and puppies." Has published poetry by Vida Chu, Carolyn Foote Edelmann, and Mary Mallery. *Kelsey Review* is about 90 glossy pages, 7×11, with paper cover. Receives about 60 submissions/year, accepts 6-10. Press run is 2,000; all distributed free to contributors, area libraries, bookstores, and schools.

How to Submit Submit up to 6 poems at a time. No previously published poems or simultaneous submissions. No fax or e-mail submissions. Manuscripts must be typed. Submit poems by May 1 deadline. Always comments on rejected poems. Guidelines available by e-mail. Responds in June of each year. Pays 5 contributor's copies. All rights revert to authors.

$☑ THE KENYON REVIEW

Walton House, Kenyon College, Gambier OH 43022. (740)427-5208. Fax: (740)427-5417. E-mail: kenyonreview@kenyon.edu. Web site: www.KenyonReview.org. Established 1939. **Contact:** David Lynn, editor.

Magazine Needs *The Kenyon Review*, published quarterly, contains poetry, fiction, essays, criticism, reviews, and memoirs. Features all styles, forms, lengths, and subject matters. Considers translations. Has published poetry by Billy Collins, Diane Ackerman, John Kinsella, Carol Muske-Dukes, Diane di Prima, and Seamus Heaney. *The Kenyon Review* is 180 pages, digest-sized, flat-spined. Receives about 4,000 submissions/year. Press run is 6,000. Sample: $12 (includes postage).

How to Submit Submit up to 6 poems at a time. No previously published poems or simultaneous submissions. Accepts submissions **through online registration only** at www.kenyon-review.org/submissions (group poems in a single document; do not submit poems individually). Reads submissions September 1-January 31 (for unsolicited work). Guidelines available on Web site. Responds in up to 4 months. Payment for accepted work is made upon publication. Author retains rights and will receive a contract upon acceptance. Does not consider unsolicited reviews.

Advice "Read recent issues of the *Review* to become familiar with the type and quality of writing being published before submitting your work."

$☐ ◎ KIDVISIONS (Specialized: fantasy, science fiction, mild horror for older children and teens)

P.O. Box 782, Cedar Rapids IA 52406-0782. E-mail: kidvisions@samsdotpublishing.com. Web site: www.samsdotpublishing.com. Established 2002. **Contact:** Lisa M. Bradley, editor. Member: The Speculative Literature Foundation.

Magazine Needs *KidVisions*, published quarterly online, prints "fantasy, science fiction, sword and sorcery, alternate history, myths/folktales, spooky short stories, poems, illustrations, puzzles, nonfiction articles, and movie and book reviews, all for a reading audience of 9-18 years old." Wants "fantasy, science fiction, spooky horror, and speculative poetry" appropriate to age group. Does not want "horror with excessive blood and gore." Considers poetry by children and teens. Has published poetry by Bruce Boston, Karen A. Romanko, Guy Belleranti, Aurelio Rico Lopez III, and Kristine Ong Muslim. Receives about 180 poems/year, accepts about 30 (16%).

How to Submit Submit up to 5 poems at a time. Lines/poem: 25 maximum. Considers previously published poems; no simultaneous submissions. Accepts e-mail submissions only (pasted into body of message). "Submission should include snail mail address and a short (1-2 lines) bio." Reads submissions year round. Submit seasonal poems 6 months in advance. Time between acceptance and publication is 1-3 months. Often comments on rejected poems. Guidelines available on Web site. Responds in 4-6 weeks. Pays $2/original poem, $1/reprint. Acquires first, exclusive worldwide electronic rights for 90 days. Reviews books/chapbooks of poetry. Send materials for review consideration to Tyree Campbell.

Advice "We prefer to see material from younger writers whenever possible."

KING LOG

E-mail: davidcase@earthlink.net. Web site: www.angelfire.com/il/kinglog. Established 1997. **Contact:** David Case, David Starkey, and Carolie Parker-Lopez, editors.

Magazine Needs *King Log*, published quarterly online, seeks "accomplished poetry by American and Anglophone writers, whether experimental, confessional, or formalist." Seeks "poetry that captures the confusion of work/writing, romantic attachments, popular and high culture, history, and political and philosophical idealism and disillusion—comedy, irony, and passion." Does not want "gushy, sentimental, macho, or precious" work. Has published poetry by Jim Daniels, Barry Spacks, Katherine Swiggart, Walt McDonald, Evelyn Perry, and Paul Willis. Receives about 400 poems/year, accepts about 60.

How to Submit Submit 3-5 poems at a time. No previously published poems or simultaneous submissions. Accepts e-mail submissions only (pasted into body of message). Cover letter is required. Reads submissions year round. Time between acceptance and publication is 3 months. Poems are read by "three editors who broadly share a consensus." Seldom comments on rejected poems. Guidelines available on Web site. Responds in 3 weeks. No payment. Acquires one-time rights.

$ THE KIT-CAT REVIEW

244 Halstead Ave., Harrison NY 10528-3611. (914)835-4833. E-mail: kitcatreview@gmail.com. Established 1998. **Contact:** Claudia Fletcher, editor.

Magazine Needs *The Kit-Cat Review*, published quarterly, is named "after the 18th-century Kit-Cat Club whose members included Addison, Steele, Congreve, Vanbrugh, and Garth. Its purpose is to promote/discover excellence and originality." Wants quality work—traditional, modern, experimental. Has published poetry by Coral Hull, Virgil Suárez, Margret J. Hoehn, Louis Phillips, Chayym Zeldis, and Marin Sorescu. *The Kit-Cat Review* is 75 pages, digest-sized, laser-printed/photocopied, saddle-stapled, with colored card cover. Receives about 1,000 poems/year. Press run is 500. "*The Kit-Cat Review* is part of the collections of the University of Wisconsin (Madison) and the State University of New York (Buffalo)." Subscription: $25. Sample: $7. Make checks payable to Claudia Fletcher.

How to Submit Submit any number of poems at a time. Considers previously published poems and simultaneous submissions. "Cover letter should contain any relevant bio." Time between acceptance and publication is 2 months. Responds within 2 months. Pays up to $100/poem plus 2 contributor's copies. Acquires first or one-time rights.

KOTAPRESS LOSS JOURNAL (Specialized: grief & healing in relation to death of a child)

(206)251-6706. E-mail: editor@kotapress.com. Web site: www.kotapress.com. Established 1999. **Contact:** Kara L.C. Jones, editor.

Magazine Needs *KotaPress Loss Journal*, published monthly online, provides support "of the grief and healing process after the death of a child. We publish *only* non-fictional poetry that somehow relates to grief and healing in relation to the death of a child. Please do not make up poems about this kind of loss and send them just to get in the magazine; it is insulting to many of our readers who are living this reality. As always, our interest is more in the content and story rather than one's ability to write in form; more in the ideas of poetry therapy rather than the academic, critique, competitive ideas normally fostered in universities.'' Has published poetry by John Fox, Poppy Hullings, Patricia Wellingham-Jones, Carol Jo Horn, and Sarah Bain.

How to Submit ''Please read current and some archived issues of the *Loss Journal* before sending anything. Then send a letter explaining your interest in contributing. We are interested in knowing how your personal experiences with death, dying, grief, and healing are playing out in the specific poems you are submitting. Include a bio if you wish to see one published with your poems after acceptance. Send your letter, poems, and bio as text all in one e-mail. Multiple e-mails will be ignored. File attachments will be deleted without ever being opened or acknoweldged. Make sure the subject line of your e-mail says 'Loss Journal Submission'—we get over 600 e-mails a day, most of them spam, so we sort and read based on the subject line.'' Reads submissions year round on a rolling basis. Time between acceptance and publication is up to 2 months. Guidelines available on Web site. Responds in 2 months. Acquires one-time electronic rights and archive rights. ''We do not remove works from our archives. Please see our Web site to find out more about us and about what we offer. We look forward to hearing from you and reading your poetry.''

Advice ''If you are interested in contributing to our *Loss Journal*, it is really important that you read the journal first. This will tell you a lot about the voice of the work we publish and how your poems might 'fit the bill' for us. Please understand that while we acknowledge that all losses are difficult, we do not equate pet loss with child loss—and we do not equate fictional ideas about loss with the reality of death and dying. Read the journal first. Then submit your poems if you feel they fit the mission of our journal.''

⊕ ☑ KRAX

63 Dixon Lane, Leeds, Yorkshire LS12 4RR England. Established 1971. **Contact:** Andy Robson, editor.

Magazine Needs *Krax*, published annually in the summer, prints contemporary poetry from England and America. Wants ''poetry that is light-hearted and witty; original ideas.'' All forms and styles considered. Does not want ''haiku, religious, or topical politics.'' Has published poetry by Arthur Winfield Knight, Eleanor Livingstone, and Salena Godden. *Krax* is 72 pages, digest-sized, offset-printed, saddle-stapled. Receives up to 700 submissions/year, accepts about 10%. Single copy: £3.50 ($7); subscription: £10 ($20). Sample: $1 (75p).

How to Submit Submit 6 poems maximum at a time. Lines/poem: 2,000 words maximum. No previously published poems or simultaneous submissions. No disk submissions. Cover letter is preferred. ''Writer's name on same sheet as poem. SASE or SAE with IRC encouraged but not vital.'' Responds in 2 months. Pays one contributor's copy. Reviews books of poetry (''brief, individual comments; no outside reviews''). Send materials for review consideration.

Advice ''Rewrite only to improve structure or format—unnecessary rewriting usually destroys the original spontaneity and rhythm.''

✪ ▣ ☑ LA PETITE ZINE

E-mail: lapetitezine@yahoo.com. Web site: www.lapetitezine.org. **Contact:** Jeffrey Salane and Danielle Pafunda, co-editors. Member: CLMP.

● Work published in *La Petite Zine* has appeared in *The Best American Poetry*.

Magazine Needs *La Petite Zine*, published 3 times/year online, features ''new and established voices in poetry, fiction, creative nonfiction, reviews, and cross-genre work. While we do not offer parameters for content, form, or style, we ask that writers submit bombastic, grotesque, excessive, destabilizing, and otherwise provocative work.'' Does not want ''writing that employs cliché in place of exploration of language, demonstrates an ignorance of contemporary poetry/literature or (especially) our publication, and/or relies on the sentimentality of its readers." Has published work by Anne Boyer, Arielle Greenberg, Johannes Goransson, Joyelle McSweeney, Joshua Marie Wilkinson, and Jonah Winter. Receives about 3,000 poems/year, accepts about 150 (5%). Sample: free online; "there is no subscription, but readers are invited to sign up for e-mail notification of new issues at the submission address."

How to Submit Submit 3-5 poems at a time ("please adhere to this guideline"). Considers simultaneous submissions, "but please notify us immediately if poems are accepted elsewhere"; no previously published poems. Accepts e-mail submissions (pasted into body of message or as attachment—Word document [preferred] or Rich Text Format); no disk submissions. "If submitting poems as an attachment, please include all poems in the same document." Cover letter is required. Include brief bio listing previous publications. "If we do not accept your work, please wait at least six months before resubmitting." Reads submissions September-May. Time between acceptance and publication is up to 6 months. "The two co-editors make all decisions by consensus." Seldom comments on rejected poems. Occasionally publishes theme issues. Upcoming themes (when applicable) and guidelines available on Web site. Responds in 2 weeks to 6 months. Always sends electronic prepublication galleys. No payment. Acquires first rights. Reviews books/chapbooks of poetry in 500 words, single- and multi-book format. "Please query lapetitezine@yahoo.com with materials for review."

Also Offers *La Petite Zine*'s home page "indexes all authors for each specific issue and offers links to past issues, as well as information about the journal, its interests and editors, and links to other sites. Art and graphics are supplied by Web del Sol. Additionally, we publish graphic poems, excerpts from graphic novels, and the like."

Advice "We are committed to severing, grafting, dissembling, eviscerating, barnstorming, rerouting, and otherwise un/rehinging language and subjectivity. Please send help."

$☐ ◎ LADYBUG MAGAZINE (Specialized: children ages 2-6)

Carus Publishing, 70 E. Lake St., Suite 300, Chicago IL 60601. Web site: www.cricketmag.com. Established 1990. **Contact:** Submissions Editor.

Magazine Needs *LADYBUG Magazine*, published monthly, is a reading and listening magazine for young children (ages 2-6). Wants poetry that is "rhythmic, rhyming; serious, humorous, active." *LADYBUG* is 40 pages, 8×10, staple-bound, with full color cover. Receives more than 1,200 submissions/month, accepts 25-30. Circulation is 120,000. Subscription: $35.97/year (12 issues). Sample: $5; sample pages available on Web site.

How to Submit Submit no more than 5 poems at a time. Lines/poem: up to 20. Considers previously published poems. Include SASE. Responds in 6 months. Guidelines available for SASE or on Web site. Pays $3/line ($25 minimum) on publication. Acquires North American publication rights for previously published poems; rights vary for unpublished poems.

Advice "In evaluating manuscripts, we look for beauty of language and a sense of joy or wonder. Before attempting to write for *LADYBUG*, be sure to familiarize yourself with this age child and with the magazine itself."

◪ LAKE EFFECT: A JOURNAL OF THE LITERARY ARTS

School of Humanities & Social Sciences, Penn State Erie, 5091 Station Rd., Erie PA 16563-1501. (814)898-6281. Fax: (814)898-6032. E-mail: gol1@psu.edu. Web site: www.pserie.psu.edu/lakeeffect. Established 1978 (as *Tempus*; renamed *Lake Effect* in 2001). **Contact:** George Looney, editor-in-chief. Member: CLMP.

Magazine Needs *Lake Effect*, published annually in March/April, provides "an aesthetic venue for writing that uses language precisely to forge a genuine and rewarding experience for our readers. *Lake Effect* wishes to publish writing that rewards more than one reading, and to present side-by-side the voices of established and emerging writers." Wants "poetry aware of, and wise about, issues of craft in forming language that is capable of generating a rich and rewarding reading experience." Does not want "sentimental verse reliant on clichés." Has published poetry by Norman Dubie, Richard Jackson, David Kirby, Susan Ludvigson, Harry Humes, and Chase Twichell. *Lake Effect* is 180 pages, digest-sized, offset-printed, perfect-bound, with gloss-by-flat film lamination cover. Receives about 3,000 poems/year, accepts about 1%. Press run is 800 (300 shelf sales); 300 distributed free to contributors and writing programs. Single copy: $6; subscription: $6. Make checks payable to The Pennsylvania State University.

How to Submit Submit 3-5 poems at a time. Considers simultaneous submissions; no previously published poems. No fax, e-mail, or disk submissions. Cover letter is required. Reads submissions year round. Time between acceptance and publication is up to 4 months. "The poetry staff reads the poems, meets and discusses them to come to a consensus. Poetry editor, along with editor-in-chief, makes final decisions." Occasionally comments on rejected poems. Guidelines available in magazine or on Web site. Responds in up to 4 months. Pays 2 contributor's copies. Acquires first North American serial rights.

Advice *"Lake Effect* strives to provide an attractive venue for the good work of both established and emerging writers. We care about the integrity of poetry, and care for the poems we accept."

⭐ 🌐 ◎ LANDFALL: NEW ZEALAND ARTS AND LETTERS (Specialized: work by & about New Zealand writers)

Otago University Press, P.O. Box 56, Dunedin New Zealand. (64)(3)479-8807. Fax: (64)(3)479-8385. E-mail: landfall@otago.ac.nz. Web site: www.otago.ac.nz/press/landfall. Established 1947; originally published by Caxton Press, then by Oxford University Press, now published by Otago University Press. **Contact:** Richard Reeve, *Landfall* coordinator.

Magazine Needs *Landfall: New Zealand Arts and Letters*, published twice/year in May and November, focuses "primarily on New Zealand literature and arts. It publishes new fiction, poetry, commentary, and interviews with New Zealand artists and writers, and reviews of New Zealand books." Single issue: $29.95 NZD; subscription: $45 NZD (2 issues) for New Zealand subscribers, $30 AUD for Australian subscribers, $30 USD for other overseas subscribers.

How to Submit No fax or e-mail submissions. "Once accepted, contributions should, if possible, also be submitted on disk." Submissions must be typed and include SASE. Publishes theme issues. Guidelines available for SASE. New Zealand poets should write for further information.

■ ◪ LANGUAGEANDCULTURE.NET

E-mail: review@languageandculture.net. Web site: www.languageandculture.net. Established 2001. **Contact:** Liz Fortini, editor.

Magazine Needs *Languageandculture.net*, published twice/year online, prints contemporary poetry in English. Also accepts translations of Spanish, French, German, Italian, and Russian; "other languages under review. Translated poems will be published side by side with the English." No restrictions on form. Considers poetry by teens. Publishes 20-40 poems/issue.

How to Submit Submit up to 5 poems at a time. Lines/poem: 70 maximum. Considers previously published poems and simultaneous submissions. Accepts e-mail submissions; no disk submissions. "Return e-mail address must be included." Cover letter is preferred. Include brief bio. Reads submissions "yearly." Time between acceptance and publication "varies; no longer than five months." Poems are circulated to an editorial board. Comments on rejected poems. No payment. Acquires one-time electronic rights. Reviews chapbooks of poetry.

Additional Information Publishes 10 online chapbooks/year. Each chapbook is posted on the Web site for one year. Send sample poems and a cover letter with brief bio and publication credits. Responds within one month.

Advice "Enrich your lives with different perspectives and poetry styles."

▢ ◎ LAURELS (Specialized: work by members only)

West Virginia Poetry Society, Rt. 2, Box 13, Ripley WV 25271. E-mail: mbush814@aol.com. Established 1996. **Contact:** Jim Bush, editor.

Magazine Needs *Laurels*, published quarterly, is the journal of the West Virginia Poetry Society, with poetry and line drawings. **Considers work from WVPS members only.** Wants "traditional forms and good free verse. If it's over 39 lines, it must be very, very good." Does not want "porn, off-color language, shape poems, doggerel, or 'broken prose.'" Considers poetry by children and teens, if members. *Laurels* is usually 62 pages, saddle-stapled, with paper cover. Receives about 2,000 poems/year, accepts about 80%. Press run is 275 (210 subscribers). Subscription: included in membership fee ($20 to Natalie J. Doty, 189 Vireo Dr., Wintersville OH 43953-4054; checks payable to WVPS Treasurer). Sample: $4 to Jim Bush at above address.

How to Submit Submit 4-5 poems at a time. Considers previously published poems. Accepts e-mail submissions. Cover letter is preferred. Include brief bio. **Writers should request and read guidelines before submitting.** Reads submissions according to the following deadlines: March 15, May 15, August 15, and November 15. Time between acceptance and publication is up to one year. Guidelines available for SASE or by e-mail. Responds "only if revision is needed or if poetry is not acceptable." Sometimes sends prepublication galleys. Acquires one-time rights.

Contest/Award Offerings West Virginia Poetry Society (WVPS) sponsors a 35-category annual contest for members. **Entry fee:** no fee for current WVPS members or K-12 students. Guidelines available to nonmembers for SASE.

Advice "Our purpose is to encourage and aid amateur poets who believe that words can be used to communicate meaning and to create beauty."

◖ THE LEDGE

40 Maple Ave., Bellport NY 11713. E-mail: tkmonaghan@aol.com. Web site: www.theledgemagazine.com. Established 1988. **Contact:** Timothy Monaghan, editor-in-chief/publisher.

Magazine Needs *The Ledge* seeks "poems that utilize language and imagery in a fresh, original fashion. We favor poems that speak to the human experience." Wants "inspired, imaginative, well-crafted verse, and we're open to all styles and schools of writing. Each issue of *The Ledge* features a wide and eclectic range of work by poets of all backgrounds and persuasions. Excellence is the ultimate criterion." Has published poetry by Elton Glaser, Robert Fanning, Jennifer Perrine, Tony Gloeggler, Melody Lacina, and Lynne Knight. *The Ledge* is 240 pages, 6×9, typeset, perfect-bound, with glossy cover. Accepts 3% of poetry received. Press run is 1,500 (750 subscribers). Single copy: $10; subscription: $18 for 2 issues, $32 for 4 issues, $42 for 6 issues.

How to Submit Submit 3-5 poems at a time. Considers simultaneous submissions; no previously published poems. Include SASE. Reads submissions September-May. Responds in 3-6 months. Pays one contributor's copy. Acquires one-time rights.

Contest/Award Offerings *The Ledge* sponsors an annual poetry chapbook contest, as well as an annual poetry contest. Details available for SASE or by e-mail.

Ⓝ ◖ LEFT BEHIND, A JOURNAL OF SHOCK LITERATURE

832 Shasta Dr., Colton CA 92324. E-mail: Jeffery@epicentermagazine.org. Established 2007. **Contact:** Jeff Green, editor.

Magazine Needs *Left Behind, A Journal of Shock Literature*, published semiannually, prints poetry, short stories, short plays, screenplays, and essays. Wants "the work you thought was too racy to ever admit you wrote. The blasphemous, erotic, misanthropic, political incorrectable, homoerotic, homophobic, homo-habilis, scatological—you know, the good stuff. Formal, free verse, experimental, visual/concrete are all welcome. Surprise us. The serious and dark are encouraged, but the humorous is prized. Make us blush and say, 'Jeez, did we print that?' Imagine your Bukowski, but without the soft fuzzy side." *Left Behind* is 80 pages, digest-sized, full-color laser-printed, perfect-bound, with color cover, includes ads. Press run is 500; distributed free. Single copy: $7. Make checks payable to Jeff Green.

How to Submit Submit 6 poems at a time. Lines/poem: "no range limit; but we are only 80 pages, so if it's long, it's got to be good." Considers previously published poems and simultaneous submissions. Accepts disk submissions; no e-mail submissions. Cover letter is preferred. Reads submissions year round. Time between acceptance and publication is 8 months. Poems are circulated to an editorial board. Sometimes comments on rejected poems. Guidelines available in magazine or for SASE. Responds in 2 months. Pays 2 contributor's copies. Acquires one-time rights. Rights revert to poets upon publication. Reviews books/chapbooks of poetry and other magazines/journals in single-book format. Send materials for review consideration to Jeff Green.

Advice "For humorous work, read it to your friends and see if they laugh before submitting it to *Left Behind*. For poetry, attend an open mic and see how the audience responds. If there are no open mics in your area, start one."

☑ ◎ LIGHT (Specialized: light verse)

P.O. Box 7500, Chicago IL 60680. Web site: www.lightquarterly.com. Established 1992. **Contact:** John Mella, editor.

Magazine Needs *Light*, published quarterly, prints "light and occasional verse, satire, wordplay, puzzles, cartoons, and line art." Does not want "greeting card verse, cloying or sentimental verse." *Light* is 64 pages, perfect-bound. Single copy: $6; subscription: $22/year, $34/2 years, $38/year international ($28/year, $46/2 years for institutions). Sample (back issue): $5 plus $2 for first-class postage.

How to Submit No previously published poems or simultaneous submissions. Submit one poem/page. Include name, address, poem title, and page number on each page. Seldom comments on rejected poems. Guidelines available for #10 SASE. Responds in 6 months or less. Always sends prepublication galleys. Pays 2 contributor's copies to domestic contributors, one to foreign contributors. Send materials for review consideration.

☑ ◎ LILLIPUT REVIEW (Specialized: poems of 10 lines or less; short Eastern forms)

282 Main St., Pittsburgh PA 15201-2807. Web site: http://donw714.tripod.com/lillieindex.html. Established 1989. **Contact:** Don Wentworth, editor.

Magazine Needs *Lilliput Review*, published 8-10 times/year, is "shipped two issues at a time, every fourth issue being a broadside that features the work of a single poet." Wants poems in any style or form, no longer than 10 lines. Has published poetry by Pamela Miller Ness, Albert Huffstickler, Charlie Mehrhoff, and Jen Besemer. *Lilliput Review* is 12-16 pages, $4\frac{1}{4} \times 3\frac{1}{2}$, laser-printed on colored paper, stapled. Press run is 400. Subscription: $5 for 6 issues, $10 for 15 issues; $12 for institutions (12 issues). Sample: $1 or SASE. Make checks payable to Don Wentworth.

How to Submit Submit up to 3 poems at a time. Lines/poem: 10 maximum. Considers previously published poems if noted as such. SASE required. Editor comments on submissions "occasionally; I always try to establish human contact." Guidelines available for SASE or on Web site. Responds within 3 months. Pays 2 contributor's copies/poem. Acquires first rights.

Additional Information The Modest Proposal Chapbook Series began in 1994, publishing one chapbook/year, 18-24 pages in length. Has published *Now Now* by Cid Corman. **Chapbook submissions are by invitation only.** Query with standard SASE. Sample chapbook: $3.

Advice "A note above my desk reads 'Clarity & resonance, not necessarily in that order.' The perfect poem for *Lilliput Review* is simple in style and language, and elusive/allusive in meaning and philosophy. *Lilliput* is open to all short poems in approach and theme, including any of the short Eastern forms, traditional or otherwise."

⬱ $⊠ ◎ THE LINK & VISITOR (Specialized: Canadian writers only; Christian; women)
E-mail: linkvis@baptistwomen.com. Web site: www.baptistwomen.com. Established 1878. **Contact:** Editor.

• **Previous editor is retiring; check Web site for new street address.**

Magazine Needs *The Link & Visitor*, published bimonthly, provides "encouragement, insight, and inspiration for Canadian Christian women with Baptist, mission, and egalitarian slant. Poetry must be grounded in a biblical Christian faith, contemporary in style and language, and upbeat, but not naïve." Does not want "anything that has already been better said in the Bible or traditional hymns." *The Link & Visitor* is 24 pages, magazine-sized, offset-printed, with self cover. Receives about 20 poems/year, accepts about 20%. Press run is 3,600. Subscription: $17 CAD, $30 USD and overseas airmail. Sample: $3 CAD.

How to Submit Submit up to 5 poems at a time. Lines/poem: 8 minimum, 30 maximum. Considers previously published poems and simultaneous submissions. Accepts e-mail submissions. Cover letter is required. Include SASE with Canadian stamps. Time between acceptance and publication is up to 2 years. Seldom comments on rejected poems. Usually publishes theme issues. Guidelines available on Web site. Pays $10-25 CAD. Acquires one-time rights.

Advice "Canadian writers only, please."

⬿ LIPS

7002 Blvd. East, #2-26G, Guttenberg NJ 07093. (201)662-1303. Fax: (201)861-2888. E-mail: LBoss79 270@aol.com. Established 1981. **Contact:** Laura Boss, poetry editor.

Magazine Needs *Lips*, published twice/year, takes pleasure "in publishing previously unpublished poets as well as the most established voices in contemporary poetry. We look for quality work: the strongest work of a poet; work that moves the reader; poems that take risks that work. We prefer clarity in the work rather than the abstract. Poems longer than 6 pages present a space problem." Has published poetry by Allen Ginsberg, Michael Benedikt, Maria Gillan, Stanley Barkan, Lyn Lifshin, and Ishmael Reed. *Lips* is about 150 pages, digest-sized, flat-spined. Receives about 16,000 submissions/year, accepts about 1%. Press run is 1,000 (200 subscribers, 100 libraries). Sample: $10 plus $2 for postage.

How to Submit Submit 6 pages maximum at a time. Poems should be typed. Reads submissions September-March only. Guidelines available for SASE. Responds in one month (but has gotten backlogged at times). Sometimes sends prepublication galleys. Pays one contributor's copy. Acquires first rights.

Advice "Remember the 2 T's: Talent and Tenacity."

⬿ THE LISTENING EYE

Kent State Geauga Campus, 14111 Claridon-Troy Rd., Burton OH 44021. (440)286-3840. E-mail: grace_butcher@msn.com. Web site: www.geocities.com/Athens/3716. Established 1970 (for student work), 1990 (as national publication). **Contact:** Grace Butcher, editor.

Magazine Needs *The Listening Eye*, published annually in early fall, prints poetry, short fiction, creative nonfiction, and art. Wants "high literary-quality poetry. Any subject, any style." Does not want "trite images or predictable rhyme." Considers poetry by children and teens if high literary quality. Has published poetry by Alberta Turner, Virgil Suárez, Walter McDonald, and Simon Perchik. *The Listening Eye* is 52-60 pages, digest-sized, professionally printed, saddle-stapled, with card stock cover with b&w or color art. Receives about 200 poems/year, accepts about 5%. Press run is 200. Single copy: $4. Make checks payable to Grace Butcher.

How to Submit Submit up to 4 poems at a time. Lines/poem: "prefer shorter poems (less than two pages), but will consider longer if space allows." Accepts previously published poems "occasionally"; no simultaneous submissions. No e-mail submissions "unless from overseas." Cover letter is required. Poems should be typed, single-spaced, one poem/page—name, address, phone number, and e-mail address in upper left-hand corner of each page—with SASE for return of work. Reads submissions January 1-April 15 only. Time between acceptance and publication is up to 6 months. Poems are circulated to the editor and 2 assistant editors who read and evaluate work separately, then meet for final decisions. Occasionally comments on rejected poems. Guidelines available in magazine or for SASE. Responds in one month. Pays 2 contributor's copies. Acquires first or one-time rights.

Contest/Award Offerings Awards $30 to the best sports poem in each issue.

Advice "I look for tight lines that don't sound like prose; unexpected images or juxtapositions; the unusual use of language; noticeable relationships of sounds; a twist in viewpoint; an ordinary idea in extraordinary language; an amazing and complex idea simply stated; play on words and with words; an obvious love of language. Poets need to read the 'Big 3'—Cummings, Thomas, Hopkins—to see the limits to which language can be taken. Then read the 'Big 2'—Dickinson to see how simultaneously tight, terse, and universal a poem can be, and Whitman to see how sprawling, cosmic, and personal. Then read everything you can find that's being published in literary magazines today, and see how your work compares to all of the above."

🔲 🗹 LITERAL LATTÉ

200 E. 10th St., Suite 240, New York NY 10003. (212)260-5532. E-mail: litlatte@aol.com. Web site: www.literal-latte.com. Established 1994. **Contact:** Dorie Davidson, assistant editor.

Magazine Needs *Literal Latté*, published continually online, is a literary journal of "pure prose, poetry, and art. Open to all styles of poetry—quality is the determining factor." Has published poetry by Allen Ginsberg, Carol Muske, Amy Holman, and John Updike. Receives about 3,000 poems/year, accepts 1%.

How to Submit Considers simultaneous submissions; no previously published poems. No e-mail submissions; postal submissions only. Cover letter is required. Include bio and SASE (or e-mail for response only). Time between acceptance and publication is within one year. Often comments on rejected poems. Guidelines available by e-mail or on Web site. Responds in 5 months.

Additional Information "We will publish an anthology in book form at the end of each year, featuring the best of our Web magazine."

Contest/Award Offerings 1) Sponsors the **Literal Latté** *Poetry Awards*, an annual contest for previously unpublished poems. Offers 1st Prize: $1,000; 2nd Prize: $300; 3rd Prize: $200; all entries considered for publication. Guidelines available for SASE, by e-mail, or on Web site. **Entry fee:** $10 for 4 poems, $15 for 8 poems. **Deadline:** July 19 (postmark). 2) Also sponsors the annual **Literal Latté** *Food Verse Contest*, featuring poems with food as an ingredient. Offers 1st Prize: $500; all entries considered for publication. Guidelines available for SASE, by e-mail, or on Web site. **Entry fee:** $10 for 4 poems, $15 for 8 poems. **Deadline:** January 15 (postmark).

✖ 🔲 🗹 ◎ LITERARY MAMA (Specialized: writing by mothers about mothering)

E-mail: poetry@literarymama.com. (submissions) or info@literarymama.com. (inquiries). Web site: www.literarymama.com. Established 2003. **Contact:** Rachel Iverson, poetry editor.

Magazine Needs *Literary Mama*, published monthly online, prints fiction, poetry, and creative nonfiction by writers of all ages who are "self-identified" mothers. "We also publish literary criticism, book reviews, and profiles about mother writers. *Literary Mama* is doing something for mama-centric literature that no one else is doing. The poetry, fiction, and creative nonfiction that may be too long, too complex, too ambiguous, too deep, too raw, too irreverent, too ironic, too body-conscious, and too full of long words for the general reader will find a home with us. While there are plenty of online literary magazines that publish writing like this, none devote themselves exclusively to writing about motherhood." Wants poems of any form that are "extraordinary for their vision, craftsmanship, integrity, and originality; centered around parenting; written by writers who are also self-identified mothers: biological, non-biological, step, transgender, adoptive." Receives about 70 poems/month, accepts about 10-15%.

How to Submit Submit 4 poems maximum at a time. Considers previously published poems (if they are not otherwise available on the Web) and simultaneous submissions. Accepts e-mail submissions (pasted into body of message; no attachments); no disk submissions. Cover letter is required. "Please include name, brief bio, and contact information." Reads submissions year round except for December and June. Time between acceptance and publication is 2-8 weeks. "The final decision about all poetry submissions is made by the poetry editor." Sometimes comments on rejected poems. Guidelines available on Web site. Responds in 6-8 weeks. No payment. Acquires first rights for previously unpublished work, non-exclusive one-time rights for reprints. Reviews books/chapbooks of poetry. Query via e-mail prior to sending materials for review consideration.

☐ THE LITERARY REVIEW: AN INTERNATIONAL JOURNAL OF CONTEMPORARY WRITING

Fairleigh Dickinson University, 285 Madison Ave., Madison NJ 07940. (973)443-8564. Fax: (973)443-8364. E-mail: tlr@fdu.edu. Web site: www.theliteraryreview.org. Established 1957. **Contact:** Walter Cummins, editor-in-chief.

Magazine Needs *The Literary Review*, published quarterly, seeks "work by new and established poets that reflects a sensitivity to literary standards and the poetic form." No specifications as to form, length, style, subject matter, or purpose. Has published poetry by David Citino, Rick Mulkey, Virgil Suárez, Gary Fincke, and Dale M. Kushner. *The Literary Review* is about 180 pages, digest-sized, professionally printed, flat-spined, with glossy color cover. Receives about 1,200 submissions/year, accepts 100-150. Press run is 2,000 (800 subscribers, one-third are overseas). Sample: $7 domestic, $8 outside U.S.; request a "general issue."

How to Submit Submit up to 5 typed poems at a time. Considers simultaneous submissions. No fax or e-mail submissions. Do not submit during the summer months of June, July, and August. Sometimes comments on rejected poems. Publishes theme issues. Responds in 4-6 months. Always sends prepublication galleys. Pays 2 contributor's copies. Acquires first rights. Reviews books of poetry in 500 words, single-book format. Send materials for review consideration.

Also Offers *TLR Online*, available on the Web site, features original work not published in the print edition. Has published poetry by Renée Ashley and Catherine Kasper.

Advice "Read a general issue of the magazine carefully before submitting."

⊞ ▣ ◯ LIVING POETS MAGAZINE

Dragonheart Press, 11 Menin Rd., Allestree, Derby DE22 2NL England. E-mail: submissions@dragonheartpress.com. Web site: www.dragonheartpress.com. Established 1995. **Contact:** Sean Woodward, executive editor.

Magazine Needs *Living Poets Magazine*, published irregularly online, provides a showcase for poetry. Wants "crafted poetry with strong imagery." Does not want "constrained rhyming structures." Receives about 400 poems/year, accepts about 20%. Sample: $10 (printable from PDF). Make checks payable to S. Woodward.

How to Submit Submit 3 poems at a time. Considers previously published poems and simultaneous submissions. Accepts e-mail submissions. Cover letter is preferred. Include bio and publication credits. Time between acceptance and publication is 1-2 months. Often comments on rejected poems. Publishes theme issues. Guidelines available for SASE, by e-mail, or on Web site. Responds in 3 months. Pays one contributor's copy. Reviews books/chapbooks of poetry or other magazines in single-book format. Send materials for review consideration to Review Editor, Dragonheart Press.

Contest/Award Offerings Sponsors Dragonheart Press Annual Poetry Competition. **Deadline:** December 31. Guidelines available for SASE (or SAE and IRC) or by e-mail (competition@dragonheartpress.com).

◳ LONE STARS MAGAZINE

4219 Flint Hill St., San Antonio TX 78230-1619. Established 1992. **Contact:** Milo Rosebud, editor/publisher.

Magazine Needs *Lone Stars,* published 3 times/year, features "contemporary poetry." Wants poetry "that holds a continuous line of thought." Does not want "profanity." Considers poetry by children and teens. Has published poetry by Bernie Bernstein, Crayton Moody, Eve J. Blohm, and Cecil Boyce. *Lone Stars* is 25 pages, magazine-sized, photocopied, saddle-stapled, bound with tape. Press run is 200 (100 subscribers, 3 libraries). Single copy: $5.50; subscription: $18. Sample: $4.50.

How to Submit Submit 3-5 poems at a time. Considers previously published poems and simultaneous submissions. Cover letter is preferred. Submit poems formatted and "typed the way you want them in print." **Charges reading fee of $1 per poem.** Time between acceptance and publication is 6 months. Publishes theme issues. Guidelines available for SASE. Responds within 3 months. Acquires one-time rights.

Contest/Award Offerings Sponsors annual "Songbook" Lyric Poetry Contest. Details available for SASE.

Advice "Submit poetry that expresses a reasonable train of thought."

▣ ◎ LONG ISLAND QUARTERLY (Specialized: Long Island, NY poets)

P.O. Box 114, Northport NY 11768. E-mail: Liquarterly@aol.com. Web site: www.poetrybay.com. Established 1990. **Contact:** George Wallace, editor/publisher.

Magazine Needs *Long Island Quarterly,* published online, is a journal of poetry (mostly lyric free verse) by people on or from Long Island. "Surprise us with fresh language. No conventional imagery, self-indulgent confessionalism, compulsive article-droppers." Has published poetry by Edmund Pennant and David Ignatow.

How to Submit Submit 3 poems at a time. Accepts e-mail submissions (preferred; pasted into body of message; "no attachments will be opened"). Include name and address on each page for postal entries; submissions without SASE are not returned. Cover letter with brief bio stating connection to Long Island region is required. Responds in 3 months.

Advice "1) Go beyond yourself; 2) Don't be afraid to fictionalize; 3) Don't write your autobiography—if you're worth it, maybe someone else will."

✪ ◎ LOS

150 N. Catalina St., No. 2, Los Angeles CA 90004. E-mail: lospoesy@earthlink.net. Web site: http://home.earthlink.net/~lospoesy. Established 1991. **Contact:** The Editors.

Magazine Needs *Los,* published 4 times/year, features poetry. Has published poetry by John P. Campbell, Jean Esteve, Mary Kasimor, Rich Murray, Shamsur Rahman and Charles Wuest. *Los* is digest-sized and saddle-stapled. Press run is 100.

How to Submit Accepts e-mail submissions (pasted into body of message or as attachment). Time between acceptance and publication is up to one month. Guidelines available on Web site. Responds in 3 months. Pays one contributor's copy.

◳ LOUISIANA LITERATURE

SLU Box 10792, Southeastern Louisiana University, Hammond LA 70402. (504)549-5022. E-mail: lalit@selu.edu. Web site: http://louisianaliterature.org. **Contact:** Jack Bedell, editor.

Magazine Needs *Louisiana Literature,* published twice/year, considers "creative work from anyone, though we strive to showcase our state's talent. We appreciate poetry that shows firm control and craft; is sophisticated yet accessible to a broad readership. We don't use highly experimental work." Has published poetry by Claire Bateman, Elton Glaser, Gray Jacobik, Vivian Shipley, D.C. Berry, and Judy Longley. *Louisiana Literature* is 150 pages, $6^3/_4 \times 9^3/_4$, handsomely printed on heavy matte stock, flat-spined, with matte card cover. Single copy: $8 for individuals; subscription: $12 for individuals, $12.50 for institutions.

How to Submit Submit 3-5 poems at a time. No simultaneous submissions. No fax or e-mail submissions. "Send cover letter, including bio to use in the event of acceptance. Enclose SASE and specify whether work is to be returned or discarded." Reads submissions year round, "although we work more slowly in summer." Publishes theme issues. Guidelines available for SASE or on Web site. Sometimes sends prepublication galleys. Pays 2 contributor's copies. Send materials for review consideration; include cover letter.

Contest/Award Offerings Sponsors The *Louisiana Literature* Prize for Poetry, offering $400 and publication. U.S. residents may submit 1-5 unpublished poems, totaling 250 lines, on any topic. All entries considered for publication in *Louisiana Literature*. **Entry fee:** $12 (includes one-year subscription). **Deadline:** April 16. Guidelines available for SASE or on Web site.

Advice "It's important to us that the poets we publish be in control of their creations. Too much of what we see seems arbitrary."

THE LOUISIANA REVIEW (Specialized: LA poets, LA-related poetry)

Division of Liberal Arts, Louisiana State University at Eunice, P.O. Box 1129, Eunice LA 70535. (337)550-1315. E-mail: bfonteno@lsue.edu. Web site: www.lsue.edu/LA-Review/. Established 1999. **Contact:** Dr. Billy Fontenot, editor.

Magazine Needs *The Louisiana Review*, published annually during the fall or spring semester, offers "Louisiana poets, writers, and artists a place to showcase their most beautiful pieces. Others may submit Louisiana- or Southern-related poetry, stories, and b&w art, as well as interviews with Louisiana writers. We want to publish the highest-quality poetry, fiction, art, and drama." Wants "strong imagery, metaphor, and evidence of craft." Does not want "sing-song rhymes, abstract, religious, or overly sentimental work." Has published poetry by Gary Snyder, Antler, David Cope, and Catfish McDaris. *The Louisiana Review* is 100-200 pages, digest-sized, professionally printed, perfect-bound. Receives up to 2,000 poems/year, accepts 40-50. Press run is 300-600. Single copy: $5.

How to Submit Submit up to 5 poems at a time. No previously published poems. No fax or e-mail submissions. "Include cover letter indicating your association with Louisiana. Name and address should appear on each page." Reads submissions year round. Time between acceptance and publication is up to 2 years. Pays one contributor's copy. Poets retain all rights.

Advice "Be true to your own voice and style."

LOVE'S CHANCE MAGAZINE (Specialized: love/romance)

Suzerain Enterprises, P.O. Box 60336, Worcester MA 01606. Established 1994. **Contact:** Milton Kerr, editor/publisher.

Magazine Needs *Love's Chance Magazine*, published 3 times/year, gives "unpublished writers a chance to be published and to be paid for their efforts." Wants romance. Does not want "porn, ageism, sexism, racism, children in sexual situations." Has published poetry by A.H. Ferguson, Wayne Adams, Robert Donald Spector, Cecil Boyce, and Ellaraine Lockie. *Love's Chance Magazine* is 15-30 pages, magazine-sized, photocopied, side-stapled, with computer-designed paper cover. Receives about 500 poems/year, accepts about 10%. Press run is 100 (70-80 subscribers). Subscription: $12/year. Sample: $4. Make checks payable to Suzerain Enterprises.

How to Submit Submit 3 poems at a time. Lines/poem: 20 maximum. Considers previously published poems and simultaneous submissions. Cover letter is preferred. "Proofread for spelling errors, neatness; must be typewritten in standard manuscript form. No handwritten manuscripts." Time between acceptance and publication is 3 months. Often comments on rejected poems. Guidelines available for SASE. Responds in 6 weeks. Acquires first or one-time rights.

Advice "Proofread your work. Edit carefully. Always include business-sized SASE with correct postage. Don't let rejection slips get you down. Keep submitting and don't give up. Don't be afraid to write something different.''

⭐ $◻ LUCIDITY POETRY JOURNAL (Specialized: submission fee required)

Bear House Press, 14781 Memorial Dr., #10, Houston TX 77079-5210. (281)920-1795. E-mail: tedbadger1@yahoo.com. Established 1985. **Contact:** Ted O. Badger, editor.

Magazine Needs *Lucidity Poetry Journal*, published semiannually, **requires a submission fee—$1/poem for "juried" selection** by a panel of judges, or **$2/poem to compete for cash awards** of $15, $10, and $5. All winners paid in both cash and copies. Also publishes 6 pages of Succint Verse—poems of 12 lines or less—in most issues. "We expect them to be pithy and significant, and there is no reading/entry fee if sent along with Cash Award or Juried poems. Just think of all poetic forms that are 12 lines or less: cinquain, limerick, etheree, haiku, senryu, lune, etc., not to mention quatrain, triolet, and couplets." In addition, a few guest contributors are invited to submit to each issue. Contributors are encouraged to subscribe or buy a copy of the magazine. No restrictions on form; space limit due to format. "We look for poetry that is life-related and has clarity and substance. We dedicate our journal to publishing those poets who express their thoughts, feelings, and impressions about the human scene with clarity and substance." Does not want "religious, butterfly, or vulgar poems." *Lucidity* is 72 pages, digest-sized, photocopied from typescript, saddle-stapled, with matte card cover. Press run is 280 (225 subscribers); some distributed free to selected winners. Subscription: $7. Sample (including guidelines): $2.

How to Submit Submit 3-5 poems in each category at a time. Lines/poem: 36 maximum (including spaces). Considers simultaneous submissions. No e-mail submissions. Time between acceptance and publication is 6 months to a year. Guidelines available for SASE or by e-mail. Responds in 12-18 months. Pays cash and one contributor's copy. Acquires one-time rights.

Additional Information Bear House Press is "**a self-publishing arrangement** by which poets can pay to have booklets published in the same format as *Lucidity* (but with perfect binding), with prices beginning at 100 copies of 32 pages for $336." Publishes about 6 chapbooks/year.

Also Offers Sponsors the *Lucidity* Poets' Ozark Retreat, a 3-day retreat held during the month of April in Eureka Springs, AR.

Advice "Small press journals offer the best opportunity to most poets for publication and recognition."

⭐ ☑ LULLWATER REVIEW

Emory University, P.O. Box 22036, Atlanta GA 30322. (404)727-6184. E-mail: LullwaterReview@yahoo.com. Established 1990. **Contact:** Acree Graham and Stephanie Yoder, Editors-in-Chief.

Magazine Needs *Lullwater Review*, published in May and December, prints poetry, short fiction, and artwork. Wants poetry of any genre with strong imagery, original voice, on any subject. Does not want profanity or pornographic material. Has published poetry by Amy Greenfield, Peter Serchuk, Katherine McCord, Virgil Suárez, and Ha Jin. *Lullwater Review* is 104-120 pages, magazine-sized, with full-color cover, includes b&w pictures. Press run is 2,500. Subscription: $12. Sample: $5.

How to Submit Submit 6 or fewer poems at a time. Considers simultaneous submissions; no previously published poems. No e-mail submissions; postal submissions only. Cover letter is preferred. Prefers poems single-spaced with name and contact info on each page. "Poems longer than one page should include page numbers. We must have a SASE with which to reply. Poems may not be returned." Reads submissions September 1-May 15 only. Time between acceptance and publication is up to 6 months. Poems are circulated to an editorial board. "A poetry editor selects approximately 16 poems per week to be reviewed by editors, who then discuss and decide on the status of each poem." Seldom comments on rejected poems. Sometimes publishes theme issues. Guidelines available for SASE. Responds in 5 months maximum. Pays 3 contributor's copies. Acquires first North American serial rights.

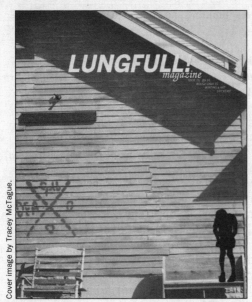

Cover image by Tracey McTague.

Editor Brendan Lorber notes that *LUNGFULL!magazine*'s cover is 100% waterproof. "Never again will you have to decide between reading and the pleaure of bathing, swimming or walking in the rain." The laminated cover of No. 15 features visual art by Tracey McTague.

Contest/Award Offerings Sponsors the annual Lullwater Prize for Poetry. Award is $500 and publication. Guidelines available for SASE. **Entry fee:** $8. **Deadline:** November 1.

Advice "Keep writing, find your voice, don't get frustrated. Please be patient with us regarding response time. We are an academic institution."

☑ LUNGFULL!MAGAZINE (Specialized: rough draft to finished poem)

316 23rd St., Brooklyn NY 11215. E-mail: lungfull @rcn.com. Web site: http://lungfull.org. Established 1994. **Contact:** Brendan Lorber, editor/ publisher.

- *LUNGFULL!* was the recipient of a multi-year grant from the New York State Council for the Arts.

Magazine Needs *LUNGFULL!magazine*, published annually, prints "the rough draft of each poem, in addition to the final, so that the reader can see the creative process from start to finish. We recommend you get a copy before submitting." Wants "any style as long as it's urgent, immediate, playful, probing, showing great thought while remaining vivid and grounded. Poems should be as interesting as conversation." Does not want "empty poetic abstractions." Has published poetry by Alice Notley, Lorenzo Thomas, Tracie Morris, Hal Sirowitz, Eileen Myles, and John Ashbery. *LUNGFULL!* is 200 pages, $8\frac{1}{2} \times 7$, offset-printed, desktop-published, perfect-bound, with glossy waterproof 2-color cover, includes ads. Receives about 1,000 poems/year, accepts 3%. Press run is 1,200 (300 subscribers, 800 shelf sales); 100 distributed free to contributors. Single copy: $9.95; subscription: $39.80 for 4 issues, $19.90 for 2 issues. Sample: $11.50. Make checks payable to Brendan Lorber, or order online.

How to Submit Submit up to 6 poems at a time. Considers previously published poems and simultaneous submissions (with notification; "however, other material will be considered first and stands a much greater chance of publication"). Accepts e-mail submissions. "We prefer hard copy by USPS—but e-submissions can be made in the body of the e-mail itself; submissions with attachments will be deleted unread." Cover letter is preferred. Time between acceptance and publication is up to 8 months. "The editor looks at each piece for its own merit and for how well it will fit into the specific issue being planned based on other accepted work." Guidelines available by e-mail. Responds in one year. Pays 2 contributor's copies.

Also Offers "Each copy of *LUNGFULL!magazine* contains a Cultural Attache Sticker—they can be removed from the magazine and placed on any flat surface to make it a little less flat. Previous stickers contain statements like 'Together we can keep the poor poor' and 'You only live once— just not as long as in countries with free healthcare.' "

Advice "Failure demands a certain dedication. Practice makes imperfection, and imperfection makes room for the amazing. Only outside the bounds of acceptable conclusions can the astounding transpire, can writing contain anything beyond twittering snack food logic and the utilitarian pistons of mundane engineering."

☑ ◎ THE LYRIC (Specialized: rhymed poetry, traditional)

P.O. Box 110, Jericho Corners VT 05465. Phone/fax: (802)899-3993. E-mail: Lyric@sover.net. Established 1921. **Contact:** Jean Mellichamp-Milliken, editor.

Magazine Needs *The Lyric*, published quarterly, is "the oldest magazine in North America in continuous publication devoted to traditional poetry." Prints about 55 poems/issue. Wants "rhymed verse in traditional forms, for the most part, with an occasional piece of blank or free verse. Our themes are varied, ranging from religious ecstasy to humor to raw grief, but we feel no compulsion to shock, embitter, or confound our readers. We also avoid poems about contemporary political or social problems—'grief but not grievances,' as Frost put it. Frost is helpful in other ways: If yours is more than a lover's quarrel with life, we are not your best market. And most of our poems are accessible on first or second reading. Frost again: 'Don't hide too far away.' " Has published poetry by Rhina P. Espaillat, Gail White, Joseph Awad, Alfred Dorn, Ruth Harrison, and Glenna Holloway. *The Lyric* is 32 pages, digest-sized, professionally printed with varied typography, with matte card cover. Press run is 750 (600 subscribers, 40 libraries). Receives about 3,000 submissions/year, accepts 5%. Subscription: $15/year, $28/2 years, $38/3 years (U.S.), $17/year for Canada and other countries (in U.S. funds only). Sample: $4.

How to Submit Submit up to 6 poems at a time. Lines/poem: 40 maximum. Considers simultaneous submissions (although "not preferred"); no previously published poems. Cover letter is "often helpful, but not required. Subscription will not affect publication of submitted poetry." Guidelines available for SASE or by e-mail. Responds in 3 months ("average; inquire after 6 months"). Pays one contributor's copy.

Contest/Award Offerings All contributors are eligible for quarterly and annual prizes totaling $750. Also offers the Lyric College Contest, open to undergraduate students. Awards prize of $400. **Deadline:** December 15. Send entries to Tanya Cimonetti, 1393 Spear St., S., Burlington VT 05403.

Advice "Our *raison d'être* has been the encouragement of form, music, rhyme, and accessibility in poetry. As we witness the growing tide of appreciation for traditional/lyric poetry, we are proud to have stayed the course for 85 years, helping keep the roots of poetry alive."

◙ THE MACGUFFIN

Schoolcraft College, 18600 Haggerty Rd., Livonia MI 48152-2696. (734)462-4400, ext. 5327. Fax: (734)462-4679. E-mail: macguffin@schoolcraft.edu. Web site: www.schoolcraft.edu/macguffin. Established 1984. **Contact:** Carol Was, poetry editor.

Magazine Needs *The MacGuffin*, published 3 times/year, prints "the best poetry, fiction, nonfiction, and artwork we find. We have no thematic or stylistic biases. We look for well-crafted poetry." Does not want "pornography, triteness, and sloppy poetry. We do not publish haiku, concrete, or light verse." Has published poetry by Susan Terris, Gabriel Welsch, Linda Nemec Foster, Conrad Hilberry, and Laurence Lieberman. *The MacGuffin* is 160 pages, 6×9, perfect-bound, with color cover. Press run is 500 (250 subscribers); the rest are local sales, contributor copies, and distribution to college offices. Subscription: $22. Sample: $6.

How to Submit Submit no more than 5 poems at a time. Lines/poem: 400 maximum. Considers simultaneous submissions if informed; no previously published poems. Accepts fax, e-mail (as Word attachment only; do not paste into body of message), and disk/CD submissions. Cover letter is required. "List titles and brief bio in cover letter. Do not staple work." Poems should be typed, single-spaced, one per page. Poet's name, address, and e-mail should appear on each page. Include SASE. Guidelines available for SASE, by fax, e-mail, or on Web site. Responds in 2-4 months. Pays 2 contributor's copies plus discount on additional copies. Rights revert to poets upon publication.

Contest/Award Offerings The National Poet Hunt Contest (see separate listing in Contests & Awards).

▣ ◙ MAD POETS REVIEW

Mad Poets Society, P.O. Box 1248, Media PA 19063-8248. E-mail: Madpoets@comcast.net. (inquiries only). Web site: www.madpoetssociety.com. Established 1987. **Contact:** Eileen M. D'Angelo, editor.

Magazine Needs *Mad Poets Review*, published annually in October/November, aims "to promote thought-provoking, moving poetry, and encourage beginning poets. We don't care if you have a 'name' or a publishing history if your poetry is well-crafted. We are anxious for work with *joie de vivre* that startles and inspires." No restrictions on subject, form, or style. "Just because our name is *Mad Poets Review* doesn't mean we want mad ramblings masquerading under the guise of poetry." Does not want obscenities simply for shock value. Has published poetry by Gerald Stern, Naomi Shihab Nye, Greg Djanikian, Harry Humes, Maria Mazziotti Gillan, and Nathalie Anderson. *Mad Poets Review* is about 180 pages, digest-sized, attractively printed, perfect-bound, with glossy, full-color laminated cover. Receives about 2,000 poems/year, accepts 100. Press run is 300. Single copy: $12. Sample: $13.50 (includes p&h). Make checks payable to either Mad Poets Society or *Mad Poets Review*.

How to Submit Submit 6 poems at a time. Considers previously published poems and simultaneous submissions. No e-mail submissions; postal submissions only. "Include 3-4 sentences about yourself suitable for our Bio Notes section. Mark envelope 'contest' or 'magazine.' Poems without a SASE with adequate postage will not be returned or acknowledged." Reads submissions January 1-June 1 only. Time between acceptance and publication is 8 months. Often comments on rejected poems. Responds in 3 months. Pays one contributor's copy. Acquires one-time rights.

Contest/Award Offerings Sponsors the annual *Mad Poets Review* Poetry Competition. Awards cash prizes determined by the number of entries received. Grand Prize winner and finalists will be published in an upcoming issue of *Mad Poets Review*. Submissions must be unpublished. See guidelines for complete entry requirements. **Entry fee:** $10 for up to 6 poems. Make checks payable to Mad Poets Society. **Deadline:** June 30. Guidelines available on Web site.

Also Offers "The Mad Poets Society is an active organization in Pennsylvania. We run 70-80 events per year and have monthly meetings for members for critique and club business; coordinate a children's contest through Delaware County School system; run an annual poetry festival the first Sunday in October; sponsor Mad Poets Bonfires for local poets and musicians; and publish newsletters that offer the most comprehensive listing available anywhere in the tri-state area. We send quarterly newsletters to members."

Advice "It is advised that if someone is going to submit, they see what kind of poetry we publish."

$ 🔲 ◎ THE MAGAZINE OF FANTASY & SCIENCE FICTION

P.O. Box 3447, Hoboken NJ 07030. E-mail: FandSF@aol.com. Web site: www.fsfmag.com. Established 1949. **Contact:** Gordon Van Gelder, editor.

- *The Magazine of Fantasy & Science Fiction* is a past winner of the Hugo Award and World Fantasy Award.

Magazine Needs *The Magazine of Fantasy & Science Fiction*, published monthly 11 times/year, is "one of the longest-running magazines devoted to the literature of the fantastic." Wants only poetry that deals with the fantastic or the science-fictional. Has published poetry by Rebecca Kavaler, Elizabeth Bear, and Robert Frazier. *The Magazine of Fantasy & Science Fiction* is 160 pages, digest-sized, offset-printed, perfect-bound, with glossy cover, includes ads. Receives about 20-40 poems/year, accepts about 1%. Press run is 35,000 (20,000 subscribers). Single copy: $4.50; subscription: $32.97. Sample: $5. Make checks payable to *The Magazine of Fantasy & Science Fiction*.

How to Submit Submit 1-3 poems at a time. No previously published poems or simultaneous submissions. No e-mail or disk submissions. Time between acceptance and publication is up to 2 years, but usually about 9 months. "I buy poems very infrequently—just when one hits me right." Seldom comments on rejected poems. Guidelines available for SASE or on Web site. Responds in up to one month. Always sends prepublication galleys. Pays $50/poem and 2 contributor's copies. Acquires first North American serial rights.

$⊘ ◎ THE MAGAZINE OF SPECULATIVE POETRY (Specialized: horror; fantasy; science fiction; science)

P.O. Box 564, Beloit WI 53512. Established 1984. **Contact:** Roger Dutcher, editor.

Magazine Needs *The Magazine of Speculative Poetry*, published biannually, features "the best new speculative poetry. We are especially interested in narrative form, but open to any form, any length (within reason); interested in a variety of styles. We're looking for the best of the new poetry utilizing the ideas, imagery, and approaches developed by speculative fiction, and will welcome experimental techniques as well as the fresh employment of traditional forms." Has published poetry by Mark Rudolph, Bruce Boston, Joanne Merriam, Sandra Lindow, and Sonya Taaffe. *The Magazine of Speculative Poetry* is 24-28 pages, digest-sized, offset-printed, saddle-stapled, with matte card cover. Receives about 500 poems/year, accepts less than 5%. Press run is 150-200. Subscription: $19/4 issues. Sample: $5.

How to Submit Submit 3-5 poems at a time. Lines/poem: "Some poems run two or three pages, but rarely anything longer. We're a small magazine, we can't print epics." No previously published poems or simultaneous submissions. "We like cover letters, but they aren't necessary. We like to see where you heard of us; the names of the poems submitted; a statement if the poetry manuscript is disposable; a big enough SASE; and if you've been published, some recent places." Poems should be double-spaced. Comments on rejected poems "on occasion." Guidelines available for SASE. Responds in up to 2 months. Pays 3¢/word ($7 minimum, $25 maximum) and one contributor's copy. Acquires first North American serial rights. "All rights revert to author upon publication, except for permission to reprint in any 'Best of' or compilation volume. Payment will be made for such publication." Reviews books of speculative poetry. Query regarding unsolicited reviews, interviews, and articles. Send materials for review consideration.

◒ MAIN STREET RAG

P.O. Box 690100, Charlotte NC 28227-7001. (704)573-2516. E-mail: editor@mainstreetrag.com. Web site: www.MainStreetRag.com. Established 1996. **Contact:** M. Scott Douglass, editor/publisher.

Magazine Needs *Main Street Rag*, published quarterly, prints "poetry, short fiction, essays, interviews, reviews, photos, art, and cartoons (political, satirical). We like publishing good material from people who are interested in more than notching another publishing credit, people who support small independent publishers like ourselves." Will consider "almost anything," but prefers "writing with an edge—either gritty or bitingly humorous. Contributors are advised to visit our Web site prior to submission to confirm current needs." Has published poetry by Silvia Curbelo, Sean Thomas Dougherty, Denise Duhamel, Cathy Essinger, Ishle Yi Park, and Dennis Must. *Main Street Rag* is about 96 pages, digest-sized, perfect-bound, with 100 lb. laminated color cover. Receives about 2,500 submissions/year; publishes 30-40 poems/issue. Press run is about 1,000 (300 subscribers, 15 libraries). "Sold nationally in bookstores." Single copy: $7; subscription: $20/year, $35 for 2 years.

How to Submit Submit 6 pages of poetry at a time. No previously published poems or simultaneous submissions. **Accepts e-mail submissions from subscribers only**. Cover letter is preferred. "No bios or credits—let the work speak for itself." Time between acceptance and publication is up to one year. Guidelines available for SASE, by e-mail, or on Web site. Responds within 6 weeks. Pays one contributor's copy. Acquires first North American print rights.

Contest/Award Offerings Main Street Rag's Annual Poetry Book Award and Main Street Rag's Annual Chapbook Contest (see separate listings in Contests & Awards).

Advice "Small press independents exist by and for writers. Without their support (and the support of readers), we have no reason to exist. Sampling first is always appreciated."

☒ $☑ THE MALAHAT REVIEW

University of Victoria, P.O. Box 1700, STN CSC, Victoria BC V8W 2Y2 Canada. (250)721-8524. Fax: (250)472-5051. E-mail: malahat@uvic.ca (inquiries only). Web site: www.malahatreview.ca. Established 1967. **Contact:** John Barton, editor.

Magazine Needs *The Malahat Review*, published quarterly, is "a high-quality, visually appealing literary journal that has earned the praise of notable literary figures throughout North America. Its purpose is to publish and promote poetry and fiction of a very high standard, both Canadian and international." Wants "various styles, lengths, and themes. The criterion is excellence." Has published poetry by Steven Heighton and Jan Zwicky. Receives about 2,000 poems/year, accepts about 100. Has 1,000 subscribers, of which 300 are libraries. Subscription: $40 CAD for individuals, $50 CAD for institutions (or U.S. equivalent). Sample: $16.45 USD.

How to Submit Submit 5-10 poems at a time. No previously published poems or simultaneous submissions. No e-mail submmissions; postal submissions only. Include SASE with Canadian stamps or IRC with each submission. Guidelines available for SASE (or SAE and IRC). Responds usually within 3 months. Pays $35 CAD per printed page, 2 contributor's copies, and one year's subscription. Acquires first world serial rights. Reviews Canadian books of poetry.

Contest/Award Offerings 1) The biennial *Long Poem Prize* offers 2 awards of $400 CAD each, plus publication and payment at $35 CAD per page, for a long poem or cycle (10-20 printed pages). Include name and address on a separate page. Guidelines available on Web site. **Entry fee:** $35 CAD, $35 USD ($40 USD for foreign entries). All entrants receive a one-year subscription to *The Malahat Review*. **Deadline:** March 1 of alternate years (2009, 2011, etc.). 2) The biennial *Far Horizons Award for Poetry* offers $500 CAD for a poem of up to 60 lines. Restricted to poets who have not yet published a full-length book (48 + pages). Submit up to 3 poems per entry. Include name and address on a separate page. Guidelines available on Web site. **Entry fee:** $25 CAD, $25 USD ($30 USD for foreign entries). All entrants receive a one-year subscription to *The Malahat Review*. **Deadline:** May 1 of alternate years (2008, 2010, etc.). 3) Presents the *P.K. Page Founders' Award for Poetry*; $1,000 to the author of the best poem or sequence of poems to be published in The *Malahat Review*'s quarterly issues during the previous calendar year.

▣ ☑ MANNEQUIN ENVY

E-mail: poetry@mannequinenvy.com. Web site: www.mannequinenvy.com. Established 2004. **Contact:** Patrick Carrington, poetry editor.

Magazine Needs *Mannequin Envy*, published quarterly online, is a journal of visual and literary arts. Wants "distilled writing that gets to the point without just painting a pretty picture. Improvisational, imperfect, innovative, quirky, non-linear, raw, brave. There is no shortage of really nice poems out there. We do not want 'nice.' We want to feel a physical reaction to your work. Nausea. Embarrassment. Arousal. Something. Make the mannequin turn and notice." Has published poetry by John Sweet, Lynn Strongin, Kelley White, Tim Mayo, and Charles Fishman. Receives about 2,000 poems/year, accepts about 10%.

How to Submit Submit 3-5 poems at a time. Considers simultaneous submissions; no previously published poems. Accepts e-mail submissions (pasted into body of message); no disk submissions. Cover letter is preferred. "Please check guidelines online." Reads submissions as follows: March 1-30 (Spring), May 1-30 (Summer), July 1-30 (Fall), and October 1-30 (Winter). "**Summer issue not open to regular submissions**. Featuring collections of the combined visual art and poetry of individual artists. Submit to Jennifer VanBuren, Editor, at editor@mannequinevy.com. See Web site for more details." Time between acceptance and publication is one month. Rarely comments on rejected poems. Guidelines available on Web site. Responds in 10 weeks. Always sends prepublication galleys. No payment. Acquires first rights; "we request the right to publish work in one anthology, in print or otherwise." Rights revert to poet upon publication. "We will nominate poets for the Pushcart Prize."

$☑ MĀNOA: A PACIFIC JOURNAL OF INTERNATIONAL WRITING

1733 Donaghho Rd., Honolulu HI 96822. Fax: (808)956-3083. E-mail: mjournal-l@hawaii.edu. Web site: http://manoajournal.hawaii.edu. Established 1989. **Contact:** Frank Stewart, poetry editor.

● Poetry published in *Mānoa* has also appeared in volumes of *The Best American Poetry*.

Magazine Needs *Mānoa*, published twice/year, is a general interest literary magazine that considers work "in many forms and styles, regardless of the author's publishing history. However, we are not for the beginning writer. It is best to look at a sample copy of the journal before submitting." Has published poetry by Arthur Sze, Ai, Linda Gregg, Jane Hirshfield, and Ha Jin. *Mānoa* is 240 pages, 7×10, offset-printed, flat-spined. Receives about 1,000 poems/year, accepts 2%. Press run is more than 2,500 (several hundred subscribers, 130 libraries, 400 shelf sales). "In addition, *Mānoa* is available through Project Muse to about 900 institutional subscribers throughout the world." Subscription: $22/year. Sample: $10.

How to Submit Submit 3-5 poems at a time. No e-mail submissions. Seldom comments on rejected poems. Guidelines available on Web site. Responds in 6 weeks. Always sends prepublication galleys. Pays "competitive" amount plus 2 contributor's copies.

Advice "We are not a regional journal, but each issue features a particular part of Asia or the Pacific; these features, which include poetry, are assembled by guest editors. The rest of each issue features work by poets from the U.S. and elsewhere. We welcome the opportunity to read poetry from throughout the country, but we are not interested in genre or formalist writing for its own sake, or in casual impressions of the Asia-Pacific region."

☆ ☑ MANY MOUNTAINS MOVING: A LITERARY JOURNAL OF DIVERSE CONTEMPORARY VOICES

549 Rider Ridge Dr., Longmont CO 80501. (303)485-0800, ext. 2. E-mail: info@mmminc.org. Web site: www.mmminc.org. Established 1994. **Contact:** Poetry Editor.

● Poetry published in *Many Mountains Moving* has also been included in volumes of *The Best American Poetry* and *The Pushcart Prize*.

Magazine Needs *Many Mountains Moving: a literary journal of diverse contemporary voices*, published annually in the fall, welcomes "previously unpublished poetry, fiction, nonfiction, reviews, and art from writers and artists of all walks of life." Wants "all forms of poetry, welcoming writing with intelligence, wit, craft, and guile, and outstanding, exciting works that reflect the diversity of our culture. Translations and book reviews are welcome." Has published Robert Bly, Lorna Dee Cervantes, Amiri Baraka, Allen Ginsberg, Yusef Komunyakaa, and Adirenne Rich. *Many Mountains Moving* is over 200 pages, digest-sized, with 4-color glossy cover. Receives 6,000 poems/year, accepts 4%. Press run is 600. Single copy: $12; subscription: $12/year.

How to Submit Submit 3-8 poems at a time. Considers simultaneous submissions; no previously published poems. Cover letter is encouraged. "See guidelines on the Web site for reading periods for paper submissions. Year-round online submissions **with a $2 reading fee** atwww.mmm-submis sions.org." Seldom comments on rejected poems. Guidelines available on Web site. Responds within 3 months; "if we are seriously considering a submission, we may take longer." Sends prepublication galleys (PDFs by e-mail). Pays one contributors copy; additional copies available at discount. Acquires first North American serial rights and "rights to publish in a future edition of the *Best of Many Mountains Moving Anthology*."

Contest/Award Offerings Many Mountains Moving Poetry Book Contest (see separate listing in Contests & Awards) and The Many Mountains Moving Poetry and Flash Fiction Contests. Guidelines available on Web site.

Advice "Although we feature many established poets, we also publish many new writers in every issue. We recommend that poets read through at least one issue to familiarize themselves with the type of work we generally publish."

◪ MARGIE/THE AMERICAN JOURNAL OF POETRY

P.O. Box 250, Chesterfield MO 63006-0250. Fax: (636)532-0539. E-mail: margiereview@aol.com. Web site: www.margiereview.com. **Established 2001. Contact:** Robert Nazarene, founding editor.

- Multiple selections from *MARGIE* have appeared in *The Best American Poetry*.

Magazine Needs *MARGIE/The American Journal of Poetry*, published annually in the fall, features "superlative poetry. No limits as to school, form, or subject matter. Imaginative, risk-taking poetry which disturbs and/or consoles is of paramount interest. A distinctive voice is prized." Has published poetry by Billy Collins, Stephen Dunn, Ted Kooser, Linda Pastan, David Wagoner, and Franz Wright. *MARGIE* is about 400+ pages, digest-sized, professionally printed, perfect-bound, with glossy cover with art/graphics, includes ads. Receives about 40,000-50,000 poems/year, accepts less than 1%. **Available by subscription only.** Single copy: $15.95 (one-year subscription) for individuals, $19.95 for institutions and foreign (prices include shipping & handling). Make checks payable to *MARGIE, Inc.*

How to Submit Submit 3-5 poems at a time. Considers simultaneous submissions (notify with cover letter). Reads submissions according to the following schedule: open reading period is June 1-July 15 (one submission/poet during this time); **subscribers only** may submit up to 4 times annually, year round ("please mark 'Subscribe' on the outside of submission envelope"). Time between acceptance and publication is up to one year. Editor makes final decision. Sometimes comments on rejected poems. Guidelines available in magazine, for SASE, or on Web site. Responds in 1-3 weeks. Pays one contributor's copy. Acquires first rights. All rights revert to poet upon publication.

Contest/Award Offerings The Marjorie J. Wilson Award for Excellence in Poetry (spring—see separate listing in Contests & Awards); "Strong Medicine" Award (fall). Guidelines available for SASE or on Web site.

Advice "Read, read, read with unwavering discipline. Then: write. Be audacious, innovative, distinctive."

✪ $▣ ◯ ◎ THE MARTIAN WAVE (Specialized: science fiction related to exploration/settlement of the Solar System)

P.O. Box 782, Cedar Rapids IA 52406-0782. E-mail: martianwave@samsdotpublishing.com. Web site: www.samsdotpublishing.com. **Established 1997. Contact:** J. Alan Erwine, editor. Member: The Speculative Literature Foundation (http://SpeculativeLiterature.org).

Magazine Needs *The Martian Wave*, published quarterly online, features "science fiction poetry and stories that are related in some way to the exploration and/or settlement of the Solar System." Does not want "anything other than science fiction." Considers poetry by children and teens. Has published poetry by Marge B. Simon, Kristine Ong Muslim, Christina Sng, Aurelio Rico Lopez III, s.c. virtes, and Tyree Campbell. Receives about 150 poems/year, accepts about 16 (12%).

How to Submit Submit up to 5 poems at a time. Lines/poem: prefers less than 100. No previously published poems or simultaneous submissions. Accepts e-mail submissions (pasted into body of message); no disk submissions. "Submission should include snail mail address and a short (1-2 lines) bio." Reads submissions year round. Submit seasonal poems 6 months in advance. Time between acceptance and publication is 1-2 months. Sometimes comments on rejected poems. Guidelines available on Web site. Responds in 4-6 weeks. Pays $5/poem. Acquires first North American serial rights.

Advice "It's up to the writer to take the first step and submit work. Some of our best poems have come from poets who weren't sure if they were good enough. Most important is our theme. The poem must be related to the exploration and/or settlement of the Solar System."

$◪ THE MASSACHUSETTS REVIEW

South College, University of Massachusetts, Amherst MA 01003. (413)545-2689. E-mail: massrev@external.umass.edu. Web site: www.massreview.org. **Established 1959. Contact:** Deborah Gorlin and Ellen Watson, poetry editors.

- Work published in *The Massacusetts Review* has been included frequently in *The Best American Poetry*.

Magazine Needs *The Massachusetts Review*, published quarterly, prints "fiction, essays, artwork, and excellent poetry of all forms and styles." Has published poetry by Catherine Barnett, Billy Collins, and Dara Wier. *The Massachusetts Review* is digest-sized, offset-printed on bond paper, perfect-bound, with color card cover. Receives about 2,500 poems/year, accepts about 25. Press run is 1,600 (1,100-1,200 subscribers, 1,000 libraries, the rest for shelf sales). Subscription: $27/year U.S., $35 outside U.S., $37 for libraries. Sample: $9 U.S., $12 outside U.S.

How to Submit No previously published poems or simultaneous submissions. Reads submissions October 1-June 30 only. Guidelines available for SASE or on Web site. Responds in 2 months. Pays 35¢/line (minimum of $10) plus 2 contributor's copies.

$☑ ◎ MATURE YEARS (Specialized: aging; Christian)

P.O. Box 801, 201 Eighth Ave. S., Nashville TN 37202. (615)749-6292. Fax: (615)749-6512. E-mail: matureyears@umpublishing.org. Established 1954. **Contact:** Marvin W. Cropsey, editor.

Magazine Needs *Mature Years*, published quarterly, aims to "help persons understand and use the resources of Christian faith in dealing with specific opportunities and problems related to aging. Poems may or may not be overtly religious. Poems should not poke fun at older adults, but may take a humorous look at them." Does not want "sentimentality and saccharine. If using rhymes and meter, make sure they are accurate." *Mature Years* is 112 pages, magazine-sized, perfect-bound, with full-color glossy paper cover. Press run is 55,000. Sample: $5.75.

How to Submit Lines/poem: 16 lines of up to 50 characters maximum. Accepts fax and e-mail submissions (e-mail preferred). Submit seasonal and nature poems for spring from December through February; for summer, March through May; for fall, June through August; and for winter, September through November. Time between acceptance and publication is up to one year. Guidelines available for SASE or by e-mail. Responds in 2 months. Pays $1/line upon acceptance.

◢ ◎ MEASURE: AN ANNUAL REVIEW OF FORMAL POETRY (Specialized: metrical poetry only)

Dept. of English, The University of Evansville, 1800 Lincoln Ave., Evansville IN 47722. (812)488-2963. E-mail: pb28@evansville.edu. Web site: http://measure.evansville.edu. Established 2005. **Contact:** The Editors.

Magazine Needs *Measure: An Annual Review of Formal Poetry* is "dedicated to publishing the best metrical, English-language verse from both the United States and abroad. In each issue we strive to bring you the best new poetry from both established and emerging writers, and we also reprint a small sampling of poems from the best books of metrical poetry published the previous year. Likewise, each issue includes interviews with some of our most important contemporary poets and offers short critical essays on the poetry that has helped to shape the craft." Wants "English-language metrical poetry with no particular stanza preference. See our Web site or a back issue for examples. *Measure* also reprints poems from books; send copy for consideration." Does not want "fixed forms written in free verse; syllabics; quantitative." Has published poetry by Timothy Steele, R.S. Gwynn, Philip Dacey, X.J. Kennedy, Rachel Hadas, and Charles Rafferty. *Measure* is 220 pages, digest-sized, perfect-bound, with glossy cover with color artwork. Receives about 1,500 poems/year, accepts about 10%. Press run is 1,000. Single copy: $10; subscription: $10 for one year, $18 for 2 years, $25 for 3 years. Make checks payable to *Measure*.

How to Submit Submit 3-5 poems at a time. Lines/poem: no minimum or maximum. No previously published poems or simultaneous submissions. No e-mail or disk submissions. Cover letter is preferred. "All submissions should be typed. Each poem should include the poet's name and phone number. A self-addressed stamped envelope must accompany the submission." Reads submissions year round. Time between acceptance and publication "depends." Never comments on rejected poems. Guidelines available in magazine, for SASE, or on Web site. Responds in 2-3 months. Pays 2 contributor's copies. Acquires one-time rights. Rights revert to poet upon publication.

Additional Information Prints the winners of the annual Howard Nemerov Sonnet Award (see separate listing in Contests & Awards).

Ⓝ Ⓤ MÊLÊE

P.O. Box 1619, Alexander City AL 35010. E-mail: info@poetrymelee.com. Web site: www.poetryme lee.com. Established 2006. **Contact:** Lisa Ann Holmes or Chris Pappas, Jr., editors. Member: CLMP.

Magazine Needs *Mêlée*, published quarterly, seeks "poetry and essays that explore the symbiotic relationships between aesthetics and political/social activism. However, our intent is to publish the best work submitted to us regardless of topic. Poetry of any style or length and short essays on any topic will be considered. Content may or may not be of overtly political intent." Does not want "tired language." Has published poetry by Amiri Baraka, Lyn Lifshin, Jennifer Abbott, Linda Frost, and Steve Davenport. *Mêlée* is 24-40 pages, newsprint tabloid, saddle-stapled, with cover with b&w photos and art, includes ads. Receives about 1,000 poems/year, accepts about 10%. Press run is 4,000 (100 subscribers, 500 shelf sales); 3,400 distributed free. Single copy: $3.95; subscription: $14 (one year), $27 (2 years). Make checks payable to *Mêlée*.

How to Submit Submit up to 5 poems at a time. Lines/poem: any length considered. Considers simultaneous submissions; no previously published poems. Accepts e-mail (as attachment in Word) and disk submissions. For e-mail submissions with Word attachments, include name, address, phone number, and e-mail address in body of message. Cover letter is unnecessary, "but welcome." Reads submissions year round. Submit seasonal poems 4 months in advance. Time between acceptance and publication is 2 months. Poems are circulated to an editorial board. "Both editors and guest readers read the poems submitted for publication." Sometimes comments on rejected poems. Sometimes publishes theme issues. Guidelines available on Web site. Responds in 2 months. E-mails acceptance/rejection notification. Always sends prepublication galleys. Pays 5 contributor's copies. Acquires first rights; acquires electronic rights "upon negotiation with individual writers." Rights revert to poets upon publication.

Additional Information Reads for *Meridian*'s anthology, *Best New Poets* (www.bestnewpoets.org).

Contest/Award Offerings "Each year two $100 prizes will be awarded to the poem and essay that we believe best supports our purpose."

$ⓘ THE MENNONITE (Specialized: Christian)

P.O. Box 347, Newton KS 67114-0347. (316)283-5155, ext. 231. Fax: (316)283-0454. E-mail: gordon h@themennonite.org. Web site: www.themennonite.org. Established 1885. **Contact:** Gordon Houser, associate editor.

Magazine Needs *The Mennonite*, published twice/month, seeks "Christian poetry—usually free verse, not too long, with multiple layers of meaning." Does not want "sing-song rhymes or poems that merely describe or try to teach a lesson." Has published poetry by Jean Janzen and Julia Kasdorf. *The Mennonite* is 32 pages, magazine-sized, with full-color cover, includes ads. Receives about 200 poems/year, accepts about 5%. Press run is 12,500 (11,000 subscribers). Single copy: $3; subscription: $41.95. Sample: $3.

How to Submit Submit up to 4 poems at a time. Considers previously published poems and simultaneous submissions. Accepts e-mail submissions (preferred). Cover letter is preferred. Time between acceptance and publication is up to one year. Seldom comments on rejected poems. Occasionally publishes theme issues. Guidelines available for SASE. Responds in 2 weeks. Pays $50-75 plus one contributor's copy. Acquires first or one-time rights.

⭐ ☑ MERIDIAN

University of Virginia, P.O. Box 400145, Charlottesville VA 22904-4145. (434)982-5798. E-mail: MeridianUVA@yahoo.com. Web site: www.readmeridian.org. Established 1998. **Contact:** Poetry Editor.

● Work published in *Meridian* has appeared in *The Best American Poetry* and *The Pushcart Prize.*

Magazine Needs *Meridian*, published semiannually, prints poetry, fiction, nonfiction, interviews, and reviews. Has published poetry by David Kirby, Charles Wright, and Joelle Biele. *Meridian* is 190 pages, digest-sized, offset-printed, perfect-bound, with color cover. Receives about 2,500 poems/year, accepts about 30 (less than 1%). Press run is 1,000 (750 subscribers, 15 libraries, 200 shelf sales); 150 distributed free to writing programs. Single copy: $7; subscription: $10/year. Make checks payable to *Meridian*.

How to Submit Submit up to 4 poems at a time. Considers simultaneous submissions (with notification of acceptance elsewhere); no previously published poems. No e-mail or disk submissions; accepts postal and online submissions (**$2 upload fee for up to 4 poems**; no fee for postal submissions). Cover letter is preferred. Reads submissions September-May primarily (do not send submissions April 15-August 15; accepts online submissions year round). Time between acceptance and publication is 1-2 months. Seldom comments on rejected poems. Guidelines available on Web site. Responds in 1-4 months. Always sends prepublication galleys and author contracts. Pays 2 contributor's copies (additional copies available at discount). Reviews books of poetry.

Contest/Award Offerings *Meridian* Editors' Prize Contest offers annual $1,000 award. Submit online only; see Web site for formatting details. **Entry fee:** $15, includes one-year subscription to *Meridian*. **Deadline:** December; see Web site for current deadline.

☐ MERIDIAN ANTHOLOGY OF CONTEMPORARY POETRY

P.O. Box 970309, Boca Raton FL 33497. E-mail: LetarP@aol.com. Web site: www.MeridianAnthology .com. Established 2002. **Contact:** Phyliss L. Geller, editor/publisher; Marilyn Krepf, literary editor.

Magazine Needs *Meridian Anthology of Contemporary Poetry*, published annually in late spring, seeks "poetry that is contemporary, insightful, and illuminating; that touches the nerves. It should have color, content, and be deciphering of existence." Does not want vulgarity, clichés. Has published poetry by Elizabeth Swados, Ann McGovern, Gladys Justin Carr, Alan Britt, and Doug Ramspeck. Has reprinted poetry (with poet's permission) by Philip Levine and Jane Hirshfield. *Meridian Anthology of Contemporary Poetry* is 110-168 pages, digest-sized, offset-printed, perfect-bound, with soft cover. Press run is 500-1,000. Single copy: $14 for Volume 4, $14 for Volume 3, $13 for Volume 2, $9 for Volume 1. Make checks payable to *Meridian Anthology of Contemporary Poetry*.

How to Submit Submit 1-5 poems at a time. Lines/poem: 78 maximum. Considers previously published poems and simultaneous submissions. No e-mail or disk submissions. Cover letter is preferred. Must include SASE. Reads submissions March-December. Time between acceptance and publication is up to one year. Seldom comments on rejected poems. Guidelines available for SASE or on Web site. Responds in 2-6 months, "depending on backlog." Pays one contributor's copy. Acquires one-time rights.

Additional Information "Volume 5, anniversary issue (late spring 2007, $15) will feature reprinted poems by Jane Hirshfield and Marie Howe."

Advice "A poem must have a reason for existence, some universal tendril."

$ ☑ MICHIGAN QUARTERLY REVIEW

University of Michigan, 3574 Rackham Bldg., 915 E. Washington St., Ann Arbor MI 48109. (734)764-9265. E-mail: mqr@umich.edu. Web site: www.umich.edu/~mqr. Established 1962. **Contact:** Laurence Goldstein, editor-in-chief.

- Poetry published in *Michigan Quarterly Review* is included frequently in volumes of *The Best American Poetry* and *The Pushcart Prize* anthologies.

Magazine Needs *Michigan Quarterly Review* is "an interdisciplinary, general interest academic journal that publishes mainly essays and reviews on subjects of cultural and literary interest." Wants all kinds of poetry except light verse. No specifications as to form, length, style, subject matter, or purpose. Has published poetry by Susan Hahn, Campbell McGrath, Carl Phillips, and Cathy Song. *Michigan Quarterly Review* is 160 pages, digest-sized, professionally printed, flat-spined, with glossy card cover. Receives about 1,400 submissions/year, accepts about 30. Press run is 2,000 (1,200 subscribers, half are libraries). Single copy: $7; subscription: $25. Sample: $4.

How to Submit No previously published poems or simultaneous submissions. No e-mail submissions. Cover letter is preferred. "It puts a human face on the manuscript. A few sentences of biography is all I want, nothing lengthy or defensive." Prefers typed mss. Publishes theme issues. Upcoming themes available in magazine and on Web site. Guidelines available for SASE or on Web site. Responds in 6 weeks. Always sends prepublication galleys. Pays $8-12/page. Acquires first rights only. Reviews books of poetry. "All reviews are commissioned."

Contest/Award Offerings The Laurence Goldstein Poetry Award, an annual cash prize of $1,000, is given to the author of the best poem to appear in *Michigan Quarterly* during the calendar year. "Established in 2002, the prize is sponsored by the Office of the President of the University of Michigan."

Advice "There is no substitute for omnivorous reading and careful study of poets past and present, as well as reading in new and old areas of knowledge. Attention to technique, especially to rhythm and patterns of imagery, is vital."

$☐ ◎ THE MID-AMERICA POETRY REVIEW (Specialized: poets living in MO, IL, AR, OK, KS, NE, IA)

The Mid-America Press, Inc., P.O. Box 575, Warrensburg MO 64093-0575. Established 1976 (press). **Contact:** Robert C. Jones, editor.

Magazine Needs *The Mid-America Poetry Review*, published 3 times/year, prints "well-crafted poetry, primarily from—but not limited to—poets living in Missouri, Illinois, Arkansas, Oklahoma, Kansas, Nebraska, and Iowa. We are open to all styles and forms; what we look for is poetry by writers who know both what they are doing and why." Has published poetry by Charles Guenther, Rhina P. Espaillat, Louis D. Brodsky, David Baker, Kate Northrop, and Gloria Vando. *The Mid-America Poetry Review* is 60-75 pages, digest-sized, offset-printed, perfect-bound, with matte paper cover. Receives about 1,000-1,500 poems/year, accepts about 15%. Press run is 750. Single copy: $6; subscription: $15/year. Make checks payable to The Mid-America Press, Inc.

How to Submit Submit 1-3 poems at a time. Lines/poem: 36 maximum. No previously published poems or simultaneous submissions. Cover letter is useful. "One-page cover letter (if included) should list items to be considered and contain brief paragraphs of information about author and previous publications. Type submissions, single- or double-spaced, on 8½ × 11 white paper; include name, address, and telephone number in top left or right corner. Enclose SASE for notification/guidelines. Do not send the only copy of your manuscript—unused submissions are recycled." Time between acceptance and publication may be up to one year. Sometimes comments on submissions. Guidelines available for SASE. Responds within 2 months. Sends prepublication galleys. Pays $5/poem on acceptance, 2 contributor's copies on publication, and one-year subscription. Acquires first North American serial rights. Staff occasionally reviews books of poetry. Send materials for review consideration.

Additional Information The Mid-America Press, Inc. publishes 1-5 book-length poetry collections/year. "**At present, the Press is not reading unsolicited book-length poetry manuscripts.**" Award-winning publications from Mid-America Press, Inc. include *Uncurling* (2000) by Jeanie Wilson, *Light and Chance* (2001) by Ardyth Bradley, *Dreaming the Bronze Girl* (2002) by Serina Allison Hearn, and

The Graveyard Picnic (2002) by William Ford. Order sample books by sending $13.95/book.
Advice "Read several copies of the magazine to see the range of subject matter and forms."

THE MIDWEST QUARTERLY

Pittsburg State University, Pittsburg KS 66762. (620)235-4689. Fax: (620)235-4686. E-mail: smeats @pittstate.edu. Web site: www.pittstate.edu/engl/mwq/MQindex.html. Established 1959. **Contact:** Stephen Meats, poetry editor.

Magazine Needs *The Midwest Quarterly* publishes "articles on any subject of contemporary interest, particularly literary criticism, political science, philosophy, education, biography, and sociology. Each issue contains a section of poetry usually 12 poems in length." Wants "well-crafted poems, traditional or untraditional, that use intense, vivid, concrete, and/or surrealistic images to explore the mysterious and surprising interactions of the natural and inner human worlds." Does not want " 'nature poems,' per se, but if a poem doesn't engage nature in a significant way, as an integral part of the experience it is offering, I am unlikely to be interested in publishing it." Has published poetry by Ted Kooser, Jim Daniels, Naomi Shihab Nye, Jonathan Holden, William Kloefkorn, and Jeanne Murray Walker. *The Midwest Quarterly* is 130 pages, digest-sized, professionally printed, flat-spined, with matte cover. Press run is 650 (600 subscribers, 500 libraries). Receives about 4,000 poems/year, accepts about 50. Subscription: $15. Sample: $5.

How to Submit Submit no more than 5 poems at a time. Lines/poem: 60 maximum ("occasionally longer if exceptional"). Considers simultaneous submissions; no previously published poems. No fax or e-mail submissions. "Manuscripts should be typed with poet's name on each page. Submissions without SASE cannot be acknowledged." Comments on rejected poems "if the poet or poem seems particularly promising." Occasionally publishes theme issues. Guidelines available on Web site. Responds in 2 months. Pays 2 contributor's copies. Acquires first serial rights. Reviews books of poetry by *Midwest Quarterly*-published poets only.

Advice "Keep writing; read as much contemporary poetry as you can lay your hands on; don't let rejection discourage you from sending your work out to editors."

MIDWIFERY TODAY (Specialized: childbirth)

P.O. Box 2672, Eugene OR 97402-0223. (541)344-7438. Fax: (541)344-1422. E-mail: editorial@mid wiferytoday.com. Web site: www.midwiferytoday.com. Established 1986. **Contact:** Cheryl K. Smith, editor.

Magazine Needs *Midwifery Today*, published quarterly, provides "a voice for midwives and childbirth educators. We are a midwifery magazine. Subject must be birth or birth profession related." Does not want poetry that is "off subject or puts down the subject." *Midwifery Today* is 75 pages, magazine-sized, offset-printed, saddle-stapled, with glossy card cover with b&w photos and b&w artwork, includes ads. Press run is 5,000 (3,000 subscribers, 1,000 shelf sales). Subscription: $50. Sample: $10.

How to Submit No previously published poems. Accepts e-mail submissions (pasted into body of message or as attachment). Cover letter is required. Time between acceptance and publication is 1-2 years. Seldom comments on rejected poems. Publishes theme issues. Upcoming themes and deadlines available on Web site. Guidelines available for SASE or on Web site. Responds in 6 months. Pays 2 contributor's copies. Acquires first rights.

Advice "With our publication, please stay on the subject."

MINAS TIRITH EVENING-STAR: JOURNAL OF THE AMERICAN TOLKIEN SOCIETY (Specialized: fantasy; middle-earth, Tolkien)

American Tolkien Society, P.O. Box 97, Highland MI 48357-0097. E-mail: editor@americantolkienso ciety.org. Web site: www.americantolkiensociety.org. Established 1967. **Contact:** Amalie A. Helms, editor.

Online Poetry Forums

A new community for poets

I t's lonely out there for a poet. Perhaps you're lucky to be surrounded by like-minded writers who can critique your work and chat about forms to the wee hours of the night. For most writers, though, it can be pretty tough to find a true community of poets who can give them the valuable feedback and intellectual discussions they crave.

That is, until now.

Many poets are discovering the joys of online poetry forums. Here, writers are able to "meet" each other and share ideas, their work and all the ups and downs of the writing life. There are countless forums on the Web, focusing on a variety of subjects, forms and skill levels. To learn more about these forums—and how to find the one that's right for you—we contacted two successful sites that shared with us all the details of their online writing communities.

The first group is The Poet Sanctuary (www.thepoetsanctuary.net). Founded in 2002, TPS is now 20,000 members strong. One of the benefits of this site is that poets can post anonymously—perfect for anyone who is shy about her work, or even prefers to write using a different persona. For this reason, you'll see in our roundtable the user names Liz80, Orpheus, LadyB, Sonne, Katriona, Scepter, ShadowDiamond, DragonsofRose, and Dragonpoe. Even with the shield of a pen name, many members form lasting friendships and have traveled across states to meet each other. In fact, two poets got married after meeting on TPS.

The second group is Wild Poetry Forum (www.wildpoetryforum.com), founded in 1998 by Debby Clowes and Michelle Petit-Sumerall, who had previously belonged to a restrictive, and sometimes abusive group. Their goal was to build an interactive community that offered a safe haven for poets who wanted to grow their skills and cultivate their creative side without fear of harsh criticism. The site has grown from 15 members to 1,000 members in 38 countries, and it's now run by M and Steve Williams.

The Poet Sanctuary and Wild Poetry Forum have a lot in common. First, they charge no fees to their members. Second, poets must be at least 13 years old to participate in the forum. Finally, members of both groups feel their experience with the forums has helped them develop as poets.

What is the main benefit of belonging to an online poetry forum?

Liz80: A forum for a poet is a place to share poetry, read poetry by other people, and get feedback on your work. It's also a place to meet other people who have the same interests as you, and some forums will even offer the opportunity to publish work.

Orpheus: The chance to have your work read by others without having to go through the trial and tribulation of being published is a major draw of poetry forums. Also, most people who belong to forums are young people who write to help deal with their feelings. For more advanced writers, showcasing your poetry on a forum and getting feedback can help you hone your skills and determine which pieces might be well received by publishers.

M: I suppose the primary attraction of poetry forums, no matter the poet's individual goal, is the ability to receive immediate exposure, feedback and critique of writing from other experienced authors. Some of our members write as an emotional outlet or hobby and simply wish to share their writing and their thoughts with other like-minded souls. Other members are published professionals, or hope to be published one day, and are more concerned with the technical aspects of improving their writing skills.

Why is a community like a poetry forum valuable for poets?

LadyB: The community is beyond valuable; it's what makes the poetry forum work. At TPS, the community is like a real community, with such a diverse array of poets. There are all sorts of personalities, and it brings us closer together.

M: At Wild Poetry Forum, a sense of community is very important and quite a valuable commodity. Members quickly learn that our community is a family, with all the privileges and responsibilities that benefit entails.

Sonne: It is very valuable—it helps poets to feel welcome and free to express themselves. TPS gives the feeling of belonging and understanding that is very important to everyone who does any creative work.

Katriona: I value the sense of community very highly, and I know many of the other poets do as well. I have in fact met several of my best friends on the TPS!

In addition to the strong sense of community, do you get valuable criticism from other members?

Liz80: That all depends on where you go and what you need. Searching out the right place for your own skill level and comfort level is very important. If you're just starting to show your work to others, you probably want somewhere more low key that focuses on the writer and less on the "rules" of writing. Then, as you grow more comfortable, you would want to seek out a more hard-hitting forum or message board/site to push your skills even further.

M: While appreciating and admiring one another's work is important, Wild Poetry Forum is a place where real critique is offered and encouraged. We have tried to design Wild Poetry Forum to address all kinds of different authors at many stages of growth and development with three main forums available.

Orpheus: I wouldn't say that everyone likes everyone else's writing, but I think everyone is of a similar mind that if you're trying, then you should be encouraged to continue and get better. On the TPS forum, there's a separate board for more rigorous critique; but overall, it's more of a supportive and encouraging forum.

Scepter: There are many types of forums for poets. The sites range from mean and angry to extremely nurturing and everything in between. New poets like to experiment with styles and techniques and get some help in improving their work. Seasoned poets like to share their work and mentor others. A forum is a great place to explore, learn, grow and mentor.

How do you find the forum that's right for you?

M: Our membership has found Wild Poetry Forum in a wide variety of ways. Most often new members come through referrals from family, friends or colleagues, or through a Google search for poetry forums. Quite a few have found us through links from other poetry or writing Web sites.

Scepter: I searched the Web for several months, looking for the right site for me. I tried the full spectrum of sites, from harsh to fluffy. In the end, I chose a site that had more than 15,000 writers on it and was organized in many different topical sections. The numbers told me that people are happy here.

Liz80: Asking friends and others you know who write is the best place to start. Once you get onto one forum, you normally will hear about several others from other members on the first board. I heard about TPS from a writer friend who posted on the site and suggested I use it to get my feet wet and to better my writing through reading and responding to it.

Sonne: I tried many forums before finding TPS. What makes it different is the fact that it's not just a place to post and do an obligatory read of someone else's work. There are discussion threads, support groups, philosophical debates and ongoing charities. There's a real sense of caring about the person behind the poem.

Do participants in your forum submit their work for publication and to outside competitions?

Liz80: It depends on the person. Sometimes published writers come into our forum to post and to help out others. Some people want the community aspect more and just want to be heard and accepted. Others want to progress in their skills with the hope of someday publishing their work.

M: Wild Poetry Forum members represent the entire spectrum, from those who write simply as a hobby or emotional outlet and are content to only share via our forum, to those who have their work published and who compete in competitions.

Scepter: Many writers start their professional work in the forum settings. They can get honest feedback from a broad sector of poetic society, by submitting developmental works on a forum. It's a great place to grow in confidence and competence.

Orpheus: Many of the members wish to be published someday and also compete in local and national competitions. Since it's a forum where most people support one another, it's only natural to see how your work will cut it outside of such a caring and safe environment.

Do you offer prizes on your forum? What purpose do they serve?

Scepter: Prizes are more of an encouragement than anything, a spur to keep us writing and give us ideas. It provides some incentive to put some real effort into our pieces.

DragonsOfRose: Prizes offer encouragement to the younger or beginner writers. Challenges teach the poet to explore their creativity. The award or prize allows them to feel accomplished and proud of what they've written.

M: Wild Poetry Forum does not sponsor a contest, per se. However, we do offer a weekly Creativity Challenge in which members write poems that adhere to specific criteria. Entries are judged and a weekly winner is announced. We also recognize a "Poem of the Week" each week that's archived in a Hall of Fame that's a permanent feature on the site.

Any final thoughts?

Dragonpoe: Being an "older" poet, I've been around many poetry forums, and TPS is the only forum I have stayed an active member of. The staff keeps the site clean and organized, lively with weekly challenges, member boards and fun boards, and keeps it mentally active with other competitions.

M: Wild Poetry Forum is a gift in all of our lives, both staff and members. We extend our sincerest thanks to all of them for sharing with us their thoughts, their words, their internal music. They've made Wild Poetry Forum a success story, and they'll remain the driving force behind all of our future endeavors.

ShadowDiamond: TPS has been an escape for me; and without it, my world would be a lot duller. The dedication of the members and staff spur me to increase my performance, and their advice on my writing has helped me more than I'd ever thought possible.

—Donya Dickerson

Donya Dickerson is an acquisitions editor focusing on business books, and she's the previous editor of *Guide to Literary Agents* (Writer's Digest Books).

Magazine Needs *Minas Tirith Evening-Star: Journal of the American Tolkien Society*, published quarterly, uses poetry of fantasy about Middle-Earth and Tolkien. Considers poetry by children and teens. Has published poetry by Thomas M. Egan, Anne Etkin, Nancy Pope, and Martha Benedict. *Minas Tirith Evening-Star* is digest-sized, offset-printed from typescript, with cartoon-like b&w graphics. Press run is 400 (350 subscribers, 10% libraries). Single copy: $3.50; subscription: $12.50. Sample: $3. Make checks payable to American Tolkien Society.

How to Submit Considers previously published poems ("maybe"); no simultaneous submissions. Accepts e-mail and disk submissions. Cover letter is preferred. Sometimes comments on rejected poems. Occasionally publishes theme issues. Guidelines available for SASE or by e-mail. Responds in 2 weeks. Sometimes sends prepublication galleys. Pays one contributor's copy. Reviews related books of poetry; length depends on the volume ("a sentence to several pages"). Send materials for review consideration.

Additional Information Under the imprint of W.W. Publications, publishes collections of poetry of fantasy about Middle-Earth and Tolkien. Books/chapbooks are 50-100 pages. Publishes 2 chapbooks/year. For book or chapbook consideration, submit sample poems.

Also Offers Membership in the American Tolkien Society is open to all, regardless of country of residence, and entitles one to receive the quarterly journal. Dues are $12.50/year to addresses in U.S., $12.50 in Canada, and $15 elsewhere. Sometimes sponsors contests.

Advice "Adhere to the guidelines and show talent."

☐ ◎ MINDPRINTS, A LITERARY JOURNAL (Specialized: writers & artists with disabilities)

Learning Assistance Program, Allan Hancock College, 800 S. College Dr., Santa Maria CA 93454-6399. (805)922-6966, ext. 3274. Fax: (805)922-3556. E-mail: pafahey@hancockcollege.edu. Web site: www.imindprints.com. Established 2000. **Contact:** Paul Fahey, editor.

Magazine Needs *Mindprints, A Literary Journal* is "a national annual publication of flash fiction, flash memoir, poetry, and black-and-white artwork. The journal is created as a forum for writers and artists with disabilities, but we also invite those who work in the field or have an interest in the population to submit their work. *Mindprints* takes great pride in showcasing new artists and giving voice to new writers. We also welcome and encourage established writers and artists." Wants all kinds of poetry. "We love anything short: haiku, haibun, cinquain; prose and rhyming poetry with unusual imagery." Considers poetry by children and teens. Has published poetry by Barbara Crooker, Linda K. Arnold, Amanda Auchter, Carol Smallwood, and Barbara Jacksha. *Mindprints* is digest-sized, perfect-bound, with gloss laminated cover. Receives about 400 submissions/year, accepts about 30.

Press run is 600. "We sell copies at book fairs and through our college bookstore." Single copy: $6 plus $2 first-class postage. Make checks payable to Allan Hancock College.

How to Submit Submit up to 3 poems at a time per reading period. Lines/poem: 34 maximum. Considers previously published poems and simultaneous submissions. Accepts e-mail submissions only if poet resides outside the U.S. and disk submissions only once the mss are accepted; no fax submissions. Cover letter is required. "Please include SASE. In cover letter, tell us something about yourself, previous publications, if applicable, and tell us why you are submitting to *Mindprints*." Reads submissions year round (begins reading collected submissions April 1). Time between acceptance and publication is 3-4 months. "We have a poetry editor who is an established poet and instructor at the college who reads the poetry and ranks it (all identifying information is removed)." Seldom comments on rejected poems. Guidelines available in magazine, for SASE, or on Web site. Responds in late May. Pays one contributor's copy. Acquires one-time rights.

Advice "We are one of the few national community college journals devoted to celebrating the work of artists and writers with disabilities. We look for a strong voice, unusual point of view, and rich imagery and description."

⭐ ☐ ◎ MINORITY LITERARY EXPO (Specialized: minority poets)

216 Avenue T. Pratt City, Birmingham AL 35214. (205)583-4617. E-mail: kervinfondren@yahoo.com. Established 1990. **Contact:** Kervin Fondren, editor.

Magazine Needs *Minority Literary Expo*, published annually, features minority poets, writers, and professionals. "Organization membership open to all minority poets nationally." Accepts poetry concerning ethnic minorities, homosexuals/bisexuals, students, women/feminism. Wants "poems from minority poets that are holistic and wholesome, any style, any form, any subject matter. Poetry that expresses holistic views and philosophies is very acceptable. Literary value is emphasized." Does not want "vulgar or hate poetry." No fee is charged for inclusion. Single copy: $25.

How to Submit Submit 1-2 poems at a time. Lines/poem: 24 or less. Accepts disk submissions; no e-mail submissions. Publishes theme issues. Guidelines available for SASE or by e-mail. Pays one contributor's copy.

Contest/Award Offerings Sponsors an annual poetry contributor's contest. Offers $150 award. **Deadline:** July annually.

Advice "We're interested in poetry, articles, and literary submissions that can be published in a professional journal."

$◎ THE MIRACULOUS MEDAL (Specialized: Catholic; Blessed Virgin Mary)

475 E. Chelten Ave., Philadelphia PA 19144-5785. (215)848-1010. Web site: www.cammonline.org. Established 1928. **Contact:** Rev. James O. Kiernan, C.M., editor.

Magazine Needs *The Miraculous Medal*, published quarterly, is a religious magazine featuring "poetry that reflects solid Catholic doctrine and experience. Any subject matter is acceptable, provided it does not contradict the teachings of the Roman Catholic Church. Poetry must have a religious theme, preferably about the Blessed Virgin Mary." Has published poetry by Gladys McKee. *The Miraculous Medal* is 32 pages, digest-sized, saddle-stapled, with 2-color cover. *The Miraculous Medal* is used as a promotional piece and is sent to all clients of the Central Association of the Miraculous Medal. Circulation is 150,000. Sample: free for postage.

How to Submit Lines/poem: 20 maximum. No previously published poems or simultaneous submissions. Poems should be double-spaced. Guidelines available for SASE. Responds in up to 3 years. Pays 50¢ and up per line, on acceptance. Acquires first North American rights.

$⬚ ◎ MODERN HAIKU (Specialized: haiku/senryu/haibun only; translations)

P.O. Box 7046, Evanston IL 60204-7046. Web site: www.modernhaiku.org. Established 1969. **Contact:** Charles Trumbull, editor.

Magazine Needs *Modern Haiku*, published 3 times/year in February, June, and October, is "the foremost international journal of English-language haiku and criticism. We are devoted to publishing only the very best haiku being written; also publish articles on haiku and have the most complete review section of haiku books.'' Wants ''contemporary haiku in English (including translations into English) that incorporate the traditional aesthetics of the haiku genre, but which may be innovative as to subject matter, mode of approach or angle of perception, and form of expression. Haiku, senryu, and haibun only. No tanka or other forms. Same considerations, pro and con, given to work by children and teens.'' Has published haiku by Billy Collins, Lawrence Ferlinghetti, Sharon Olds, Paul Muldoon, and Gary Snyder. *Modern Haiku* is 100 pages (average), digest-sized, printed on heavy quality stock, with full-color cover illustrations. Receives about 12,000-14,000 submissions/year, accepts about 500. Press run is 800. Subscription: $26 ppd. Sample: $10 ppd.

How to Submit Submit ''any number of haiku per 8½×11 sheet.'' No previously published haiku or simultaneous submissions. Put name and address on each sheet. Include SASE. Guidelines available for SASE or on Web site. Responds in 2-6 weeks. Pays $1/haiku (but no contributor's copy). Acquires first North American serial rights. Staff reviews books of haiku in 350-1,000 words, single-book format. Send materials for review consideration with complete ordering information.

Contest/Award Offerings Sponsors the annual Robert Spiess Memorial Haiku Competition. Guidelines available for SASE or on Web site.

Advice ''Study what haiku really are. We do not want sentimentality, pretty-pretty, or pseudo-Japanese themes. Juxtaposition of seemingly disparate entities that nonetheless create harmony is very desirable.''

◪ MONKEY'S FIST

Pathfinder Press, P.O. Box 316, Madison ME 04950-0316. Established 2001. **Contact:** Robin Merrill, editor.

Magazine Needs *Monkey's Fist*, published annually, seeks ''accessible poetry that lives in the real world. Have something to say and say it well.'' Considers poetry by teens. *Monkey's Fist* is 32 pages, digest-sized, professionally printed. Receives hundreds of poems/year, accepts about 5%. Press run is 100 (50 subscribers). Single copy: $6. Make checks payable to Robin Lindeman.

How to Submit Submit 3 poems at a time. Considers simultaneous submissions. No disk submissions. Poems should be submitted one to a page on plain white 8½×11 paper, with name and address on each page. Send in white #10 envelope and include SASE. ''We like creases and dislike big brown envelopes and wasted stamps.'' Time between acceptance and publication is up to one year. ''Do not send for guidelines. Just be courteous and professional and follow the guidelines here.'' Responds in up to 2 months. Sometimes sends prepublication galleys. Pays one contributor's copy. Acquires one-time rights.

◪ ◪ MOUNT OLIVE REVIEW

634 Henderson St., Mount Olive NC 28365. (919)658-2502. Established 1987. **Contact:** Dr. Pepper Worthington, editor.

Magazine Needs *Mount Olive Review* features ''literary criticism, poetry, short stories, essays, and book reviews.'' Wants ''modern poetry.'' Receives about 2,000 poems/year, accepts 8%. Press run is 500. Single copy: $10. Make checks payable to Mount Olive College Press.

How to Submit Submit 6 poems at a time. No previously published poems or simulatneous submissions. Cover letter is preferred. Time between acceptance and publication varies. Poems are circulated to an editorial board. Seldom comments on rejected poems. Responds in 6 months. Sometimes sends prepublication galleys. Acquires first rights. Reviews books/chapbooks of poetry and other magazines/journals. Send materials for review consideration.

◪ ◪ ◎ MR. MARQUIS' MUSELETTER (Specialized: poems by/for/about children)

Kwil Kids Publishing, Box 29556, Maple Ridge BC V2X 2V0 Canada. E-mail: kwilville@shaw.ca. Established 1996. **Contact:** Mr. Marquis, editor.

Magazines/Journals

Magazine Needs *Mr. Marquis' Museletter*, published quarterly, is a newsletter that prints "stories and poems to encourage and celebrate writers, readers, and researchers." Wants poetry that is "gentle, with compassionate truth and beauty, peace, humor; for children, by children, about children." Does not want "profane, hurtful, violent, political, or satirical work." Has published poetry by Matthew Stasinski Schnitzler, Annunziata Militano, Raanan Burd, Pamela Bond, Bryan Wilson, and Cathy Porter. *Mr. Marquis' Museletter* is 10 pages. Receives about 400 poems/year, accepts about 80%. Press run is 200 (150 subscribers). Subscription: $20 CAD ("includes newsletter and newspaper publishing opportunities, and encouragement galore"). Sample: $2 CAD and SASE (or SAE and IRC). Make checks payable to Mr. Marquis.

How to Submit Submit 5 poems at a time. Accepts e-mail submissions (pasted into body of message; no attachments). Cover letter is preferred. Include SASE and parent's signature. Submit seasonal poems 3 months in advance. Time between acceptance and publication is up to 3 months. Always comments on rejected poems. "Kwil always provides encouragement and personalized response with SASE (or SAE and IRC)." Occasionally publishes theme issues. Guidelines available for SASE (Canadian-stamped envelope, or IRC, or $1 USD for Canadian postage) or by e-mail. Responds in April, August, and December. Pays one contributor's copy. Acquires one-time rights.

Advice "Submit best and submit often; provide Canadian-stamped envelope; sign permission card; have fun writing."

▣ ◪ MUDLARK: AN ELECTRONIC JOURNAL OF POETRY & POETICS

Dept. of English, University of North Florida, Jacksonville FL 32224-2645. (904)620-2273. Fax: (904)620-3940. E-mail: mudlark@unf.edu. Web site: www.unf.edu/mudlark. Established 1995. **Contact:** William Slaughter, editor.

Magazine Needs *Mudlark: An Electronic Journal of Poetry & Poetics*, published online "irregularly, but frequently," offers 3 formats: issues of *Mudlark* "are the electronic equivalent of print chapbooks; posters are the electronic equivalent of print broadsides; and flash poems are poems that have news in them, poems that feel like current events. The poem is the thing at *Mudlark*, and the essay about it. As our full name suggests, we will consider accomplished work that locates itself anywhere on the spectrum of contemporary practice. We want poems, of course, but we want essays, too, that make us read poems (and write them?) differently somehow. Although we are not innocent, we do imagine ourselves capable of surprise. The work of hobbyists is not for *Mudlark*." Has published poetry by Sheila E. Murphy, John Kinsella, Chris Semansky, Diane Wald, Ian Randall Wilson, and Jeffrey Little. *Mudlark* is archived and permanently on view at www.unf.edu.

How to Submit Submit any number of poems at a time. Considers previously published poems ("inasmuch as issues of *Mudlark* are the electronic equivalent of print chapbooks, some of the individual poems in them might, or might not, have been previously published; if they have been, that previous publication must be acknowledged"); no simultaneous submissions ("because of our short turn-around time"). "Only poems that have not been previously published will be considered for *Mudlark* posters, the electronic equivalent of print broadsides, or for *Mudlark* flash poems." Accepts e-mail submissions; no fax submissions. Cover letter is optional. Time between acceptance and publication is up to 3 months. Seldom comments on rejected poems. Guidelines available for SASE, by e-mail, or on Web site. Responds in "one day to one month, depending.." Always sends prepublication galleys "in the form of inviting the author to proof the work on a private Web site that *Mudlark* maintains for that purpose." No payment; however, "one of the things we can do at *Mudlark* to 'pay' our authors for their work is point to it here and there. We can tell our readers how to find it, how to subscribe to it, and how to buy it—if it is for sale. Toward that end, we maintain A-Notes (on the authors) we publish. We call attention to their work." Acquires one-time rights.

Advice "*Mudlark* has been reviewed well and often. At this early point in its history, *Mudlark* has established itself, arguably, as one of the few serious rivals in the first generation of the electronic medium, to print versions of its kind. Look at *Mudlark*, visit the Web site, spend some time there. Then make your decision: to submit or not to submit.''

$◨ ◎ MYTHIC DELIRIUM (Specialized: science fiction; fantasy; horror; surreal; cross-genre)

3514 Signal Hill Ave. NW, Roanoke VA 24017-5148. E-mail: mythicdelirium@gmail.com. Web site: www.mythicdelirium.com. Established 1998. **Contact:** Mike Allen, editor. Member: Science Fiction Poetry Association, Science Fiction & Fantasy Writers of America.

Magazine Needs *Mythic Delirium*, published biannually, is ''a journal of speculative poetry for the new millennium. All forms considered. Must fit within the genres we consider, though we have published some mainstream verse.'' Does not want ''forced rhyme, corny humor, jarringly gross sexual material, gratuitous obscenity, handwritten manuscripts.'' Has published poetry by Sonya Taaffe, Theodora Goss, Joe Haldeman, Ursula K. Le Guin, Ian Watson, and Jane Yolen. *Mythic Delirium* is 32 pages, digest-sized, saddle-stapled, with color cover art, includes house ads. Receives about 750 poems/year, accepts about 5%. Press run is 150. Subscription: $9/year, $16/2 years. Sample: $5. Make checks payable to Mike Allen.

How to Submit Submit up to 6 poems at a time. No previously published poems or simultaneous submissions. Accepts e-mail submissions; no disk submissions. Cover letter is preferred. Time between acceptance and publication is 9 months. Often comments on rejected poems. Guidelines available for SASE, by e-mail, or on Web site. Responds in 5 weeks. Pays $5/poem, plus one contributor's copy. Acquires first North American serial rights.

Advice ''*Mythic Delirium* isn't easy to get into, but we publish newcomers in every issue. Show us how ambitious you can be, and don't give up.''

◨ NASSAU REVIEW

English Dept., Nassau Community College, Garden City NY 11530-6793. (516)572-7792. Established 1964. **Contact:** Editorial Board.

Magazine Needs *Nassau Review*, published annually in September, is a ''creative and research vehicle for Nassau College faculty and the faculty of other colleges.'' Wants ''serious, intellectual poetry of any form or style. Submissions from adults only. No college students; graduate students acceptable. Want only poems of high quality.'' Does not want ''light or satiric verse.'' Has published poetry by Patti Tana, Dick Allen, David Heyen, Joan Sevick, and Mario Susko. *Nassau Review* is about 190 pages, digest-sized, flat-spined. Receives up to 1,900 poems/year, accepts about 20-25. Press run is 1,100 (about 1,100 subscribers, 200 libraries). Sample: free.

How to Submit Submit 3 poems at a time (only once per yearly issue). No previously published poems or simultaneous submissions. Submit 3 copies of each poem. SASE required for reply. ''Manuscripts will not be returned unless SASE includes sufficient postage.'' Reads submissions November 1-March 1 only. Guidelines available for SASE. Responds in up to 4 months. Pays 2 contributor's copies.

Contest/Award Offerings Sponsors an annual poetry contest with $200 award. **Deadline:** March 31. **Advice** ''We want professional-level, high-quality work!''

$◨ THE NATION

33 Irving Place, New York NY 10003. Web site: www.thenation.com. Established 1865. **Contact:** John Palattella, poetry editor.

● Poetry published by *The Nation* has been included in *The Best American Poetry*.

Magazine Needs *The Nation*, published weekly, is a journal of left/liberal opinion, with arts coverage that includes poetry. The only requirement for poetry is ''excellence.'' Has published poetry by W.S. Merwin, Maxine Kumin, James Merrill, May Swenson, Edward Hirsch, and Charles Simic.

How to Submit Submit up to 3 poems at a time. No simultaneous submissions. No e-mail or disk submissions. Send by First-Class Mail, include SASE.

◖ THE NATIONAL POETRY REVIEW

P.O. Box 2080, Aptos CA 95001-2080. Web site: www.nationalpoetryreview.com. Established 2003. **Contact:** C.J. Sage, editor.

- Poetry appearing in *The National Poetry Review* has also appeared in *The Pushcart Prize*.

Magazine Needs *The National Poetry Review* seeks ''the most stunning, memorable poems available. The editors agree with Frost's declaration that the best poems begin in delight and end in wisdom. *TNPR* considers both experimental and 'mainstream' work.'' Does not want ''overly self-centered or confessional poetry, simple autobiography, prose poems, or vulgarity.'' Has published poetry by Bob Hicok, Jennifer Michael Hecht, Larissa Szplorluk, Margot Schilpp, Sarah Hannah, and Ted Kooser. *The National Poetry Review* is 64 pages, perfect-bound, with full-color cover. Accepts less than 1% of submissions received. Single copy: $7; subscription: $12/year. Make checks payable to C.J. Sage only.

How to Submit Submit 3-5 poems at a time. Considers simultaneous submissions ''with notification only''; no previously published poems. No disk submissions. ''E-mail submissions are allowed only from those following all guidelines; send to tnprsubmissions@yahoo.com.'' Cover letter is preferred. ''Submit poems with brief bio, contact information including e-mail address if you have one (e-mail addresses will be kept confidential), and SASE. Please write your own address in the return address area of your SASE as well as in the addressee area. Subscribers and benefactors may submit any time during the year (please write 'subscriber' or 'benefactor' on your envelope). Reading period for non-subscribers is June through August only. See Web site before submitting.'' Time between acceptance and publication is no more than one year. ''The editor makes all publishing decisions.'' Seldom comments on rejected poems. Guidelines available in magazine or on Web site. Usually responds in about 8 weeks. Pays one contributor's copy ''and small honorarium if funds are available.'' Acquires first rights.

Contest/Award Offerings The Annie Finch Prize for Poetry, The Laureate Prize for Poetry, and *The National Poetry Review* Book Prize (see separate listings in Contests & Awards).

Advice ''Read an issue or two before submitting. Send only your very best work.''

◖ NERVE COWBOY

P.O. Box 4973, Austin TX 78765. Web site: www.jwhagins.com/nervecowboy.html. Established 1995. **Contact:** Joseph Shields and Jerry Hagins, co-editors.

Magazine Needs *Nerve Cowboy*, published semiannually, features contemporary poetry, short fiction, and b&w drawings. ''Open to all forms, styles, and subject matter, preferring writing that speaks directly and minimizes literary devices.'' Wants ''poetry of experience and passion which can find that raw nerve and ride it. We are always looking for that rare writer who inherently knows what word comes next.'' Has published poetry by Fred Voss, Gerald Locklin, Suellen Luwish, Joan Jobe Smith, Heather Abner, and David J. Thompson. *Nerve Cowboy* is 64 pages, $7 \times 8^{1}/_{2}$, attractively printed, saddle-stapled, with matte card cover with b&w art. Accepts about 5% of submissions received. Press run is 300 (175 subscribers). Subscription: $16/4 issues. Sample: $6.

How to Submit Submit 3-7 poems at a time. Considers previously published poems with notification; no simultaneous submissions. Cover letter is preferred. Inclue bio and credits. Put name on each page of ms. Seldom comments on rejected poems. Guidelines available for SASE or on Web site. Responds in 3 months. Pays one contributor's copy. Acquires first or one-time rights.

Contest/Award Offerings The Nerve Cowboy Chapbook Contest (see separate listing Contests & Awards).

$⬛ NEW ENGLAND REVIEW

Middlebury College, Middlebury VT 05753. (802)443-5075. E-mail: nereview@middlebury.edu. (inquiries only). Web site: http://go.middlebury.edu/nereview. Established 1978. **Contact:** Poetry Editor.

● Work published in *New England Review* is frequently included in *The Best American Poetry*.

Magazine Needs *New England Review*, published quarterly, is a prestigious, nationally distributed literary journal. Has published poetry by Carl Phillips, Lucia Perillo, Linda Gregerson, and William Logan. *New England Review* is 200+ pages, 7×10, printed on heavy stock, flat-spined, with glossy cover with art. Receives 3,000-4,000 poetry submissions/year, accepts about 70-80 poems/year. Subscription: $25. Sample: $8.

How to Submit Submit up to 6 poems at a time. No previously published poems or simultaneous submissions. Accepts submissions by postal mail only; accepts questions by e-mail. "Brief cover letters are useful." Address submissions to Poetry Editor. Reads submissions postmarked September 1-May 31 only. Time between acceptance and publication is 3-6 months. Responds in up to 3 months. Always sends prepublication galleys. Pays $10/page ($20 minimum) plus 2 contributor's copies. Send materials for review consideration.

Advice "Read a few copies of the magazine before submitting work. Our response time is reasonable, so please do not send simultaneous submissions."

▣ ⬛ THE NEW HAMPSHIRE REVIEW

E-mail: submissions@tnhr.org. Web site: www.tnhr.org. Established 2005. **Contact:** Seth D. Abramson, poetry editor. Editor-in-chief: Virginia M. Heatter.

Magazine Needs *The New Hampshire Review*, published irregularly online, seeks "ambitious work from both new and established writers." Has published poetry by Dan Beachy-Quick, Jason Schneiderman, C. Dale Young, Peter Campion, and Paula Bohince. Receives more than 1,500 submissions/year, accepts less than 4%.

How to Submit Submit 3-5 poems at a time. Considers simultaneous submissions "if stated in cover letter; we ask that you notify us immediately upon acceptance elsewhere"; no previously published poems. Accepts e-mail submissions (see Web site for specific submission instructions); no disk submissions. Cover letter is required. "E-mail submissions without an appropriate cover letter will not receive a response. Cover letter must include full name, address, and phone number." Reads submissions year round. Time between acceptance and publication is 3-6 months. Seldom comments on rejected poems. Guidelines available on Web site. Responds in 2-4 months. Always sends prepublication galleys "as HTML sample page(s)." Acquires first North American serial rights. Reviews books of poetry. Send materials for review consideration to Review Editor (reviews@tnhr.org).

⬛ NEW LETTERS

University of Missouri-Kansas City, 5101 Rockhill Rd., Kansas City MO 64110. (816)235-1168. Fax: (816)235-2611. E-mail: newletters@umkc.edu. Web site: www.newletters.org. Established 1934 (as University Review), 1971 (as New Letters). **Contact:** Robert Stewart, editor.

Magazine Needs *New Letters*, published quarterly, "is dedicated to publishing the best short fiction, contemporary poetry, literary articles, photography, and artwork by both established writers and new talents." Wants "fresh, new writing of all types. Short works are more likely to be accepted than very long ones." Has published poetry by Naomi Shihab Nye, Albert Goldbarth, Quincy Troupe, Ellen Bass, Joseph Millar, and Mia Leonin. *New Letters* is about 180 pages, digest-sized, professionally printed, flat-spined, with glossy 4-color cover with art. Press run is 3,600 (2,600 subscribers, about 40% libraries). Subscription: $22. Sample: $10.

How to Submit Submit no more than 6 poems at a time. No previously published poems. No e-mail submissions. Short cover letter is preferred. Guidelines available on Web site.

Contest/Award Offerings The annual *New Letters* Poetry Prize awards $1,500 to the best group of

3-6 poems. All entries will be considered for publication in the magazine. **Entry fee:** $15 (includes one-year subscription). **Deadline:** May 18. Guidelines available for SASE or on Web site.

Advice "Write with originality and freshness in language, content, and style. Avoid clichés in imagery and subject."

⛝ $⌑ NEW ORLEANS REVIEW

Box 195, Loyola University, New Orleans LA 70118. (504)865-2295. Fax: (504)865-2294. Web site: www.loyno.edu/~noreview. Established 1968. **Contact:** Katie Ford, poetry editor.

Magazine Needs *New Orleans Review*, published twice/year, is an international journal of poetry, fiction, essays, book reviews, and interviews. Wants "dynamic writing that demonstrates attention to the language and a sense of the medium; writing that engages, surprises, moves us. We subscribe to the belief that in order to truly write well, one must first master the rudiments: grammar and syntax, punctuation, the sentence, the paragraph, the line, the stanza." Has published poetry by Chrisopher Howell, Martha Zweig, Lee Upton, Jeffrey Levine, Carlie Rosemurgy, and D.C. Berry. *New Orleans Review* is 120-200 pages, elegantly printed, perfect-bound, with glossy card cover. Receives about 3,000 mss/year. Press run is 1,500. Single copy: $7. Sample: $5.

How to Submit Submit 3-6 poems at a time. Considers simultaneous submissions "if we're notified immediately upon acceptance elsewhere"; no previously published poems. No fax submissions. Brief cover letter is preferred. Guidelines available on Web site. Responds in 2-4 months. Pays 2 contributor's copies and honorarium. Acquires first North American serial rights.

⛝ ⌑ NEW ORPHIC REVIEW

New Orphic Publishers, 706 Mill St., Nelson BC V1L 4S5 Canada. (250)354-0494. Fax: (250)352-0743. Established 1995 (New Orphic Publishers), 1998 (*New Orphic Review*). **Contact:** Margrith Schraner, associate editor. Editor-in-Chief: Ernest Hekkanen.

Magazine Needs *New Orphic Review*, published in May and October, is run "by an opinionated visionary who is beholden to no one, least of all government agencies like the Canada Council or institutions of higher learning. He feels Canadian literature is stagnant, lacks daring, and is terribly incestuous." Publishes poetry, novel excerpts, mainstream and experimental short stories, and articles on a wide range of subjects. Each issue includes a Featured Poet section. "*New Orphic Review* publishes authors from around the world as long as the pieces are written in English and are accompanied by a SASE with proper Canadian postage and/or U.S. dollars to offset the cost of postage." Wants "tight, well-wrought poetry over leggy, prosaic poetry. No 'fuck you' poetry; no rambling pseudo Beat poetry." Has published poetry by Robert Cooperman, Step Elder, Louis E. Bourgeios, and Art Joyce. *New Orphic Review* is 120-140 pages, magazine-sized, laser-printed, perfect-bound, with color cover, includes ads. Receives about 400 poems/year, accepts about 10%. Press run is 500 (250 subscribers, 20 libraries). Subscription: $30 CAD for individuals, $35 CAD for institutions. Sample: $20 CAD.

How to Submit Submit 6 poems at a time. Lines/poem: 5 minimum, 30 maximum. Considers simultaneous submissions; no previously published poems. Cover letter is preferred. "Make sure a SASE (or SAE and IRC) is included." Time between acceptance and publication is up to 8 months. "The managing editor and associate editor refer work to the editor-in-chief." Seldom comments on rejected poems. Occasionally publishes theme issues. Guidelines available for SASE (or SAE and IRC). Responds in 2 months. Pays one contributor's copy. Acquires first North American serial rights.

Additional Information New Orphic Publishers publishes 4 paperbacks/year. However, **all material is solicited**.

Advice "Read the magazine before submitting."

$⬛ THE NEW RENAISSANCE

26 Heath Rd. #11, Arlington MA 02474-3645. E-mail: marccreate@aol.com. (inquiries only). Web site: www.tnrlitmag.net. Established 1968. **Contact:** Frank Finale, poetry editor. Editor-in-Chief: Louise T. Reynolds.

Magazine Needs *the new renaissance*, published spring and fall ("resources permitting"), is "intended for the 'renaissance' person—the generalist, not the specialist. We publish the best new writing and translations and offer a forum for articles on political, sociological topics; feature established as well as emerging visual artists and writers; highlight reviews of small press; and offer essays on a variety of topics from visual arts and literature to science. Open to a variety of styles, including traditional." Has published poetry by Anita Susan Brenner, Anne Struthers, Marc Widershien, Miguel Torga (trans. Alexis Levetin), Stephen Todd Booker, and Rabindranath Togore (trans. Wendy Barker and S. Togore). *the new renaissance* is 144-182 pages, digest-sized, professionally printed on heavy stock, flat-spined, with glossy color cover. Receives about 650 poetry submissions/year, accepts about 40. Press run is 1,500 (760 subscribers, 132 libraries). Single copy: $12.50 (current), $11.50 (recent), $7.50 (back issue); subscription: $30 for 3 issues in U.S., $35 in Canada, $38 all others. "All checks in U.S. dollars. A three-issue subscription covers 18-22 months."

How to Submit Submit 3-6 poems at a time, "unless a long poem—then one." Considers simultaneous submissions, if notified; no previously published poems "unless magazine's circulation was under 250." Always include SASE or IRC. Accepts submissions by postal mail only; "when accepted, we ask if a disk is available, and we prefer accepted translations to be available in the original language on disk. **All poetry submissions are tied to our Awards Program for poetry published in a three-issue volume; judged by independent judges."** **Entry fee:** $16.50 for non-subscribers, $11.50 for subscribers, "for which they receive 2 back issues or a recent issue or an extension of their subscription. Submissions without entry fee are returned unread." Reads submissions January 2-June 30. Guidelines available for SASE. Responds in 5 months. Pays $21-40 (more for the occasional longer poem), plus one contributor's copy/poem. Acquires all rights but returns rights provided *the new renaissance* retains rights for any *the new renaissance* collection. Reviews books of poetry.

Contest/Award Offerings The Awards Program offers 3 prizes of $250, $125, and $50, with 3-4 Honorable Mentions of $25 each; all submissions are tied to the Awards Program (see above for entry fee).

Advice "Read, read, read! And support the literary magazines that support serious writers and poets. In 2002, more than 350 separate submissions came in, all without the required fee. Since our Poetry Awards Program has been in effect since 1995, and since we've notified all markets about our guidelines and entry fee, this just shows an indifferent, careless reading of our magazine's requirements."

⬛ ⬛ ⬛ ⬛ THE NEW VERSE NEWS (Specialized: current news, issues, & events)

E-mail: editor@newversenews.com. Web site: www.newversenews.com. Established 2005. **Contact:** James Penha, editor.

Magazine Needs *The New Verse News*, published online and updated "every day or two," has "a clear liberal bias, but will consider various visions and views." Wants "poems, both serious and satirical, on current events and topical issues; will also consider prose poems and short-short stories and plays." Does not want "work unrelated to the news." Has published poetry by Rochelle Ratner, Bill Costley, Rochelle Owens, A.D. Winans, Mary Saracino, and Dave Lordan. Receives about 700 poems/year, accepts about 300.

How to Submit Submit 1-5 poems at a time. Lines/poem: no length restrictions. No previously published poems or simultaneous submissions. Accepts e-mail submissions (pasted into body of message); no disk submissions. Reads submissions year round. Submit seasonal poems one month in advance. "Normally, poems are published immediately upon acceptance." Poems are circulated to an editorial board. Sometimes comments on rejected poems. Guidelines available on Web site. Responds in 1-3 weeks. No payment. Acquires first rights. Rights revert to poet upon publication.

⊕ $⬚ THE NEW WRITER

P.O. Box 60, Cranbrook, Kent TN17 2ZR England. (44)(1580)212626. Fax: (44)(1580)212041. E-mail: admin@thenewwriter.com. Web site: www.thenewwriter.com. Established 1996. **Contact:** Catherine Smith, poetry editor.

Magazine Needs *The New Writer*, published 6 times/year, is "aimed at writers with a serious intent, who want to develop their writing to meet the high expectations of today's editors. The team at *The New Writer* is committed to working with its readers to increase the chances of publication through masses of useful information and plenty of feedback. More than that, we let you know about the current state of the market with the best in contemporary fiction and cutting-edge poetry, backed up by searching articles and in-depth features." Wants "short and long unpublished poems, provided they are original and undeniably brilliant. No problems with length/form, but anything over two pages (150 lines) needs to be brilliant. Cutting edge shouldn't mean inaccessible. No recent disasters—they date." Does not want " 'my baby/doggie' poems, God poems that sound like hymns, dum-dum rhymes, or comic rhymes (best left at the pub)." *The New Writer* is 56 pages, A4, professionally printed, saddle-stapled, with paper cover. Press run is 1,500 (1,350 subscribers); 50 distributed free to publishers, agents. Single copy: £6.25 in U.S. (5 IRCs required); subscription: £37.50 in U.S. "We have a secure server for subscriptions and entry into the annual Prose and Poetry Prizes on the Web site. Monthly e-mail newsletter included free of charge in the subscription package."

How to Submit Submit up to 6 poems at a time. Lines/poem: 150 maximum. Considers previously published poems. Accepts e-mail submissions (pasted into body of message). Time between acceptance and publication is up to 6 months. Often comments on rejected poems. **Offers criticism service: £12/6 poems.** Guidelines available for SASE (or SAE with IRC) or on Web site. Pays £3 voucher plus one contributor's copy. Acquires first British serial rights. Reviews books/chapbooks of poetry and other magazines. Send materials for review consideration.

Contest/Award Offerings Sponsors *The New Writer* Prose & Poetry Prizes annually. "All poets writing in the English language are invited to submit an original, previously unpublished poem or a collection of six to ten poems. Up to 25 prizes will be presented, as well as publication for the prize-winning poets in an anthology, plus the chance for a further ten shortlisted poets to see their work published in *The New Writer* during the year." Guidelines available by e-mail or on Web site.

⬚ NEW YORK QUARTERLY

P.O. Box 693, Old Chelsea Station, New York NY 10113. Web site: www.nyquarterly.com. Established 1969. **Contact:** Raymond Hammond, editor.

Magazine Needs *New York Quarterly*, published 3 times/year, seeks to print "a cross-section of the best of contemporary American poetry." Has published poetry by Charles Bukowski, James Dickey, Lola Haskins, Lyn Lifshin, Elisavietta Ritchie, and W.D. Snodgrass. *New York Quarterly* is digest-sized, elegantly printed, flat-spined, with glossy color cover. Subscription: $20.

How to Submit Submit 3-5 poems at a time. Considers simultaneous submissions with notification. Include your name and address on each page. "Include SASE; no international postage coupons." Guidelines available on Web site. Responds within 6 weeks. Pays in contributor's copies.

$⬚ THE NEW YORKER

4 Times Square, New York NY 10036. E-mail: poetry@newyorker.com. Web site: www.newyorker. com. Established 1925. **Contact:** Poetry Editor.

● Poems published in *The New Yorker* often have been included *The Best American Poetry*.

Magazine Needs *The New Yorker*, published weekly, prints poetry of the highest quality (including translations). Subscription: $47/year (47 issues), $77 for 2 years (94 issues).

How to Submit Submit no more than 6 poems at a time. No previously published poems or simultaneous submissions. Accepts e-mail submissions (pasted into body of message or as attachment). Include poet's name in the subject line and as the title of attached document. "We prefer to receive no more than two submissions per writer per year." Pays top rates.

NEW ZOO POETRY REVIEW

P.O. Box 36760, Richmond VA 23235. Web site: http://members.aol.com/newzoopoet. Established 1997. **Contact:** Angela Vogel, editor.

Magazine Needs *New Zoo Poetry Review*, published annually in January, tends to print "free verse in well-crafted lyric and narrative forms. Our goal is to publish established poets alongside lesser-known poets of great promise." Wants "serious, intellectual poetry of any form, length, or style. Rhyming poetry only if exceptional." Does not want "light verse, song lyrics, or greeting card copy. If you're not reading the best of contemporary poetry, then *New Zoo Poetry Review* is not for you." Has published poetry by Heather McHugh, Leonard Gontarek, Frannie Lindsay, Marlys West, Natasha Sajé, and Martha Collins. *New Zoo Poetry Review* is 30-40 pages, digest-sized, photocopied, saddle-stapled, with card cover with with illustration or photo. Receives about 1,000 poems/year, accepts about 4%. Press run is 200. Single copy: $5.

How to Submit Submit 3-5 poems at a time. Considers simultaneous submissions; no previously published poems. Cover letter is required. Include SASE and brief bio. Seldom comments on rejected poems. Responds in 2 months. Pays one contributor's copy. Acquires first North American serial rights. "Poets are discouraged from submitting more than once in a 12-month period. Please do not write to us for these submission guidelines. We understand and encourage simultaneous submissions and think threatening to 'blacklist' poets who do so responsibly is unfortunate. *NZPR* responds to submissions in an appropriate timeframe and seeks thereby to gather the best work out there."

NEXUS LITERARY JOURNAL

016 Student Union, Wright State University, Dayton OH 45435. (937)775-5533. E-mail: wsu_nexus @yahoo.com. Established 1967. **Contact:** Dave Nichols, editor.

Magazine Needs *Nexus Literary Journal*, published 3 times/year in fall, winter, and spring, is a student-operated magazine of mainstream and street poetry. Wants "truthful, direct poetry. Open to poets anywhere. We look for contemporary, imaginative work." *Nexus* is 80-96 pages. Receives about 1,000 submissions/year, accepts about 50-70. Circulation is 3,000. Sample: free for 10×15 SAE with 5 first-class stamps.

How to Submit Submit up to 5 poems at a time. Considers simultaneous submissions ("due to short response time, we want to be told it's a simultaneous submission"). Cover letter is required. Include brief bio. Reads submissions year round. Sometimes comments on rejected poems. Upcoming themes and guidelines available in magazine, for SASE, or by e-mail. Responds in 5 months except during summer. Pays 2 contributor's copies. Acquires first rights.

NIMROD: INTERNATIONAL JOURNAL OF POETRY AND PROSE

University of Tulsa, 600 S. College Ave., Tulsa OK 74104-3189. (918)631-3080. Fax: (918)631-3033. E-mail: nimrod@utulsa.edu. Web site: www.utulsa.edu/nimrod. Established 1956. **Contact:** Manly Johnson, poetry editor.

- Poetry published in *Nimrod* has been included in *The Best American Poetry*.

Magazine Needs *Nimrod: International Journal of Poetry and Prose*, published 2 times/year, is "an active 'little magazine,' part of the movement in American letters which has been essential to the development of modern literature." Publishes an awards issue in the fall, featuring the prizewinners of its national competition, and a thematic issue each spring. "Poems in non-award issues range from formal to freestyle with several translations." Wants "vigorous writing that is neither wholly of the academy nor the streets; typed manuscripts." Has published poetry by Diane Glancy, Judith Strasser, Steve Lautermilch, Virgil Suárez, and Jen-Mark Sens. *Nimrod* is about 200 pages, digest-sized, professionally printed on coated stock, perfect-bound, with full-color glossy cover. Receives about 2,000 submissions/year, accepts 1%. Press run is 2,500 (subscribers, 200 public and university libraries). Subscription: $17.50/year U.S., $19 foreign. Sample: $10. "Specific back issues available. Please send check or money order."

How to Submit Submit 5-10 poems at a time. No fax or e-mail submissions. Publishes theme issues. Guidelines available for SASE, by e-mail, or on Web site. Responds in up to 3 months. "During the months that the *Nimrod*/Hardman Awards competition is being conducted, reporting time on non-contest manuscripts will be longer." Pays 2 contributor's copies, plus reduced cost on additional copies.

Contest/Award Offerings The annual *Nimrod*/Hardman Writing Awards include The Pablo Neruda Prize for Poetry (see separate listing in Contests & Awards).

Also Offers Sponsors the *Nimrod*/Hardman Awards Workshop, a one-day workshop held annually in October. Cost is about $50. Send SASE for brochure and registration form.

$☑ NINTH LETTER

Dept. of English, University of Illinois, 608 S. Wright St., Urbana IL 61801.E-mail: ninthletter@uiuc.edu. Web site: www.ninthletter.com. Established 2004. **Contact:** Jodee Stanley, editor. Member: CLMP; CELJ.

- *Ninth Letter* won Best New Literary Journal 2005 from the Council of Editors of Learned Journals (CELJ) and has had poetry selected for *The Pushcart Prize*, *Best New Poets*, and *The Year's Best Fantasy and Horror*.

Magazine Needs *Ninth Letter*, published semiannually, is "dedicated to the examination of literature as it intersects with various aspects of contemporary culture and intellectual life." Open to all forms of poetry. Wants "exceptional literary quality." Has published poetry by Cate Marvin, L.S. Asekoff, William Wenthe, Sharmila Voorakkara, Geri Doran, and T.R. Hummer. *Ninth Letter* is 176 pages, 9×12, offset-printed, perfect-bound, with 4-color cover with graphics. Receives about 9,000 poems/year, accepts about 40. Press run is 3,500 (500 subscribers, 1,000 shelf sales); 1,500 distributed free, 500 to contributors, media, and fundraising efforts. Single copy: $12.95; subscription: $19.95/year. Sample: $8.95 (back issue). Make checks payable to *Ninth Letter*.

How to Submit Submit no more than 6 poems or 10 pages at a time. No previously published poems or simultaneous submissions. No e-mail or disk submissions. Cover letter is preferred. "SASE must be included for reply." Reads submissions September 1-April 30 (inclusive postmark dates). Time between acceptance and publication is 5-6 months. Poems are circulated to an editorial board. Sometimes comments on rejected poems. Guidelines available for SASE, by e-mail, or on Web site. Responds in 2 months. Always sends prepublications galleys. Pays $25/page and 2 contributor's copies. Acquires first North American serial rights. Rights revert to poet upon publication.

☑ NOMAD'S CHOIR

% Meander, 30-15 Hobart St., F4H, Woodside NY 11377. Established 1989. **Contact:** Joshua Meander, editor.

Magazine Needs *Nomad's Choir*, published quarterly, seeks "love poems, protest poems, mystical poems, nature poems, poems of humanity, poems with solutions to world problems and inner conflict, poems with hope; simple words, careful phrasing." Wants "free verse, rhymed poems, sonnets, half-page parables, myths and legends, song lyrics." Does not want "curse words in poems; little or no name-dropping; no naming of consumer products; no 2-page poems; no humor, no bias writing, no poems untitled." Has published poetry by David Lo, Marta Rosario, Tim Divito, and Lily Georgick. *Nomad's Choir* is 12 pages, magazine-sized, typeset, saddle-stapled. Receives about 150 poems/year, accepts 50. Press run is 400; all distributed free. Subscription: $5. Sample: $1.50. Make checks payable to Joshua Meander.

How to Submit Submit 4 poems at a time, each on a different topic. Lines/poem: 9 minimum, 30 maximum. Guidelines available for SASE. Responds in 2 months. Pays one contributor's copy. **Advice** "Social commentary with beauty and hope gets first consideration."

$⬛ NORTH AMERICAN REVIEW

University of Northern Iowa, 1222 West 27th St., Cedar Falls IA 50614-0516. (319)273-6455. Fax: (319)273-4326. E-mail: nar@uni.edu. Web site: http://webdelsol.com/NorthAmReview/NAR. Established 1815. **Contact:** Vince Gotera, poetry editor.

Magazine Needs *North American Review*, published 5 times/year, is "the oldest literary magazine in America." Wants "poetry of the highest quality; poems that are passionate about subject, language, and image. Especially interested in work that addresses contemporary North American concerns and issues, particularly with the environment, race, ethnicity, gender, sexual orientation, and class." Has published poetry by Debra Marquart, Nick Carboó, Yusef Komunyakaa, Virgil Suárez, Nance Van Winckel, and Dara Wier. *North American Review* is about 48 pages, magazine-sized, professionally printed, saddle-stapled, with glossy full-color paper cover. Receives about 10,000 poems/year, accepts 100. Press run is 2,500 (1,500 subscribers, 1,000 libraries). Subscription: $22 in U.S., $29 in Canada, $32 foreign. Sample: $5.

How to Submit Submit 3-6 poems at a time. No previously published poems or simultaneous submissions. No fax, e-mail, or disk submissions. Cover letter is preferred. Include brief bio and list poem titles. Include SASE. Time between acceptance and publication is up to one year. Guidelines available in magazine, for SASE, by e-mail, or on Web site. Responds in 4 months. Always sends prepublication galleys. Pays $1/line ($20 minimum, $100 maximum) and 2 contributor's copies. Acquires first North American serial rights only. Rights revert to poets upon publication.

Contest/Award Offerings The annual James Hearst Poetry Prize (see separate listing in Contest & Awards).

✦ $⬚ NORTH CAROLINA LITERARY REVIEW (Specialized: NC topics, work by NC authors)

Dept. of English, East Carolina University, Greenville NC 27858-4353. (252)328-1537. E-mail: bauerm@mail.ecu.edu. Web site: www.ecu.edu/nclr. Established 1992. **Contact:** Margaret Bauer, editor.

Magazine Needs *North Carolina Literary Review*, published annually in the summer, contains "articles and other works about North Carolina topics or by North Carolina authors." Wants "poetry by writers currently living in North Carolina, those who have lived in North Carolina, or those using North Carolina for subject matter." Has published poetry by Betty Adcock, James Applewhite, and A.R. Ammons. *North Carolina Literary Review* is 200 pages, magazine-sized. Receives about 100 submissions/year, accepts about 10%. Press run is 1,000 (350 subscribers, 100 libraries, 100 shelf sales); 100 distributed free to contributors. Subscription: $20 for 2 years, $36 for 4 years. Sample: $15.

How to Submit Submit 3-5 poems at a time. No e-mail submissions. Cover letter is required. "Submit two copies and include SASE or e-mail address for response." Reads submissions August 1-April 30 only. Time between acceptance and publication is up to one year. Often comments on rejected poems. Guidelines available for SASE, by e-mail, or on Web site. Responds in 3 months within reading period. Sometimes sends prepublication galleys. Pays 2-year subscription plus 1-2 contributor's copies. Acquires first or one-time rights. Reviews books of poetry by North Carolina poets in up to 2,000 words, multi-book format. Poets from North Carolina may send books for review consideration. Rarely reviews chapbooks.

◻ ⬚ NORTH CENTRAL REVIEW (Specialized: undergraduate writers)

North Central College, CM #235, 30 N. Brainard St., Naperville IL 60540. (630)637-5291. Fax: (630)637-5221. E-mail: nccreview@noctrl.edu. Established 1936. **Contact:** The Editors ("editors change year to year, but postal and e-mail addresses don't").

Magazine Needs *North Central Review*, published semiannually, considers "work in all literary genres, including occasional interviews, from undergraduate writers globally. The journal's goal is for college-level, emerging creative writers to share their work publicly and create a conversation with each other. ALL styles and forms are welcome as submissions. The readers tend to value attention to form (but not necessarily fixed form), voice, and detail. Very long poems or sequences (running more than four or five pages) may require particular excellence because of the journal's space and budget constraints." Does not want "overly sentimental language and hackneyed imagery. These are all-too-common weaknesses that readers see in submissions; we recommend revision and polishing before sending work." Considers poetry by teens (undergraduate writers only). *North Central Review* is 120 pages, digest-sized, perfect-bound, with cardstock cover with 4-color design. Press run is about 750, distributed free to contributors and publication reception attendees. Single copy: $5; subscription: $10. Make checks payable to *North Central Review*.

How to Submit Submit 2-5 poems at a time. Lines/poem: "no limit, but poems running more than 4-5 pages may undergo particular scrutiny." No previously published poems or simultaneous submissions. Accepts e-mail submissions (as Word attachments only); no fax submissions. Cover letter is preferred. Include name, postal address, phone number, and e-mail address (.edu address as proof of student status). If necessary (i.e., .edu address not available), include a photocopy of student ID with number marked out as proof of undergraduate status. Reads submissions September-March, with deadlines of February 15 and October 15. Time between acceptance and publication is 1-4 months. Poems are circulated to an editorial board. "All submissions are read by at least three staff members, including an editor." Sometimes comments on rejected poems. Guidelines available in magazine, for SASE, or by e-mail. Responds in 1-4 months. Pays 2 contributor's copies. Acquires one-time rights. Rights revert to poet upon publication.

Also Offers "For every issue, the staff holds a Publication Celebration and Reading featuring the work in the journal. Contributors are welcome to attend, but the staff recognizes that distance prohibits most contributors from joining in. So, NCC student contributors read their work, and staff also read selections from undergraduates elsewhere. Refreshments are served, and copies of the issue are free to those in attendance."

Advice "Don't send anything you just finished moments ago—rethink, revise, and polish. Avoid sentimentalitity and abstraction. That said, the *North Central Review* publishes beginners, so don't hesitate to submit and, if rejected, submit again."

◖ NORTH DAKOTA QUARTERLY

Merrifield Hall Room 110, 276 Centennial Dr. Stop 7209, Grand Forks ND 58202-7209. E-mail: ndq@und.nodak.edu. Web site: www.und.nodak.edu/org/ndq. Established 1910. **Contact:** Robert Lewis, editor.

Magazine Needs *North Dakota Quarterly* is published by the University of North Dakota. Seeks material related to the arts and humanities—essays, fiction, interviews, poems, reviews, and visual art. Wants poetry "that reflects an understanding not only of the difficulties of the craft, but of the vitality and tact that each poem calls into play." Has published poetry by Maxine Kumin, Paul Muldoon, Robert Bagg, James Scully, Patricia Schneider, and Marianne Boruch. *North Dakota Quarterly* is about 200 pages, digest-sized, professionally designed and printed, perfect-bound, with full-color artwork on white card cover. Has 550 subscribers. Subscription: $25/year. Sample: $8.

How to Submit Submit 5 poems at a time. No previously published poems or simultaneous submissions. No e-mail submissions; accepts only typed hard-copy submissions by postal mail. Time between acceptance and publication varies. Responds in up to 6 weeks. Always sends prepublication galleys. Pays 2 contributor's copies. Acquires first serial rights.

Advice "We look to publish the best fiction, poetry, and essays that, in our estimation, we can. Our tastes and interests are best reflected in what we have been recently publishing, and we suggest that you look at some current numbers."

◖ NORTHEAST ARTS MAGAZINE

P.O. Box 4363, Portland ME 04101. Established 1990. **Contact:** Mr. Leigh Donaldson, editor/publisher.

Magazine Needs *Northeast Arts Magazine*, published biannually, seeks poetry, short fiction, essays, reviews, art, and photography that is "honest, clear, with a love of expression through simple language. We maintain a special interest in work that reflects cultural diversity in New England and throughout the world." Has published poetry by Steve Lutrell, Eliot Richman, Elizabeth R. Curry, Bob Begieburg, and Alisa Aran. *Northeast Arts Magazine* is 32 or more pages, digest-sized, professionally printed, with one-color coated card cover. Accepts 10-20% of submissions. Press run is 500-1,000 (150 subscribers, 75 libraries); 50 distributed to arts organizations. Subscription: $10. Sample: $4.50.

How to Submit Lines/poem: 30 maximum. "A short bio is helpful." Reads submissions November 1-February 1 only. Guidelines available for SASE. Responds in 3 months. Pays 2 contributor's copies. Acquires first North American serial rights.

◻ NORTHERN STARS MAGAZINE

North Star Publishing, N17285 Co. Rd. 400, Powers MI 49874. Established 1997. **Contact:** Beverly Kleikamp, editor.

Magazine Needs *Northern Stars Magazine*, published bimonthly, welcomes submissions of fiction, nonfiction, and poetry on any subject or style. "The main requirement is good clean family reading material—nothing you can't read to your child or your mother." Does not want "smut or filth." Considers poetry by children and teens. Has published poetry by Terri Warden, Gary Edwards, Sheila B. Roark, and C.L. Rymer. *Northern Stars Magazine* is 32 pages, magazine-sized, photocopied, saddle-stapled, with cardstock cover. Single copy: $5; subscription: $21. Make checks payable to Beverly Kleikamp or *Northern Stars Magazine*.

How to Submit Submit up to 5 poems at a time. Lines/poem: 25 maximum. "Shorter poems stand a better chance of timely publication." Considers previously published poems; no simultaneous submissions. Cover letter is preferred. "Manuscripts must be typed; please do not submit handwritten material." Often comments on rejected poems. Guidelines available for SASE. "No payment, but nonsubscribers are notified of publication." All rights return to authors on publication.

Additional Information "I also publish chapbooks **for an 'affordable' price to the author**." Has published more than 100 chapbooks to date, including *Beholden* by Paul Truttman and *Butterfly Descending Sunlight* by Nancy M. Ryan. Chapbook prices and information available for SASE.

Contest/Award Offerings 1) Sponsors contests for poetry and fiction/nonfiction in alternating issues (i.e., poetry contest in March-April issue, fiction/nonfiction in May-June). Guidelines available for SASE. **Entry fee:** $2.50/poem for nonsubscribers, $1/poem for subscribers. **Deadline:** 20th of month preceding publication. Publishes an annual chapbook of contest winners and honorable mentions in January. 2) Also sponsors an annual chapbook contest, offering 1st Prize: 50 copies; 2nd Prize: 25 copies; 3rd Prize: 10 copies. Submit 24-page poetry chapbooks only. All copy must be typewritten with name and address at the top of each page. Guidelines available for SASE. **Entry fee:** $20. **Deadline:** December 31. Winner announced January 30.

Advice "Keep it clean, short, and interesting."

◖ NORTHWEST REVIEW

369 PLC, University of Oregon, Eugene OR 97403. (541)346-3957. Fax: (541)346-1509. E-mail: jwitte@uoregon.edu. (inquiries only). Web site: http://nwr.uoregon.edu. Established 1957. **Contact:** John Witte, poetry editor.

- Poetry published by *Northwest Review* has been included in *The Best American Poetry*.

Magazine Needs *Northwest Review*, published 3 times/year in May, September, and January, states, "The only criterion for acceptance of material for publication is that of excellence. There are no restrictions on length, style, or subject matter, but we smile on originality.'' Has published poetry by Alan Dugan, Charles Bukowski, Ted Hughes, Olga Broumas, Gary Snyder, and William Stafford. *Northwest Review* is digest-sized, flat-spined. Receives about 3,500 submissions/year, accepts about 4%. Press run is 1,300 (1,200 subscribers, 600 libraries). Single copy: $8; subscription: $22/year (3 issues). Sample: $4.

How to Submit Submit 6-8 poems at a time. No simultaneous submissions. No e-mail submissions; postal submissions only. Send only clear, clean copies. Guidelines available on Web site. Responds within 3 months. Pays 3 contributor's copies.

Advice ''Persist.''

$⊘ NORTHWOODS JOURNAL

Northwoods Press, P.O. Box 298, Thomaston ME 04861-0298. (207)354-0998. E-mail: cal@america nletters.org. (inquiries only). Web site: www.americanletters.org. Established 1972 (Northwoods Press), 1993 (*Northwoods Journal*). **Contact:** Robert Olmsted, editor.

Magazine Needs *Northwoods Journal*, published quarterly, is a literary magazine for writers that publishes fiction, essays, reviews, nonfiction, and poetry. Interested in ''all writers who feel they have something to say and who work to say it well. We have no interest in closet writers or credit-seekers. All writers seeking an audience, working to improve their craft, and determined to 'get it right' are welcome here.'' *Northwoods Journal* is about 40 pages, digest-sized. Subscription: available only through membership in the Conservatory of American Letters (CAL) ($25/year). Sample: $6.50 and 6×9 SASE with $1.31 postage affixed.

How to Submit No previously published poems or simultaneous submissions. No e-mail submissions; submit by postal mail only. **Reading fee: $1 for 2 poems for CAL members, $1/poem for nonmembers.**'' CAL offers one free read (up to 5 poems) per year if poetry is submitted simultaneously with membership or renewal.'' Make checks payable to CAL. Guidelines available for SASE or on Web site. ''See guidelines before submitting anything.'' Pays 10¢ per line on average; ''we do not provide free issues.''

Additional Information Northwoods Press considers ''books by working poets only. No subsidy permitted. No closet poets or credit-seekers. All accepted books offer opportunity to include CD of author (or others) reading the book, or selections from the book. Original CD to be produced by author as we have no recording studio. No reading fee for book-length works. We would like to publish up to 12 books per year, but never receive enough quality manuscripts.'' Requires a personal marketing plan of prospective authors and **membership in the Conservatory of American Letters (CAL)**.

Also Offers Publishes *The Northwoods Anthology*. Considers poetry and fiction. **Deadline:** October 31. Guidelines available for #10 SASE or on Web site. Pays cash on acceptance.

Advice ''Reading fees hold submissions down to a level that someone with 'yes' authority can actually read. They limit competition in a big way. We never get enough of anything. Reading this blurb does not equal 'knowing your market.' Read a few issues. Anyone who submits to a magazine or anthology they've never seen deserves whatever happens.''

$⊘ NOTRE DAME REVIEW/ND[RE]VIEW

840 Flanner Hall, University of Notre Dame, Notre Dame IN 46556. (574)631-7562. Fax: (574)631-4795. E-mail: english.ndreview.1@nd.edu. Web site: www.nd.edu/~ndr/review.htm. Established 1994. **Contact:** Managing Editor.

Magazine Needs *Notre Dame Review*, published semiannually, aims ''to present a panoramic view of contemporary art and literature—no one style is advocated over another. We are especially interested in work that takes on big issues by making the invisible seen.'' Has published poetry by W.S. Merwin, R.T. Smith, Moira Egan, Michael Harper, Floyd Skloot, and Kevin Ducey. *Notre Dame Review* is 170 pages, magazine-sized, perfect-bound, with 4-color glossy cover, includes ads.

Receives about 400 poems/year, accepts 10%. Press run is 2,000 (500 subscribers, 150 libraries, 1,000 shelf sales); 350 distributed free to contributors, assistants, etc. Single copy: $8; subscription: $15/year. Sample: $6 (back issue).

How to Submit Submit 3-5 poems at a time. Considers simultaneous submissions; no previously published poems. Cover letter is required. Reads submissions September-November and January-March only. Time between acceptance and publication is 3 months. Seldom comments on rejected poems. Publishes theme issues. Guidelines available on Web site. Responds in 3 months. Always sends prepublication galleys. Pays small gratuity on publication, plus 2 contributor's copies. Acquires first rights. Staff reviews books of poetry in 500 words, single- and multi-book format. Send materials for review consideration.

Additional Information *nd[re]view* is the online companion to *Notre Dame Review*, offering "interviews, critique, and commentary on authors and artists showcased within the pages of the print magazine." See Web site for more details.

Contest/Award Offerings The Ernest Sandeen Prize in Poetry (see separate listing in Contests & Awards).

Advice "Read magazine before submitting."

⊕ ▣ ☑ NTHPOSITION

E-mail: toddswift@clara.co.uk. Web site: www.nthposition.com. Established 2002. **Contact:** Todd Swift, poetry editor.

Magazine Needs *nthposition*, published monthly online, is an eclectic, London-based journal dedicated to poetry, fiction, and nonfiction "with a weird or innovative edge." Wants "all kinds of poetry—from spoken word to new formalist to linguistically innovative. We also publish political poetry." Does not want poetry from never-before-published authors. Has published poetry by Charles Bernstein, George Szirtes, Stephanie Bolster, and Mimi Khalvati. Receives about 3,000 poems/year, accepts about 5%.

How to Submit Submit 2-6 poems at a time. No previously published poems or simultaneous submissions. Accepts e-mail submissions only (pasted into body of message, no attachments). Cover letter is required. "A brief author's bio is appreciated." Reads submissions throughout the year. Time between acceptance and publication is 3 months. "Poems are read and selected by the poetry editor, who uses his own sense of what makes a poem work online to select." Never comments on rejected poems. Occasionally publishes theme issues. Guidelines available by e-mail or on Web site. Responds in one week. No payment. Does not request rights.

Also Offers Publishes special theme e-books from time to time, such as *100 Poets Against the War*.

Advice "Never give up; keep writing. Poetry is a life's work."

▢ ◎ NUTHOUSE (Specialized: humor)

Twin Rivers Press, P.O. Box 119, Ellenton FL 34222. Web site: http://hometown.aol.com/Nuthous 499/index2.html. Established 1989 (Twin Rivers Press) and 1993 (*Nuthouse*). **Contact:** Ludwig VonQuirk, editor.

Magazine Needs *Nuthouse*, published every 3 months, uses humor of all kinds, including homespun and political. Wants "humorous verse; virtually all genres considered." Has published poetry by Holly Day, Daveed Garstenstein-Ross, and Don Webb. *Nuthouse* is 12 pages, digest-sized, photocopied from desktop-published originals. Receives about 500 poems/year, accepts about 100. Press run is 100 (50 subscribers). Subscription: $5/4 issues. Sample: $1.25. Make checks payable to Twin Rivers Press.

How to Submit Considers previously published poems and simultaneous submissions. Time between acceptance and publication is 6 months to one year. Often comments on rejected poems. Responds within one month. Pays one contributor's copy/poem. Acquires one-time rights.

☐ THE OAK

1530 Seventh St., Rock Island IL 61201. (309)788-3980. Established 1991. **Contact:** Betty Mowery, poetry editor.

Magazine Needs *The Oak*, published quarterly, is a "publication for writers, featuring poetry and fiction." No restrictions as to form and style. Does not want "pornography or love poetry." Receives about 100 poems/year, accepts more than 50%. Press run is 250 (10 libraries). Subscription: $10. Sample: $3. Make all checks payable to *The Oak*.

How to Submit Submit 5 poems at a time. Lines/poem: 35 maximum. Considers previously published poems and simultaneous submissions. "Include a SASE or manuscripts will not be returned." Responds in one week. "*The Oak* does not pay in dollars or copies, but you need not purchase to be published." Acquires first or second rights.

Contest/Award Offerings Sponsors numerous poetry contests. Guidelines available for SASE.

Also Offers Established in 1991, *The Gray Squirrel* is included in *The Oak* and accepts poetry and fiction from writers 60 years of age and older.

Advice "Write tight poems with a message; don't write about lost loves or crushes. Study the markets for word limit and subject. Always include SASE, or rejected manuscripts will not be returned."

⊞ ☐ OBSESSED WITH PIPEWORK

8 Abbot's Way, Pilton, Somerset BA4 4BN England. (44)(1749)890019. E-mail: cannula.dementia@virgin.net. Established 1995. **Contact:** Charles Johnson, editor.

Magazine Needs *Obsessed with Pipework*, published quarterly, is "very keen to publish strong new voices—'new poems to surprise and delight' with somewhat of a high-wire aspect." Wants "original, exploratory poems—positive, authentic, oblique maybe—delighting in image and in the dance of words on the page." Does not want "the predictable, the unfresh, the rhyme-led, the clever, the didactic, the sure-of-itself. No formless outpourings, please." Has published poetry by David Hart, Jennifer Compton, Susan Wicks, Carol Burns, Lucille Gang Shulklapper, and Maria Jastrzebska. *Obsessed with Pipework* is 49 pages, A5, stapled, with card cover. Receives about 1,500 poems/year, accepts about 10%. Press run is 70-100. Single copy: £3.50; subscription: £12. Sample: £2 if available. Make checks payable in pounds to Flarestack Publishing. Back issues are also available online at www.poetrymagazines.org.uk.

How to Submit Submit maximum of 6 poems at a time. No previously published poems or simultaneous submissions. Accepts e-mail submissions ("paste a maximum of three poems in the body of the message, as attached files may become lost or corrupted"). Cover letter is preferred. Often comments on rejected poems. Guidelines available for SASE or by e-mail. Responds in 2 months. Pays one contributor's copy. Acquires first rights.

Advice "Most beginning poets show little evidence of reading poetry before writing it! Join a poetry workshop. For chapbook publishing, we are looking for coherent first collections that take risks, make leaps, and show evidence of being written by a human being living in the 21st century."

☑ OFF THE COAST

P.O. Box 205, Bristol ME 04539. (207)677-2840. E-mail: arge109@midcoast.com. Web site: www.ofthecoast.com. Established 1989. **Contact:** George V. Van Deventer, editor.

Magazine Needs *Off the Coast*, published 3 times/year in January, May, and September, prints all styles and forms of poetry. Does not want pornography or profanity. Considers poetry by children and teens. Has published poetry by Kate Barnes, Henry Braun, Wesley McNair, Baron Wormser, Betsy Sholl, and Robert Cording. *Off the Coast* is 68+ pages, digest-sized, copied, perfect-bound, with stock cover with original art. Receives about 1,500 poems/year, accepts about 175. Press run is 300 (247 subscribers, 6 shelf sales); occasional complimentary copies offered. Single copy: $8; subscription: $25. Make checks payable to *Off the Coast*.

How to Submit Submit 4-6 poems at a time. Lines/poem: prefers 32 maximum. Considers previously published poems. No e-mail or disk submissions. Cover letter is preferred. "Put name and address on every page; include SASE." Reads submissions year round. Time between acceptance and publication is 3-6 months. Sometimes comments on rejected poems. Guidelines available in magazine or on Web site. Responds in 1-3 months. Pays one contributor's copy. "The rights to each individual poem and print are retained by each individual artist." Reviews books/chapbooks of poetry and other magazines/journals in 500 words. Send materials for review consideration to George V. Van Deventer.

🖥 ☑ OFFERTA SPECIALE

Bertola Carla Press, Corso De Nicola 20, Torino 10128 Italy. Established 1988. **Contact:** Carla Bertola, editor/director.

Magazine Needs *Offerta Speciale*, published semiannually in May and November, is an international journal. Has published poetry by Federica Manfredini (Italy), Bernard Heidsieck (France), Richard Kostelanetz, and E. Mycue (U.S.). *Offerta Speciale* is 56 pages, digest-sized, neatly printed, saddle-stapled, with glossy card cover. Receives about 300 poems/year, accepts about 40%. Press run is 500 (60 subscribers). Single copy: $25; subscription: $110. Make checks payable to Carla Bertola.

How to Submit Submit 3 poems at a time. No previously published poems or simultaneous submissions. Time between acceptance and publication is one year. Often comments on rejected poems. Guidelines available for SASE (or SAE and IRC). Pays one contributor's copy.

🔷 ◎ OPEN MINDS QUARTERLY (Specialized: writing by those who have experienced mental illness)

The Writer's Circle, 680 Kirkwood Dr., Building 1, Sudbury ON P3E 1X3 Canada. (705)675-9193, ext. 8286. Fax: (705)675-3501. E-mail: openminds@nisa.on.ca. Web site: www.nisa.on.ca. Established 1997. **Contact:** Dinah Laprairie, editor.

Magazine Needs *Open Minds Quarterly* provides a "venue for individuals who have experienced mental illness to express themselves via poetry, short fiction, essays, first-person accounts of living with mental illness, book/movie reviews." Wants "unique, well-written, provocative poetry." Does not want overly graphic or sexual violence. Considers poetry by children and teens. Has published poetry by Pamela MacBean, Sophie Soil, Alice Parris, and Kurt Sass. *Open Minds Quarterly* is 24 pages, magazine-sized, saddle-stapled, with 100 lb. stock cover with original artwork, includes ads. Receives about 300 poems/year, accepts about 30%. Press run is 750 (300 subscribers, 4-5 libraries, 5 shelf sales); 400 distributed free to potential subscribers, published writers, advertisers. Single copy: $5.40 CAD, $5 USD; subscription: $35 CAD, $28.25 USD (special rates also available). Make checks payable to NISA/Northern Initiative for Social Action.

How to Submit Submit 1-5 poems at a time. Considers previously published poems and simultaneous submissions. Accepts fax, e-mail, and disk submissions. Cover letter is required. "Info in cover letter: indication as to 'consumer/survivor' of the mental health system status." Reads submissions year round. Submit seasonal poems at least 8 months in advance. Time between acceptance and publication is 6-18 months. "Poems are first reviewed by poetry editor, then accepted/rejected by the editor. Sometimes, submissions are passed on to a third party for input or a third opinion." Seldom comments on rejected poems. Guidelines available for SASE, by fax, e-mail, or on Web site. Responds in up to 4 months. "Rarely" sends prepublication galleys. "All authors own their work—if another publisher seeks to reprint from our publication, we request they cite us as the source."

Also Offers "All material not accepted for our journal will be considered for The Writer's Circle Online, our Internet publication forum. Same guidelines apply. Same contact person."

Contest/Award Offerings "The Brainstorm Poetry Contest runs in first two months of each year. Contact the editor for information."

Advice "We are unique in that our outlets help to reduce the stigma surrounding mental illness by illustrating the creative talents of individuals suffering from mental illness."

✅ OPEN SPACES

6327 C SW Capitol Hwy., Suite 134, Portland OR 97239. (503)227-5764. Fax: (503)227-3401. E-mail: info@open-spaces.com. (inquiries only). Web site: www.open-spaces.com. Established 1997. **Contact:** Susan Juve-Hu Bucharest, poetry editor.

Magazine Needs *Open Spaces*, published quarterly, "gives voice to the Northwest on issues that are regional, national, and international in scope. Our readership is thoughtful, intelligent, widely read, and appreciative of ideas and writing of the highest quality. With that in mind, we seek thoughtful, well-researched articles and insightful fiction, reviews, and poetry on a variety of subjects from a number of different viewpoints. Although we take ourselves seriously, we appreciate humor as well. Poetry is presented with care and respect." Has published poetry by Vern Rutsala, Pattiann Rogers, Lou Masson, and William Jolliff. *Open Spaces* is 64 pages, magazine-sized, sheet-fed-printed, with cover art. Press run is 5,000-10,000. Subscription: $25/year. Sample: $10. Make checks payable to Open Spaces Publications, Inc.

How to Submit Submit 3-5 poems at a time. Considers simultaneous submissions. No fax or e-mail submissions; accepts submissions by postal mail only. Cover letter is required. Time between acceptance and publication is 2-3 months. Poems are circulated to an editorial board. Seldom comments on rejected poems. Guidelines available on Web site. Responds in up to 4 months. Payment varies. Reviews books/chapbooks of poetry.

🌐 ◯ ORBIS: AN INTERNATIONAL QUARTERLY OF POETRY AND PROSE

17 Greenhow Ave., West Kirby, Wirral CH48 5EL England. E-mail: carolebaldock@hotmail.com. Established 1968. **Contact:** Carole Baldock, editor.

Magazine Needs *Orbis: An International Quarterly of Poetry and Prose* features "news, reviews, views, letters, prose, and quite a lot of poetry." Wants "more work from young people (this includes 20-somethings) and women writers." *Orbis* is 84 pages, digest-sized, professionally printed, flat-spined, with full-color glossy card cover. Receives "thousands" of submissions/year. Single copy: £4 UK, £5 overseas (€10, $11 USD); subscription: £15 UK, £20 overseas (€30, $38 USD).

How to Submit Submit up to 4 poems at a time. Accepts e-mail submissions "from outside UK only; send no more than 2 poems, pasted into body of message (no attachments)." For postal submissions, "one poem/page; enclose SASE (or SAE and 2 IRCs) with all correspondence." Responds in up to one month. Reviews books and other magazines. Send books for review consideration to Nessa O'Mahony, 28 The Glen, Blacon, Chester CH1 5GA England. Send magazines for review consideration to Nathan Jones, Belvedere Rd., Princes Park, Liverpool L8 3TF England.

Contest/Award Offerings Prizes in each issue: £50 for featured writer (3-4 poems); £50 Readers' Award for piece receiving the most votes; £50 split among 4 (or more) runners-up.

🌐 $◻️ ◎ OUTPOSTS POETRY QUARTERLY

22 Whitewell Rd., Frome, Somerset BA11 4EL England. Phone/fax: (44)(1373)466653. Established 1943. **Contact:** Roland John, poetry editor.

Magazine Needs *Outposts Poetry Quarterly* "is a general poetry magazine that welcomes all work, from either the recognized or the unknown poet." Wants "fairly mainstream poetry." Does not want "concrete poems or very free verse." Has published poetry by Jared Carter, John Heath-Stubbs, Lotte Kramer, and Peter Russell. *Outposts* is 60-120 pages, A5, litho-printed, perfect-bound, with laminated card cover, includes ads. Receives about 46,000 poems/year, accepts about 1%. Press run is 1,800 (1,200 subscribers, 400 libraries, 400 shelf sales). Single copy: $8; subscription: $26. Sample: $6 (includes guidelines). Make checks payable to Hippopotamus Press. "We prefer credit cards because of bank charges."

How to Submit Submit 5 poems at a time. Considers simultaneous submissions; no previously published poems. Accepts fax submissions. Cover letter is required. "IRCs must accompany U.S. submissions." Time between acceptance and publication is 9 months. Comments on rejected poems "only if asked." Occasionally publishes theme issues. Upcoming themes available for SASE (or SAE and IRC). Responds in 2 weeks "plus post time." Sometimes sends prepublication galleys. Pays £8/poem plus one contributor's copy. Copyright remains with author. Staff reviews books of poetry in 200 words for "Books Received" page. Also uses full essays up to 4,000 words. Send materials for review consideration to M. Pargitter.

OVER THE TRANSOM

825 Bush St. #203, San Francisco CA 94108. (415)928-3965. E-mail: jsh619@earthlink.net. Established 1997. **Contact:** Jonathan Hayes, editor.

Magazine Needs *Over The Transom*, published 2 times/year, is a free publication of art and literature. Open to all styles of poetry. "We look for the highest quality poetry and art that best fits the issue." Considers poetry by children and teens. Has published poetry by A.D. Winans, Glen Chesnut, W.B. Keckler, Gerald Locklin, Alan Catlin, and Simon Perchik. *Over The Transom* is 32 pages, magazine-sized, saddle-stapled, with cardstock cover. Receives about 1,000 poems/year, accepts about 5%. Press run is 300 (100 subscribers); 150 distributed free to cafes, bookstores, universities, and bars. Single copy: free. Sample: $3. Make checks payable to Jonathan Hayes.

How to Submit Submit 5 poems at a time. Considers previously published poems and simultaneous submissions. Accepts e-mail submissions; no disk submissions. Must include a SASE with postal submissions. Reads submissions year round. Time between acceptance and publication is 2-6 months. Never comments on rejected poems. Occasionally publishes theme issues. Guidelines available for SASE or by e-mail. Responds in 2 months. Sometimes sends prepublication galleys. Pays one contributor's copy. Acquires first rights.

Advice "Editors have differing tastes, so don't be upset by rejection. Always send a SASE for response."

PACIFIC COAST JOURNAL

P.O. Box 56, Carlsbad CA 92018. E-mail: paccoastj @frenchbreadpublications.com. (inquiries only). Web site: www.frenchbreadpublications.com/pcj. Established 1992. **Contact:** Stillson Graham, editor.

Magazine Needs *Pacific Coast Journal*, published quarterly, is an "unprofessional literary magazine. Whatever you think that means, go with it." Has published poetry by Tom Holmes, Anne Babson, and A.D. Winans. *Pacific Coast Journal* is 40 pages, digest-sized, photocopied, saddle-stapled, with cardstock cover. Receives 400-500 poems/year, accepts about 5%. Press run is 200 (100 subscribers). Single copy: $3; subscription: $12. Sample: $2.50.

How to Submit Submit up to 6 poems or 12 pages at a time. Considers simultaneous submissions; no previously published poems. No e-mail submissions. Cover letter is preferred. Encourages the inclusion of e-mail address in lieu of SASE for response. Time between acceptance and publication is 3-18 months. Seldom comments on rejected poems. Guidelines available for SASE, by

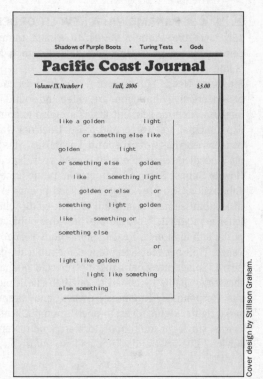

Shadows of Purple Boots • Turing Tests • Gods

Pacific Coast Journal

Volume IX Number 1   *Fall, 2006*   *$3.00*

```
like a golden         light
        or something else like
golden        light
or something else       golden
    like      something light
      golden or else       or
something     light     golden
like      something or
something else
                      or
light like golden
      light like something
else something
```

Cover design by Stillson Graham.

For *Pacific Coast Journal* #34, the cover image is a poem by Patrick Hartigan. "I liked the poem a lot," says editor Stillson Graham, "and it had a nice visual and contextual impact with the rest of the issue—and with the magazine in general."

e-mail, or on Web site. Responds in 6-9 months (usually). Pays one contributor's copy. Acquires one-time rights.

Advice "We like experiments."

⭐ $▣ ⬚ PAINTED BRIDE QUARTERLY

Drexel University, Dept. of English and Philosophy, 3141 Chestnut St., Philadelphia PA 19104. E-mail: pbq@drexel.edu. (inquiries only). Web site: http://pbq.drexel.edu. Established 1973. **Contact:** Poetry Editors.

Magazine Needs *Painted Bride Quarterly*, published online, "aims to be a leader among little magazines published by and for independent poets and writers nationally. We have no specifications or restrictions. We'll look at anything." Has published poetry by Robert Bly, Charles Bukowski, S.J. Marks, and James Hazen. *Painted Bride Quarterly* is printed as one hardcopy anthology annually. Single copy: $15.

How to Submit Submit up to 5 poems at a time. Lines/poem: any length. No previously published poems. No e-mail submissions. "Submissions must be original, typed, and should include a short bio." Time between acceptance and publication is 6-9 months. Seldom comments on rejected poems. Occasionally publishes theme issues. Guidelines available on Web site. Pays one-year subscription, one half-priced contributor's copy, and $5/accepted piece. Publishes reviews of poetry books.

Contest/Award Offerings Sponsors an annual poetry contest and a chapbook competition. **Entry fee:** required for both. Guidelines available for SASE or on Web site.

ⓝ ▣ ⬚ ◎ PANAMOWA: A NEW LIT ORDER

152 Davis Ave., Auburn ME 04210. E-mail: mmpottlehill@yahoo.com. Web site: http://web.mac.com/newlitorder/. Established 2007. **Contact:** Michelle Morgan, editor; Christina Thibault, arts editor.

Magazine Needs *panamowa: a new lit order*, published quarterly online, features "poetry, short fiction, creative nonfiction, art, video and sound files; preference given to emerging and established female writers/artists, but males are also encouraged to submit." Wants narrative, confessional, experimental, free verse, and prose. Does not want "song lyrics, blatant rhyme." Considers poetry by teens "on basis of exceptional promise." Has published poetry by PJ Nights and Cynthia Brackett-Vincent. Accepts about 50 poems/year. Number of unique visitors: about 500 in first month.

How to Submit Submit 3-5 poems at a time. Lines/poem: 20-60 preferred. Considers simultaneous submissions; no previously published poems. Accepts e-mail (pasted into body of message) and disk submissions. "If unusual format, editor will request e-mail attachment upon interest." Cover letter is required. "Include bio/previous publications (if any) in cover letter. SASE required with postal submissions." Reads submissions year round. Submit seasonal material 4-6 months in advance. Time between acceptance and publication is 4-6 months. Poems are circulated to an editorial board. Sometimes comments on rejected poems. Sometimes publishes theme issues. Upcoming themes available by e-mail or on Web site. Guidelines available for SASE, by e-mail, or on Web site. Responds in 4 months. Always sends prepublication galleys. Acquires first North American serial rights. Rights revert to poets upon publication. Reviews books/chapbooks of poetry in 1,000 words, single- or multi-book format. Send materials for review consideration to Michelle Morgan.

Advice "Literary trends come and go; but if you're proud of your work and it is high quality, send it in!"

◎ PARADOXISM (Specialized: avant-garde, experimental)

University of New Mexico, Gallup NM 87301. E-mail: smarand@unm.edu. Web site: www.gallup.unm.edu/ ~ smarandache/a/Paradoxism.htm. Established 1990. **Contact:** Florentin Smarandache, editor.

Magazine Needs *Paradoxism*, published annually, prints "avant-garde poetry, experiments, poems without verses, literature beyond the words, anti-language, non-literature and its literature, as well as the sense of the non-sense; revolutionary forms of poetry. Paradoxism, a 1980s movement of anti-totalitarian protest, is based on excessive use of antitheses, antinomies, contradictions, paradoxes in creation." Wants "avant-garde poetry, 1-2 pages, any subject, any style (lyrical experiments)." Does not want "classical, fixed forms." Has published poetry by Paul Georgelin, Mircea Monu, Ion Rotaru, Michéle de LaPlante, and Claude LeRoy. *Paradoxism* is 52 pages, digest-sized, offset-printed, with soft cover. Press run is 500; distributed "to its collaborators, U.S. and Canadian university libraries, and the Library of Congress as well as European, Chinese, Indian, and Japanese libraries."

How to Submit No previously published poems or simultaneous submissions. Do not submit during the summer. "We do not return published or unpublished poems or notify the author of date of publication." Responds in up to 3 weeks. Pays one contributor's copy.

Additional Information Paradoxism Association also publishes 2 poetry paperbacks and 1-2 chapbooks/year, including translations. "The poems must be unpublished and must meet the requirements of the Paradoxism Association." Responds to queries in 2 months; to mss in up to 3 weeks. Pays 50 author's copies. Sample e-books available on Web site at www.gallup.unm.edu/~smarandache/eBooksLiterature.htm.

Advice "We mostly receive traditional or modern verse, but not avant-garde (very different from any previously published verse). We want anti-literature and its literature, style of the non-style, poems without poems, non-words and non-sentence poems, very upset free verse, intelligible unintelligible language, impersonal texts personalized, transformation of the abnormal to the normal. Make literature from everything; make literature from nothing!"

✒ PASSAGES NORTH

English Dept., Northern Michigan University, 1401 Presque Isle Ave., Marquette MI 49855. (906)227-1203. E-mail: passages@nmu.edu. Web site: http://myweb.nmu.edu/~passages. Established 1979. **Contact:** Austin Hummell, poetry editor.

Magazine Needs *Passages North*, published annually in spring, prints poetry, short fiction, creative nonfiction, essays, and interviews. Publishes work by established and emerging writers. Has published poetry by Moira Egan, Frannie Lindsay, Ben Lerner, Bob Hicok, and Gabe Gudding. *Passages North* is 250 pages. Circulation is 1,500. Single copy: $13; subscription: $13/year, $23 for 2 years. Sample: $3 (back issue).

How to Submit Submit up to 6 poems at a time. Considers simultaneous submissions. Time between acceptance and publication is 6 months. Reads submissions September-May only. Responds in 2 months. Pays 2 contributor's copies.

Contest/Award Offerings Sponsors the Elinor Benedict Poetry Prize every other year. 1st Prize: $1,000, plus 2 Honorable Mentions. **Entry fee:** $10 for 1-3 poems (each entrant receives the contest issue of *Passages North*). Make checks payable to Northern Michigan University. **Deadline:** reads entries October 15-January 22. Guidelines available for SASE, by e-mail, or on Web site.

✒ PATERSON LITERARY REVIEW

Poetry Center, Passaic County Community College, Cultural Affairs Dept., One College Blvd., Paterson NJ 07505-1179. (973)684-6555. Fax: (973)523-6085. E-mail: mgillan@pccc.edu. Web site: www.pccc.edu/poetry. Established 1979. **Contact:** Maria Mazziotti Gillan, editor/executive director.

• The Poetry Center Library at Passaic County Community College has an extensive collection of contemporary poetry and seeks small press contributions to help keep it abreast.

Magazine Needs *Paterson Literary Review*, published annually, is produced by the The Poetry Center at Passaic County Community College. Wants poetry of "high quality; clear, direct, powerful work." Has published poetry by Diane di Prima, Ruth Stone, Marge Piercy, and Laura Boss. *Paterson*

Literary Review is 320 pages, magazine-sized, professionally printed, saddle-stapled, with glossy 2-color card cover. Press run is 1,000 (100 subscribers, 50 libraries). Sample: $13.

How to Submit Submit up to 5 poems at a time. Lines/poem: 100 maximum. Considers simultaneous submissions. Reads submissions December 1-March 31 only. Responds within one year. Pays one contributor's copy. Acquires first rights.

Contest/Award Offerings The Allen Ginsberg Poetry Awards and The Paterson Poetry Prize (see separate listings in Contests & Awards).

Also Offers Publishes *The New Jersey Poetry Resource Book* ($5 plus $1.50 p&h) and *The New Jersey Poetry Calendar*. The Distinguished Poets Series offers readings by poets of international, national, and regional reputation. Poetryworks/USA is a series of programs produced for UA Columbia-Cablevision. See Web site for details about these additional resources.

⭐ 🌐 ◐ ◎ PATTAYA POETRY REVIEW (Specialized: work from subscribers only)

Classic Village, 95/31 Moo 10 Nong Phrue, Banglamung, Chonburi 20260 Thailand. (661)7177 941. E-mail: nasomhong@yahoo.com. Established 2003. **Contact:** Jiraporn Sutta, editor.

Magazine Needs *Pattaya Poetry Review*, published quarterly, prints poetry, short stories, and reviews. Wants "all types and styles, especially traditional forms." *Pattaya Poetry Review* is 16 pages, digest-sized, with cardstock cover. Receives about 200 poems/year, accepts about 20%. Press run is 70. Single copy: $9; subscription: $16. Make checks payable to Jiraporn Sutta.

How to Submit Submit 3 poems at a time. Considers previously published poems and simultaneous submissions. No e-mail or disk submissions. Reads submissions year round. Time between acceptance and publication is 3 months. Sometimes comments on rejected poems. **Subscription required to submit work.** Guidelines available for SASE. Responds in 3 months. Always sends prepublication galleys. Pays one contributor's copy. Acquires all rights. Returns rights upon written request. Reviews books/chapbooks of poetry. Send materials for review consideration to Jiraporn Sutta.

◪ PAVEMENT SAW

Pavement Saw Press, P.O. Box 6291, Columbus OH 43206-0291. E-mail: info@pavementsaw.org. Web site: www.pavementsaw.org. Established 1992. **Contact:** David Baratier, editor.

Magazine Needs *Pavement Saw*, published annually in August, wants "letters and short fiction, and poetry on any subject, especially work." Does not want "poems that tell; no work by a deceased writer, and no translations." Dedicates 15-20 pages of each issue to a featured writer. Has published poetry by Simon Perchik, Sofia Starnes, Alan Catlin, Adrianne Kalfopoulou, Jim Daniels, and Mary Weems. *Pavement Saw* is 88 pages, digest-sized, perfect-bound. Receives about 9,000 poems/year, accepts less than 1%. Press run is 550 (about 300 subscribers, about 250 shelf sales). Single copy: $8; subscription: $14. Sample: $7. Make checks payable to Pavement Saw Press.

How to Submit Submit 5 poems at a time. Lines/poem: 1-2 pages. Considers simultaneous submissions, "as long as poet has not published a book with a press run of 1,000 or more"; no previously published poems. No e-mail submissions; postal submissions only. Cover letter is required. "No fancy typefaces." Seldom comments on rejected poems. Guidelines available in magazine or for SASE. Responds in 4 months. Sometimes sends prepublication galleys. Pays at least 2 contributor's copies. Acquires first rights.

Additional Information Pavement Saw Press also publishes books of poetry. "Most are by authors who have been published in the journal." Published "seven titles in 2005 and seven titles in 2006; five were full-length books ranging from 80 to 240 pages."

Contest/Award Offerings Transcontinental Poetry Award and Pavement Saw Press Chapbook Award (see separate listings in Contests & Awards).

▣ ◻ ◎ PEACE & FREEDOM (Specialized: submissions from subscribers only)

Peace & Freedom Press, 17 Farrow Rd., Whaplode Drove, Spalding, Lincs PE12 0TS England. E-mail: p_rance@yahoo.co.uk. Web site: http://uk.geocities.com/p_rance/pandf.htm. Established 1985. **Contact:** Paul Rance, editor.

Magazine Needs *Peace & Freedom*, published semiannually, emphasizes social, humanitarian, and environmental issues. **Considers submissions from subscribers only.** "Those new to poetry are welcome. The poetry we publish is pro-animal rights/welfare, anti-war, environmental; poems reflecting love; erotic, but not obscene; humorous; spiritual, humanitarian; with or without rhyme/meter." Considers poetry by children and teens. Has published poetry by Dorothy Bell-Hall, Freda Moffatt, Bernard Shough, Mona Miller, and Andrew Savage. *Peace & Freedom* has a varied format. Subscription: $20 U.S., £10 UK for 6 issues. Sample: $5 U.S., £1.75 UK. "Sample copies can be purchased only from the above address. Advisable to buy a sample copy before submitting. Banks charge the equivalent of $5 to cash foreign checks in the UK, so please only send bills, preferably by registered post."

How to Submit Lines/poem: 32 maximum. No previously published poems or simultaneous submissions. Accepts e-mail submissions (pasted into body of message, no attachments; no more than 3 poems/e-mail); no fax submissions. Include bio. Reads submissions year round. Publishes theme issues. Upcoming themes available in magazine, for SAE with IRC, by e-mail, or on Web site. Responds to submissions in less than a month ("usually"), with SAE/IRC. "Work without correct postage will not be responded to or returned until proper postage is sent." Pays one contributor's copy. Reviews books of poetry.

Contest/Award Offerings "*Peace & Freedom* holds regular poetry contests as does one of our other publications, *Eastern Rainbow*, which is a magazine concerning 20th-century popular culture using poetry up to 32 lines." Subscription: $20 U.S., £10 UK for 6 issues. Further details of competitions and publications available for SAE with IRC or on Web site.

Also Offers Publishes anthologies. Guidelines and details of upcoming anthologies available in magazine, for SAE with IRC, by e-mail, or on Web site.

Advice "Too many writers have lost the personal touch that editors generally appreciate. It can make a difference when selecting work of equal merit."

◖ PEARL

3030 E. Second St., Long Beach CA 90803-5163. (562)434-4523 or (714)968-7530. E-mail: pearlmag @aol.com. (inquiries only). Web site: www.pearlmag.com. Established 1974. **Contact:** Joan Jobe Smith, Marilyn Johnson, and Barbara Hauk, poetry editors.

Magazine Needs *Pearl*, published semiannually in May and November, is interested "in accessible, humanistic poetry that communicates and is related to real life. Humor and wit are welcome, along with the ironic and serious. No taboos, stylistically or subject-wise." Does not want "sentimental, obscure, predictable, abstract, or cliché-ridden poetry. Our purpose is to provide a forum for lively, readable poetry that reflects a wide variety of contemporary voices, viewpoints, and experiences—that speaks to real people about real life in direct, living language, profane or sublime. Our Spring/Summer issue is devoted exclusively to poetry, with a 12- to 15-page section featuring the work of a single poet." Has published poetry by Fred Voss, David Hernandez, Lisa Glatt, Jim Daniels, Nin Andrews, and Frank X. Gaspar. *Pearl* is 112-136 pages, digest-sized, offset-printed, perfect-bound, with glossy cover. Press run is 700 (150 subscribers, 7 libraries). Subscription: $21/year (includes a copy of the Pearl Poetry Prize-winning book). Sample: $8.

How to Submit Submit 3-5 poems at a time. Lines/poem: no longer than 40 lines preferred, each line no more than 10-12 words, to accommodate page size and format. Considers simultaneous submissions ("must be acknowledged as such"); no previously published poems. No e-mail submissions; postal submissions only. Cover letter is appreciated. "Handwritten submissions and unreadable printouts are not acceptable." Reads submissions September-May only. Time between acceptance and publication is up to one year. Guidelines available for SASE or on Web site. Responds in 2 months. Sometimes sends prepublication galleys. Pays one contributor's copy. Acquires first serial rights.

Additional Information Pearl Editions publishes the winner of the Pearl Poetry Prize only (see separate listing in Contests & Awards). All other books and chapbooks are by invitation only.

Advice "Advice for beginning poets? Just write from your own experience, using images that are as concrete and sensory as possible. Keep these images fresh and objective. Always listen to the music."

◕ PEBBLE LAKE REVIEW

15318 Pebble Lake Dr., Houston TX 77095. E-mail: submissions@pebblelakereview.com. Web site: www.pebblelakereview.com. Established 2002. **Contact:** Amanda Auchter, editor.

• Poems published in *Pebble Lake Review* appear regularly on Verse Daily (www.versedaily.org) and were included in *Pushcart Prize XXXI: Best of the Small Presses.*

Magazine Needs *Pebble Lake Review*, published 3 times/year in April, August, and December, seeks "high-quality, image-rich poetry that demonstrates attention to language, form, and craft. Looking for more experimental work." Does not want "anything cliché, Hallmark-style, racist, or erotic." Has published poetry by Kelli Russell Agodon, Denise Duhamel, Jeannine Hall Gailey, Ilya Kaminsky, Dzvinia Orlowsky, and Marge Piercy. *Pebble Lake Review* is 200 pages, digest-sized, perfect-bound, with color cover. Receives about 10,000 poems/year, accepts less than 5%. Single copy: $10; subscription: $24/year. Make checks payable to *Pebble Lake Review.*

How to Submit Submit 3-5 poems at a time. Considers simultaneous submissioins with notification; no previously published poems. Accepts e-mail submissions (pasted into body of message; attachments accepted if Word documents); no disk submissions. Cover letter is required. Include SASE. Reads submissions year round. Time between acceptance and publication is 3-6 months. "Poems are circulated between the editors, and the decision is finalized by the editor-in-chief." Seldom comments on rejected poems. Guidelines available in magazine, for SASE, by e-mail, or on Web site. Sometimes sends prepublication galleys. Pays one contributor's copy. Acquires one-time rights; rights are returned to author upon publication. Reviews books/chapbooks of poetry in 500-1,000 words, single-book format. Send materials for review consideration.

Also Offers Selects poets to read work as part of the *Pebble Lake Review* Audio Project. E-mail the online editor at webmaster@pebblelakereview for details.

$ ▣ ◕ THE PEDESTAL MAGAZINE

E-mail: pedmagazine@carolina.rr.com. (inquiries only; make submissions through online submission form). Web site: www.thepedestalmagazine.com. Established 2000. **Contact:** John Amen, editor-in-chief. Member: CLMP.

Magazine Needs *The Pedestal Magazine*, published bimonthly online, prints "12-15 poems per issue, as well as fiction, interviews, and book reviews. We are open to a wide variety of poetry, ranging from the highly experimental to the traditionally formal." Has published poetry by W.S. Merwin, Philip Levine, Nikki Giovanni, and Sharon Olds. Receives about 5,000 poems/year, accepts about 1%. "We have a readership of approximately 13,000 per month."

How to Submit Submit up to 6 poems at a time. Lines/poem: open. Considers simultaneous submissions; no previously published poems. No e-mail or disk submissions. "Submissions are accepted via a submission form provided in the 'Submit' section of the Web site. Our submissions schedule is posted in the guidelines section." Time between acceptance and publication is 2-4 weeks. Poems are circulated to an editorial board. Sometimes comments on rejected poems. Sometimes publishes theme issues. Guidelines available on Web site. Responds in 4-6 weeks. Always sends prepublication galleys (by e-mail). Pays $30/poem. Acquires first rights. Reviews books/chapbooks of poetry in 850-1,000 words. "Please query via e-mail prior to sending books or related materials."

☑ PEGASUS

P.O. Box 61324, Boulder City NV 89006. Established 1986. **Contact:** M.E. Hildebrand, editor.

Magazine Needs *Pegasus*, published quarterly, is "for serious poets who have something to say and know how to say it using sensory imagery." Does not want "religious, political, and pornographic themes." Has published poetry by John Grey, Elizabeth Perry, Diana K. Rubin, Lyn Lifshin, Robert K. Johnson, and Nikolas Macioci. *Pegasus* is 32 pages, digest-sized, desktop-published, saddle-stapled, with colored paper cover. Publishes 10-15% of the poetry received. Circulation is 200. Subscription: $20. Sample: $6.

How to Submit Submit 3-5 poems at a time. Lines/poem: 3 minimum, 40 maximum. Considers previously published poems, provided poet retains rights; no simultaneous submissions. Guidelines available for SASE. Responds in 2 weeks. Publication is payment. Acquires first or one-time rights.

☑ PENNSYLVANIA ENGLISH

Penn State DuBois, DuBois PA 15801-3199. (814)375-4814. E-mail: ajv2@psu.edu. (inquiries only). Established 1988. **Contact:** Antonio Vallone, editor.

Magazine Needs *Pennsylvania English*, published annually, is "sponsored by the Pennsylvania College English Association." Wants poetry of "any length, any style." Has published poetry by Liz Rosenberg, Walt MacDonald, Amy Pence, Jennifer Richter, and Jeff Schiff. *Pennsylvania English* is up to 200 pages, digest-sized, perfect-bound, with full-color cover. Press run is 500. Subscription: $10/year.

How to Submit Submit 3 or more poems at a time. Considers simultaneous submissions; no previously published poems. No e-mail submissions. Submissions must be typed. Include SASE. Guidelines available for SASE. Responds in 6 months. Pays 2 contributor's copies.

Advice "Poetry does not express emotions; it evokes emotions. Therefore, it should rely less on statements and more on images."

☑ ◎ THE PENWOOD REVIEW (Specialized: spirituality, the sacred)

P.O. Box 862, Los Alamitos CA 90720-0862. E-mail: submissions@penwoodreview.com. Web site: www.penwoodreview.com. Established 1997. **Contact:** Lori M. Cameron, editor.

Magazine Needs *The Penwood Review*, published semiannually, seeks "to explore the spiritual and sacred aspects of our existence and our relationship to God." Wants "disciplined, high-quality, well-crafted poetry on any subject. Rhyming poetry must be written in traditional forms (sonnets, tercets, villanelles, sestinas, etc.)." Does not want "light verse, doggerel, or greeting card-style poetry. Also, nothing racist, sexist, pornographic, or blasphemous." Has published poetry by Kathleen Spivack, Anne Babson, Hugh Fox, Anselm Brocki, Nina Tassi, and Gary Guinn. *The Penwood Review* is about 40 pages, magazine-sized, saddle-stapled, with heavy card cover. Press run is 50-100. Single copy: $6; subscription: $12.

How to Submit Submit 3-5 poems at a time. Lines/poem: less than 2 pages preferred. No previously published poems or simultaneous submissions. Accepts e-mail submissions (pasted into body of message). Cover letter is preferred. One poem to a page with the author's full name, address, and phone number in the upper right corner. Time between acceptance and publication is up to one year. "Submissions are circulated among an editorial staff for evaluations." Never comments on rejected poems. Responds in up to 4 months. Pays with subscription discount of $10 and, with subscription, one additional contributor's copy. Acquires one-time rights.

⚒ ☑ PEREGRINE

Amherst Writers & Artists, 190 University Dr., Suite 1, Amherst MA 01002. (413)253-3307. E-mail: peregrine@amherstwriters.com. Web site: www.amherstwriters.com. Established 1983. **Contact:** Nancy Rose, editor.

Magazine Needs *Peregrine*, published annually in November, features poetry and fiction. Open to all styles, forms, and subjects except greeting card verse. *"Peregrine* has provided a forum for national and international writers since 1983, and is committed to finding excellent work by new writers as well as established authors. We publish what we love, knowing that all editorial decisions are subjective." Has published poetry by Willie James King, Virgil Suárez, Susan Terris, Janet Aalfs, Dianalee Velie, and Ralph Hughes. *Peregrine* is 104 pages, digest-sized, professionally printed, perfect-bound, with glossy cover. Press run is 1,000. Single copy: $15. Sample: $12. Make checks payable to AWA Press.

How to Submit Submit 3-5 poems at a time. Lines/poem: 50 maximum (including spaces). Considers simultaneous submissions; no previously published poems. No e-mail submissions. Include cover letter with bio, 30 words maximum; indicate line count for each poem. Reads submissions February 1-June 1 (postmark) only. Each ms read by several readers; final decisions made by the editor. Guidelines available for #10 SASE or on Web site. Pays 2 contributor's copies. Acquires first rights.

⬙ ◎ PERSPECTIVES (Specialized: Christian)

Dept. of English, Hope College, Holland MI 49422-9000. **Contact:** Rhoda Janzen, poetry editor.

Magazine Needs *Perspectives*, published 10 times/year, aims "to express the Reformed faith theologically; to engage in issues that Reformed Christians meet in personal, ecclesiastical, and societal life; and thus to contribute to the mission of the church of Jesus Christ." Wants "poems excellent in craft and significant in subject, both traditional and free in form. We publish 1-2 poems every other issue." Has published poetry by Ann Hostetler, Paul Willis, and Priscilla Atkins. *Perspectives* is 24 pages, magazine-sized, web offset-printed, saddle-stapled, with paper cover containing b&w illustration. Receives about 300 poems/year, accepts 6-20. Press run is 3,300 (3,000 subscribers, 200 libraries). Subscription: $30. Sample: $3.50.

How to Submit No previously published poems or simultaneous submissions. Cover letter is preferred. Include SASE. "Submissions without SASE will not be returned." Time between acceptance and publication is 3-12 months. Responds in 3-6 months. Pays 5 contributor's copies. Acquires first rights.

✪ ◻ ◎ PHILADELPHIA STORIES (Specialized: submissions from PA, NJ, DE resident poets)

2021 S. 11th St., Philadelphia PA 19148. E-mail: info@philadelphiastories.org. Web site: www.philadelphiastories.org. Established 2003. **Contact:** Conrad Weiser. Member: CLMP.

Magazine Needs *Philadelphia Stories*, published quarterly, strives "to publish the finest literary fiction, poetry, and art from Pennsylvania, New Jersey, and Delaware—and provide it to the general public free of charge." Wants "polished, well crafted poems." Does not want "first drafts." Considers poetry by teens. Has published poetry by Daniel Abdal-Hayy Moore, Scott Edward Anderson, Sandy Crimmins, Liz Dolan, Alison Hicks, and Margaret A. Robinson. *Philadelphia Stories* is 24 pages, magazine-sized, saddle-stapled, with 4-color cover with original art, includes ads. Receives about 300 poems/year, accepts about 15%. Press run is 12,000/quarter, distributed free. Subscription: "we offer $20 memberships that include home delivery." Make checks payable to *Philadelphia Stories*.

How to Submit Submit 3 poems at a time. Lines/poem: 36. Considers simultaneous submissions; no previously published poems. Accepts submissions through online submission form at www.philadelphiastories.org/submissions; no disk submissions. Cover letter is preferred. Reads submissions year round. Time between acceptance and publication is 3 months. Poems are circulated to an editorial board. "Each poem is reviewed by a preliminary board that decides on a final list; the entire board discusses this list and chooses the mutual favorites for print and Web." Guidelines available on Web site. Responds in 3 months. "We send a layout proof to check for print poems." Acquires one-time rights. Rights revert to poets upon publication. Reviews books of poetry.

⚏ ✑ PHOEBE: A JOURNAL OF LITERATURE AND ART

MSN 2D6, George Mason University, 4400 University Dr., Fairfax VA 22030-4444. (703)993-2915. E-mail: phoebe@gmu.edu. (inquiries only). Web site: www.gmu.edu/pubs/phoebe. Established 1970. **Contact:** Poetry Editor.

Magazine Needs *Phoebe: A Journal of Literature and Art*, published semiannually in September and February, looks "for imagery that will make your thumbs sweat when you touch it." Has published poetry by C.D. Wright, Russell Edson, Yusef Komunyakaa, Rosemarie Waldrop, and Leslie Scalapino. Press run is 3,000, with 35-40 pages of poetry in each issue. Receives 4,000 submissions/year. Single copy: $6; subscription: $12/year.

How to Submit Submit up to 5 poems at a time. No simultaneous submissions. No e-mail submissions; postal submissions only. Include SASE and a short bio. Reads submissions September 1-April 15 (postmark); mss postmarked April 16-August 31 will not be read. Guidelines available for SASE or on Web site. Responds in up to 3 months. Pays 2 contributor's copies or one-year subscription.

Additional Information Check http://phoebejournal.blogspot.com. for additional information and commentary about *Phoebe*.

Contest/Award Offerings Sponsors the Greg Grummer Poetry Award, offering $1,000 and publication for winner, possible publication for finalists, and a copy of awards issue to all entrants. Submissions must be unpublished. Submit up to 4 poems (not to exceed 20 pages total), any subject, any form, with name on cover page only. Include SASE for results only; mss will not be returned. Guidelines available for SASE or on Web site. **Entry fee:** $15/entry. Make checks/money orders payable to *Phoebe*/GMU. **Deadline:** December 1 (postmark). Contest receives 300-400 submissions. Awards issue (back copy): $6.

✑ THE PIKEVILLE REVIEW

Humanities Division, Pikeville College, 147 Sycamore St., Pikeville KY 41501. (606)218-5602. Fax: (606)218-5225. E-mail: sengland@pc.edu. (inquiries only). Web site: http://humanities.pc.edu/review/. Established 1987. **Contact:** Sydney C. England, editor.

Magazine Needs *The Pikeville Review*, published annually in late fall, has "no editorial bias, though we recognize and appreciate style and control in each piece." Does not want "emotional gushing." *The Pikeville Review* is 94 pages, digest-sized, professionally printed, perfect-bound, with glossy card cover with b&w illustration. Accepts about 10% of poetry received. Press run is 500. Sample: $4.

How to Submit No previously published poems or simultaneous submissions. No e-mail submissions; postal submissions only. SASE required. Sometimes comments on rejected poems. Guidelines available for SASE or on Web site. Pays 5 contributor's copies.

✑ THE PINCH

Dept. of English, University of Memphis, Memphis TN 38152-6176. (901)678-4591. Fax: (901)678-2226. E-mail: thepinch@memphis.edu. Web site: www.thepinchjournal.com. orwww.mfainmemphis.com. Established 1980. **Contact:** Kristen Iversen, editor-in-chief.

Magazine Needs *The Pinch*, published semiannually (fall and spring), prints fiction, poetry, interviews, creative nonfiction, and visual art. Has published poetry by Albert Goldbarth, Maxine Kumin, Jane Hirshfield, Terrance Hayes, S. Beth Bishop, and Naomi Shahib Nye. *The Pinch* is 160 pages, 7×10, professionally printed, perfect-bound, with colorful glossy cover. Press run is 1,500. Sample: $10.

How to Submit Submit no more than 5 poems at a time. No e-mail submissions. Include SASE. Reads submissions according to these deadlines only: August 15-November 1 (Spring issue) and January 15-March 15 (Fall issue). Guidelines available for SASE, by e-mail, or on Web site. Responds in up to 3 months. Pays 2 contributor's copies.

Contest/Award Offerings Offers an annual award in poetry. 1st Prize: $1,000 and publication; 2nd-

and 3rd-Prize poems will also be published. Any previously unpublished poem of up to 2 pages is eligible. No simultaneous submissions. Poems should be typed and accompanied by a cover letter. Author's name should not appear anywhere on ms. Manuscripts will not be returned. Guidelines available for SASE, by e-mail, or on Web site. **Entry fee:** $15 for up to 3 poems (includes one-year subscription). **Deadline:** January 15-March 15 (inclusive postmark dates). Winners will be notified in June; published in Spring issue.

▣ ◻ THE PINK CHAMELEON—ONLINE

E-mail: dpfreda@juno.com. Web site: www.geocities.com/thepinkchameleon/index.html. Established 1985 (former print version), 1999 (online version). **Contact:** Mrs. Dorothy P. Freda, editor.
Magazine Needs *The Pink Chameleon—Online* publishes "family-oriented, upbeat poetry, any genre in good taste that gives hope for the future." Wants "poems about nature, loved ones, rare moments in time." Does not want "pornography, cursing, swearing; nothing evoking despair." Considers poetry by children and teens. Receives about 50 poems/year, accepts about 50%.
How to Submit Submit 1-4 poems at a time. Lines/poem: 6 minimum, 24 maximum. Considers previously published poems; no simultaneous submissions. Accepts e-mail submissions only (pasted into body of message; "please, no attachments"). Use plain text and include a brief bio. Reads submissions January-April and September-October. Time between acceptance and publication is 2 months. "As editor, I reserve the right to edit for grammar, spelling, sentence structure, flow; omit redundancy and any words or material I consider in bad taste." Often comments on rejected poems. Guidelines available by e-mail or on Web site. Responds in one month. No payment. Acquires one-time, one-year publication rights. All rights revert to poet in 6 months to a year, depending on date of acceptance.
Advice "Always keep a typed hard copy or a back-up disk of your work for your files. Mail can go astray. And I'm human, I can accidentally delete or lose the submission."

◪ PINYON

Dept. of Languages, Literature & Communications, Mesa State College, 1100 North Ave., Grand Junction CO 81051. E-mail: pinyonpoetry@hotmail.com. Established 1995. **Contact:** Randy Phillis, editor.
Magazine Needs *Pinyon*, published annually in June, prints "the best available contemporary American poetry and fiction. No restrictions other than excellence. We appreciate a strong voice." Does not want "inspirational, light verse, or sing-song poetry." Has published poetry by Mark Cox, Barry Spacks, Wendy Bishop, and Anne Ohman Youngs. *Pinyon* is about 120 pages, magazine-sized, perfect-bound. Receives about 4,000 poems/year, accepts 2%. Press run is 300 (150 subscribers, 5 libraries, 50 shelf sales); 100 distributed free to contributors, friends, etc. Subscription: $8/year. Sample: $4.50. Make checks payable to Pinyon, MSC.
How to Submit Submit 3-5 poems at a time. No previously published poems or simultaneous submissions. Cover letter is preferred. "Name, address, e-mail, and phone number on each page. SASE required." Reads submissions August 1-December 1. "Three groups of assistant editors, led by an associate editor, make recommendations to the editor." Seldom comments on rejected poems. Guidelines available for SASE. Responds in February. Pays 2 contributor's copies. Acquires one-time rights.
Advice "Send us your best work!"

◪ ◎ PLAINSONGS (Specialized: Great Plains poems encouraged)

Dept. of English, Hastings College, Hastings NE 68902-0269. (402)461-7352. Fax: (402)461-7756. E-mail: plainsongs@hastings.edu. (inquiries only). Established 1980. **Contact:** Laura Marvel Wunderlich, editor.
Magazine Needs *Plainsongs*, published 3 times/year, considers poems "on any subject, in any

style, but free verse predominates. Plains region poems encouraged." *Plainsongs'* title suggests not only its location on the Great Plains, but its preference for the living language, whether in free or formal verse. *"Plainsongs* is committed to poems only, to make space without visual graphics, bios, reviews, or critical positions." Has published poetry by Phillip Belcher, Michael Kriesel, W. Dale Nelson, Judith Tate O'Brien, and Danielle Sellers. *Plainsongs* is 40 pages, digest-sized, laser-set, printed on thin paper, saddle-stapled, with one-color matte card cover with generic black logo. "Published by the English department of Hastings College, the magazine is partially financed by subscriptions. Although editors respond to as many submissions with personal attention as they have time for, the editor offers specific observations to all contributors who also subscribe." Subscription: $15 for 3 issues. Sample: $5.

How to Submit Submit up to 6 poems at a time, with name and address on each page. No fax, e-mail, or disk submissions; postal submissions only. Reads submissions according to the following deadlines: July 15 for Winter issue; November 15 for Spring issue; March 15 for Fall issue. Responds 7-8 weeks after deadline. Guidelines available for SASE. Pays 2 contributor's copies and one-year subscription. Acquires first rights.

Contest/Award Offerings Three poems in each issue receive a $25 prize. "A short essay in appreciation accompanies each award poem."

Advice "We like poems that seem to be aware of modernist and post-modernist influences during the last hundred years, not necessarily by imitation or allusion, but by using the tools provided by that rich heritage. Poets need to read and absorb the work of other poets."

$☑ PLEIADES

Pleiades Press, Dept. of English, Central Missouri State University, Warrensburg MO 64093. (660)543-8106. E-mail: kdp8106@cmsu2.cmsu.edu. Web site: www.cmsu.edu/englphil/pleiades. Established 1990. **Contact:** Kevin Prufer, editor.

• Poems published in *Pleiades* have appeared in *The Best American Poetry* and *The Pushcart Prize.*

Magazine Needs *Pleiades*, published semiannually in April and October, prints poetry, fiction, literary criticism, belles lettres (occasionally), and reviews. Open to all writers. Wants "avant-garde, free verse, and traditional poetry, and some quality light verse." Does not want anything "pretentious, didactic, or overly sentimental." Has published poetry by James Tate, Joyce Carol Oates, Brenda Hillman, Wislawa Szymborska, Carl Phillips, and Jean Valentine. *Pleiades* is 160 pages, digest-sized, perfect-bound, with heavy coated cover with color art. Receives about 3,000 poems/year, accepts 1-3%. Press run is 2,500-3,000 (several hundred shelf sales); about 200 distributed free to educational institutions and libraries across the country. Single copy: $6; subscription: $12. Sample: $5. Make checks payable to Pleiades Press.

How to Submit Submit 3-5 poems at a time. Considers simultaneous submissions with notification; no previously published poems. Cover letter is preferred. Include brief bio. Time between acceptance and publication "can be up to one year. Each poem published must be accepted by two readers and approved by the poetry editor." Seldom comments on rejected poems. Guidelines available for SASE or on Web site. Responds in up to 3 months. Payment varies. Acquires first and second serial rights.

Contest/Award Offerings The annual Lena-Miles Wever Todd Poetry Series Book Competition (see separate listing in Contests & Awards).

$☑ PLOUGHSHARES

Emerson College, 120 Boylston St., Dept. P, Boston MA 02116. (617)824-8753. Web site: www.pshares.org. Established 1971. **Contact:** Poetry Editor.

● Work published in *Ploughshares* has been selected frequently for *The Best American Poetry*.

Magazine Needs *Ploughshares*, published 3 times/year, is "a journal of new writing guest-edited by prominent poets and writers to reflect different and contrasting points of view. Translations are welcome if permission has been granted." Editors have included Carolyn Forché, Gerald Stern, Rita Dove, Chase Twichell, and Marilyn Hacker. Has published poetry by Donald Hall, Li-Young Lee, Robert Pinsky, Brenda Hillman, and Thylias Moss. *Ploughshares* is 200 pages, digest-sized. Receives about 2,500 poetry submissions/year. Press run is 7,000. Subscription: $24 domestic, $36 foreign. Sample: $10.95 current issue, $8.50 back issue.

How to Submit Submit 1-3 poems at a time. Considers simultaneous submissions if indicated as such; no previously published poems. Postal submissions only, include SASE. Cover letter is preferred. Reads submissions August 1-March 31 (postmark); mss submitted April 1-July 31 will be returned unread. "We suggest you read a few issues (online or in print) before submitting. Check our Web site for any special guidelines." Responds in up to 5 months. Always sends prepublication galleys. Pays $25/printed page ($50 minimum, $250 maximum), plus 2 contributor's copies and a subscription.

$□ ◎ POCKETS (Specialized: Christian; poetry by/for children; thematic issues)

1908 Grand Av., P.O. Box 340004, Nashville TN 37203-0004. E-mail: pockets@upperroom.org. Web site: www.pockets.org. **Contact:** Lynn W. Gilliam, editor.

Magazine Needs *Pockets*, published monthly (except February), is an interdenominational magazine for children ages 6-11. "Each issue is built around a specific theme, with material (including poetry) that can be used by children in a variety of ways. Submissions do not need to be overly religious; they should help children experience a Christian lifestyle that is not always a neatly wrapped moral package but is open to the continuing revelation of God's will." Considers poetry by children.

How to Submit Lines/poem: 24 maximum. Considers previously published poems (first reprint only). No fax or e-mail submissions. Submissions should be typed, double-spaced, on $8^{1}/_{2} \times 11$ paper, accompanied by SASE for return. "Those who wish to save postage and are concerned about paper conservation may send a SASP for notification of accepted manuscripts; we will recycle the paper the submission is printed on. Please list the title of the submission(s) on the postcard." Reads submissions year round. Publishes theme issues; themes are available each year in December. Guidelines available on Web site (under Adults/Writer's Corner). Pays $2/line ($25 minimum). Pays on acceptance; may place mss on long-term hold for specific issues. Acquires newspaper, periodical, and electronic rights.

✪ ◩ POEM

Huntsville Literary Association, P.O. Box 2006, Huntsville AL 35804. Web site: www.hla-hsv.org. Established 1967. **Contact:** Rebecca Harbor, editor.

Magazine Needs *Poem*, published twice/year in May and November, consists entirely of poetry. "We publish both traditional forms and free verse." Wants poems "characterized by compression, rich vocabulary, significant content, and evidence of 'a tuned ear and practiced pen.' We want coherent work that moves through the particulars of the poem to make a point. We equally welcome submissions from established poets as well as from less-known and beginning poets." Does not want translations. Has published poetry by Kathryn Kirkpatrick, Peter Serchuk, and Kim Bridgford. *Poem* is 90 pages, digest-sized, flat-spined, printed on good stock paper, with a clean design and a matte cover. Prints more than 60 poems/issue, generally featured one to a page. Press run is 500 (all subscriptions, including libraries). Single copy: $10; subscription: $20. Sample: $7 (back issue).

How to Submit Send 3-5 poems at a time. No previously published poems or simultaneous submissions. Include SASE. Reads submissions year round. Guidelines available for SASE or on Web site. Respond in 1-2 months. Pays 2 contributor's copies. Acquires first serial rights.

ⓐ POEMS & PLAYS

English Dept., Middle Tennessee State University, Murfreesboro TN 37132. (615)898-2712. Established 1993. **Contact:** Gaylord Brewer, editor.

Magazine Needs *Poems & Plays*, published annually in the spring, is an "eclectic publication for poems and short plays." No restrictions on style or content of poetry. Has published poetry by Naomi Wallace, Kate Gale, James Doyle, and Charles Harper Webb. *Poems & Plays* is 88 pages, digest-sized, professionally printed, perfect-bound, with coated color card cover. Receives 1,500 poems per issue, publishes 30-35 "typically." Press run is 800. Subscription: $10 for 2 issues. Sample: $6.

How to Submit No previously published poems or simultaneous submissions. Reads submissions October-November only. "Work is circulated among advisory editors for comments and preferences. All accepted material is published in the following issue." Sometimes comments on rejected poems. Responds in 2 months. Pays one contributor's copy. Acquires first publication rights only.

Contest/Award Offerings Considers chapbook mss (poems or short plays) of 20-24 pages for The Tennessee Chapbook Prize. "Any combination of poems or plays, or a single play, is eligible. The winning chapbook is printed within *Poems & Plays*." Winning author receives 50 copies of the issue. SASE required. **Entry fee:** $10 (includes one copy of the issue). **Deadline:** same as for the magazine (October-November). Past winners include Julie Lechevsky and Nancy Naomi Carlson. "The chapbook competition annually receives over 150 manuscripts from the U.S. and around the world."

ⓐ ⓖ POESY MAGAZINE (Specialized: Boston, MA & Santa Cruz, CA)

P.O. Box 7823, Santa Cruz CA 95061. (831)239-4419. E-mail: info@poesy.org. Web site: www.poes y.org. Established 1991. **Contact:** Brian Morrisey, editor/publisher.

Magazine Needs *POESY Magazine*, published quarterly, is "an anthology of American poetry. *POESY*'s main concentrations are Boston, Massachusetts and Santa Cruz, California, two thriving homesteads for poets, beats, and artists of nature. Our goal is to unite the two scenes, updating poets on what's happening across the country." Wants to see "original poems that express observational impacts with clear and concise imagery. Acceptence is based on creativity, composition, and relation to the format of *POESY*." Does not want "poetry with excessive profanity. We would like to endorse creativity beyond the likes of everyday babble." Has published poetry by Lawrence Ferlinghetti, Jack Hirschman, Edward Sanders, Todd Moore, Diane Di Prima, and Julia Vinograd. *POESY* is 16 pages, magazine-sized, newsprint, glued/folded, includes ads. Receives about 1,000 poems/year, accepts about 10%. Press run is 1,000; most distributed free to local venues. Single copy: $1; subscription: $12/year. Sample: $2. Make checks payable to Brian Morrisey.

How to Submit Submit 3-5 poems at a time. Lines/poem: 32 maximum. No previously published poems or simultaneous submissions. Accepts e-mail (submissions@poesy.org) and disk submissions. "Snail mail submissions are preferred with a SASE." Cover letter is preferred. Reads submissions year round. Time between acceptance and publication is one month. "Poems are accepted by the Santa Cruz editor/publisher based on how well the poem stimulates our format." Guidelines available in magazine, for SASE, by e-mail, or on Web site. Responds in one month. Sometimes sends prepublication galleys. Pays 3 contributor's copies. Acquires one-time rights. Reviews books/chapbooks of poetry and other magazines/journals in 1,000 words, single-book format. Send materials for review consideration to *POESY*, % Brian Morrisey.

Advice "Stay away from typical notions of love and romance. Become one with your surroundings and discover a true sense of natural perspective."

ⓐ POET LORE

The Writer's Center, 4508 Walsh St., Bethesda MD 20815. (301)654-8664. Fax: (801)730-6233. E-mail: postmaster@writer.org. Web site: www.writer.org. Established 1889. **Contact:** Jason DeYoung, managing editor.

Magazine Needs *Poet Lore*, published biannually, is "dedicated to the best in American and world poetry as well as timely reviews and commentary." Wants "fresh uses of traditional forms and devices, but any kind of excellence is welcome." Has published poetry by Ai, Denise Duhamel, Jefferey Harrison, Eve Jones, Carl Phillips, and Ronald Wallace. *Poet Lore* is 144 pages, digest-sized, professionally printed, perfect-bound, with glossy card cover. Receives about 4,200 poems/year, accepts 125. Press run is at least 800 (600 subscribers, 200 libraries). Single copy: $9; subscription: $18. "Add $1/single copy for shipping; add $5 postage for subscriptions outside U.S."

How to Submit Considers simultaneous submissions "with notification in cover letter." No e-mail or disk submissions. "Submit typed poems, with author's name and address on each page; SASE is required." Guidelines available for SASE or on Web site. Responds in 3 months. Pays 2 contributor's copies. Reviews books of poetry. Send materials for review consideration.

◩ POETALK

P.O. Box 11435, Berkeley CA 94712-2435. E-mail: poetalk@aol.com. Web site: www.bayareapoetsc oalition.org. Established 1974. **Contact:** Maggie Morley, editor.

Magazine Needs *POETALK*, published 2-4 times/year, is the poetry journal of the Bay Area Poets Coalition (BAPC) and publishes about 65 poets in each issue. "*POETALK* is open to all. No particular genre. Rhyme must be well done." *POETALK* is 36 pages, digest-sized, photocopied, saddle-stapled, with heavy card cover. Press run is 400 for members, subscribers, and contributors. Subscription: $8/year. Sample: $2.

How to Submit Submit 3-5 poems at a time, no more than twice/year. Lines/poem: under 35 preferred; longer poems of outstanding quality considered. Considers previously published poems and simultaneous submissions, but must be noted. Cover letter is preferred. Include SASE. "Manuscripts should be clearly typed, single-spaced, and include author's name and mailing address on every page. Include e-mail address if you have one." Responds in up to 6 months. Pays one contributor's copy. All rights revert to author upon publication.

Contest/Award Offerings Sponsors yearly contest. **Deadline:** submit October 1-November 15 (postmark). Guidelines available in early September for SASE or by e-mail.

Also Offers Bay Area Poets Coalition holds monthly readings (in Berkeley, CA). BAPC has 150 members. BAPC Membership: $15/year (includes subscription to *POETALK* and other privileges); extra outside U.S.

Advice "If you don't want suggested revisions, you need to say so clearly in your cover letter or indicate on each poem submitted."

▦ ▢ ◎ POETIC HOURS (Specialized: subscriptions encouraged; raises money for charity)

43 Willow Rd., Carlton, Nolts NG4 3BH England. E-mail: erranpublishing@hotmail.com. Web site: www.poetichours.homestead.com. Established 1993. **Contact:** Nicholas Clark, editor.

Magazine Needs *Poetic Hours*, published biannually, aims "to encourage and publish new poets, i.e., as a forum where good but little known poets can appear in print; and **to raise money for third world and other charities**. *Poetic Hours* features articles and poetry by subscribers and others." Wants "any subject; rhyme preferred but not essential; suitable for wide-ranging readership." Does not want "gothic, horror, extremist, political, self-interested." *Poetic Hours* is 40 pages, A4, saddle-stapled. Receives about 500 poems/year, accepts about 40%. Press run is about 400 (300 subscriptions and shelf sales, 12 libraries). Subscription: £7 sterling; overseas payments in sterling (Europe and EC) or U.S. dollars ($20 from U.S. or Canada). Subscribe online from Web site or send bankers checks (UK only) or cash. Sample: £3.75. Make checks payable to Erran Publishing.

How to Submit Submit 3-4 poems at a time. Lines/poem: 30 maximum. Considers previously published poems; no simultaneous submissions. Accepts e-mail (preferred; pasted into body of

Magazines/Journals

message) and disk (non-returnable) submissions. Cover letter is required. "Poets are encouraged to subscribe or buy a single copy, though not required." Time between acceptance and publication is 3 months. "Poems are read by editors and, if found suitable, are used." Always comments on rejected poems. Responds "within a week, whenever possible." Acquires one-time rights.

Additional Information *Poetic Hours* is non-profit-making; all proceeds go to various charities, particularly well-building and children's charities. A page of each issue is set aside for reporting how money is spent.

Also Offers Poetic Hours Online (www.poetichours.homestead.com/PoeticHoursOnline.html) features original content **by invitation of editor only.**

Advice "We welcome newcomers and invite those just starting out to have the courage to submit work. The art of poetry has moved from the hands of book publishers down the ladder to the new magazines. This is where all the best poetry is found."

◎ POETIC LOGIC (Specialized: FL resident poets; renga; radio feature)

E-mail: poeticlogic@earthlink.net. Web site: www.wmfe.org/907/arts/poetry.asp. Established 2002. **Contact:** Sara Schlossman, producer/editor; Charlene L. Edge, associate reader.

Magazine Needs *Poetic Logic*, broadcast weekly, is a "radio feature that runs on National Public Radio (NPR) Affiliate WMFE 90.7FM. In addition, we post the poems on our Web site for one week, then archive the audio readings, which are accessible to all who search the site. The poets listed below reach across a broad spectrum and indicate the different sensiblities we like to present. We feature poets from the state of Florida, especially central Florida, and poets who are visiting our state for a reading, teaching position, book tour, vacation, etc. We have had U.S. Poets Laureate and many internationally known poets on our program in addition to Florida's resident poets." Considers poetry by children and teens, "but if child is under 11th-grade level, work must be submitted by teacher on behalf of student." Has published poetry by Billy Collins, Philip F. Deaver, Terry Godbey, Russ Kesler, Ilyse Kusnetz, and Campbell McGrath.

How to Submit Submit 5 poems at a time. Lines/poem: prefers no more than 40. Considers previously published poems and simultaneous submissions. Accepts e-mail submissions (preferred; pasted into body of message); no disk submissions. "If submission is accepted, we request an electronic document in MS Word." Cover letter is preferred. Include short bio. Reads submissions year round "but slower in summer and in winter holiday season." Submit seasonal poems 2 months in advance. Time between acceptance and publication is 1-3 months. Sometimes comments on rejected poems. Guidelines available on Web site. Responds in 2-4 months. Acquires electronic rights. "We like to post a printed version of chosen poem(s) on our Web site for one week; all rights revert to author."

Also Offers "The Poetic Logic Renga Chain began in April of 2005 and is still going strong. Contributors sign up, are assigned a sequence number, and when their number is up, compose a tanka to link with the previous contributor's work. Guidelines for joining this work-in-progress are on the Web site. We do prefer Florida poets, but if you are from out-of-state and would like to contribute to the renga only, send your request to the producer as there may be an opportunity for non-resident contributors in the near future."

Advice "Read the work of the poets we have listed as it shows our broad spectrum of preferences. We are open to talented writers."

✪ ▣ ◪ POETIC MATRIX, A PERIODIC LETTER

P.O. Box 1223, Madera CA 93639. (559)673-9402. E-mail: poeticmatrix@yahoo.com. Web site: www.poeticmatrix.com. Established 1997 in Yosemite. **Contact:** John Peterson, editor/publisher.

Magazine Needs *Poetic Matrix, a periodic letteR*, published 2 times/year online, seeks poetry that "creates a 'place in which we can live' rather than telling us about the place; poetry that draws from the imaginal mind and is rich in the poetic experience—hence the poetic matrix." Does not want poetry that talks about the experience. Has published poetry by Lyn Lifshin, Tony White, Gail Entrekin, James Downs, Joan Michelson, and Brandon Cesmat.

How to Submit Accepts e-mail submissions (pasted into body of message). Guidelines available for SASE, by e-mail, or on Web site. Acquires one-time rights. Occasionally reviews books of poetry and online magazines/journals in 500-1,000 words, single- and multi-book format. Send materials for review consideration to John Peterson, editor.

Additional Information *"Poetic Matrix* has a call for manuscripts for the Slim Volume Series once a year. See Web site for when reading dates are set and for additional guidelines and awards. The Slim Volume Series is for manuscripts of 65-75 pages." **Charges reading fee of $17.**

Advice "Write with quality, passion, and intelligence."

◎ POETICA MAGAZINE, REFLECTIONS OF JEWISH THOUGHT

P.O. Box 11014, Norfolk VA 23517. Fax: (757)399-3936. E-mail: poeticamag@aol.com. Web site: www.poeticamagazine.com. Established 2002. **Contact:** Michal Mahgerefteh, publisher/editor.

Magazine Needs *Poetica Magazine, Reflections of Jewish Thought*, published 3 times/year, offers "an outlet for the many writers who draw from their Jewish backgrounds and experiences to create poetry/prose/short stories, giving both emerging and recognized writers the opportunity to share their work with the larger community." Does not want long pieces, haiku, rhyming poetry. Considers poetry by children and teens, grades 6-12. *Poetica* is 40-60 pages, digest-sized, desktop-published, saddle-stapled, with glossy cardstock cover with b&w art, includes some ads. Receives about 500 poems/year, accepts about 60%. Press run is 200 (80 subscribers). Single copy: $4; subscription: $12.

How to Submit Submit 3 poems at a time. Lines/poem: 2 pages maximum. Considers simultaneous submissions. No e-mail or disk submissions. Cover letter is optional. Reads submissions year round. Time between acceptance and publication is 6 months to a year. Seldom comments on rejected poems. Occasionally publishes theme issues. Guidelines available for SASE or on Web site. Responds in one month. Pays one contributor's copy. Poet retains all rights.

Contest/Award Offerings Offers annual poetry contest with up to $50 awarded for First Prize; up to 5 Honorable Mentions. Selected poems will be published in future issues of *Poetica*. Accepts simultaneous submissions. No limit on number of entries (3 poems constitute an entry). Submit 2 copies of each poem, single-spaced, no more than one poem/page. Include poet's name on all pages. No e-mail submissions. Include SASE for results only; mss will not be returned. Guidelines available on Web site. **Entry fee:** $12 for up to 3 poems. **Deadline:** March 31 annually. Judge: editors and visiting editors of *Poetica Magazine.* Notifies winners by June.

Advice " 'A fierce light beats upon the Jew'—reflect it in your writings. Tikun Olam is encouraged."

——$◙ POETRY

444 N. Michigan Ave., Suite 1850, Chicago IL 60611. E-mail: poetry@poetrymagazine.org. (send Letters to the Editor to editors@poetrymagazine.org). Web site: www.poetrymagazine.org. Established 1912. **Contact:** The Editors.

● Work published in *Poetry* is frequently included in *The Best American Poetry* and *The Pushcart Prize: Best of the Small Presses.*

Magazine Needs *Poetry*, published monthly by The Poetry Foundation, "has no special manuscript needs and no special requirements as to form or genre: We examine in turn all work received and accept that which seems best." Has published poetry by the major voices of our time as well as new talent. Poetry is $5\frac{1}{2} \times 9$, elegantly printed, flat-spined. Receives 90,000 submissions/year, accepts about 300-350. Press run is 16,000 (11,500 subscribers, 20% libraries). Single copy: $3.75; subscription: $35 ($38 for institutions). Sample: $5.50.

How to Submit Submit no more than 4 poems at a time. No previously published poems or simultaneous submissions. No e-mail submissions. Submit by postal mail only, with return address on outside of envelope; include SASE. Submissions must be typed, single-spaced, with poet's name and address on every page. Guidelines available for SASE. Responds in 1-2 months. Pays $10/line (with a minimum payment of $150). Reviews books of poetry in multi-book formats of varying lengths. Does not accept unsolicited reviews.

Contest/Award Offerings Seven prizes (Bess Hokin Prize, Levinson Prize, Frederick Bock Prize, J. Howard and Barbara M.J. Wood Prize, John Frederick Nims Memorial Prize, Friends of Literature Prize, Union League Civic and Arts Poetry Prize) ranging from $300 to $5,000 are awarded annually to poets whose work has appeared in the magazine that year. Only verse already published in *Poetry* is eligible for consideration; no formal application is necessary.

Also Offers *Poetry*'s Web site offers featured poems, letters, reviews, interviews, essays, and Web-exclusive features.

THE POETRY CHURCH MAGAZINE (Specialized: subscribers only; Christian)

Feather Books, P.O. Box 438, Shrewsbury SY3 0WN England. Phone/fax: (44)(174)387-2177. E-mail: john@waddysweb.freeuk.com. (inquiries only). Web site: www.waddysweb.freeuk.com. Established 1982 (Feather Books); 1996 (*The Poetry Church Magazine*). **Contact:** Rev. John Waddington-Feather, editor.

Magazine Needs *The Poetry Church Magazine*, published quarterly, contains Christian poetry, prayers, and hymns. Wants "Christian or good religious poetry." Does not want "unreadable blasphemy." **Publishes subscribers' work only.** Considers poetry by children over age 10. Has published poetry by Laurie Bates, Joan Sheridan Smith, Idris Caffrey, Isabella Strachan, Walter Nash, and Susan Glyn. *The Poetry Church Magazine* is 40 pages, digest-sized, photocopied, saddle-stapled, with illustrated cover. Receives about 1,000 poems/year, accepts about 500. Press run is 1,000 (400 subscribers, 10 libraries). Single copy: free; subscription: £12 for 4 issues ($20 USD). Make checks payable in sterling to Feather Books. Payment can also be made through Web site.

How to Submit Submit 2 poems at a time. Lines/poem: usually around 20, "but will accept longer." Considers previously published poems and simultaneous submissions. Cover letter is preferred (with information about the poet). No e-mail submissions; postal submissions only. Include SASE, or SAE and IRC. Submissions must be typed. **Publishes "only subscribers' poems as they keep us solvent."** Time between acceptance and publication is 4 months. "The editor does a preliminary reading, then seeks the advice of colleagues about uncertain poems." Responds within one week. Poets retain copyright.

Additional Information Feather Books publishes the Feather Books Poetry Series, collections of around 20 Christian poems and prayers. Has recently published the Glyn family, Walter Nash, David Grieve, and Rosie Morgan Barry. "We have now published 300 poetry collections by individual Christian poets." Books are usually photocopied, saddle-stapled, with illustrated covers. "We do not insist, but **most poets pay for their work. Enquire for current costs.** If they can't afford it, but are good poets, we stand the cost. We expect poets to read *The Poetry Church Magazine* to get some idea of our standards."

Also Offers Each winter and summer, selected poems appear in *The Poetry Church Collection*, the leading Christian poetry anthology used in churches and schools.

Advice "We find it better for poets to master rhyme and rhythm before trying free verse. Many poets seem to think that if they write 'down' a page they're writing poetry, when all they're doing is writing prose in a different format. But good free verse is accpted."

THE POETRY EXPLOSION NEWSLETTER (THE PEN)

P.O. Box 4725, Pittsburgh PA 15206-0725. (866)234-0297. E-mail: arthurford@hotmail.com. Established 1984. **Contact:** Arthur C. Ford, Sr., editor.

Magazine Needs *The Poetry Explosion Newsletter (The PEN)*, published quarterly, is "dedicated to the preservation of poetry." Wants "all forms and subject matter with the use of good imagery, symbolism, and honesty. Rhyme and non-rhyme." Does not want "vulgarity." Considers poetry by children and teens; "if under 18 years old, parent or guardian should submit!" Has published poetry by Iva Fedorka. *The PEN* is 12-16 pages, saddle-stapled, mimeographed on both sides. Receives about 300 poems/year, accepts 80. Press run is 850 (735 subscribers, 5 libraries). Subscription: $20/year. Send $4 for sample copy and more information. Make checks payable to Arthur C. Ford.

How to Submit Submit up to 5 poems at a time. Lines/poem: 40 maximum. Considers previously published poems and simultaneous submissions. No e-mail submissions. Include large SASE if you want work returned. **Reading fee:** $1. Sometimes publishes theme issues. Guidelines available for SASE. Responds in up to 3 weeks. Comments on rejected poems "sometimes, but not obligated." **Poetry critiques available for 15¢/word.** Pays one contributor's copy. Send materials for review consideration.

Advice "Be fresh, honest, and legible!"

🌐 ✏ POETRY KANTO

Kanto Gakuin University, Kamariya-cho 3-22-1, Kanazawa-ku, Yokohama 236-8502 Japan. E-mail: alan@kanto-gakuin.ac.jp. Web site: http://home.kanto-gakuin.ac.jp/~kg061001/. Established 1984 by William I. Elliott. **Contact:** Alan Botsford, editor.

Magazine Needs *Poetry Kanto*, published annually in September by the Kanto Gakuin University, is Japan's leading annual bilingual, bicultural poetry magazine. Features "outstanding poetry that navigates the divide of ocean and language. We seek exciting, well-crafted contemporary poetry in English and also encourage and publish high-quality English translations of modern and emerging Japanese poets. All translations must be accompanied by the original poems." See Web site for sample poems. Has published poetry by W.S. Merwin, Seamus Heaney, Harryette Mullen, Tanikawa Shuntaro, and Sarah Arvio. *Poetry Kanto* is 100 pages, 6×9, professionally printed on coated stock, perfect-bound, with glossy cover. Press run is 1,000; many are distributed free to schools, poets, and presses. The magazine is unpriced. Sample: send SAE with IRCs.

How to Submit Submit 5 poems at a time maximum. No previously published poems or simultaneous submissions. Prefers e-mail submissions (as attachment in Word). Cover letter is required. Include brief bio. All postal submissions require SAE and IRCs. Reads submissions September-April. Guidelines available on Web site. Pays 3-5 contributor's copies.

Advice "From forebears, learn; from the future, write; in the present, live."

🖥 ✏ POETRY MIDWEST

(913)469-8500, ext. 4705. E-mail: submit@poetrymidwest.org. (submissions); editors@poetrymidwest.org. (queries). Web site: www.poetrymidwest.org. Established 2000. **Contact:** Matthew W. Schmeer, editor/publisher.

Magazine Needs *Poetry Midwest*, published 3 times/year online (winter, spring/summer, fall), features poetry, nongenre microfiction, and brief creative nonfiction from new and established writers. Wants free verse, traditional Western forms, traditional Asian forms other than haiku and senryu, prose poems, long poems, nongenre microfiction (up to 300 words), and brief creative nonfiction (up to 300 words). Does not want science fiction, fantasy, inspirational, religious, or children's verse or fiction; anything of an overtly political or religious nature; or spoken word poetry. Has published poetry by Philip Dacey, Cherryl Floyd-Miller, Rhoda Janzen, J. Patrick Lewis, Adrian Matejka, and Matt Rasmussen. *Poetry Midwest* is 20-100 pages, published online as a (free) downloadable Adobe Acrobat PDF file. Receives about 1,500 poems/year, accepts about 7%.

How to Submit Submit 3 poems at a time. Lines/poem: 3 minimum, 10 pages maximum. Considers simultaneous submissions; no previously published poems. "Submit via e-mail only. Submissions should be pasted into the body of an e-mail message with 'Poetry Midwest Submission' in subject line (omit quotation marks). Absolutely no e-mail file attachments. E-mail messages containing attachments will be deleted upon receipt. Do not send submissions via postal mail; they will be returned unread.'' Reads submissions year round. Submit seasonal poems 3-6 months in advance. Time between acceptance and publication is 3 months to one year. ''I read submissions as they are received, deciding whether or not to use a piece based on its own literary merits and whether it fits in with other poems selected for an issue in progress.'' Seldom comments on rejected poems. Guidelines available by e-mail or on Web site. Responds in up to 6 months. Acquires first rights or first North American serial rights as well as first electronic rights, reprint rights, and electronic archival rights.

Advice ''Submissions to online journals should reflect the same attention to detail that goes into submissions to traditional print journals. Fancy display fonts, distracting animated graphics, and pictures of you and/or your significant other and/or pets do not increase the likelihood of a piece being accepted; in fact, they almost ensure your piece will be automatically rejected. There are professional standards for submitting to literary journals which can be found on many Web sites and in most handbooks for creative writers. Follow those guidelines and any market-specific requests if you want your submission seriously considered.''

POETRY NORTHWEST

4232 SE Hawthorne Blvd., Portland OR 97215. (503)236-0615. E-mail: editors@poetrynw.org. Web site: www.poetrynw.org. Established 1959. **Contact:** David Biespiel, editor.

Magazine Needs *Poetry Northwest*, published semiannually in March and October, reappeared in 2006 after a 4-year hiatus. ''The mission of *Poetry Northwest* is to publish the best poetry written in English. In the words of founding editor Carolyn Kizer, we aim to 'encourage the young and the inexperienced, the neglected mature, and the rough major talents and the fragile minor ones.' All styles and aesthetics will find consideration.'' Has published poetry by Theodore Roethke, Czeslaw Milosz, Anne Sexton, Harold Pinter, Thom Gunn, and Philip Larkin. *Poetry Northwest* is 40 + pages, magazine-sized, Web press-printed, saddle-stapled, with 4-color cover, includes ads. Receives about 5,000 poems/year, accepts about 1%. Press run is 2,000 (1,000 subscribers, 400 libraries). Single copy: $8. Sample: $9. Make checks payable to *Poetry Northwest*.

How to Submit Submit 4 poems at a time maximum. No previously published poems or simultaneous submissions. No e-mail or disk submissions. Cover letter is required. Time between acceptance and publication is 2 months. Sometimes comments on rejected poems. Sometimes publishes theme issues. Upcoming themes available in magazine or by e-mail. Guidelines available on Web site. Responds in 4-6 weeks (''except during July and August; submissions sent during these months will be considered in September''). Always sends prepublication galleys. Pays 2 contributor's copies. Acquires all rights. Returns rights to poets upon request. Reviews books of poetry in single- and multi-book format. Send materials for review consideration to Garth Weber, senior editor.

POETRY NOTTINGHAM

11 Orkney Close, Stenson Fields, Derbyshire DE24 3LW England. Established 1946. Web site: http://nottinghampoetrysociety.co.uk. **Contact:** Adrian Buckner, editor.

Magazine Needs *Poetry Nottingham*, published 4 times/year, features articles and reviews in addition to poetry. Open to submissions from anyone. Has published poetry by Martin Stannard, Edmund Skellings, Helena Nelson, Lorna Dowell, Lucie McKee, and C.J. Allen. *Poetry Nottingham* is 6 × 8, professionally printed. Receives about 1,500 submissions/year, accepts about 120. Press run is 300 (200 subscribers). Single copy: £2.75; subscription: £17 sterling. (Subscriptions and individual copies can be purchased in U.S. dollars by sending check payable to Karen Crosbie at 827½ Santa Barbara St., Santa Barbara CA 93101. Single copy: $7 current issue, $4 back issue; subscription: $25/year.)

How to Submit Submit up to 6 poems at a time. No previously published poems. Cover letter is required. ''Send SAE and 3 IRCs for stamps. No need to query.'' Responds in 2 months. Pays one contributor's copy. Staff reviews books of poetry. Send materials for review consideration.

Contest/Award Offerings The Nottingham Open Poetry Competition offers cash prizes, annual subscriptions, and publication in *Poetry Nottingham*. Open to all. Guidelines available on Web site.
Advice "We seek to provide an uncluttered environment for poems of wit, poems of concise lyrical intensity, and poems that are bold enough to expand on a theme."

◯ POETRY OF THE PEOPLE

3341 SE 19th Ave., Gainesville FL 32641. (352)375-0244. E-mail: poetryforaquarter@yahoo.com. Web site: www.angelfire.com/fl/poetryofthepeople. Established 1986. **Contact:** Paul Cohen, poetry editor.

Magazine Needs *Poetry of the People*, published semimonthly or monthly as a leaflet, is open to all forms of poetry. Wants "humorous poetry, love poetry, nature poetry, and fantasy." Does not want "racist or highly ethnocentric poetry. We do not like poetry that lacks images or is too personal or contains rhyme to the point that the poem has been destroyed." Also considers poetry written in French and Spanish. Considers poetry by children and teens. Has published poetry by Laura Stamps, Dan Matthews, Jenica Deer, Shannon Dixon, Kristi Castro, and Peggy C. Hall. *Poetry of the People* is 4 pages, magazine-sized. Sample: $4 for 11 pamphlets.

How to Submit Submit "as many poems as you want" at a time. Accepts e-mail and disk submissions. Include SASE with postal submissions. Cover letter is required (often publishes the cover letter). Include bio. "Autobiographical information is important in understanding the poetry." Often comments on rejected poems. Guidelines available by e-mail or on Web site. Responds within 18 months. Pays 10 contributor's copies. Acquires first rights.

Advice "You should appeal to as broad an audience as possible. Nature makes people happy."

🌐 ☑ POETRY SALZBURG REVIEW

University of Salzburg, Dept. of English, Akademiestrasse 24, Salzburg A-5020 Austria. (43)(662)8044-4422. Fax: (43)(662)8044-167. E-mail: editor@poetrysalzburg.com. Web site: www. poetrysalzburg.com. Established 2001. **Contact:** Dr. Wolfgang Goertschacher, editor.

Magazine Needs *Poetry Salzburg Review*, published twice/year, contains "articles on poetry, mainly contemporary, and 60 percent poetry. Also includes essays on poetics, review-essays, interviews, artwork, and translations. We tend to publish selections by authors who have not been taken up by the big poetry publishers. Nothing of poor quality." Has published poetry by John Kinsella, Michael Hamburger, Aidan Andrew Dunn, Glen Cavaliero, and Sue Walker. *Poetry Salzburg Review* is about 200 pages, A5, professionally printed, perfect-bound, with illustrated card cover. Receives about 5,000 poems/year, accepts 5%. Press run is 500 (200 subscribers, 15% libraries). Single copy: $11; subscription: $20 (cash only for those sending U.S. funds). Make checks payable to Wolfgang Goertschacher. "No requirements, but it's a good idea to subscribe to *Poetry Salzburg Review*."

How to Submit No previously published poems or simultaneous submissions. Accepts e-mail submissions (as attachment). Time between acceptance and publication is 6 months. Seldom comments on rejected poems. Occasionally publishes theme issues. Responds in 2 months. No payment. Acquires first rights. Reviews books/chapbooks of poetry as well as books on poetics. Send materials for review consideration.

🖥 ☺ POETRYBAY

P.O. Box 114, Northport NY 11768. (631)427-1950. Fax: (631)367-0038. E-mail: poetrybay@aol.com. Web site: www.poetrybay.com. Established 2000. **Contact:** George Wallace, editor.

Magazine Needs *Poetrybay*, published biannually online, seeks "to add to the body of great contemporary American poetry by presenting the work of established and emerging writers. Also, we consider essays and reviews." Has published poetry by Robert Bly, Yevgeny Yevtushenko, Marvin Bell, Diane Wakoski, Cornelius Eady, and William Heyen.

How to Submit Submit 5 poems at a time. Considers simultaneous submissions; no previously published poems. Accepts e-mail submissions (pasted into body of message); no disk submissions. Time between acceptance and publication is 2 months. Seldom comments on rejected poems. Occasionally publishes theme issues. Guidelines available on Web site. Sometimes sends prepublication galleys. Acquires first-time electronic rights. Reviews books/chapbooks of poetry and other magazines/journals. Send materials for review consideration.

▣ ◯ THE POET'S HAVEN

Web site: www.PoetsHaven.com. Established 1997. **Contact:** Vertigo Xi'an Xavier, publisher.
Magazine Needs *The Poet's Haven* is a Web site "featuring poetry, artwork, stories, reviews, essays, and much more." Wants work that's "emotional, personal, and intimate with the author or subject. Topics can cover just about anything." Does not want "material that is obscene, excessively vulgar, pornographic, racist, or religious." Has published poetry by Danielle Briganti, Jacob Erin-Cilberto, Rebecca Guile Hudson, Elisha Porat, and Katherine Zaleski. Work published on *The Poet's Haven* is left on the site permanently. Receives about 1,000 poems/year, accepts about 80%.
How to Submit Considers previously published poems and simultaneous submissions. Accepts submissions through online form only. Time between acceptance and publication is about 2 weeks. Never comments on rejected poems. Guidelines available on Web site. No payment for online publication; pays one contributor's copy for print edition. Acquires rights to publish on the Web site permanently and in any future print publications. Poet retains rights to have poems published elsewhere, "provided the other publishers do not require first-time or exclusive rights."
Additional Information Has published print editions as *The Poet's Haven Digest*. On indefinite hiatus as of April 2007. Check Web site for updated information or to order sample copies.
Also Offers Message forums, chat room, publisher's blog, an online store, and Web site hosting for authors and artists.

Ⓝ ▣ ◯ POET'S INK

E-mail: poet_Kelly@yahoo.com. Web site: www.PoetsInk.com. Established 2005. **Contact:** Kelly Morris.
Magazine Needs *Poet's Ink,* published monthly online, seeks "poetry of all kinds. Work by new poets is published alongside that of more experienced poets." Does not want "bad rhyme, clichés, poetry riddled with abstractions." Considers poetry by teens. "Will be judged by the same standards as poetry by adults." Has published poetry by Alexandria Webb, Julie Allen, Colin Baker, Jessica Healy, and Shelby Norris. Receives about 150 poems/year, accepts about 20%.
How to Submit Submit 3-5 poems at a time. Lines/poem: 2 minimum, 100 maximum ("longer poems better not be long-winded!"). Considers previously published poems and simultaneous submissions. Accepts e-mail submissions (as attachment); no disk submissions. Cover letter is preferred. "No funky formatting of poems!" Reads submissions year round. Time between acceptance and publication is one month. Often comments on rejected poems. Sometimes publishes theme issues. Guidelines available by e-mail or on Web site. Responds in 1-2 weeks. Acquires one-time rights. Rights revert to poets upon publication.
Advice "Read guidelines carefully before submitting. Take advantage of all the advice you get, but also follow your heart."

▣ ▨ POETS ON THE LINE

P.O. Box 20292, Brooklyn NY 11202-0292. E-mail: llerner@mindspring.com. Web site: www.echonyc.com/ ~ poets. Established 1995 (founded by Andrew Gettler and Linda Lerner). **Contact:** Linda Lerner, editor.
  • **Currently not accepting unsolicited work.**

Christine Swanberg

Living the well-imagined life

Photo by Jeffrey Swanberg

I n the following discussion, Christine Swanberg asks "What gifts do you bring to the table?" as she contemplates poetry writing and exploring life's possibilities. A review of her background reveals that Swanberg herself fills the table with a treasure trove of gifts.

She's a widely published poet with several collections in print, including her most recent books, *The Red Lacquer Room* (Chiron Press, 2001) and *Who Walks Among the Trees with Charity* (Wind Publications, 2005). Her readings and workshops have led her throughout the United States, and she's traveled globally pursuing further adventures with her husband of 35 years, Jeffrey. A liturgist and lyricist as well as a poet, Swanberg has sung with The Mendelssohn Chorale and Womansong Chorale as well as the Christ United choir, Court Street Sanctuary choir, and Revelation Praise Team (all in Rockford, Illinois).

Poet, lyricist, singer, teacher, editor, literary judge . . . Christine Swanberg's greatest gift of all may be her ability to recognize and explore her talents—and generously share them with everyone.

In their review of your book *Who Walks Among the Trees with Charity*, J. Glenn and Barbara Evans at *Poets*West say, "Christine's praise poems are a gift for a life 'lived well' and the 'fire of a life imagined well.'" Could you address the relationship between a "life lived well" and a "life imagined well" and its impact on your work?

The fire of a "life imagined well" has to do with living deliberately and discerning the gifts you've been given and what to do with them.

A few decades ago, I began to imagine the kind of life I wanted to live. I wondered if my own life would be "lived well" if I didn't follow various musings such as traveling, teaching, writing, riding horses, publishing, singing, and involvement in spiritual endeavors.

I imagined the places I would see, discerned the kind of writing I would do, pushed myself toward publishing, risked singing in front of large audiences, bought a horse and learned to ride it, and defined myself through spiritual pursuits.

Being part of the horse culture is rather like being part of the poetry culture. There's a sense of romance, adventure, and risk in both. Both have a "secret language" and a process to master. Since riding in the country was an integral part of my life, I did write many poems dealing with the experience. Riding in the country through cornfields and forests and by the river, I learned the language of the terrain—a language that became integrated into my poetry. Many of my poems name various plants and birds by exact species. In addition, I learned the language of horses, which is really the language of touch.

Ultimately, the horse experience enlarged my world in many ways. "Before Grooming the Horse in Winter," "For Lee, Who Shoes Horses," "Pasture," and "Prairie Burner" are among my poems inspired by the experience of owning, training, and riding a horse for nearly two decades.

How would you characterize a "praise poem"?

Sometimes the world seems like a wondrous place. Although I may not consciously set out to write a praise poem, as I begin writing on that blank page, the poem may evolve into some sort of praise. It may praise a good neighbor, a tree, prairie grass, the ocean, a marriage that lasts, a friendship, or Indian summer. I hadn't realized that some of my work was ardently praiseful until J. Glenn and Barbara Evans said so in their review.

Your bio on the *Poets*West Web site (www.poetswest.com) states "many wild and wacky jobs, places, people, and coincidences that have happened to her have shaped her poetry." Can you describe some of these unusual circumstances and locations and their impact on your work?

I began working at a very early age. I was a short order cook, a carhop, a nurse's aide, a factory worker, a nightshift worker in a mental institution, and I did a one-day stint as a clown, all before I was 20. Then I began a long and arduous career as a teacher, which lasted 35 years and encompassed high school, college and post-graduate teaching.

As a teacher, summers were spent trekking through Europe, Central America, the Caribbean, Canada and most of the United States. Many of these experiences have found their ways into poems. "Night Shift," "Mallory Pier, Key West," "A Remembrance for Panajachel," "The Bath in Koblenz," and "Paris on $5 a Day" are a few such poems that have been published in various journals and in my own collections. Most of these poems have a narrative line that tells the story of these "wild and wacky jobs, places, and people" that have shaped some of my work.

Could you give an example of one of these unusual people or experiences that inspired a poem?

"The Man at the Pool" is really a person that I see regularly where I swim. He has always intrigued me because he has no legs. Amazingly, he's always cheerful. I welcome seeing him there because he's easy to swim with. I've wondered how he lost his legs, but this has never come up in our greetings. It seems intrusive to ask him questions, so the mystery of the man at the pool prevails. One day I learned that he has a rather bizarre sense of humor, which turned out to be the "punch line" of the poem.

The Man at the Pool

The man with no legs swims today.
He lowers himself into the pool from his wheelchair,
balancing one hand at a time
like a Russian acrobat or master Yogi.
The arms of Vulcan.
The torso of Zeus.
The body of a porpoise.
We must be the same age, so I wonder

> *if he lost his legs in Viet Nam.*
> *I love swimming with him in parallel lines,*
> *how his body undulates like an S.*
> *I love swimming with him*
> *because he doesn't chop and slash*
> *like other alpha swimmers*
> *who send my measured back stroke*
> *flailing against the guard ribbon.*
> *Today one huge arm hugs the pool's rim.*
> *The other holds a renegade razor.*
> *He says, "Look what I found in the pool."*
> *I say, "What on earth . . . ?"*
> *He says, "Gee. You think maybe*
> *I should shave my legs?"*

(from *Who Walks Among the Trees with Charity* [Wind Publications, ©2005]; reprinted with permission)

Your husband is a photographer and did the photos for your book *The Tenderness of Memory* (Plainview Press, 1995). Do you collaborate often?

Jeff's photographs were used both as the cover and inside of *The Tenderness of Memory*. That was our first collaboration—and it wasn't even our idea! Susan Bright, the publisher of Plainview Press, visited us and was taken with Jeff's photographs. It was her idea to use them throughout the book; she chose the inside photographs herself. Jeff has since supplied the cover work for other presses and books, including *Who Walks Among the Trees with Charity*.

Together you established Prints and Poet Studio in your home and host "arts and poetry gatherings" as well. What do these involve? Who participates?

A few years ago, we moved into a house partly because the basement had potential to be a studio/gallery. We whimsically named it The Prints and Poet. We built a few walls, hung bright curtains, and used bright Moderno rugs—so it was pretty low budget. Our first collaborations were loosely thematic with names such as "Seeing Red," "Scapes," and "A-Muse-ing." I used my inventory of poems to play on the theme of Jeff's photos. For example, for "Seeing Red," I picked out the ones that alluded to red (or shades of red).

We recently started having group cooperative shows, under the title "Poetry in Motion." The last show featured 10 visual artists of various media as well as about 10 poets. Each is responsible for sending out invitations and hosting for an hour for the weekend. In this case, both visual artists and poets have a wide range of themes and can interpret "Poetry in Motion" any way that moves them. We found this worked best.

Most of the 100 or so guests really come to see a particular artist or hear a particular poet. We organize it in time frames, so that guests know when a certain poet is reading. We were thrilled with the reception of the poets and the attention that was given to them. All the seats were taken and folks actually sat on the stairs to listen.

Although Jeff has the artist's eye for composition and contrast, we do have "artistic conflicts" over how to hang the shows. While he tends to want to measure inches between art pieces, I tend to want to group by "vignette" and not worry about exact spacing. Since we don't have a month to hang the shows, I usually prevail.

You've written "commissioned" poems for several occasions as well as song lyrics. How does a poet approach a commissioned piece? How does writing lyrics compare to writing poetry?

Writing commissioned pieces is another form of collaboration. When writing a poem for a particular event, institution, or person, it's important to consider who is likely to read it or hear it. Poetic license is not the key to writing commissions but rather occasion, intent and audience.

I interview first to determine the expectations of the commission, taking notes to find key phrases, themes and possible key images that might play into the commission. Sometimes the repetition of a key phrase paces the poem, and *voila!*—there it is. This process uses the left brain in terms of logical sequence and structure more than personal poems, which are often right-brained and more intuitive.

The same is true with writing lyrics, especially for choral groups who depend on meter and prefer the comfort of end rhyme. When writing commissioned pieces and lyrics that have a specific audience or choral group, the poet has to step out of her skin and write for *them*, not for herself. Personal poetry is self-revelatory, sometimes candid and even confessional. It strives for originality—phrases that surprise and form that challenges.

Lyrics, on the other hand, need a comfort zone for the singers, who often have very few practices before they perform the piece.

Explain some of the differences in reaching an audience with the performance of your lyrics as opposed to readers enjoying your poems in print. What are the special satisfactions and frustrations (if any) unique to each?

When I first began writing seriously and sending out my work over 20 years ago, nothing could match the thrill of publication. After accumulating a number of acceptances, I used to think that at any given time, someone could possibly be reading my poetry. Eventually I came to see that as a literary network. Of course, the only major feedback you get is from the editor who accepts the work; or, perhaps, winning a prize.

Most poets don't really get to know if their poetry has been well received. From time to time, I did get notes from strangers about certain poems, but certainly not many. Yet the published poem invites the reader to return to it, again and again, and that is very satisfying. I do worry, however, that the "audience" is limited to other writers.

Performances involving lyrics or commissioned pieces have immediate large one-time audiences. For example, this year I wrote lyrics for a collaboration entitled "Music for my Eyes." This was collaboration in the truest sense, involving several community organizations, visual artists and individual soloists. The culmination was a "walk across the street" to a large, old church (Second Congregational, Rockford, Illinois) for the performance of the musical pieces.

The entire church was packed for the "debut." As a member of Womansong Chorale, I experienced singing the commissioned piece, "Not for Us Alone." It was scary and exhilarating at the same time. I believe my hair was standing on end when the organ began and we started singing.

Fortunately, the piece was well-received, thanks to the brilliance of the musical composer, Donald Fraser. We received a standing ovation and exuberant kudos for the evening. The thrill was very intense, though short-lived. We did sing it again on the Coronado stage for the Mayor's Art Award, and again at my church. So far, there is no CD. The worry here is that it was a "flash in the pan."

Did singing in chorales lead you to writing lyrics? How does having your life so closely entwined with music affect your poetry?

Singing in chorales and choirs has indeed influenced my poetry. One subtle way is that I now tend to think of lines of poems the same as a line of music. Breath control and flow create a stronger line, when reading aloud. Also, I have come to expect a certain amount of "music" in all poetry, whether it is rhymed or not.

Singing has also made me realize that most people want immediate delight with words they are singing or hearing. Serious modern poetry often depends on originality, intellectual subtleties, self-revelation and psychological depth. These arduous luxuries do not vigorously inform musical lyrics in general. Rhythm (meter) and rhyme are often expected, and I have learned not to shy away from them. I remember a benediction that I wrote which involved a string of unrhymed, unmetered similes. The choir struggled with them—and who could blame them when they had only a week to learn the piece?

You're a liturgist as well. What does that mean and what makes up a "liturgy"?

Lyrics are written for the public, either for secular or non-secular performance. Liturgy is written specifically for public worship. The liturgical writing that I have done is also a form of collaboration. I don't write liturgy for publication, although some liturgists do. I write strictly for a specific church with a specific need.

For example, I might be asked to write the liturgical poetry for a Lenten series. I have written several of these. The pastors and worship team supply the theme and Biblical context. We brainstorm. Themes might incorporate characters of the Bible, social justice issues or the stories behind the [church's] stained glass windows.

The lyrics to a song I was asked to write for Advent on the theme of expectation has been sung several times. The music again was composed by Donald Fraser. My church, Christ United Methodist, had sent a sizable troop of helpers to Mississippi in the wake of Hurricane Katrina. This helped inspire the words of "There's Something Coming" with its reference to "a storm of love." It has been a great joy to hear the entire congregation sing this song many times.

Faith and spirituality appear to be a very important part of your life. How do they influence your poetry? Do you consciously write "spiritual" poetry? Are spiritual poetry and religious poetry the same thing?

Though I don't wear religion on my sleeve, faith and spirituality have always been among the things I seek ardently. However, most of my poems really wouldn't be considered religious.

Since attending several academic writers' programs, including a year of post-graduate poetry at Vermont College at Norwich University, I also "swim in that pool," striving to write poems that are intellectually stimulating, narrative, musical and quirky. *Who Walks Among the Trees with Clarity* is certainly not overtly religious, though I hope a sense of praise and charity inform the collection. *The Tenderness of Memory* and *Invisible String* (Erie St., 1990) definitely do not have a religious flavor. *Slow Miracle* (Lake Shore, 1992) is more overtly spiritual as it was written during a time of recovery from a badly broken leg.

Yet, I personally have little interest in religious poetry outside of liturgy. I don't believe I have ever bought a book of religious poems. I do believe strongly in a sort of poetic "separation of church and state." I would not send a liturgical poem to a strictly literary magazine, nor would I read an overtly erotic poem to a church group of elderly men and women. I don't mind "shape shifting" if it fosters the enjoyment of poetry. Though I have written some stridently political pieces such as "To Love My Country is to Say No" and "The Tree Trimmers," I save those for the right magazines and appropriate readings.

Could you share a few perspectives on the subject of collaboration? In what ways does it excite and inspire you? Is it for everyone?

Collaboration and "shape shifting" aren't for everyone. You have to have thick skin when you send out your poems, which are likely to be rejected. You have to have thick skin when collaborating, too—but probably not as thick! For one thing, you know that whatever you're working on will come to fruition; you know the date, if and what you are being paid, who is likely to be there, and generally what is expected.

For me, the greatest joy is how the words are enhanced and enlarged in an artistic setting or by a brilliant composer. However, if you can't step out of your own skin and let the others involved have their own "license," collaboration might seem like a compromise. I have never felt it was a compromise; in fact, I've found collaboration invigorating and satisfying. You have to be completely open to the possibilities and "go with the flow." Collaboration is not for divas, that's for sure.

It all goes back to the notion of exploring your gifts. At some point you have to truly ask the question: What kind of poet are you going to be? What gifts do you bring to the table? What would happen if you explored them? Then you have to follow the answers wherever they lead. Who knows? They might lead you somewhere more interesting and exciting than you ever dreamed.

—Nancy Breen

Nancy Breen writes and publishes poetry and edits *Poet's Market*. Her chapbooks include *Rites and Observances* (Finishing Line Press) and *How Time Got Away* (Pudding House Publications).

Magazines/Journals

☑ ◎ THE POET'S PEN (Specialized: members/subscribers preferred)

The Society of American Poets (SOAP), 309 Cork Pond Rd., Sylvania GA 30467. (912)564-2722. E-mail: DrRev@alltel.net. Established 1984. **Contact:** Dr. Charles E. Cravey, editor.

Magazine Needs *The Poet's Pen*, published quarterly by The Society of American Poets, is "open to all styles of poetry and prose—both religious and secular." Does not want "gross or 'X-rated' poetry without taste or character." Has published poetry by Najwa Salam Brax, Henry Goldman, Henry W. Gurley, William Heffner, Linda Metcalf, and Charles Russ. *The Poet's Pen* uses poetry **primarily by members and subscribers**, but outside submissions are also welcome. Subscription: included in membership, $30/year ($25 for students). Sample: $10.

How to Submit Submit 3 poems at a time/quarter. Considers simultaneous submissions and previously published poems, if permission from previous publisher is included. Include name and address on each page. "Submissions or inquiries will not be responded to without a #10 business-sized SASE. We do stress originality and have each new poet and/or subscriber sign a waiver form verifying originality." Publishes seasonal/theme issues. Guidelines available in magazine, for SASE, or by e-mail. Sometimes sends prepublication galleys. Always comments on rejected poems.

Contest/Award Offerings Sponsors several contests each quarter, with prizes totaling $100-250. Also offers Editor's Choice Awards each quarter. The President's Award for Excellence is a prize of $50. **Deadline:** November 1. Also publishes a quarterly anthology from poetry competitions in several categories with prizes of $25-100. Guidelines available for SASE or by e-mail.

Advice "Be honest with yourself above all else. Read the greats over and again and study styles, grammar, and what makes each unique. Meter, rhythm, and rhyme are still the guidelines that are most acceptable today."

◑ PORCUPINE LITERARY ARTS MAGAZINE

P.O. Box 259, Cedarburg WI 53012. E-mail: ppine259@aol.com. Web site: www.porcupineliterarya rts.com. Established 1996. **Contact:** W.A. Reed, managing editor.

Magazine Needs *Porcupine*, published semiannually, contains featured artists, poetry, short fiction, and visual art. "There are no restrictions as to theme or style. Poetry should be accessible and highly selective. If a submission is not timely for one issue, it will be considered for another." Has published poetry by Carol Hamilton, James Grabill, and George Wallace. *Porcupine* is 100-150 pages, digest-sized, offset-printed, perfect-bound, with full-color glossy cover. Receives about 500 poems/year, accepts 10%. Press run is 1,500 (500 subscribers, 50 libraries, 500 shelf sales); 100 distributed free. Single copy: $8.95; subscription: $15.95. Sample: $5.

How to Submit Submit up to 3 poems at a time. No previously published poems or simultaneous submissions. Accepts e-mail submissions (pasted into body of message). For postal submissions, one poem/page with name and address on each; include SASE. "The outside of the envelope should state: 'Poetry.' " Time between acceptance and publication is 6 months. "Poems are selected by editors, then submitted to managing editor for final approval." Seldom comments on rejected poems. Guidelines available for SASE or on Web site. Responds in 3 months. Pays one contributor's copy. Acquires one-time rights.

☑ ◎ POST POEMS (Specialized: poems under 7 lines; poetry postcard series)

Raw Dog Press, 151 S. West St., Doylestown PA 18901-4134. Web site: http://rawdogpress.braveho st.com. Established 1977. **Contact:** R. Gerry Fabian, poetry editor.

Magazine Needs Post Poems, published annually by Raw Dog Press, is a postcard series. Wants "short poetry (3-7 lines) on any subject. The positive poem or the poem of understated humor always has an inside track. No taboos, however. All styles considered. Anything with rhyme had better be immortal." Has published poetry by Don Ryan, John Grey, and the editor, R. Gerry Fabian. Send SASE for catalog to buy samples.

How to Submit Submit 3-5 poems at a time. Lines/poem: 3-7. Cover letter is optional. SASE is required. Always comments on rejected poems. Guidelines available on Web site. Pays in contributor's copies. Acquires all rights. Returns rights on mention of first publication. Sometimes reviews books of poetry.

Additional Information Raw Dog Press welcomes new poets and detests second-rate poems from "name" poets. "We exist because we are dumb like a fox, but even a fox takes care of its own." Send SASE for catalog to buy samples.

Also Offers Offers criticism for a fee; "if someone is desperate to publish and is willing to pay, we will use our vast knowledge to help steer the manuscript in the right direction. We will advise against it, but as P.T. Barnum said."

Advice "I get poems that do not fit my needs. At least one quarter of all poets waste their postage because they do not read the requirements. Also, there are too many submissions without a SASE and they go directly into the trash!"

✖ ◻ ◎ POTLUCK CHILDREN'S LITERARY MAGAZINE (Specialized: poetry by & for children/teens)

P.O. Box 546, Deerfield IL 60015-0546. (847)948-1139. Fax: (847)317-9492. E-mail: susan@potluck magazine.org. Web site: http://potluckmagazine.org. Established 1997. **Contact:** Susan Napoli Picchietti, founder/editor-in-chief.

Magazine Needs *Potluck Children's Literary Magazine*, published quarterly, provides "a forum which encourages young writers to share their voices and to learn their craft. Open to all styles, forms, and subjects—we just want well-crafted poems that speak to the reader." Does not want "poems so abstract they only have meaning to the writer. Violent, profane, or sexually explicit poems will not be accepted." Considers poetry by children and teens. *Potluck* is 48 pages, digest-sized, photocopied, saddle-stapled, with 60-lb. glossy paper cover with original artwork. Receives about 350 poems/quarter. Press run is over 1,110 (150 subscribers, 800 shelf sales). Single copy:

$5.80 USD ($7.80 CAD); subscription: $21.99 USD ($31.99 CAD). Sample: $4.25 USD (includes guidelines).

How to Submit Submit up to 3 poems at a time. Lines/poem: 30 maximum. No previously published poems or simultaneous submissions. Accepts fax and e-mail (pasted into body of message) submissions. Cover letter is optional. "Submissions without a SASE or an e-mail address will not be considered." Poems are circulated to an editorial board. "We each review every poem, make our remarks on them, then discuss our view of each—the best works make the issue." Always comments on rejected poems. Guidelines available in magazine, for SASE, by fax, e-mail, or on Web site. Responds 6 weeks after deadline. Pays one contributor's copy. Acquires first rights. Reviews chapbooks of poetry.

Advice "Be present; write what you see, hear, taste, smell, observe, and what you feel/experience. Be honest, clear, and choose your words with great care. Enjoy."

⊡ ▣ ☑ THE POTOMAC

2020 Pennsylvania Ave. NW, Suite 443, Washington DC 20006. E-mail: nathan_21045@yahoo.com. Web site: www.webdelsol.com/The_Potomac. Established 2004. **Contact:** Nathan Leslie, editor. Member: Web del Sol.

Magazine Needs *The Potomac*, published quarterly online, features political commentary, cutting-edge poetry, flash fiction, and reviews. Open to all forms of poetry by new and established writers. Has published poetry by Jim Daniels, Elaine Equi, Maurice Oliver, Holly Iglesias, and Ilya Kaminsky. Receives a "variable" number of poems/year, accepts about 50-60. Sample: free online.

How to Submit Submit any number of poems at a time. Considers simultaneous submissions; no previously published poems. Accepts e-mail submissions (as attachment) only; no postal or disk submissions. Cover letter is preferred. Reads submissions year round. Time between acceptance and publication is 3 months. Often comments on rejected poems. Guidelines available on Web site. Responds in 2 months. Sometimes sends prepublication galleys. No payment. Acquires one-time rights. Reviews books/chapbooks of poetry and other magazines/journals in up to 2,000 words, single- and multi-book format. Send materials for review consideration.

Advice "We welcome the opportunity to read work from new writers."

⊠ $☑ ◎ THE PRAIRIE JOURNAL

Prairie Journal Press, P.O. Box 61203, Brentwood Post Office, 217-3630 Brentwood Rd. NW, Calgary AB T2L 2K6 Canada. E-mail: prairiejournal@yahoo.com. Web site: www.geocities.com/prairiejour nal. Established 1983. **Contact:** A. Burke, editor.

Magazine Needs *The Prairie Journal*, published twice/year, seeks poetry "of any length; free verse, contemporary themes (feminist, nature, urban, non-political), aesthetic value, a poet's poetry." Does not want to see "most rhymed verse, sentimentality, egotistical ravings. No cowboys or sage brush." Has published poetry by Liliane Welch, Cornelia Hoogland, Sheila Hyland, Zoe Lendale, and Chad Norman. *The Prairie Journal* is 40-60 pages, digest-sized, offset-printed, saddle-stapled, with card cover, includes ads. Receives about 1,000 poems/year, accepts 10%. Press run is 600 (200 subscribers, 50% libraries); the rest are sold on newsstands. Subscription: $10 for individuals, $18 for libraries. Sample: $8 ("use postal money order"). No U.S. stamps.

How to Submit No previously published poems or simultaneous submissions. No e-mail submissions. "We will not be reading submissions until such time as an issue is in preparation (twice yearly), so be patient and we will acknowledge, accept for publication, or return work at that time." Guidelines available for postage ("no U.S. stamps, please"; get IRCs from USPS) or on Web site. Sometimes sends prepublication galleys. Pays $10-50 and one contributor's copy. Acquires first North American serial rights. Reviews books of poetry, "but must be assigned by editor. Query first."

Additional Information For chapbook publication by Prairie Journal Press, **Canadian poets only**

(preferably from the plains region). Has published *Voices From Earth*, selected poems by Ronald Kurt and Mark McCawley, and *In the Presence of Grace* by McCandless Callaghan. "We also publish anthologies on themes when material is available." Query first, with 5 sample poems and cover letter with brief bio and publication credits. Responds to queries in 2 months; to mss in 6 months. Payment in modest honoraria.

Also Offers Publishes "Poems of the Month" online. Submit up to 4 poems **with $1 reading fee** by postal mail.

Advice "Read recent poets! Experiment with line length, images, metaphors. Innovate."

◪ PRAIRIE SCHOONER

201 Andrews Hall, P.O. Box 880334, University of Nebraska, Lincoln NE 68588-0334. (402)472-0911. Fax: (402)472-9771. E-mail: kgrey2@unl.edu. Web site: http://prairieschooner.unl.edu. Established 1926. **Contact:** Kelly Grey Carlisle, managing editor.

• Poetry published in *Prairie Schooner* has been selected for inclusion in *The Best American Poetry* and *The Pushcart Prize*.

Magazine Needs *Prairie Schooner*, published quarterly, prints poetry, fiction, personal essays, interviews, and reviews. Wants "poems that fulfill the expectations they set up." No specifications as to form, length, style, subject matter, or purpose. Has published poetry by Alicia Ostriker, Marilyn Hacker, D.A. Powell, Stephen Dunn, and David Ignatow. *Prairie Schooner* is about 200 pages, digest-sized, flat-spined. Receives about 5,500 submissions/year, uses about 300 pages of poetry. Press run is 2,500. Single copy: $9; subscription: $28. Sample: $6.

How to Submit Submit 5-7 poems at a time. No simultaneous submissions. No fax or e-mail submissions; postal submissions only. Reads submissions September 1-May 1 (mss must be received during that period). Guidelines available for SASE or on Web site. Responds in 4 months, "sooner if possible." Always sends prepublication galleys. Pays 3 contributor's copies. Acquires all rights. Returns rights upon request without fee. Reviews books of poetry. Send materials for review consideration.

Contest/Award Offerings "All manuscripts published in *Prairie Schooner* automatically will be considered for our annual prizes." These include The Strousse Award for Poetry ($500), the Bernice Slote Prize for Beginning Writers ($500), the Hugh J. Luke Award ($250), the Edward Stanley Award for Poetry ($1,000), the Virginia Faulkner Award for Excellence in Writing ($1,000), the Glenna Luschei Prize for Excellence ($1,500), the Jane Geske Award ($250), and the Larry Levis Prize for Poetry ($1,000). Also, each year 10 Glenna Luschei Awards ($250 each) are given for poetry, fiction, and nonfiction. All contests are open only to those writers whose work was published in the magazine the previous year. Editors serve as judges. Also sponsors The *Prairie Schooner* Book Prize (see separate listing Contests & Awards).

Also Offers Editor-in-Chief Hilda Raz also promotes poets whose work has appeared in her pages by listing their continued accomplishments in a special section (even when their work does not concurrently appear in the magazine).

▢ ◎ PRAYERWORKS (Specialized: praying; the elderly)

P.O. Box 301363, Portland OR 97294-9363. (503)761-2072. E-mail: jay4prayer@aol.com. Established 1988. **Contact:** V. Ann Mandeville, editor.

Magazine Needs *PrayerWorks*, published weekly, is a newsletter "encouraging elderly people to recognize their value to God as prayer warriors." Established as a ministry to people living in retirement centers, *PrayerWorks* features "prayers, ways to pray, stories of answered prayers, teaching on a Scripture portion, articles that build faith, and poems." *PrayerWorks* is 4 pages, digest-sized, desktop-published, photocopied, folded. Receives about 50 poems/year, accepts about 25%. Press run is 1,000 (1,000 subscribers). Subscription: free.

How to Submit Submit 5 poems at a time. Considers previously published poems and simultaneous submissions. Accepts e-mail submissions (WordPerfect or Microsoft Word attachments). Cover letter is preferred. One poem/page. Time between acceptance and publication is usually within one month. Seldom comments on rejected poems. Publishes theme issues relating to the holidays (submit holiday poetry 2 months in advance). Guidelines available for SASE. Responds in 3 weeks. Pays 5 or more contributor's copies.

⬆ $◩ PRISM INTERNATIONAL

Creative Writing Program, University of British Columbia, Buchanan E462, 1866 Main Mall, Vancouver BC V6T 1Z1 Canada. E-mail: prism@interchange.ubc.ca. Web site: http://prism.arts.ubc.ca. Established 1959. **Contact:** Editor (rotating title).

● *PRISM international* is one of the top literary journals in Canada.

Magazine Needs *PRISM international*, published quarterly, prints poetry, drama, short fiction, creative nonfiction, and translation into English in all genres. "We have no thematic or stylistic allegiances: Excellence is our main criterion for acceptance of manuscripts." Wants "fresh, distinctive poetry that shows an awareness of traditions old and new. We read everything." Considers poetry by children and teens. "Excellence is the only criterion." Has published poetry by Marlene Cookshaw, Warren Heiti, Don McKay, Bill Bissett, and Stephanie Bolster. *PRISM international* is 88 pages, digest-sized, elegantly printed, flat-spined, with original color artwork on a glossy card cover. Receives 1,000 submissions/year, accepts about 80. Circulation is for 1,100 subscribers (200 libraries). Subscription: $25/year, $35 for 2 years. Sample: $10. "Subscribers outside of Canada, please pay in U.S. dollars."

How to Submit Submit up to 6 poems at a time. No previously published poems or simultaneous submissions. No e-mail submissions. Cover letter is required. Include brief introduction and list of previous publications. Poems must be typed or computer-generated (font and point size open). Include SASE (or SAE with IRCs). "Note: American stamps are not valid postage in Canada. No SASEs with U.S. postage will be returned. Translations must be accompanied by a copy of the original." Guidelines available for SASE (or SAE with IRCs), by e-mail, or on Web site. Responds in up to 6 months. Pays $40/printed page (for poetry) and one-year subscription; plus an additional $10/printed page to selected authors for publication online. Editors sometimes comment on rejected poems. Acquires first North American serial rights.

Contest/Award Offerings The editorial board awards an annual $500 prize to an outstanding poetry contributor in each volume.

Advice "While we don't automatically discount any kind of poetry, we prefer to publish work that challenges the writer as much as it does the reader. We are particularly looking for poetry in translation."

$◩ ◎ PROVINCETOWN ARTS (Specialized: Cape Cod & area art colony culture)

P.O. Box 35, 650 Commercial St., Provincetown MA 02657. (508)487-3167. E-mail: cbusa@comcast. net. Web site: www.provincetownarts.org. Established 1985. **Contact:** Christopher Busa, editor.

Magazine Needs *Provincetown Arts*, published annually in July, prints quality poetry, focusing "broadly on the artists and writers who inhabit or visit the tip of Cape Cod." Seeks to "stimulate creative activity and enhance public awareness of the cultural life of the nation's oldest continuous art colony. Drawing upon a century-long tradition rich in visual art, literature, and theater, *Provincetown Arts* publishes material with a view towards demonstrating that the artists' colony, functioning outside the urban centers, is a utopian dream with an ongoing vitality." Has published poetry by Bruce Smith, Franz Wright, Sandra McPherson, and Cyrus Cassells. *Provincetown Arts* is about 170 pages, magazine-sized, perfect-bound, with full-color glossy cover. Press run is 10,000 (500 subscribers, 20 libraries, 6,000 shelf sales). Sample: $10.

How to Submit Submit up to 3 poems at a time. No e-mail submissions; "all queries and submissions should be sent via postal mail." Submissions must be typed. Reads submissions October-February.

Guidelines available for SASE. Responds in 3 months. Usually sends prepublication galleys. Pays $25-100/poem plus 2 contributor's copies. Acquires first rights. Reviews books of poetry in 500-3,000 words, single- or multi-book format. Send materials for review consideration.

Additional Information The Provincetown Arts Press has published 8 volumes of poetry. The Provincetown Poets Series includes *At the Gate* by Martha Rhodes, *Euphorbia* by Anne-Marie Levine (a finalist in the 1995 Paterson Poetry Prize), and *1990* by Michael Klein (co-winner of the 1993 Lambda Literary Award).

◖ ◎ PUDDING MAGAZINE: THE INTERNATIONAL JOURNAL OF APPLIED POETRY (Specialized: popular culture; virtual journalism)

Shadymere Lane, Columbus OH 43213. (614)986-1881. E-mail: info@puddinghouse.com. Web site: www.puddinghouse.com. Established 1979. **Contact:** Jennifer Bosveld, editor.

Magazine Needs *Pudding Magazine: The International Journal of Applied Poetry*, published "every several months," seeks "what hasn't been said before. Speak the unspeakable. Long poems okay as long as they aren't windy." *Pudding* also serves as "a forum for poems and articles by people who take poetry arts into the schools and the human services." Wants "poetry on popular culture, rich brief narratives, i.e. 'virtual journalism' (see Web site)." Does not want "preachments or sentimentality; obvious traditional forms without fresh approach." Has published poetry by Knute Skinner, David Chorlton, Mary Winters, and Robert Collins. *Pudding* is 70 pages, digest-sized, offset-composed on Microsoft Word PC. Press run is 1,500 (1,100 subscribers). Subscription: $29.95/4 issues. Sample: $8.95.

How to Submit Submit 3-10 poems at a time. Previously published submissions "respected, but include credits"; no simultaneous submissions. Cover letter is preferred ("cultivates great relationships with writers"). "Submissions without SASEs will be discarded. No postcards." Sometimes publishes theme issues. Guidelines available on Web site only. Responds on same day (unless traveling). Pays one contributor's copy; $10 and 4 contributor's copies to featured poets. Returns rights "with *Pudding* permitted to reprint." Send materials for review consideration or listing as recommended.

Also Offers "Our Web site is one of the greatest poetry Web sites in the country—calls, workshops, publication list/history, online essays, games, guest pages, calendars, poem of the month, poet of the week, much more." The Web site also links to the site for The Unitarian Universalist Poets Cooperative and American Poets Opposed to Executions, both national organizations.

Advice "Editors have pet peeves. I won't respond to postcards. I require SASEs. I don't like cover letters that state the obvious, poems with trite concepts, or meaning dictated by rhyme. Thoroughly review our Web site; it will give you a good idea about our publication history and editorial tastes."

⊕ ◖ PULSAR POETRY MAGAZINE

Ligden Publishers, 34 Lineacre, Grange Park, Swindon, Wiltshire SN5 6DA England. (44)(01793)875941. E-mail: pulsar.ed@btopenworld.com. Web site: www.pulsarpoetry.com. Established 1992. **Contact:** David Pike, editor.

Magazine Needs *Pulsar Poetry Magazine*, published every March and September, "encourages the writing of poetry from all walks of life. Contains poems, reviews, and editorial comments." Wants "hard-hitting, thought-provoking work; interesting and stimulating poetry." Does not want "racist material. Not keen on religious poetry." Has published poetry by A.C. Evans, Chris Hardy, Kate Edwards, Elizabeth Birchall, and Michael Newman. *Pulsar* is 40-44 pages, A5, professionally printed, saddle-stapled, with glossy full-color cover, includes ads. Press run is 300 (100 subscribers, 40 libraries); several distributed free to newspapers, etc. Subscription: $18 (£8 UK). Sample: $9. Make checks payable to Ligden Publishers.

How to Submit Submit 3 poems at a time. No previously published poems or simultaneous submissions. Accepts e-mail submissions (pasted into body of message). "Send no more than two poems via e-mail; file attachments will not be read." Cover letter is preferred. Include SAE with IRCs. Manuscripts should be typed. Time between acceptance and publication is about one month. "Poems can be published in next edition if it is what we are looking for. The editor and assistant read all poems." Seldom comments on rejected poems. Guidelines available for SASE (or SAE and IRC) or on Web site. Responds within one month. Pays one contributor's copy. Acquires first rights. "Originators retain copyright of their poems." Staff reviews poetry books and audio tapes, CDs (mainstream); word count varies. Send materials for review consideration.

Advice "Give explanatory notes if poems are open to interpretation. Be patient and enjoy what you are doing. Check grammar, spelling, etc. (should be obvious). Note: we are a nonprofit-making society."

$ ◙ PURPOSE (Specialized: Mennonite; poetry for young adults & adults)

Mennonite Publishing Network, 616 Walnut Ave., Scottdale PA 15683-1999. (724)887-8500. E-mail: horsch@mph.org. **Contact:** James E. Horsch, editor.

Magazine Needs *Purpose*, published by Mennonite Publishing Network (the official publisher for the Mennonite Church in the U.S. and Canada), is a "religious young adult/adult monthly in weekly parts." Focuses on "action-oriented, discipleship living." *Purpose* is digest-sized with 4-color printing throughout. Press run is 8,000. Receives about 2,000 poems/year, accepts 150. Sample: (with guidelines) $2 and 9×12 SAE.

How to Submit Lines/poem: up to 12. Considers simultaneous submissions. Accepts e-mail submissions (preferred). Postal submissions should be double-spaced, typed on one side of sheet only. Responds in 6 months. Guidelines available for SASE. Pays $7.50 to $20/poem plus 2 contributor's copies.

⊕ $ ◻ QUANTUM LEAP (Specialized: subscribers favored)

Q.Q. Press, York House, 15 Argyle Terrace, Rothesay, Isle of Bute PA20 0BD Scotland. Established 1997. **Contact:** Alan Carter, editor.

Magazine Needs *Quantum Leap*, published quarterly, uses "all kinds of poetry—free verse, rhyming, whatever—as long as it's well written and preferably well punctuated, too. We rarely use haiku." Has published poetry by Pamela Constantine, Ray Stebbing, Leigh Eduardo, Sky Higgins, Norman Bissett, and Gordon Scapens. *Quantum Leap* is 40 pages, digest-sized, desktop-published, saddle-stapled, with card cover. Receives about 2,000 poems/year, accepts about 15%. Press run is 200 (180 subscribers). Single copy: $12; subscription: $38. Sample: $9. Make checks payable to Alan Carter. "All things being equal in terms of a poem's quality, **I will sometimes favor that of a subscriber (or someone who has at least bought an issue) over a nonsubscriber**, as it is they who keep us solvent."

How to Submit Submit 6 poems at a time. Lines/poem: 36 ("normally"). Considers previously published poems (indicate magazine and date of first publication) and simultaneous submissions. Cover letter is required. "Within the UK, send a SASE; outside it, send IRCs to the value of what has been submitted." Time between acceptance and publication is usually 3 months "but can be longer now, due to magazine's increasing popularity." Sometimes comments on rejected poems. Guidelines available for SASE (or SAE and 2 IRCs). Responds in 3 weeks. Pays £2 sterling. Acquires first or second British serial rights.

Additional Information Under the imprint "Collections," Q.Q. Press offers **subsidy arrangements** "to provide a cheap alternative to the 'vanity presses'—poetry only." Charges **£150 sterling ($300 USD) plus postage** for 50 32-page (A4) books. Write for details. Order sample books by sending $12 (postage included). Make checks payable to Alan Carter.

Contest/Award Offerings Sponsors open poetry competitions as well as competitions for subscribers only. Send SAE and IRC for details.

Advice "Submit well thought-out, well presented poetry, preferably well punctuated, too. If rhyming poetry, make it flow and don't strain to rhyme. I don't bite, and I appreciate a short cover letter, but not a long, long list of where you've been published before! Please do not add U.S. stamps to IRCs. They have no validity here. If you want to increase the value, just send extra IRCs.''

◢ QUARTERLY WEST

Dept. of English/LNCO 3500, University of Utah, 255 S. Central Campus Dr., Salt Lake City UT 84112-9109. (801)581-3938. E-mail: quarterlywest@yahoo.com. (inquiries only). Web site: www.u tah.edu/quarterlywest. Established 1976. **Contact:** Susan Goslee and Brenda Sieczkowski, poetry editors. Editors: Paul Ketzle and Mike White.

• Poetry published in *Quarterly West* has appeared in *The Best American Poetry* and in numerous Pushcart Prize anthologies.

Magazine Needs *Quarterly West*, published semiannually, seeks ''original and accomplished literary verse—free or formal.'' Also considers translations (include originals with submissions). No greeting card or sentimental poetry. Has published poetry by Quan Barry, Medbh McGuckian, James Harms, Bob Hicok, David Kirby, and Linh Dinh. *Quarterly West* is 160 pages, digest-sized, offset-printed, with 4-color cover art. Receives 2,500 submissions/year, accepts less than 1%. Press run is 1,500 (500 subscribers, 300-400 libraries). Subscription: $14/year, $25 for 2 years. Sample: $8.50.

How to Submit Submit 3-5 poems at a time. Considers simultaneous submissions, with notification; no previously published poems. No e-mail submissions; postal submissions only. Reads submissions September 1-May 1. Seldom comments on rejected poems. Guidelines available on Web site. Responds in up to 6 months. Pays 2 contributor's copies and money when possible. Acquires first North American serial rights. Returns rights with acknowledgment and right to reprint. Reviews books of poetry in 1,000-3,000 words.

$◻ ◎ ELLERY QUEEN'S MYSTERY MAGAZINE (Specialized: mystery/suspense)

475 Park Ave. S., 11th Floor, New York NY 10016. E-mail: elleryqueen@dellmagazines.com. (inquries only). Web site: www.themysteryplace.com. Established 1941. **Contact:** Janet Hutchings.

Magazine Needs *Ellery Queen's Mystery Magazine*, published 10 times/year, uses primarily short stories of mystery, crime, or suspense—little poetry. *Ellery Queen's Mystery Magazine* is 144 pages (double-issue, published twice/year, is 240 pages), digest-sized, professionally printed on newsprint, flat-spined, with glossy paper cover. Single copy: $5 by check to publisher, available for $3.99 on newsstands; subscription: $43.90.

How to Submit Considers simultaneous submissions; no previously published poems. No e-mail submissions; postal submissions only. Include SASE with submissions. Guidelines available for SASE or on Web site. Responds in 3 months. Pays $15-65 and 3 contributor's copies.

◢ QUERCUS REVIEW

Quercus Review Press, Modesto Junior College, Division of Literature & Language Arts, 435 College Ave., Modesto CA 95350. (209)575-6183. E-mail: pierstorffs@mjc.edu. Web site: www.quercusrevi ew.com. Established 1999. **Contact:** Sam Pierstorff, editor.

Magazine Needs *Quercus Review*, published annually in May/June, prints high-quality poetry, fiction, and b&w art. ''We publish numerous nationally recognized and award-winning writers from across the nation.'' Wants ''writing with a pulse. Writing that reflects a unique voice.'' Does not want ''rhyme, religious, or cliché writing.'' Considers poetry by children and teens. Has published poetry by X.J. Kennedy, Gerald Locklin, Naomi Shihab Nye, Amiri Baraka, Charles Harper Webb, and Dorianne Laux. *Quercus Review* is 112 pages, digest-sized, professionally printed, perfect-bound, with full-color cover. Receives about 3,500 poems/year, accepts less than 10%. Press run is 500 (50 subscribers, 10 libraries, 350 shelf sales); 100 distributed free to contributors and local bookstores. Single copy: $8; subscription: $20 for 2 years (includes 2 issues of *Quercus Review*, plus annual book award winner). Make checks payable to "MJC (QR)."

How to Submit Submit 3-5 poems at a time. Lines/poem: prefers 40 maximum, but will consider longer. No previously published poems or simultaneous submissions. No e-mail or disk submissions. Cover letter is required. Include brief bio and SASE. Reads submissions year round. Time between acceptance and publication is usually 3 weeks to 3 months. "Poems are selected by five-person staff of editors, which rotates annually." Guidelines available on Web site. Sometimes sends prepublication galleys. Pays one contributor's copy, 30% discount on additional copies. Acquires first rights.

Contest/Award Offerings Quercus Review Press publishes one poetry book/year, selected through competition only. Winner of the Quercus Review Poetry Series Annual Book Award receives $500 and 50 author's copies. Books are 50-112 pages, professionally printed, perfect-bound, with full-color covers. Submit 46-96 pages in ms format. Include cover letter and SASE. Book mss may include previously published poems. **Entry fee:** $20 ($25 to receive a copy of winning book). **Deadline:** submit August 1-October 15 (postmark). Guidelines available on Web site. 2006 winner was Neil Carpathios (*At the Axis of Imponderables*).

Advice "Avoid overusing the world 'soul,' but feel free to drown us in fresh imagery and bold language. We like poems with a pulse. Make us laugh or cry, but don't bore or try too hard to impress us."

◲ QUEST

Freiburger Hall, Lynn University, 3601 N. Military Trail, Boca Raton FL 33431. E-mail: lkeiley@lynn .edu. Established 1997. **Contact:** Dr. Lizbeth Keiley, editor.

Magazine Needs *Quest*, published annually in April, is a literary and arts journal. Wants "poems with a clear voice that use careful diction to create poetry in which sound and sense work together, creating fresh perception." Does not want "poems that rely on profanity or shock value." Has published poetry by Eugene Martel, Andrea Best, Fred Cichocki, Johanne Perron, Rosalie Schwartz, and Diane Richard-Allerdyce. *Quest* is digest-sized, laser-printed, saddle-stapled, with 32 lb. bright white coverstock cover printed with 4-color process. Receives about 100 poems/year, accepts about 25. Press run is 200 (one library subscriber); 150 distributed free to Lynn University faculty, staff, and students. Single copy: $5. Make checks payable to Lizbeth Keiley.

How to Submit Submit up to 5 poems at a time. No previously published poems or simultaneous submissions. No e-mail or disk submissions. Cover letter is preferred. "Include adequate SASE if you want work returned." Reads submissions mid-September to mid-January. Time between acceptance and publication is up to 7 months. "English Department faculty review submissions." Seldom comments on rejected poems. Guidelines available for SASE. Responds in up to 4 months. Pays one contributor's copy. Acquires one-time rights.

Advice "Even the freest of verse has its roots in the formal elements."

◲ RAINBOW CURVE

P.O. Box 93206, Las Vegas NV 89193-3206. E-mail: rainbowcurve@sbcglobal.net. Web site: www.r ainbowcurve.com. Established 2001. **Contact:** Julianne Bonnet, poetry editor.

Magazine Needs *Rainbow Curve*, published biannually, is a forum for short fiction and poetry. Wants "well-crafted poetry that works both on the surface and beneath it." Does not want rhyme, traditional forms, Hallmark greeting card sentiment. Has published poetry by Virgil Suárez and Terry Ehret. *Rainbow Curve* is 100 pages, digest-sized, offset-printed, perfect-bound, with 4-color glossy 10 pt. CS1 cover. Receives about 3,500 poems/year, accepts about 2%. Press run is 250. Single copy: $8; subscription: $16. Sample: $6. Make checks payable to *Rainbow Curve*.

How to Submit Submit 3 poems at a time. Considers simultaneous submissions; no previously published poems. Accepts e-mail submissions (as attachment; must be MS Word 6.0 or higher format only). Cover letter is preferred. "Include SASE with sufficient postage for reply and return of manuscript. If return of manuscript is not desired, we will respond via e-mail, if requested." Reads submissions year round. Time between acceptance and publication is 6 months. Seldom comments on rejected poems. Guidelines available in magazine, for SASE, or on Web site. Responds in 3 months. Always sends prepublication galleys. Pays one contributor's copy. Acquires first North American serial rights.

Advice "It is always a good idea to read a magazine before submitting to it—that way you have a good idea if your writing style fits with the editorial slant of the publication."

THE RAINTOWN REVIEW (Specialized: formal/traditional poetry)

E-mail: h_stanbrough@yahoo.com. Web site: www.StoneThread.com. Established 1996. **Contact:** Harvey Stanbrough, editor.

Magazine Needs *The Raintown Review*, published 2 times/year in February and August, contains poetry "and the occasional literary criticism or review." Wants well-crafted poems. "We are primarily a venue for formal/traditional poetry." Has published poetry by William Baer, Joseph S. Salemi, Richard Moore, Annie Finch, and many others. *The Raintown Review* is 120 pages, perfect-bound. Receives about 900 poems/year, accepts 10-15%. Press run is 150 (most go to subscribers and contributors). Subscription: $24/year, $45 for 2 years, $65 for 3 years. Sample: $12. Make checks/money orders payable to Central Ave Press, 2132A Central SE #144, Albuquerque NM 87106.

How to Submit Submit 3-5 poems at a time. Lines/poem: no restrictions. Considers previously published poems (with acknowledgment of previous publication) and simultaneous submissions. Accepts e-mail submissions only (pasted into body of message); no postal submissions. Comments on rejected poems if requested at the time of submission. Guidelines available on Web site. Usually responds in 2 weeks, if possible. Pays one contributor's copy. Acquires one-time rights.

RATTAPALLAX (Specialized: the diversity of world cultures)

532 La Guardia Place, Suite 353, New York NY 10012. E-mail: info@rattapallax.com. Web site: www.rattapallax.com. Established 1998. **Contact:** Poetry Editor.

Magazine Needs *Rattapallax*, published biannually, is named for "Wallace Steven's word for the sound of thunder. The magazine includes a DVD featuring poetry films and audio files. *Rattapallax* is looking for the extraordinary in modern poetry and prose that reflect the diversity of world cultures. Our goals are to create international dialogue using literature and focus on what is relevant to our society." Has published poetry by Anthony Hecht, Sharon Olds, Lou Reed, Marilyn Hacker, Billy Collins, and Glyn Maxwell. *Rattapallax* is 112 pages, magazine-sized, offset-printed, perfect-bound, with 12-pt. CS1 cover. Receives about 5,000 poems/year, accepts 2%. Press run is 2,000 (100 subscribers, 50 libraries, 1,200 shelf sales); 200 distributed free to contributors, reviews, and promos. Single copy: $7.95; no subscriptions. Make checks payable to *Rattapallax*.

How to Submit Submit 3-5 poems at a time. Considers simultaneous submissions; no previously published poems. Accepts e-mail submissions (sent as simple text) from outside the U.S. and Canada; all other submissions must be sent via postal mail (SASE required). Cover letter is preferred. Reads submissions year round; issue deadlines are June 1 and December 1. Time between acceptance and publication is 6 months. "The editor-in-chief, senior editor, and associate editor review all the submissions and then decide on which to accept every week. Near publication time, all accepted work is narrowed, and unused work is kept for the next issue." Often comments on rejected poems. Guidelines available by e-mail or on Web site. Responds in 2 months. Always sends prepublication galleys. Pays 2 contributor's copies. Acquires first rights.

RATTLE

12411 Ventura Blvd., Studio City CA 91604. (818)505-6777. E-mail: timgreen@rattle.com. Web site: www.rattle.com. Established 1994. **Contact:** Timothy Green, editor.

Magazine Needs *RATTLE*, published semiannually in June and December, includes poems, essays, reviews, interviews with poets, and a tribute section dedicated to a specific ethnic or vocational group. Wants "high-quality poetry of any form. Nothing unintelligible." Considers some poetry by children and teens (ages 10-18). Has published poetry by Lucille Clifton, Charles Simic, Mark Doty, Sharon Olds, Billy Collins, and Stephen Dunn. *RATTLE* is 196 pages, digest-sized, neatly printed, perfect-bound, with 4-color coated card cover. Receives about 8,000 submissions/year, accepts 200. Press run is 4,000. Subscription: $16/year, $28/2 years, $34/3 years. Sample: $10. Make checks payable to *RATTLE*.

How to Submit Submit up to 5 poems at a time. Considers simultaneous submissions "if notified immediately by e-mail or phone should they be taken elsewhere." Accepts e-mail submissions (pasted into body of message). Cover letter is required (with e-mail address, if possible). Include bio. For postal submissions, put name, address, and phone number on each page in upper right corner; include SASE. Reads submissions year round. Seldom comments on rejected poems (unless requested by the author). Guidelines available in magazine, by e-mail, or on Web site. Responds in up to 2 months. Pays 2 contributor's copies. Rights revert to poet upon publication. Reviews books of poetry in 375 words or less. Send materials for review consideration.

Additional Information Welcomes essays up to 2,000 words on poetry or the writing process. Publishes a biannual electronic issue in March and September, e-mailed as a PDF to 4,000 subscribers, featuring excerpts from poetry collections, chapbooks, reviews, and print issue previews.

Contest/Award Offerings The *RATTLE* Poetry Prize (see separate listing in Contests & Awards).

✓ RB'S POETS' VIEWPOINT

330 S. Third St., Lot 67, Coleman MI 48618-9587. Established 1989. **Contact:** Robert Bennett, editor.

Magazine Needs *RB's Poets' Viewpoint*, published bimonthly, features poetry and cartoons. Wants "general and religious poetry, sonnets, and sijo." Does not want "vulgar language." Has published poetry by Robert D. Spector, Ruth Ditmer Ream, Ruth Halbrooks, and Delphine Ledoux. *RB's Poets' Viewpoint* is 34 pages, digest-sized, photocopied, saddle-stapled. Receives about 400 poems/year, accepts about 90%. Press run is 60. Subscription: $8. Sample: $2. Make checks payable to Robert Bennett.

How to Submit Submit 3 poems at a time. Lines/poem: 21 maximum. Considers previously published poems and simultaneous submissions. Submissions should be typed single-spaced. **Reading fee: $1.50/poem.** Reads submissions February, April, June, August, October, and December only. Time between acceptance and publication is one month. "Poems are selected by one editor." Often comments on rejected poems. Guidelines available for SASE. Responds in one month. Pays one contributor's copy. Acquires one-time rights.

Contest/Award Offerings Sponsors contests for general poetry, religious poetry, sonnets, and sijo with 1st Prizes of $20, $6, and $5, respectively, plus publication in *RB's Poets' Viewpoint*. **Entry fee:** 50¢/poem (sijo), $1.50/poem (all others). Guidelines available for SASE.

$ ◎ RED LIGHTS (Specialized: English-language tanka)

33 Riverside Dr., Suite 4-G, New York NY 10023-8025. (212)875-9342. E-mail: deucedk@aol.com. Established 2004. **Contact:** Pamela Miller Ness, editor.

Magazine Needs *red lights*, published semiannually in January and June, is devoted to English-language tanka and tanka sequences. Wants "print-only tanka, mainly 'free-form' but also strictly syllabic 5-7-5-7-7; will consider tanka sequences and tan-renga." Considers poetry by children and teens. Has published poetry by Sanford Goldstein, Michael McClintock, Laura Maffei, Linda Jeannette Ward, Jane Reichhold, and Michael Dylan Welch. *red lights* is 28-36 pages, $8^{1}/_{2} \times 3^{3}/_{4}$, offset-printed, saddle-stapled, with Japanese textured paper cover; copies are numbered. Receives about 1,200 poems/year, accepts about 20%. Press run is 150. Single copy: $6; subscription: $12 U.S., $13 USD Canada, $15 USD foreign. Make checks payable to Pamela Miller Ness.

How to Submit Submit 10 tanka or 2 sequences at a time (maximum). No previously published poems or simultaneous submissions. No e-mail or disk submissions. Include SASE. Reads submissions year round. Time between acceptance and publication "depends on submission time." Often comments on rejected poems. Guidelines available for SASE. Responds in 2 weeks. Pays $1/tanka. Acquires first rights.

Contest/Award Offerings "Each issue features a '*red lights* featured tanka' on the theme of 'red lights.' Poet whose poem is selected receives one contributor's copy in addition to $1."

Additional Information "The center four pages are devoted to the 'Featured Tanka Poet,' selected by invitation. Twelve previously published poems are featured."

⚡ $⃠ ◪ ◎ THE RED MOON ANTHOLOGY OF ENGLISH LANGUAGE HAIKU

P.O. Box 2461, Winchester VA 22604-1661. (540)722-2156. E-mail: jim.kacian@redmoonpress.com. Web site: www.redmoonpress.com. Established 1996. **Contact:** Jim Kacian, editor/publisher.

Magazine Needs *The Red Moon Anthology of English Language Haiku*, published annually in February, is "a collection of the best haiku published in English around the world." Considers poetry by children and teens. Has published haiku and related forms by Lee Gurga, Michael Dylan Welch, William J. Higginson, and Gary Snyder. *The Red Moon Anthology of English Language Haiku* is 184 pages, digest-sized, offset-printed on quality paper, with 4-color heavy-stock cover. Receives several thousand submissions/year, accepts less than 2%. Print run is 1,000 for subscribers and commercial distribution. Subscription: $16.95 plus $4 p&h. Sample available for SASE or by e-mail.

How to Submit Submit up to 5 haiku or related works at a time, published within the calendar year. **Considers previously published poems only.** Accepts e-mail and disk submissions. Include SASE for postal submissions. Time between acceptance and publication varies according to time of submission. Poems are circulated to an editorial board. "Only haiku published within the calendar year will be considered." Guidelines available for SASE or by e-mail. Pays $1/page. Acquires North American serial rights.

Also Offers *contemporary haibun*, "an annual volume of the finest English-language haibun and haiga published anywhere in the world." (See separate listing in this section.)

Advice "Haiku is a burgeoning and truly international form. It is nothing like what your fourth-grade teacher taught you years ago, and so it is best if you familiarize yourself with what is happening in the genre (and its close relatives) today before submitting. We strive to give all the work we publish plenty of space in which to resonate, and to provide a forum where the best of today's practitioners can be published with dignity and prestige."

◪ RED ROCK REVIEW

English Dept. J2A, Community College of Southern Nevada, 3200 E. Cheyenne Ave., North Las Vegas NV 89030. (702)651-4094. Fax: (702)651-4639. E-mail: richard.logsdon@ccsn.nevada.edu. Web site: www.ccsn.edu/english/redrockreview/index.html. Established 1994. **Contact:** Dr. Richard Logsdon, editor. Poetry Editor: T.D. Eliopulos. Associate Editor: Todd Moffett.

Magazine Needs *Red Rock Review*, published semiannually in May and December, prints "the best poetry available," as well as fiction, creative nonfiction, and book reviews. Has published poetry by Dorianne Laux, Kim Addonizio, Ellen Bass, Cynthia Hogue, and Dianne di Prima. *Red Rock Review* is about 130 pages, magazine-sized, professionally printed, perfect-bound, with 10-pt. CS1 cover. Accepts about 15% of poems received/year. Press run is 750. Sample: $5.50.

How to Submit Submit 2-3 poems at a time. Lines/poem: 80 maximum. Considers simultaneous submissions; no previously published poems. Accepts disk submissions. Cover letter and SASE are required. Submissions should be "mailed flat, not folded, into a letter-sized envelope." Reads submissions September-May. Time between acceptance and publication is 3-5 months. "Poems go to poetry editor, who then distributes them to three readers." Seldom comments on rejected poems. Guidelines available for SASE or on Web site. Responds in 3-5 months. Pays 2 contributor's copies.

Acquires first North American serial rights. Reviews books/chapbooks of poetry in 500-1,000 words, multi-book format. Send materials for review consideration.

☑ RED WHEELBARROW

De Anza College, 21250 Stevens Creek Blvd., Cupertino CA 95014. (408)864-8600. E-mail: SplitterRandolph@deanza.edu. Web site: www.deanza.edu/redwheelbarrow. Established 1976 (as *Bottomfish Magazine*). **Contact:** Randolph Splitter, editor, or Poetry Editor.

● "**Please note:** We are not affiliated with Red Wheelbarrow Press or any similarly named publication."

Magazine Needs *Red Wheelbarrow*, published annually in spring or summer, is a college-produced, national magazine. Wants "diverse voices." Has published poetry by Mark Brazaitis, K.S. Hardy, Liza Porter, Anthony Walstorm, Ulys Yates, and Jianquin Zheng. *Red Wheelbarrow* is 175-225 pages, book-sized, printed on heavy stock with b&w graphics, perfect-bound. Press run is on demand. Single copy: $10. Sample: $2.50 (for back issue).

How to Submit Submit up to 5 poems at a time. Accepts e-mail submissions. Include SASE or e-mail address for reply. Reads submissions September-January (January 31 deadline). Responds in 2-6 months, depending on backlog. Pays 2 contributor's copies.

Advice "We seek diverse voices from around the country and the world."

☑ REDIVIDER

Dept. of Writing, Literature, and Publishing, Emerson College, 120 Boylston St., Boston MA 02118. E-mail: redivider@emerson.edu. Web site: www.redividerjournal.org. Established 1990 (as *Beacon Street Review*). **Contact:** Poetry Editor (changes annually, see Web site). Member: CLMP.

Magazine Needs *Redivider*, published semiannually, prints high-quality poetry, art, fiction, and creative nonfiction. Wants "all styles of poetry. Most of all, we look for language that seems fresh and alive on the page, that tries to do something new. Read a sample copy for a good idea." Does not want "greeting card verse or inspirational verse." Has published poetry by Noah Falck, Joe Wenderoth, Dorianne Laux, David Lawrence, Bob Hicok, and Timothy Liu. *Redivider* is 100+ pages, digest-sized, offset-printed, perfect-bound, with 4-color artwork on cover. Receives about 1,000 poems/year, accepts about 30%. Press run is 1,000. Single copy: $6; subscription: $10. Make checks payable to *Redivider* at Emerson College.

How to Submit Submit 3-6 poems at a time. Considers simultaneous submissions, but requires notification if your work is taken elsewhere; no previously published poems. No e-mail or disk submissions. Cover letter is required. Reads submissions year round. Seldom comments on rejected poems. Guidelines available in magazine, for SASE, by e-mail, or on Web site. Responds in 5 months. Pays 2 contributor's copies. Acquires first North American serial rights. Reviews books of poetry in 500-2,000 words, single-book format.

The Issue 4, Volume 1 cover of *Redivider* features "Stronger than Will," an acrylic on canvas by Hungarian artist Zsófia Ötvös (www.zsofiaotvos.com).

Artwork by Zsófia Ötvös; cover design by Jamie Kerry.

Send materials for review consideration, Attn: Review Copies. "Book reviews and interviews are internally generated."

Advice "Consider subscribing and supporting your fellow writers!"

✪ ▣ ◪ ◎ THE REDNECK REVIEW, AN ONLINE POETRY JOURNAL

P.O. Box 8718, Atlanta GA 31106. E-mail: editor@redneckreview.com. Web site: www.redneckrevi ew.com. Established 2000. **Contact:** Penya Sandor, editor.

Magazine Needs *The Redneck Review*, published semiannually online, is "born out of the rich literary tradition of the South." Wants "writing that is interesting, has energy, and doesn't feel like homework." Considers poetry by children and teens. Has published poetry by Denise Duhamel, Marie Howe, Walt McDonald, Hal Sirowitz, Ben Satterfield, and Jean Trounstine. Publishes about 15-20 poems/issue.

How to Submit Submit no more than 5 poems at a time. Considers previously published poems and simultaneous submissions. Accepts e-mail and disk submissions. Cover letter is preferred. "If sending submissions by postal mail, include SASE unless you have an e-mail address. Poems won't be returned." Time between acceptance and publication "depends." Often comments on rejected poems. Guidelines available on Web site. Response time varies. Sometimes sends prepublication galleys. No payment. "Authors retain rights, but we ask that they mention our journal if they publish the poem again." Send materials for review consideration to *The Redneck Review*.

Advice "There are many respectable literary journals that publish well-written but dull writing. We would prefer to read literature that is electric, not just technically well crafted."

◪ ◎ REFLECTIONS LITERARY JOURNAL (Specialized: work from NC resident/native poets)

P.O. Box 1197, Roxboro NC 27573. (336)599-1181, ext. 231. E-mail: reflect@piedmontcc.edu. Established 1999. **Contact:** Ernest Avery, editor.

Magazine Needs *Reflections Literary Journal*, published annually in spring, prints poetry, short fiction, and creative nonfiction. Wants any styles and forms of poetry, including translations. Does not want material using obscenities, or culturally insensitive material. **Accepts submissions from NC authors only (residents or natives).** "If time and space permit, we'll consider submissions from southeastern U.S. authors and from authors we've previously published." Has published poetry by Robert Cooperman, Fredrick Zydek, Bruce Bennett, Fred Chappell, Shari O'Brien, and Daniel Green. *Reflections Literary Journal* is 100-150 pages, digest-sized. Receives about 400 poems/ year, accepts about 5%. Press run is 250 (20 subscribers, 4 libraries, 150 shelf sales); 75 distributed free to contributors, editors, advisors, local schools, and cultural sites. Single copy: $7; subscription: $7. Sample: $5 (back issue). Make checks payable to *Reflections Literary Journal*.

How to Submit Submit 5 poems maximum at a time. Lines/poem: no longer than one page (single-spaced). Considers previously published poems and simultaneous submissions (if notified). Accepts e-mail submissions (pasted into body of message or as attachment in MS Word). "Include a 25-word bio with submission. Include two copies of each poem—one with name and address, one without. Affix adequate postage to SAE for return of manuscript if desired, or use First-Class stamps on SAE for notification." Reads submissions September 1-December 31. "Poems are read by an 8- to 12-member editorial board who rank submissions through 'blind' readings. Board members refrain from ranking their own submissions." Sometimes comments on rejected poems. Guidelines available in magazine, for SASE, or by e-mail. Responds in up to 9 months (in March or April). Pays one contributor's copy. Acquires first North American serial rights (if poem is unpublished) or one-time rights (if poem is previously published).

✪ ◪ RHINO

P.O. Box 591, Evanston IL 60204. Web site: www.rhinopoetry.org. Established 1976. **Contact:** Kathleen Kirk or Jackie White, co-editors.

• *RHINO* poems have been reprinted in *The Best American Poetry*, nominated for Pushcart Prizes, and won repeated Illinois Arts Council awards.

Magazine Needs *RHINO*, published annually in spring, prints poetry, short-shorts, and translations. Wants "work that reflects passion, originality, engagement with contemporary culture, and a love affair with language. We welcome free verse, formal poetry, innovation, and risk-taking." Has published poetry by Geoffrey Forsyth, Daniel Gutstein, Michael Hettich, Alexis Levitin, Maureen Seaton, and Martha Silano. *RHINO* is 150 pages, 7×10, printed on high-quality paper, with card cover with art. Receives 8,000-10,000 submissions/year, accepts 90-100, or 1%. Press run is 1,000. Single copy: $10. Sample: $5 (back issue).

How to Submit Submit 3-5 poems or 1-3 short-shorts once during reading period. Considers simultaneous submissions with notification; no previously published poems. Include SASE. Expects electronic copy upon acceptance; sends proofs. Reads submissions April 1-October 1. Guidelines available for SASE or on Web site. Responds in up to 3-6 months. Pays 2 contributor's copies. Acquires first rights only.

▣ ⊘ ◎ RHODE ISLAND ROADS (Specialized: RI/New England themes)

E-mail: asurkont@local.net. Web site: www.riroads.com. Established 2000. **Contact:** Amanda Surkont, poetry editor.

Magazine Needs *Rhode Island Roads*, published monthly online, features work with Rhode Island and New England themes. Open to all forms and styles, although "rhyme will have difficulty finding a home here." Considers poetry by children and teens. Has published poetry by Audrey Friedman, Barbara Schweitzer, Michele F. Cooper, Pat Hagneur, Lauri Burke, and Peggy Conti. Receives about 150 poems/year, accepts 12-16/year. Has about 70,000 readers/month. Sample: can view sample pages for free online.

How to Submit Submit up to 5 poems at a time. Lines/poem: "We are flexible." Considers previously published poems and simultaneous submissions. Accepts e-mail submissions only (pasted into body of message). "We'll ask for a bio if we use your work." Reads submissions year round. Submit seasonal poems 3 months in advance. Time between acceptance and publication is 2 months "unless seasonal, then it could be several months." Sometimes comments on rejected poems. Sometimes publishes theme issues. Upcoming themes available by e-mail. Guidelines available by e-mail or on Web site. "I try to respond within a week or two." Pays free subscription. Acquires one-time rights and electronic rights. "We archive." Rights revert to poet upon publication. "Electronic rights returned to author if requested."

Advice "Know your market. Read the publication before submitting poems. Get a feel for what we like. We sometimes suggest an alternative market for work. We suggest poets make a commitment to subscribing to five lit mags per year; we have more writers of poetry than readers. This is not a good balance."

▣ $⊘ THE RIALTO

P.O. Box 309, Alysham, Norwich, Norfolk NR11 6LN England. Web site: www.therialto.co.uk. Established 1984. **Contact:** Michael Mackmin, editor.

Magazine Needs *The Rialto*, published 3 times/year, seeks "to publish the best new poems by established and beginning poets. We seek excellence and originality." Has published poetry by Alice Fulton, Jenny Joseph, Les Murray, George Szirtes, Philip Gross, and Ruth Padel. *The Rialto* is 64 pages, A4, with full-color cover. Receives about 12,000 poems/year, accepts about 1%. Press run is 1,500 (1,000 subscribers, 50 libraries). Single copy: £7.50; subscription: £23 (prices listed are for U.S. and Canada). Make checks payable to *The Rialto*. "Checks in sterling only, please. Online payment also available on Web site."

How to Submit Submit up to 6 poems at a time. Considers simultaneous submissions; no previously published poems. Cover letter is preferred. "SASE or SAE with IRCs essential. U.S. readers please note that U.S. postage stamps are invalid in UK.'' Time between acceptance and publication is up to 4 months. Seldom comments on rejected poems. Responds in up to 4 months. ''A large number of poems arrive every week, so please note that you will have to wait at least 10 weeks for yours to be read.'' Pays £20/poem. Poet retains rights.

Additional Information *''The Rialto* has recently commenced publishing first collections by poets. Please do not send book-length manuscripts. Query first.''

Contest/Award Offerings Sponsors an annual young poets competition. Details available in magazine and on Web site.

Advice Before submitting, ''you will probably have read many poems by many poets, both living and dead. You will probably have put aside each poem you write for at least three weeks before considering it afresh. You will have asked yourself, 'Does it work technically?'; checked the rhythm, the rhymes (if used), and checked that each word is fresh and meaningful in its context, not jaded and tired. You will hopefully have read *The Rialto*.''

⬛ ◎ RIBBONS: TANKA SOCIETY OF AMERICA JOURNAL

P.O. 3267, La Pine OR 97739. E-mail: anya@bendnet.com. Web site: www.tankasocietyofamerica.com. Established 2000. **Contact:** an'ya, editor.

Magazine Needs *Ribbons: Tanka Society of America Journal*, published quarterly, seeks and regularly prints ''the best tanka poetry being written in English, together with reviews, critical and historical essays, commentaries, and translations.'' Wants ''poetry that exemplifies the very best in English-language tanka, which we regard as 'the queen of short form poetry,' having a significant contribution to make to the short poem in English. All schools and approaches are welcome.'' Tanka should ''reflect contemporary life, issues, values, and experience, in descriptive, narrative, and lyrical modes.'' Does not want ''work that merely imitates the Japanese masters.'' Considers poetry by children and teens. ''We have no age restrictions.'' Has published poetry by Cherie Hunter Day, Marianne Bluger, Sanford Goldstein, Larry Kimmel, John Stevenson, and George Swede. *Ribbons* is 28-32 pages, magazine-sized, offset-printed, saddle-stapled, with fine coverstock cover on acid-free paper. Receives about 2,000 poems/year, accepts about 20%. Press run is 275 (225 subscribers, 3 libraries); 15 distributed free. Single copy: $10; subscription: $25. Make checks payable to Tanka Society of America.

How to Submit Submit 1-8 poems at a time. Lines/poem: 5 minimum; sequences of up to 50 total lines considered. No previously published poems or simultaneous submissions. Prefers e-mail submissions (pasted into body of message); no disk submissions. ''Postal submissions must include SASE.'' Reads submissions year round. ''See the publication or contact the editor for specific deadlines for each issue.'' Time between acceptance and publication is 2 months. Sometimes comments on rejected poems. Regularly publishes theme issues. Guidelines available in magazine or on Web site. Responds in 4-8 weeks. No payment. Acquires one-time rights. Rights revert to poet upon publication. Reviews books/chapbooks of poetry and other magazines/journals in 250-1,200 words, single- or multi-book format. Send materials for review consideration to the editor or to Michael McClintock, President, Tanka Society of America, 9230 N. Stoneridge Lane, Fresno CA 93720.

Additional Information ''Features in each issue include 'Poet and Tanka' (various writers); 'Tanka Cafe' by Michael McClintock; 'Tanka Favorites,' essays by various writers, book reviews, and topical and historical essays and commentaries. About 200 new tanka appear in each issue. McClintock's 'Tanka Cafe' uses up to 45 poems per issue on a given theme, with critical commentary relating to contemporary tanka in English trends, styles, techniques, and subject matter.''

Contest/Award Offerings Sponsors the annual Tanka Society of America International English-Language Tanka Competition, offering cash prizes for 1st, 2nd, and 3rd places. Guidelines available in magazine, by e-mail, or on Web site. ''Potential entrants should consult the Web site or magazine for details pertaining to submissions to the annual tanka competition. Additionally, a Members'

Choice Award of $25 is given each quarter for a poem appearing in the 'Tanka Cafe' feature; non-cash Editor's Choice Awards are also featured in each issue.''

Advice ''Work by beginning as well as established English-language tanka poets is welcome; first-time contributors are encouraged to study the tanka form and contemporary examples before submitting. No particular school or style of tanka is preferred over another; our publications seek to showcase the full range of English-language tanka expression and subject matter through the work of new and established poets in the genre from around the world.''

✪ ▣ ☑ ◎ ROADRUNNER HAIKU JOURNAL (Specialized: haiku, senryu, short haiku-like poetry)

E-mail: roadrunner_haiku@cox.net or ztemttocs@gmail.com. Web site: www.roadrunnerjournal.net. Established 2004. **Contact:** Jason Sanford Brown, Scott Metz, editors; Richard Gilbert, translation editor.

Magazine Needs *Roadrunner Haiku Journal*, published quarterly online, is ''an international Web journal that publishes the most innovative modern haiku written today.'' Wants haiku, senryu, and short haiku-like poetry. Does not want tanka, haiga, or haibun. Considers poetry by children and teens. Has published poetry by Fay Aoyagi, Dhugal Lindsay, Dietmar Tauchner, and Diane Wakoski. Receives about 5,000 poems/year, accepts about 5%. Distributed free online. Number of unique visitors: 25,000/year.

How to Submit Submit 5-15 poems at a time. Lines/poem: ''less than 5 or so.'' No previously published poems or simultaneous submissions. Accepts e-mail submissions (pasted into body of message, with ''Roadrunner Submission'' and poet's name in subject line); no disk submissions. Cover letter is unnecessary. ''Please include a short bio.'' Reads submissions year round. Time between acceptance and publication is less than 3 months. Poems are circulated to an editorial board. Sometimes comments on rejected poems. Guidelines available on Web site. Responds in 2 weeks. Sometimes sends prepublication galleys. Acquires first rights. Rights revert to poets upon publication.

☑ ROANOKE REVIEW

English Dept., Roanoke College, 221 College Lane, Salem VA 24153. E-mail: review@roanoke.edu. Web site: www.roanoke.edu/roanokereview/. Established 1967. **Contact:** Paul Hanstedt, poetry editor.

Magazine Needs *Roanoke Review*, published annually in June, uses poetry that is ''grounded in strong images and unpretentious language.'' Has published poetry by David Citino, Jeff Daniel Marion, and Charles Wright. *Roanoke Review* is 200 pages, digest-sized, professionally printed, with matte card cover with full-color art. Receives 400-500 submissions of poetry/year, accepts 40-60. Press run is 250-300 (150 subscribers, 50 libraries). Single copy: $8; subscription: $13/2 years. Sample: $5.

How to Submit Submit original typed mss, no photocopies. Guidelines available on Web site. Responds in 3 months. Pays 2 contributor's copies ''plus cash when budget allows.''

Advice ''Be real. Know rhythm. Concentrate on strong images.''

☑ THE ROCKFORD REVIEW

P.O. Box 858, Rockford IL 61105. E-mail: daveconnieross@aol.com. Web site: http://writersguild1.tripod.com. Established 1971. **Contact:** David Ross, editor.

Magazine Needs *The Rockford Review*, published twice/year by the Rockford Writers' Guild, features poetry and prose by members and other contributors from across the country and abroad. Wants ''experimental or traditional poetry that provides fresh insight into the human condition in a literal or satirical voice.'' Open to veterans and novices alike. ''We delight in discovering new talent.'' Considers poetry by children and teens. *The Rockford Review* is about 100 pages, digest-sized, professionally printed, perfect-bound. Press run is 350. Single copy: $9; subscription: $20 (includes the Guild's monthly newsletter, *Write Away*).

How to Submit Submit up to 3 poems at a time. Lines/poem: 50 maximum. Considers simultaneous submissions; no previously published poems (including those published on the Internet). No e-mail submissions; accepts postal submissions only. Cover letter is required. "Include your name, address, phone number, e-mail address (if available), a three-line bio, and an affirmation that the poems are unpublished electronically or in print." SASE required for return. Guidelines available for SASE or on Web site. Responds in 2 months. Pays one contributor's copy and an invitation to be a guest of honor at annual summer Gala Reading & Reception in July. Acquires first North American serial rights.

Contest/Award Offerings Editor's Choice Prizes of $25 are awarded each issue. Also sponsors an Ides of March Poetry and Prose Contest for adults and youth, with cash prizes and publication in the summer *Rockford Review*. Details available on Web site.

Also Offers Rockford Writers' Guild is a nonprofit corporation established 60 years ago "to promote good writing of all forms and to nurture literary artists of all stages." Monthly meetings and newsletters offer practical tips on writing/marketing from professional guest poets, and open mics for contests/works in progress. Levels of membership/dues: $35/year. Further information available for SASE, by e-mail, or on Web site.

Advice "If the heart/soul of your poetry raises/answers questions about coping with the human condition, try us first—we're on the same page."

⊠ $⊠ ◎ ROCKY MOUNTAIN RIDER MAGAZINE (Specialized: horses; cowboy poetry; Northern Rockies region)

P.O. Box 1011, Hamilton MT 59840. (406)363-4085 or (800)509-1537. Fax: (406)363-1056. E-mail: info@rockymountainrider.com. Web site: www.rockymountainrider.com. Established 1993. **Contact:** Natalie Riehl, editor.

Magazine Needs *Rocky Mountain Rider Magazine*, published monthly, is a regional all-breed horse magazine. Wants "cowboy poetry; western or horse-themed poetry." *Rocky Mountain Rider Magazine* is 64 + pages, magazine-sized, web offset-printed on newsprint, stapled. Publishes 1-2 poems/issue. Press run is 16,000; distributed free through 500 locations in 11 states.

How to Submit Submit 1-10 poems at a time. Lines/poem: keep length to no more than 5 stanzas. Considers previously published poems and simultaneous submissions. No e-mail submissions; postal submissions only. Cover letter is preferred. Include SASE. Seldom comments on rejected poems. Occasionally publishes theme issues. Guidelines available for SASE. Pays $10/poem. Acquires one-time rights. Reviews books of poetry. Send materials for review consideration.

ℕ ⊠ THE ROGUE

P.O. Box 484, Pocatello ID 83204. Established 2006. **Contact:** Martin Vest or Anne Vest, co-editors.

Magazine Needs *The Rogue*, published annually in June, seeks "well-crafted work with plenty of open windows. No stuffy manors, please. We like crash landings, poems that hit the page belly-first and slide to a halt with all the passengers still alive. We have nothing against haiku, but *we do not like / one placid leaf / in the birdbath / or the old tree shedding its plums*. Please do not *nasturtium* and *begonia* us to death with every blossom in your garden. This having been said, we have nothing against flowers. But we prefer them wild. We like darkness. But think Anne Sexton, not Anne Rice. We like humor, but try to remember that humor is funny. We have nothing against war, peace, devil, or priest. We simply want work that is written in earnest. And speaking of Ernest, we'll leave you with these words from *Death in the Afternoon*: 'A serious writer is not to be confounded with a solemn writer. A serious writer may be a hawk or a buzzard or even a popinjay, but a solemn writer is always a bloody owl.' " *The Rogue* is 30-40 pages, "professionally printed on quality papers and hand-sewn in a variety of sizes and formats," includes ads. Receives about 6,000 poems/year, accepts about 1%. Press run is 350-500 (2 libraries). Single copy: $12; subscription: $20 (2 issues). Make checks payable to Martin and/or Anne Vest.

How to Submit Submit no more than 10 poems at a time. Lines/poem: no more than 100. Considers previously published poems and simultaneous submissions. Cover letter is preferred. Include SASE. Reads submissions year round. Often comments on rejected poems. Sometimes publishes theme issues. Guidelines available for SASE. Responds in 2 months. Pays one contributor's copy. Acquires first rights and one-time rights. Rights revert to poets upon publication. Reviews books/chapbooks of poetry and other magazines/journals in 1-2 pages. Send materials for review consideration to Martin and/or Anne Vest.

◯ ◎ RUAH: A JOURNAL OF SPIRITUAL POETRY (Specialized: poetry of a spiritual nature)

Power of Poetry, 5890 Birch Ct., Oakland CA 94618-1627. Fax: (510)596-1860. E-mail: cjrenzop@yahoo.com. Web site: http://popruah.opwest.org. Established 1990. **Contact:** C.J. Renz, O.P., general editor.

Magazine Needs *Ruah: A Journal of Spiritual Poetry*, published annually in June, provides "a 'non-combative forum' for poets who have had few or no opportunities to publish their work." Theme: spiritual poetry. Has 3 sections: general poems, featured poet, and chapbook contest winners. Wants "poetry that is of a 'spiritual nature,' i.e., describes an experience of the Transcendent. No religious affiliation preferences; no style/format limitations." Does not want "Satanic verse." Has published poetry by Jean Valentine, Alberto Rios, Luci Shaw, and Wendell Berry. *Ruah* is 60-80 pages, digest-sized, photocopied, perfect-bound, with glossy cardstock cover with color photo. Receives about 350 poems/year, accepts 10-20%. Press run is 250 (about 100 subscribers, 7 libraries, 10 shelf sales); 50 distributed free to authors, reviewers, and inquiries. Subscription: donated cost of $10 plus $1.75 s&h. Sample: $5 plus $1.75 s&h. Make checks payable to Power of Poetry/ DSPT.

How to Submit Submit 3-5 poems at a time. Lines/poem: no more than 4 typed pages. Considers simultaneous submissions; no previously published poems. Accepts fax, e-mail (as MS Word 97 file attachments or pasted into body of message), and disk submissions. Submit poems January 1-March 31 only; reads submissions April-June only. Time between acceptance and publication is up to 6 months. "Poems are reviewed by writers and/or scholars in field of creative writing/literature." Guidelines available for SASE or by e-mail. Responds in 2 weeks. Pays one contributor's copy/poem. Acquires first rights, including right to publish poems on Web site.

Contest/Award Offerings The New Eden Chapbook Competition (see separate listing in Contests & Awards).

Advice "*Ruah* is a gathering place in which new poets can come to let their voices be heard alongside and in the context of 'more established' poets. The journal hopes to provide some breakthrough experiences of the Divine at work in our world."

⊕ ◪ S.W.A.G., THE MAGAZINE OF SWANSEA'S WRITERS AND ARTISTS

Dan-y-Bryn, 74 CWM Level Rd., Brynhyfryd, Swansea SA5 9DY Wales. Established 1992. **Contact:** Peter Thabit Jones, chairman/editor.

Magazine Needs *S.W.A.G., The Magazine of Sansea's Writers and Artists*, published biannually, contains poetry, prose, articles, and illustrations. "Our purpose is to publish good literature." Wants "first-class poetry—any style." Has published poetry by Adrian Mitchell, Alan Llwyd, Mike Jenkins, and Dafydd Rowlands. *S.W.A.G.* is 48 pages, A4, professionally printed on coated paper, saddle-stapled, with glossy paper cover. Press run is 500 (120 subscribers, 50 libraries). Subscription: £5. Sample (including guidelines): £2.50 plus postage.

How to Submit Submit 6 poems at a time. Lines/poem: 40 maximum. No previously published poems or simultaneous submissions. Cover letter is required. Submissions must be typed. Time between acceptance and publication is 4-6 months. Poems are circulated to an editorial board. ''Editor chooses/discusses choices with board.'' Guidelines available for SASE (or SAE with IRCs). Responds ASAP. Pays 2 contributor's copies plus a copy of S.W.A.G.'s newsletter. Staff reviews books of poetry (half page to full page). Send materials for review consideration.

Also Offers The Swansea Writers and Artists Group (S.W.A.G.) also publishes a newsletter containing information on the group's events. Send SASE for details on the organization. ''We also publish Welsh-language poetry.''

Advice ''Interested poets should obtain sample beforehand (to see what we offer).''

☑ ◎ SACRED JOURNEY: THE JOURNAL OF FELLOWSHIP IN PRAYER (Specialized: multifaith spirituality)

291 Witherspoon St., Princeton NJ 08542. (609)924-6863. Fax: (609)924-6910. E-mail: editorial@sacredjourney.org. (inquiries) and submissions@sacredjourney.org. (submissions). Web site: www.sacredjourney.org. Established 1950. **Contact:** The Editor.

Magazine Needs *Sacred Journey*, published bimonthly, is ''concerned with prayer, meditation, spiritual life, and service to others.'' Wants short poetry ''with a spiritual and/or religious nature that reflects personal experience and is accessible to people of all faith traditions.'' *Sacred Journey* is 48 pages, digest-sized, professionally printed, saddle-stapled, with glossy card cover. Accepts about 10% of submissions received. Press run is 6,000. Subscription: $18. Sample: free.

How to Submit Submit 1-5 poems at a time. Considers previously published poems ''sometimes, if reprint permission is readily available'' and simultaneous submissions. Accepts e-mail submissions at submissions@sacredjourney.org (preferred; pasted into body of message or as MS Word attachment). Cover letter is required. Make sure contact information includes ''mailing address, phone number, and e-mail address, if applicable.'' Poems should be single-spaced. Responds within 2 months. Pays 5 contributor's copies.

☑ ◎ SAHARA (Specialized: poetry of Central New England; subscribers preferred)

P.O. Box 20705, Worcester MA 01602. (508)798-5672. E-mail: SaharaJournal@aol.com. Established 2000. **Contact:** Lydia Mancevice, managing editor.

Magazine Needs *Sahara*, published annually at the end of the year, is ''dedicated to the poetry of our region, Central New England.'' Wants ''unaffected, clear writing in any style. Poems may exist, but they should mean something, too.'' Does not want ''pointless obscenities.'' Considers poetry by children and teens. Has published poetry by Robert Cording, Martin Espada, Laura Jehn Menides, Judith Ferrara, Wally Swist, and John Hodgen. *Sahara* is 90 pages, digest-sized, offset-printed, perfect-bound, with b&w printed card cover with graphics. Receives about 600 poems/year, accepts about 10%. Press run is 300 (70 subscribers, 10 libraries, 100-150 shelf sales). Single copy: $12; subscription: $20 for 2 years. Make checks payable to Elizabethan Press.

How to Submit Submit 5 poems at a time. No previously published poems or simultaneous submissions. No fax, e-mail, or disk submissions. Cover letter is required. ''Please state the titles of the poems and include a bio.'' Reads submissions continually. Submit seasonal poems 6 months in advance. Time between acceptance and publication is at least 6 months. ''Material is circulated among several editors and must find at least one strong advocate to be considered.'' Seldom comments on rejected poems. **''Subscribers are preferred.''** Responds in up to 9 months. Sometimes sends prepublication galleys. Pays one contributor's copy. Acquires one-time rights. Reviews books/chapbooks of poetry in 300-600 words. Send materials for review consideration.

Advice ''Keep revising and submitting your work.''

☑ THE SAME

P.O. Box 494, Mount Union PA 17066. E-mail: riverfrontreadings@yahoo.com. Web site: http://tsmag.itgo.com. Established 2000. **Contact:** Philip Miller, editor.

Magazine Needs *The Same*, published semiannually, prints nonfiction (essays, reviews, literary criticism), poetry, and short fiction. Wants "eclectic to formal to free verse, traditional to experimental, all subject matter." Considers poetry by children and teens. Has published poetry by Kathy Allen, Carl Bettis, Donna Biffar, Wayne Lanter, Patricia Lawson, and Robert Weaver. *The Same* is 24-32 pages, desktop-published, saddle-stapled, with cardstock cover. Receives about 2,000 poems/year, accepts about 5%. Press run is 250 (125 subscribers/shelf sales). Single copy: $5; subscription: $9 for 2 issues, $18 for 4 issues. Make checks payable to Philip Miller.

How to Submit Submit 1-7 poems at a time. Lines/poem: 120 maximum. No previously published poems or simultaneous submissions "without query." Prefers e-mail submissions (pasted into body of message). Cover letter is optional. "Include SASE if you want a snail mail response. If you don't want your manuscript returned, you may omit the SASE if we can respond by e-mail." Reads submissions year round. Time between acceptance and publication can be up to 11 months. Sometimes comments on rejected poems. Guidelines available for SASE, by e-mail, or on Web site. Responds within 2 months. Pays one contributor's copy. Acquires first North American serial rights and online rights for up to 9 months; returns rights to poet.

Additional Information Publishes 1-3 chapbooks/year. **Solicited mss only.** Chapbooks are 24-32 pages, desktop-published, saddle-stapled, with cardstock covers. Pays 25 author's copies (out of a press run of 100).

Advice "Our motto is 'Everyone else is different, but we're the same!' We are eclectic and non-doctrinaire."

○ SANSKRIT

UNC Charlotte, Cone University Center, Charlotte NC 28223. (704)687-2326. Fax: (704)687-3394. E-mail: sanskrit@email.uncc.edu. Web site: http://cone.uncc.edu. (click Student Media Publications). Established 1965. **Contact:** Samantha Webster, editor.

Magazine Needs *Sanskrit*, published annually in April, seeks "to encourage and promote beginning and established artists and writers. No restrictions as to form or genre, but we do look for maturity and sincerity in submissions." Does not want anything "lewd or sentimental." Has published poetry by Kimberleigh Luke-Stallings. *Sanskrit* is 64 pages. Press run is 3,500 (about 100 subscribers, 2 libraries). Sample: $10.

How to Submit Submit up to 15 poems at a time. Considers simultaneous submissions. Accepts e-mail submissions. Cover letter is required. "Include 30- to 70-word bio. Please do not list previous publications as a bio." Reads submissions by the first Friday in November (deadline). Never comments on rejected poems. Guidelines available for SASE or by e-mail. Responds in 2 months. Pays one contributor's copy.

○ THE SARANAC REVIEW

CVH, Plattsburgh State University, 101 Broad St., Plattsburgh NY 12901. (518)564-5151. E-mail: saranacreview@plattsburgh.edu. Web site: http://research.plattsburgh.edu/saranacreview. Established 2004. **Contact:** Poetry Editor.

Magazine Needs *The Saranac Review*, published annually in the fall, wants poetry from both U.S. and Canadian writers. Does not want "amateurish or 'greeting card' poetry." Has published poetry by Neil Shepard, Don Revell, Jim Daniels, and Naomi Ayala. *The Saranac Review* is magazine-sized, with color photo or painting on cover, includes ads. Press run is 750. Single copy: $9; subscription: $8/year, $15 for 2 years, $27 for 3 years, $32 for 5 years ($15/year for institutions— multi-year subscriptions receive 15% institutional discount); all Canadian subscriptions add $3/year. Make checks payable to *The Saranac Review*.

How to Submit Submit no more than 5 poems at a time. Considers simultaneous submissions if notified; no previously published poems. No e-mail or disk submissions. Cover letter is appreciated. Include phone and e-mail contact information (if possible) in cover letter. Manuscripts will not be returned without SASE. Reads submissions September-February. Poems are circulated to an editorial board. Sometimes comments on rejected poems. Guidelines available by e-mail or on Web site. Responds in 3-6 months. Pays 2 contributor's copies. Acquires first rights.

SEAM

P.O. Box 1051, Sawston, Cambridge CB22 3WT England. E-mail: seam.magazine@googlemail.com. (inquiries only). Web site: www.seampoetry.co.uk. Established 1994. **Contact:** Anne Berkeley, editor.

Magazine Needs *Seam*, published twice/year in January and July, seeks "good contemporary poetry." Wants "high-quality poems that engage the reader." Has published poetry by Annemarie Austin, Vernon Scannell, Kim Bridgford, Caroline Natzler, and Angus MacMillan. *Seam* is 64 pages, A5, perfect-bound, with b&w cover. Receives about 2,000 poems/year, accepts about 5%. Press run is 300. Subscription: £8/year (£12 or $18 overseas). Sample: £4.50 (£5.50 or $9 overseas). Payments accepted through PayPal.

How to Submit Submit 5-6 poems at a time. No simultaneous submissions or previously published poems (if published in UK). No e-mail submissions. Type each poem on one sheet of paper (A4 size). Sometimes comments on rejected poems. Pays one contributor's copy.

Contest/Award Offerings *Seam* is affiliated with the annual Essex Poetry Festival Competition. Write for details or visit www.essex-poetry-festival.co.uk.

SEEMS

P.O. Box 359, Lakeland College, Sheboygan WI 53082-0359. (920)565-1276 or (920)565-3871. Fax: (920)565-1206. E-mail: kelder@excel.net. Web site: www1.lakeland.edu/seems. Established 1971. **Contact:** Karl Elder, editor.

Magazine Needs *SEEMS*, published irregularly, prints poetry, fiction, and essays. Two of the issues are considered chapbooks, and the editor suggests sampling *SEEMS* #14, "What Is The Future Of Poetry?" ($5), consisting of essays by 22 contemporary poets; "if you don't like it, return it, and we'll return your $5." "Explain That You Live: Mark Strand with Karl Elder" (*SEEMS* #29) is available for $3. Has published poetry by Philip Dacey, William Hathaway, William Heyen, Sapphire, and Frank Stanford. *SEEMS* is handsomely printed, nearly square ($7 \times 8^{1}/_{4}$), saddle-stapled. Publishes less than .5% of submissions received. Press run is 500 (more than 250 subscribers, 20 libraries). Single copy: $4; subscription: $16 for 4 issues.

How to Submit Lines/poem: open. No simultaneous submissions. No fax or e-mail submissions. Cover letter is optional. Include biographical information, SASE. Reads submissions year round. There is a 1- to 2-year backlog. "People may call or fax with virtually any question, understanding that the editor may have no answer." Guidelines available on Web site. Responds in up to 3 months (slower in summer). Pays one contributor's copy. Acquires first North American serial rights and permission to publish online. Returns rights upon publication.

Additional Information See the editor's Web site atwww.karlelder.com. "Links to my work and an interview may provide insight for the potential contributor."

Advice "Visit the *SEEMS* Web site."

$ THE SEWANEE REVIEW

University of the South, 735 University Ave., Sewanee TN 37383-1000. (931)598-1246. E-mail: lcouch@sewanee.edu. Web site: www.sewanee.edu/sewanee_review. Established 1892 ("thus being our nation's oldest continuously published literary quarterly"). **Contact:** George Core, editor.

Magazine Needs *Sewanee Review*, published quarterly, is open "to all styles and forms: formal sequences, metered verse, structured free verse, sonnets, and lyric and narrative forms—all accessible and intelligent. Fiction, criticism, and poetry are invariably of the highest establishment standards. Many of our major poets appear here from time to time." Has published poetry by Wendell

Berry, George Bilgere, Catherine Savage Brosman, David Mason, Leslie Norris, and Christian Wiman. *The Sewanee Review* is nearly 200 pages, conservatively bound in matte paper, always of the same typography. Press run is 2,600. Subscription: $25/year for individuals, $33/year for institutions. Sample: $8.50 U.S., $9.50 foreign.

How to Submit Submit up to 6 poems at a time. Lines/poem: 40 maximum. No simultaneous submissions. No e-mail submissions; postal submissions only. ''Unsolicited works should not be submitted between June 1 and August 31. A response to any submission received during that period will be greatly delayed.'' Guidelines available in magazine or on Web site. Responds in 2 months. Pays per line, plus 2 contributor's copies (and reduced price for additional copies). Solicits brief, standard, and essay-reviews.

Contest/Award Offerings Winners of the Allen Tate Prize and the Aiken Taylor Award for Modern American Poetry are determined by the editorial board and a prize committee; poets cannot apply for these awards.

Advice ''Please keep in mind that for each poem published in *The Sewanee Review*, approximately 250 poems are considered.''

✵ $✉ ◎ SHELTER: FOR RENEGADE PRIESTS (Specialized: experimental poetry)

Independent Press, 1120 W4, #1A, Erie PA 16507. (814)453-7777. Established 1991. **Contact:** Gary Wykoff, editor/publisher.

Magazine Needs *Shelter: For Renegade Priests*, published semiannually, uses ''very high quality material to present experimental poetry.'' Wants ''experimental, spiritual, art.'' Does not want ''explicit sexuality.'' Considers poetry by teens (''write well!''). *Shelter* is 150 pages, magazine-sized, desktop-published, journal-style binding, includes ads. Receives about 200 poems/year, accepts about 50%. Press run is 100. Single copy: $12.95; subscription: $19.95. Make checks payable to Independent Press.

How to Submit Lines/poem: 10-50. Considers previously published poems and simultaneous submissions. Accepts disk submissions; no e-mail submissions. Cover letter is unnecessary. Reads submissions year round. **Charges $1/poem reading fee.** Time between acceptance and publication is 6 months. Sometimes comments on rejected poems. Guidelines available for SASE. Responds in 6 months. Pays $5. Acquires one-time rights. Rights revert to poets upon publication. Reviews chapbooks of poetry in single-book format.

Advice ''Simply dig inside as deeply as possible and write well.''

◯ ◎ SHEMOM (Specialized: parenting)

2486 Montgomery Ave., Cardiff CA 92007. E-mail: pdfrench@cox.net. Established 1997. **Contact:** Peggy French, editor.

Magazine Needs *Shemom*, published 3 times/year, is a zine that ''celebrates parenting and the joys and struggles that present themselves on that journey.'' Includes poetry, essays, book and CD reviews, recipes, art, and children's poetry. Open to any style, but prefers free verse. ''We showcase writers of all ages that reflect on life's varied experiences. We often feature hiaku.'' *Shemom* is 10-20 pages. Receives about 100 poems/year, accepts 50%. Press run is 60 (30 subscribers). Single copy: $3.50; subscription: $12/4 issues. Make checks payable to Peggy French.

How to Submit Submit 3 poems at a time. Considers previously published poems and simultaneous submissions. Accepts e-mail submissions (as attachment or pasted into body of message). ''Prefer e-mail submission, but not required; if material is to be returned, please include a SASE.'' Time between acceptance and publication is 3 months. Guidelines available for SASE or by e-mail. Responds in 2 months. Pays one contributor's copy. Acquires one-time rights.

✪ $☑ SHENANDOAH

Mattingly House, 2 Lee Ave., Washington and Lee University, Lexington VA 24450-0303. (540)458-8765. Fax: (540)458-8461. E-mail: lleech@wlu.edu. Web site: http://shenandoah.wlu.edu. Established 1950. **Contact:** Lynn Leech, managing editor.

• Poetry published in *Shenandoah* has been included in *The Best American Poetry*.

Magazine Needs *Shenandoah*, published triannually at Washington and Lee University, is open to all styles and forms. Has published poetry by Mary Oliver, Andrew Hudgins, W.S. Merwin, and Rita Dove. *Shenandoah* is 224+ pages, digest-sized, professionally printed, perfect-bound, with full-color cover. Press run is 2,000+. Subscription: $22/year, $40 for 2 years, $54 for 3 years. Sample: $8.

How to Submit Considers simultaneous submissions "only if we are immediately informed of acceptance elsewhere." No e-mail submissions. All submissions should be typed on one side of the paper only, with name and address clearly written on the upper right corner of the ms. Include SASE. Reads submissions September 1-May 30 only. Responds in 3 months. Pays $2.50/line, one-year subscription, and one contributor's copy. Acquires first publication rights. Staff reviews books of poetry in 7-10 pages, multi-book format. Send materials for review consideration. (Most reviews are solicited.)

Contest/Award Offerings Sponsors the annual James Boatwright III Prize for Poetry, a $1,000 prize awarded to the author of the best poem published in *Shenandoah* during a volume year.

☑ ◎ THE SHEPHERD (Specialized: religious; inspirational)

1530 Seventh St., Rock Island IL 61201. (309)788-3980. Established 1996. **Contact:** Betty Mowery, poetry editor.

Magazine Needs *The Shepherd*, published quarterly, features inspirational poetry from all ages. Wants "something with a message but not preachy." Subscription: $10. Sample: $3. Make all checks payable to *The Oak*.

How to Submit Submit 5 poems at a time. Lines/poem: 35 maximum. Considers previously published poems. Include SASE with all submissions. Responds in one week. "*The Shepherd* does not pay in dollars or copies, but you need not purchase to be published." Acquires first or second rights. All rights revert to poet upon publication.

☑ SHIP OF FOOLS

Ship of Fools Press, University of Rio Grande, Box 1028, Rio Grande OH 45674-9989. (740)992-3333. Web site: http://meadhall.homestead.com/Ship.html. Established 1983. **Contact:** Jack Hart, editor. Review Editor: James Doubleday.

Magazine Needs *Ship of Fools*, published "more or less quarterly," seeks "coherent, well-written, traditional or modern, myth, archetype, love—most types." Does not want "concrete, incoherent, or greeting card poetry." Considers poetry by children and teens. Has published poetry by Rhina Espaillat and Gale White. *Ship of Fools* is digest-sized, offset-printed, saddle-stapled, includes cover art and graphics. Press run is 179 (43 subscribers, 5 libraries). Subscription: $8/4 issues. Sample: $2.

How to Submit No previously published poems or simultaneous submissions. Cover letter is preferred. Often comments on rejected poems. Guidelines available for SASE. Responds in one month. "If longer than six weeks, write and ask why." Pays 1-2 contributor's copies. Reviews books of poetry.

Additional Information "We have no plans to publish chapbooks in the next year due to time constraints."

Advice "Forget yourself; it is not you that matters, but the words."

◎ SHIRIM, A JEWISH POETRY JOURNAL (Specialized: reflections of Jewish living)

259 St. Joseph Ave., Long Beach CA 90803. (310)476-2861. Established 1982. **Contact:** Marc Dworkin, editor.

Magazine Needs *Shirim, A Jewish Poetry Journal*, published biannually, prints "poetry that reflects

Jewish living without limiting to specific symbols, images, or contents." Has published poetry by Robert Mezcy, Karl Shapiro, and Grace Schulmon. *Shirim* is 40 pages, 4×5, desktop-published, saddle-stapled, with cardstock cover. Press run is 200. Subscription: $7. Sample: $4.

How to Submit Submit 4 poems at a time. No previously published poems or simultaneous submissions. Cover letter is preferred. Seldom comments on rejected poems. Regularly publishes theme issues. Responds in 3 months. Acquires first rights.

SIERRA NEVADA COLLEGE REVIEW

999 Tahoe Blvd., Incline Village NV 89451. E-mail: sncreview@sierranevada.edu. Web site: www.sierranevada.edu/zSNCReview/. Established 1990. **Contact:** June Sylvester Saraceno, advisory editor.

Magazine Needs *Sierra Nevada College Review*, published annually in May, features poetry and short fiction by new writers. Wants "image-oriented poems with a distinct, genuine voice. Although we don't tend to publish 'light verse,' we do appreciate, and often publish, poems that make us laugh. No limit on length, style, etc." Does not want "sentimental, clichéd, or obscure poetry." Has published poetry by Virgil Suárez, Simon Perchik, Carol Frith, and Marisella Veiga. *Sierra Nevada College Review* is about 75 pages, with art on cover. Receives about 500 poems/year, accepts about 50. Press run is 500. Subscription: $10/year. Sample: $5.

How to Submit Submit up to 5 poems at a time. Considers simultaneous submissions; no previously published poems. Accepts e-mail submissions (pasted into body of message, no attachments). Reads submissions September 1-March 1 only. Sometimes comments on rejected poems. Guidelines available for SASE, by e-mail, or on Web site. Responds in about 3 months. Pays 2 contributor's copies.

Advice "We're looking for poetry that shows subtlety and skill."

THE SILT READER

Temporary Vandalism, P.O. Box 6184, Orange CA 92863-6184. E-mail: tvrec@yahoo.com. Web site: http://home.surewest.net/aphasiapress. Established 1991 (Temporary Vandalism Recordings), 1999 (*The Silt Reader*). **Contact:** Robert Roden and Barton M. Saunders, editors.

Magazine Needs *The Silt Reader*, published semiannually in January and August, is a small print magazine. "Form, length, style, and subject matter can vary. It's difficult to say what will appeal to our eclectic tastes." Does not want "strictly rants, overly didactic poetry." Has published poetry by M. Jaime-Becerra, Gerald Locklin, Simon Perchik, Margaret Garcia, and Don Winter. *The Silt Reader* is 32 pages, 4¼×5½, photocopied, saddle-stapled, with colored card cover, includes ads. Accepts less than 5% of poems received. Press run is 500. Sample: $2. Make checks payable to Robert Roden.

How to Submit Submit 5 poems at a time. Considers previously published poems and simultaneous submissions. No e-mail submissions. Cover letter is preferred. Submissions should be neatly typed. Time between acceptance and publication is 12-16 months. "Two editors' votes required for in-

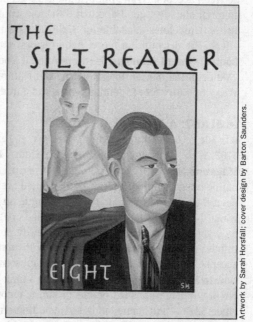

The Issue 8 cover of *The Silt Reader* features "Business Lunch" by Sarah Horsfall (www.shorsfall.com). "The image struck us with its disinterested intimacy, how the viewer is brought to the gaze of each man because they are avoiding each other's gaze," explains co-editor Barton Saunders.

clusion.'' Seldom comments on rejected poems. Responds in up to 6 months. Guidelines available for SASE or on Web site. Pays 2 contributor's copies. Acquires one-time rights.

Additional Information Temporary Vandalism publishes 2 chapbooks/year. **"We are not currently accepting any unsolicited full-length manuscripts for publishing."** Chapbooks are usually 40 pages, photocopied, saddle-stapled, with an initial press run of 100 (reprint option if needed). For sample chapbooks, send $5 to the above address.

☐ ◎ SKIPPING STONES: A MULTICULTURAL MAGAZINE (Specialized: poetry by young writers by young writers under 18; bilingual; multicultural and social issues nature/ecology

P.O. Box 3939, Eugene OR 97403. (541)342-4956. E-mail: editor@skippingstones.org. Web site: www.skippingstones.org. Established 1988. **Contact:** Arun Toké, editor.

- *Skipping Stones* has been the recipient of EdPress, NAME, and Parent's Guide Awards, among others.

Magazine Needs *Skipping Stones: A Multicultural Magazine*, published bimonthly during the school year (5 issues), ''encourages cooperation, creativity, and celebration of cultural and ecological richness.'' Wants ''poetry by young writers under age 18, on multicultural and social issues, family, freedom—uplifting. No adult poetry, please.'' *Skipping Stones* is magazine-sized, saddle-stapled, printed on recycled paper. Receives about 500-1,000 poems/year, accepts 10%. Press run is 2,500 (1,700 subscribers). Subscription: $25. Sample: $5.

How to Submit Submit up to 5 poems at a time. Lines/poem: 30 maximum. Considers simultaneous submissions; no previously published poems. Accepts e-mail submissions. Cover letter is preferred. ''Include your cultural background, experiences, and the inspiration behind your creation.'' Time between acceptance and publication is 6-9 months. ''A piece is chosen for publication when all the editorial staff feel good about it.'' Seldom comments on rejected poems. Publishes multi-theme issues. Guidelines available for SASE. Responds in up to 4 months. Pays one contributor's copy, offers 25% discount for more. Acquires first serial rights and non-exclusive reprint rights.

Contest/Award Offerings Sponsors Annual Youth Honor Awards for 7- to 17-year-olds. Theme is ''Multicultural, Social, International, and Nature Awareness.'' Guidelines available for SASE or on Web site. **Entry fee:** $3 (entitles entrant to a free issue featuring the 10 winners). **Deadline:** June 25.

◙ SLANT: A JOURNAL OF POETRY

Box 5063, University of Central Arkansas, 201 Donaghey Ave., Conway AR 72035-5000. (501)450-5107. Web site: www.uca.edu/english/Slant/. Established 1987. **Contact:** James Fowler, editor.

Magazine Needs *Slant: A Journal of Poetry*, published annually in May, aims ''to publish a journal of fine poetry from all regions of the United States and beyond.'' Wants ''traditional and 'modern' poetry, even experimental; moderate length, any subject on approval of Board of Readers.'' Doesn't want ''haiku, translations.'' Has published poetry by Susan H. Case, Philip Dacey, Elizabeth Howard, Timothy Martin, Gilbert Wesley Purdy, and Nancy Scott. *Slant* is 120 pages, professionally printed on quality stock, flat-spined, with matte card cover. Receives about 1,400 poems/year, accepts 70-80. Press run is 175 (70-100 subscribers). Sample: $10.

How to Submit Submit up to 5 poems at a time. Lines/poem: poems should be of moderate length. No previously published poems or simultaneous submissions. Submissions should be typed; include SASE. ''Put name, address (including e-mail if available), and phone number at the top of each page.'' Reads submissions September 1-November 15. Comments on rejected poems ''on occasion.'' Guidelines available in magazine, for SASE, or on Web site. Responds in 3-4 months from November 15 deadline. Pays one contributor's copy. Poet retains rights.

Advice ''We tend to publish those poems whose execution, line by line, does full justice to their conception. Often the decision to accept comes down to the matter of craft, language.''

☐ ◎ SLATE & STYLE (Specialized: by & for blind writers)

2704 Beach Dr., Merrick NY 11566. (516)868-8718. E-mail: LoriStay@aol.com. Web site: http://
home.earthlink.net/~uinen/writers_division/. Established 1982. **Contact:** Loraine Stayer, editor.
Magazine Needs *Slate & Style*, published quarterly, is the magazine of the Writers' Division of the
National Federation of the Blind. Published for blind writers, *Slate & Style* is available on cassette,
in large print, in Braille, and by e-mail, and includes resources and articles of interest to blind
writers. "We prefer contributors be blind writers, or at least writers by profession or inclination.
New writers welcome. No obscenities. Will consider all forms of poetry including haiku. Interested
in new talent." Considers poetry by children and teens, "but please specify age." Has published
poetry by Mary Brunoli, Kerry Elizabeth Thompson, Katherine Barr, and Nancy Scott. *Slate &
Style* (print format) is 28-32 pages, magazine-sized, stapled. Press run is 200 (160 subscribers, 4-5
libraries). Subscription/membership: $10/year (regardless of format). Sample: $3.
How to Submit Submit 3 poems at a time once or twice/year. Lines/poem: 5-36. No previously
published poems or simultaneous submissions. Accepts submissions by e-mail (pasted into body
of message). "On occasion we receive poems in Braille. I prefer print, since Braille slows me down.
Typed is best." Cover letter is preferred. Reads submissions according to the following deadlines:
February 16, May 15, August 15, November 15; "do not submit manuscripts in July." Comments
on rejected poems "if requested." Guidelines available in magazine, for SASE, by e-mail, or on
Web site. Responds in 2 weeks "if I like it." Pays one contributor's copy. Reviews books of poetry.
Send materials for review consideration.
Contest/Award Offerings Sponsors an annual poetry contest, awarding 1st Prize: $30; 2nd Prize:
$20; 3rd Prize: $10. Honorable mentions may also be awarded, and winning poems will be pub-
lished in magazine. **Entry fee:** $5 for up to 3 poems. Make check or money order payable to NFB
Writers' Division. **Deadline:** June 1. Guidelines available for SASE, by e-mail, or on Web site.
Advice "Before you send us a poem, read it aloud. Does it sound good to you? We put our poetry
into tape format, so we want it to sound and look good."

☐ SLEEPINGFISH

202 E. 7th St., New York NY 10009. E-mail: white@sleepingfish.net. Web site: www.sleepingfish.n
et. Established 2003. **Contact:** Derek White, editor.
Magazine Needs *SleepingFish*, published 1-2 times/year, is "a print magazine of experimental
visual and prose poetry and 'textual art.' Some online features, including *5cense Reviews*." Wants
"art, visual poetry, prose poems, experimental texts, graffiti, collage, multi-cultural, cross-genre
work—anything that defies categorization." Does not want "conventional 'lined' or rhyming poetry
(anything that looks like a 'poem'), conventional stories, genre fiction or poetry, political, religious,
New Age, anything with an agenda." Considers poetry by teens. Has published writings by Brian
Evenson, Norman Lock, Peter Markus, Daryl Scroggins, Malcolm de Chazal, and John Olson. *SleepingFish* is 100-120 pages, magazine-sized, digitally printed, perfect-bound or with other binding,
with 110 lb. cardstock cover in full color. Receives about 500 poems/year, accepts about 25 (5%).
Press run is 400 (10 libraries, 300 shelf sales, 100 online sales); 50 distributed free to contributors.
Single copy: $12. Make checks payable to Calamari Press.
How to Submit Submit 1-5 prose or visual poems at a time. Lines/poem: 1-3 pages (prose less than
1,000 words). Considers simultaneous submissions; no previously published poems. Accepts e-
mail submissions only (pasted into body of message or as small attachments [less than 2 MB] in
DOC, RTF, JPG, GIF, or PDF format); no disk submissions. Cover letter is preferred. "Please send
submissions by e-mail. If sending by postal mail, query first by e-mail. Reading period varies; see
Web site for details." Time between acceptance and publication is 2-6 weeks. "Currently, a two-
person lo-fi operation. Tastes and whims vary and are subject to change. Sometimes there is a
loose theme, and acceptance may also be dependent on whether the admission fits in with other
work in the issue." Sometimes comments on rejected poems. "Poet should be familiar with *Sleep-*

ingFish. Online samples and work on site (www.sleepingfish.net) if you can't afford a copy." Sometimes publishes theme issues. Guidelines available on Web site. Responds in 1-3 months. Sometimes sends prepublication galleys. Pays one contributor's copy, with additional contributor copies available at half price. "Payment depends on funds." Acquires first rights. Returns all rights "as long as *SleepingFish* is acknowledged as first place of publication." Reviews books/chapbooks of poetry and other magazines/journals. "Reviews are usually published underwww.5cense.com. as 'sensory reviews' and are usually not conventional or objective." Send materials for review consideration to Derek White by e-mail.

Advice "Keep it real."

SLIPSTREAM

Dept. W-1, P.O. Box 2071, Niagara Falls NY 14301-0071. (716)282-2616 (after 5 PM, EST). E-mail: editors@slipstreampress.org. Web site: www.slipstreampress.org. Established 1980. **Contact:** Dan Sicoli, Robert Borgatti, and Livio Farallo, poetry editors.

Magazine Needs *Slipstream*, published annually in spring, is "about 95% poetry, with some artwork. We like new work with contemporary urban flavor. Writing must have a cutting edge to get our attention. We like to keep an open forum, any length, subject, style. Best to see a sample to get a feel. Like city stuff as opposed to country." Wants "poetry that springs from the gut, screams from dark alleys, inspired by experience." Does not want "pastoral, religious, traditional, rhyming" poetry. Has published poetry by Terry Godbey, Gerald Locklin, David Chorlton, Martin Vest, Beth Royer, and Mofolasayo Ogundiran. *Slipstream* is 80-100 pages, $7 \times 8^{1}/_{2}$, professionally printed, perfect-bound. Receives more than 2,500 poetry submissions/year, accepts less than 10%. Press run is 500 (400 subscribers, 10 libraries). Subscription: $20 for 2 issues and 2 chapbooks. Sample: $7.

How to Submit No e-mail submissions. Sometimes comments on rejected poems. Publishes theme issues. Guidelines available for SASE or on Web site. Responds in up to 2 months "if SASE included." Pays 1-2 contributor's copies.

Contest/Award Offerings *Slipstream* Poetry Contest (see separate listing in Contests & Awards).

Advice "Do not waste time submitting your work 'blindly.' Sample issues from the small press first to determine which ones would be most receptive to your work."

SMALL BRUSHES

Adept Press, P.O. Box 5, Allamuchy NJ 07820. Established 1999. **Contact:** Jan Epps Turner or John Chadsey Turner.

Magazine Needs *Small Brushes*, published twice/year in April and October, "looks for poetry of literary quality, including humor and nostalgia. We value unity, coherence, emphasis, accessibility, and want to see poetry expressed without the use of vulgarity. Striving for universality and ageless connections of the human spirit, we avoid issues of a narrow religious, social, or political character as well as overly sentimental or personal poems." Considers poetry by children and teens. Has published poetry by John P. Kristofco, Laverne Frith, Carol Hamilton, David Napolin, Robert Lowenstein, and Lyn Lifshin. *Small Brushes* is 28 pages, digest-sized, desktop-published, photocopied, saddle-stapled, with heavyweight paper cover. Receives more than 1,000 poems/year, accepts about 8%. Press run is 100. Single copy: $3; subscription: $10 for 2 years (4 issues). Make checks payable to Adept Press. "Subscriptions are for a few loyal readers and a way for contributors to get extra copies at a savings by specifying the issues or any four copies they want. Otherwise, we neither require nor expect contributors to subscribe. Subscription purchase does not affect our choice of poetry, so please do not send a check with first submissions. Samples (old issues), with our guidelines enclosed, can be obtained by sending a self-addressed catalog envelope (6×9) with $1.14 postage attached."

How to Submit Submit 3-4 poems at a time. No previously published poems or simultaneous submissions. Cover letter is preferred. "Please include a brief bio in your cover letter, and place your name and address at the top of each manuscript page. Send SASE if you want any manuscript returned (standard envelope and first-class postage only)." Time between acceptance and publication is up to 18 months. Guidelines available for SASE. Responds in up to 3 months. Pays one contributor's copy. Rights remain with authors and artists.

Advice "Read carefully our needs and preferences in this listing. Submit poetry to us only if your style and subject matter are an exact fit. Please send submissions to us in standard letter envelopes."

◙ SMARTISH PACE

P.O. Box 22161, Baltimore MD 21203. E-mail: sreichert@smartishpace.com. Web site: www.smarti shpace.com. Established 1999. **Contact:** Stephen Reichert, editor.

Magazine Needs *Smartish Pace*, published in, contains poetry and translations. "*Smartish Pace* is an independent poetry journal and is not affiliated with any institution." No restrictions on style or content of poetry. Has published poetry by Linda Gregerson, Paul Muldoon, Rosanna Warren, Susan Howe, and Tony Hoagland. *Smartish Pace* is about 140 pages, digest-sized, professionally printed, perfect-bound, with full-color cover featuring contemporary artwork. Receives about 3,000 poems/year, accepts 2%. Press run is 1,100. Subscription: $20. Sample: $10.

How to Submit Submit no more than 6 poems at a time. Considers simultaneous submissions; no previously published poems. Cover letter with bio and SASE required. Submit seasonal poems 8 months in advance. Time between acceptance and publication is up to one year. Guidelines available for SASE or on Web site. Responds in up to 8 months. Pays one contributor's copy. Acquires first rights. Encourages unsolicited reviews, essays, and interviews. Send materials for review consideration. All books received will also be listed in the Books Received section of each issue and on the Web site along with ordering information and a link to the publisher's Web site.

Contest/Award Offerings *Smartish Pace* hosts the annual Erskine J. Poetry Prize and the Beullah Rose Poetry Prize (for women) (see separate listings in Contests & Awards).

Also Offers Also available on Web site: Poets Q&A, where readers can ask questions of poets and read their responses. Recent participants have included Robert Pinsky, Jorie Graham, Stephen Dunn, Carl Dennis, Eavan Boland, Campbell McGrath, and Robert Hass.

Advice "Visit our Web site. Read a few issues."

⊕ ◙ SMOKE

First Floor, Liver House, 96 Bold St., Liverpool L1 4HY England. (44)(151)709-3688. Web site: www.windowsproject.demon.co.uk. Established 1974. **Contact:** Dave Ward, editor.

Magazine Needs *Smoke*, published semiannually, contains poetry and graphics. Wants "short, contemporary poetry, expressing new ideas through new forms." Has published poetry by Carol Ann Duffy, Roger McGough, Jackie Kay, and Henry Normal. *Smoke* is 24 pages, A5, offset-litho-printed, stapled, with paper cover. Receives about 3,000 poems/year, accepts about 40. Press run is 750 (350 subscribers, 18 libraries, 100 shelf sales); 100 distributed free to contributors/other magazines. Subscription: $10. Sample: $2. Make checks payable to Windows Project (cash preferred—exchange rate on cheques not viable).

How to Submit Submit 6 poems at a time. Considers previously published poems and simultaneous submissions. Cover letter is preferred. Time between acceptance and publication is 6 months. Seldom comments on rejected poems. Responds in 2 weeks. Pays one contributor's copy.

$◙ ◎ SNOWY EGRET (Specialized: nature-oriented poetry)

P.O. Box 29, Terre Haute IN 47808. Web site: www.snowyegret.net. Established 1922 by Humphrey A. Olsen. **Contact:** Philip Repp, editor.

Magazine Needs *Snowy Egret*, published in spring and autumn, specializes in work that is "nature-oriented: poetry that celebrates the abundance and beauty of nature or explores the interconnections between nature and the human psyche." Has published poetry by Conrad Hilberry, Lyn

Lifshin, Gayle Eleanor, James Armstrong, and Patricia Hooper. *Snowy Egret* is 60 pages, magazine-sized, offset-printed, saddle-stapled. Receives about 500 poems/year, accepts about 30. Press run is 400 (250 subscribers, 50 libraries). Sample: $8; subscription: $15/year, $25/2 years.

How to Submit Guidelines available for #10 SASE. Responds in one month. Always sends prepublication galleys. Pays $4/poem or $4/page plus 2 contributor's copies. Acquires first North American and one-time reprint rights.

Advice "First-hand, detailed observation gives poetry authenticity and immediacy."

☑ ◎ SO TO SPEAK: A FEMINIST JOURNAL OF LANGUAGE AND ART (Specialized: women/feminism)

George Mason University, 4400 University Dr., MS 2D6, Fairfax VA 22030-4444. (703)993-3625. E-mail: sts@gmu.edu. (inquiries only). Web site: www.gmu.edu/org/sts. Established 1991. **Contact:** Gretchen Sullivan, poetry editor.

Magazine Needs *So to Speak*, published semiannually, prints "high-quality work relating to feminism, including poetry, fiction, nonfiction (including book reviews and interviews), photography, artwork, collaborations, lyrical essays, and other genre-questioning texts." Wants "poetry that speaks to and/or interconnects with issues of significance to women's lives and movements for equality." Has published poetry by Eleni Sikelianos, Michelle Tea, Marcella Durand, Jean Donnelly, Heather Fuller, and Carolyn Forché. *So to Speak* is 100-128 pages, digest-sized, photo-offset-printed, perfect-bound, with glossy cover, includes ads. Receives about 800 poems/year, accepts 10%. Press run is 1,000 (75 subscribers, 100 shelf sales); 500 distributed free to students/contributors. Subscription: $12. Sample: $7.

How to Submit Submit 3-5 poems at a time. Considers simultaneous submissions; no previously published poems. No e-mail submissions. "Please submit poems as you wish to see them in print. Be sure to include a cover letter with full contact info, publication credits, and awards received." Reads submissions August 15-October 15 and December 31-March 15. Time between acceptance and publication is 6-8 months. Seldom comments on rejected poems. Responds in 3 months if submissions are received during reading period. Pays 2 contributor's copies. Acquires one-time rights.

Contest/Award Offerings *So to Speak* holds an annual poetry contest that awards $500. Guidelines available for SASE, by e-mail, or on Web site.

☑ ◎ SONG OF THE SAN JOAQUIN (Specialized: subjects pertinent to the San Joaquin Valley)

P.O. Box 1161, Modesto CA 95353-1161. E-mail: SSJQ03psj@yahoo.com. Web site: www.Chaparral Poets.org/SSJ.html. Established 2003. **Contact:** The Editor.

Magazine Needs *Song of the San Joaquin*, published quarterly, features "subjects about or pertinent to the San Joaquin Valley of Central California. This is defined geographically as the region from Fresno to Stockton, and from the foothills on the west to those on the east." Wants all forms and styles of poetry. "Keep subject in mind." Does not want "pornographic, demeaning, vague, or trite approaches." Considers poetry by children and teens. Has published poetry by Joyce Odam, Wilma Elizabeth McDaniel, Margarita Engle, Marnelle White, Frederick Zydek, and Nancy Haskett. *Song of the San Joaquin* is 60 pages, digest-sized, direct-copied, saddle-stapled, with cardstock cover with glossy color photo. Press run is 200 (25 copies to libraries); 40 distributed free to contributors.

How to Submit Submit up to 3 poems at a time. Lines/poem: open ("however, poems under 40 lines have the best chance"). Considers previously published poems; no simultaneous submissions. Accepts e-mail submissions; no disk submissions. Cover letter is preferred. "SASE required. All submissions must be typed on one side of the page only. Proofread submissions carefully. Name, address, phone number, and e-mail address should appear on all pages. Cover letter should include any awards, honors, and previous publications for each poem, and a biographical sketch of 75 words or less." Reads submissions "periodically throughout the year." Submit seasonal poems at least 3 months in advance. Time between acceptance and publication is 3-6 months. "Poems are circulated to an editorial board of five who then decide on the final selections." Seldom comments on rejected poems. Occasionally publishes theme issues. Upcoming themes available for SASE, by e-mail, or on Web site. Guidelines available in magazine, for SASE, by e-mail, or on Web site. Responds in up to 3 months. Pays one contributor's copy. Acquires one-time rights.

Additional Information "Poets of the San Joaquin, which sponsors this publication, is a chapter of California Federation of Chaparral Poets, Inc., and publishes an annual anthology of members' works. Information available for SASE or by e-mail."

Contest/Award Offerings Poets of the San Joaquin holds an annual local young poets' contest as well as regular poetry contests. Guidelines available for SASE or by e-mail.

Advice "Know the area about which you write. Poems do not need to be agricultural or nature-oriented but should reflect the lifestyles of the California Central Valley."

◗ SOUL FOUNTAIN

90-21 Springfield Blvd., Queens Village NY 11428. (718)479-2594. E-mail: davault@aol.com. Web site: www.TheVault.org. Established 1997. **Contact:** Tone Bellizzi, editor.

Magazine Needs *Soul Fountain*, published 3 times/year, is produced by The Vault, a not-for-profit arts project of the Hope for the Children Foundation, "committed to empowering young and emerging artists of all disciplines at all levels to develop and share their talents through performance, collaboration, and networking." Prints poetry, art, photography, short fiction, and essays. Open to all. "We publish quality submitted work, and specialize in emerging voices. We favor visionary, challenging, and consciousness-expanding material." Does not want "poems about pets, nature, romantic love, or the occult. Sex and violence themes not welcome." Considers poetry by teens. *Soul Fountain* is 28 pages, magazine-sized, offset-printed, saddle-stapled. Subscription: $18. Sample: $6. Make checks payable to Hope for the Children Foundation.

How to Submit Submit 2-3 poems at a time. Lines/poem: one page maximum. Considers previously published poems and simultaneous submissions. Accepts e-mail submissions (pasted into body of message). Poems should be camera-ready. "When e-mailing a submission, it is necessary to include your mailing address. Cover letter not needed. SASE with postal mail submissions is not necessary, but $2 in postage is appreciated." Time between acceptance and publication is up to one year. Guidelines available for SASE or on Web site. Pays one contributor's copy.

◗ THE SOUTH CAROLINA REVIEW

Center for Electronic & Digital Publishing, Strode Tower Room 611, Box 340522, Clemson SC 29634-0522. (864)656-3151 or 656-5399. Fax: (864)656-1345. Web site: www.clemson.edu/caah/cedp/scrintro.htm. Established 1968. **Contact:** Wayne Chapman, editor.

Magazine Needs *The South Carolina Review*, published semiannually, is a literary magazine "recognized by the *New York Quarterly* as one of the top 20 of this type." Wants "any kind of poetry as long as it's good. Interested in seeing more traditional forms." Does not want "stale metaphors, uncertain rhythms, or lack of line integrity." Has published poetry by Stephen Cushman, Alberto Ríos, and Virgil Suárez. *The South Carolina Review* is 200 pages, digest-sized, professionally printed, flat-spined. Receives about 1,000 submissions of poetry/year, accepts about 60. Press run is 600 (400 subscribers, 250 libraries). Sample: $12.

How to Submit Submit 3-10 poems at a time. No previously published poems or simultaneous submissions. Cover letter is preferred. "Editor prefers a chatty, personal cover letter plus a list of publishing credits. Manuscript format should be according to new MLA Stylesheet." Submissions should be sent "in an 8×10 manila envelope so poems aren't creased." Do not submit during June, July, August, or December. Publishes theme issues. Responds in 2 months. Pays in contributor's copies. Staff reviews books of poetry.

☑ ◎ SOUTH DAKOTA REVIEW (Specialized: American West subjects & work by Western authors)

Dept. of English, University of South Dakota, 414 E. Clark St., Vermillion SD 57069. (605)677-5184 or 677-5966. Fax: (605)677-6409. E-mail: bbedard@usd.edu. Web site: www.usd.edu/sdreview/. Established 1963. **Contact:** Brian Bedard, editor.

Magazine Needs *South Dakota Review*, published quarterly, prints "poetry, fiction, criticism, and scholarly and personal essays. When material warrants, emphasis is on the American West; writers from the West; Western places or subjects. There are frequent issues with no geographical emphasis; periodic special issues on one theme, one place, or one writer." Wants "originality, sophistication, significance, craft—i.e., professional work." Has published poetry by Allan Safarik, Joanna Gardner, Nathaniel Hansen, and Jeanine Stevens. Press run is 500-600 (450 subscribers, half libraries). Single copy: $10; subscription: $30/year, $45/2 years. Sample: $8.

How to Submit Submit 3-5 poems at a time. No e-mail submissions. Cover letter is required. Must include SASE. Reads submissions year round. Time between acceptance and publication is up to 6 months. Sometimes comments on rejected poems. Publishes theme issues. Guidelines available for SASE or on Web site. Responds in 2-3 months ("sometimes longer if still considering manuscript for possible use in a forthcoming issue"). Pays one contributor's copy and a one-year subscription. Acquires first North American serial rights and reprint rights.

Advice "We tend to favor the narrative poem, the concrete crafted lyric, the persona poem, and the meditative place poem. Yet we try to leave some room for poems outside those parameters to keep some fresh air in our selection process."

☑ SOUTHERN HUMANITIES REVIEW

9088 Haley Center, Auburn University, Auburn AL 36849-5202. E-mail: shrengl@auburn.edu. Web site: www.auburn.edu/english/shr/home.htm. Established 1967. **Contact:** Dan Latimer and Virginia M. Kouidis, co-editors.

Magazine Needs *Southern Humanities Review*, published quarterly, is "interested in poems of any length, subject, genre. Space is limited, and brief poems are more likely to be accepted. Translations welcome, but also send written permission from the copyright holder." Has published poetry by Donald Hall, Andrew Hudgins, Margaret Gibson, Stephen Dunn, Walt McDonald, and R.T. Smith. *Southern Humanities Review* is 100 pages, digest-sized. Press run is 800. Subscription: $15/year. Sample: $5.

How to Submit Submit 3-5 poems at a time. No previously published poems or simultaneous submissions. No e-mail submissions. "Send poems in a business-sized envelope. Include SASE. Avoid sending faint computer printout." Responds in 2 months, "possibly longer in summer." Always sends prepublication galleys. Pays 2 contributor's copies. Copyright reverts to author upon publication. Reviews books of poetry in approximately 750-1,000 words. Send materials for review consideration.

Contest/Award Offerings Sponsors the Theodore Christian Hoepfner Award, a $50 prize for the best poem published in a given volume of *Southern Humanities Review*.

Advice "For beginners, we recommend study and wide reading in English and classical literature, and, of course, American literature—the old works, not just the new. We also recommend study of or exposure to a foreign language and a foreign culture. Poets need the reactions of others to their work: criticism, suggestions, discussion. A good creative writing teacher would be desirable here, and perhaps some course work, too; and then submission of work, attendance at workshops. And again, the reading: history, biography, verse, essays—all of it. We want to see poems that have gone beyond the language of slippage and easy attitudes."

✖ $☑ THE SOUTHERN REVIEW

Louisiana State University, Old President's House, Baton Rouge LA 70803. (225)578-5108. Fax: (225)578-5098. E-mail: southernreview@lsu.edu. Web site: www.lsu.edu/thesouthernreview. Established 1935 (original series), 1965 (new series). **Contact:** The Editors.

- Work published in *The Southern Review* has been included frequently in *The Best American Poetry* and *The Pushcart Prize* as well as *The Beacon's Best of 1999*.

Magazine Needs *The Southern Review*, published quarterly, prints "fiction, poetry, critical essays, and book reviews, with emphasis on contemporary literature in the U.S. and abroad. Selections are made with careful attention to craftsmanship and technique and to the seriousness of the subject matter." Wants "any variety of poetry that is well crafted, though we cannot normally accommodate excessively long poems (i.e., 10 pages and over)." Has published poetry by Mary Oliver, Sydney Lea, Madeline DeFrees, Brendan Galvin, Claudia Emerson, and Jay Rogoff. *The Southern Review* is 240 pages, digest-sized, flat-spined, with matte card cover. Receives about 6,000 poetry submissions/year. Press run is 2,900 (2,100 subscribers, 70% libraries). Subscription: $25. Sample: $8.

How to Submit Submit up to 1-4 pages of poetry at a time. No previously published poems. No fax or e-mail submissions. "We do not require a cover letter, but we prefer one giving information about the author and previous publications." Reads submissions September-May. Guidelines available for SASE or on Web site. Responds in 1-2 months. Pays $30/printed page plus 2 contributor's copies. Acquires first North American serial rights. Staff reviews books of poetry in 3,000 words, multi-book format. Send materials for review consideration.

$☑ SOUTHWEST REVIEW

Southern Methodist University, P.O. Box 750374, Dallas TX 75275-0374. (214)768-1037. Fax: (214)768-1408. E-mail: swr@mail.smu.edu. Web site: www.southwestreview.org. Established 1915. **Contact:** Willard Spiegelman, editor.

- Poetry published in *Southwest Review* has been included in *The Best American Poetry* and *The Pushcart Prize*.

Magazine Needs *Southwest Review*, published quarterly, prints fiction, essays, poetry, and occasional interviews. "We always suggest that potential contributors read several issues of the magazine to see for themselves what we like. We demand very high quality in our poems; we accept both traditional and experimental writing, but avoid unnecessary obscurity and private symbolism. We place no arbitrary limits on length but find shorter poems easier to fit into our format than longer ones. We have no specific limitations as to theme. Poems tend to be lyric and narrative free verse combining a strong voice with powerful topics or situations. Diction is accessible and content often conveys a strong sense of place." Has published poetry by Albert Goldbarth, John Hollander, Mary Jo Salter, James Hoggard, Dorothea Tanning, and Michael Rosen. *Southwest Review* is 144 pages, digest-sized, professionally printed, perfect-bound, with matte text stock cover. Receives about 1,000 poetry submissions/year, accepts about 32. Press run is 1,500 (1,000 subscribers, 600 libraries). Subscription: $24. Sample: $6.

How to Submit No previously published poems or simultaneous submissions. No fax or e-mail submissions. Manuscripts must be typed; include SASE. Guidelines available for SASE or on Web site. Responds within one month. Always sends prepublication galleys. Pays cash plus contributor's copies.

Contest/Award Offerings 1) The annual *Elizabeth Matchett Stover Memorial Award* presents $250 to the author of the best poem or groups of poems (chosen by editors) published in the preceding year. 2) The annual *Morton Marr Poetry Prize* presents 1st Prize: $1,000 and 2nd Prize: $500 for a poem by a writer who has not yet published a first book. Submit 6 poems in a "traditional" form. Guidelines available on Web site. **Deadline:** September 30.

☑ THE SOW'S EAR POETRY REVIEW

217 Brookneill Dr., Winchester VA 22602. E-mail: errol@kitenet.net. (inquiries only). Web site: www.sows-ear.kitenet.net. Established 1988. **Contact:** Kristin Zimet, submissions editor.

Magazine Needs *The Sow's Ear Poetry Review*, published quarterly, wants fine poetry of all styles and lengths. "Excellent art in black and white complements the poems. We often take more than one poem by an author we like. The 'Community of Poets' feature presents group submissions; define 'community' as broadly as you like. The 'Crossover' feature showcases works that marry the written word with another art form (for example, lyrics with music, word collages, or special calligraphy)." Has published poetry by Robert Morgan, Elizabeth Spires, Virgil Suárez, Susan Terris, and Franz Wright. *The Sow's Ear Poetry Review* is 32 pages, magazine-sized, professionally printed, saddle-stapled, with matte card cover. Receives about 3,000 poems/year, accepts about 75. Press run is 700 (600 subscribers, 15 libraries). Subscription: $20. Sample: $5. For subscriptions, contact Errol Hess, Managing Editor, 355 Mt. Lebanon Rd., Donalds SC 29638.

How to Submit Submit up to 5 poems at a time. Considers simultaneous submissions "if you tell us promptly when work is accepted elsewhere"; no previously published poems, although will consider poems from chapbooks if they were never published in a magazine. No e-mail submissions; postal submissions only. Include brief bio and SASE. Guidelines available for SASE, by e-mail, or on Web site. Responds in 3 months. Pays 2 contributor's copies. Acquires first publication rights. Inquire about reviews, interviews, and essays.

Contest/Award Offerings *The Sow's Ear* Poetry Competition and *The Sow's Ear* Chapbook Contest (see separate listings in Contests & Awards).

Advice "Four criteria help us judge the quality of submissions: 1) Does the poem make the strange familiar or the familiar strange, or both? 2) Is the form of the poem vital to its meaning? 3) Do the sounds of the poem make sense in relation to the theme? 4) Does the little story of the poem open a window on the Big Story of the human situation?"

☑ SP QUILL QUARTERLY MAGAZINE

Shadow Poetry, 1209 Milwaukee St., Excelsior Springs MO 64024. Phone/fax: (208)977-9114. E-mail: spquill@shadowpoetry.com. Web site: www.shadowpoetry.com/magazine/spquill.html. Established 2000 (Shadow Poetry Web site), 2003 (*SP Quill*). **Contact:** Marie Summers, chief editor. Poetry Editor: Andrea Dietrich.

Magazine Needs *SP Quill Quarterly Magazine* is "an interactive chapbook-style magazine for poets and writers, filled with poetry, flash fiction, book reviews, articles, contests, profiles/bios, quotes, and more." Wants high-quality poetry, flash fiction, and quotes. Does not want "anything in poor taste, or poorly crafted poetry." Considers poetry by children (parental permission required) and teens. *SP Quill Quarterly Magazine* is 52-60 pages, digest-sized, saddle-stapled, with cardstock cover with b&w artwork (cover design remains the same from issue to issue). Receives about 500 poems/quarter, accepts less than 10%. Single copy: $8 U.S., $10 international; subscription: $25/year U.S., $30/year international. Make checks/money orders payable to Shadow Poetry.

How to Submit Submit up to 3 poems at a time. Lines/poem: 3 minimum, 30 maximum. No previously published poems or simultaneous submissions. Accepts fax, e-mail, disk, and postal submissions as well as submissions through online form. Cover letter is preferred. "Name of author, street address, and e-mail address must accompany all submissions, no exceptions. A small author bio may accompany submission. If work is accepted, participants will be contacted by mail or e-mail before magazine release date." Reads submissions by the following deadlines: November 20 (Winter issue), February 28 (Spring issue), May 31 (Summer issue), and August 31 (Fall issue). Welcomes seasonal poems for the appropriate issue. Time between acceptance and publication is 3 weeks or more. "Poems are decided upon and edited by the poetry editor and chief editor. Final drafts will be e-mailed or mailed to the accepted poet." Never comments on rejected poems. Publishes special issues; "submit up to eight cinquain for a special Spring issue and/or 3 etheree for a special Fall issue. For definitions of these poetry types, please visit the Shadow Poetry Web site." Guidelines available in magazine or on Web site. Acquires first rights. Reviews books/chapbooks of poetry.

Additional Information Shadow Poetry sponsors The Little Bitty Poetry Competition, Rhyme Time Poetry Contest, Seasonal Poetry Competition, Shadow Poetry's Biannual Chapbook Competition, and *White Lotus* Haiku Competition (see separate listings in Contests & Awards).

🖾 ◻ SPEEDPOETS ZINE

86 Hawkwood St., Brisbane QLD 4122 Australia. (61)(7)3420-6092. E-mail: speedpoets@speedpoet s.org. Web site: www.speedpoets.org. Established 2002. **Contact:** Graham Nunn, editor.

Magazine Needs *SpeedPoets Zine*, published monthly, showcases "the community of poets that perform at the monthly SpeedPoets readings in Brisbane, as well as showcasing poets from all around the world." Wants "shorter, experimental pieces." Does not want long submissions. Has published poetry by Robert Smith, Steve Kilbey, Brentley Frazer, Jayne Fenton Keane, Graham Nunn, and Marie Kazalia. *SpeedPoets Zine* is 28 pages, digest-sized, photocopied, folded and stapled, with color cover. Press run is 50. Single copy: $2.50 AUD. Make checks payable to Graham Nunn.

How to Submit Submit 2 poems at a time. Lines/poem: 25 maximum. Considers previously published poems. Accepts e-mail submissions (pasted into body of message); no disk submissions. Cover letter is preferred. Reads submissions year round. Time between acceptance and publication is 2 weeks. Sometimes comments on rejected poems. Guidelines available by e-mail. Responds in 2 weeks. Rights revert to poet upon publication.

$◻ ◎ SPIDER MAGAZINE (Specialized: children ages 6-9)

Carus Publishing, 70 E. Lake St., Suite 300, Chicago IL 60601. Web site: www.cricketmag.com. Established 1994. **Contact:** Submissions Editor.

Magazine Needs *SPIDER Magazine*, published monthly, is a reading and activity magazine for children ages 6-9. "It's specially written and edited for children who have reached that amazing age when they first get excited about reading on their own." Wants "serious and humorous poetry, nonsense rhymes." *SPIDER* is 38 pages, 8×10, staple-bound. Receives more than 1,200 submissions/month, accepts 25-30. Circulation is 70,000. Subscription: $35.97/year (12 issues). Sample: $5; sample pages available on Web site.

How to Submit Submit no more than 5 poems at a time. Lines/poem: no more than 20. Considers previously published poems. Responds in 6 months. Guidelines available for SASE or on Web site. Pays up to $3/line on publications. Acquires North American publication rights for previously published poems; rights vary for unpublished poems.

Advice "Our standards are very high, and we will accept only top-quality material. Before attempting to write for *SPIDER*, be sure to familiarize yourself with this age child and with the magazine itself."

◻ SPIKY PALM

Dept. of General Academics, Texas A&M University at Galveston, P.O. Box 1675, Galveston TX 77553. E-mail: spikypalm@tamug.edu. Web site: www.tamug.edu/spikypalm. Established 2004. **Contact:** Carol Cotten and Chuck Wemple, co-editors.

Magazine Needs *Spiky Palm*, published quarterly, is open to "all forms, styles, and subject matter." Has published poetry by Alan Birkelbach, Larry Thomas, John Gorman, and Janet McCann. *Spiky Palm* is 4 pages, magazine-sized (11×17 center-folded to $8\frac{1}{2} \times 11$), photocopied, with 70 lb. cover. (Also available as PDF download from Web site.) Receives about 1,000 poems/year, accepts about 6%. Press run is 1,000-1,500 (90 subscribers); 25 distributed free to bookstores, coffeehouses, and by request. Sample: free to anyone who sends a SASE or by download from Web site.

How to Submit Submit up to 5 poems at a time. Lines/poem: "will consider all poems, but prefer poems under 50 lines.'' Considers previously published poems and simultaneous submissions. Accepts e-mail (pasted into body of message or as attachment) and disk submissions. ''Either format is okay, but document must be in Microsoft Word.'' Cover letter is preferred. ''Please submit two copies of each poem along with a #10 SASE; on a separate page include name, address, e-mail, a brief three-line biography, and titles of submissions.'' Reads submissions year round. Submit seasonal poems 4 months in advance. Time between acceptance and publication is up to 3 months. ''Co-editors read separately and negotiate choices. One editor reads copies with names removed.'' Sometimes comments on rejected poems. Guidelines available in magazine, for SASE, by e-mail, or on Web site. Responds in 1-2 months. Pays 2 contributor's copies. Acquires one-time rights. Rights revert to poet upon publication.

◙ SPILLWAY

P.O. Box 7887, Huntington Beach CA 92615-7887. (714)968-0905. E-mail: spillway@tebotbach.org. Web site: www.tebotbach.org. Established 1991. **Contact:** Mifanwy Kaiser, publisher/senior editor; J.D. Lloyd, editor; or Catherine Turner, managing editor.

Magazine Needs *Spillway*, published annually in August, celebrates ''writing's diversity and power to affect our lives.'' Open to all voices, schools, and tendencies. ''We publish poetry, translations, reviews, essays, and black-and-white photography.'' Has published poetry by David Lehman, Richard Jones, Virgil Suárez, Gerry Locklin, Charles Harper Webb, and Eleanor Wilner. *Spillway* is about 176 pages, digest-sized, attractively printed, perfect-bound, with 2-color or 4-color card cover. Press run is 2,000. Single copy: $11; subscription: $20 for 2 issues, $32 for 4 issues. All prices include s&h. Make checks payable to *Spillway*.

How to Submit Submit 3-6 poems at a time (6 pages maximum total). Considers previously published poems (''only in rare instances'') and simultaneous submissions (''say where also submitted''). Accepts e-mail submissions; no disk submissions. Cover letter is required. Include brief bio and SASE. ''No cute bios.'' Reads submissions year round. Responds in up to 6 months. Pays one contributor's copy. Acquires one-time rights. Reviews books of poetry in 500-2,500 words. Send materials for review consideration.

◙ SPINNING JENNY

% Black Dress Press, P.O. Box 1373, New York NY 10276. Web site: www.spinning-jenny.com. Established 1994. **Contact:** C.E. Harrison, editor.

Magazine Needs *Spinning Jenny*, published once/year in the fall (usually September), has published poetry by Tina Cane, Kaya Oakes, Tony Tost, and Ian Randall Wilson. *Spinning Jenny* is 96 pages, digest-sized, perfect-bound, with heavy card cover. ''We accept less than 5% of unsolicited submissions.'' Press run is 1,000. Single copy: $8; subscription: $15 for 2 issues.

How to Submit Submit up to 6 poems at a time. No previously published poems or simultaneous submissions. Accepts e-mail submissions (pasted into body of message, no attachments; see Web site for address). Reads submissions September 15-May 15 only. Seldom comments on rejected poems. Guidelines available for SASE, by e-mail, or on Web site. Responds within 4 months. Pays 3 contributor's copies. Authors retain rights.

⊠ ◙ ◎ SPITBALL: THE LITERARY BASEBALL MAGAZINE (Specialized: writing about baseball)

5560 Fox Rd., Cincinnati OH 45239. Web site: www.angelfire.com/oh5/spitball. Established 1981. **Contact:** Mike Shannon, editor-in-chief.

Magazine Needs *Spitball: The Literary Baseball Magazine*, published biannually, is ''a unique magazine devoted to poetry, fiction, and book reviews exclusively about baseball. Newcomers are very welcome, but remember that you have to know the subject; we do, and our readers do. Perhaps a good place to start for beginners is one's personal reactions to the game, a game, a player, etc., and take it from there." **Writers submitting to *Spitball* for the first time must buy a sample copy (waived for subscribers).** "This is a one-time-only fee, which we regret, but economic reality dictates that we insist those who wish to be published in *Spitball* help support it, at least at this minimum level." *Spitball* is 96 pages, digest-sized, computer-typeset, perfect-bound. Receives about 1,000 submissions/year, accepts about 40. Press run is 1,000 (750 subscribers, 25 libraries). Subscription: $12. Sample: $6.

How to Submit Submit a "batch" of poems at a time ("we prefer to use several of same poet in an issue rather than a single poem"). Lines/poem: open. No previously published poems or simultaneous submissions. Cover letter is required. Include brif bio and SASE. "Many times we are able to publish accepted work almost immediately." Pays 2 contributor's copies.

Additional Information "All material published in *Spitball* will be automatically considered for inclusion in the next *Best of Spitball* anthology."

Contest/Award Offerings 1) Poems submitted to *Spitball* will be considered automatically for Poem of the Month, to appear on the Web site. 2) "We sponsor the Casey Award (for best baseball book of the year) and hold the Casey Awards Banquet in late February or early March. Any chapbook of baseball poetry should be sent to us for consideration for the 'Casey' plaque that we award to the winner each year."

Advice "Take the subject seriously. We do. In other words, get a clue (if you don't already have one) about the subject and about the poetry that has already been done and published about baseball. Learn from it—think about what you can add to the canon that is original and fresh—and don't assume that just anybody with the feeblest of efforts can write a baseball poem worthy of publication. And most importantly, stick with it. Genius seldom happens on the first try."

SPLIZZ

4 St. Marys Rise, Burry Port, Carms SA16 0SH Wales. E-mail: splizzmag@yahoo.co.uk. Established 1993. **Contact:** Amanda Morgan, editor.

Magazine Needs *Splizz*, published quarterly, features poetry, prose, reviews of contemporary music, and background to poets. Wants "any kind of poetry. We have no restrictions regarding style, length, subjects." Does not want "anything racist or homophobic." Has published Colin Cross (UK), Anders Carson (Canada), Paul Truttman (U.S.), Jan Hansen (Portugal), and Gregory Arena (Italy). *Splizz* is 60-64 pages, A5, saddle-stapled, includes ads. Receives about 200-300 poems/year, accepts about 90%. Press run is 150 (35 subscribers). Single copy: £2 UK, 6 IRCs or $7 elsewhere; subscription: £8 UK, 24 IRCs or $28 elsewhere. Make checks payable to Amanda Morgan (British checks only).

How to Submit Submit 5 poems at a time. No previously published poems or simultaneous submissions. Accepts e-mail submissions (as attachment). Cover letter is required. Include short bio. Typed submissions preferred. Name and address must be included on each page of submitted work. Include SAE with IRCs. Time between acceptance and publication is 4 months. Often comments on rejected poems. **Charges criticism fee.** "Just enclose SAE/IRC for response, and allow 1-2 months for delivery. For those sending IRCs, please ensure that they have been correctly stamped by your post office." Guidelines available in magazine, for SASE (or SAE and IRC), or by e-mail. Responds in 2 months. Sometimes sends prepublication galleys. Reviews books/chapbooks of poetry or other magazines in 50-300 words. Send materials for review consideration. E-mail for further enquiries.

Advice "Beginners seeking to have their work published, send your work to *Splizz*, as we specialize in giving new poets a chance to see their work published alongside more established writers."

THE SPOON RIVER POETRY REVIEW

4241/English Dept., Illinois State University, Normal IL 61790-4241. Web site: www.litline.org/spoon. Established 1976. **Contact:** Bruce Guernsey and Tara Reeser, editors.

Magazine Needs *The Spoon River Poetry Review*, published semiannually, features "newer and well-known poets from around the country and world." Also features one Illinois poet per issue at length for the magazine's Illinois Poet Series. Wants "interesting and compelling poetry that operates beyond the ho-hum, so-what level, in any form or style, about anything; language that is fresh, energetic, committed; a poetics aware of itself and of context." Also uses translations of poetry. Has published poetry by Stuart Dybek, Brad Telford, Phyllis Stowell, Dorothea Grünzweig, and Alicia Ostriker. *The Spoon River Poetry Review* is 128 pages, digest-sized, laser-set, with card cover, includes ads. Receives about 3,000 poems/month, accepts 1%. Press run is 1,500 (800 subscribers, 100 libraries). Subscription: $16. Sample: $10 (includes guidelines).

How to Submit Submit 3-5 poems at a time. No simultaneous submissions "unless we are notified immediately if a submission is accepted elsewhere. Include name and address on every poem." Do not submit mss April 15-September 15. Comments on rejected poems "many times, if a poet is promising." Guidelines available in magazine or on Web site. Responds in 3 months. Pays a year's subscription. Acquires first North American serial rights. Reviews books of poetry. Send materials for review consideration.

Contest/Award Offerings Sponsors the Editor's Prize Contest for previously unpublished work. One poem will be awarded $1,000, and 2 runners-up will receive $100 each. Winning poem, runners-up, and honorable mentions will be published in the fall issue of *The Spoon River Poetry Review*. Entries must be previously unpublished. **Entry fee:** $16 (includes one-year subscription). **Deadline:** April 15. Guidelines available for SASE or on Web site. 2005 winner was Salita S. Bryant.

Advice "Read. Workshop with poets who are better than you. Subscribe to at least five literary magazines per year, especially those you'd like to be published in."

SPOUT MAGAZINE

P.O. Box 581067, Minneapolis MN 55458-1067. E-mail: spoutpress@hotmail.com. Web site: www.spoutpress.com. Established 1989. **Contact:** Michelle Filkins, poetry editor.

Magazine Needs *Spout*, published approximately 3 times/year, aims to provide "a paper community of unique expression." Wants "poetry of the imagination; poetry that surprises. We enjoy the surreal, the forceful, the political, the expression of confusion." No light verse, archaic forms or language. Has published poetry by Gillian McCain, Larissa Szporluk, Matt Hart, Joanna Fuhrman, Josie Rawson, and Richard Siken. *Spout* is 40-60 pages, saddle-stapled, with cardstock or glossy cover (different color each issue). Receives about 400-450 poems/year, accepts about 10%. Press run is 200-250 (35-40 subscribers, 100-150 shelf sales). Single copy: $4; subscription: $15.

How to Submit Submit up to 5 poems at a time. Considers previously published poems and simultaneous submissions. Accepts e-mail submissions. Cover letter is preferred. Time between acceptance and publication is 2-3 months. "Poems are reviewed by two of three editors; those selected for final review are read again by all three." Seldom comments on rejected poems. Guidelines available for SASE or on Web site. Responds in 4 months. Pays one contributor's copy.

Advice "Read a copy of the magazine to understand our editorial biases."

SPRING: THE JOURNAL OF THE E.E. CUMMINGS SOCIETY (Specialized: poems in the spirit of E.E. Cummings; submissions from subscribers only)

129 Lake Huron Hall, Grand Valley State University, Allendale MI 49401-9403. (616)331-3071. Fax: (616)331-3430. E-mail: websterm@gvsu.edu. Web site: www.gvsu.edu/english/cummings/Index.html. **Contact:** Michael Webster, editor.

Magazine Needs *Spring: The Journal of the E.E. Cummings Society*, published annually (usually in the fall), is designed "to maintain and broaden the audience for E.E. Cummings, and to explore various facets of his life and art." **Contributors are required to subscribe.** Wants poems in the spirit of Cummings, primarily poems of one page or less. Does not want "amateurish" work. Has published poetry by John Tagliabue, Jacqueline Vaught Brogan, and Gerald Locklin. *Spring* is about

180 pages, digest-sized, offset-printed, perfect-bound, with light cardstock cover. Press run is 500 (200 subscribers, 25 libraries, 300 shelf sales). Subscription or sample: $17.50.

How to Submit No previously published poems or simultaneous submissions. Accepts fax and e-mail (as attachment) submissions. Cover letter is required. Reads submissions May-August only. Seldom comments on rejected poems. Guidelines available for SASE. Responds in 6 months. Pays one contributor's copy.

$☐ ◎ ST. ANTHONY MESSENGER (Specialized: Catholic; spirituality/inspirational)

28 W. Liberty St., Cincinnati OH 45202-6498. Fax: (513)241-0399. Web site: www.americancatholic .org. **Contact:** Christopher Heffron, poetry editor.

- *St. Anthony Messenger* poetry occasionally receives awards from the Catholic Press Association Annual Competition.

Magazine Needs *St. Anthony Messenger*, published monthly, is a mgazine for Catholic families, mostly with children in grade school, high school, or college. Some issues feature a poetry page that uses poems appropriate for their readership. Poetry submissions are always welcome despite limited need. "We seek to publish accessible poetry of high quality. Spiritual/inspirational in nature a plus, but not required." Considers poetry by young writers, ages 14 and older. *St. Anthony Messenger* is 56-pages. Press run 310,000. Sample: free for 9×12 SASE.

How to Submit Submit "a few" poems at a time. Lines/poem: under 25. No previously published poems. Accepts fax and e-mail submissions. "Do not send us your entire collection of poetry. Poems must be original . Please include your social security number with your submission." Submit seasonal poems several months in advance. Guidelines available for SASE, by fax, or on Web site. Pays $2/line on acceptance plus 2 contributor's copies. Acquires first worldwide serial rights.

⊕ $☑ STAPLE

114-116 St. Stephen's Rd., Sneinton, Nottingham NG2 4FJ England. Established 1982 (redesigned 2001). **Contact:** Wayne Burrows, editor.

Magazine Needs *Staple*, published 3 times/year, accepts "poetry, short fiction, and articles about the writing process and general culture in relation to writing." *Staple* is about 100 pages, perfect-bound. Press run is 500 (350 subscribers). Single copy: £5; subscription: £15/year. Sample: £3.50 (back issue).

How to Submit Submit 6 poems at a time. No previously published poems or simultaneous submissions. Cover letter is preferred. Include SAE and 2 IRCs. Reads submissions by the following deadlines: end of March, July, and November. Sometimes comments on rejected poems. Responds in up to 3 months. Pays £5/poem.

$◎ STAR*LINE (Specialized: science fiction, fantasy, horror)

Science Fiction Poetry Association, 1412 NE 35th St., Ocala FL 34479. E-mail: SFPASL@aol.com. Web site: www.sfpoetry.com. Established 1978. **Contact:** Marge Simon, editor.

Magazine Needs *Star*Line*, published bimonthly by the Science Fiction Poetry Association (see separate listing in Organizations), is a newsletter and poetry magazine. "Open to all forms—free verse, traditional forms, light verse—as long as your poetry shows skilled use of the language and makes a good use of science fiction, science, fantasy, horror, or speculative motifs." Considers poetry by children and teens. Has published poetry by Lawrence Schimel, Kendall Evans, Charlie Jacob, Terry A. Garey, and Timons Esaias. *Star*Line* is digest-sized, photocopied, saddle-stapled. Receives about 300-400 submissions/year, accepts about 80. Has 250 subscribers (one library). Subscription: $13 for 6 issues. Sample: $2. Send requests for copies/membership information to Helena Bell, SFPA Treasurer, 1225 West Freeman St., Apt. #12, Carbondale IL 62901. Send submissions to *Star*Line* only.

How to Submit Submit 3-5 poems at a time. Lines/poem: preferably under 50. No simultaneous submissions. Accepts e-mail submissions (preferred; pasted into body of message, no attachments). Cover letter is preferred (brief). Submissions must be typed. Responds in one month. Pays $3 for 10 lines or less; $5 for 11-50 lines; 10 cents/line rounded to the next dollar for 51+ lines. Buys first North American serial rights. Reviews books of poetry "within the science fiction/fantasy field" in 50-500 words. Open to unsolicited reviews. Send materials for review consideration.

Also Offers The Association also publishes *The Rhysling Anthology*, a yearly collection of nominations from the membership "for the best science fiction/fantasy long and short poetry of the preceding year."

$ ▣ ◐ STICKMAN REVIEW: AN ONLINE LITERARY JOURNAL

721 Oakwater Lane, Port Orange FL 32128. E-mail: poetry@stickmanreview.com. Web site: www.stickmanreview.com. Established 2001.

Magazine Needs *Stickman Review*, published semiannually online, is dedicated to printing great poetry, fiction, nonfiction, and artwork. Wants poetry "that is literary in intent; no restrictions on form, subject matter, or style." Does not typically want "rhyming poetry."

How to Submit Submit 5 poems at a time. Considers simultaneous submissions; no previously published poems. Accepts e-mail submissions only (as attachment in Word, .rtf or .txt, or pasted into body of message); no postal submissions. Cover letter is preferred. Reads submissions year round. Time between acceptance and publication is 4-6 months. "Currently, the editors-in-chief review all submissions." Sometimes comments on rejected poems. Guidelines available on Web site. Responds in up to 4 months. Pays $10/poem, up to $20/author. Acquires first rights.

Advice "Keep writing and submitting. A rejection is not necessarily a reflection upon the quality of your work. Be persistent, trust your instincts, and sooner or later, good things will come."

Ⓝ ◐ ◎ STILL CRAZY (Specialized: writing by & about people over 50)

271 Chriswood Ct., Columbus OH 43235. E-mail: bkussow@hotmail.com. Web site: coming soon. Established 2007. **Contact:** Barbara Kussow.

Magazine Needs *Still Crazy*, published annually, prints "poetry, short stories, and some short nonfiction pieces by and about people over fifty years of age." Wants "poems that tell a story." Does not want "rhyming poetry, or poetry that is too sentimental." *Still Crazy* is magazine-sized. Single copy: $8; subscription: $10/year. Make checks payable to Barbara Kussow.

How to Submit Submit 3-5 poems at a time. Lines/poem: 30 maximum. Considers previously published poems and simultaneous submissions. Accepts e-mail submissions only (as attachment). Cover letter is preferred. Reads submissions year round. Time between acceptance and publication is one year. Sometimes comments on rejected poems. Sometimes publishes theme issues. Guidelines available by e-mail. Responds in 6 months. Sometimes sends prepublication galleys. Pays one contributor's copy. Acquires one-time rights. Rights revert to poet upon publication.

$ ◐ ◎ STONE SOUP, THE MAGAZINE BY YOUNG WRITERS AND ARTISTS (Specialized: poetry by/for children 13 or younger)

Submissions Dept., P.O. Box 83, Santa Cruz CA 95063. (831)426-5557. Fax: (831)426-1161. E-mail: editor@stonesoup.com. Web site: www.stonesoup.com. Established 1973. **Contact:** Ms. Gerry Mandel, editor.

• *Stone Soup* has received Parents' Choice and Edpress Golden Lamp Honor Awards.

Magazine Needs *Stone Soup*, published 6 times/year, showcases writing and art by children ages 13 and under. Wants free verse poetry. Does not want rhyming poetry, haiku, or cinquain. *Stone Soup* is 48 pages, 7×10, professionally printed in color on heavy stock, saddle-stapled, with coated cover with full-color illustration. Receives 5,000 poetry submissions/year, accepts about 12. Press run is 20,000 (14,000 subscribers, 5,000 shelf sales, 1,000 other). Subscription: membership in the Children's Art Foundation includes a subscription, $34/year. Sample: $5.

How to Submit No simultaneous submissions. No e-mail submissions. "Submissions can be any number of pages, any format. Include name, age, home address, and phone number. Don't include SASE; we respond only to those submissions under consideration and cannot return manuscripts." Guidelines available for SASE, by e-mail, or on Web site. Responds in up to 6 weeks. Pays $40, a certificate, and 2 contributor's copies plus discounts. Acquires all rights. Returns rights upon request. Open to reviews by children.

◻ THE STORYTELLER

2441 Washington Rd., Maynard AR 72444. (870)647-2137. E-mail: storyteller1@hightowercom.com. Web site: www.freewebs.com/fossilcreek. Established 1996. **Contact:** Regina Williams, editor.

Magazine Needs *The Storyteller*, published quarterly, "is geared to, but not limited to, new writers and poets." Wants "any form, any subject, any style, but must have a meaning. Do not throw words together and call it a poem." Does not want "explicit sex, violence, horror, or explicit language. I would like it to be understood that I have young readers, ages 9-18." Considers poetry by children and teens. Has published poetry by Patrick Lobrutto, Bryan Byrd, and Gerald Zipper. *The Storyteller* is 72 pages, magazine-sized, desktop-published, with slick cover with original pen & ink drawings, includes ads. Receives about 300 poems/year, accepts about 40%. Press run is 700 (more than 600 subscribers). Single copy: $6 U.S., $8 Canada and foreign; subscription: $20 U.S., $24 Canada & foreign.

How to Submit Submit 3 poems at a time. Lines/poem: up to 40. Considers previously published poems and simultaneous submissions, "but must state where and when poetry first appeared." No e-mail submissions; postal submissions only. "However, if accepted, you will be asked to send material by e-mail, if possible." Cover letter is preferred. Manuscripts must be typed and double-spaced. "Make sure name and address are on each page submitted. We are getting many submissions without names." Time between acceptance and publication is 9 months. "Poems are read and discussed by staff." Sometimes comments on rejected poems. Guidelines available for SASE or on Web site. Responds in one week. Pays ¼ cent/word; does not provide contributor's copies. Acquires first or one-time rights. Reviews books/chapbooks of poetry by subscribers only. Send materials for review consideration to Jamie Johnson, assistant editor.

Contest/Award Offerings Sponsors a quarterly contest. "Readers vote on their favorite poems. Winners receive a copy of the magazine and a certificate. We also nominate for the Pushcart Prize." See www.storyteller1.UPCsites.org. for yearly contest announcements and winners.

Advice "Be professional. Do not send four or five poems on one page. Send us poetry written from the heart."

◻ STRAYLIGHT

University of Wisconsin-Parkside, English Dept., 900 Wood Rd., P.O. Box 2000, Kenosha WI 53141. (262)595-2139. Fax: (262)595-2271. E-mail: straylight@litspot.net. Web site: www.litspot.net/straylight. Established 2005. **Contact:** Poetry Editor.

Magazine Needs *Straylight*, published semiannually, seeks "poetry of almost any style as long as it's inventive." *Straylight* is digest-sized. Single copy: $4; subscription: $7. Make checks payable to *Straylight*.

How to Submit Submit 3-6 poems at a time. No previously published poems or simultaneous submissions. Accepts e-mail submissions (preferred, as .rtf or .doc attachment); no fax or disk submissions. Cover letter is required. "Include contact information on all pages of submission." Reads submissions August 15-April 15. Submit seasonal poems 3 months in advance. Time between acceptance and publication is 6 months. Never comments on rejected poems. Sometimes publishes theme issues. Upcoming themes available on Web site. Guidelines available for SASE or on Web site. Responds in 2 months. Pays 2 contributor's copies. Acquires first North American serial rights. Rights revert to poet upon publication.

Advice "We suggest you buy a sample copy to get a feel for what we publish."

⊕ ▣ ⊘ STRIDE MAGAZINE

Stride Publications, 4b Tremayne Close, Devoran, Cornwall TR3 6QE England. E-mail: submissions @stridemagazine.co.uk (submissions) or editor@stridemagazine.co.uk (inquiries). Web site: www .stridemagazine.co.uk. Established 1982. **Contact:** Rupert Loydell, editor.

Magazine Needs *Stride Magazine*, published online, is "a gathering of new poetry, short prose, articles, news, reviews, and whatever takes our fancy. *Stride* is regularly updated with new contributions."

How to Submit Submit 4-5 poems at a time. Accepts e-mail submissions (pasted into body of message; no attachments). "Attachments or snail mail without SAEs will not be considered or replied to."

Additional Information "At the moment, **Stride Publications is unable to consider any manuscript submissions.**" Check www.stridebooks.co.uk for updates.

▢ ◎ STRUGGLE: A MAGAZINE OF PROLETARIAN REVOLUTIONARY LITERATURE (Specialized: working class, social issues)

P.O. Box 13261, Detroit MI 48213-0261. (313)273-9039. E-mail: timhall11@yahoo.com. Web site: www.strugglemagazine.net. Established 1985. **Contact:** Tim Hall, editor.

Magazine Needs *Struggle: A Magazine of Proletarian Revolutionary Literature*, published quarterly, focuses "on the struggle of the working people and all oppressed against the rich, dealing with such issues as racism, poverty, women's rights, aggressive wars, workers' struggle for jobs and job security, the overall struggle for a non-exploitative society, a genuine socialism." The poetry and songs printed are "generally short, any style; subject matter must criticize or fight—explicitly or implicitly—against the rule of the billionaires. We welcome experimentation devoted to further-ing such content. We are open to both subtlety and direct statement." Has published poetry by Luis Cuauhtemoc Berriozabal, J.L. Torres, Niki Bell de Castenon, Bob Vance, Sreeman Barua, and Chicago Red (Albert Thomas Coleman). *Struggle* is 36 pages, digest-sized, photocopied. Subscrip-tion: $10/year (4 issues). Sample: $3. Make checks payable to "Tim Hall—Special Account."

How to Submit Submit up to 8 poems at a time. Accepts e-mail submissions (pasted into body of message, no attachments), but prefers postal mail. "Writers must include SASE. Name and address must appear on the opening page of each poem." Accepted work usually appears in the next or following issue. Comments on rejected poems "with every submission." Responds in 4 months, if possible, but often becomes backlogged. Pays one contributor's copy. "If you are unwilling to have your poetry published on our Web site, please inform us."

Advice "Show passion and fire. Humor also welcome. Prefer powerful, colloquial language over academic timidity. Look to Neruda, Lorca, Bly, Whitman, Braithwaite, Tupac Shakur, Muriel Ru-keyser. Experimental, traditional forms both welcome. Especially favor: works reflecting rebellion by the working people against the rich; works against racism, sexism, militarism, imperialism; works critical of our exploitative culture; works showing a desire for—or fantasy of—a non-exploit-ative society; works attacking the Republican 'anti-terrorism' war frenzy and the Democrats' surren-der to it."

⊕ ⊘ ◎ STUDIO, A JOURNAL OF CHRISTIANS WRITING (Specialized: Christian; spirituality)

727 Peel St., Albury NSW 2640 Australia. Phone/fax: (61)(2)6021-1135. E-mail: studio00@bigpond. net.au. Established 1980. **Contact:** Paul Grover, publisher.

Magazine Needs *Studio, A Journal of Christians Writing*, published quarterly, prints "poetry and prose of literary merit, offering a venue for previously published, new, and aspiring writers, and seeking to create a sense of community among Christians writing." Also publishes occasional articles as well as news and reviews of writing, writers, and events of interest to members. Wants "shorter pieces [of poetry] but with no specification as to form or length (necessarily less than 200 lines), subject matter, style, or purpose. People who send material should be comfortable being published under this banner: *Studio, A Journal of Christians Writing.*" Has published poetry by John Foulcher, Les Murray, and other Australian poets. *Studio* is 36 pages, digest-sized, professionally printed on high-quality recycled paper, saddle-stapled, with matte card cover. Press run is 300 (all subscriptions). Subscription: $60 AUD for overseas members. Sample: $10 AUD (airmail to U.S.).

How to Submit Lines/poem: less than 200. Considers simultaneous submissions. Cover letter is required. Include brief details of previous publishing history, if any. SAE with IRC required. "Submissions must be typed and double-spaced on one side of A4 white paper. Name and address must appear on the reverse side of each page submitted." Response time is 2 months. Time between acceptance and publication is 9 months. Pays one contributor's copy. Acquires first Australian rights. Reviews books of poetry in 250 words, single-book format. Send materials for review consideration.

Contest/Award Offerings Conducts a biannual poetry and short story contest.

Advice "The trend in Australia is for imagist poetry and poetry exploring the land and the self. Reading the magazine gives the best indication of style and standard, so send for a sample copy before sending your poetry. Keep writing, and we look forward to hearing from you."

◪ STUDIO ONE

Mary Commons, College of St. Benedict, St. Joseph MN 56374. E-mail: studio1@csbsju.edu. Web site: http://clubs.csbsju.edu/studio1. Established 1976. **Contact:** Editor (changes yearly).

Magazine Needs *Studio One*, published annually in May, is a "literary and visual arts magazine designed as a forum for local, regional, and national poets/writers. No specifications regarding form, subject matter, or style of poetry submitted." Considers poetry by children and teens. Has published poetry by Bill Meissner, Eva Hooker, and Larry Schug. *Studio One* is 50-80 pages, typeset, with soft cover. Receives 600-800 submissions/year. No subscriptions, but a sample copy can be obtained by sending a self-addressed, stamped manilla envelope and $6 for p&h. Make checks payable to *Studio One*.

How to Submit Submit no more than 5 poems at a time. Lines/poem: "poetry no more than 2 pages stands a better chance of publication." Considers simultaneous submissions; no previously published poems. Accepts e-mail submissions (pasted into body of message); "clearly show page breaks and indentations." Reads submissions by March 1 deadline for spring publication. Seldom comments on rejected poems.

◖ SULPHUR RIVER LITERARY REVIEW

P.O. Box 19228, Austin TX 78760-9228. (512)292-9456. Established 1978, re-established 1987. **Contact:** James Michael Robbins, editor/publisher.

Magazine Needs *Sulphur River Literary Review*, published semiannually in March and September, prints poetry, prose, and artwork. "No restrictions except quality." Does not want poetry that is "trite or religious, or verse that does not incite thought." Has published poetry by Carol Frith, Ken Meisel, Diane Shipley DeCillis, George Gott, E.G. Burrows, and Robert Wynne. *Sulphur River* is digest-sized, perfect-bound, with glossy cover. Receives about 4,000 poems/year, accepts 2%. Press run is 350 (200 subscribers, 100 shelf sales). Subscription: $12. Sample: $7.

How to Submit No previously published poems or simultaneous submissions. Responds in one month. Always sends prepublication galleys. Pays 2 contributor's copies.

Additional Information *Sulphur River* also publishes full-length volumes of poetry.

Advice "Read everything."

$⬛ THE SUN

107 N. Roberson St., Chapel Hill NC 27516. Web site: www.thesunmagazine.org. Established 1974. **Contact:** Sy Safransky, editor.

Magazine Needs *The Sun*, published monthly, is "noted for honest, personal work that's not too obscure or academic. We avoid traditional, rhyming poetry, as well as limericks and haiku. We're open to almost anything else: free verse, prose poems, short and long poems." Has published poetry by Ellen Bass, Christopher Bursk, Steve Kowit, Alison Luterman, Kim Stafford, and Janine Pommy Vega. *The Sun* is 48 pages, magazine-sized, offset-printed on 50 lb. paper, saddle-stapled. Press run is 80,000 (70,000 subscribers, 500 libraries). Receives 3,000 submissions of poetry/year, accepts about 30. Subscription: $36. Sample: $5.

How to Submit Submit up to 6 poems at a time. Considers previously published poems; no simultaneous submissions. "Poems should be typed and accompanied by a cover letter and SASE." Guidelines available for SASE or on Web site. Responds within 3-6 months. Pays $75-250 on publication plus contributor's copies and subscription. Acquires first serial or one-time rights.

⬛ ◯ SUNKEN LINES

E-mail: dogger@sunkenlines.com. Web site: www.sunkenlines.com. Established 2005. **Contact:** Dogger Banks, poetry editor.

Magazine Needs *Sunken Lines*, published quarterly online, is a magazine of poetry, fiction, essays, and artwork "intended as a forum for talented writers looking for more exposure, and as entertainment for our readers. We also print an annual 'best of' edition." Wants "poems that evoke a strong response in the reader, whether it be laughter, empathy, the conjuring of a strong image, or admiration of a witty line. Formal or (accessible) free verse." Does not want "poems that are excessively religious, offensive, or miserable." Has published poetry by Larry Rapant, Tony Gruenewald, Suzanne Harvey, Anna Evans, Paul Lench, and Bruce Niedt. *Sunken Lines* (the print annual) is 24 pages, A4-sized, laser-printed, saddle-stapled. Receives about 500 poems/year, accepts about 20%. Press run is 150. Single copy: $5. Make checks payable to R. Grainger.

How to Submit Submit up to 5 poems at a time. Lines/poem: 40 maximum. Considers simultaneous submissions; no previously published poems. Accepts e-mail submissions (pasted into body of message or as attachment in MS Word or RTF format); no disk submissions. Cover letter is required. "Please be prepared to supply a short biography and optional photo upon notification of acceptance." Reads submissions year round. Time between acceptance and publication is up to 3 months. Poems are circulated to an editorial board. Sometimes comments on rejected poems. Guidelines available on Web site. Responds in one month. Acquires one-time rights. Rights revert to poet upon publication.

Advice "Check out current and back issues on Web site."

⬛ SUNSTONE

343 N. Third W., Salt Lake City UT 84103-1215. (801)355-5926. Established 1974. **Contact:** Dixie Partridge, poetry editor.

Magazine Needs *Sunstone*, published 5 times/year, prints "scholarly articles of interest to an open, Mormon audience; personal essays; fiction and poetry." Wants "both lyric and narrative poetry that engages the reader with fresh, strong images, skillful use of language, and a strong sense of voice and/or place." Does not want "didactic poetry, sing-song rhymes, or in-process work." Has published poetry by Susan Howe, Anita Tanner, Robert Parham, Ryan G. Van Cleave, Robert Rees, and Virgil Suárez. *Sunstone* is 80 pages, magazine-sized, professionally printed, saddle-stapled, with semi-glossy paper cover. Receives more than 500 poems/year, accepts 40-50. Press run is 5,000 (4,000 subscribers, 300 libraries, 700 shelf sales). Subscription: $36/6 issues. Sample: $8 postpaid.

How to Submit Submit up to 5 poems at a time. Lines/poem: 40 maximum. No previously published poems or simultaneous submissions. Include name and address on each poem. Time between acceptance and publication is 2 years or less. Seldom comments on rejected poems. Guidelines available for SASE. Responds in 3 months. Pays 5 contributor's copies. Acquires first North American serial rights.

Advice "Poems should not sound like a rewording of something heard before. Be original; pay attention to language, sharp imagery. Contents should deepen as the poem progresses. We've published poems rooted strongly in place, narratives seeing life from another time or culture, poems on religious belief or doubt—a wide range of subject matter."

⊙ ◎ SUPERIOR CHRISTIAN NEWS (Specialized: Christian; translations into English; Rocky Mountain West)

Superior Poetry Press, P.O. Box 424, Superior MT 59872. Established 1995. **Contact:** Ed and Guna Chaberek, editors.

Magazine Needs *Superior Christian News*, published quarterly, prints "the best and most interesting of new Christian poets, as well as mainstream poets, we can find. Also, we encourage lively translation into English from any language." Wants "Christian, Western, or humorous poetry; translations." Considers poetry by children and teens; the only restriction is quality, not age. Has published poetry by Bob Kimm, Dr. Kelley White, John Grey, makyo, and Charles L. Wright. *Superior Christian News* is 12-24 pages, digest-sized, photocopied. Receives about 1,500 poems/year, accepts 5-10%. Press run is 100 (50 subscribers); 5 distributed free to libraries. Single copy: $2; subscription: $6/4 issues.

How to Submit Submit 3-5 poems at a time. Lines/poem: 40 maximum. No previously published poems or simultaneous submissions (unless stated). Cover letter is preferred. Include short bio. Time between acceptance and publication is 3 months. Seldom comments on rejected poems. Guidelines available for SASE. Responds in one week. Pays one contributor's copy. Acquires first rights.

Additional Information *Superior Christian News* is now repositoried at the University of Wisconsin (Madison) Memorial Library.

Advice "Original—be original."

⊠ ▣ ◎ SWELL (Specialized: gay/lesbian/bisexual/transgendered)

E-mail: swelleditor@gmail.com. Web site: www.swellzine.com. Established 1980. **Contact:** Kevin Standifer, editor.

Magazine Needs *Swell*, published quarterly online by NewTown Writers (see separate listing in Organizations), aims "to reach beyond the traditional boundaries of the printed word, exploring the limits of form, structure, and content, while giving a voice to emerging writers." Wants "work that reflects a spectrum of perspectives as diverse as the community from which it was born. Ideal publication candidates approach GLBT issues in a fresh way or present universal topics from a unique point of view."

How to Submit Lines/poem: no works over 3,000 words total. Welcomes multiple submissions as long as the total submitted is under the maximum word count. Accepts e-mail submissions only (as attachment in Word). Responds in 1-2 months. Rights revert to poet upon publication.

⊠ ⊕ $⊙ TAKAHE

P.O. Box 13 335, Christchurch 8001 New Zealand. (64)(3)359-8133. Web site: www.takahemagazin e.ne1.net. Established 1990. **Contact:** James Norcliffe, poetry editor.

Magazine Needs *Takahe*, published 3-4 times/year, features stories and poetry by both established and emerging writers. "While insisting on correct British spelling (or recognized spellings in foreign languages), smart quotes, and at least internally consistent punctuation, we, nonetheless, try to allow some latitude in presentation. Any use of foreign languages must be accompanied by an

Hank Hudepohl

Making connections

Poetry has always been an essential part of Hank Hudepohl's life. "My mom introduced me to poetry when I was very young, and I've been writing poems ever since," he says. "I won a prize in a national poetry contest when I was ten or so, and that encouraged me to keep writing." More than simply continuing to write, Hudepohl has taught poetry, edited a literary journal, and published a collection of his poems. He's also had some worldly experiences that have inspired his writing as well as shaped his character.

As an English major at Harvard University, Hudepohl studied with legendary Irish poet Seamus Heaney. "I was fortunate enough to be selected both years that I was eligible," says Hudepohl, who was chosen based on the poems he submitted to Heaney when he registered for the class, which admitted only about 10 students. Hudepohl also attended a summer program in Ireland thanks to a Ford research grant. After earning his Bachelor of Arts degree with Honors in 1992, Hudepohl began a four-year stint in the U.S. Navy, a commitment he made as the recipient of an ROTC college scholarship.

In 1996, a teaching scholarship allowed Hudepohl to work toward a PhD at the University of Kentucky. He left the program after a year, however, to pursue a business venture as an executive that kept him busy for about seven years. Hudepohl returned to academia in 2004 as an MFA student at Hollins University in Roanoke, Virginia, where he currently resides with his wife and two young daughters. While attending the two-year MFA program, Hudepohl taught undergraduate creative writing courses in fiction and poetry, won several school writing awards, and served as assistant poetry editor of *The Hollins Critic*, the university's literary journal. He also earned publishing credits in journals such as *Appalachian Heritage*, *Limestone*, *Cargoes* and *Ghoti*.

Hudepohl completed his MFA degree in June of 2006; his poetry thesis earned him high marks as well as a publishing contract. *The Journey of Hands*, his first collection of poems, was published by Word Press in July 2007. "Composed primarily of recent work, it does include a few poems that are older," Hudepohl says. "The subject matter varies from childhood reverie to fatherhood to poems about paintings by Andrew Wyeth and Grant Wood. It's a book about passages."

Here, Hudepohl discusses his writing process, the pros and cons of MFA programs, the ins and outs of publishing and the life passages that have inspired him and his writing.

How did you obtain the competitive Ford research grant to study in Ireland? Do you think it's a good idea for writers to apply for grants?

I applied for the grant to complete my senior thesis on W.B. Yeats. Of course, Ireland is a great destination under any circumstance, so it was a bonus to be there on the premise of my poetry studies. The grant gave me access to an archive of material not available in the United States, but more importantly, it put me in touch with a community of scholars with whom I could discuss the poetry and the life of the poet. I still have friendships from that trip.

I received the grant through the help of an academic advisor and a professor; I had never applied for one before. If poets are interested in grant opportunities, they should look to local universities for support and information. It might help to contact a professor or someone who has won a similar grant and ask him or her about the process. I suggest doing more than sending an e-mail and hoping for a response. Campus events such as poetry readings offer great opportunities to make informal and personal connections.

How did your experience in the Navy influence you—in general and as a writer?

To my surprise, the active duty commitment I had once dreaded became one of the best experiences of my life. It informs my writing the same way any pivotal experience will: sometimes by direct address, but most often less perceptibly through the quieter manifestation of a profound change. All that time at sea entices even the most lighthearted person to be reflective and philosophical. For a poet, the voyage can be a little dangerous that way; and like Odysseus, my homecoming was a long way off even after the actual deployment had ended.

What inspires your writing?

Sometimes I'm inspired by the way light falls across the kitchen floor, or by one of my wife's long, curly hairs on the sleeve of my sweater, or by the way my youngest daughter calls everything "blue" as she practices her knowledge of colors. For me, inspiration is a mix of imagination and observation; it's the outcome of paying attention to the world around you. Landscape and history—what they mean, what they become—are also thematic interests.

My mother is a Hatfield with ties to the Hatfield-McCoy region of Eastern Kentucky. Growing up, family vacation meant a trip to the coal-mining region of Pike County to a mountain farm in Little Blue Springs holler, my grandfather's home. Experiences there, and my reflections upon them, have been important to my poetry. Lately I find myself writing about fatherhood, though the ideas of place and memory are never far away. Keeping the observation antennae up comes at a price, however; I have a difficult time making my way through grocery stores, and crowds tire me out.

Reading is a great inspiration to my writing. Once in a while, I come upon a poem that hits such a pure note it makes me say, "I wish I had written that." These poems are a pleasure to find because I can read them over and over and still feel the strange tingle at the tips of my fingers and the top of my head. Lately, I've been reading nursery rhymes to my oldest daughter at bedtime, and I've enjoyed rediscovering the rhythms and images of those verses.

The Fair

Before the gates opened, before popcorn
and cotton candy drifted down throats

like sweet and salty summer evenings
of childhood, before the townspeople

confessed to the music and lights,
the Ferris wheel baskets swung empty

in a slow arc, one by one, offering color
to the sky—red, yellow, orange, blue.

Just roving boys, what else could we do
but follow the sandaled feet of girls

out to the fair to buy them rides
until our pockets turned up penniless,

until we lost them in the dark
the way sparrows will fly from you,

until our last walk past the fun house
mirrors stretched our bodies like gum,

when we caught ourselves looking
back at ourselves for the first time.

(from *The Journey of Hands* [Word Press, ©2007]; reprinted with permission)

What is your writing process like? Do you have any "rituals" that define it?

I'm a late-night writer and have always been this way. I like to write poems out in longhand because I find it useful to have all the words in front of me, even the ones I cross out. Sometimes I'll write toward one poem, but out comes the pieces of two or three different poems.

I usually begin writing with a couple of words or a phrase that comes into my head that day, or an observation I jotted down in a notepad sometime earlier. I like the idea of writing by candlelight, but this hasn't actually helped me write better poems, as I had hoped. I usually end up staring at the candle.

How have your roles as teacher and editor affected and informed you as a writer?

Teaching uses a different kind of energy than writing. For me, the reward as a teacher is connecting with other writers and helping them along their way. My teaching experiences have made me a better reader and listener, though I make no excuse to my students for being an opinionated writer like them. Teaching keeps my hands in the soil, though my own writing does not come easily during the time that I'm teaching.

In my two-year role as assistant poetry editor for *The Hollins Critic*, I learned a great deal about journal submissions. It surprised me that so many people ignored submission guidelines regarding number of poems, format, return envelope, etc. We received a large percentage of work that wasn't suited for the journal—I doubt whether these poets had ever read it. But I can only be so righteous, because I've been guilty of doing the same thing. Still, the experience made me realize how important it is for a poet to become familiar with a publication before submitting to it.

The best way to get to know a journal is by reading it and getting a feel for the kinds of poems inside. Then pay attention to the guidelines; they really do matter. Be selective about where you aim to publish, and send out fewer, more qualified submissions. You'll do yourself a favor, and the journals will be grateful as well.

Do poets need to publish extensively in journals before attempting to get an entire book published?

Literary journals are in many ways the life support system of American poetry, if not the poets. It's common for poets to first publish a number of poems in journals before publishing a book, and this has been my experience. Journals are not only a sort of proving ground for young poets, however; they are a place for poets to publish at any stage of their careers. Journals also provide a way to market an upcoming book.

What advice can you offer about dealing with rejections?

In my experience at *The Hollins Critic*, I came to realize that the practice of sending out form letters, though impersonal, is at least equitable. State poet laureates and prize-winning poets were sent the same rejection letter that went to the unpublished writers. You will rarely ever (or never) receive a special editor's note with a rejection letter, so don't feel that you're in the minority if all you get back is a form letter. It's just the way things are done. Many journals receive hundreds of letters and thousands of poems to consider for each issue.

Also, any kind of editor feedback by way of critique or suggestion, no matter how well-intentioned, might be misunderstood by the poet as a formula for getting published with the journal. The poet then makes the changes, resubmits the poem, and says, "I did what you asked me to do," with the strong expectation that the finished work will resonate with the editor. The matter of selecting poems is a little more mercurial than that.

I always found that the easiest poems to select were the ones that made the ends of my fingertips tingle as I held them. Most editors simply want good writing, so don't feel like you need a special pass to get through the front door. Just keep your cover letter courteous and succinct.

I recently learned that a well-known literary journal now accepts submissions by e-mail, and if you don't hear back in six weeks you should assume you've been rejected. That seems to be the harshest treatment of all. I do wonder if there's something kinder and gentler that journals could do for their writers. When I receive a rejection letter, for instance, I'd like to know if my poem just missed the mark or if I never really had a chance. Did the editors discuss my poem for twenty minutes, or did they simply shake their heads disapprovingly? Maybe journals will consider implementing a rejection scale—circle a number from one to ten—so the poets have a bread crumb of sense about how their work fares.

Does having an MFA increase a poet's chances for success?

The MFA in Creative Writing is a fairly recent invention, though apprenticeship has always been important to the art form. The MFA is a way to formalize that mentoring process. There are those who believe that MFA programs are raising up poets who produce a kind of poetry by committee. What prevents this from actually happening is the artistic conviction of each writer and the diversity of voices in the programs.

But can poetry be taught? Certainly the history of poetry, the forms of poetry and the habits that seem to benefit successful poets can be taught. The act of writing poetry is ultimately a solo sport, like golf. No one can write the poem (or sink the putt) for you. A good MFA program with good teachers should help you become a better, more avid reader of poetry—both your own and that of others—and should help you learn the optimal habits for writing well.

When you consider schools, look closely at the faculty roster. Read their work. Talk to graduates and current students. Ask yourself if you think there is something to learn from these writers. I was lucky enough to find a connection with several people at Hollins.

That said, it's not a setting for everyone; and for those who choose to attend, they get out of it what they put into it, like anything else. I certainly don't value a poem any more or any less because the poet does, or does not, have an MFA. I don't need to know a poet's credentials to enjoy a poem.

How long after you began submitting the manuscript did it take to get your first book published?

The total process took about a year. I submitted the manuscript to several contests prior to my success with Word Press. It seems that the most available route to publication for a first-time poet is via the contest circuit. The problem with this approach is that a contest usually awards only a single manuscript when several might be outstanding. Also, contest sponsors often charge sizeable entry fees, and apparently some presses use the entry fees for profit and to fund the publication of the winning manuscript. Word Press appealed to me because they choose manuscripts by open submission and do not charge a reading fee.

What are your feelings about self-publishing? Is it an avenue worth exploring if contests and open submissions don't pan out?

The best poetry books will sell the way they've always sold—by word of mouth. If you never publish your book, you will never know if there is an audience for it. Most poets have heard the story of how Walt Whitman self-published *Leaves of Grass*, which is now considered by many as the book that helped define the American voice in poetry. That said, the challenge with self-publishing is that it places the book's success (both business and artistic) squarely upon the poet's shoulders. Few people are capable of managing that weight on their own.

Do you have any other advice to offer aspiring/struggling poets and writers?

Take it one small accomplishment at a time. Do something every day that makes you a writer. Jot down an interesting phrase or word in a notebook. Read a poem. I've lost a lot of days waiting around for the big moment to come—waiting for an acceptance letter, a first book, or simply the right time and place to put words to the page. I believe it was Toni Morrison who said you have to write around the vomit (in reference to the time her child got sick on a manuscript). So, do it. Have you written anything today? Put down this book and get started.

—Erika O'Connell

Erika O'Connell is the editor of *Artist's & Graphic Designer's Market* as well as an aspiring poet and artist. She is former assistant editor of *Poet's Market* and *Photographer's Market*. E-mail her at artdesign@fwpubs.com, or check out www.artists-market.com for more information.

English translation." No style, subject, or form restrictions. Has published poetry by Virgil Suárez, Keith Flynn, Steve de Franco, Elizabeth Smithers, and Michael Harlow. *Takahe* is 60 pages, A4 size. Receives about 500 poems/year, accepts about 10%. Press run is 400 (300 subscribers, 30 libraries, 40 shelf sales). Single copy: $6.50 NZD; subscription: $25 NZD within New Zealand, $35 NZD elsewhere.

How to Submit No simultaneous submissions. No e-mail submissions. "**Please note:** U.S. stamps should not be used on SAEs. They do not work in New Zealand. Please enclose IRCs or supply e-mail address." Cover letter is required. "Advise if you have e-mail." Time between acceptance and publication is 4 months. Often comments on rejected poems. Guidelines available for SASE. Responds in 4 months. "Payment varies, but currently $30 NZD total for any and all inclusions in an issue, plus 2 contributor's copies. Overseas contributors receive a year's subscription in lieu of cash." Acquires first or one-time rights.

Additional Information *Takahe* is published by Takahe Collective Trust, a nonprofit organization formed to help new writers and get them into print alongside established poets.

Contest/Award Offerings The Takahe Poetry Competition awards 1st Prize: $250 NZD; 2nd Prize: $100 NZD; plus one-year subscriptions to *Takahe* to 2 runners-up. Submit as many poems as you wish, but each much be named separately on the entry form. Submissions must be unpublished and may not be entered in other contests. Poems must be in English and typed on A4 paper, with no identifying information on the the ms. Include SASE with entry for results and/or return of entries (or SAE with IRCs for overseas entrants; may also add $2 NZD to entry fee for handling and postage). All entries considered for publication in *Takahe*. Guidelines and entry form available on Web site. **Entry fee:** $5 NZD/poem. **Deadline:** was September 30 for 2006. 2006 judge: David Howard. Winners announced in December.

$☐ ◎ TALES OF THE TALISMAN (Specialized: science fiction; fantasy; horror)

P.O. Box 2194, Mesilla Park NM 88047-2194. E-mail: hadrosaur@zianet.com. Web site: www.hadro saur.com. Established 1995. **Contact:** David Lee Summers, editor.

Magazine Needs *Tales of the Talisman*, published quarterly, prints "well-written, thought-pro-voking science fiction and fantasy." Wants "strong visual imagery. Strong emotion from a sense of fun to more melancholy is good." Does not want "graphic/gory violence or poetry that strays too far from the science fiction/fantasy genre." Has published poetry by Bruce Boston, Deborah P. Kolodji, Karen A. Romanko, and Kendall Evans. *Tales of the Talisman* is 86 pages, $8\frac{1}{4} \times 10\frac{1}{2}$, printed on 60 lb. white paper, perfect-bound, with full-color cardstock cover. Receives about 100 poems/year, accepts up to 25%. Press run is 200 (100 subscribers). Single copy: $8; subscription: $20/year. Make checks payable to Hadrosaur Productions.

How to Submit Submit 1-5 poems at a time. Considers previously published poems; no simultaneous submissions. Accepts e-mail submissions (pasted into body of message); no disk submissions. "For e-mail submissions, place the word 'Hadrosaur' in the subject line. Submissions that do not include this will be destroyed unread. Postal submissions will not be returned unless sufficient postage is provided." Cover letter is preferred. Time between acceptance and publication is one year. Often comments on rejected poems. Guidelines available for SASE or on Web site. Responds in one month. Sends prepublication galleys on request. Pays $4/poem plus one contributor's copy. Acquires one-time rights.

Advice "Read absolutely everything you can get your hands on, especially poetry outside your genre of choice, and ask 'What if?' This is a great source for original speculative poems."

✦ ☐ ◎ TAPESTRIES (Specialized: for senior citizen audience)

MWCC Life Program, 444 Green St., Gardner MA 01440. (978)630-9176. Fax: (978)632-6155. E-mail: alanahb@earthlink.net. or p_cosentino@mwcc.mass.edu. Web site: www.mwcc.mass.edu/LLL/tapestriesGuidelines.html. Established 2001. **Contact:** Patricia B. Cosentino, editor.

Magazine Needs *Tapestries*, published annually in November, is an anthology for senior citizens of poetry, short stories, features on family, heritage, tradition, and folklore. Wants any style poetry; no restrictions on form. Does not want "political, propaganda, pornographic, or sexually explicit material as this is a 'family' magazine. We do not exclude religious poems, but they must have non-sectarian universality." Has published poetry by Maxine Kumin, Victor Howes, Diana Der-Hovanessian, Marge Piercy, bg Thurston, and FD Reeve. *Tapestries* is 100 pages, magazine-sized, offset-printed, tape-bound, with card stock/offset cover. Receives about 500 poems/year, accepts about 10%. Press run is 500. Single copy: $5 plus $5 postage. Make checks payable to MWCC Life Program.

How to Submit Submit 3-5 poems at a time. Lines/poem: 30. Considers previously published poems and simultaneous submissions. Accepts disk submissions; no fax or e-mail submissions. Cover letter is preferred (only if work is previously published). "Prefer hard copy submissions. Submit two copies, with name and address on only one copy. Include SASE." Reads submissions by March 31 deadline. Time between acceptance and publication is 4 months. Poems are circulated to an editorial board of 3-4 judges. Occasionally publishes theme issues. Upcoming themes available on Web site. Guidelines available in magazine, for SASE, by fax, e-mail (life@mwcc.mass.edu), or on

Web site. Responds in 3 months. No payment. Acquires first North American serial rights.

Advice "As an anthology, we accept original and/or previously published material, but prefer original. Our authors range in age from 50-92. We want humor and wisdom in our writings. Experiment with point of view—too many poems use first-person speaker."

☑ TAPROOT LITERARY REVIEW

P.O. Box 204, Ambridge PA 15003. (724)266-8476. E-mail: taproot10@aol.com. Established 1986. **Contact:** Tikvah Feinstein, editor.

Magazine Needs *Taproot Literary Review*, published annually, is "a very respected anthology with increasing distribution. We publish some of the best poets in the U.S. We enjoy all types and styles of poetry from emerging writers to established writers to those who have become valuable and old friends who share their new works with us." Has published poetry by Ellen Hyatt, Lyn Lifshin, Taylor Graham, Shari O'Brien, Vera Schwarcz, and Patricia Rose. *Taproot Literary Review* is about 95 pages, offset-printed on white stock, with one-color glossy cover. Circulation is 500. Single copy: $8.95; subscription: $7.50. Sample: $5.

How to Submit Submit up to 5 poems at a time. Lines/poem: 35 maximum. No previously published poems or simultaneous submissions. Accepts submissions by e-mail (pasted into body of message), but "we would rather have a hard copy. Also, we cannot answer without a SASE." Cover letter is required (with general information). Reads submissions September 1-December 31 only. Guidelines available for SASE. Sometimes sends prepublication galleys. Pays one contributor's copy; additional copies are $6.50 each. Open to receiving books for review consideration. Send query first.

Contest/Award Offerings Sponsors the annual Taproot Writer's Workshop Annual Writing Contest. 1st Prize: $25 and publication in *Taproot Literary Review*; 2nd and 3rd Prizes: publication. Submit 5 poems of literary quality, in any form, on any subject except porn. **Entry fee:** $12/5 poems (no longer than 35 lines each); fee includes copy of *Taproot*. **Deadline:** December 31. Winners announced the following March.

Advice "We publish the best poetry we can in a variety of styles and subjects, so long as it's literary quality and speaks to us. We love poetry that stuns, surprises, amuses, and disarms."

☑ TAR RIVER POETRY

Erwin Building Mailroom, East Carolina University, Greenville NC 27858-4353. (252)328-6783. E-mail: TarRiverPoetry@gmail.com. Web site: http://core.ecu.edu/engl/trp. Established 1978. **Contact:** Luke Whisnant, editor; Carolyn Elkins, associate editor.

Magazine Needs *Tar River Poetry*, published twice/year, is an " 'all-poetry' magazine that publishes 40-50 poems per issue, providing the talented beginner and experienced writer with a forum that features all styles and forms of verse." Wants "skillful use of figurative language; poems that appeal to the senses." Does not want "sentimental, flat-statement poetry." Has published poetry by William Stafford, Sharon Olds, Carolyn Kizer, A.R. Ammons, and Claudia Emerson. Has also published "many other well-known poets, as well as numerous new and emerging poets." *Tar River Poetry* is 64 pages, digest-sized, professionally printed on salmon stock, with matte card cover with photo. Receives 6,000-8,000 submissions/year, accepts 80-100. Press run is 900 (500 subscribers, 125 libraries). Subscription: $12. Sample: $6.50.

How to Submit Submit no more than 5 poems at a time. No previously published poems or simultaneous submissions. Accepts e-mail submissions only; no print submissions. "Detailed submission instructions appear on the Web site, along with writer's guidelines." Reads submissions September 1-April 30 only; "we do not read manuscripts from May through August—submissions will be returned unread." Rarely comments on rejections "due to volume of submissions." Guidelines available for SASE or on Web site. Responds in 6 weeks. Pays 2 contributor's copies. Acquires first rights. Reviews books of poetry in 4,000 words maximum, single- or multi-book format. Send materials for review consideration.

Advice "Writers of poetry should first be readers of poetry. Read and study traditional and contemporary poetry."

▣ ⬧ TARPAULIN SKY

E-mail: editors@tarpaulinsky.com. (inquiries) or submissions@tarpaulinsky.com. (submissions). Web site: www.tarpaulinsky.com. Established 2002. **Contact:** Poetry Editors. Editor: Christian Peet.

Magazine Needs *Tarpaulin Sky*, published quarterly in print and online, features "highest-quality poetry, prose, cross-genre work, art, photography, interviews, and reviews. We are open to all styles and forms, providing the forms appear inevitable and/or inextricable from the poems. We are especially fond of inventive/experimental and cross-/trans-genre work. The best indication of our aesthetic is found in the journal we produce: Please read it before submitting your work. Also, hardcopy submissions may be received by different editors at different times; check guidelines before submitting." Has published poetry by Jenny Boully, Matthea Harvey, Bin Ramke, Eleni Sikelianos, Juliana Spahr, and Joshua Marie Wilkinson. Receives about 3,000 poems/year.

How to Submit Submit 4-6 poems at a time. Considers simultaneous submissions; no previously published poems. Accepts e-mail submissions ("best received as attachments in .rtf or .pdf formats"); no disk submissions. Cover letter is preferred. Reads submissions year round. Time between acceptance and publication is 2-6 months. "Poems are read by all editors. We aim for consensus." Rarely comments on rejected poems. Guidelines available for SASE, by e-mail, or on Web site. Responds in 1-4 months. Always sends prepublication galleys (electronic). Acquires first rights. Reviews books/chapbooks of poetry.

▣ ⬛ TATTOO HIGHWAY

E-mail: submissions@tattoohighway.org. Web site: www.tattoohighway.org. Established 1998. **Contact:** Sara McAulay, editor.

Magazine Needs *Tattoo Highway*, published biannually online, is a journal of poetry, literary prose, new media, and art. "We're open to most styles; only criterion is quality." Wants "language that is fresh, vivid, and original; writing that is smart and a little edgy, that engages with the world beyond the writer's own psyche. We like formal poetry if well handled." Does not want "self-pity, navel-contemplation, clichés, workshop hackery." Has published poetry by Judith Skillman, Barry Spacks, Kelley White, Taylor Graham, Erin Murphy, and Corey Mesler. Receives about 800 poems/year, accepts about 50.

How to Submit Submit up to 5 poems at a time. Considers previously published poems (if they've appeared in small-circulation print journals; unpublished work preferred) and simultaneous submissions ("but please let us know promptly if you place your piece elsewhere"). Accepts e-mail submissions (pasted into body of message) only. "For hypertext or New Media (Flash, etc.) submissions, please provide a URL where we may view the work." Reading periods vary; "typically last about three months. Blind readings by editorial board. Several rounds of 'triage' during the reading period, usually handled by e-mail. Face-to-face editorial meeting shortly after submission deadline, where final selections are made. Editor and poetry editor have final say." Sometimes comments on rejected poems. "If a poem has its moments, though it doesn't quite work, we try to acknowledge that. We encourage near-misses to try us again." Regularly publishes theme issues. Guidelines available on Web site. Responds in up to 3 months ("usually within one week of deadline"). Always sends prepublication galleys. No payment. Acquires first electronic rights; rights revert to author 90 days after online publication date.

Contest/Award Offerings "Picture Worth 500 Words" contest for poetry/prose. No entry fee; small prizes. See guidelines on Web site.

Advice "Read some past issues before submitting."

☑ ◎ THE TEACHER'S VOICE (Specialized: the American teacher experience, from pre-K to university professor)

P.O. Box 150384, Kew Gardens NY 11415. E-mail: editor@the-teachers-voice.org. Web site: www.the-teachers-voice.org. Established 2005. **Contact:** Andrés Castro, founder/managing editor.

Magazine Needs *The Teacher's Voice*, published twice/year in spring and fall (beginning in 2008), is "a nonprofit magazine supported by an all-volunteer staff and subscribers, founded as a venue for teachers and others with a strong interest in American education and its development. We publish poetry, short-short stories/microfiction, and creative nonfiction." Wants "all styles and forms. We welcome work that ranges from 'art for art's sake' to radically social/political. Writing that illuminates the most pressing/urgent issues in American education and the lives of teachers gets special attention. We also would like to receive pre-1923 poetry that is in the public domain for our 'Distinguished Professor' category." Has published poetry by Edward Francisco Sapphire, Hal Sirowitz, and Walt Whitman. *The Teacher's Voice* is 60-64 pages, digest-sized, highest quality color laser-printed (POD), saddle-stapled, with textured, linen, or glossy heavy card cover. Receives about 1,000 poems/year, accepts about 10%. Press run is "up to 1,000 copies of each issue we print on demand" (50 subscribers). Single copy: $10; subscription: $18/year. Make checks payable to *The Teacher's Voice*.

How to Submit Submit 3-5 poems at a time. Lines/poem: no limits. Considers previously published poems and simultaneous submissions. No e-mail or disk submissions. Cover letter is required "stating engagement with American education: Are you a teacher, administrator, librarian, coach, custodian, student, parent, etc.? Work that is not accompanied by a SASE with the appropriate postage is recycled." Reads submissions year round. Time between acceptance and publication is 1-6 months. Poems are circulated to an editorial board. Sometimes comments on rejected poems. "We respond if the author asks for feedback that addresses a specific aspect or issue." Guidelines available in magazine, for SASE, or on Web site. Sometimes sends prepublication galleys "if requested." Pays 2 contributor's copies. Acquires first rights and electronic reprint rights. "If your work is accepted, we may include it in the sampling of work on our online version of the magazine." Rights revert to poet upon publication.

Additional Information "A 'best of 2005-2008' anthology is being planned (professionally printed or publishing house, flat spine)."

Contest/Award Offerings Sponsors *The Teacher's Voice* Annual Chapbook Contest and *The Teacher's Voice* Annual Poetry Contest for Unpublished Poets. Guidelines for both contests available for SASE, by e-mail, or on Web site.

Also Offers "*The Teacher's Voice*'s sibling Don Quixote Poetry Project was established to bring free workshops to schools, libraries, and community centers in underserved communities in New York City. Information is available on our Web site."

Advice "We highly recommend that you purchase at least one issue before submitting your work. If you are a teacher, become a poet. If you are a poet, become a teacher. And please, be daring and take some risks! This being said, many teachers are afraid of truth-telling work putting their positions at risk when working in an unaccepting or punitive education environment: If you must, include a pseudonym with your real name."

▦ ☑ 10TH MUSE

33 Hartington Rd., Southampton, Hants SO14 0EW England. E-mail: andyj@noplace.screaming.net. Established 1990. **Contact:** Andrew Jordan, editor.

Magazine Needs *10th Muse* "includes poetry and reviews, as well as short prose and graphics." Has published poetry by Richard Caddel, Stephen M. Dickey, Andrew Duncan, Carrie Etter, Becky Gould Gibson, and Bill Griffiths. *10th Muse* is 48-72 pages, A5, photocopied, saddle-stapled, with card cover. Press run is 200. Single copy: £3.50 (UK); subscription: £9/3 issues (UK). Make checks payable to *10th Muse*. "U.S. subscribers: Send $10 in bills for single copy (including postage)."

How to Submit Submit up to 6 poems at a time. No e-mail submissions. Include SASE (or SAE with IRCs). Responds in 3 months. Pays one contributor's copy. Staff reviews books of poetry. Send materials for review consideration.

Advice "Poets should read a copy of the magazine first."

▨ ◎ TEXAS POETRY CALENDAR (Specialized: poems with a TX connection)

Dos Gatos Press, 1310 Crestwood Rd., Austin TX 78722. (512)467-0678. Fax: (408)580-8523. E-mail: editors@dosgatospress.org. Web site: www.dosgatospress.org. Established 2004 (under current editorship). **Contact:** Scott Wiggerman or David Meischen, co-editors.

Magazine Needs *Texas Poetry Calendar*, published annually in August, features a "week-by-week calendar side-by-side with poems with a Texas connection." Wants "a wide variety of styles, voices, and forms, including rhyme—though a Texas connection is preferred. Humor is welcome! Poetry *only*!" Does not want "children's poetry, erotic poetry, profanity, obscure poems, previously published work, or poems over 35 lines." *Texas Poetry Calendar* is about 130 pages, digest-sized, offset-printed, spiral-bound, with 2-color cardstock cover. Receives about 500 poems/year, accepts about 60. Press run is 1,500; 60 distributed free to contributors. Single copy: $12.95 plus $3 shipping. Make checks payable to Dos Gatos Press.

How to Submit Submit 3 poems at a time. Lines/poem: 35 maximum, "including spaces and title." Considers simultaneous submissions; no previously published poems. No fax, e-mail, or disk submissions. Cover letter is required. "Include a short bio (100 words or less) and poem titles in cover letter. Also include e-mail address and phone number. Do not include poet's name on the poems themselves!" Reads submissions year round. Time between acceptance and publication is 3-4 months. Poems are circulated to an editorial board. Never comments on rejected poems. "**Entry fee for the** *Texas Poetry Calendar* Awards is required for all submissions—all poems submitted are eligible for cash awards." (See Contest/Award Offerings below.) Guidelines available in magazine, by e-mail, or on Web site. Responds "only once a year, in spring." Sometimes sends prepublication galleys. Pays one contributor's copy. Acquires first, electronic, and reprint rights.

Contest/Award Offerings Sponsors the annual Texas Poetry Calendar Awards, offering 1st Prize: $150; 2nd Prize: $75; 3rd Prize: $40. "Award-winning poems receive special recognition in the calendar in which they are printed." Submit 3 poems. Guidelines available in magazine, by e-mail, or on Web site. **Entry fee:** $5. **Deadline:** March 20 (postmark). "Judged by a nationally known poet—Robert McDowell, Naomi Shihab Nye, etc."

$▨ ◎ THEMA (Specialized: specific theme per issue)

Thema Literary Society, P.O. Box 8747, Metairie LA 70011-8747. E-mail: thema@cox.net. Web site: http://members.cox.net/thema. Established 1988. **Contact:** Gail Howard, poetry editor.

● *THEMA* is supported by a grant from the Louisiana Division of the Arts, Office of Cultural Development, Department of Culture, Recreation and Tourism, in cooperation with the Louisiana State Arts Council as administered by Art Council of New Orleans.

Magazine Needs *THEMA*, published triannually, uses poetry related to specific themes. "Each issue is based on an unusual premise. Please, please send SASE for guidelines before submitting poetry to find out the upcoming themes." Does not want "scatologic language, alternate lifestyle, explicit love poetry." Has published poetry by James Penha, Louis Gallo, Nancy G. Westerfield, and L.G. Mason. *THEMA* is 150 pages, digest-sized, professionally printed, with matte card cover. Receives about 400 poems/year, accepts about 8%. Press run is 500 (270 subscribers, 30 libraries). Subscription: $16. Sample: $8.

How to Submit Submit up to 3 poems at a time. Include SASE. "All submissions should be typewritten on standard 8½×11 paper. Submissions are accepted all year, but evaluated after specified deadlines." Editor comments on submissions. Upcoming themes and guidelines available in magazine, for SASE, by e-mail, or on Web site. Pays $10/poem and one contributor's copy. Acquires one-time rights.

Advice "Do not submit to *THEMA* unless you have one of *THEMA*'s upcoming themes in mind. And be sure to specify which one!"

▣ ◻ THICK WITH CONVICTION

E-mail: sarablanton10@yahoo.com. or karinablondie11@hotmail.com. Web site: www.angelfire. com/poetry/thickwithconviction. Established 2005. **Contact:** Sara Blanton or Karina Bowman, editors.

Magazine Needs *Thick With Conviction*, published quarterly online, is "run by two quirky twenty-something women who are desperately searching for new and interesting ideas in poetry. We'd like to be moved to anger or tears." Wants all genres of poetry, "poems that make us exhale a deep sigh after reading them. Basically, if we can't feel the words in front of us, we're not going to be happy. We'd like to expose the world to poets who may not get the kind of exposure that more experienced poets do." Does not want "teen angst poems, religious poems, or greeting card tripe." Considers poetry by teens. Has published poetry by Taylor Graham, Corey Mesler, Kendall A. Bell, Tanya Ranta, Rachel Bunting, and Simon Perchik. Receives about 300 poems/year, accepts about 15%.

How to Submit Submit 3-5 poems at a time. Lines/poem: no limit. Considers previously published poems; no simultaneous submissions. Accepts e-mail submissions (pasted into body of message; "any attachments will be deleted"); no disk submissions. Cover letter is required. Reads submissions year round. Submit seasonal poems 3 months in advance. Time between acceptance and publication is 3 months. Never comments on rejected poems. Guidelines available on Web site. Responds in "roughly one to two weeks." Acquires one-time rights. Rights revert to poet upon publication.

Advice "Take the time to read the poems on our Web site. If your style is similar, we'll most likely enjoy your work. The most important thing a writer can do is read, read, read. The more you read, the more your writing will grow and blossom. Be sure to have thick skin, and don't let rejections get you down."

◨ THIRD COAST

Dept. of English, Western Michigan University, Kalamazoo MI 49008-5331. (269)387-2675. Web site: www.wmich.edu/thirdcoast. Established 1995. **Contact:** Poetry Editors.

Magazine Needs *Third Coast*, published semiannually in March and September, is a national literary magazine of poetry, prose, creative nonfiction, translations, and drama. Wants "excellence of craft and originality of thought. Nothing trite." Has published poetry by Myronn Hardy, Sean Thomas Dougherty, Terrance Hayes, Margo Schlipp, Mark Halliday, and Philip Levine. *Third Coast* is 176 pages, digest-sized, professionally printed, perfect-bound, with 4-color cover with art. Receives about 2,000 poems/year, accepts about 1%. Press run is 3,500 (850 subscribers, 50 libraries, 2,400 shelf sales). Single copy: $8; subscription: $14/year, $26 for 2 years, $38 for 3 years. Sample: $6 (back issue).

How to Submit Submit up to 5 poems at a time. Considers simultaneous submissions with notification; no previously published poems. No electronic submissions. Cover letter is preferred. "Poems should be typed single-spaced, with the author's name on each page. Stanza breaks should be double-spaced." Poems are circulated to assistant poetry editors and poetry editors; poetry editors make final decisions. Seldom comments on rejected poems. Guidelines available on Web site. Responds in 4 months. Pays 2 contributor's copies plus one-year subscription. Acquires first rights.

Contest/Award Offerings Sponsors an annual poetry contest. 1st Prize: $1,000 and publication; 4 finalists receive notification in prize-winners issue, possible publication, and a 3-year subscription. Guidelines available on Web site. **Entry fee:** $15, includes one-year subscription to *Third Coast*.

⬧ 🌐 ○ THE THIRD HALF

K.T. Publications, 16 Fane Close, Stamford, Lincolnshire PE9 1HG United Kingdom. (44)(1780)754193. Established 1989. **Contact:** Kevin Troop, editor.

Magazine Needs *The Third Half*, published regularly, is a literary magazine containing "free-flowing and free-thinking material on most subjects. Open to all ideas and suggestions." Showcases 4 poets/issue. "Each poet has 24 pages with illustrations." Does not want "badly written or obscene scribbling." Has published poetry by Gillian Bence-Jones, R. Tomas, Raymond Humphreys, and Mario Petrucci. *The Third Half* is neatly printed, perfect-bound, with glossy cover. Press run is 100-500. Single copy: £5.50 in UK. Sample: £10 overseas. Make checks payable to K.T. Publications.

How to Submit Submit 6 poems at a time. No previously published poems. Accepts disk submissions. Cover letter is preferred. Include SAE. Time between acceptance and publication "depends on the work and circumstances." **There is a £5 reading fee to cover costs.** Seldom comments on rejected poems. Sometimes publishes theme issues ("as themes present themselves"). Responds in 2 days. Always sends prepublication galleys. Pays 1-6 contributor's copies. "Copyright belongs to the poets/authors throughout."

Also Offers A "reading and friendly help service to writers. Costs are reasonable." Write for details.

Advice "Keep writing; be patient."

⬧ ▣ ♥ THE 13TH WARRIOR REVIEW

Asterius Press, P.O. Box 5122, Seabrook NJ 08302-3511. E-mail: theeditor@asteriuspress.com. Web site: www.asteriuspress.com. Established 1997. **Contact:** John C. Erianne, editor.

Magazine Needs *The 13th Warrior Review*, published irregularly online, seeks "excellent literary-quality poetry as well as fiction, essays, and reviews. All excellent poetry will be given serious consideration." Has published poetry by P.Q. Perron, Cindy Rosmus, B.Z Niditch, Genine Hanns, John Sweet, and Corey Ginsberg.

How to Submit Submit no more than 5 poems at a time. Considers simultaneous submissions, but "not encouraged"; no previously published poems. Accepts e-mail submissions (encouraged; pasted as text into body of message—no attachments). "Use 'submission' as the subject header. Any submission that comes as a file attachment will be deleted without reply." Cover letter is preferred; "should be brief and to the point." Include SASE for postal submissions. Time between acceptance and publication is up to one year. Seldom comments on rejected poems. Guidelines available on Web site. No payment. Acquires first rights, first electronic rights, and non-exclusive anthology rights.

Advice "Write from love; don't expect love in return, don't take rejection personally, and don't let anyone stop you."

◖ ◉ THOUGHTS FOR ALL SEASONS: THE MAGAZINE OF EPIGRAMS (Specialized: epigrams; rhyming poetry; humor; themes)

86 Leland Rd., Becket MA 01223. Established 1976. **Contact:** Prof. Em. Michel Paul Richard, editor.

Magazine Needs *Thoughts for All Seasons*, published irregularly, is "designed to preserve the epigram as a literary form; satirical. All issues are commemorative. Volume 6 celebrates the centennial of the publication of *The Devil's Dictionary* by Ambrose Bierce." Has published poetry by Kendal Bush, William D. Barney, and Jill Williams. *Thoughts for All Seasons* is 80 pages, offset-printed from typescript, saddle-stapled, with card cover. Accepts about 15% of material submitted. Press run is 500-1,000. "There are several library subscriptions, but most distribution is through direct mail or local bookstores and newsstand sales." Single copy: $6 (includes p&h).

How to Submit Submit at least one or 2 pages (10-12 epigrams or 2-4 poems) at a time. Considers simultaneous submissions; no previously published epigrams "unless a thought is appended which alters it." Include SASE and one-paragraph bio. Comments on rejected poems. Publishes theme issues. Guidelines available in magazine or for SASE. Responds in one week. Pays one contributor's copy, additional discounted copies.

Advice "Preference given to rhyming poetry, including original limericks. Nonsense verse with good imagery also acceptable. No haiku!"

$⬚ THE THREEPENNY REVIEW

P.O. Box 9131, Berkeley CA 94709. (510)849-4545. Web site: www.threepennyreview.com. Established 1980. **Contact:** Wendy Lesser, editor.

- Work published in *The Threepenny Review* has been included in *The Best American Poetry* and *The Pushcart Prize*.

Magazine Needs *The Threepenny Review*, published quarterly, is "a national review of literature, performing and visual arts, and social articles aimed at the intelligent, well-read (but not necessarily academic) reader." Wants "formal, narrative, short poems (and others). No bias against formal poetry; in fact, a slight bias in favor of it." Has published poetry by Anne Carson, Frank Bidart, Seamus Heaney, Robert Pinsky, and Louise Glück. *The Threepenny Review* is a 36-page tabloid. Receives about 4,500 submissions of poetry/year, accepts about 40 poems. Press run is 10,000 (8,000 subscribers, 150 libraries). Subscription: $25. Sample: $12.

How to Submit Submit up to 5 poems at a time. Lines/poem: 100 maximum ("exceptions are possible"). No previously published poems or simultaneous submissions. **Do not submit mss September-December.** Guidelines available for SASE or on Web site. Responds in up to 2 months. Pays $200/poem plus one-year subscription. Acquires first serial rights. Guidelines available for SASE.

⬚ $⬚ TICKLED BY THUNDER

14076-86A Ave., Surrey BC V3W 0V9 Canada. E-mail: info@tickledbythunder.com. Web site: www. tickledbythunder.com. Established 1990. **Contact:** Larry Lindner, editor/publisher.

Magazine Needs *Tickled by Thunder*, published up to 4 times/year, uses poems "about fantasy particularly; writing or whatever. Require original images and thoughts. Welcome humor and creative inspirational verse." Does not want "anything pornographic, childish, unimaginative." Has published poetry by Laleh Dadpour Jackson and Helen Michiko Singh. *Tickled by Thunder* is 24 pages, digest-sized, published on Macintosh. Has 1,000 readers/subscribers. Subscription: $12 CAD/4 issues. Sample: $2.50 CAD.

How to Submit Submit 3-5 poems at a time. Lines/poem: up to 40 ("keep them short—not interested in long, long poems"). No e-mail submissions. Cover letter is required. Include "a few facts about yourself and brief list of publishing credits." Comments on rejected poems "80% of the time." Guidelines available for SASE or on Web site. Responds in up to 6 months. Pays 2¢/line, $2 CAD maximum. Acquires first rights. Reviews books of poetry in up to 300 words. Open to unsolicited reviews. Send materials for review consideration.

Contest/Award Offerings Offers a poetry contest 4 times/year. Prize: cash, publication, and subscription. **Entry fee:** $5 CAD for one poem; free for subscribers. **Deadlines:** the 15th of February, May, August, and October.

Additional Information Publishes **author-subsidized chapbooks**. "We are interested in student poetry and publish it in our center spread: *Expressions*." Send SASE (or SAE and IRC) for details.

⬚ TIGER'S EYE: A JOURNAL OF POETRY

Tiger's Eye Press, P.O. Box 2935, Eugene OR 97402. E-mail: tigerseyepoet@yahoo.com. Web site: www.tigerseyejournal.com. Established 2001. **Contact:** Colette Jonopulos and JoAn Osborne, editors.

Magazine Needs *Tiger's Eye: A Journal of Poetry*, published semiannually, features both established and undiscovered poets. "Besides publishing the work of several exceptional poets in each issue, we feature two poets in interviews, giving the reader insight into their lives and writing habits." Wants "both free verse and traditional forms; no restrictions on subject or length. Poems with distinct imagery and viewpoint are read and re-read by the editors and considered for publication." Has published poetry by Taylor Graham, Robert Schuler, Andrea L. Watson, Susan Kenyon, Laura LeHew, and Amy E. Van Orden. *Tiger's Eye* is digest-sized, saddle-stapled. Receives about 1,000 poems/year, accepts about 100. Press run is 300. Single copy: $5; subscription: $10 for 2 issues. Make checks payable to Tiger's Eye Press.

How to Submit Submit 3-5 poems at a time. Considers simultaneous submissions with notification if a poem is accepted elsewhere; no previously published poems. No e-mail or disk submissions. Cover letter is required. Include brief bio. SASE for notification only; no submissions are returned. Reads submissions year round; deadlines are February 28 and August 31. Time between acceptance and publication is 3 months. "All poems are read by the editors, then filed as poems we definitely want to publish, those we are still considering, and those we aren't publishing. Our two featured poets are chosen, then letters and e-mails are sent out." Seldom comments on rejected poems. Guidelines available in magazine or on Web site. Responds in 6 months. Always sends prepublication galleys. Pays one contributor's copy to each poet, 2 to featured poets. Acquires one-time rights.

Additional Information *Tiger's Eye* now nominates for The Pushcart Prize.

Contest/Award Offerings *Tiger's Eye* Annual Poetry Contest offers prizes of $500, $100, and $50 for 3 winning poems. No previously published poems; accepts simultaneous submissions. No restriction on form, subject, or length. "We welcome haiku, haibun, sonnets, villanelles, etc., as well as free verse and experimental poetry." Submit up to 3 poems with a cover letter and short bio. Guidelines available on Web site. **Entry fee:** $10. **Deadline:** February 28, 2008. "Winning poems will appear in our Mid-Spring issue."

Advice "We accept poems from new poets with as much enthusiasm as from established poets. Poems with clean images, unique subjects, and strong voices have a good chance of being published in *Tiger's Eye*."

TIME OF SINGING, A MAGAZINE OF CHRISTIAN POETRY (Specialized: literary Christian poetry)

P.O. Box 149, Conneaut Lake PA 16316. E-mail: timesing@zoominternet.net. Web site: www.timeo fsinging.bizland.com. Established 1958-1965, revived 1980. **Contact:** Lora H. Zill, editor.

Magazine Needs *Time of Singing, A Magazine of Christian Poetry*, published 4 times/year, seeks "poems that 'show' rather than 'tell.' The viewpoint is unblushingly Christian—but in its widest and most inclusive meaning." Wants free verse and well-crafted rhyme; would like to see more forms. Does not want "collections of uneven lines, sermons that rhyme, unstructured 'prayers,' and trite sing-song rhymes." Has published poetry by John Grey, Luci Shaw, Bob Hostetler, Frances P. Reid, Barbara Crooker, and Charles Waugaman. *Time of Singing* is 44 pages, digest-sized, offset from typescript. Receives more than 800 submissions/year, accepts about 175. Press run is 300 (150 subscribers). Subscription: $17 USD, $21 USD Canada, $30 USD overseas. Sample: $4, or 2 for $6 (postage paid).

How to Submit Submit up to 5 poems at a time. Lines/poem: prefers less than 40, "but will publish up to 60 lines if exceptional." Considers previously published poems (indicate when/where appeared) and simultaneous submissions. Accepts e-mail submissions (pasted into body of message or as attachment). Poems should be single-spaced. Time between acceptance and publication is up to one year. Comments "with suggestions for improvement if close to publication." Guidelines available for SASE, by e-mail, or on Web site. Responds in 2 months. Pays one contributor's copy.

Contest/Award Offerings Sponsors theme contests for specific issues. Guidelines available for SASE, by e-mail, or on Web site.

Advice "Study the craft. Be open to critique. A poet is often too close to his/her work and needs a critical, honest eye. *Time of Singing* publishes more literary-style verse, not greeting card style."

⊿ ◎ TO TOPOS: POETRY INTERNATIONAL (Specialized: humanism; pacifism; altermondialism)

OSU Dept. of Foreign Languages & Literatures, 210 Kidder Hall, Corvallis OR 97331. (541)737-2146. Fax: (541)737-3563. E-mail: jkrause@oregonstate.edu. Web site: http://oregonstate.edu/dept/forei gn_lang/totopos/index.html. Established 1997. **Contact:** Joseph Krause, editor.

• *To Topos* is funded through Poetry Enterprises, a nonprofit association.

Magazine Needs *To Topos: Poetry International*, published semiannually in June and December, is "committed to fostering human rights on an environmentally fragile planet. Its focus is altermondialist, recognizing that the causes of poverty and injustice are often related to race, gender, nationality, and the effacement of earth-given resources. Most issues are thematically focused. Previous themes have included Incarceration, Peace and the Sea, Forests, North African Voices (guest-edited by Nabil Boudraa), Contemporary Hungarian Poets (guest-edited by Eniko Bollobaso), and Indigenous American Voices (guest-edited by Allison Hedge Coke). *To Topos* is open to both aspiring and recognized poets, and primarily interested in living poets who believe words carry the gift of positive social change. We particularly invite submissions from refugees and the borderless. The harmony of craft and message should be the primary consideration prior to submitting texts. Black and white photography and imagery are particularly welcome to complement specific themes." Wants "poetry from all over the world and in any language, so long as it is accompanied by an English translation. The journal espouses a vision of pacifism and human rights but is not anchored in a political current." Does not want "self-serving poetry." Has published poetry by Leonard Cirino, Khadija Al Mourabit, Gérard Bocholier, Sándor Csooóri, Joy Harjo, and Mairead Byrne. *To Topos* is 50-120 pages, digest-sized, docutech-printed, perfect-bound, with cardstock cover with graphics, includes ads (from Amnesty International only). Receives 100-300 poems/issue "depending on the theme," accepts 30-50%. Press run is 250-300; distributed to the international poetry community and to contributors. Single copy: $9; subscription: $18.

How to Submit Submit no more than 6 poems at a time. Considers previously published poems (with the permission of the original copyright holder) and simultaneous submissions. Accepts e-mail (as attachment) and disk submissions; no fax submissions. Cover letter is preferred. "Include brief bio (2-4 lines) and SASE." Reads submissions year round. Time between acceptance and publication is 1-6 months. Poems are circulated to an editorial board. "Guest Editor makes initial selection; co-editors finalize, often seeking advice from consulting editors." Rarely comments on rejected poems. Regularly publishes theme issues. Guidelines available in magazine or on Web site. Pays one contributor's copy. Acquires one-time rights. Rights revert to poet upon publication. Reviews books of poetry in 250 words, single-book format. "We review books relevant to theme. Books reviewed are selected by the editors. Contact editors to suggest titles."

Advice "The mission of this journal is to reveal the human face of poetry as a statement of urgency in today's world. *To Topos* is open to all aesthetic and stylistic orientations, but submissions should be a seed for social change along humanist principles without indulging in political or nationalist rhetoric."

Ⓝ ▣ ⊿ ◎ TORCH: POETRY, PROSE, AND SHORT STORIES BY AFRICAN AMERICAN WOMEN

E-mail: info@torchpoetry.org. (inquiries); poetry@torchpoetry.org. (submissions). Web site: www .torchpoetry.org. Established 2006. **Contact:** Amanda Johnston, editor.

Magazine Needs *Torch: Poetry, Prose, and Short Stories by African American Women*, published semiannually online, provides "a place to celebrate contemporary poetry, prose, and short stories by experienced and emerging writers alike. We prefer our contributors to take risks, and offer a diverse body of work that examines and challenges preconceived notions regarding race, ethnicity, gender roles, and identity." Has published poetry by Sharon Bridgforth, Patricia Smith, Shia Shabazz, Ana-Maurine Lara, and Remica L. Bingham. Receives about 250+ submissions/year, accepts about 20. Number of unique visitors: 300+/month.

How to Submit Submit 3-7 poems at a time. Lines/poem: 40 maximum. No previously published poems or simultaneous submissions. Accepts e-mail submissions only (as one attachment). Send to poetry@torchpoetry.org with "Poetry Submission" in subject line. "Poems should be individually typed on separate pages." Cover letter is preferred (in the body of the e-mail). Reads submissions June 1-August 31 only. Time between acceptance and publication is 2-7 months. Sometimes comments on rejected poems. Sometimes publishes theme issues. Guidelines available on Web site. Always sends prepublication galleys. No payment. Acquires rights to publish accepted work in online issue and in archives. Rights revert to poets upon publication.

Also Offers "Within *Torch*, we offer a special section called Flame that features an interview, biography, and work sample by an established writer as well as an introduction to their Spark—an emerging writer who inspires them and adds to the boundless voice of creative writing by Black women." A free online newsletter is available; see Web site.

Advice "Black women, write freely. Know that your words are wanted, needed, and safe here. Read the previous issues online for examples of the type of writing *Torch* publishes."

✉ ◎ TOUCHSTONE LITERARY JOURNAL (Specialized: traditional forms, sonnets; translations)

P.O. Box 130233, The Woodlands TX 77393-0233. E-mail: panthercreek3@hotmail.com. Web site: www.panthercreekpress.com. Established 1975. **Contact:** Guida Laufer, poetry editor.

● *"At present we are overstocked and will accept no new submissions until 2008."*

Magazine Needs *Touchstone Literary Journal*, published annually in December, prints "experimental or well-crafted traditional forms, including sonnets, and translations." Does not want "light verse or doggerel." Has published poetry by Chuck Taylor, Chris Ellery, Jan Epton Seale, Paul Christensen, Walter McDonald, and Paul Ramsey. *Touchstone* is 100 pages, digest-sized, professionally printed in small, dark type, flat-spined, with glossy card cover. Subscription: $9.

How to Submit Submit 5 poems at a time. Cover letter is preferred. "Telling us something about the poet piques our interest and makes the submission seem less like a mass mailing." Sometimes sends prepublication galleys. Pays 2 contributor's copies. Reviews books of poetry. Send materials for review consideration to Review Editor.

✉ TRESTLE CREEK REVIEW

English Dept., North Idaho College, 1000 W. Garden Ave., Coeur d'Alene ID 83814-2199. (208)769-7877. Fax: (208)769-3431. E-mail: tcr@nic.edu. Established 1982-83. **Contact:** Lori Wallin, editor.

Magazine Needs *Trestle Creek Review*, published annually by North Idaho College, features poetry, fiction, creative nonfiction, and b&w art. "We're fairly eclectic and favor poetry strong on image and sound." Does not want "the romantic, the formulaic, and the clichéd." Has published poetry by Sean Brendan-Brown, E.G. Burrows, Ron McFarland, and Mary Winters. *Trestle Creek Review* is 57 pages, digest-sized, professionally printed on heavy buff stock, saddle-stapled, with matte cover with art. Receives 300 submissions/year, accepts about 30. Press run is 500. Single copy: $8.40. Sample: $5.25 (back issue).

How to Submit Submit 3-5 poems at a time. No previously published poems or simultaneous submissions. Accepts e-mail submissions; no fax submissions. Cover letter is required. Include address, phone number, e-mail address, brief bio, and SASE with all submissions; electronic submissions must include this information as well. Accepts submissions to January 31 deadline (for May publication). Responds by May 30. Pays 5 contributor's copies.

Advice "Be neat; be precise; don't romanticize or cry in your beer; strike the surprising, universal note. Know the names of things."

▢ ◎ TRIBUTARIES: A JOURNAL OF NATURE WRITING

% Cuyahoga Valley National Park Association, 1403 West Hines Hill Rd., Peninsula OH 44264. Web site: www.cvnpa.org. Established 1997.

Magazine Needs *TRIBUTARIES: A Journal of Nature Writing*, published annually by Cuyahoga Valley Nature Writers, seeks poems "addressing some aspect of nature or human relationships with the natural world." *TRIBUTARIES* is about 50 pages, digest-sized, saddle-stapled, with color cardstock cover. Single copy: $8. Available from Cuyahoga Valley National Park Association (see Web site).

How to Submit Submit up to 5 poems at a time. Lines/poem: no more than 60, including spaces between stanzas. Considers simultaneous submissions if identified as such; no previously published poems. Cover letter is required. Include name, mailing address, phone number, e-mail address, and titles of all submissions. Submit two copies of each poem, single-spaced in plain font on 8 × 11 pages. One copy should have title and author's name at the top of the page; the second copy should have only the title of the poem. Include a SASE. Reads submissions by July 31 deadline for publication the following year. **Reading fee:** $5. Make checks payable to Cuyahoga Valley National Park Association. Editorial committee reviews all submissions. Guidelines available for SASE. "We respond by letter in November. Writers whose work is accepted will be asked to supply a brief biographical note and sign a release certifying the work is their own and has not been published elsewhere."

Also Offers "Cuyahoga Valley Nature Writers is a volunteer group of local and regional writers. It provides workshop opportunities for writers in the area to present and discuss their prose and poetry. In keeping with the mission of the park, the principal focus of the group is on the natural world and all living things on our planet. Cuyahoga Valley Nature Writers is co-sponsored by the National Park Service at Cuyahoga Valley National Park and Cuyahoga Valley National Park Association."

✫ ▣ ◪ ◎ TRIPLOPIA (Specialized: thematic issues)

E-mail: editor@triplopia.org. Web site: www.triplopia.org. Established 2001. **Contact:** Tara A. Elliott, poetry editor.

Magazine Needs *TRIPLOPIA* is "an internationally oriented, Web-based quarterly with a solid emphasis on excellence and accessibility. We favor work that is both accessible and of significant use to the working writer." Wants "attention to craft as well as a range of voice." Does not want "poetry that has to force its way through an overt agenda." Considers poetry by teens. Has published poetry by Joy Harjo, Steve Kowit, Bob Holman, Angie Estes, Barbara Crooker, and Frannie Lindsay. Receives about 1,600 poems/year, accepts about 100. Number of unique visitors: 31,350/issue. "Each issue is widely publicized on Internet poetry sites/forums and individually to our large mailing list."

How to Submit Submit 5-6 poems at a time. Lines/poem: "no preference." Considers previously published poems; no simultaneous submissions. Accepts e-mail submissions; no disk submissions. "For work in special formats, please paste into body of e-mail and include an explanatory note in your submission. We will invite you to send an attachment once your material is under consideration." Cover letter is unnecessary. Reads submissions January 15-February 20; April 15-May 20; July 15-August 20; and October 15-November 20. Time between acceptance and publication is one month. Poems are circulated to an editorial board. Sometimes comments on rejected poems. Regularly publishes theme issues. Upcoming themes and guidelines available on Web site. Responds in 2 months. Always sends prepublication galleys. No payment, but provides links to contributor's other publications and maintains work in archives. Acquires one-time rights. Rights revert to poets upon publication.

Contest/Award Offerings Sponsors the Best of the Best Competition (see separate listing in Contests & Awards).

Advice ''We at *TRIPLOPIA* do everything in our power and imagination to promote and honor our contributors. We publish multiple pieces; contribute to major competitions including Pushcart and Best of the Net; offer our own competition (see Best of the Best in the Contests & Awards section); respond to submissions quickly; invite contributors back as reviewers; link to their work and Web sites in extensive bio notes; keep their work accessible in our archive; and are meticulous about galley proofs. We believe that we are there to support artists, not the other way around.''

✅ ◎ THE TULE REVIEW (Specialized: poets living in the greater Sacramento area)

Sacramento Poetry Center, 1719 25th St., Sacramento CA 95816. (916)451-5569. E-mail: tulereview @sacramentopoetrycenter.org. Web site: www.sacramentopoetrycenter.org. **Contact:** Brad Buchanan, managing editor.

Magazine Needs *The Tule Review*, published biannually, uses ''poetry, book reviews, and essays concerning contemporary poetry; occasionally includes an audio CD.'' Wants ''all styles and forms of poetry.'' Primarily publishes poets living in the greater Sacramento area, but accepts work from anywhere. Has published poetry by Gary Snyder, Diane DiPrima, Jack Hirschman, Julia Connor, Eve West Bessier, and Douglas Blazek. *The Tule Review* is 24-32 pages, digest-sized, saddle-stapled, with b&w cover artwork. Receives about 500 poems/year, accepts about 10-20%. Press run is 500 (300 subscribers, 20 libraries, 100 shelf sales); 80 distributed free to contributors and for review. Single copy: $6 ppd; subscription: $25/year (includes *Poetry Now*, a monthly publication). Make checks payable to Sacramento Poetry Center.

How to Submit Submit 3-6 poems at a time. Lines/poem: 96 maximum. Considers previously published poems; no simultaneous submissions. Accepts e-mail (pasted into body of message or as attachment) and disk submissions. ''If you attach poems, put all poems into one attachment.'' Cover letter is required. Reads submissions year round. Submit seasonal poems 6 months in advance. Time between acceptance and publication is 1-6 months. Poems are circulated to an editorial board. Sometimes comments on rejected poems. Sometimes publishes theme issues. Upcoming themes available in magazine, by e-mail, or on Web site. Guidelines available in magazine, for SASE, by e-mail, or on Web site. Responds in 4-6 weeks. Pays 2 contributor's copies. Acquires first North American serial rights. Rights revert to poet upon publication. Reviews books/chapbooks of poetry and other magazines/journals.

Also Offers ''Audio submissions are also accepted. Please submit all audio on CD. Recordings must be clear and high quality. Recordings of live performances must have minimal background noise.''

Advice ''Send us your best work!''

◑ ◎ TUNDRA: THE JOURNAL OF THE SHORT POEM (Specialized: poems of 13 or fewer lines, including haiku and tanka)

22230 NE 28th Place, Sammamish WA 98074-6408. E-mail: WelchM@aol.com. Web site: http://hometown.aol.com/welchm/Tundra.html. Established 1999. **Contact:** Michael Dylan Welch, editor/publisher.

Magazine Needs *Tundra: The Journal of the Short Poem* showcases all short poetry, including haiku, tanka, and other genres. Wants ''short poems of 13 or fewer lines rooted in immediate and objective imagery, including haiku and tanka.'' Does not want religious, topical, or confessional poetry. Has published poetry by Dana Gioia, X.J. Kennedy, Jane Hirshfield, Peter Pereira, Robert Bly, and Madeleine DeFrees. *Tundra* is 128 pages, digest-sized, offset-printed, perfect-bound, with glossy cover. Receives about 14,000 poems/year, accepts less than 1%. Press run is 1,200 (700 subscribers, 10 libraries, 50 shelf sales); 10 distributed free to such places as poetry centers. Single copy: $9; subscription: $21 for 3 issues. Make checks payable to Michael Dylan Welch.

How to Submit Submit 3-5 poems at a time (''up to ten is okay if as short as haiku''). No previously published poems or simultaneous submissions. Accepts e-mail submissions (pasted into body of message; no attachments); no disk submissions. ''Always include your full postal address with each e-mail submission." Cover letter is optional; "okay the first time you submit, but unnecessary thereafter unless you write something you are sure the editor needs to know. *Tundra* does not publish bios, so there's no need to include them except for the editor's information. Please include a #10 SASE with sufficient postage for return of the manuscript or for a response." Reads submissions year round. Time between acceptance and publication "varies, but is sometimes up to a year. The editor makes the sole decision, and may occasionally offer suggestions on poems whether accepted or returned. The editor will clearly indicate if he wants to see a revision." Recommends reading an issue before submitting, "but no purchase or subscription is required." Guidelines available for SASE, by e-mail, or on Web site. Responds in 1-2 months. Sometimes sends prepublication galleys. Pays one contributor's copy. Acquires first rights. "Rights revert to author after publication, but we may want to include selected poems on a Web site in the future." Reviews books/chapbooks of poetry in 500-2,000 words, single- and multi-book format. Send materials for review consideration to Michael Dylan Welch.

Advice "If your work centers on immediate and objective imagery, *Tundra* is interested. All poems must be 13 or fewer lines, with only very rare exceptions (where each line is very short). If you think that a haiku is merely 5-7-5 syllables, then I do not want to see your work (see 'Becoming a Haiku Poet' online at www.haikuworld.org/begin/mdwelch.apr2003.html. for reasons why). Due to the excessive volume of inappropriate submissions for *Tundra* in the past, I now encourage only well-established poets to submit."

$⊚ TURTLE MAGAZINE FOR PRESCHOOL KIDS (Specialized: ages 2-5; health-related themes)

Children's Better Health Institute, 1100 Waterway Blvd., Indianapolis IN 46202. Web site: www.cbhi.org. or www.turtlemag.org.

Magazine Needs *Turtle Magazine for Preschool Kids*, published by Childen's Better Health Institute, is a magazine for children ages 2-5. "Colorful and entertaining . . . perfect for reading aloud." Wants poetry appropriate for the age group with health-related themes. " 'Health' is a broad topic that includes exercise, sports, safety, nutrition, hygiene, and drug education." **Does not encourage writing submissions from children.** Reviews submissions for possible use in all Children's Better Health Institute publications. Subscription: $15.95/year each ($23.95 outside U.S.). Sample: $2.95.

How to Submit No simultaneous submissions. Manuscripts must be typewritten with poet's contact information in upper right-hand corner of each poem's page. SASE required. Submit seasonal material at least 8 months in advance. Guidelines available for SASE or on Web site. Responds in about 3 months. Pays $25 minimum for poetry. Acquires all rights.

Advice "We receive too many poetry submissions that are about kids, not for kids. Or, the subject matter is one that adults think children would or should like. Reading our guidelines is not enough. Careful study of current issues will acquaint writers with each title's 'personality.' "

⊘ 24.7

30 Forest St., Providence RI 02906. (401)521-4728. Established 1994. **Contact:** David Church, poetry editor.

• **Considers solicited submissions only.**

⊿ U.S. 1 WORKSHEETS

P.O. Box 127, Kingston NJ 08528-0127. Established 1973. **Contact:** Nancy Scott, managing editor.

Magazine Needs *U.S. 1 Worksheets*, published annually, uses high-quality poetry and, on occasion, short fiction. "We prefer complex, well-written work." Has published poetry by Alicia Ostriker, BJ Ward, James Richardson, Lois Marie Harrod, and Baron Wormser. *U.S. 1 Worksheets* is 96 pages, perfect-bound, with b&w cover art. Press run is 500. Subscription: $8/year, $14/2 years. Sample: $6.

How to Submit Submit up to 5 poems at a time. No previously published poems; no simultaneous submissions unless indicated. "We use a rotating board of editors. We read April through June, and can no longer return manuscripts. Enclose SASE for reply." Pays one contributor's copy.

Also Offers The U.S. 1 Poets' Cooperative co-sponsors (with the Princeton Public Library) a series of poetry readings (U.S. 1 Poets Invite) at the Princeton Public Library. "There is no formal membership, only the willingness of participants to share their work."

Advice "Send us your best. Please note submission dates. We receive many good poems we cannot consider because they arrive far outside our reading period."

UGLY ACCENT: A LITERARY ADVERSARIA BROUGHT TO YOU BY THE MIDWEST

2310 40th Pl. NW, #302, Washington DC 20007. E-mail: poetry@uglyaccent.com. Web site: www.uglyaccent.com. Established 2006. **Contact:** Matt Friauf and Gabe Gossett, poetry editors.

Magazine Needs *UGLY ACCENT: A Literary Adversaria Brought to You by the Midwest*, published quarterly in print and online, seeks "to publish new talent, specifically those with some degree of separation to the Midwest. We wish to glorify the cesspool of talent that this part of the nation breeds." Has published poetry by Ron Czerwien, Eddie Kilowatt, Gene Tanta, Paul Gaszak, Karla Huston, and Bronwen Tate. *UGLY ACCENT* (print version) is 40 pages, magazine-sized, newsprint with glued binding, with newsprint cover with artwork, includes ads. Receives about 350 poems/ year, accepts about 80 (22%). Press run is 2,000; distributed free to local bookstores, cafes, food co-ops, libraries, and universities. Single copy: $4; subscription: $10/year. Make checks payable to *UGLY ACCENT*.

How to Submit Submit 5 poems at a time. Lines/poem: open. Considers previously published poems and simultaneous submissions. Accepts e-mail submissions (as attachment); no disk submissions. Cover letter is preferred. Include 50-word bio with submission. Reads submissions year round. Time between acceptance and publication is 6 months. Poems are circulated to an editorial board. Often comments on rejected poems. Sometimes publishes theme issues. Guidelines available on Web site. Responds in 3-4 months. Pays one contributor's copy. Acquires one-time rights and right to publish work in online archives. Rights revert to poets upon publication. Reviews books/ chapbooks of poetry. Send materials for review consideration to the attention of Gabe Gossett.

Advice "We are looking for writers with subtlety and a predilection for experimentation with language and form. We believe that poetry should test the elasticity of language and utilize the form for all its worth. Self-absorbed poems will not be tolerated; sure, all poems are autobiographical to some extent, but at least pretend to care about something else."

UNDERSTANDING MAGAZINE

127 Milton Rd. W., 7 Duddingston House Courtyard, Edinburgh EH15 1JG Scotland. Phone/fax: (44)(131)661-1156. Established 1989. **Contact:** Denise Smith.

Magazine Needs *Understanding Magazine*, published annually, features "poetry, short stories, parts of plays, reviews, and articles." Wants "original poetry." Has published poetry by Susanna Roxman, D. Zervanou, Thom Nairn, Alexis Stamatis, Byron Leodaris, and Keith Bennett. *Understanding* is A5, perfect-bound. Receives 2,000 poems/year. Press run is 1,000 (500 subscribers). Single copy: £5.50; subscription: £11. Sample: £3. Make checks payable to Dionysia Press Ltd.

How to Submit Submit up to 5 poems at a time. No previously published poems or simultaneous submissions. No fax submissions. Time between acceptance and publication is 6 months to a year. Poems are circulated to an editorial board. Often comments on rejected poems. Guidelines available for SASE or by fax. Responds in 6 months or more. Always sends prepublication galleys. Pays one contributor's copy. Acquires all rights. Returns rights after publication. Staff reviews books/ chapbooks of poetry or other magazines. Send materials for review consideration.

Contest/Award Offerings Sponsors poetry competitions with cash prizes. Guidelines and themes available for SASE.

Advice "Be original."

✪ ◙ UNMUZZLED OX

105 Hudson St., New York NY 10013. Established 1971. **Contact:** Michael Andre, poetry editor.

Magazine Needs Unmuzzled Ox, published biannually, is a literary tabloid. Each edition is built around a theme or specific project. **"The chances of an unsolicited poem being accepted are slight since I always have specific ideas in mind."** Has published poetry by Allen Ginsberg, Robert Creeley, and Denise Levertov. Subscription: $20.

How to Submit Only unpublished work will be considered, but poems may be in French as well as English.

Advice "I suggest contributors read carefully an issue before sending in an unsolicited manuscript."

▣ ◪ VALPARAISO POETRY REVIEW: CONTEMPORARY POETRY AND POETICS

Dept. of English, Valparaiso University, Valparaiso IN 46383-6493. (219)464-5278. Fax: (219)464-5511. E-mail: vpr@valpo.edu. Web site: www.valpo.edu/english/vpr/. Established 1999. **Contact:** Edward Byrne, editor.

Magazine Needs *Valparaiso Poetry Review: Contemporary Poetry and Poetics*, published semiannually online, accepts "submissions of unpublished or previously published poetry, book reviews, author interviews, and essays on poetry or poetics that have not yet appeared online and for which the rights belong to the author. Query for anything else." Wants poetry of any length or style, free verse or traditional forms. Has published poetry by Charles Wright, Jonathan Holden, Janet Mc-Cann, Laurence Lieberman, Beth Simon, and Margot Schilpp. Receives about 2,000 poems/year, accepts about 7%.

How to Submit Submit 3-5 poems at a time (no more than 5). Considers previously published poems ("original publication must be identified to ensure proper credit") and simultaneous submissions. Accepts e-mail submissions (pasted into body of message, no attachments); no fax or disk submissions. **Postal submissions preferred.** Cover letter is preferred. Include SASE. Reads submissions year round. Time between acceptance and publication is 6-12 months. Seldom comments on rejected poems. Guidelines available on Web site. Responds in up to 6 weeks. Acquires one-time rights. "All rights remain with author." Reviews books of poetry in single- and multi-book format. Send materials for review consideration.

🌐 ◪ VAN GOGH'S EAR: BEST WORLD POETRY & PROSE

French Connection Press, 12 rue Lamartine, Paris 75009 France. (33)(1)4016-0535. Fax: (33)(1)4016-0701. E-mail: frenchcx@tiscali.fr. Web site: www.frenchcx.com. Established 2002. **Contact:** Ian Ayres, founder/editor.

● Poetry published in *VAN GOGH'S EAR* has appeared in *The Best American Poetry*.

Magazine Needs *VAN GOGH'S EAR*, published annually in April, is an anthology series "devoted to publishing powerful poetry and prose in English and English translations by major voices and innovative new talents from around the globe." Has published poetry by Marilyn Monroe, Tony Curtis, Yoko Ono, James Dean, Xaviera Hollander, and Charles Manson. *VAN GOGH'S EAR* is 280 pages, digest-sized, offset-printed, perfect-bound, with 4-color matte cover with commissioned artwork. Receives about 1,000 poems/year, accepts about 30%. Press run is 2,000 (105 subscribers, 25 libraries, 1,750 shelf/online sales); 120 distributed free to contributors and reviewers. Single copy: $19; subscription: $36 for 2 years. "As a 501(c)(3) nonprofit enterprise, *VAN GOGH'S EAR* needs the support of individual poets, writers, and readers to survive. Any donation, large or small, will help *VAN GOGH'S EAR* continue to publish the best cross-section of contemporary poetry and prose. Because of being an anglophone publication based in France, *VAN GOGH'S EAR* is unable to get any grants or funding. Your contribution will be tax-deductible. Make donation checks payable to Committee on Poetry-*VGE*, and mail them (donations **only**) to the Allen Ginsberg Trust, P.O. Box 582, Stuyvesant Station, New York NY 10009. All U.S. checks/money orders for reading fees, subscriptions, and purchases must be made out to French Connection Press and sent to Michael Hathaway, 522 E. South Ave., St. John KS 67576-2212.''

How to Submit Submit 6 poems or 2 prose pieces at a time. Lines/poem: 165 maximum (1,500 words maximum for prose). No previously published poems or simultaneous submissions. No fax, e-mail, or disk submissions. Cover letter is preferred. ''**Send to the French Connection Press address only!** Please include SASE (or SAE with IRCs) or e-mail address along with a brief bio of up to 120 words.'' Reads submissions May 1-October 31. **Charges $10 (USD) reading fee for non-subscribers.** Time between acceptance and publication is one year. ''Every submission is closely read by all members of the editorial board and voted upon.'' Seldom comments on rejections. ''Our continued existence, and continued ability to read your work, depends mainly on subscriptions/donations. Therefore, we must ask that you at least purchase a sample copy before submitting work.'' Guidelines available in anthology or on Web site. Responds in 9 months. Always sends prepublication galleys. Pays one contributor's copy. Acquires one-time rights.

Advice ''The goal of *VAN GOGH'S EAR* is for each volume to transport all who experience it into multifaceted realities that transcend color and culture through the uncensored pens of legendary and new talents from all walks of life. 'Intensity' is the key. And we are more than open to poets/writers who haven't been published before. Being published isn't as important as the work itself.''

VERSAL

Amsterdam, The Netherlands. E-mail: versal@wordsinhere.com. (inquiries only). Web site: www.wordsinhere.com. Established 2002. **Contact:** Megan M. Garr, editor.

Magazine Needs *Versal*, published annually by wordsinhere, is the only English-language literary magazine in The Netherlands and publishes new poetry, prose, and art from around the world. Wants work ''that is urgent, involved, and unexpected. Send us your best.'' Has published poetry by Russell Edson, Naomi Shihab Nye, Marilyn Hacker, and Aleida Rodriguez. *Versal* is 100 pages, 20cm×20cm, offset-printed, perfect-bound, with acid-free full-color cover. Receives about 1,000+ poems/year, accepts about 4%. Single copy: $10 USD or €8. Ordering information available on Web site.

How to Submit Submit 3-5 poems at a time. Considers simultaneous submissions ''as long as you inform us as soon as your work has been accepted elsewhere''; no previously published poems. Accepts e-mail submissions only (as attachment, all poems in a single Word document). **NOTE:** See Web site for submission e-mail address, which is removed from site between reading periods. Cover letter is required (in body of e-mail). Reads submissions September 15-January 15. Time between acceptance and publication is 4-6 months. Poems are circulated to an editorial board. Sometimes comments on rejected poems. Guidelines available on Web site. Responds in 4 months. Sends prepublication PDF galleys. Pays one contributor's copy. Acquires one-time rights. Rights revert to poet upon publication.

Advice ''Write as much as you can. Follow the guidelines. Resist the urge to send us poems about tulips, windmills, or sex and drug adventures. Support independent literary publishing: Buy copies of *Versal* and any other lit mag you find.''

VERSE

Dept. of English, University of Richmond, Richmond VA 23173. Web site: http://versemag.blogspot.com. Established 1984. **Contact:** Brian Henry and Andrew Zawacki, editors.

● **NOTE:** *Verse* **is closed to submissions for the rest of 2007; check Web site for latest submission details.** Poetry published in *Verse* has also appeared in *The Best American Poetry* and *The Pushcart Prize*.

Magazine Needs *Verse*, published 3 times/year, is "an international poetry journal which also publishes interviews with poets, essays on poetry, and book reviews." Wants "no specific kind; we look for high-quality, innovative poetry. Our focus is not only on American poetry, but on all poetry written in English, as well as translations." Has published poetry by James Tate, John Ashbery, Barbara Guest, Gustaf Sobin, and Rae Armantrout. *Verse* is 128-416 pages, digest-sized, professionally printed, perfect-bound, with card cover. Receives about 5,000 poems/year, accepts 1%. Press run is 1,000 (600 subscribers, 200 libraries, 200 shelf sales). Single copy: $10; subscription: $18 for individuals, $39 for institutions. Sample: $6.

How to Submit Submit up to 5 poems at a time, no more than twice/year. Considers simultaneous submissions; no previously published poems. Cover letter is required. Time between acceptance and publication is up to 18 months. Occasionally comments on rejected poems. "The magazine often publishes special features—recent features include younger American poets, Mexican poetry, prose poetry, the poetic sequence, women Irish poets, and Australian poetry—but does not publish 'theme' issues." Guidelines available on Web site. Responds within 4 months. Always sends prepublication galleys. Pays 2 contributor's copies plus a one-year subscription. Send materials for review consideration.

Advice "Read widely and deeply. Avoid inundating a magazine with submissions; constant exposure will not increase your chances of getting accepted."

✖ ▣ ◨ VIGIL

2 Rougemont Terrace, Axminster, Devon EX13 5JP England. Established 1986. **Contact:** John Howard-Greaves, poetry editor.

Magazine Needs *Vigil*, published semiannually, seeks "poetry with a high level of emotional force or intensity of observation. Color, imagery, and appeal to the senses should be important features. Form may be traditional or experimental." Does not want "whining self-indulgent, neurotic soul-baring poetry." Has published poetry by Michael Newman, Claudette Bass, David Flynn, Sheila Murphy, and Karen Rosenberg. *Vigil* is usually 40 pages, digest-sized, professionally printed, saddle-stapled, with colored matte card cover. Receives about 400 poems/year, accepts about 60. Press run is 250 (85 subscribers, 6 libraries). Subscription: £8. Sample: £3.

How to Submit Submit up to 6 poems at a time. Lines/poem: 40 maximum. No previously published poems. Submissions should be typed. Sometimes comments on rejected poems. Guidelines available in magazine or for SASE (or SAE and IRC). Sometimes sends prepublication galleys. Pays 2 contributor's copies.

Additional Information Query regarding book publication by Vigil Publications. **Offers "appraisal" for £15** for a sample of a maximum of 6 poems.

$▣ THE VIRGINIA QUARTERLY REVIEW

P.O. Box 400223, Charlottesville VA 22904-4223. (434)924-3124. Fax: (434)924-1397. Web site: www.vqronline.org. Established 1925.

Magazine Needs *The Virginia Quarterly Review* uses about 45-50 pages of poetry in each issue. No length or subject restrictions. Issues have largely included lyric and narrative free verse, most of which features a strong message or powerful voice. *The Virginia Quarterly Review* is 200-300 pages, digest-sized, flat-spined. Press run is 6,500.

How to Submit Submit up to 5 poems at a time. No simultaneous submissions. Accepts postal submissions only; include SASE ("you will not be notified otherwise"). Responds in 3 months or longer, "due to the large number of poems we receive." Guidelines available for SASE, by e-mail, or on Web site; do not request by fax. Pays $5/line.

Contest/Award Offerings Sponsors the Emily Clark Balch Prize for Poetry, an annual award of $1,000 given to the best poem or group of poems published in the *Review* during the year. 2006 winner was Susan B. A. Somers-Willett.

◪ VOICINGS FROM THE HIGH COUNTRY

4920 S. Oak St., Casper WY 82601. Established 2000. **Contact:** Ella J. Cvancara, editor.

Magazine Needs *Voicings from the High Country*, published annually in the spring, seeks "poetry with substance, not just pretty words; understandable, rather than obscure; poetry that goes beyond the self. Biased toward free verse that is worldly rather than introspective, tells a story, and uses many/most/all of the five senses." Also considers haiku, senryu, and tanka (for a haiku page). Does not want "rhyming, pornography, violent language, 'Hallmark' verse, political poems, or overtly religious poetry. No poetry that's unsure of why it was written, is demeaning to the human spirit, or untitled." Has published poetry by guest poets David Lee, the first poet laureate of Utah, and Robert Roripaugh, former poet laureate of Wyoming. *Voicings from the High Country* is 35-40 pages, digest-sized, computer-generated, stapled, with 110 lb. cardstock cover. Receives about 200 poems/year, accepts about 15%. Press run is 75 (45 shelf sales); 30 distributed free to contributors. Single copy: $6. Make checks payable to Ella J. Cvancara.

How to Submit Submit 3 poems at a time. Lines/poem: 35 maximum. Considers previously published poems; no simultaneous submissions. Accepts submissions by postal mail only; no disk submissions. Cover letter is required. Include a 3- to 5-line bio. "Submit each poem on a separate page with name and address in upper right corner; typed or computer-generated. Include SASE for response." Reads submissions July 1-February 1 only. Time between acceptance and publication is 3 months. "Poems are circulated to a three-member editorial board with the names of the poets removed. Poems are ranked according to a system." Seldom comments on rejected poems. Guidelines available for SASE. Responds in 6 months. Pays one contributor's copy. Acquires one-time rights.

Advice "Beginners often write about themselves. Reach beyond yourself, avoid clichés, search for fresh language. Use metaphor and simile. Strike a spark with words."

◪ VOX

P.O. Box 527, Oxford MS 38655. E-mail: voxjournal@hotmail.com. Established 2004. **Contact:** Louis E. Bourgeois, Max B. Hipp, and J.E. Pitts, editors.

Magazine Needs *VOX*, published semiannually, seeks "new voices that truly stand out from the crowd." Wants "lyrical/experimental anti-narrative [poetry]. Originality is key." Does not want "workshop conformity, watered-down Dada and Surrealism, or greeting card verse. Rhymed verse is discouraged unless exceptional." Has published poetry by André Breton, Anne Baker, Cyril Wong, Steve Kistulentz, and George Trakl. *VOX* is 100 pages, digest-sized, laser-printed, perfect-bound, with glossy cover. Receives about 2,000 poems/year, accepts about 1%. Press run is 500. Single copy: $7.50; subscription: $15. Make checks payable to VOX Publications.

How to Submit Submit 3-5 poems or 3 short prose pieces at a time. Lines/poem: 60 maximum (1,000 words maximum for prose poems). Considers previously published poems and simultaneous submissions. Accepts e-mail submissions (pasted into body of message or as attachment); no disk submissions. Cover letter is preferred. Include SASE. Reads submissions year round. Time between acceptance and publication is 6 months. Poems are circulated to an editorial board. Sometimes comments on rejected poems. Guidelines available in magazine or by e-mail. Responds in up to 4 months. Sometimes sends prepublication galleys. Pays one contributor's copy and a discount on additional issues. Acquires one-time rights. Reviews books/chapbooks of poetry and other magazines/journals in 500 words, single-book format. Send materials for review consideration to J.E. Pitts.

◻ ◎ WATERWAYS: POETRY IN THE MAINSTREAM (Specialized: thematic issues)

Ten Penny Players, Inc., 393 Saint Pauls Ave., Staten Island NY 10304-2127. (718)442-7429. E-mail: tenpennyplayers@si.rr.com. Web site: www.tenpennyplayers.org. Established 1977. **Contact:** Barbara Fisher and Richard Spiegel, poetry editors.

Magazine Needs *Waterways: Poetry in the Mainstream*, published 11 times/year, prints work by adult poets. "We publish theme issues and are trying to increase an audience for poetry and the printed and performed word. While we do 'themes,' sometimes an idea for a future magazine is inspired by a submission, so we try to remain open to poets' inspirations. Poets should be guided, however, by the fact that we are children's and animal rights advocates and are a NYC press. We are open to reading material from people we have never published, writing in traditional and experimental poetry forms." Does not want "haiku or rhyming poetry; never use material of an explicit sexual nature." Has published poetry by Ida Fasel, Robert Cooperman, and Joan Payne Kincaid. *Waterways* is 40 pages, $4\frac{1}{4} \times 7$, photocopied from various type styles, saddle-stapled, with matte card cover. Accepts 60% of poems submitted. Press run is 150 (58 subscribers, 12 libraries). Subscription: $33. Sample: $3.50.

How to Submit Submit less than 10 poems at a time (for first submission). Considers simultaneous submissions. Accepts e-mail submissions (pasted into body of message). "Since we've taken the time to be very specific in our response, writers should take seriously our comments and not waste their emotional energy and our time sending material that isn't within our area of interest. Sending for our theme sheet and a sample issue and then objectively thinking about the writer's own work is practical and wise. Manuscripts that arrive without a return envelope are not sent back." Sometimes comments on rejected poems. Guidelines available for SASE or on Web site. Responds in less than one month. Pays one contributor's copy. Acquires one-time publication rights.

Additional Information Ten Penny Players publishes chapbooks "by children and young adults only—not by submission—they come through our workshops in the library and schools. Adult poets are published through our Bard Press imprint, **by invitation only**. Books evolve from the relationship we develop with writers we publish in *Waterways* and to whom we would like to give more exposure."

Advice "We suggest that poets attend book fairs and check our Web site. It's a fast way to find out what we're publishing. Without meaning to sound 'precious' or unfriendly, the writer should understand that small press publishers doing limited editions and all production work in-house are working from their personal artistic vision and know exactly what notes will harmonize, effectively counterpoint, and meld. Many excellent poems submitted to *Waterways* are sent back to the writers because they don't relate to what we are trying to create in a given month."

☑ WAVELENGTH: POEMS IN PROSE AND VERSE

1753 Fisher Ridge Rd., Horse Cave KY 42749-9706. Established 1999. **Contact:** David P. Rogers, editor/publisher.

Magazine Needs *Wavelength: Poems in Prose and Verse*, published twice /year, seeks "poems that use lively images, intriguing metaphor, and original language. Long poems OK; would like to see more prose poems. Rhyme is almost always a liability. All subjects and styles considered as long as the poem is thought-provoking or uses language in an innovative way." Does not want "rhymed, very religious—anything that sacrifices creativity for convention." Has published poetry by Robert Cooperman, Lyn Lifshin, Francis Blessington, Ann Taylor, Albert Haley, and Virgil Suárez. *Wavelength* is 35 (or more) pages, digest-sized, laser-printed, perfect-bound, with heavy cardstock cover with illustration. Receives about 450 poems/year, accepts 5-10%. Press run is 100 (25 subscribers, 20-25 shelf sales); 50 distributed free to the public. Single copy: $6; subscription: $15 for 3 issues. Make checks payable to Dr. David P. Rogers.

How to Submit Submit 1-5 poems at a time. Considers previously published poems and simultaneous submissions, "but please do not withdraw the poem after we've accepted it." No disk submissions. Cover letter is required. "Brief bio preferred. Poet's name and address must appear on every page. SASE or no response. Poets who want poems returned should include sufficient postage." Submit seasonal poems 3 months in advance. Time between acceptance and publication is up to one year. Seldom comments on rejected poems. "Please do not write for guidelines. Just send a courteous submission following the guidelines in this listing." Responds in 4 months. Pays one contributor's copy. Acquires one-time rights. Reviews books/chapbooks of poetry in 100-150 words, single-book format. Send materials for review consideration.

Advice "Read and write every day. If a poem still seems good a year after you wrote it, send it out. Be original. Say something clever, and ask what will the reader get out of it? Editor has a weakness for synesthesia. The cover letter will not get your poems published if they're not what we need, but it gives you a chance to create interest in them—why not take it?"

$◙ WEBER STUDIES—VOICES AND VIEWPOINTS OF THE CONTEMPORARY WEST

Weber State University, 1214 University Circle, Ogden UT 84408-1214. (801)626-6473. E-mail: webe rstudies@weber.edu. Web site: http://weberstudies.weber.edu. Established 1983. **Contact:** Brad L. Roghaar, editor.

• Poetry published in *Weber Studies* has appeared in *The Best American Poetry*.

Magazine Needs *Weber Studies—Voices and Viewpoints of the Contemporary West*, published 3 times/year, is "an interdisciplinary journal interested in relevant works covering a wide range of topics." Wants "three or four poems; we publish multiple poems from a poet." Does not want "poems that are flippant, prurient, sing-song, or preachy." Has published poetry by William Kloefkorn, Gailmarie Pahmeier, Mark Strand, Janet Sylvester, David Lee, and Robert Dana. *Weber Studies* is 144 pages, $7\frac{1}{2} \times 10$, offset-printed on acid-free paper, perfect-bound, with color cover. Receives about 250-300 poems/year, accepts 30-40. Press run is 1,200 (1,000 subscribers, 90 libraries). Subscription: $20 ($30 for institutions). Sample: $10 (back issue).

How to Submit Submit 3-4 poems at a time, 2 copies of each (one without name). Considers simultaneous submissions; no previously published poems. Cover letter is preferred. Time between acceptance and publication is 15 months. Poems are selected by an anonymous (blind) evaluation. Seldom comments on rejected poems. Publishes theme issues. Guidelines available in magazine, for SASE, by e-mail, or on Web site. Responds in up to 6 months. Always sends prepublication galleys. Pays $30-50/poem (depending on fluctuating grant monies) and 2 contributor's copies. Acquires all rights. Copyright reverts to author after first printing.

Contest/Award Offerings The Dr. Sherwin W. Howard Poetry Award, a $500 cash prize, is awarded annually to the author of the best set of poems published in *Weber Studies* during the previous year. The competition is announced each year in the Spring/Summer issue.

Advice "This journal is refereed by established poets—beginners not encouraged."

◪ ◎ WESTVIEW: A JOURNAL OF WESTERN OKLAHOMA (Specialized: particularly interested in Southwest writers)

Southwestern Oklahoma State University, 100 Campus Dr., Weatherford OK 73096. Established 1981. **Contact:** James Silver, editor.

Magazine Needs *Westview: A Journal of Western Oklahoma*, published semiannually, is "particularly interested in writers from the Southwest; however, we are open to quality work by poets from elsewhere. We publish free verse, prose poems, and formal poetry." Has published poetry by Carolynne Wright, Miller Williams, Walter McDonald, Robert Cooperman, Alicia Ostriker, and James Whitehead. *Westview* is 64 pages, magazine-sized, perfect-bound, with full-color glossy card cover. Receives about 500 poems/year, accepts 7%. Press run is 700 (300 subscribers, about 25 libraries). Subscription: $15/2 years. Sample: $5.

How to Submit Submit 5 poems at a time. Cover letter is required. Including biographical data for contributor's note. Comments on submissions "when close." Manuscripts are circulated to an editorial board. Responds within 4-6 months. Pays one contributor's copy.

☐ WESTWARD QUARTERLY: THE MAGAZINE OF FAMILY READING

Laudemont Press, P.O. Box 250, Kirkland IL 60146. (800)440-4043. E-mail: wwquarterly@aol.com. Web site: http://members.aol.com/wwquarterly. Established 1999. **Contact:** Shirley Anne Leonard, editor.

Magazine Needs *WestWard Quarterly: The Magazine of Family Reading* prints poetry and occasional short stories. Wants "all forms, including rhyme—we welcome inspirational, positive, reflective, humorous material promoting nobility, compassion, and courage." Does not want "experimental or avant-garde forms, offensive language, depressing or negative poetry." Considers poetry by children and teens. Has published poetry by Bruce Adkins, Margaret Been, Joseph Fecher, Brian Felder, Michael Keshigian, and d.n. simmers. *WestWard Quarterly* is 32 pages, digest-sized, laser-printed, saddle-stapled, with inkjet color cover with scenic photos, includes ads. Receives about 2,000 poems/year, accepts about 8%. Press run is 120 (60 subscribers). Single copy: $4; subscription: $15/year ($18 foreign). Make checks payable to Laudemont Press.

How to Submit Submit up to 5 poems at a time. Lines/poem: 40 maximum. Considers previously published poems and simultaneous submissions. Prefers e-mail submissions (pasted into body of message); no disk submissions. Reads submissions year round. Submit seasonal poems 3 months in advance. Time between acceptance and publication is "months." Often comments on rejected poems. Guidelines available for SASE, by e-mail, or on Web site. Responds in "weeks." Pays one contributor's copy. Acquires one-time rights.

Contest/Award Offerings Offers a quarterly prize of one-half of entry fees per contest. Submit poems up to 40 lines. **Entry fee:** $1 for subscribers, $2 for nonsubscribers. **Deadline:** March 31, June 30, September 30, December 31. Guidelines available in magazine, for SASE, by e-mail, or on Web site.

Also Offers "Every issue has an article on improving writing skills and/or writing different forms of poetry."

☑ WHISKEY ISLAND MAGAZINE

English Dept., Cleveland State University, Cleveland OH 44115. (216)687-2056. Fax: (216)687-6943. E-mail: whiskeyisland@csuohio.edu. Web site: www.csuohio.edu/whiskey_island. Established 1968. **Contact:** Poetry Editor. (Student editors change yearly.)

Magazine Needs *Whiskey Island Magazine*, published semiannually, prints poetry, fiction, nonfiction, drama, and art. Wants "writing that engages the reader immediately. It's always good to be interesting early." Has published poetry by Nin Andrews, Jim Daniels, Denise Duhamel, Alison Luterman, and Maureen McHugh. *Whiskey Island Magazine* is about 80 pages, digest-sized, professionally printed, perfect-bound, with glossy stock cover. Receives 1,000-1,500 poetry mss/year, accepts 6%. Press run is 1,200 (200 subscribers, 20 libraries, about 300 shelf sales). Subscription: $12 domestic, $20 overseas. Sample: $6. Make checks payable to *Whiskey Island Magazine*.

How to Submit Submit 3-5 poems at a time. No previously published poems. Cover letter is required. Include brief bio and SASE for reply only, with name, address, e-mail, and phone number on each page of ms. Reads submissions year round. Poems are circulated to an editorial committee. Guidelines available in magazine, for SASE, by e-mail, or on Web site. Responds within 4 months. Pays 2 contributor's copies and one-year subscription.

Contest/Award Offerings Sponsors an annual poetry contest. 1st Prize: $300; 2nd Prize: $200; 3rd Prize: $100. **Entry fee:** $10. **Deadline:** entries accepted October 1-March 31. Guidelines available by e-mail or on Web site.

☑ ◎ WHITE LOTUS: A JOURNAL OF SHORT ASIAN VERSE AND HAIGA

Shadow Poetry, 1209 Milwaukee St., Excelsior Springs MO 64024. Phone/fax: (208)977-9114. E-mail: whitelotus@shadowpoetry.com. Web site: www.shadowpoetry.com/magazine/whitelotus.h

tml. Established 2005 (Shadow Poetry Web site established 2000). **Contact:** Marie Summers, chief editor. Associate Editor: Kathy Lippard Cobb.

Magazine Needs *White Lotus*, published semiannually, is a "specialized journal of haiku, senryu, tanka, and haiga. Editors'/readers' choice awards are also featured. Articles, book reviews, and sumi-e are welcome." Wants "only haiku, senryu, tanka, haiga, and sumi-e of the highest quality from poets ages 13 and up. The top ten placing entries in Shadow Poetry's annual *White Lotus* Haiku Competition are published in the Spring/Summer issue." *White Lotus* is 32-60 pages, digest-sized, saddle-stapled, with glossy b&w cover; back cover reserved for a color-printed haiga. Receives about 500 haiku/senryu per issue, prints less than 10%. Single copy: $7.95 U.S., $8.95 Canada, $10 USD international; subscription: $15/year U.S., $20/year international. Make checks/money orders payable to Shadow Poetry.

How to Submit Submit up to 10 haiku/senryu/tanka at a time, with correct seasonal theme (if applicable) in accordance with the next issue to be released. No previously published poems or simultaneous submissions. Accepts fax, e-mail, and disk submissions, as well as submissions through online form and by postal mail. Cover letter is preferred. "Name of author, street address, and e-mail address must accompany all submissions, no exceptions. If work is accepted, participants will be contacted by mail or e-mail within one month of submissions." Reads submissions according to the following deadlines: June 30 (Fall/Winter issue) and December 31 (Spring/Summer issue). Never comments on rejected poems. Guidelines available in magazine or on Web site. Sends prepublication galleys. "Final drafts will be e-mailed or mailed to the accepted poet." Acquires first rights.

Additional Information Shadow Poetry sponsors The Little Bitty Poetry Competition, Rhyme Time Poetry Contest, Seasonal Poetry Competition, Shadow Poetry's Biannual Chapbook Competition, and *White Lotus* Haiku Competition (see separate listings in Contests & Awards.

WHITE PELICAN REVIEW

P.O. Box 7833, Lakeland FL 33813. Established 1999. **Contact:** Nancy Wiegel, editor.

Magazine Needs *White Pelican Review*, published semiannually in April and October, is dedicated to printing poetry of the highest quality. Wants "writing that goes beyond competency to truly masterful acts of imagination and language." Has published poetry by Paul Hostovsky, Michael Hettich, Corrine De Winter, James Doyle, and Lou Suarez. *White Pelican Review* is about 48 pages, digest-sized, photocopied from typescript, saddle-stapled, with matte cardstock cover. Receives about 5,000 poems/year, accepts 3%. Circulation is 500. Single copy: $4; subscription: $8/year for individuals, $10/year for institutions. Make checks payable to *White Pelican Review*.

How to Submit Submit 3-5 poems at a time. Lines/poem: "optimal length is 32 lines plus title, although longer poems are given full consideration." No previously published poems or simultaneous submissions. Cover letter is required. SASE is a must. "Please include name, address, telephone number, and (if available) e-mail address on each page. No handwritten poems." Reads submissions year round. Time between acceptance and publication is 1-6 months. Poems are circulated to an editorial board. Seldom comments on rejected poems. Guidelines available for SASE. Responds in 6 months. Pays one contributor's copy. Acquires one-time rights.

Contest/Award Offerings The Hollingsworth Prize of $100 is offered to the most distinguished poem published in each issue. No contest or fee is involved.

WILD GOOSE POETRY REVIEW

Central Piedmont Community College, Levine Campus, P.O. Box 35009, Charlotte NC 28235-5009. (704)330-4397. E-mail: Patricia.Bostian@cpcc.edu. Web site: www.wildgoosepoetryreview.com. Established 2005. **Contact:** Patricia Kennedy Bostian, editor.

Magazine Needs *Wild Goose Poetry Review*, published quarterly online, is a poetry journal with essays, reviews, and interviews. Wants "poetry that exudes a sense of place, that is well-crafted, with an eye to imagery and an ear to music." Does not want "erotica, abstract stream-of-consciousness, or gratuitous obscenities." Has published poetry by Anthony Abbott. Receives about 1,000 poems/year, accepts about 12%.

How to Submit Submit 3-5 poems at a time. Lines/poem: "no poems longer than two pages accepted." Considers simultaneous submissions; no previously published poems. Accepts e-mail submissions only (pasted into body of message); no disk submissions. Cover letter is preferred. Reads submissions year round. Time between acceptance and publication is up to 6 months. Poems are circulated to an editorial board. Comments on rejected poems. Guidelines available on Web site. Responds in 4-6 weeks. Rights revert to poet upon publication. Reviews books/chapbooks of poetry in 500 words. Send materials for review consideration to Patricia Bostian.

Advice "Read, read, read. Inspiration does not a poem make. Revise, revise, revise."

▣ ⬭ WILD VIOLET

P.O. Box 39706, Philadelphia PA 19106-9706. E-mail: wildvioletmagazine@yahoo.com. Web site: www.wildviolet.net. Established 2001. **Contact:** Alyce Wilson, editor.

Magazine Needs *Wild Violet*, published quarterly online, aims "to make the arts more accessible, to make a place for the arts in modern life." Wants "poetry that is well crafted, that engages thought, that challenges or uplifts the reader. We have published free verse, haiku, blank verse, and other forms. If the form suits the poem, we will consider any form." Does not want "abstract, self-involved poetry; poorly managed form; excessive rhyming; self-referential poems that do not show why the speaker is sad, happy, or in love." Has published poetry by Lyn Lifshin, Erik Kestler, Anselm Brocki, Berwyn Moore, and Doug Bolling. Accepts about 15% of work submitted.

How to Submit Submit 3-5 poems at a time. Considers simultaneous submissions; no previously published poems. Accepts e-mail submissions (pasted into body of message, or as text or Word attachment); no disk submissions. Cover letter is preferred. Reads submissions year round. Submit seasonal poems 3 months in advance. Time between acceptance and publication is 3 months. "Decisions on acceptance or rejection are made by the editor." Seldom comments on rejected poems, unless requested. Occasionally publishes theme issues. Guidelines available by e-mail or on Web site. Responds in up to 6 weeks. Pays by providing a bio and link on contributor's page. Requests electronic rights to publish and archive accepted works. Reviews books/chapbooks of poetry in 250 words, single-book format. Query for review consideration.

Contest/Award Offerings Sponsors an annual poetry contest, offering 1st Prize: $100 and publication in *Wild Violet*; 2 Honorable Mentions will also be published. Guidelines available by e-mail or on Web site. **Entry fee:** $5/poem. Judged by independent judges.

Advice "Read voraciously; experience life and share what you've learned. Write what is hardest to say; don't take any easy outs."

✖ ⬭ WILLARD & MAPLE

163 S. Willard St., Box 34, Burlington VT 05401. E-mail: willardandmaple@champlain.edu. Established 1996. **Contact:** Poetry Editor.

Magazine Needs *Willard & Maple*, published annually in spring, is "a student-run literary magazine from Champlain College's Professional Writing Program that publishes a wide array of poems, short stories, creative essays, short plays, pen & ink drawings, photos, and computer graphics." Wants "creative work of the highest quality." Does not want any submissions over 5 typed pages in length; all submissions must be in English. Considers poetry by children and teens. Has published poetry by Robert Cooperman, Robert James Berry, Cheryl Burghdurf, Gerald Zipper, and Kenneth DiMaggio. *Willard & Maple* is 125 pages, digest-sized, digitally printed, perfect-bound. Receives about 500 poems/year, accepts about 20%. Press run is 600 (80 subscribers, 4 libraries); 200 are distributed free to the Champlain College writing community. Single copy: $12. Make checks payable to Champlain College.

How to Submit Submit up to 5 poems at a time. Lines/poem: 100 maximum. Considers simultaneous submissions; no previously published poems. Accepts e-mail and disk submissions. Cover letter is required. "Please provide current contact information including an e-mail address. Single-space submissions, one poem/page." Reads submissions September 1 -March 31. Time between acceptance and publication is less than one year. "All editors receive a blind copy to review. They meet weekly throughout the academic year. These meetings consist of the submissions being read aloud, discussed, and voted upon." Seldom comments on rejected poems. Occasionally publishes theme issues. Upcoming themes available by e-mail. Responds in less than 6 months. Pays 2 contributor's copies. Acquires one-time rights. Reviews books/chapbooks of poetry and other magazines/journals in 1,200 words. Send materials for review consideration to the poetry editor.
Advice "The power of imagination makes us infinite."

THE WILLIAM AND MARY REVIEW

Campus Center, The College of William and Mary, P.O. Box 8795, Williamsburg VA 23187-8795. (757)221-3290. E-mail: review@wm.edu. Web site: www.wm.edu/so/wmreview/. Established 1962. **Contact:** Poetry Editors.
Magazine Needs *The William and Mary Review*, published annually in May, is "dedicated to publishing new work by established poets as well as work by new and vital voices." Has published poetry by Cornelius Eady, Minnie Bruce Pratt, Edward Field, Dan Bellm, Forrest Gander, and Walter Holland. *The William and Mary Review* is about 105 pages, digest-sized, professionally printed on coated paper, perfect-bound, with 4-color card cover. Receives about 5,000 poems/year, accepts 12-15. Press run is 1,600 (100 library subscriptions, about 500 shelf sales). Sample: $5.50.
How to Submit Submit up to 6 poems at a time. Accepts submissions by postal mail only. Cover letter is required. Include address, phone number, e-mail address (if available), and brief bio note. SASE required. Type one poem/page. Reads submissions September 1-February 1 only. Responds in up to 6 months. Pays 5 contributor's copies.
Advice "Submit considered, well-crafted poetry. Seeking originality of topic and clarity of language. New writers are encouraged to submit."

THE WILLOW

The Smithtown Poetry Society, P.O. Box 793, Nesconset NY 11767. (631)656-6690. Fax: (631)656-6690. E-mail: editor@thesmithtownpoetrysociety.com. Web site: www.thesmithtownpoetrysociety.com. Established 1991. **Contact:** Sheryl Minter.
Magazine Needs *The Willow*, published quarterly online, features "new and upcoming poets alongside known poets. We also feature art, short stories, and poetry, regardless of length, that inspire intelligent thought and originality." Wants all forms of poetry. Does not want "poetry written without thought or in sing-song rhyme." Considers poetry by children and teens. Has published poetry by Marian Ford and Najwa Brax. Receives about 1,000 poems/year, accepts about 15%. Press run is 600 (100 subscribers, 200 libraries); 300 distributed free to coffee shops. Single copy: $7; subscription: $20. Make checks payable to S. Minter.
How to Submit Submit up to 3 poems at a time. Lines/poem: 30 maximum (longer poems are considered but may take longer to publish, depending on magazine space; query before submitting). Considers previously published poems; no simultaneous submissions. Accepts disk submissions; no fax or e-mail submissions. Cover letter is preferred. "All submissions must be typed, double-spaced, with submitter's name and address clearly printed. Please include a SASE for all submissions if you would like your original work returned." Reads submissions year round. Submit seasonal poems 6 months in advance. **Charges $1 reading fee.** Time between acceptance and publication is up to one year. Poems are circulated to an editorial board. Sometimes comments on rejected poems. Guidelines available in magazine, for SASE, by e-mail, or on Web site. Responds in one month.

Contest/Award Offerings The Smithtown Poetry Society Yearly Contest is open to all poets and offers 50% of the contest proceeds as first prize; "the other half goes to the distribution of *The Willow*." Submit up to 3 poems, 20 lines maximum each. **Entry fee:** $5. **Deadline:** June 1. Guidelines available in magazine, for SASE, or on Web site. "All submissions may be edited for grammar and punctuation."

◑ WILLOW REVIEW

College of Lake County, 19351 W. Washington St., Grayslake IL 60030-1198. (847)543-2956. Fax: (847)543-3956. E-mail: com426@clcillinois.edu. Web site: www.clcillinois.edu/community/willowreview.asp. Established 1969. **Contact:** Michael F. Latza, editor.

● *Willow Review* is partially supported by a grant from the Illinois Arts Council, a state agency.

Magazine Needs *Willow Review*, published annually, is interested in poetry, creative nonfiction, and fiction of high quality. "We have no preferences as to form, style, or subject, as long as each poem stands on its own as art and communicates ideas." Has published poetry by Lisel Mueller, Lucien Stryk, David Ray, Louis Rodriguez, John Dickson, and Patricia Smith. *Willow Review* is 88-96 pages, digest-sized, professionally printed, flat-spined, with a 4-color cover featuring work by an Illinois artist. Press run is 1,000. Subscription: $18 for 3 issues, $30 for 5 issues. Sample: $5 (back issue).

How to Submit Submit up to 5 poems at a time. Considers simultaneous submissions "if indicated in the cover letter"; no previously published poems. No e-mail submissions; postal submissions only. Include SASE; **"manuscripts will not be returned unless requested."** Reads submissions September-May. Guidelines available on Web site. Pays 2 contributor's copies. All rights remain with the author.

Contest/Award Offerings Prizes totaling $400 are awarded to the best poetry and short fiction/creative nonfiction in each issue.

Also Offers The College of Lake County Reading Series (4-7 readings/academic year) has included Thomas Lux, Isabel Allende, Donald Justice, Galway Kinnell, Lisel Mueller, Amiri Baraka, and others. One reading is for contributors to *Willow Review*. Readings, usually held on Thursday evenings and widely publicized in Chicago and suburban newspapers, are presented to audiences of about 150 students and faculty of the College of Lake County and other area colleges, as well as residents of local communities.

◑ ◎ WINDFALL: A JOURNAL OF POETRY OF PLACE (Specialized: poetry of place, specifically in the Pacific Northwest)

Windfall Press, P.O. Box 19007, Portland OR 97280-0007. E-mail: bsiverly@comcast.net. Web site: www.hevanet.com/windfall. Established 2002. **Contact:** Bill Siverly and Michael McDowell, co-editors.

Magazine Needs *Windfall: A Journal of Poetry of Place*, published biannually in March and September, is "looking for poems of place, specifically places in the Pacific Northwest (the broad bioregion extending from the North Slope of Alaska to the San Francisco Bay Area, and from the Rocky Mountains to the Pacific Coast). 'Place' can be named or unnamed; but if unnamed, then location should be clearly implied or suggested by observed detail. The poet does not have to be living in the Pacific Northwest, but the poem does. We favor poetry based on imagery derived from sensory observation. *Windfall* also favors poetry that occurs in lines and stanzas." Does not want "language poetry, metapoetry, surrealism, 'Internet poetry' (constructed from search engine information rather than experience), abstract, or self-centered poetry of any kind." Has published poetry by Judith Barrington, Gloria Bird, Barbara Drake, Clem Starck, Tom Wayman, and Robert Wrigley. *Windfall* is 52 pages, digest-sized, stapled, with art on covers ("all are drawings or prints by Portland artist Sharon Bronzan"). Receives about 160 poems/year, accepts about 60. Press run is 250. Single copy: $5; subscription: $10/year. Make checks payable to Windfall Press.

How to Submit Submit 5 poems at a time. Lines/poem: up to 50. Considers simultaneous submissions; no previously published poems. Accepts e-mail submissions (as attachment). Cover letter is preferred. "SASE required for submissions by U.S. mail." Reads submissions "after the deadlines for each issue: February 1 for Spring, and August 1 for Fall." Time between acceptance and publication is 2 months. Never comments on rejected poems. Guidelines available in magazine or on Web site. Responds in 2 weeks to 6 months ("depends on when poems are submitted in the biannual cycle"). Pays 2 contributor's copies. Acquires first North American serial rights. "Poem may appear in sample pages on *Windfall* Web site." Rights revert to poet upon publication.

Advice "In every issue of *Windfall*, editors Siverly and McDowell present an afterword that explores some aspect or tradition of poetry of place in the spirit of informing and inspiring new poems. Poets submitting to *Windfall* should check our Web site where all afterwords are posted and can be downloaded. Sample pages from most issues are also available. We are serious about our emphasis on poetry of place in the Pacific Northwest, and we are looking for poems that are based in direct experience and close observation in built or natural settings. At the end of the age of oil, we want to encourage poetry that goes back to its roots."

$ ◨ ◎ WISTERIA: A JOURNAL OF HAIKU, SENRYU, & TANKA

P.O. Box 150932, Lufkin TX 75915-0932. E-mail: wisteriajournal@gmail.com. (inquiries only). Web site: www.wistaria.blogspot.com. Established 2006. **Contact:** T.A. Thompson, founder.

Magazine Needs *Wisteria: A Journal of Haiku, Senryu, & Tanka*, published quarterly, is a small journal printing only haiku, senryu, and tanka forms. *Wisteria* is 24 pages, $4^1/4 \times 5^1/2$, self-published, laser-printed, saddle-stapled, with cardstock cover with photo. Press run is 200; 25 distributed free to poetry publishers and small presses that publish haiku, senryu, and tanka. Single copy: $3; subscription: $10/year. Make checks payable to T.A. Thompson (cash and money orders also accepted).

How to Submit Submit 5-7 poems at a time. No previously published poems or simultaneous submissions. No e-mail or disk submissions; postal submissions only. "Please include name, address, e-mail in upper right corner of manuscript. SASE required for reply." Reads submissions year round. Time between acceptance and publication is 6 months. Sometimes comments on rejected poems. Guidelines available in magazine or on Web site. Responds in one month. Pays $1 maximum and one contributor's copy. Acquires first rights. Rights revert to poet upon publication.

Contest/Award Offerings The Pinewood Haiku Contest (see separate listing in Contests & Awards).

Advice "We look forward to being a part of the small press scene that specializes in haiku, senryu, and tanka."

◨ THE WORCESTER REVIEW

Worcester County Poetry Association, Inc., 1 Ekman St., Worcester MA 01607. (508)797-4770. E-mail: wcpaboard@yahoo.com. Web site: www.geocities.com/wreview. Established 1973. **Contact:** Rodger Martin, managing editor.

Magazine Needs *The Worcester Review*, published annually by the Worcester County Poetry Association, encourages "critical work with a New England connection; no geographic limitation on poetry and fiction." Wants "work that is crafted, intuitively honest and empathetic, not work that shows the poet little respects his work or his readers." Has published poetry by May Swenson, Cleopatra Mathis, and Walter McDonald. *The Worcester Review* is 160 pages, digest-sized, professionally printed in dark type on quality stock, perfect-bound, with matte card cover. Press run is 750 (300 subscribers, 50 libraries, 300 shelf sales). Subscription: $25 (includes membership in WCPA). Sample: $6.

How to Submit Submit up to 5 poems at a time ("I recommend 3 or less for most favorable readings"). Considers previously published poems "only on special occasions" and simultaneous submissions "if indicated." Cover letter is required. Include brief bio. Poems should be typed on

$8\frac{1}{2} \times 11$ paper, with author's name in upper left corner of each page. Include SASE for return of ms. Comments on rejected poems "if manuscript warrants a response." Guidelines available for SASE or on Web site. Responds in up to 9 months. Pays 2 contributor's copies plus subscription. Acquires first rights.

Advice "Read some. Listen a lot."

$□ ◎ THE WRITE CLUB (Specialized: work by members only)

P.O. Box 1454, Conover NC 28613. (828)256-3821. Established 2001. **Contact:** Nettie C. Blackwelder, editor/president.

Magazine Needs *The Write Club*, published quarterly, prints "one original poem from each of our members in each quarterly club booklet. These poems are voted on by all members. We pay $1 to each member for each vote his/her poem receives. Each booklet also contains four assignments for all members who want to do them (usually poetry assignments). Our poetry specifications are open as to form, subject matter, style, or purpose. Just send your best. We don't print anything indecent or offensive." Has published poetry by Claudia Nelson, Gary Edwards, Mary Ports, David Bell, and Karen O'Leary. *The Write Club* is 48 pages, $4\frac{1}{4} \times 11$, computer-printed, saddle-stapled, with color cardstock cover. Receives about 800 poems/year, accepts about 90%. Press run is 72 (60 subscribers). Subscription: $15 (included in membership). Sample: $1 or 3 First-Class stamps. Make checks payable to Nettie C. Blackwelder.

How to Submit Submit one poem at a time. Lines/poem: 3 minimum, 30 maximum. Considers previously published poems and simultaneous submissions. Cover letter is preferred. "Send SAE and 3 First-Class stamps (or $1) for information and sample booklet before submitting poetry." Reads submissions year round. Submit seasonal poems 3 months in advance. Time between acceptance and publication is 3 months. "Poems are voted on by our members. Each vote is worth $1 to that poem's author." **Membership required** (all members receive subscription to club booklet). Guidelines available for SASE. Responds in 3 months. Pays $1 per vote, per poem. Acquires one-time rights.

Advice "Writing is work; writing is fun. A good combination of both will usually achieve very pleasing results."

◢ WRITE ON!! POETRY MAGAZETTE

P.O. Box 901, Richfield UT 84701-0901. E-mail: jimnipoetry@yahoo.com. Established 1998. **Contact:** Jim Garman, editor.

Magazine Needs *Write On!! Poetry Magazette*, published monthly, features "poetry from poets around the world." Wants poetry of "any style; all submissions must be suitable for all ages to read." Does not want "adult or vulgar material." Considers poetry by children and teens. Has published poetry by Cathy Porter, B.Z. Niditch, Gerald Zipper, and Betty Shelley. *Write On!!* is 24 pages, digest-sized, photostat-copied, saddle-stapled. Receives about 500 poems/year, accepts about 50%. Press run is 50 (10 subscribers, one library, 10 shelf sales). Single copy: $4. Sample: $3. Make checks payable to Jim Garman.

How to Submit Submit 1-6 poems at a time. Lines/poem: 6 minimum, 28 maximum. Considers previously published poems and simultaneous submissions. Accepts e-mail submissions (pasted into body of message, no attachments). Reads submissions year round. Submit seasonal poems 2 months in advance. Time between acceptance and publication is one month. Never comments on rejected poems. Occasionally publishes theme issues. Guidelines available by e-mail. Responds in "approximately" 3 weeks. No payment. Acquires one-time rights, "which return to author upon publication."

Advice "Send only your best material after it has been refined."

☑ WRITER'S BLOC

Dept. of Language & Literature, Texas A&M University-Kingsville, MSC 162, Kingsville TX 78363-8202. E-mail: c-downs@tamuk.edu. (inquiries only). Web site: www.tamuk.edu/langlit/writer's.htm. Established 1980. **Contact:** C. Downs, faculty sponsor.

Magazine Needs *Writer's Bloc*, published annually in September, prints poetry, fiction, creative nonfiction, and graphic art. "About half of our pages are devoted to the works of Texas A&M University-Kingsville students and half to the works of writers and artists from all over the world." Wants quality poetry; no restrictions on content or form. *Writer's Bloc* is 80-96 pages, digest-sized. Press run is 300-500. Subscription: $7. Sample: $7.

How to Submit Submit no more than 3 pages of poetry at a time ("prose poems okay"). Lines/poem: 50 maximum. No previously published poems or simultaneous submissions. No e-mail submissions; postal submissions only. "Submissions should be typed, double-spaced; SASE required for reply." Reads submissions September-January only. "Manuscripts are published upon recommendation by a staff of students and faculty." Seldom comments on rejected poems. Guidelines available in magazine or for SASE. "Acceptance letters are sent out in October." Pays one contributor's copy.

✪ $☑ ◎ WRITERS' JOURNAL

P.O. Box 394, Perham MN 56573. (218)346-7921. Fax: (218)346-7924. E-mail: writersjournal@writersjournal.com. Web site: www.writersjournal.com. Established 1980. **Contact:** Esther M. Leiper, poetry editor.

Magazine Needs *Writers' Journal*, published bimonthly, offers "advice and guidance, motivation, and inspiration to the more serious and published writers and poets." Features 2 columns for poets: "Esther Comments" offers critiques of poems sent in by readers, and "Every Day with Poetry" discusses a wide range of poetry topics, often—but not always—including readers' work. Wants "a variety of poetry: free verse, strict forms, concrete, Oriental. Since we appeal to those of different skill levels, some poems are more sophisticated than others, but those accepted must move, intrigue, or otherwise positively capture me. 'Esther Comments' is never used as a negative force to put a poem or a poet down. Indeed, I focus on the best part of a given work and seek to suggest means of improvement on weaker aspects." Does not want anything "vulgar, preachy, or sloppily written." Considers poetry by children (school-age). Has published poetry by Lawrence Schug, Diana Sutliff, and Eugene E. Grollmes. *Writers' Journal* is 64 pages, magazine-sized, professionally printed, with paper cover. Receives about 900 submissions/year, accepts about 25 (including those used in columns). Press run is 26,000. Single copy: $5.99; subscription: $19.97/year U.S., add $15 for Canada/Mexico, $30 for Europe, all others add $35. Sample: $5.

How to Submit Submit 3-4 poems at a time. Lines/poem: 25 maximum. No e-mail submissions; postal submissions only. Responds in up to 5 months. Pays $5/poem plus one contributor's copy.

Contest/Award Offerings Sponsors poetry contests for previously unpublished poetry. Submit serious verse only, on any subject or in any form, 25 lines maximum. "Submit in duplicate: one with name and address, one without." Received 300 entries/contest. Winners announced in *The Writers' Journal* and on Web site. **Entry fee:** $3/poem for each contest. **Deadline:** April 30, August 30, and December 30. Guidelines available for SASE or on Web site.

☑ ◎ XAVIER REVIEW (Specialized: focus on African American, Caribbean, Southern literature)

Xavier University, 1 Drexel Dr., New Orleans LA 70125-1098. (504)520-7303. Fax: (504)520-7917. Web site: www.xula.edu/review. Established 1980 (review), 1988 (press). **Contact:** Dr. Richard Collins, editor (review) or Dr. Thomas Bonner, executive editor (press).

Magazine Needs *Xavier Review*, published biannually, is a journal of poetry, fiction, translations, essays, and reviews (contemporary literature) for professional writers, libraries, colleges, and uni-

Cover art by Herbert Kearney; cover design by Plamen Arnaudov.

VOL 25 NO 2   FALL 2005

Xavier Review's first issue published after Hurricane Katrina (Vol. 25, No. 2) features cover art by Herbert Kearney ("We're Only Sleeping"). Managing editor Robert E. Skinner says, "Much of the issue's content was inspired by the storm and its devastating effect on New Orleans and its people."

versities. "Our content includes a focus on African American, Caribbean, and Southern literature, as well as works that touch on issues of religion and spirituality. We do, however, consider quality works on all themes." Has published poetry by Chris Waters, Lisa Sisk, Mark Taksa, Glenn Sheldon, Christine DeSimone, and Holly Pettit. Press run is 300. Subscription: $10/year for individuals, $15/year for institutions. Sample: $5. **How to Submit** Submit 3-5 poems at a time. Include SASE. "Overseas authors only may submit by e-mail attachment." Pays 2 contributor's copies; offers 40% discount on additional copies.

Additional Information Xavier Review Press publishes book-length works of poetry and prose. Recent publications include *Turning Up the Volume* by Patrice Melnick and *Vespers at Mount Angel* by Stella Nesanovich. Books are available through Web site or by e-mailing rskinner@xula.edu. Query via e-mail: tbonner@xula.edu. "**Manuscripts should not be sent without permission of the editor.**"

⊠ ☑ YALOBUSHA REVIEW

University of Mississippi, Dept. of English, Bondurant Hall, P.O. Box 1848, University MS 38677-1848. E-mail: yalobush@olemiss.edu (inquiries only). Web site: www.olemiss.edu/yalobusha. Established 1995. **Contact:** Poetry Editor.

Magazine Needs *Yalobusha Review*, published annually in April, promotes "new writing and art, creative nonfiction, fiction, and poetry." Does not want anything over 10 pages. Has published poetry by Charles Wright, Tom Chandler, and Claude Wilkinson. *Yalobusha Review* is 126 pages, digest-sized, with matte cover. Receives 300-400 poems/year, accepts about 15%. Press run is 1,000; 50 are distributed free to chosen writers/artists. Single copy: $10. Sample: $8. Make checks payable to *Yalobusha Review*.

How to Submit Submit 10 poems at a time maximum. Lines/poem: one page minimum, 10 pages maximum. No previously published poems. No e-mail or electronic submissions; postal submissions only. Cover letter is required. Include SASE. Reads submissions July 15-November 15. Submit seasonal poems 4 months in advance. Time between acceptance and publication is 4 months. Poems are circulated to an editorial board: from reader to specific editor (prose/poetry) to editor-in-chief to editorial board (including advisors). Never comments on rejected poems. Occasionally publishes theme issues. Guidelines available for SASE or on Web site. Responds in up to 4 months. Pays 2 contributor's copies. Acquires all rights. Returns full rights upon request.

Advice "It seems as though poetry has become so regional, leaving us to wonder, 'Where is the universal?' "

☑ YEMASSEE

Dept. of English, University of South Carolina, Columbia SC 29208. (803)777-2085. E-mail: yemassee@gwm.sc.edu. Web site: www.cla.sc.edu/ENGL/yemassee. Established 1993. **Contact:** Melissa Pluta and Brian Ray, co-editors.

Magazine Needs *Yemassee*, published semiannually, features "primarily fiction and poetry, but we are also interested in one-act plays, brief excerpts of novels, essays, reviews, and interviews with literary figures. Our essential consideration for acceptance is the quality of the work; we are open to a variety of subjects and writing styles." Does not want "poems of such a highly personal nature that their primary relevance is to the author; bad Ginsberg." Has published poetry by Nick Finney, Kwame Dawes, Pamela McClure, Rafael Campo, David Kirby, and Susan Ludvigson. *Yemassee* is 80-100 pages, perfect-bound. Receives about 400 poems/year, accepts about 10%. Press run is 750 (120 subscribers, 10 shelf sales); 275-300 distributed free to English department heads, creative writing chairs, agents and publishers. Subscription: $15/2 issues ($10 for students). Sample: $5. Make checks payable to Education Foundation/English Literary Magazine Fund.

How to Submit Submit up to 5 poems at a time. Lines/poem: less than 50, "but poems of exceptional quality are considered regardless of length." No previously published poems. No fax or e-mail submissions. Cover letter is required. "Each issue's contents are determined on the basis of blind selections. Therefore, we ask that all works be submitted without the author's name or address anywhere on the manuscript. Include this information along with the title(s) of the work(s) in a cover letter. For longer submissions, please include an approximate word count." Reads submissions August 15-May 15. Time between acceptance and publication is up to 4 months. "Staff reads and votes on 'blind' submissions." Often comments on rejected poems. Guidelines available for SASE or on Web site. Responds in up to 2 months after submission deadline. Pays 2 contributor's copies with the option to purchase additional copies at a reduced rate. Acquires first rights.

Contest/Award Offerings Sponsors the Yemassee Awards when funding permits. Prizes total $400/issue, usually $200 each for poetry and fiction. Details of annual poetry competition posted on Web site in early spring .

▣ ▨ ◎ ZEEK: A JEWISH JOURNAL OF THOUGHT AND CULTURE (Specialized: Jewish writers/themes preferred)

330 Seventh Ave., 21st Floor, New York NY 10001. E-mail: zeek@zeek.net. Web site: www.zeek.net. Established 2002. **Contact:** Jay Michaelson, poetry editor. Associate Editor: Dan Friedman.

Magazine Needs *Zeek: A Jewish Journal of Thought and Culture*, published monthly online and in print, seeks poetry that is "poetically daring, with shades of the numinous as it manifests in moments non-poets would ignore." Does not want "clichéd, 'inspirational,' or ethnocentric writing; something that could serve as a greeting card, political poster, etc.; cynicism." Has published poetry by Hal Sirowitz, Matthue Roth, Abraham Mezrich, David Goldstein, and Sara Seinberg. *Zeek* (print version) is 96 pages, digest-sized, perfect-bound, includes photography. Receives about 500 poems/year, accepts about 7. Press run (print) is 2,000 (200 subscribers); online version gets 60,000 hits/month. Single copy: $7; subscription: $14/year. Make checks payable to Zeek Media Inc.

How to Submit Submit 3 poems at a time. Considers simultaneous submissions; no previously published poems. Accepts e-mail submissions only (pasted into body of message). Cover letter is preferred. Reads submissions year round. Time between acceptance and publication varies. "Poetry editor has final approval, but editorial board of four can propose or reject." Seldom comments on rejected poems. Occasionally publishes theme issues. Guidelines available on Web site. Responds in one month. Pays 5 contributor's copies (to poets published in print edition). Acquires one-time rights. Reviews books of poetry.

Advice "If someone else can say it, let them. If no one else can say it, say *that*."

Book/Chapbook Publishers

Every poet dreams of publishing a collection of his or her work. However, it's surprising how many poets still envision putting out a thick, hardbound volume containing hundreds of poems. In reality, poetry books are usually slim, often paperback, with varying levels of production quality, depending on the publisher.

More common than full-length poetry books (i.e., 50-150 pages by modern standards) are poetry *chapbooks*, small editions of approximately 24-32 pages. They may be printed on quality paper with beautiful cover art on heavy stock; or they may be photocopied sheets of plain typing paper, folded and stapled or hand-sewn along the spine.

In this section you'll find a variety of presses and publishers of poetry books and chapbooks. However, it's a reflection of how poetry publishing works in the early 21st century that many book/chapbook publishing opportunities appear in the Contest & Awards section instead. To thoroughly search for a publisher/press, consult the Chapbook Publishers index (starting on page 480) and the Book Publishers index (starting on page 483) for a complete roundup of publishers that are listed in this edition of *Poet's Market*.

HOW LISTINGS ARE FORMATTED

Content of each listing was provided or verified by a representative of the press or publisher (poetry editor, managing editor, owner, etc.). Here is how that content is arranged in each listing:

Symbols. Icons at the beginning of each listing offer visual signposts to specific information about the book/chapbook publisher: ( ) this market is recently established and new to *Poet's Market*; ( ) this market did not appear in the 2007 edition; ( ) this market publishes primarily online (some books and chapbooks are indeed published online, sometimes as a PDF that can be printed out); ( ) this market is located in Canada or ( ) outside the U.S. and Canada; ($) this market pays a monetary amount (as opposed to a given number of author's copies); ( ) this market welcomes submissions from beginning poets; ( ) this market prefers submissions from skilled, experienced poets, will consider work from beginning poets; ( ) this market prefers submissions from poets with a high degree of skill and experience; ( ) this market has a specialized focus (listed in parentheses after publisher/press name); ( ) this market does not consider unsolicited submissions; and ( ) this market is closed to *all* submissions. (Keys to these symbols are listed on the inside covers of this book and on page 6.)

Contact information. Next you'll find the information you need to contact the press or publisher, according to what was provided for each listing: name (in bold) of the publisher/ press (with areas of specialization noted in parentheses where appropriate); regular mail address; telephone number; fax number; e-mail address; Web site address; year the publisher/press was established; the name of the person to contact (or an editorial title); and membership in small press/publishing organization(s). (**Note:** If a publisher or press wants electronic submissions exclusively, no street address may be given.)

Book/Chapbook Needs. This section provides an overview of the publisher/press, including such helpful information as editorial preferences; how manuscripts are considered; the number and kinds of books and/or chapbooks produced; a list of recently published titles; and production information about the titles (number of pages, printing/binding details, type of cover, press run).

How to Submit. This section states whether a poet should query with samples or send the complete manuscript; possible reading periods; reading fees, if applicable; response time; payment amount/terms; and how to order sample copies.

Additional Information. Editors/publishers may use this section to explain other types of publishing activities (such as broadsides, postcards or anthologies), elaborate on some aspect of production—anything beyond the basic details of the submission process that readers may find of interest.

Contest/Award Offerings. This section discusses prizes and competitions associated with the publisher, with either brief guidelines or a cross-reference to a separate listing in the Contests & Awards section.

Also Offers. Describes other offerings associated with this publisher (i.e., sponsored readings, Web site activities such as blogs and forums, related poetry groups, etc.).

Advice. Provides direct quotes from the editor/publisher about everything from pet peeves to tips on writing to views on the state of poetry today.

GETTING STARTED, FINDING A PUBLISHER

If you don't have a publisher in mind, read randomly through the listings, making notes as you go. (Don't hesitate to write in the margins, underline, use highlighters; it also helps to flag markets that interest you with Post-It Notes). Browsing the listings is an effective way to familiarize yourself with the kind of information presented and the publishing opportunities that are available at various skill levels.

If you're thinking of a specific publisher by name, however, begin with the General Index. Here all *Poet's Market* listings are alphabetized along with publishers from the 2007 edition that don't appear in this book (the latter are accompanied by a two-letter code explaining the publisher's absence; a key to these codes appears at the beginning of the General Index.) In addition, publishers/presses that have changed names since the 2007 edition are listed in the General Index, cross-referenced to the new names.

REFINE YOUR SEARCH

To supplement the General Index, we provide several more specific indexes to help you refine your marketing plan for your manuscript. Not every listing appears in one of these indexes, so use them only to reinforce your other research efforts. As mentioned earlier, the Chapbook Publishers Index and Book Publishers Index are good places to start when you have a poetry collection to submit. In addition, the following indexes may be helpful:

Openness to Submissions Index breaks out markets according to the symbols (☐ ☑ ☒ ◎) that appear at the beginning of each listing—signposts that indicate the level of writing an editor/publisher prefers to see. (For an explanation of these symbols, see page 6, the inside covers of this book, or the handy tear-out bookmark just inside the front cover.)

Geographical Index sorts publishers/presses by state and by countries outside the U.S. Some publishers are more open to poets from their region, so use this index when you're pinpointing local opportunities.

Subject Index groups all markets into categories according to areas of special focus. These include all specialized markets (appearing with the ◉ symbol) as well as broader categories such as online markets, poetry for children, markets that consider translations, and others. Save time when looking for a specific type of publisher/press by checking this index first.

THE NEXT STEP

Once you know how to interpret the listings in this section and identify markets for your work, the next step is to start submitting your poetry collection. See ''Getting Started (and Using This Book)'' on page 4 and ''Frequently Asked Questions'' on page 9 for advice, guidelines for preparing your manuscript and proper submissions procedures.

ADDITIONAL INFORMATION

The Book/Chapbook Publishers section includes an Insider Report about **Stanley Barkan**, founder and head of Cross-Cultural Communications (CCC), which specializes in bilingual poetry and translation.

AHSAHTA PRESS

MFA Program in Creative Writing, Boise State University, 1910 University Dr., Boise ID 83725-1525. (208)426-2195. Fax: (208)426-4373. E-mail: ahsahta@boisestate.edu. Web site: http://ahsahtapress.boisestate.edu. Established 1976. **Contact:** Janet Holmes, editor.

Book/Chapbook Needs Ahsahta Press, which originally published contemporary poets of the American West, has since expanded its scope "to publish poets nationwide, seeking out and publishing the best new poetry from a wide range of aesthetics—poetry that is technically accomplished, distinctive in style, and thematically fresh." Has published *Quarantine* by Brian Henry, *Knowledge, Forms, The Aviary* by Karla Kelsey, *The Violence* by Ethan Paquin, *Fence Above the Sea* by Brigitte Byrd, *Spell* by Dan Beachy-Quick, and *Saving the Appearances* by Liz Waldner.

How to Submit Considers multiple and simultaneous submissions. Submit only during March 1-May 1 reading period. Send complete ms and letter-sized SASE for reply. Responds in up to 3 months. Forthcoming, new, and backlist titles available on Web site. Most backlist titles: $9.95; most current titles: $16.

Contest/Award Offerings The Sawtooth Poetry Prize (see separate listing in Contests & Awards).

Advice "Ahsahta seeks distinctive, non-imitative, unpredictable, and innovatively crafted work. Please check our Web site for examples of what we publish."

ARC PUBLICATIONS (Specialized: UK writers; world and overseas poets; translations)

Nanholme Mill, Shaw Wood Rd., Todmorden, Lancashire OL14 6DA England. E-mail: arc.publications@btconnect.com. Web site: www.arcpublications.co.uk. Established 1969. **Contact:** Tony Ward, managing editor/senior partner.

Book/Chapbook Needs Publishes "contemporary poetry from new and established writers from the UK and abroad, specializing in the work of world poets writing in English, and the work of overseas poets in translation."

How to Submit *"At present we are not accepting submissions."*

$ AUSABLE PRESS

1026 Hurricane Rd., Keene NY 12942-9719. E-mail: editor@ausablepress.org. Web site: www.ausablepress.org. Established 1999. **Contact:** Chase Twichell, editor. Member: CLMP.

Book/Chapbook Needs Ausable Press wants poetry "that investigates and expresses human consciousness in language that goes where prose cannot." Interested in work by new poets. Does not want "children's poetry or poetry for children, chapbooks, light verse, inspirational poetry, illustrated poetry, or peviously self-published work." Has published poetry by C.K. Williams, Steve Orlen, Linton Kwesi Johnson, Bruce Weigl, Laura Kasischke, and Laure-Anne Bosselaar. Publishes 4-6 books/year, paperback, offset-printed; number of pages varies.

How to Submit Considers unsolicited mss **in June only**. Responds to queries in one week; to mss in up to 4 months. Pays royalties of 10%, advance of $1,000, and 10 author's copies (out of a press run of 1,000). Guidelines available for SASE or on Web site. "Please do not submit a manuscript without first reading the guidelines."

Advice "This is not a contest. Ausable Press is under no obligation to publish any of the manuscripts submitted. Response time can be as long as three to four months, so please be patient."

THE BACKWATERS PRESS

3502 N. 52nd St., Omaha NE 68104-3506. (402)451-4052. E-mail: gkosmicki@cox.net. Web site: www.thebackwaterspress.homestead.com. **Contact:** Greg Kosmicki, editor.

Book/Chapbook Needs "The Backwaters Press continues to accept manuscripts for consideration for publication through the Open Submissions category. We're looking for manuscripts between 65 and 80 pages in length. **There is a $25 reading fee.**"

How to Submit "Please see the Web site for complete details, or send a self-addressed, stamped envelope to 'Guidelines' at the above address, or e-mail with a subject line of 'Open Submission Guidelines.' " Books available through The Backwaters Press or Amazon.com.

Advice "The Backwaters Press is dedicated to publishing the best new literature we can find. Send your best work."

BARNWOOD PRESS

4604 47th Ave., S, Seattle WA 98118-1824. (206)225-6887. E-mail: barnwoodpress@earthlink.net. Web site: www.barnwoodpress.org. Established 1975. **Contact:** Tom Koontz, editor.

Book/Chapbook Needs Barnwood Press publishes one paperback and one chapbook of poetry/year. Has recently published *Hitler's Mustache* by Peter Davis, *Gone So Far* by Martha Collins, and *Whatever You Can Carry* by Stephen Herz. Chapbooks are usually 12-32 pages, offset-printed, saddle-stapled, with paper covers with art; size varies.

How to Submit Query first with a few sample poems and cover letter with brief bio and publication credits. Responds to queries and mss in one month. Order sample books/chapbooks through Web site.

BELHUE PRESS (Specialized: gay male poetry)

2501 Palisade Ave., Suite A1, Riverdale, Bronx NY 10463. E-mail: belhuepress@earthlink.net. Web site: www.perrybrass.com. Established 1990. **Contact:** Tom Laine, editor.

Book/Chapbook Needs Belhue Press is a small press specializing in gay male poetry. "We are especially interested in books that get out of the stock poetry market." Wants "hard-edged, well-crafted, fun, and often sexy poetry. No mushy, self-pitying, confessional, boring, indulgent, teary, or unrequited love poems—yuck! Poet must be willing to promote book through readings, mailers, etc." Publishes 3 paperbacks/year; no chapbooks. **"We have a $10 sample and guideline fee. Please send this before submitting any poetry. We have had to initiate this due to a deluge of bad, amateur, irrelevant submissions. After fee, we will give constructive criticism when necessary."**

How to Submit Query first, with 6 pages of poetry and cover letter with brief bio and publication credits. Considers previously published poems and simultaneous submissions. Time between acceptance and publication is one year. Often comments on rejected poems. Will request criticism fees "if necessary." Responds "fast" to queries and submitted mss. No payment information provided.

Advice "The only things we find offensive are stupid, dashed off, 'fortune cookie' poems that show no depth or awareness of poetry. We like poetry that, like good journalism, tells a story."

BIRCH BROOK PRESS

P.O. Box 81, Delhi NY 13753. Fax: (607)746-7453. E-mail: birchbrook@usadatanet.net (inquiries only). Web site: www.birchbrookpress.info. Established 1982. **Contact:** Tim Tolnay, poetry editor. Member: American Academy of Poets, Small Press Center, Publishers Marketing Association, American Typefounders Fellowship.

Book/Chapbook Needs Birch Brook Press "is a letterpress book printer/typesetter/designer that uses monies from these activities to publish several titles of its own each year with cultural and literary interest." Specializes in literary work, flyfishing, baseball, outdoors, anthologies, translations of classics, and books about books. Has published *Daimonion Sonata* by Steven Owen Shields, *Human/Nature* by Lance Lee, *Confessions of a Rational Lunatic* by Marcus Rome, *Jack's Beans* by Tom Smith, and *The Garden of Detritus* by Stanley Nelson. Publishes 4 paperbacks and/or hardbacks/year. Specializes "mostly in anthologies with specific themes." Books are "handset letterpress editions printed in our own shop." **Offers occasional co-op contract.**

How to Submit Query first with sample poems, or send entire ms. No e-mail submissions; submissions by postal mail only. "Must include SASE with submissions." Occasionally comments on rejected poems. Guidelines available for SASE. Pays from $5-25 for publication in anthology. Order sample books by sending SASE for free catalog.

Advice "Send your best work, and see other Birch Brook Press books."

$⬚ BLACK LAWRENCE PRESS

P.O. Box 9, Watertown NY 13601. E-mail: info@blacklawrencepress.com. Web site: www.blacklawrencepress.com. Established 2003. **Contact:** Colleen Ryor, editor.

Book/Chapbook Needs Black Lawrence Press seeks "to publish intriguing books of literature: novels, short story collections, poetry. Will also publish the occasional translation (from the German and French)." Has published poetry by Frank Matagrano, D.C. Berry, Marcel Jolley, James Owens, James Reidel, and Helen Marie Casey. Publishes 4-8 books/year, mostly poetry and fiction. Manuscripts are selected through open submission and competition (see below). Books are 48-400 pages, offset-printed or high-quality POD, perfect-bound, with matte 4-color cover.

How to Submit "Regular submissions are considered on a year-round basis. Please check the general submissions page on our Web site for the most up-to-date guidelines information before submitting." Responds in up to 4 months for mss, "sometimes longer depending on backlog." Pays royalties of 7% and/or other negotiable contract. Sample books available through Web site.

Contest/Award Offerings The St. Lawrence Book Award, The Ontario Prize, and The Black River Chapbook Competition (see separate listings in Contests & Awards).

⬚ BLUE LIGHT PRESS

3600 Lyon St., San Francisco CA 94123. (415)440-8668 or (641)472-7882. E-mail: bluelightpress@aol.com. Established 1988. **Contact:** Diane Frank, chief editor.

Book/Chapbook Needs Blue Light Press publishes 3 paperbacks, 2 chapbooks/year. "We like poems that are imagistic, emotionally honest, and push the edge—where the writer pushes through the imagery to a deeper level of insight and understanding. No rhymed poetry." Has published poetry by Alice Rogoff, Ken McCullough, Becky Sakellariou, Tom Centolella, Stewart Florsheim, and Christopher Buckley. Chapbooks are 30 pages, digest-sized, professionally printed, with original art on an elegant matte cover. Chapbooks available for $8 plus $2 p&h; books for $15.95 plus $2 p&h.

How to Submit Submission guidelines for non-contest submissions available for SASE or by e-mail. Does not accept e-mail submissions. Deadline: December 15, 2007.

Contest/Award Offerings Offers the Blue Light Poetry Prize and Chapbook Contest. The winner "will be published by Blue Light Press and receive a $100 honorarium and 50 copies of his or her book, which can be sold for $8 each, for a total of $500." Submit ms of 10-24 pages, typed or printed with a laser or inkjet printer. No e-mail submissions. Include SASP for notification of receipt of ms, SASE for contest results only; no mss will be returned. Guidelines available for SASE or by e-mail. **Entry fee:** $10. Make checks payable to Blue Light Press. **Deadline:** June 1 for 2007. Winner announced on or before September 1.

Also Offers "We have an online poetry workshop with a wonderful group of American and international poets—open to new members three times per year. Send an e-mail for info. We work in person with local poets, and will edit/critique poems by mail; $40 for four poems."

Advice "Read some of the books we publish, especially one of the anthologies. We like to publish poets with a unique vision and gorgeous or unusual language; poems that push the edge. Stay in the poem longer and see what emerges in your vision and language."

$⬚ BOA EDITIONS, LTD.

260 East Ave., Rochester NY 14604. (585)546-3410. Web site: www.boaeditions.org. Established 1976. **Contact:** Thom Ward, poetry editor.

Book/Chapbook Needs BOA Editions, a Pulitzer Prize-winning, not-for-profit publishing house acclaimed for its work, reads poetry mss for the American Poets Continuum Series (new poetry by distinguished poets in mid- and late career), the Lannan Translations Selection Series (publication of 2 new collections of contemporary international poetry annually, supported by The Lannan Foundation of Santa Fe, NM), and The A. Poulin, Jr. Poetry Prize (to honor a poet's first book; mss considered through competition). Has published poetry by W.D. Snodgrass, John Logan, Isabella Gardner, Richard Wilbur, and Lucille Clifton. Also publishes introductions by major poets of those less well-known (Gerald Stern wrote the foreword for Li-Young Lee's *Rose*, for example).

How to Submit Check Web site for reading periods for the American Poets Continuum Series and The Lannan Translation Selection Series. "Please adhere to the general submission guidelines for each series." Guidelines available for SASE or on Web site. Pays advance plus 10 author's copies.

Contest/Award Offerings The A. Poulin, Jr. Poetry Prize (see separate listing in Contests & Awards).

Also Offers Available for download from Web site are reading and teaching guides for selected titles; and Season Sampler chapbooks, which provide introductions to BOA poets and their work.

✅ ◎ ☑ BOTTOM DOG PRESS, INC. (Specialized: writing from the Midwest; working lives; Zen Buddhism)

P.O. Box 425, Huron OH 44839. (419)433-5560, ext. 20784. E-mail: LsmithDog@aol.com. Web site: http://members.aol.com/lsmithdog/bottomdog. **Contact:** Larry Smith, director. Associate Editors: David Shevin and Laura Smith.

- Imprint: Bird Dog Publishing

Book/Chapbook Needs Bottom Dog Press, Inc., "is a nonprofit literary and educational organization dedicated to publishing the best writing and art from the Midwest." Has published poetry by Jeff Gundy, Jim Daniels, Maj Ragain, Diane di Prima, and Sue Doro. Publishes the Midwest Series, Working Lives Series, and Harmony Series (95 books to date).

How to Submit Guidelines available on Web site.

Advice "Please read some of our books and send us a query before submitting anything."

✅ BRICKHOUSE BOOKS, INC.

306 Suffolk Rd., Baltimore MD 21218. (410)235-7690. E-mail: charriss@towson.edu. Web site: www.towson.edu/~harriss/!bhbwebs.ite/bhb.htm. Established 1970. **Contact:** Clarinda Harriss, editor/director.

- Imprints: New Poets Series, Chestnut Hills Press, and Stonewall.

Book/Chapbook Needs BrickHouse Books "is open to submissons of all kinds (poetry, novellas, plays, etc.), so long as they do not exceed 128 pages." New Poets Series brings out first books by promising new poets. Poets who have previously had book-length mss published are not eligible. Prior publication in journals and anthologies is strongly encouraged. Wants "excellent, fresh, non-trendy, literate, intelligent poems. Any form (including traditional), any style." BrickHouse Books and New Poets Series pay 20 author's copies (out of a press run of 500), the sales proceeds going back into the corporation to finance the next volume. "BrickHouse has been successful in its effort to provide writers with national distribution; in fact, The New Poets Series was named an Outstanding Small Press by the prestigious Pushcart Awards Committee, which judges some 5,000 small press publications annually." Chestnut Hills Press publishes **author-subsidized books**; "high-quality work only, however. Chestnut Hills Press has achieved a reputation for prestigious books, printing only the top 10% of manuscripts Chestnut Hills Press and New Poets Series receive." Chestnut Hills Press authors receive proceeds from sale of their books. The Stonewall series publishes work with a gay, lesbian, or bisexual perspective. BrickHouse Books and its subdivisions have published books by Rane Aroyo, Gale Acuff, Harris George, Jan-Mitchell Sherrill, Donald Richardson, and Richard Fein. Books are 42-200 pages. Chapbooks available for $10; full-length books for $15-25.

How to Submit Send a 50- to 55-page manuscript, **$10 reading fee**, and cover letter including bio and publication credits. "Do not query by phone or fax; e-mail or postal mail queries only. Do not send anything by certified mail; BHB is unable to sign for such deliveries." Considers simultaneous submissions. No e-mail submissions. "Cover letters should be very brief, businesslike, and include an accurate list of published work. Indicate if manuscript is to be considered for BrickHouse, New Poets Series, Chestnut Hills Press, or Stonewall." Manuscripts accepted for publication must be available on a CD provided by the author. Sometimes comments briefly on rejected poems. Responds in up to one year. Manuscripts "are circulated to an editorial board of professional, publishing poets. BrickHouse is backlogged, but the best 10% of the manuscripts it receives are automatically eligible for Chestnut Hills Press consideration," **a subsidy arrangement**. Send $5 and a 7×10 SASE for a sample volume.

☐ ☑ CALAMARI PRESS

202 E. 7th St., Apt. 1D, New York NY 10009. E-mail: white@sleepingfish.net. Web site: www.calamaripress.com. Established 2003. **Contact:** Derek White, editor.

Book/Chapbook Needs Calamari Press publishes books of literary text and art. Recent publications include *Good, Brother* by Peter Markus, *The Night I Dropped Shakespeare on the Cat* by John Olson, *Trilce* by James Wagner, and *Land of the Snow Men* by Norman Lock. Publishes 3-5 books/year. Manuscripts are selected through open submission or by invitation. Books are 30-200 pages, digitally printed, perfect-bound or saddle-stapled, with 110 lb. cardstock covers with art/graphics.

How to Submit Query first, with a few sample pieces and a cover letter with brief bio and publication credits. Book mss may include previously published pieces. "Should be familiar with and interested in other Calamari Press titles and *SleepingFish* (www.sleepingfish.net; see separate listing in Magazines/Journals). Helps to be published in *SleepingFish* first." Responds to queries in up to 6 months. Pays about 50 author's copies (out of a press run of about 200; "negotiable"). Order books through the Web site, Powell's, or SPD.

☑ ◎ CAROLINA WREN PRESS (Specialized: women; minorities; gay/lesbian)

120 Morris St., Durham NC 27701. (919)560-2738. Fax: (919)560-2759. E-mail: carolinawrenpress@earthlink.net. Web site: www.carolinawrenpress.org. Established 1976. **Contact:** Andrea Selch, president.

Book/Chapbook Needs Publishes one poetry book/year, "usually through our poetry series. Primarily women and minorities, though men and majorities also welcome." Has published *Churchboys and Other Sinners* by Preston L. Allen, as well as poetry by William Pitt Root, George Elliott Clarke, Jaki Shelton Green, Evie Shockley, and Erica Hunt.

How to Submit Query first, with 10 pages of sample poems and cover letter with brief bio and publication credits. Include SASE for reply only. Accepts e-mail queries, but send **only** letter and description of work; no large files. Reads unsolicited poetry submissions February 1-June 1. "Your best bet is to submit as part of our biennial poetry contest held in autumn of even-numbered years (e.g., 2008, 2010)." Guidelines available for SASE, by e-mail, or on Web site. Responds to queries in 3 months; to mss in 6 months. Payment varies.

Contest/Award Offerings Carolina Wren Press Poetry Contest for a First Book is open only to poets who have *not* published a full-length collection (48 pages or more). Submissions must be unpublished as a collection, but individual poems may have been previously published in journals or a chapbook; manuscripts that have been previously self-published are not eligible. Submissions may be entered as a collection in other contests (notify immediately of acceptance elsewhere). Submit 2 copies of a poetry ms of 48-60 pages. Page count should include title page, table of contents, and optional dedication page. See guidelines for complete formatting and submission details. Include SASE for results; mss will not be returned. Guidelines available for SASE, by e-mail, or on Web site. **Entry fee:** $18. **Deadline:** December 1 (postmark). 2007 judge: Evie Shockley. Copies of winning books available through Web site, Amazon, or local bookstore.

Book/Chapbook Publishers

⚡ $⊘ CC. MARIMBO

P.O. Box 933, Berkeley CA 94701-0933. Established 1996. **Contact:** Peggy Golden, editor.

• **"We are currently closed to all submissions as we are scheduled into 2008!"**

Book/Chapbook Needs CC. Marimbo "promotes the work of underpublished poets/artists by providing a well-crafted, cheap (people's prices), and therefore affordable/accessible collection." Publishes 2-3 poetry titles/year. "Books are issued as 'minichaps' to introduce underpublished poets/artists to the public. Runs done by alphabet, lettered A-Z, AA-ZZ, etc. Short poems for the small format, styles, and content welcome in whatever variation. We do not want to see already published work, unless poems previously in print in magazines (attributed); i.e., poems okay, reprintable books not okay." Considers poetry by children and teens. Has published poetry by Guy R. Beining, Joan McNair Gatten, and Mark Schwartz. Chapbooks are usually 40 pages, $4^1/_4 \times 5^1/_4$, offset-printed, photocopied, with matte covers.

How to Submit Query first, with a few sample poems and cover letter with brief bio and publication credits. Include SASE. Lines/poem: 25 maximum. Responds to queries in 3 months; to mss in 6 months. Pays 5 author's copies (out of a press run of 26). Additional copies paid for larger press runs. "Author gets 10% of cover price on all copies sold, except for copies sold to author." Order sample chapbooks by sending $5 (5¢ for p&h).

⚡ ☑ CLEVELAND STATE UNIVERSITY POETRY CENTER

2121 Euclid Ave., RT1841, Cleveland OH 44115-2214. (216)687-3986 or (888)278-6473. Fax: (216)687-6943. E-mail: poetrycenter@csuohio.edu. Web site: www.csuohio.edu/poetrycenter. Established 1962 (first publications in 1971). **Contact:** Rita Grabowski, manager.

Book/Chapbook Needs The Poetry Center publishes "the CSU Poetry Series for poets national and international, and the Cleveland Poets Series for Ohio poets. Open to many kinds of form, length, subject matter, style, and purpose. Should be well-crafted, clearly of professional quality, ultimately serious (even when humorous). No light verse, devotional verse, or verse in which rhyme and meter seem to be of major importance." Recent CSU Poetry Series publications include *Piece Work* by Barbara Presnell and *Sunflower Brother* by Sam Witt. Publications in the Cleveland Poets Series include *One of Everything* by Diane Gilliam Fisher.

Contest/Award Offerings Books are chosen for publication from the entries to 2 contest categories: First Book and Open Competition, the latter for poets who have published a collection of a least 48 pages with a press run of at least 500. Winners receive $1,000, publication, and 50 author's copies. The Cleveland Poets Series (for Ohio poets) offers 50 copies (out of a press run of 500). Considers simultaneous submissions (if notified of acceptance elsewhere). Manuscripts should be "clear and contain a minimum of 40 pages of poetry and a table of contents, pages numbered." Include 2 cover sheets: one with ms title, poet's name, address, phone number, and e-mail; the second with ms title only. Poet's name should appear on first cover sheet and nowhere else on ms. Do not send acknowledgments, cover letters, or bio. Manuscripts cannot be returned. No e-mail submissions. Guidelines available for SASE, by e-mail, fax, or on Web site. **Entry fee:** $20. **Deadline:** submit for all series between November 1 and February 1 (postmark) only. Responds to all submissions for the year by the end of summer.

⚑ ☑ COFFEE HOUSE PRESS

27 N. Fourth St., Suite 400, Minneapolis MN 55401. (612)338-0125. Web site: www.coffeehousepress.org. Established 1984. **Contact:** Christopher Fischbach, senior editor.

• Books published by Coffee House Press have won numerous honors and awards. Example: *The Book of Medicines* by Linda Hogan won the Colorado Book Award for Poetry and the Lannan Foundation Literary Fellowship.

Book/Chapbook Needs Publishes 4-5 poetry books/year. Wants poetry that is "challenging and lively; influenced by the Beats, the NY School, LANGUAGE and post-LANGUAGE, or Black Mountain." Has published poetry collections by Victor Hernandez Cruz, Anne Waldman, Eleni Sikelianos, and Paul Metcalf.

How to Submit Query first, with 8-12 sample poems and cover letter with brief bio and publication credits. "Please include a SASE for our reply and/or the return of your manuscript. Absolutely no phone, fax, or e-mail queries." Seldom comments on rejected poems. Responds to queries in one month; to mss in up to 8 months. Always sends prepublication galleys. Catalog available for SASE.

Also Offers Online sign-up for free e-newsletter.

$⬛ $☑ ◎ COTEAU BOOKS (Specialized: Canadian writers only)

Thunder Creek Publishing Co-op, 2517 Victoria Ave., Regina SK S4P 0T2 Canada. (306)777-0170. Fax: (306)522-5152. E-mail: coteau@coteaubooks.com. Web site: www.coteaubooks.com. Established 1975. **Contact:** Acquisitions Editor.

Book/Chapbook Needs Coteau Books is a "small literary press that publishes poetry, fiction, drama, anthologies, criticism, young adult novels—**by Canadian writers only**." Has published *Blue Marrow* by Louise Bernice Halfe, *The Gift of the Hawk* by Randy Lundy, and *The Names Leave the Stones* by Steven Michael Berzensky.

How to Submit Submit 30-50 poems "and indication of whole manuscript," typed with at least 12-point font. No simultaneous or non-Canadian submissions. No e-mail or fax submissions. Cover letter is required. Include publishing credits and bio, and SASE for return of ms. Responds to queries and mss in 4 months. Always sends prepublication galleys. Author receives 10% royalties and 10 author's copies. Order samples by sending 9×12 SASE for catalog.

Additional Information Web site includes title and ordering information, author interviews, awards, news and events, submission guidelines, and links.

Advice "Generally, poets should have a number of publishing credits (single poems or series) in literary magazines and anthologies before submitting a manuscript."

⬛ ☑ ◎ CROSS-CULTURAL COMMUNICATIONS (Specialized: bilingual, translations, multicultural)

239 Wynsum Ave., Merrick NY 11566-4725. (516)868-5635. Fax: (516)379-1901. E-mail: cccpoetry @aol.com. Web site: www.cross-culturalcommunications.com. Established 1971. **Contact:** Stanley H. and Bebe Barkan.

Book/Chapbook Needs "*Cross-Cultural Review* began as a series of chapbooks (6-12 per year) of collections of poetry translated from various languages, and continues as the Holocaust, Women Writers, Latin American Writers, African Heritage, Italian Heritage, International Artists, Art & Poetry, Jewish, Israeli, Yiddish, Hebrew, American, Bengali, Bulgarian, Cajun, Catalan, Chicano, Chinese, Dutch, Estonian, Finnish, Gypsy (Roma), Korean, Macedonian, Polish, Russian, Serbian, Sicilian, Swedish, Scandinavian, Turkish, Ukrainian, Welsh, and Long Island and Brooklyn Writers Chapbook Series (with a number of other permutations in the offing)—issued simultaneously in palm-sized and regular paperback and cloth-binding editions, and boxed and canned editions, as well as audiocassette, CD, DVD, and videocassette. The Cross-Cultural International Writers Series, focusing on leading poets from various countries, includes titles by Leo Vroman (Holland) and Pablo Neruda (Chile). The Holocaust series is for survivors. In addition to publications in these series, Cross-Cultural Communications has published anthologies and postcard and broadside portfolio collections by dozens of poets from many countries, a number in special biligual limited editions, including such poets and translators as Joan Alcover, Bohdan Boychuk, Stanley Kunitz, Vinícius de Moraes, Gregory Rabassa, Rainer Maria Rilke, Louis Simpson, William Stafford, and Daniel Weissbort, with complementary artwork by various international artists such as Eduardo Arranz-Bravo (Catalonia), Nicoló; D'Alessandro (Sicily), Picasso (Spain), Tchouki (Bulgaria), and Alfred Van Loen (Holland/USA)." Sample chapbook: $10 postpaid.

How to Submit Guidelines available for SASE. Pays 10% of print run.

Additional Information New: *Cross-Cultural Review Chapbook* (CCRCB), an occasional series of 16-48 page limited edition chapbooks (print runs of 100-150 copies) focusing on poetry (bilingual preferred). Sample: $15 postpaid. Pays 5-10 copies.

Also Offers "Cross-Cultural Communications continues, on an occasional basis, to organize events for international poets and writers. In April 2008, CCC will host a national tour for two Welsh poets: Peter Thabit Jones, editor of *The Seventh Quarry*, and Aeronwy Thomas (daughter of Dylan Thomas)."

$ ☑ ☑ JOHN DANIEL & COMPANY

Daniel & Daniel Publishers, Inc., P.O. Box 2790, McKinleyville CA 95519. (707)839-3495. Fax: (707)839-3242. E-mail: dandd@danielpublishing.com. Web site: www.danielpublishing.com. Established 1980; reestablished 1985. **Contact:** John Daniel, editor.

Book/Chapbook Needs John Daniel & Company, an imprint of Daniel & Daniel Publishers, Inc., is a general small press publisher, specializing in literature, both prose and poetry. "Book-length manuscripts of any form or subject matter will be considered, but we do not want to see pornographic, libelous, illegal, or sloppily written poetry." Has published *Angelus* by Jeanne Shannon, *The Light at the Edge* by Marilyn Chandler, and *Hunger for Light* by Stephen Browning. Publishes about 6 flat-spined poetry paperbacks/year. Books average 80 pages. Press runs average between 500-1,000. No longer issues a print catalog, but all books are shown and described on Web site.

How to Submit Query first, with 12 sample poems and cover letter with brief bio and publication credits. Considers simultaneous submissions. No fax or e-mail submissions. Responds to queries in 2 weeks; to mss in 2 months. Always sends prepublication galleys. Pays 10% royalties of net receipts. Acquires English-language book rights. Returns rights upon termination of contract.

Advice "We receive over 5,000 unsolicited manuscripts and query letters per year. We publish only a few books per year, of which fewer than half are received unsolicited. Obviously the odds are not with you. For this reason, we encourage you to send out multiple submissions, and we do not expect you to tie up your chances while waiting for our response. Also, poetry does not make money, alas. It is a labor of love for both publisher and writer. But if the love is there, the rewards are great."

🌐 ☑ ☑ DIONYSIA PRESS LTD.

127 Milton Rd. W., 7 Duddingston House Courtyard, Edinburgh EH15 1JG Scotland. Phone/fax: (44)(131)661-1156. Established 1989. **Contact:** Denise Smith.

Book/Chapbook Needs Dionysia Press Ltd. publishes 2-10 paperbacks and chapbooks of poetry/year. "Sometimes we select from submissions or competitions." Has published *Chagall Takes a Fall* by Thom Nairn; *Imagining Seals* by Susanne Roxman; *The Stone Moon* by D. Zervanou; *Psychostasia* by Byron Leodaris; *Like Words and the Body Without a Passkey* by Zefi Daraki (author), Tom Nairn and D. Zervanou (translators); and *Rattlesnake Road* by Tom Bryan. Books are usually A5, perfect-bound, with hard covers with art.

How to Submit Query first, with a few sample poems and a cover letter with brief bio and publication credits. Responds to queries in 2-6 months. Pays in author's copies. "We usually get arts council grants, or poets get grants for themselves." For sample books or chapbooks, write to the above address.

✪ ☑ ☑ DOLPHIN-MOON PRESS

P.O. Box 22262, Baltimore MD 21203. Established 1973. **Contact:** James Taylor, president.

Book/Chapbook Needs Dolphin-Moon is "a limited-edition (500-1,000 copies) press that emphasizes quality work (regardless of style), often published in unusual/'radical' format." The writer is usually allowed a strong voice in the look/feel of the final piece. "We've published magazines, anthologies, chapbooks, pamphlets, perfect-bound paperbacks, records, audio cassettes, and comic books. All styles are read and considered, but the work should show a strong spirit and voice. Although we like the feel of 'well-crafted' work, craft for its own sake won't meet our standards either." Has published work by Teller, Michael Weaver, John Strausbaugh, Josephine Jacobsen, and William Burroughs.

How to Submit Query first, with 6-10 sample poems and a cover letter with brief bio and publication credits. "Please, no submission of complete manuscripts unless requested." No fax or e-mail submissions. Responds to queries and full-length submissions (if invited) in up to one month. Always sends prepublication galleys. Pays in author's copies (negotiable, usually 10% of the press run). Acquires first edition rights. Send SASE for catalog to purchase samples, or send $15 for a "sampler" (guaranteed to be up to $25 worth of publications).

Advice "Our future plans are to continue as we have since 1973, publishing the best work we can by local, up-and-coming, and nationally recognized writers—in a quality package."

◗ ◎ FLOATING BRIDGE PRESS (Specialized: WA poets)

% Richard Hugo House, 1634 11th Ave., Seattle WA 98122. E-mail: floatingbridgepress@yahoo.com. Web site: www.scn.org/arts/floatingbridge. Established 1994. **Contact:** The Editor.

Book/Chapbook Needs Floating Bridge Press publishes chapbooks and anthologies by Washington State poets, selected through an annual contest (see below). Has published *In the Convent We Become Clouds* by Annette Spaulding-Convy, *Toccata & Fugue* by Timothy Kelly, and *The Former St. Christopher* by Michael Bonacci, among others. The press also publishes *Pontoon*, an annual anthology featuring the work of Washington State poets. *Pontoon* is 86-144 pages, digest-sized, offset-printed, perfect-bound, with glossy cardstock cover. For a sample chapbook or anthology, send $13 postpaid.

Contest/Award Offerings For consideration, **Washington State poets only** should submit a chapbook ms of 20-24 pages of poetry. In addition to publication, the winner receives $500, 15 author's copies, and a reading in the Seattle area. All entrants receive a copy of the winning chapbook and will be considered for inclusion in *Pontoon*. Poet's name must not appear on the ms. Include a separate page with ms title, poet's name, address, phone number, and acknowledgments of any previous publications. Include SASE for results only; mss will not be returned. **Entry fee:** $12. **Deadline:** usual reading period is November 1-February 15 (postmark). Considers previously published individual poems and simultaneous submissions. Manuscripts are judged anonymously.

✪ ◗ ◎ GERTRUDE PRESS (Specialized: gay, lesbian, bisexual, transgendered, queer-identified & allied)

P.O. Box 83948, Portland OR 97283. E-mail: editor@gertrudepress.org. Web site: www.gertrudepress.org. Established 1998. **Contact:** Eric Delehoy, founding editor.

Book/Chapbook Needs Gertrude Press, a nonprofit 501(c)(3) organization, showcases and develops "the creative talents of lesbian, gay, bisexual, trans, queer-identified, and allied individuals." Has published *Bone Knowing* by Kate Grant. Gertrude Press publishes 2 chapbooks/year (one fiction, one poetry) as well as *Gertrude*, a semiannual literary journal (see separate listing in Magazines/Journals). Manuscripts are chosen through competition only (see below). Chapbooks are 20-24 pages, offset-printed, saddle-stapled, with cardstock cover with art.

How to Submit Refer to guidelines for Gertrude Press Poetry Chapbook Contest (see separate listing in Contests & Awards). Order sample chapbooks for $10.

Contest/Award Offerings The Gertrude Press Poetry Chapbook Contest (see separate listing in Contests & Awards).

⊕ ◻ ⊘ GINNINDERRA PRESS

P.O. Box 6753, Charnwood ACT 2615 Australia. E-mail: smgp@optusnet.com.au. Web site: www.ginninderrapress.com.au. Established 1996. **Contact:** Stephen Matthews, publisher.

Book/Chapbook Needs Ginninderra Press works "to give publishing opportunities to new writers." Has published poetry by Alan Gould and Geoff Page. Books are usually up to 72 pages, A5, laser-printed, saddle-stapled or thermal-bound, with board covers.

How to Submit Query first, with a few sample poems and a cover letter with brief bio and publication credits. Considers previously published poems; no simultaneous submissions. No fax or e-mail submions. Time between acceptance and publication is 2 months. Seldom comments on rejected poems. Responds to queries in one week; to mss in 2 months.

$ GOOSE LANE EDITIONS (Specialized: Canadian poets only)

500 Beaverbrook Court, Fredericton NB E3B 5X4 Canada. (506)450-4251. Fax: (506)459-4991. Web site: www.gooselane.com. Established 1954. **Contact:** Ross Leckie, poetry editor.

Book/Chapbook Needs Goose Lane is a small literary press publishing Canadian fiction, poetry, and nonfiction. **Considers mss by Canadian poets only.** Receives about 400 mss/year, publishes 15-20 books/year, 4 of which are poetry collections. Has published *Transformations* by John Reibetanz and *Take Us Quietly* by Tammy Armstrong.

How to Submit "Call to inquire whether we are reading submissions." Accepts submissions by postal mail only. Guidelines available on Web site. Always sends prepublication galleys. Authors may receive royalties of up to 10% of retail price on all copies sold. Copies available to author at 40% discount.

Advice "Many of the poems in a manuscript accepted for publication will have been previously published in literary journals such as *The Fiddlehead*, *The Dalhousie Review*, or *The Malahat Review*."

GRAYWOLF PRESS

2402 University Ave., Suite 203, Saint Paul MN 55114. Web site: www.graywolfpress.org. Established 1974. **Contact:** Jeff Shotts, poetry editor.

- Poetry published in Graywolf Press collections has been included in *The Pushcart Prize*, and many books have won major awards.

Book/Chapbook Needs Graywolf Press is considered one of the nation's leading nonprofit literary publishers. "We have claimed our piece of the literary landscape by introducing and promoting the most exciting and creative writers of our times." Considers only mss by poets widely published in magazines and journals of merit; **does not consider unsolicited mss**. Has published poetry by Vijay Seshadri, Tess Gallagher, Tony Hoagland, Linda Gregg, Carl Phillips, Dana Gioia, and many more. Publishes around 9 collections of poetry, 1-2 collections of poetry in translation, and 1-2 collections of essays on poetry/year.

How to Submit Query first, with 10 pages of poetry (as a sample from the ms) and cover letter with brief bio and publication credits. SASE required for reply. No e-mail queries. Reads queries postmarked January 15-December 1 only. Responds to queries in 3-6 months. Order sample books through Web site, or request catalog through online submission form.

GREENHOUSE REVIEW PRESS

3965 Bonny Doon Rd., Santa Cruz CA 95060. Established 1975.

Book/Chapbook Needs Publishes a series of poetry chapbooks and broadsides.

How to Submit *"Unsolicited manuscripts are not accepted."*

HELIKON PRESS

120 W. 71st St., New York NY 10023. Established 1972. **Contact:** Robin Prising and William Leo Coakley, poetry editors.

Book/Chapbook Needs "We try to publish the best contemporary poetry in the tradition of English verse. We read (and listen to) poetry and ask poets to build a collection around particular poems. We print fine editions illustrated by good artists."

How to Submit *"Unfortunately, we cannot encourage submissions."*

◎ HIGH LYRICAL EXPERIMENTS (formerly American Research Press) (Specialized: experimental; paradoxism; outer-art)

P.O. Box 141, Rehoboth NM 87322. E-mail: M_L_Perez@yahoo.com. Web site: www.gallup.unm.e du ~ smarandache/ebooksliterature.htm. Established 1990. **Contact:** Minh Perez, publisher.

Book/Chapbook Needs High Lyrical Experiments publishes 2-3 poetry paperbacks/year. Wants experimental poetry dealing with paradoxism. No classical poetry. See Web site for poetry samples. Has published poetry by Anatol Ciocanu, Nina Josu, and Al Bantos.

How to Submit Submit 3-4 poems at a time. No previously published poems or simultaneous submissions. Cover letter is preferred. Submit seasonal poems one month in advance. Time between acceptance and publication is one year. Seldom comments on rejected poems. Responds to queries in one month. Pays 100 author's copies. Order sample books by sending SASE.

Also Offers Free e-books available on Web site.

$◻ ◎ ◻ HIGH PLAINS PRESS (Specialized: WY and the American West)

P.O. Box 123, Glendo WY 82213. (307)735-4370. Fax: (307)735-4590. E-mail: editor@highplainspre ss.com. Web site: www.highplainspress.com. Established 1985. **Contact:** Nancy Curtis, poetry editor.

Book/Chapbook Needs High Plains Press considers books of poetry "about Wyoming and the American West, particularly poetry based on historical people/events or nature. We mainly publish historical nonfiction, but do publish one book of poetry every year." Has published *Cloud Seeding* by Stacy Coyle, *Bitter Creek Junction* by Linda Hasselstrom, and *Beasts in Snow* by Jane Wohl.

How to Submit Query first with 3 sample poems (from a 50-poem ms). Accepts submissions by e-mail (as attachment); no fax or disk submissions. Time between acceptance and publication is up to 2 years. Guidelines available for SASE or by fax or e-mail. Responds in 2 months. Always sends prepublication galleys. Pays 10% of sales. Acquires first rights. Catalog available on request; sample books: $5.

Advice "Look at our previous titles."

▦ ◎ ◻ HILLTOP PRESS (Specialized: science fiction, dark fantasy)

4 Nowell Place, Almondbury, Huddersfield, West Yorkshire HD5 8PB England. Web site: www.bbr-online.com/catalogue (online catalog). Established 1966. **Contact:** Steve Sneyd, editor.

Book/Chapbook Needs Hilltop Press publishes mainly science fiction poetry, plus some dark fantasy poetry. Publications include: a series of books on poetry in U.S. and UK SFanzines; collections, new and reprint, by individual science fiction poets including Andrew Darlington, Gavin Salisbury, Mary Ladd, Mark Sonnenfeld, John F. Haines, and William Dearden; anthology of SF poetry from Oxford reading that includes Brian Aldiss, etc.; Medusa poems anthology, a cross-section of leading U.S. and UK speculative poets. Orders from the U.S. can be placed through the Web site of BBR Solutions Ltd. (see above).

How to Submit Query (with SAE/IRC) with proposals for relevant projects. **Does not accept unsolicited mss.**

Advice "My advice for beginning poets is: a) Persist—don't let any one editor discourage you. 'In poetry's house are many mansions.' What one publication hates another may love; b) Be prepared for long delays between acceptance and appearance of work—the small press is mostly self-financed and part-time, so don't expect it to be more efficient than commercial publishers; c) Always keep a copy of everything you send out, put your name and address on everything you send, and always include adequately stamped SAE."

▦ $◻ ◎ ◻ HIPPOPOTAMUS PRESS (Specialized: Modernism)

22 Whitewell Rd., Frome, Somerset BA11 4EL England. Phone/fax: (44)(1373)466653. E-mail: rjhip popress@aol.com. Established 1974. **Contact:** Roland John, poetry editor.

Stanley Barkan

Translating the essence of a culture

Photo by Mark Polyakov

There's an old Italian expression: *Traduttore, traditore*. Translator, traitor. The sentiment—that to translate a work is to somehow betray its original meaning—is a familiar one, common to many cultures. But for Stanley Barkan, the founder and head of Cross-Cultural Communications (CCC), a Merrick, New York-based publisher that specializes in translating poets from all across the world, translation is the key to unlocking the truth of poetry.

"The translator to me and CCC is more important than a Nobel Prize winner," says Barkan, himself a poet. "The latter is only one author, while the former is a key to a whole language, a whole culture." CCC has translated poets and authors from more than 50 different languages; translators who have collaborated with CCC have included such renowned names as Gregory Rabassa, the translator for Gabriel Garcia Marquez's seminal *One Hundred Years of Solitude*.

Poet's Market spoke to Barkan about the mission of CCC, how living in close contact with other cultures has broadened his own poetry and where his explorations will take him next.

How has being involved so deeply with translations and poetry from other cultures affected your own poetry? For instance, has it helped you become more nuanced and refined, more aware of the subtleties of language?

Most significantly, the exposure to other cultures, either via the other languages or directly by traveling to where those cultures are based and their languages are spoken, has broadened my perspective on the range of humanity. This broadening, coupled by my senses being stirred by a panoply of different things to see, smell, touch, taste and hear, have concretized and particularized how I express myself much more than prior to this kind of exploration. Early in my writing career, I wondered if I had anything worthwhile to say for others to read, since I had so little experience of the world; the exploration of other cultures and languages gave me confidence in what I had to say and how I would say it.

Translating and co-translating poetry from other languages has acutely heightened my awareness of the nuances and subtleties of how words can affect the reader/listener. I think translation is really transmutation. It is a process of adapting to a different worldview. The translator must shed his own skin and put on the skin of the author he is translating, at least during the process of such transmutation. Translating or arranging for the translation of poetry from English into other languages has, for me, frequently resulted in a kind of linguistic epiphany.

You've said that the mission of Cross-Cultural Communications is to help preserve poetry from cultures endangered by the hegemony of dominant languages such as English. Why do you feel that's important?

I think that some languages are more endangered than the humpback whale. I think of poetry (representative of all the arts) as the essence of a culture. It is a vital artifact of humanity.

Given the language barriers, is it difficult to work with authors throughout the translation process, or do you find there's sort of a "universal language" among poets and poetry lovers?

Actually, I've found it easier to work with authors whose native language is not English, particularly when that language is not among the dominant ones (e.g., French and German). And especially easier with those whose language is among the more threatened ones (e.g., Catalan, Macedonian, Provençal). Perhaps this is because they're grateful that their work is being exposed to a larger audience. It is also possible that it's because most of them function in a multilingual environment and, thus, are more likely to be simpatico. Finally, I would say it's because of the camaraderie that is felt among poets, struggling to be heard via a medium that has little or no commercial value in our time.

Cross-Cultural Communications has translated literature from such a vast diversity of countries and cultures, from Bulgarian to Korean. What are some of the cultures you'd like to explore in the future?

To be accurate, we've translated from 50 different languages and cultures to date. In 2007, I'm going to be publishing a bilingual edition of classical Persian (Farsi) by Hafez. I'd like to study it, while producing the book. But Chinese has been on the agenda for some time now, especially since my trip down the Yangtze and through the Three Gorges. Also, a translation of a Norwegian novel is on the agenda for this spring. And I hope one day to work with some of the languages that Jews used during their long dispersion, like Ladino, Targumic, Shuabit, Yevanic, Judeo-Arabic.

Many of your authors are barely known outside of their countries. How do you find them?

Basically, I find them via the translator. But usually they find me. The translator to me and CCC is more important than a Nobel Prize winner. The latter is only one author, while the former is a key to a whole language, a whole culture. But, when looking for someone to translate something special like "The Layers," Stanley Kunitz's signature poem, into a language I don't have (currently I have it in 46 languages), or a book by John Steinbeck for our John Steinbeck-in-Translation Center in Sag Harbor (curated by Vince Clemente), then I seek out translators via ALTA (American Literary Translators Association), of which I am a member. Since most ALTA members devote their lives to a particular language or foreign author, they are a very good source for providing an author from that language who would be willing and able to do it.

You're a great admirer and tireless advocate of the great American poet Stanley Kunitz, and have brought out translations of his work in many different languages. What is it about Kunitz's work that resonates so profoundly for you?

To date, I've published five bilingual editions of his poetry (Bulgarian, Italian, Polish, Ukrainian, and, the latest, French, in a large broadside portfolio with complementary lithographs by Bulgarian artist, Tchouki) and have had his signature poem, "The Layers," translated into 46 different languages, ranging from Albanian and Armenian through Tagalog and Turkish to Welsh and Yiddish. (When I have 50, I will produce a special multilingual edition.) In Kunitz's poetry, I've found a universality and profundity that, in many ways, crosses linguistic and media boundaries. Generally, a painting or a symphony is unencumbered by the so-called language barrier. I've discovered that some really significant poetry, like "The Layers," can cross over the languages barrier, when subjected to the multilingual translation process. It becomes a kind of prism that, when held up to the light, breaks down all the constituent parts of meaning and feeling. Though it would take a Mario Pei, who mastered some 50 different languages, to attest to this result most provably.

"Traduttore, tradittore" (translator, traitor), says the old Italian expression. Care to refute that?

It's a cliché. But because it is, it is no less true. Yes, I can refute it to some degree, since sometimes there can be a gain in translation.

There's a line in a poem, "On the Death of a Day Old Child," originally written in English by Menke Katz: "The wind will sing my lullabies to you." In Italian, that translates as "Il vento ti canterà la mia ninna-nanna." Say both aloud, and I'm sure you will agree that the Italian is more musical.

Another line from the same poem: "You are the beginning when light is wise." The word "light" here in English does not resonate the full meaning in this context. In English, "light" is a very general word: it can stand for candlelight, moonlight, sunlight, the artificial light from a bulb. In Jewish tradition, when a child is born, it is believed that his soul comes from Heaven knowing everything. This knowledge has to be removed by either an angel kissing it from his eyes or by the removal of the piece of skin between the nose and the upper lip, the space known as the philtrum. In the poem, here "light" means this light of understanding. In Swahili, the word *nuru* means "the light of understanding." Thus, the Swahili translation is more precise. In one, the translation is more musical; in the other, more precise. Both are gains in translation.

Then, again and finally, there is the "prism" possibility in a multilingual translation process, with its yielding a range of meaning and feeling, much more than only in a single language.

—*Travis Adkins*

Travis Adkins is a freelance writer living in Brooklyn, New York.

Book/Chapbook Needs Hippopotamus Press publishes 6 books/year. "The Hippopotamus Press is specialized, with an affinity with Modernism. No Typewriter Poetry, Concrete Poetry, or Surrealism."

How to Submit Query first, with a few sample poems and cover letter with brief bio and publication credits. Considers simultaneous submissions and previously published poems. Responds in 6 weeks. Pays 7½-10% royalties plus author's copies. Request book catalog to purchase sample books.

☑ ◎ ☑ HOLIDAY HOUSE, INC. (Specialized: poetry for children/teens)

Editorial Dept., 425 Madison Ave., New York NY 10017. Web site: www.holidayhouse.com. Established 1936.

Book/Chapbook Needs A trade children's book house. Has published hardcover books for children by John Updike and Walter Dean Myers. Publishes one poetry book/year, averaging 32 pages.

How to Submit *"The acceptance of complete book manuscripts of high-quality children's poetry is limited."* Send a query with SASE before submitting.

✪ ☑ THE JOHNS HOPKINS UNIVERSITY PRESS

2715 N. Charles St., Baltimore MD 21218. Web site: www.press.jhu.edu. Established 1878.

Book/Chapbook Needs "One of the largest American university presses, Johns Hopkins publishes primarily scholarly books and journals. We do, however, publish short fiction and poetry in the series Johns Hopkins: Poetry and Fiction, edited by John Irwin."

How to Submit *"Unsolicited submissions are not considered."*

✪ 🌐 ◯ ◎ ☑ KITE BOOKS (Specialized: poetry for children)

K.T. Publications, 16 Fane Close, Stamford, Lincolnshire PE9 1HG England. (44)(1780)754193. Established 1989. **Contact:** Kevin Troop, editor.

Book/Chapbook Needs K.T. Publications and Kite Books publish "as much as possible each year" of poetry, short stories, and books for children—"at as high a standard as humanly possible." Has published *Freezing the Frame* by Michael Bangerter and *Insect Nights* by Hannah Welfare. Books are usually 50-60 pages, A5, perfect-bound, with glossy covers.

How to Submit Query first, with up to 6 sample poems and a cover letter with brief bio and publication credits. "Also include suitable SAE with IRCs—so that I do not end up paying return postage every time."

Also Offers A "reading and friendly help service to writers. Costs are reasonable." Write for details.

Advice "Keep writing; be patient."

☑ LINTEL

24 Blake Lane, Middletown NY 10940. Phone/fax: (845)342-5224. Established 1977.

● **Not currently accepting unsolicited mss.**

◖ ◎ ☑ LONE WILLOW PRESS (Specialized: theme-driven chapbooks)

P.O. Box 31647, Omaha NE 68131-0647. (402)551-0343. E-mail: lonewillowpress@aol.com. Established 1993. **Contact:** Fredrick Zydek, editor.

Book/Chapbook Needs Lone Willow Press publishes 2-3 chapbooks/year. "We publish chapbooks on single themes and are open to all themes. The only requirement is excellence." Does not want "doggerel or greeting card verse." Has published *Cave Poems* by Marjorie Power, *Things Like This Happen All the Time* by Eric Hoffman, *Monsters We Give Our Children* by Carolyn Riehle, and *From the Dead Before* by Clif Mason. Chapbooks are 36-50 pages, digest-sized, neatly printed on fine paper, saddle-stapled, with cardstock covers.

How to Submit Query first, with 5 sample poems and a cover letter with brief bio and publication credits. No simultaneous submissions. No fax or e-mail submissions. Guidelines available for SASE. Responds to queries in one month; to mss (if invited) in up to 3 months. Pays 25 author's copies. "We also pay a small royalty if the book goes into a second printing." Order sample chapbooks by sending $7.95 (check or money order).

Advice "If you don't know the work of Roethke, DeFrees, and Hugo, don't bother sending work our way. We work with no more than two poets at a time."

✪ ◐ ◎ ☑ LOONFEATHER PRESS (Specialized: for MN-area writers)

P.O. Box 1212, Bemidji MN 56619. (218)444-4869. E-mail: books@loonfeatherpress.com. Web site: http://loonfeatherpress.com Established 1979. **Contact:** Poetry Editors.

Book/Chapbook Needs Loonfeather Press publishes a limited number of quality poetry books. Has published *Imaginarium* by Lynn Levin (a 2005 ForeWord Finalist); *The Rhubarb King* by Sharon

Chmielarz; and *Traces in Blood, Bone, & Stone: Contemporary Ojibwe Poetry*, edited by Kimberly Blaeser.

How to Submit *Does not accept unsolicited mss.* Check Web site for updates.

⬤ LOUISIANA STATE UNIVERSITY PRESS

P.O. Box 25053, Baton Rouge LA 70894-5053. (225)578-6434. Fax: (225)578-6461. E-mail: jeaster@lsu.edu. Web site: www.lsu.edu/lsupress. Established 1935. **Contact:** John Easterly, executive editor.

Book/Chapbook Needs A highly respected publisher of collections by poets such as Claudia Emerson, Brendan Galvin, Lisel Mueller, Fred Chappell, Marilyn Nelson, and Henry Taylor. Publisher of the Southern Messenger Poets series edited by Dave Smith.

How to Submit *"Currently accepting poetry submissions, but the lists are full through 2009."*

◐ ◎ ☑ LUNA BISONTE PRODS (Specialized: experimental, avant-garde)

137 Leland Ave., Columbus OH 43214-7505. Web site: www.johnmbennett.net. Established 1967. **Contact:** John M. Bennett, editor/publisher.

Book/Chapbook Needs Luna Bisonte Prods considers book submissions. "Interested in avant-garde and highly experimental work only." Has published poetry by Jim Leftwich, Sheila E. Murphy, Al Ackerman, Richard Kostelanetz, Ivan Argüelles, Peter Ganick, and many others.

How to Submit Query first, with a few sample poems and cover letter with brief bio and publication credits. "Keep it brief. Chapbook publishing usually depends on grants or other subsidies, and is usually by solicitation. **Will also consider subsidy arrangements on negotiable terms.**" A sampling of various Luna Bisonte Prods products is available for $20.

Advice "Be blank."

✖ ☑ MAD RIVER PRESS

State Road, Richmond MA 01254. (413)698-3184. Established 1986. **Contact:** Barry Sternlieb, editor.

Book/Chapbook Needs Mad River publishes 2 broadsides and one chapbook/year, "all types of poetry, no bias."

How to Submit *Does not read unsolicted submissions.*

◐ ◎ MARYMARK PRESS (Specialized: experimental, avant-garde)

45-08 Old Millstone Dr., East Windsor NJ 08520. (609)443-0646. Established 1994. **Contact:** Mark Sonnenfeld, editor/publisher.

Book/Chapbook Needs Marymark Press's goal is "to feature and promote experimental writers. I will most likely be publishing broadsides, give-out sheets, and chapbooks this year. I want to see experimental writing of the outer fringe. Make up words, sounds, whatever, but say something you thought never could be explained. Disregard rules, if need be." No traditional, rhyming, or spiritual verse; no predictable styles. Has published poetry by Jose Roberto Sechi, Charles Plymell, Kris Coontz, Richard Kostelanetz, and Jeffrey D. Moore.

How to Submit Submit 3 poems at a time. Considers previously published poems and simultaneous submissions. Cover letter is preferred. "Copies should be clean, crisp, and camera-ready. I do not have the means to accept electronic submissions. A SASE should accompany all submissions, and include a telephone number if at all possible." Time between acceptance and publication is one month. Seldom comments on rejected poems. Guidelines available for SASE. Responds to queries and mss in up to 2 weeks. Pays at least 10 author's copies (out of a press run of 200-300). **May offer subsidy arrangements.** "It all depends upon my financial situation at the time. Yes, I might ask the author to subsidize the cost. It could be worth their while. I have good connections in the international small press." Order sample publications by sending a 6×9 SAE. "There is no charge for samples."

Advice "Experiment with thought, language, the printed word."

☐ ⊘ MAVERICK DUCK PRESS (formerly Powerscore Press)

E-mail: maverickduckpress@yahoo.com. Web site: www.maverickduckpress.com. Established 2005. **Contact:** Kendall A. Bell, editor.

Book/Chapbook Needs Maverick Duck Press is a "publisher of chapbooks from undiscovered talent. We are looking for fresh and powerful work that shows a sense of innovation or a new take on passion or emotion. Previous publication in print or online journals will increase your chances of us accepting your manuscript." Does not want "unedited work." Recently published *The Mathematics of Frustration and Loss* by Kendall A. Bell, *Hazy Expressions* by Katrina Guarascio, *House of Fame* by Kristina Marie Darling, *Wire To The Heart* by Bruce Niedt, and *Mid-Range* by Leisa Pierce. Publishes 5-10 chapbooks/year. Manuscripts are selected through open submission. Chapbooks are 25-40 pages, photocopied, saddle-stapled, with cardstock covers (poet must provide desired cover art).

How to Submit Query first, with a few sample poems and a cover letter with brief bio and publication credits. Chapbook mss may include previously published poems. "Previous publication is always a plus, as we may be more familiar with your work. Chapbook manuscripts should have at least 20 poems." Pays 20 author's copies (out of a press run of 50).

Advice "Write and revise often. Read a lot of other poets. Your manuscript should be the strongest of your work."

$ ⊘ ◎ MEADOWBROOK PRESS (Specialized: anthologies; children; humor)

5451 Smetana Dr., Minnetonka MN 55343. Web site: www.meadowbrookpress.com. Established 1975. **Contact:** Poetry Editor.

Book/Chapbook Needs Meadowbrook Press is "currently seeking poems to be posted on our Web site and to be considered for future funny poetry book anthologies for children." Wants humorous poems aimed at children ages 6-12. "Poems should be fun, punchy, and refreshing. We're looking for new, hilarious, contemporary voices in children's poetry that kids can relate to." Has published poetry by Shel Silverstein, Jack Prelutsky, Jeff Moss, Kenn Nesbitt, and Bruce Lansky. Published anthologies include *Kids Pick the Funniest Poems*, *A Bad Case of the Giggles*, and *Miles of Smiles*.

How to Submit "Please take time to read our guidelines, and send your best work." Submit up to 10 poems at a time; one poem to a page with name and address on each; include SASE. Lines/poem: 25 maximum. Considers simultaneous submissions. Time between acceptance and publication is 1-2 years. Poems are tested in front of grade school students before being published. Guidelines available for SASE or on Web site. Responds only if interested. Pays $50-100/poem plus one contributor's copy.

✪ ⊘ MELLEN POETRY PRESS

P.O. Box 450, Lewiston NY 14092-0450. (716)754-2266. Fax: (716)754-4056. Web site: www.mellen press.com. Established 1973. **Contact:** Patricia Schultz, poetry editor.

• **"Mellen Poetry Press is currently on indefinite 'hold.' We are not accepting proposals or manuscripts at this time."**

◎ ⊘ MIDWEST VILLAGES & VOICES (Specialized: Midwestern poetry)

P.O. Box 40214, St. Paul MN 55104. (612)822-6878. Established 1979.

Book/Chapbook Needs Midwest Villages & Voices is a cultural organization and small press publisher of Midwestern poetry and prose.

How to Submit "We encourage and support Midwestern writers and artists. However, **at this time submissions are accepted by invitation only.** Unsolicited submissions are not accepted."

◪ MILKWEED EDITIONS

1011 Washington Ave. S., Suite 300, Minneapolis MN 55415-1246. (612)332-3192. Fax: (612)215-2550. E-mail: editor@milkweed.org. Web site: www.milkweed.org. Established 1984. **Contact:** Poetry Reader.

Book/Chapbook Needs Milkweed Editions is "looking for poetry manuscripts of high quality that embody humane values and contribute to cultural understanding." Not limited in subject matter. Open to writers with previously published books of poetry or a minimum of 6 poems published in nationally distributed commercial or literary journals. Considers translations and bilingual mss. Has published *Furia* by Orlando Ricardo Menes, *Music for Landing Planes By* by Eireann Lorsung, *Atlas* by Katrina Vandenberg, and *Willow Room, Green Door* by Deborah Keenan.

How to Submit Submit 60 pages or more, typed on high-quality white paper. No fax or e-mail submissions. Do not send originals. Include SASE for reply. Reads unsolicited mss in January and June **only**, but accepts mss all year. "In the event that manuscripts are not accepted for publication, we prefer to recycle them. If you need your work returned, **please enclose a check for $5 rather than a stamped mailer**." Guidelines available for SASE or on Web site. Responds in up to 6 months. Order sample books through Web site.

◪ ◪ MOUNT OLIVE COLLEGE PRESS

634 Henderson St., Mount Olive NC 28365. (919)658-2502. Established 1990. **Contact:** Dr. Pepper Worthington, editor.

Book/Chapbook Needs Mount Olive Press publishes 2 books/year. Books are usually digest-sized.

How to Submit Submit 12 sample poems. Guidelines available for SASE. Responds to queries and mss in 3 months. Obtain sample books by writing to the above address.

◉ ◪ MOVING PARTS PRESS (Specialized: translations; Latino/Chicano)

10699 Empire Grade, Santa Cruz CA 95060-9474. (831)427-2271. E-mail: frice@movingpartspress.com. Web site: www.movingpartspress.com. Established 1977. **Contact:** Felicia Rice, poetry editor.

Book/Chapbook Needs Moving Part Press publishes handsome, innovative books, broadsides, and prints that "explore the relationship of word and image, typography and the visual arts, the fine arts and popular culture." Published *Codex Espangliensis: from Columbus to the Border Patrol* (1998) with performance texts by Guillermo Gómez-Peña and collage imagery by Enrique Chagoya; *Cosmogonie Intime/An Intimate Cosmogony* (2005), a limited edition artists' book with poems by Yves Peyré, translated by Elizabeth R. Jackson, and drawings by Ray Rice.

How to Submit *Does not accept unsolicited mss.*

◪ ◪ ◪ MULTICULTURAL BOOKS

Suite 307, 6311 Gilbert Rd., Richmond BC V7C 3V7 Canada. (604)277-3864. E-mail: jrmbooks@hotmail.com. Web site: www.thehypertexts.com. Established 1985. **Contact:** Joe M. Ruggier, publisher.

Book/Chapbook Needs Multicultural Books publishes poetry and related literature as well as fiction and various forms of nonfiction. Publishes 1-6 books/year "depending on availability and quality." Manuscripts are selected through open submission. Books are 120+ pages, digitally photocopied, perfect-bound, with heavy color cardstock cover.

How to Submit Query first, with a few sample poems and a cover letter with brief bio and publication credits. Book mss may include previously published poems. "The only criteria is quality of work and excellence." Responds to queries in 2 months; to mss in 2 months. **Offers author-subsidy as well as publisher-subsidy options**; the selection process for the latter is extremely competitive and quality-conscious. "Authors who feel their work may be up to standard are welcome to query us with a sample or else submit an entire manuscript. All interested parties may consult our guidelines as well as our sample publication contract on www.thehypertexts.com." Order sample books/chapbooks by contacting Joe M. Ruggier.

◎ ☑ NEW NATIVE PRESS (Specialized: translations; marginalized & endangered languages)

P.O. Box 661, Cullowhee NC 28723. (828)293-9237. E-mail: newnativepress@hotmail.com. Web site: www.newnativepress.com. Established 1979. **Contact:** Thomas Rain Crowe, publisher.

Book/Chapbook Needs New Native Press has "selectively narrowed its range of contemporary 20th- and 21st-century literature to become an exclusive publisher of writers in marginalized and endangered languages. All books published are bilingual translations from original languages into English." Publishes about 2 paperbacks/year. Has published *Kenneth Patchen: Rebel Poet in America* by Larry Smith; Gaelic, Welsh, Breton, Cornish, and Manx poets in an all-Celtic-language anthology of contemporary poets from Scotland, Ireland, Wales, Brittany, Cornwall, and Isle of Man, entitled *Writing The Wind: A Celtic Resurgence* (The New Celtic Poetry); and *Selected Poems* by Kusumagraj (poet from Bombay, India) in the Marathi language. Books are sold by distributors in 4 foreign countries, and in the U.S. by Baker & Taylor, Amazon.com, library vendors, and Small Press Distribution. Books are typically 80 pages, offset-printed on glossy 120 lb. stock, perfect-bound, with professionally designed color cover.

How to Submit Query first, with 10 sample poems and cover letter with brief bio and publication credits. Considers previously published poems and simultaneous submissions. Time between acceptance and publication is up to one year. Always comments on rejected poems. Responds in 2 weeks. Pays in author's copies ("amount varies with author and title").

Advice "We are looking for work indicative of rare and unique talent—and original voices—using language experimentally and symbolically, if not subversively."

✖ ❷ NEW ORLEANS POETRY JOURNAL PRESS

2131 General Pershing St., New Orleans LA 70115. (504)891-3458. Established 1956. **Contact:** Maxine Cassin, publisher/editor. Co-Editor: Charles de Gravelles.

● **"For the present, due to Hurricane Katrina, all correspondence should be sent to Maxine Cassin at 140 Wylie Dr., #4, Baton Rouge LA 70808."**

Book/Chapbook Needs "We prefer to publish relatively new and/or little-known poets of unusual promise or those inexplicably neglected." Does not want to see "cliché or doggerel, anything incomprehensible or too derivative, or workshop exercises. First-rate lyric poetry preferred (not necessarily in traditional forms)." Has published books by Everette Maddox, Charles Black, Malaika Favorite, Martha McFerren, Paul Petrie, and Charles de Gravelles.

How to Submit *This market is currently closed to all submissions.*

Advice "Read as much as possible! Write only when you must, and don't rush into print! No poetry should be sent without querying first! Publishers are concerned about expenses unnecessarily incurred in mailing manuscripts. *Telephoning is not encouraged.*"

$ ☑ ◎ ☑ OOLIGAN PRESS (Specialized: gives preference to translated poetry, prose poetry, traditional verse, and works from local poets)

Portland State University, P.O. Box 751, Portland OR 97207-0751. Web site: www.publishing.pdx.edu. Established 2001. **Contact:** Acquisitions Committee.

Book/Chapbook Needs As a general trade press, Ooligan Press is "open to publishing limited collections of poetry (this genre represents only a small percentage of the overall list)." Open to "all forms of style and verse; however, we give special preference to translated poetry, prose poetry, and traditional verse. We place special value on collections of works from local poets. Although spoken word, slam, and rap poetry are of interest to the press, we will not consider such work if it does not translate well to the written page." Has published *American Scream & Palindrome*

Apocalypse by Durbravaka Oraic-Tolid, translated by Julienne Eden Busic, and *Deer Drinks the Moon*, edited by Liz Nakazawa. Manuscripts are selected through open submission. Books are offset-printed, perfect-bound, with soft covers.

How to Submit Query by postal mail, with a few sample poems, a brief bio including poet's publication credits, and a SASE. Book mss may include previously published poems. Accepts simultaneous submissions. See Web site for explanation of acquisition process and complete submission guidelines. Responds to queries in 3 months. Payment varies, but generally 6-12% of retail price and 25 author's copies. Order sample books through Web site.

◔ ☑ PANTHER CREEK PRESS

P.O. Box 130233, Panther Creek Station, Spring TX 77393-0233. E-mail: panthercreek3@hotmail.com. Web site: www.panthercreekpress.com. Established 1975. **Contact:** Guida Jackson, managing editor.

- **"At present we are overstocked and will accept no new submissions until 2007."**

Book/Chapbook Needs Panther Creek Press no longer publishes chapbooks. Recent book-length titles include *This Light We Live In* by Chris Ellery, *You Give Me Fever* by Chuck Taylor, *Living on the Hurricane Coast* by Robb Jackson, *The Mottled Air* by Paul Christensen, and *Under a Riverbed Sky* by Christopher Woods.

How to Submit Query first, with a few sample poems and cover letter with brief bio and publication credits. Include SASE. "Absolutely no mail is answered without SASE or e-mail address."

$ ◔ ◎ ☑ PELICAN PUBLISHING COMPANY (Specialized: regional/various; poetry books for children)

1000 Burmaster St., Gretna LA 70053. E-mail: editorial@pelicanpub.com. Web site: www.pelicanpub.com. Established 1926. **Contact:** Nina Kooij, editor-in-chief.

Book/Chapbook Needs Pelican Publishing Company is a moderate-sized publisher of cookbooks, travel guides, regional books, and inspirational/motivational books. Considers poetry for "hardcover children's books only, preferably with a regional focus. However, our needs for this are very limited; we publish 22 juvenile titles per year, and most of these are prose, not poetry." Has published *Nurse's Night Before Christmas* by David Davis and *Santa's Revenge* by James Rice. Two of Pelican's popular series are prose books about Gaston the Green-Nosed Alligator by James Rice, and Clovis Crawfish by Mary Alice Fontenot. Has a variety of books based on "The Night Before Christmas," adapted to regional settings such as Cajun, prairie, and Texas. Books are 32 pages, magazine-sized, include illustrations.

How to Submit *Currently not accepting unsolicited mss.* Query first with a cover letter including "work and writing backgrounds and promotional connections." No previously published poems or simultaneous submissions. Guidelines available for SASE or on Web site. Responds to queries in one month; to mss (if invited) in 3 months. Always sends prepublication galleys. Pays royalties. Acquires all rights. Returns rights upon termination of contract. Typically, Pelican books sell for $15.95. Write for catalog or visit Web site to buy samples.

Advice "We try to avoid rhyme altogether, especially predictable rhyme. Monotonous rhythm can also be a problem."

$ ◔ ☑ THE PEOPLE'S PRESS

4810 Norwood Ave., Baltimore MD 21207-6839. Fax: (410)448-0254. Established 1997. **Contact:** Submissions Editor.

Book/Chapbook Needs "The goal of the types of material we publish is simply to move people to think and perhaps act to make the world better than when we inherited it." Wants "meaningful poetry that is mindful of human rights/dignity." Considers poetry by children and teens; parental consent is mandatory for publication. Has published *Untouchable Jivan* by Aasha Sunar; *Familiar,* works by various artists; *Late* by Kelley Jean White, MD; *Hard Hooved Hussy* by Mary Alice Ramsey; *Sweet Somethings* by Garrett Flagg and Marvin Pirila; *Braids* by Rasheed Adero Merritt; and *2000 Here's to Humanity* by various artists. Books are at least 50 pages, usually perfect-bound, with soft covers.

How to Submit Query first with 1-5 sample poems and a cover letter with brief bio and publication credits. SASE required for return of work and/or response. No fax submissions. Time between acceptance and publication is 6 months to one year. Seldom comments on rejected poems. Guidelines available for SASE. Responds to queries within 6 weeks; to mss within 3 months. Pays royalties of 5-20% and 30 author's copies (out of a press run of 500). Order sample books by sending $8.

Contest/Award Offerings The People's Press sponsors an annual Poetry Month Contest in April. "Prizes and/or publication possibilities vary from contest to contest." Details available for SASE.

Advice "Expound on something that moves you within the realm of human rights/dignity, and hopefully we will be moved also."

☑ PERUGIA PRESS (Specialized: first or second poetry book by a woman)

P.O. Box 60364, Florence MA 01062. E-mail: info@perugiapress.com. Web site: www.perugiapress. com. Established 1997. **Contact:** Susan Kan, director.

Book/Chapbook Needs Perugia Press publishes one collection of poetry each year, by a woman at the beginning of her publishing career (first or second books only). "Our books appeal to people who have been reading poetry for decades, as well as those who might be picking up a book of poetry for the first time. Slight preference for narrative poetry." Has published *Kettle Bottom* by Diane Gilliam Fisher, *Lamb* by Frannie Lindsay, *The Disappearing Letters* by Carol Edelstein, *Seamless* by Linda Tomol Pennisi, and *Red* by Melanie Braverman. Books are an average of 88 pages, offset-printed, perfect-bound. Print run is 500-1,200. Order sample books through Web site.

How to Submit "We are not accepting general submissions at this time." *Manuscripts are selected through competition only.*

Contest/Award Offerings The Perugia Press Prize (see separate listing in Contests & Awards).

☑ ◎ ☑ PLAN B PRESS (Specialized: experimental, concrete, visual poetry)

3412 Terrace Dr., #1731, Alexandria VA 22302. (215)732-2663. E-mail: teammay@att.net. Web site: www.planbpress.com. Established 1999. **Contact:** stevenallenmay, president.

Book/Chapbook Needs Plan B Press is a "small publishing company with an international feel. Our intention is to have Plan B Press be part of the conversation about the direction and depth of literary movements and genres. Plan B Press's new direction is to seek out authors rarely-to-never published, sharing new voices that might not otherwise be heard. Plan B Press is determined to merge text with image, writing with art." Publishes poetry and short fiction. Wants "experimental poetry, concrete/visual work." Does not want "sonnets, political or religious poems, work in the style of Ogden Nash." Has published poetry by Lamont B Steptoe, Michele Belluomini, Jim Mancinelli, Lyn Lifshin, Robert Miltner, and stevenallenmay. Publishes one poetry book/year and 5-10 chapbooks/year. Manuscripts are selected through open submission and through competition (see below). Books/chapbooks are 24-48 pages, with covers with art/graphics.

How to Submit Query first, with a few sample poems and a cover letter with brief bio and publication credits. Book/chapbook mss may include previously published poems. Guidelines available on Web site. Responds to queries in one month; to mss in 3 months. Author keeps royalties. Pays varying number of author's copies; press run varies per book. **About 10-25% of books are author subsidy-published each year.** Order sample books/chapbooks by writing to Plan B. Press or through Web site.

Contest/Award Offerings Sponsors the annual Plan B Press Poetry Chapbook Contest. Winner receives $150 and 50 author's copies. Submit 15-20 poems (48 pages total maximum). Poems may be previously published, but must be written primarily in English. Include e-mail address or SASE for notification of winner; mss will not be returned. Author retains copyright of poems, but Plan B reserves rights to layout and/or cover art and design. Guidelines available on Web site. **Entry fee:** $15. Multiple submissions accepted, with multiple fees. **Deadline:** March 15.

Advice "Writing reveals the mirror to your soul. Don't think about words until you are in the editing phase, and then only look for errors. Whatever sense your work makes is for the reader to ascertain, not you. You are a beacon, a transmitter."

✪ ◻ PLATONIC 3WAY PRESS

P.O. Box 844, Warsaw IN 46581. (317)457-3505. E-mail: mail@platonic3waypress.com. Web site: www.Platonic3WayPress.com. Established 2005. **Contact:** Steve Henn, Oren Wagner, and Don Winter, co-editors.

Book/Chapbook Needs Platonic 3Way Press wants "poetry that celebrates honesty and humor, poetry with some bite to it." Does not want "cute bunny poems, overtly political poems, knee-jerk, poorly executed anti-(fill in the blank) poems." Publishes one chapbook/year. Manuscript selected through the Evil Genius Chapbook Contest only (see separate listing). "Winners selected by votes of the three editors." Chapbooks are 16-30 pages, high resolution photocopied, usually saddle-stapled, with cardstock cover and graphics that "vary according to the project."

How to Submit Submissions accepted through the Evil Genius Chapbook Contest only (see separate listing in Contests & Awards).

Also Offers *Fight These Bastards*, a journal of literature and art (see separate listing in Magazines/Journals) as well as the Painfully Platonic chapbook series (submissions by invitation only).

Advice "Looking for the poetry of revolt—against the Academy, against the poetic mainstream. Looking for poetry accessible beyond the ivory towers of academia and outside the bonds of religious or politically correct restrictions."

🌐 ☑ ☑ POETRY SALZBURG

University of Salzburg, Dept. of English, Akademiestrasse 24, Salzburg A-5020 Austria. (43)(662)8044-4422. Fax: (43)(662)8044-167. E-mail: editor@poetrysalzburg.com. Web site: www.poetrysalzburg.com. Established 1971 (as University of Salzburg Press). **Contact:** Dr. Wolfgang Goertschacher, editor.

Book/Chapbook Needs Poetry Salzburg publishes "collections of at least 100 pages by mainly poets not taken up by big publishers." Publishes 6-8 paperbacks/year. Books are usually 100-350 pages, A5, professionally printed, perfect-bound, with card covers.

How to Submit Query first, with a few sample poems and a cover letter with brief bio and publication credits. Suggests authors publish in *Poetry Salzburg Review* (see separate listing in Magazines/Journals) first. Responds to queries in 4 weeks; to mss in about 3 months. Payment varies.

◖ ◎ ☑ PRESS HERE (Specialized: haiku, tanka)

22230 NE 28th Place, Sammamish WA 98074-6408. E-mail: WelchM@aol.com. Established 1989. **Contact:** Michael Dylan Welch, editor/publisher.

• Press Here publications have won the 1st-place Merit Book Award and other awards from the Haiku Society of America.

Book/Chapbook Needs Press Here publishes award-winning books of haiku, tanka, and related poetry by the leading poets of these genres, as well as essays, criticism, and interviews about these genres. "We publish work only by those poets who are already frequently published in the leading haiku and tanka journals." Does not want any poetry other than haiku, tanka, and related genres. Has published poetry by Lee Gurga, paul m., Paul O. Williams, Pat Shelley, Cor van den Heuvel, and William J. Higginson. Publishes 2-3 poetry books/year, plus occasional books of essays or interviews. Manuscripts are selected through open submission. Books are 32-112 pages, offset-printed, perfect-bound, with glossy paperback covers.

How to Submit Query first, with a few sample poems and a cover letter with brief bio and publication credits. Book mss may include previously published poems ("previous publication strongly preferred"). "All proposals must be by well-established haiku or tanka poets, and must be for haiku or tanka poetry, or criticism/discussion of these genres. If the editor does not already know your work well from leading haiku and tanka publications, then he is not likely to be interested in your manuscript." Responds to queries in up to one month; to mss in up to 2 months. Pays a negotiated percentage of author's copies (out of a press run of 200-1,000). Catalog available for #10 SASE.

Advice "Press Here publishes only 2-3 titles per year by leading haiku and tanka poets. For Press Here to publish your book, you will likely already know other Press Here books and the work of their authors, and the editor would most likely already know you and your work. If not, then establish yourself in these genres first by publishing extensively in the leading haiku or tanka journals."

◎ PRINCETON UNIVERSITY PRESS (Specialized: poetry in translation only)

41 William St., Princeton NJ 08540. (609)258-4900. Fax: (609)258-6305. Web site: www.press.princ eton.edu. **Contact:** Hanne Winarsky, editor.

Book/Chapbook Needs "In the Lockert Library series, we publish simultaneous cloth and paperback editions for each poet. Clothbound editions are printed on acid-free paper, and binding materials are chosen for strength and durability. Each book is given individual design treatment rather than stamped into a series mold. We have published a wide range of poets from other cultures, including well-known writers such as Hölderlin and Cavafy, and those who have not yet had their due in English translation, such as Göran Sonnevi. Manuscripts are judged with several criteria in mind: the ability of the translation to stand on its own as poetry in English; fidelity to the tone and spirit of the original, rather than literal accuracy; and the importance of the translated poet to the literature of his or her time and country."

How to Submit Submit hard copy of proposal with sample poems or full ms. Cover letter is required. Reads submissions year round. Manuscripts will not be returned. Comments on finalists only. Responds in 3-4 months.

✪ ◪ THE PUDDIN'HEAD PRESS

P.O. Box 477889, Chicago IL 60647. (708)656-4900. E-mail: phbooks@compuserve.com. Web site: www.puddinheadpress.com. Established 1985. **Contact:** David Gecic, editor-in-chief.

Book/Chapbook Needs The Puddin'head Press is interested in "well-rounded poets who can support their work with readings and appearances." Wants "quality poetry by active poets who read and lead interesting lives. We occasionally publish chapbook-style anthologies and let poets on our mailing lists know what type of work we're interested in for a particular project." Does not want experimental, overly political poetry, or poetry with overt sexual content; no shock or novelty poems. Has published poetry by Jared Smith, Carol Anderson, Larry Janowski, Sandy Goldsmith, and Norman Porter. Puddin'head Press publishes 2-3 books and 2-3 chapbooks per year. Books/chapbooks are 30-100 pages, perfect-bound or side-stapled ("we use various formats").

How to Submit "Please e-mail us for submission guidelines." Poets must include SASE with submission. Responds to queries in one month; to mss in 3 months. Pays various royalty rates "depending on the publication. We usually have a press run of 500 books." **About 10% of books are author subsidy-published.** Terms vary. Order sample books/chapbooks by sending $10 (price plus postage) to The Puddin'head Press (also available through Amazon).

Additional Information "In the last several years we have been increasingly active across the country. There are numerous readings and events that we sponsor. We do our own distribution, primarily in the Midwest, and also do distribution for other small presses. Please send a SASE for a list of our current publications and publication/distribution guidelines."

Also Offers "Extensive Web site with rare and used books, extensive links to who's who in poetry and online marketing."

Advice "It is difficult to find a quality publisher. Poets must have patience and find a press that will work with them. The most important part of publication is the relationship between poet and publisher. Many good books will never be seen because the poet/publisher relationship is not healthy. If a poet is involved in the literary world, he will find a publisher, or a publisher will find him."

☑ ◎ PUDDING HOUSE PUBLICATIONS (Specialized: social issues; popular culture reflected in poetry arts)

Shadymere Lane, Columbus OH 43213. (614)986-1881. E-mail: info@puddinghouse.com. Web site: www.puddinghouse.com. Established 1979. **Contact:** Jennifer Bosveld, editor.

Book/Chapbook Needs Pudding House Publications prints chapbooks, anthologies, and broadsides. Has nearly 900 titles in print. Provides "a sociological looking glass through poems that speak to the pop culture, struggle in a consumer and guardian society, and more—through 'felt experience.' Speaks for the difficulties and the solutions." Pudding House is also the publisher of the respected national archive, POETS' GREATEST HITS—an invitational. Has recently published *The Allegories* by Dan Sicoli, *Barb Quill Down* by Bill Griffin, *Sonnets to Hamlet* by David Rigsbee, *Mischief* by Charlene Fix, and over 200 others.

How to Submit Chapbooks considered outside of competitions, no query. Send complete ms and a cover letter with publication credits and bio. **Reading fee:** $12. Sometimes comments; "no more critiquing, too busy now."

Contest/Award Offerings Pudding House offers an annual chapbook competition. **Entry fee:** $15. **Deadline:** September 30. Guidelines available on Web site.

Also Offers "Our Web site is one of the greatest poetry Web sites in the country—calls, workshops, publication list/history, online essays, games, guest pages, calendars, poem of the month, poet of the week, much more." The Web site also links to the site for The Unitarian Universalist Poets Cooperative and American Poets Opposed to Executions, both national organizations.

Advice "Editors have pet peeves. I won't respond to or on postcards. I require SASEs. Love cover letters that are genuine, friendly, and don't state the obvious. Don't like poems with trite concepts or meaning dictated by rhyme. Thoroughly review our Web site; it will give you a good idea about our publication history and editorial tastes."

$☑ ☑ QED PRESS/CYPRESS HOUSE

155 Cypress St., Fort Bragg CA 95437. (800)773-7782. Fax: (707)964-7531. E-mail: joeshaw@cypres shouse.com. Web site: www.cypresshouse.com. Established 1985. **Contact:** Joe Shaw, editor.

Book/Chapbook Needs QED Press publishes "clear, clean, intelligent, and moving work." Wants "concrete, personal, and spare writing. No florid rhymed verse." Has published poetry by Victoria Greenleaf, Luke Breit, Paula Tennant (Adams), and Cynthia Frank. Publishes 1-2 paperback poetry books/year. Books are usually about 100 pages (75-80 poems), digest-sized, offset-printed, perfect-bound, with full-color covers.

How to Submit "We prefer to see ten representative poems." Considers simultaneous submissions. Cover letter and SASE for return of materials are required. Time between acceptance and publication is up to one year. Poems are circulated to an editorial board. Responds to queries and mss in one month. Pays royalties of 7-12% and 25 author's copies (out of a press run of 500-1,000). Order sample books through Web site.

Also Offers Book packaging, and promotion and marketing services to start-up publishers. "We are not a vanity press."

$ ☑ ◎ ☑ RATTAPALLAX PRESS (Specialized: the diversity of world cultures)

532 La Guardia Place, Suite 353, New York NY 10012. E-mail: info@rattapallax.com. Web site: www.rattapallax.com. Established 1998. **Contact:** Poetry Editor.

Book/Chapbook Needs Rattapallax Press publishes "contemporary poets and writers with unique, powerful voices." Publishes 5 paperbacks and 3 chapbooks/year. Books are usually 64 pages, digest-sized, offset-printed, perfect-bound, with 12-pt. CS1 covers.

How to Submit Query first, with a few sample poems and cover letter with brief bio and publication credits. Include SASE. Requires authors to first be published in *Rattapallax*. Responds to queries in one month; to mss in 2 months. Pays royalties of 10-25%. Order sample books from Web site.

☑ RED DRAGON PRESS

P.O. Box 19425, Alexandria VA 22320-0425. Web site: www.reddragonpress.com. Established 1993. **Contact:** Laura Qa, editor/publisher.

Book/Chapbook Needs Red Dragon Press is a proponent "of works that represent the nature of man as androgynous, as in the fusing of male and female symbolism, and we support works that deal with psychological and parapsychological topics." Wants "innovative, progressive, and experimental poetry and prose using literary symbolism and aspiring to the creation of meaningful new ideas, forms, and methods." Has published *The Distance of Ducks* by Louis Bourgeois, *Spectator Turns Witness* by George Karos, and *The Crown of Affinity* by Laura Qa. Publishes 3-4 chapbooks/year. Chapbooks are usually 64 pages, digest-sized, offset-printed on trade paper, perfect-bound.

How to Submit Submit up to 5 poems at a time with SASE. Considers previously published poems and simultaneous submissions. Cover letter with brief bio is preferred. **Reading fee: $5 for poetry and short fiction, $10 for novels.** Make checks or money orders payable to Red Dragon Press. Time between acceptance and publication is 8 months. "Poems are selected for consideration by the publisher, then circulated to senior editor and/or poets previously published for comment. Poems are returned to the publisher for further action, i.e., rejection or acceptance for publication in an anthology or book by a single author. Frequently, submission of additional works is required before final offer is made, especially in the process for a book by a single author." Often comments on rejected poems. **Charges criticism fee of $10/page on request.** Responds to queries in 10 weeks, to mss in one year. Purchase sample books at bookstores, or mail-order direct from Red Dragon Press at the above address.

☑ ◎ ☑ RED MOON PRESS (Specialized: English-language haiku & related forms)

P.O. Box 2461, Winchester VA 22604-1661. (540)722-2156. E-mail: jim.kacian@redmoonpress.com. Web site: www.redmoonpress.com. Established 1993. **Contact:** Jim Kacian, editor/publisher.

Book/Chapbook Needs Red Moon Press "is the largest and most prestigious publisher of English-language haiku and related work in the world." Publishes 6-8 volumes/year, usually 3-5 anthologies and individual collections of English-language haiku, as well as 1-3 books of essays, translations, or criticism of haiku. Under other imprints, the press also publishes chapbooks of various sizes and formats.

How to Submit Query with book theme and information, and 30-40 poems or draft of first chapter. Responds to queries in 2 weeks, to mss (if invited) in 3 months. "Each contract separately negotiated."

Advice "Haiku is a burgeoning and truly international form. It is nothing like what your fourth-grade teacher taught you years ago, and so it is best if you familiarize yourself with what is happening in the genre (and its close relatives) today before submitting. We strive to give all the work we publish plenty of space in which to resonate, and to provide a forum where the best of today's practitioners can be published with dignity and prestige. All our books have either won awards or are awaiting notification. We intend to work hard to keep it that way."

⊠ $ ⬛ ◎ ⊠ RONSDALE PRESS (Specialized: Canadian poets only)

3350 W. 21st Ave., Vancouver BC V6S 1G7 Canada. (604)738-4688. Fax: (604)731-4548. E-mail: ronsdale@shaw.ca. Web site: www.ronsdalepress.com. Established 1988. **Contact:** Ronald B. Hatch, director.

Book/Chapbook Needs Publishes 3 flat-spined paperbacks of poetry per year—**by Canadian poets only**—classical to experimental. "Ronsdale looks for poetry manuscripts that show the writer reads and is familiar with the work of some of the major contemporary poets. It's also essential that you have published some poems in literary magazines. We have never published a book of poetry when the author has not already published a goodly number in magazines." Has published *Free Will* by Harold Rhenisch, *Rilke's Late Poetry*, translated by Graham Good, *Cobalt 3* by Kevin Roberts, *Poems for a New World* by Connie Fife, *Steveston* by Daphne Marlatt, and *After Ted & Sylvia* by Crystal Hurdle.

How to Submit Query first, with a few sample poems and cover letter with brief bio and publication credits. Considers previously published poems and simultaneous submissions. Often comments on rejected poems. Responds to queries in 2 weeks, to mss in 2 months. Pays 10% royalties and 10 author's copies. Write for catalog to purchase sample books.

Advice "Ronsdale looks for Canadian poetry with echoes from previous poets. To our mind, the contemporary poet must be well-read."

⊠ ROSE ALLEY PRESS

4203 Brooklyn Ave. NE, #103A, Seattle WA 98105-5911. (206)633-2725. E-mail: rosealleypress@juno.com. Web site: www.rosealleypress.com. Established 1995. **Contact:** David D. Horowitz, editor/publisher.

- **"We presently do not read unsolicited manuscripts."**

◻ ⊠ SEAWEED SIDESHOW CIRCUS

P.O. Box 234, Jackson WI 53037. (414)791-1109. Fax: (262)644-0249. E-mail: sscircus@aol.com. Web site: http://hometown.aol.com/SSCircus/sscweb.html. Established 1994. **Contact:** Andrew Wright Milam, editor.

Book/Chapbook Needs Seaweed Sideshow Circus is "a place for young or new poets to publish a chapbook." Has published *Main Street* by Steven Paul Lansky and *The Moon Incident* by Amy McDonald. Publishes one chapbook/year. Chapbooks are usually 30 pages, digest-sized, photocopied, saddle-stapled, with cardstock covers.

How to Submit Query first, with 5-10 sample poems and cover letter with brief bio and publications credits. Responds to queries in 3 weeks; to mss in 3 months. Pays 10 author's copies (out of a press run of 100). Order sample chapbooks by sending $6.

🌐 ⊠ SECOND AEON PUBLICATIONS

19 Southminster Rd., Roath, Cardiff CF23 5AT Wales. Phone/fax: (44)(29)2049-3093. E-mail: peter @peterfinch.co.uk. Web site: www.peterfinch.co.uk. Established 1966. **Contact:** Peter Finch, poetry editor.

- **Does not accept unsolicited mss.**

🌐 ◻ ⊠ SOUTH PATTAYA PRESS

95/31 Moo 10 Classic Village, Nongphrue Banglamung, Chonburi 20150 Thailand. (661)7177 941. E-mail: nasomhong@yahoo.com. Established 2003. **Contact:** Jiraporn Sutta, editor.

Book/Chapbook Needs South Pattaya Press publishes 6 chapbooks/year. Manuscripts are selected through open submission. Chapbooks are 12 pages, stapled, with cardstock covers.

How to Submit Query first, with a few sample poems and a cover letter with brief bio and publication credits. Chapbook mss may include previously published poems. Responds to queries in 3 months.

Pays 3 author's copies. **"We publish chapbooks only by partial author subsidy."** Order sample chapbooks by sending $16 to Jiraporn Sutta.

☑ STEEL TOE BOOKS

Western Kentucky University, 1906 College Heights Blvd. #11086, Bowling Green KY 42101-1086. (270)745-5769. E-mail: tom.hunley@wku.edu. Web site: www.steeltoebooks.com. Established 2003. **Contact:** Dr. Tom C. Hunley, director.

Book/Chapbook Needs Steel Toe Books publishes "full-length, single-author poetry collections. Our books are professionally designed and printed. We look for workmanship (economical use of language, high-energy verbs, precise literal descriptions, original figurative language, poems carefully arranged as a book); a unique style and/or a distinctive voice; clarity; emotional impact; humor (word plays, hyperbole, comic timing); performability (a Steel Toe poet is at home on the stage as well as on the page)." Does not want "dry verse, purposely obscure language, poetry by people who are so wary of being called 'sentimental' they steer away from any recognizable human emotions, poetry that takes itself so seriously that it's unintentionally funny." Has published poetry by James Doyle, Jennifer Gresham, Ken Waldman, Mary Biddinger, John Guzlowski, and Jeannine Hall Gailey. Publishes 1-3 poetry books/year. Manuscripts are selected through open submission. Books are 48-64 pages, perfect-bound, with full-color covers with art/graphics.

How to Submit "Check the Web site for news about our next open reading period." Book mss may include previously published poems. Responds to mss in 3 months. Pays 20% royalties and 10 author's copies. Order sample books by sending $12 to Steel Toe Books.

☑ SWAN SCYTHE PRESS

2052 Calaveras Ave., Davis CA 95616-3021. E-mail: sandyjmc@mindspring.com. Web site: www.swanscythe.com. Established 1999. **Contact:** Sandra McPherson, editor/publisher.

- Swan Scythe Press has been awarded a California Arts Council Multicultural Entry Grant and a Fideicomiso para la Cultura Mexico-EUA/US-Mexico Fund for Culture Grant.

Book/Chapbook Needs "After publishing 25 chapbooks, a few full-sized poetry collections, and one anthology, Swan Scythe Press is resting. **We cannot at this time consider manuscripts**, but our books are still for sale. A multi-ethnic press primarily publishing emerging writers, we have also published established poets such as Ted Joans and Jordan Smith." Has published poetry by Emmy Pérez, Maria Melendez, John Olivares Espinoza, Karen An-hwei Lee, Pos Moua, and Walter Pavlich. Order sample books/chapbooks by sending $11 to Swan Scythe Press or order through Web site.

How to Submit *Not considering mss at this time.*

Ⓝ ☑ ◎ TARPAULIN SKY PRESS (Specialized: cross- and trans-genre work)

P.O. Box 190, Saxtons River, VT 05154. E-mail: editors@tarpaulinsky.com (inquiries). Web site: www.tarpaulinsky.com. Established 2006. **Contact:** Elena Georgiou and Christian Peet, editors.

Book/Chapbook Needs Tarpaulin Sky Press publishes cross-/trans-genre works as well as innovative poetry and prose. Produces full-length books and chapbooks, hand-bound books and trade paperbacks, and offers both hand-bound and perfect-bound paperback editions of full-length books. "We're a small, author-centered press endeavoring to create books that, as objects, please our authors as much their texts please us." Has published books and chapbooks by Jenny Boully, Danielle Dutton, Joyelle McSweeney, Chad Sweeney, Andrew Michael Roberts, and Max Winter, as well as a collaborative book by Noah Eli Gordon as Joshua Marie Wilkinson.

How to Submit Writers whose work has appeared in or been accepted for publication in *Tarpaulin Sky* (see separate listing in Magazines/Journals) may submit chapbook or full-length manuscripts at any time, with no reading fee. Tarpaulin Sky Press also considers chapbook and full-length manuscripts from writers whose work has not appeared in the journal, but **asks for a $10 (chap-**

book) or $20 (full-length) reading fee. Make checks/money orders to Tarpaulin Sky Press. Cover letter is preferred. Reads submissions year round.

◐ ☑ TEBOT BACH

P.O. Box 7887, Huntington Beach CA 92615-7887. (714)968-0905. E-mail: info@tebotbach.org. Web site: www.tebotbach.org. **Contact:** Mifanwy Kaiser, editor/publisher.

Book/Chapbook Needs Tebot Bach (Welsh for "little teapot") publishes books of poetry. Has published *Whatever Lasts in Winter* by Michael Clifton, *48 Questions* by Richard Jones, *The Way In* by Robin Chapman, and *Written in Rain: New and Selected Poems 1985-2000* by M.L. Liebler.

How to Submit Query first, with a few sample poems and cover letter with brief bio and publication credits. Include SASE. Responds to queries and mss, if invited, in one month. Time between acceptance and publication is up to 2 years. Write to order sample books.

Contest/Award Offerings The Patricia Bibby First Book Award (see separate listing in Contests & Awards).

Also Offers An anthology of California poets, published annually in April. Must be current or former resident of California in order to submit, but no focus or theme required for poetry. Submit up to 6 poems with "California Anthology" written on lower left corner of envelope. Accepts submissions by e-mail (pasted into body of message or as attachment in Word). Deadline for submission is in August. Also publishes *Spillway: A Literary Journal* (see separate listing in Magazines/Journals).

$◐ TOKYO ROSE RECORDS/CHAPULTEPEC PRESS (formerly Chapultepec Press)

4222 Chambers, Cincinnati OH 45223. E-mail: chapultepecpress@hotmail.com. Web site: www.TokyoRoseRecords.com. Established 2001. **Contact:** David Garza.

Book/Chapbook Needs Chapultepec Press publishes books of poetry/literature, essays, social/political issues, art, music, film, history, popular science; library/archive issues, and bilingual works. Wants "poetry that works as a unit, that is caustic, fun, open-ended, worldly, mature, relevant, stirring, evocative. Bilingual. Looking for authors who have a publishing history. No poetry collections without a purpose, that are mere collections. Also looking for broadsides/posters/illuminations." Publishes 1-2 books/year. Books are usually 1-100 pages.

How to Submit Query first with a few sample poems, or a complete ms, and a cover letter with brief bio and publication credits. Pays advance or author's copies. Order sample books by sending $4 payable to David Garza.

✪ ☑ THE UNIVERSITY OF CHICAGO PRESS

1427 E. 60th St., Chicago IL 60637. (773)702-7700. Fax: (773)702-2705. Web site: www.press.uchicago.edu. Established 1891. **Contact:** Randolph Petilos, poetry editor.

● **Submissions by invitation only!**

Book/Chapbook Needs The University of Chicago Press publishes scholarly books and journals. "We may only publish four books of new poems in the Phoenix Poets series per year, and perhaps four books of poetry in translation per year. We occasionally publish a book of poems outside Phoenix Poets, or as a reprint from other houses." Has published poetry by Liam Rector, Joshua Weiner, Stephen Yenser, Maggie Dietz, Daniel Hall, and Peg Boyers.

How to Submit *By invitation only.* No unsolicited mss.

✪ ✪ ◐ ◎ ☑ VEHICULE PRESS (Specialized: work by Canadian poets only)

P.O. Box 125 Station Place du Parc, Montreal QC H2X 4A3 Canada. (514)844-6073. Fax: (514)844-7543. E-mail: vp@vehiculepress.com. Web site: www.vehiculepress.com. **Contact:** Carmine Starnino, poetry editor.

Book/Chapbook Needs Vehicle Press is a "literary press with a poetry series, Signal Editions, publishing the work of Canadian poets only." Publishes flat-spined paperbacks. Has published

White Stone: The Alice Poems by Stephanie Bolster (winner of the 1998 Governor-General's Award for Poetry), *Merrybegot* by Mary Dalton, and *Reaching for Clear* by David Solway. Publishes Canadian poetry that is "first-rate, original, content-conscious."
How to Submit Query before submitting.

⬙ ⬙ WARTHOG PRESS
77 Marlboro St., Belmont MA 02478. (617)484-0336. Established 1979. **Contact:** Patricia Fillingham, poetry editor.
Book/Chapbook Needs Warthog Press publishes paperback books of poetry "that are understandable, poetic." Has published *From the Other Side of Death* by Joe Lackey, *Wishing for the Worst* by Linda Portnay, *Enemies of Time* by Donald Lev, and *Hanging On* by Joe Benevento. Wants book-length mss only.
How to Submit Query with 5 samples, cover letter, and SASE. "A lot of the submissions I get seem to be for a magazine. I don't publish anything but books." Considers simultaneous submissions. Manuscript should be "readable." Comments on rejected poems, "if asked. People really don't want criticism."
Advice "The best way to sell poetry still seems to be from poet to listener."

$⬙ ⬙ WASHINGTON WRITERS' PUBLISHING HOUSE (Specialized: Washington, D.C.- and Baltimore-area poets only)
12 Mallow Hill Rd., Baltimore MD 21229. E-mail: moirae333@earthlink.net. Web site: www.wwph. org. Established 1973. **Contact:** Moira Egan, president. Member: CLMP.
   • Winner of the Towson University Prize; finalist in the *ForeWord Magazine* Book of the Year Award.
Book/Chapbook Needs Washington Writers' Publishing House publishes books by Washington, D.C.- and Baltimore-area poets through its annual book competition. "No specific criteria, except literary excellence." Has published books by Carly Sachs, Piotr Gwiazda, Moira Egan, Jane Satterfield, Jean Nordhaus, and Gray Jacobik. Publishes 1-2 poetry books/year.
How to Submit Washington Writers' Publishing House considers book-length mss for publication by poets living within 60 driving miles of the U.S. Capitol (Baltimore area included) through competition only (see below).
Contest/Award Offerings Offers $500 and 100 copies of published book. Manuscripts may include previously published poems. Submit 3 copies of a poetry ms of 50-60 pages, single-spaced (poet's name should not appear on ms pages). Include separate page of publication acknowledgments plus 2 cover sheets: one with ms title, poet's name, address, telephone number, and e-mail address, the other with ms title only. Include SASE for results only; mss will not be returned (will be recycled). Guidelines available for SASE or on Web site. **Entry fee:** $20. **Deadline:** July 1-November 1 (postmark). Order sample books by sending $12 plus $2 s&h to Washington Writers' Publishing House, P.O. Box 15271, Washington DC 20003.
Advice "Washington Writers' Publishing House is a nonprofit cooperative poetry press reflecting the cultural and racial diversity of the Greater Washington-Baltimore area. The winning poet becomes a member of the organization and should be prepared to participate actively in the work of the press, including such areas as publicity, distribution, production, and fundraising. Our tradition of poets actively working on behalf of other poets is essential to the continued vitality and success of WWPH. Contest entrants should be willing to make this commitment should their work be selected for publication."

⬙ $⬙ ⬙ WEST END PRESS (Specialized: social/political concerns; multicultural)
P.O. Box 27334, Albuqueque NM 87125. (505)345-5729. Established 1976. **Contact:** John Crawford, publisher.

Book/Chapbook Needs West End Press publishes poetry, fiction, and drama with a social/cultural interest. Open as to form. Does not want "purely aesthetic, precious, self-involved poetry." Has published poetry by Laura Tohe, Joseph Bruchac, Charles Potts, and Michael Henson. Publishes 2 poetry books/year; occasional chapbooks and anthologies. Books/chapbooks are 48-96 pages, off-set-printed, perfect-bound, with glossy 4-color covers.

How to Submit Query first, with a few sample poems and a cover letter with brief bio and publication credits. Book/chapbook mss may include previously published poems. Responds to queries in 6 weeks; to mss in 3 months. Pays royalties of 6%; 10% author's copies (out of a press run of 600-1,500). Order sample books/chapbooks postage-free by sending $8.95 to West End Press.

Advice "We prefer crude vigor to polished banality."

☑ ☑ WHITE EAGLE COFFEE STORE PRESS

P.O. Box 383, Fox River Grove IL 60021-0383. E-mail: WECSPress@aol.com. Web site: http://members.aol.com/wecspress. Established 1992.

Book/Chapbook Needs White Eagle is a small press publishing 2-3 chapbooks/year. "Alternate chapbooks are published by invitation and by competition. Author published by invitation becomes judge for next competition." Wants "any kind of poetry. No censorship at this press. Literary values are the only standard." Does not want "sentimental or didactic writing." Has published poetry by Timothy Russell, Connie Donovan, Scott Lumbard, Linda Lee Harper, Scott Beal, and Jill Peléz Baumgaertner. Sample: $5.95.

How to Submit *Regular submissions by invitation only.*

Contest/Award Offerings Winner receives $300 and 25 author's copies. All entrants will receive a copy of the winning chapbook. Considers previously published poems and simultaneous submissions, with notice. Submit complete chapbook ms (20-24 pages), paginated, with table of contents. Poet's name should not appear on ms pages. Include 2 cover sheets: one with ms title, poet's name, address, phone number, and brief biography; second with ms title and 125-word statement about poet's work to be included in chapbook (poet's name should not appear on second cover sheet). Include list of credits for previously published poems. No e-mail submissions. Include SASE for results only; mss will not be returned. Guidelines available for SASE or on Web site. **Entry fee:** $15. **Deadline:** October 31 (postmark) for 2007. "Each competition is judged by either the author of the most recent chapbook published by invitation or by previous competition winners." Responds 3 months after deadline.

Advice "Poetry is about a passion for language. That's what we're about. We'd like to provide an opportunity for poets of any age who are fairly early in their careers to publish something substantial. We're excited by the enthusiasm shown for this press and by the extraordinary quality of the writing we've received."

☑ ◎ WOODLEY MEMORIAL PRESS (Specialized: work by KS poets)

English Dept., Washburn University, 1700 SW College Ave., Topeka KS 66621. E-mail: paul.fecteau @washburn.edu. Web site: www.washburn.edu/reference/woodley-press. Established 1980. **Contact:** Paul Fecteau, managing editor.

Book/Chapbook Needs Woodley Memorial Press publishes 1-2 flat-spined paperbacks/year, "most being collections of poets from Kansas or with Kansas connections. Terms are individually arranged with author on acceptance of manuscript." Has published *Retrieving Old Bones* by William Sheldon, *Thailand Journal* by Denise Low, and *Kansas Poems of William Stafford*. Sample books may be ordered from Woodley Memorial Press.

How to Submit Guidelines available on Web site. Responds to queries in 2 weeks; to mss in 6 months. Time between acceptance and publication is one year.

Advice "We look for experienced writers who are part of their writing and reading communities."

☑ ◎ ☑ ZOMBIE LOGIC PRESS (Specialized: avant-garde; zombie subculture)

3032 Ruth St., Rockford IL 61103. E-mail: zombielogic@insightbb.com. Web site: www.zombielogicpress.com. Established 1997. **Contact:** Thomas L. Vaultonburg, publisher.

Book/Chapbook Needs Zombie Logic Press publishes avant-garde, small press poetry. Wants "poems written by and for the zombie subculture." Does not want "traditional or rhyming poems." Recently published *Detached Retinas* by Thomas L. Vaultonburg. Publishes one poetry book/year. Manuscripts are selected through open submission. Books are 72 pages, professionally printed, perfect-bound, with glossy covers.

How to Submit Query first, with a few sample poems and a cover letter with brief bio and publication credits. Book mss may include previously published poems. "Electronic submissions are preferred." Guidelines available on Web site. Responds to queries in one month. Pays 100 author's copies (out of a press run of 1,000). Order sample books by sending $6 to Thomas L. Vaultonburg at Zombie Logic Press.

Contests & Awards

This section contains a wide array of poetry competitions and literary awards. These range from state poetry society contests (with a number of modest monetary prizes) to prestigious honors bestowed by private foundations, elite publishers and renowned university programs. Because these listings reflect such a variety of skill levels and degrees of competitiveness, it's important to read each carefully and note its unique requirements. *Never* enter a contest without consulting the guidelines and following directions to the letter (including manuscript formatting, number of lines or pages of poetry accepted, amount of entry fee, entry forms needed and other details).

Important note: As we gathered information for this edition of *Poet's Market*, we found that some competitions hadn't yet established their 2008 fees and deadlines. In such cases, we list the most recent information available as a general guide. Always consult current guidelines for updates before entering any competition.

WHERE TO ENTER?

While it's perfectly okay to "think big," being realistic may improve your chances of winning a prize for your poetry. Many of the listings in the Contests & Awards section begin with symbols that reflect their level of difficulty:

Contests ideal for beginners and unpublished poets are coded with the (◻) symbol. That's not to say these contests won't be highly competitive—there may be a large number of entries. However, you may find these entries are more on a level with your own, increasing your chances of being "in the running" for a prize. Don't assume these contests reward low quality, though. If you submit less than your best work, you're wasting your time and money (in postage and entry fees).

Contests for poets with more experience are coded with the (◖) symbol. Beginner/unpublished poets are usually still welcome to enter, but the competition is keener here. Your work may be judged against that of widely published, prize-winning poets, so consider carefully whether you're ready for this level of competition. (Of course, nothing ventured, nothing gained—but those entry fees *do* add up.)

Contests for accomplished poets are coded with the (◕) symbol. These may have stricter entry requirements, higher entry fees and other conditions that signal these programs are not intended to be "wide open" to all poets.

Specialized contests are coded with the (◉) symbol. These may include regional contests; awards for poetry written in a certain form or in the style of a certain poet; contests for women, gay/lesbian, ethnic, or age-specific poets (for instance, children or older adults); contests for translated poetry only; and many others.

There are also symbols that give additional information about contests. The (N) symbol indicates the contest is newly established and new to *Poet's Market*; the (★) symbol indicates this contest did not appear in the 2007 edition; the (✦) symbol identifies a Canadian contest or award and the (🌐) symbol an international listing. Sometimes Canadian and international contests require that entrants live in certain countries, so pay attention when you see these symbols.

ADDITIONAL CONTESTS & AWARDS

Contest information also appears in listings in other sections of the book (Magazines/Journals, Book/Chapbook Publishers, Conferences, Workshops & Festivals and Organizations). To make sure you don't overlook these opportunities, we've cross-referenced them under Additional Contests & Awards at the back of this section. For details about a contest associated with a market in this list, go to that market's page number.

WHAT ABOUT ENTRY FEES?

Most contests charge entry fees, and these are usually quite legitimate. The funds are used to cover expenses such as paying the judges, putting up prize monies, printing prize editions of magazines and journals, and promoting the contest through mailings and ads. If you're concerned about a poetry contest or other publishing opportunity, see "Is It a 'Con'?" on page 36 for advice on some of the more questionable practices in the poetry world.

OTHER RESOURCES

Widen your search for contests beyond those listed in *Poet's Market*. Many Internet writer's sites have late-breaking announcements about competitions old and new (see Additional Resources on page 463). Often these sites offer free electronic newsletter subscriptions, sending valuable information right to your e-mail inbox.

The writer's magazines at your local bookstore regularly include listings for upcoming contests, as well as deadlines for artist's grants at the state and national level. (See Additional Resources on page 463 for a few suggestions; also, Grants on page 419.) The Association of Writers & Writing Programs (AWP) is a valuable resource, including its publication, *Writer's Chronicle*. (See Organizations, page 443.) State poetry societies are listed throughout this book; they offer many contests, as well as helpful information for poets (and mutual support). To find a specific group, search the General Index for listings under your state's name or look under "poetry society" or "society."

Don't overlook your local connections. City and community newspapers, radio and TV announcements, bookstore newsletters and bulletin boards, and your public library can be terrific resources for competition news, especially regarding regional contests.

$⬚ AKRON POETRY PRIZE

The University of Akron Press, Akron OH 44325-1703. (330)972-5342. Fax: (330)972-8364. E-mail: uapress@uakron.edu. Web site: www.uakron.edu/uapress. **Contact:** Elton Glaser, award director. Offers annual award of $1,000 plus publication of a book-length ms. Submissions must be unpublished and may be entered in other contests (with notification of acceptance elsewhere). Submit 60-100 pages maximum, typed, single-spaced or double-spaced, with SASE for results. Manuscripts will not be returned. Do not send mss bound or enclosed in covers. Guidelines available for SASE or by fax, e-mail, or on Web site. **Entry fee:** $25. **Deadline:** entries accepted May 15-June 30 only. Competition receives 450-550 entries. 2006 winner ws Alison Pelegrin (*Big Muddy River of Stars*). 2007 judge: Stephen Dunn. Winner will be announced in September by letter (if SASE enclosed with entry) or on Web site. Copies of winning books are available from UAP or through your local bookstore. The University of Akron Press "is committed to publishing poetry that, as Robert Frost said, 'begins in delight and ends in wisdom.' Books accepted must exhibit three essential qualities: mastery of language, maturity of feeling, and complexity of thought."

$⬚ AGHA SHAHID ALI PRIZE IN POETRY

The University of Utah Press, 1795 E. South Campus Dr., #101, Salt Lake City UT 84112. (801)581-6771. Fax: (801)581-3365. E-mail: sarah.hoffman@utah.edu. Web site: www.uofupress.com/Agha-Shahid-Ali. Established 2003. The University of Utah Press and the University of Utah Department of English offer an annual award of $1,000, publication of a book-length poetry ms, and a reading in the Guest Writers Series. Poems must be unpublished as a collection, but individual poems may have been previously published in journals, anthologies, or chapbooks. Collection may be entered simultaneously in other ms contests. "However, entrants must notify the Press immediately if the collection submitted is accepted for publication elsewhere during the competition." Submit 48-64 typed pages of poetry, with no names or other identifying information appearing on title page or within ms. Include cover sheet with complete contact information (name, address, telephone, e-mail address). Submissions must be in English. Mss will not be returned; include SASE for notification only. Guidelines available on Web site. **Entry fee:** $25/book submission. **Deadline:** submit February 1-March 1. Competition receives over 300 mss/year. 2006 winner was Jane Springer. 2006 judge: J.D. McClatchy. Winner announced on press Web site after September 1; series editor contacts winning poet. Copies of winning books are available for $12.95 from University of Utah Press ((800)621-2736 for order fulfillment) or through Web site.

$ ALLIGATOR JUNIPER'S NATIONAL WRITING CONTEST

Prescott College, Prescott AZ 86301. E-mail: aj@prescott.edu. Web site: www.prescott.edu/highlights/alligator_juniper/index.html. Established 1995. *Alligator Juniper*, published annually in May, awards $500 each to first prize winners in poetry, fiction, and creative nonfiction. Additional winners selected for publication are paid 4 contributor's copies. Submissions must be unpublished; may be entered in other contests ("inform us in your cover letter and contact us immediately if your work is accepted elsewhere"). Submit up to 5 poems at a time with reading fee (separate fee for each additional entry). Submissions must be typed with numbered pages; single-spaced okay for poetry entries. Cover letter is required with the following statement: "I have read and understand the guidelines for *Alligator Juniper*'s national writing contest." Include SASE for response only; mss are not returned. "All entrants receive a personal letter from one of our staff regarding the status of their submissions." No e-mail submissions. Guidelines available for SASE, by e-mail, or on Web site. **Entry fee:** $10/entry (5 poems or 5 pages of poetry). Each entrant receives a copy of *Alligator Juniper*, a $10 value. **Deadline:** submit May 1-October 1 (postmark). 2007 winner was Elton Glaser. Winner announced in late January. *Alligator Juniper* is available for $10.

$ ☑ THE AMERICAN POETRY JOURNAL BOOK PRIZE

P.O. Box 2080, Aptos CA 95001-2080. E-mail: editor@americanpoetryjournal.com. Web site: www.americanpoetryjournal.com. Established 2004. **Contact:** J.P. Dancing Bear, editor. *The American Poetry Journal* Book Prize awards $500 and book publication. Submit 48-60 paginated pages of poetry, table of contents, acknowledgments, bio, and e-mail address (for results). No SASE required; mss will be recycled. Guidelines available on Web site. **Entry fee:** $20. Make checks payable to J.P. Dancing Bear. **Deadline:** February 28 (check Web site for updates). 2006 winner was Theodore Worozbyt (*The Dauber Wings*).

$ ☑ THE AMERICAN POETRY REVIEW/HONICKMAN FIRST BOOK PRIZE

117 S. 17th St., Suite 910, Philadelphia PA 19103. (215)496-0439. Fax: (215)569-0808. Web site: www.aprweb.org. Established 1972. Annual award to encourage excellence in poetry, and to provide a wide readership for a deserving first book of poems. Offers $3,000, publication of a book-length ms, and distribution by Copper Canyon Press through Consortium. Open to U.S. citizens writing in English and who have not yet published a book-length collection of poems which was assigned an ISBN. Guidelines available on Web site. **Entry fee:** $25/book ms. **Deadline:** October 31. 2007 winner was Gregory Pardlo (*Totem*). 2007 judge: Tony Hoagland.

☆ $ ☐ ◎ THE AMY AWARD FOR POETRY (Specialized: women age 30 & under living in NYC metropolitan area & Long Island; lyric poems)

Poets & Writers, 72 Spring St., New York NY 10012. Web site: www.pw.org/prizes. Established 1996. The Amy Award, sponsored by Poets & Writers, Inc. (see separate listing in Organizations), offers honorarium, books, plus a reading in NYC. **Entrants must be women 30 years of age or under who reside on Long Island or in the New York metropolitan region.** Submit 3 lyric poems of no more than 50 lines each, with SASE and brief biography. Guidelines available on Web site (posted in Feburary). **Entry fee:** none. **Deadline:** to be announced (check Web site). Past winners include Alexandra Cordera, Dorene Evans, and Shannon Holman. "The Amy Award was established by Edward Butscher and Paula Trachtman of East Hampton in memory of Mrs. Trachtman's daughter, Amy Rothholz, an actor and poet who died at age 25."

$ ☑ ANABIOSIS PRESS CHAPBOOK CONTEST

2 S. New St., Bradford MA 01835. (978)469-7085. E-mail: rsmyth@anabiosispress.org. Web site: www.anabiosispress.org. **Contact:** Richard Smyth, editor. The Anabiosis Press Chapbook Contest offers $100 plus publication of the winning chapbook and 75 copies of the first run. Submit 16-20 pages of poetry on any subject. Include separate pages with a biography, table of contents, and acknowledgments for any previous publications. Include SASE with correct postage for return of ms. **Entry fee:** $11 (all entrants receive a copy of the winning chapbook). Make checks payable to The Anabiosis Press. **Deadline:** June 30 (postmark). Winners announced by September 30. 2006 winner was Jackie White (*Bestiary Charming*).

$ ☑ THE ANHINGA PRIZE FOR POETRY

Anhinga Press, Tallahassee FL 32302. (850)442-1408. Fax: (850)442-6323. E-mail: info@anhinga.org. Web site: www.anhinga.org. Established 1973. **Contact:** Rick Campbell, poetry editor. The annual Anhinga Prize awards $2,000 and publication to a book-length poetry ms. Guidelines available for SASE or on Web site. **Entry fee:** $20. **Deadline:** submit February 15-May 1. Past judges include Donald Hall, Joy Harjo, Robert Dana, Reginald Shepherd, and Sidney Wade.

$ ARIZONA LITERARY CONTEST & BOOK AWARDS

Arizona Authors Association, P.O. Box 87857, Phoenix AZ 85080-7857. (623)847-9343. E-mail: info@azauthors.com. Web site: www.azauthors.com. **Contact:** Toby Heathcotte, president. Arizona Authors Association sponsors annual literary contest in poetry, short story, essay, unpublished novels, and published books (fiction, nonfiction, and children's literature). Awards publication in *Arizona Literary Magazine*, publication of novel by AuthorHouse, and $100 1st Prize, $50 2nd Prize, and $25 3rd Prize in each category. Poetry submissions must be unpublished and may be entered in other contests. Submit any number of poems on any subject up to 42 lines. Entry form and guidelines available for SASE. **Entry fee:** $10/poem. **Deadline:** reads submissions January 1-July 1. Competition receives 1,000 entries/year. Recent poetry winners include Catherine Crawford and Marijane Datson. Judges: Arizona authors, editors, and reviewers. Winners announced at an award banquet by November 15.

$⬚ ARIZONA STATE POETRY SOCIETY ANNUAL CONTEST

7041 West Cavalier Dr., Glendale AZ 85303. Web site: www.azpoetry.org. **Contact:** Kristen Kerrick Morton. Offers a variety of cash prizes in several categories ranging from $10-125; 1st, 2nd, and 3rd Prize winners are published in *Sandcutters*, ASPS's quarterly publication, which also lists names of Honorable Mention winners. See guidelines for detailed submission information (available for SASE or on Web site). **Entry fee:** varies according to category; see guidelines. **Deadline:** approximately September 15 (postmark). Competition receives over 1,000 entries/year. "ASPS sponsors a variety of monthly contests for members. Membership is available to anyone anywhere."

$⬚ ◎ THE ART OF MUSIC ANNUAL WRITING CONTEST (Specialized: music-related writing)

Piano Press, Del Mar CA 92014-0085. (619)884-1401. Fax: (858)755-1104. E-mail: pianopress@pian opress.com. Web site: www.pianopress.com. Established 1998. **Contact:** Elizabeth C. Axford, M.A., owner, Piano Press. The Art of Music Annual Writing Contest offers cash prizes and publication in *The Art of Music: A Collection of Writings*. 1st Prize: $150; 2nd Prize: $100; 3rd Prize: $50; also presents winners with a copy of each anthology, an engraved trophy, and a certificate. In addition, the top 75 entries are published in the anthology. Open to all writers ages 4 and up; signature of a parent or guardian is required for entrants under 18 years old. Entry may consist of an original, unpublished music-related poem, short story, essay, song lyric, or cover illustration. Manuscripts must be titled and typed, with no identifying information on any page. No entries will be returned. Each entry must be accompanied by an official form. Guidelines and entry form available on Web site. **Entry fee:** $20. Make checks/money orders payable to Piano Press. All entrants receive a copy of *The Art of Music: A Collection of Writings*, Volume 1 or Volume 2 (designate preference on entry form). **Deadline:** June 30 (postmark). Judges: published poets, authors, and songwriters. Winners announced by mail by October 31. Copies of anthologies available through Web site.

$⬚ ◎ ARTIST TRUST (Specialized: WA resident artists)

1835 12th Ave., Seattle WA 98122. (206)467-8734. Fax: (206)467-9633. E-mail: info@artisttrust.org. Web site: www.artisttrust.org. **Contact:** Heather Helbach-Olds, Director of Programs. Artist Trust is a nonprofit arts organization that provides grants to artists (including poets) who are residents of the state. Applications for Grants for Artist Projects (GAP) are accepted each year in February; awards grants of up to $1,500. Applications for Fellowship Program are accepted in June of odd-numbered years; awards $6,000 merit-based awards. **Deadline:** GAP, last Friday of February annually; Fellowship, second Friday of June in odd-numbered years. Each competition receives 200-300 literary entries/year. Most recent winners include Stacey Levine, Ann Pancake, and Brenda Miller. Also publishes a newsletter (4 times/year) full of information on arts-related topics and cultural issues; *Possibilities* (published 6 times/year), full of listings of opportunities for artists of all disciplines; and *Artists' Assets* (published annually) full of resources for artists of all disciplines.

$✓ AUTUMN HOUSE POETRY PRIZE

Autumn House Press, P.O. Box 60100, Pittsburgh PA 15211. (412)381-4261. E-mail: simms@duq.e du. Web site: http://autumnhouse.org. Established 1999. **Contact:** Michael Simms, editor. Offers annual prize of $2,500 and publication of book-length ms with national promotion. Submission must be unpublished as a collection, but individual poems may have been previously published in journals. Submissions may be entered simultaneously in other ms contests. Submit 50-80 pages of poetry ("blind judging—2 cover sheets requested"). Guidelines available for SASE, by e-mail, or on Web site. **Entry fee:** $25/ms. **Deadline:** June 30 annually. Competition receives 700 entries/ year. 2006 winner was Nancy Pagh. 2007 judge: Mark Doty. Winners announced through mailings and through ads in *Poets & Writers*, *American Poetry Review*, and *Writer's Chronicle* (extensive publicity for winner). Copies of winning books available from Amazon.com, Barnes & Noble, Borders, and other retailers. "Autumn House is a nonprofit corporation with the mission of publishing and promoting poetry. We have published books by Gerald Stern, Ed Ochester, Julie Suk, Jo McDougall, and others." Advice: "Include only your best poems."

$☐ BACKWARDS CITY REVIEW POETRY CHAPBOOK CONTEST

Backwards City Publications, Greensboro NC 27404-1317. E-mail: editors@backwardscity.net. Web site: www.backwardscity.net. Established 2004. **Contact:** Tom Christopher, editor. Member: CLMP. The *Backwards City Review* Poetry Chapbook Contest offers $250 and publication, plus 25 limited edition copies of winning ms as well as 25 standard edition copies. All chapbook contest entries considered for the Backwards City Chapbook Series and for *Backwards City Review*. Submit 18-62 pages of poetry. Include cover letter, acknowledgments page, and short bio (see guidelines for complete submission details). Accepts multiple entries (separate entry fee for each) and simultaneous submissions with notification. Guidelines available in magazine, for SASE, or on Web site. **Entry fee:** $15. **Deadline:** submit October 1-March 15. Judges: the editors.

$✓ THE MURIEL CRAFT BAILEY MEMORIAL AWARD

4956 St. John Dr., Syracuse NY 13215. (315)488-8077. E-mail: poetry@comstockreview.org. Web site: www.comstockreview.org. The annual Muriel Craft Bailey Memorial Award offers 1st Prize: $1,000; 2nd Prize: $250; 3rd Prize: $100; Honorable Mentions; plus publication of winners and selected finalists in *The Comstock Review* (see separate listing in Magazines/Journals). May offer discounted copies or subscriptions to entrants. Submissions must be unpublished and not under consideration elsewhere at the time of the contest. Submit poems of 40 lines each, single-spaced. Put poet's name, address, phone number, and e-mail address on reverse side (back) of each page. "We read each poem 'blind,' so we do not want to see your name on the front of the poem." Poems with identification visible to judges on the front side of page will not be read. Include SASE for results only; no poems will be returned. Guidelines available for SASE or on Web site. **Entry fee:** $4/poem. Make checks payable to *The Comstock Review* (combine fees on a single check for multiple entries). **Deadline:** reads April 1-July 1 (postmark). 2006 winners were Allan Peterson (1st), Greg Larson (2nd), and Lynn Levin (3rd). 2007 judge: Carolyn Forché; initial screening by editorial team from *The Comstock Review*. Winners notified in September.

ℕ ☐ ◎ THE BAILEY PRIZE (Specialized: open to upper-level undergraduate & graduate-level writing students)

The Chrysalis Reader, 1745 Gravel Hill Rd., Dillwyn VA 23936. (434)983-3021. Fax: (434)983-1074. E-mail: chrysalis@hovac.com. Web site: www.swedenborg.com/chrysalis. Established 2007. **Contact:** The Editor. The Swedenborg Foundation celebrates *The Chrysalis Reader*'s 20 years of publishing established and emerging writers by offering the annual Bailey Prize for undergraduate and graduate writing students. Winners will be published in the Autumn 2008 issue of *The Chrysalis Reader* (see separate listing in Magazines/Journals), receive 3 copies of the issue, and have their work available online after print publication. The Bailey Prize is open to nominations by instructors of upper-level undergraduate and graduate-level courses. Instructors may submit a maximum of 3 nominations from their students' output within a period of one year (2007). Nominations may be any combination of previously unpublished poetry (100 lines maximum) or fiction or nonfiction (3,100 words maximum). "We welcome both traditional and experimental writing with an emphasis on insightful writing related to *The Chrysalis Reader* annual theme, which changes every year. The 2008 theme is 'Renewal.' " Submit one copy of each entry with writer's contact information. Include a cover letter from the instructor on official stationery and SASE. No e-mail or disk submissions. No nominated entries will be returned. Guidelines available on Web site. **Entry fee:** none. **Deadline:** all entries must be dated on or before December 1, 2007.

$ BAKELESS LITERARY PUBLICATION PRIZES

Break Loaf Writers' Conference, Middlebury College, Middlebury VT 05753. (802)443-2018. E-mail: bakeless@middlebury.edu. Web site: www.middlebury.edu/blwc/bakeless. **Contact:** Mr. Ian Pounds, contest coordinator. The Bread Loaf Writers' Conference sponsors the Bakeless Literary Publication Prizes for new authors of literary works in poetry, fiction, and creative nonfiction. Awards publication by Houghton Mifflin of a book-length ms, and a fellowship to attend the Bread Loaf Writers' Conference. Submissions must be unpublished as a collection, but individual poems may have been previously published elsewhere; may be entered in other contests, "but contestants are asked to notify the contest coordinator immediately if a manuscript has been accepted for publication elsewhere." Submit at least 50 pages of poetry, typed double- or single-spaced on letter-size paper. Good-quality photocopies or letter-quality printed mss acceptable. Include 2 cover pages: one with poet's name, address, phone number, ms title, and genre (poetry) indicated; one with only ms title and genre. Poet's name must not appear on any ms page. Do not include author's note, bio, or acknowledgments page. Include SASP for confirmation of ms receipt and SASE for results only; mss will not be returned. Guidelines available on Web site. **Entry Fee:** $10/submission. Make checks payable to Middlebury College. **Deadline:** November 1, 2007. Winners announced in May.

$ THE WILLIS BARNSTONE TRANSLATION PRIZE (Specialized: translations from any language)

1800 Lincoln Ave., Evansville IN 47722. Phone/fax: (812)488-1042. E-mail: evansvillereview@evansville.edu. Web site: http://english.evansville.edu/EvansvilleReview.htm. Established 1989. **Contact:** Corinna McClanahan, poetry editor. The annual Willis Barnstone Translation Prize offers an annual award of $1,000 and publication in *The Evansville Review* for translated poems from any language and any time period, ancient to contemporary. Submissions must be unpublished. Each translated poem must not exceed 200 lines. "Please staple the translation to a copy of the original (which identifies the original poet) and put the name, address, and phone number of the translator(s) on the back of the translation page." Accepts multiple entries (up to 10/translator). Include SASE for results; mss will not be returned. Guidelines available for SASE or on Web site. **Entry fee:** $5 for the first poem, $3 for each subsequent poem. Make checks payable to The University of Evansville. **Deadline:** December 1. Competition receives 400 entries/year. Winner will be announced in April in *The Evansville Review* and to entrants who provided SASEs.

$ BARROW STREET PRESS BOOK CONTEST

P.O. Box 1831, New York NY 10156. E-mail: info@barrowstreet.org. Web site: www.barrowstreet.org. Established 2002. **Contact:** Contest Coordinator. Barrow Street Press publishes one poetry book/year through the annual Barrow Street Press Book Contest. Winner receives $1,000 and publication. Submit a 50- to 70-page ms of original, previously unpublished poetry in English. Manuscript should be typed, single-spaced on white $8\frac{1}{2} \times 11$ paper. Clear photocopies acceptable. Include 2 title pages and an acknowledgments page listing any poems previously published in journals or anthologies.

Author's name, address, and daytime phone number should appear on first title page only, and nowhere else in ms. Include SASE for results only; no mss will be returned. **Entry fee:** $25; include mailer with $1.59 postage for copy of winning book. Make checks payable to Barrow Street. **Deadline:** June 30. Guidelines available on Web site. 2006 winner was Richard Hoffman (*Golden Star Road*). 2007 judge: Carl Phillips.

⬛ $⬛ THE SHAUNT BASMAJIAN CHAPBOOK AWARD

P.O. Box 340, Station B, London ON N6A 4W1 Canada. Phone/fax: (519)660-0548. E-mail: cpa@sympatico.ca. Web site: www3.sympatico.ca/cpa. Established 1996. **Contact:** Wayne Ray, contest director. The Shaunt Basmajian Chapbook Award, named in honor of one of the founding members of the Canadian Poetry Association, offers $100 CAD and publication, plus 50 copies. Submissions must be unpublished as a collection, but individual poems may have been previously published elsewhere. Accepts simultaneous submissions. Submit up to 20 pages of poetry, typed single-spaced and paginated, with collection title on each page. Include separate sheet with ms title, poet's name, address, and phone number (poet's name must not appear on ms pages). Manuscripts will not be returned. Guidelines available for SASE and on Web site. **Entry fee:** $15 CAD. Make checks/money orders payable to the Canadian Poetry Association. **Deadline:** April 30 (postmark) annually. Judge: members of the London Chapter committee. Winning chapbooks available for $6 CAD.

$⬛ ◎ BEST OF OHIO WRITERS WRITING CONTEST (Specialized: OH resident writers)

12200 Fairhill Rd., Cleveland OH 44120. (216)421-0403. E-mail: pwlgc@yahoo.com. Web site: www.pwlgc.com/ohiowriter.html. Offers annual contest for poetry, fiction, creative nonfiction, and "Writers on Writing" (any genre). 1st Prize: $150; 2nd Prize: $50; plus publication for 1st-prize winner of each category in a special edition of *Ohio Writer*. Submit up to 3 typed poems, no more than 2 pages each, unpublished mss only. Open only to Ohio residents. "Entries will be judged anonymously, so please do not put name or other identification on manuscript. Attach entry form (or facsimile) to submission. Manuscripts will not be returned." Include SASE for list of winners. Entry form and guidelines available for SASE, by e-mail, or on Web site. **Entry fee:** $15/first entry in each category (includes one-year subscription or renewal to *Ohio Writer*); $2 for each additional entry in same category (limit 3/category). **Deadline:** July 31. Judges have included Larry Smith, Richard Hague, Ron Antonucci, and Sheila Schwartz. Winners announced in the November/December issue of *Ohio Writer*.

Ⓝ $⬛ ◎ BEST OF THE BEST COMPETITION (Specialized: poems that have won first place in other competitions)

E-mail: bestofthebest@triplopia.org. Web site: www.triplopia.org. Established 2006. **Contact:** Tracy Koretsky, contest coordinator. *TRIPLOPIA* (see separate listing in Magazines/Journals) sponsors an annual award of $100, Pushcart Prize nomination, author interview, and publication for a poem that has previously won first place in other competitions. Poem may be previously published. Submit one poem of 2 pages maximum, any subject, form, or style. **Must specify what competition the poem won previously.** Guidelines available on Web site. **Entry fee:** none. **Deadline:** enteries accepted ONLY April 15-June 1. Will consider only the first 100 eligible entries. 2006 winner was Jan Steckel ("Tiresias"). See poem and interview at www.triplopia.org/inside.cfm?ct = 674. Annual judge: Tracy Koretsky with *TRIPLOPIA* editors Gene Justice and Tara A. Elliott. Winner will be contacted by e-mail by August 1. Interview and poem will be published in the October 15th issue of *TRIPLOPIA*. "*TRIPLOPIA* is an internationally oriented, Web-based quarterly with a solid emphasis on excellence and accessibility."

Ⓝ $⬛ THE PATRICIA BIBBY FIRST BOOK AWARD

Tebot Bach, P.O. Box 7887, Huntington Beach CA 92615-7887. E-mail: info@tebotbach.org. Web site: www.tebotbach.org. Established 2005. **Contact:** Mifanwy Kaiser. The Patricia Bibby First Book

Award offers $1,000 and publication of a book-length poetry manuscript by Tebot Bach (see separate listing in Book/Chapbook Publishers). Open to "all poets writing in English who have not committed to publishing collections of poetry of 36 poems or more in editions of over 400 copies." Submissions must be unpublished as a collection, but individual poems may have been previously published elsewhere. Accepts simultaneous submissions, but Tebot Bach must be notified immediately by e-mail if the collection is accepted for publication. Submit 50-84 pages of poetry, letter-quality, single-spaced; clear photocopies acceptable. Use binder clip; no staples, folders, or printer-bound copies. Include 2 title pages: one (not fastened to ms) with ms title, poet's name, address, phone number, and e-mail address; the second (fastened to ms) with ms title only. Also include acknowledgments page and table of contents. Include SASP for notification of receipt of entry and SASE for results only; no mss will be returned. Guidelines available by e-mail or on Web site. **Entry fee:** $25. Make checks/money orders payable to Tebot Bach. **Deadline:** October 31 (postmark) annually. Winner announced each year in April. Judges are selected annually.

$ ✉ ◎ BINGHAMTON UNIVERSITY MILT KESSLER POETRY BOOK AWARD (Specialized: poets over 40)

Binghamton University Creative Writing Program, P.O. Box 6000, Binghamton NY 13902. (607)777-2713. Fax: (607)777-2408. E-mail: cwpro@binghamton.edu. Web site: http://english.binghamton.edu/cwpro. Established 2001. **Contact:** Maria Mazziotti Gillan, award director. Offers annual award of $1,000 and a reading at the university for a book of poetry judged best of those published that year by a poet over the age of 40. "Submit books published that year; do not submit manuscripts." Entry form and guidelines available for SASE, by e-mail, or on Web site. **Entry fee:** none; "just submit three copies of book." **Deadline:** March 1. Competition receives 500 books/year. 2006 winner was Christopher Bursk. Winner will be announced in June in *Poets & Writers* and on Web site, or by SASE if provided. (**NOTE:** Not to be confused with the Milton Kessler Memorial Prize for Poetry sponsored by *Harpur Palate*).

$ ✉ THE BLACK RIVER CHAPBOOK COMPETITION

Black Lawrence Press, P.O. Box 9, Watertown NY 13601. E-mail: info@blacklawrencepress.com. Web site: www.blacklawrencepress.com. Established 2003. **Contact:** Colleen Ryor, editor. The semiannual Black River Chapbook Competition awards $300, publication, and 25 copies to the winner. Accepts simultaneous submissions, but notify immediately if ms is accepted elsewhere. Submit 16-40 pages of poetry, paginated, with cover letter with brief bio and contact information (include valid e-mail address), acknowledgments page (if applicable), and table of contents. No e-mail submissions. Include SASE or e-mail address for results only; mss will not be returned. Guidelines available on Web site. **Entry fee:** $15/entry; multiple submissions accepted with entry fee for each. Make checks/money orders payable to Black Lawrence Press. **Deadline:** November 30 (fall) and May 31 (spring) (postmark).

✪ $ ✉ SUSAN BLALOCK POETRY CHAPBOOK CONTEST

Permafrost, Chapbook Division, % English Dept., University of Alaska Fairbanks, P.O. Box 755720, Fairbanks AK 99775. E-mail: fbpfrost@uaf.edu. Web site: www.uaf.edu/english/permafrost. Established 1977. **Contact:** Poetry Editor. The Susan Blalock Poetry Chapbook Contest offers $100, publication, and 30 author's copies. Submit a ms of no more than 34 pages. Include SASE. Guidelines available for SASE or on Web site. **Entry fee:** $10, includes a one-issue subscription to *Permafrost*. **Deadline:** March 15.

$ ✉ THE BRIAR CLIFF REVIEW FICTION, POETRY AND CREATIVE NONFICTION CONTEST

3303 Rebecca St., Sioux City IA 51104-2100. Web site: www.briarcliff.edu/bcreview. **Contact:**

Jeanne Emmons, poetry editor. *The Briar Cliff Review* (see separate listing in Magazines/Journals) sponsors an annual contest offering $1,000 and publication to each First Prize winner in fiction, poetry, and creative nonfiction. Previous year's winner and former students of editors ineligible. Winning pieces accepted for publication on the basis of First-Time Rights. Accepts simultaneous submissions, "but notify us immediately upon acceptance elsewhere." Submit 3 poems, single-spaced on $8^{1}/_{2} \times 11$ paper, no more than one poem/page. Include separate cover sheet with author's name, address, e-mail, and poem title(s); no name on ms. Include SASE for notification only; mss will not be returned. Guidelines available on Web site. **Entry fee:** $15 for 3 poems. "All entrants receive a copy of the magazine with winning entries." **Deadline:** November 1. Judge: the editors of *The Briar Cliff Review*.

$⊘ BRIGHT HILL PRESS POETRY BOOK AWARD

P.O. Box 193, 94 Church St., Treadwell NY 13846-0193. (607)829-5055. Fax: (607)829-5054. E-mail: wordthur@stny.rr.com. Web site: www.brighthillpress.org. Established 1992. **Contact:** Bertha Rogers, editor-in-chief/founding director. Member: Council of Literary Magazines and Presses, NYC. The annual Bright Hill Press Poetry Book Award offers $1,000, publication of a book-length ms, and 25 author's copies. Submissions must be unpublished as a collection, but individual poems may have been previously published elsewhere. Accepts simultaneous submissions if Bright Hill Press is notified of acceptance elsewhere. Submit 48-65 pages of poetry, paginated and secured with bulldog or spring clip. Include bio, table of contents, and acknowledgments page. Include 2 title pages: one with ms title, poet's name, address, and phone number; one with ms title only. Include SASE for results only; mss are not returned. Guidelines available for SASE, by e-mail, or on Web site. **Entry fee:** $20 for Word Thursdays/Bright Hill Press members; $22 for nonmembers. **Deadline:** was November 30 (postmark) for 2006. Competition receives over 300 entries/year. Winners will be announced in summer of the year following the contest. Copies of winning books available from Bright Hill Press (see Web site); include **with entry only** a sturdy 6×8 or 9×12 envelope with $1.65 postage affixed to receive a free copy of an award-winning Bright Hill Press poetry book (affix $2 postage for padded envelope). "Publish your poems in literary magazines before trying to get a whole manuscript published. Publishing individual poems is the best way to hone your complete manuscript."

$⊘ BRIGHT HILL PRESS POETRY CHAPBOOK AWARD

P.O. Box 193, 94 Church St., Treadwell NY 13846-0193. (607)829-5055. Fax: (607)829-5054. E-mail: wordthur@stny.rr.com. Web site: www.brighthillpress.org. Established 1992. **Contact:** Bertha Rogers, editor-in-chief/founding director. Member: Council of Literary Magazines and Presses, NYC. The annual Bright Hill Press Chapbook Award offers $300, publication of a chapbook-length ms, and 25 author's copies. Submissions must be unpublished as a collection, but individual poems may have been previously published elsewhere. Accepts simultaneous submissions if Bright Hill Press is notified of acceptance elsewhere. Submit 16-24 pages of poetry, paginated and secured with bulldog or spring clip. Include bio, table of contents, and acknowledgments page. Include 2 title pages: one with ms title, poet's name, address, and phone number; one with ms title only. Include SASE for results only; mss are not returned. Guidelines available for SASE, by e-mail, or on Web site. **Entry fee:** $10 for Word Thursdays/Bright Hill Press members; $12 for nonmembers. Multiple entries accepted with separate fee for each. **Deadline:** July 31 (postmark). Competition receives over 300 entries/year. Copies of winning chapbooks available from Bright Hill Press (see Web site); include **with entry only** a 5×7 SASE with $1.31 postage affixed and receive a free copy of a recent winning Bright Hill Press poetry chapbook. "Publish your poems in literary magazines before trying to get a whole manuscript published. Publishing individual poems is the best way to hone your complete manuscript."

✪ $☑ BRITTINGHAM PRIZE IN POETRY

University of Wisconsin Press, Dept. of English, 600 N. Park St., University of Wisconsin, Madison WI 53706. E-mail: rwallace@wisc.edu. Web site: www.wisc.edu/wisconsinpress/index.html. Established 1985. **Contact:** Ronald Wallace, poetry series editor. The annual Brittingham Prize in Poetry is one of 2 prizes awarded by The University of Wisconsin Press (see separate listing for the Felix Pollak Prize in Poetry). Offers $1,000 plus publication, with an additional $1,500 honorarium to cover expenses of a reading in Madison. Submissions must be unpublished as a collection, but individual poems may have been published elsewhere (publication must be acknowledged). Considers simultaneous submissions if notified of selection elsewhere. Submit 50-80 unbound ms pages, typed single-spaced (with double spaces between stanzas) or double-spaced. Clean photocopies are acceptable. Include title page with poet's name, address, and telephone number. No translations. Include SASE for results only; mss will not be returned. Guidelines available for SASE or on Web site. **Entry fee:** $25. **NOTE:** $25 fee applies to consideration of same entry for the Felix Pollak Prize in Poetry—one fee for 2 contest entries. Make checks/money orders payable to University of Wisconsin Press. **Deadline:** submit September 1-30 (postmark). 2005 Brittingham Prize winner was Susanna Childress (*Jagged with Love*). Qualified readers will screen all mss. Judge: "a distinguished poet who will remain anonymous until the winners are announced in mid-February."

$☑ ◎ BROKEN BRIDGE POETRY PRIZE (Specialized: students enrolled in independent secondary schools, grades 9-12)

398 Pomfret St., Pomfret CT 06258-0128. (860)963-5220. E-mail: eds@brokenbridge.us. Web site: www.brokenbridge.us. Established 2005. **Contact:** Brad Davis, editor. The annual Broken Bridge Poetry Prize awards $500 plus full scholarship to Broken Bridge Summer Writing Workshops. Winner and finalists published in *Broken Bridge Review* (see separate listing in Magazines/Journals). "**Open only to students enrolled in independent secondary schools, grades 9-12.**" Submit up to 3 poems. Guidelines available by e-mail or on Web site. **Entry fee:** none. **Deadline:** November 15.

$◎ BURNING BUSH POETRY PRIZE (formerly People Before Profits Poetry Prize) (Specialized: community-centered values, democratic processes)

Burning Bush Publications, P.O. Box 4658, Santa Rosa CA 95402. Web site: www.bbbooks.com. Offers annual award of $200 plus publication in online e-zine, *In Our Own Words* (see separate listing in Magazines/Journals), to a poet whose writing "inspires others to value human life and the natural world instead of values based on short-term economic advantage; speaks for community-centered values and democratic processes, especially those whose voices are seldom heard; demonstrates poetic excellence; and educates readers of the relevance of the past to the present and future." Submit 3 poems maximum, any style or form. "We prefer unpublished work, but published poems may be submitted. If published before, please include where, when, and any acknowledgment information we may need." Include index card with name, address, e-mail, phone, and title of each poem submitted. Also include SASE with sufficient postage for return of work. "Submissions without SASE will not be returned. If your poem is selected for the Poetry Prize, we will need a brief (50 words) biographical statement from you." Guidelines available on Web site. **Entry fee:** $10. **Deadline:** was June 1 for 2007. Competition receives 100 entries/year. 2006 winner was Laura LeHew. Winner announced in late June.

$☑ BURNSIDE REVIEW CHAPBOOK COMPETITION

P.O. Box 1782, Portland OR 97207. E-mail: sid@burnsidereview.org. Web site: www.burnsidereview.org. Established 2004. **Contact:** Sid Miller, editor. The annual *Burnside Review* Chapbook Competition awards $200, publication, and 25 author's copies to winning poet. Guidelines available for SASE or on Web site. **Entry fee:** $15. **Deadline:** March 15-June 30. 2006 winner was John Surowiecki (*Bolivia Street*). (See separate listing for *Burnside Review* in Magazines/Journals.)

$THE WITTER BYNNER FOUNDATION FOR POETRY, INC.

P.O. Box 10169, Santa Fe NM 87504. (505)988-3251. Fax: (505)986-8222. E-mail: bynnerfoundation @aol.com. Web site: www.bynnerfoundation.org. **Contact:** Steven Schwartz, executive director. Awards grants, ranging from $1,000 to $10,000, exclusively to nonprofit organizations for the support of poetry-related projects in the area of: 1) support of individual poets through existing nonprofit institutions; 2) developing the poetry audience; 3) poetry translation and the process of poetry translation; and 4) uses of poetry. "May consider the support of other creative and innovative projects in poetry." Letters of intent accepted annually August 1-December 31; requests for application forms should be submitted to Steven Schwartz, executive director. Additional information available by fax, e-mail, or on Web site. **Deadline:** Applications, if approved, must be returned to the Foundation postmarked by February 1.

$ CAA POETRY AWARD (Specialized: Canadian poets)

Canadian Authors Association, Box 419, Campbellford ON K0L 1L0 Canada. (705)653-0323. Fax: (705)653-0593. E-mail: admin@CanAuthors.org. Web site: www.CanAuthors.org. **Contact:** Alec McEachern, national director. The CAA Poetry Award offers $1,000 CAD and a silver medal to Canadian writers for a poetry collection (by a single poet) published during the year. Guidelines available on Web site. **Entry fee:** $35 CAD/title. **Deadline:** December 15; except for works published after December 1, in which case the postmark deadline is January 15. Competition receives 100 entries/year. 2006 winner was Barry Dempster (*The Burning Alphabet*). All awards are given at the CAA Awards Banquet at the annual conference.

THE CATHOLIC ACADEMY OF LETTERS PRIZE IN POETRY

Catholic Institute of Arts and Letters, P.O. Box 8401, Albuquerque NM 87198. E-mail: cathinst@com cast.net. Web site: www.cathinst.com. Established 2006. **Contact:** Joseph Charles McKenzie. The annual Catholic Academy of Letters Prize in Poetry awards a certificate, medal, trophy, and honors. Poems may be previously published; may be entered in other contests and/or under consideration elsewhere. Submit any number of poems of any length "on a lofty subject worthy of universal attention, in a form which exploits the grand traditions of poetry." Entry form and guidelines available for SASE or by e-mail. **Entry fee:** $25/poem. **Deadline:** December 8, 2007. Judges: members of the Catholic Academy of Letters, the Chancellor of the Catholic Institute, and invited scholars. Winner announced/notified by press release and mail 2 weeks before the official ceremony. "The Catholic Academy of Letters defends the highest, most noble aspirations of human letters. Poets must rise to the level of literary tradition with genius, virtue, and originality."

$ CAVE CANEM POETRY PRIZE (Specialized: African American)

Cave Canem Foundation, Inc., 584 Broadway, Suite 508, New York NY 10012. Fax: (212)941-5724. E-mail: ccpoets@verizon.net. Web site: www.cavecanempoets.org. Established 1999 (prize) and 1996 (foundation). **Contact:** Alison Meyers, Cave Canem director. Offers "annual first book award dedicated to presenting the work of African American poets who have not been published by a professional press. The winner will receive $500 cash, publication, and 50 copies of the book." **U.S. poets only.** "Send two copies of manuscript of 50-75 pages. The author's name should not appear on the manuscript. Two title pages should be attached to each copy. The first must include the poet's name, address, telephone number, and the title of the manuscript; the second should list the title only. Number the pages. Manuscripts will not be returned, but a SASE postcard may be included for notice of manuscript receipt. Simultaneous submissions should be noted. If the manuscript is accepted for publication elsewhere during the judging, immediate notification is requested." Guidelines available for SASE or on Web site. **Entry fee:** $15. **Deadline:** May 15 annually. 2006 winner was Dawn Lundy Martin (*A Gathering of Matter/A Matter of Gathering*, The University of Georgia Press). 2007 judge: Claudia Rankine. Winners will be announced by press release in October of year of contest. Copies of winning books are available from "any bookseller, because the publishers are Graywolf Press, University of Georgia, and University of Pittsburgh. Cave Canem sponsors a weeklong retreat each summer and a regional workshop in New York. It sponsors readings in various parts of the country. The winner of the prize and the judge are featured in an annual reading." Recommends "being at a stage in your development where some of your poems have already been published in literary journals. Manuscripts not adhering to guidelines will not be forwarded to judge nor returned to applicant."

$✎ CIDER PRESS REVIEW BOOK AWARD

777 Braddock Lane, Halifax PA 17032. E-mail: editor@ciderpressreview.com. (inquiries only). Web site: http://ciderpressreview.com/bookaward. Established 1999. **Contact:** Contest Director. The annual Cider Press Review Book Award offers $1,000, publication, and 25 author's copies. Submissions must be unpublished as a collection, but individual poems may have been previously published elsewhere. Submit book-length ms of 48-80 pages. "Submissions can be made online using the submission form on the Web site or by mail. If sending by mail, include two cover sheets—one with title, author's name, and complete contact information; and one with title only, all bound with a spring clip. Online submissions must be in Word for PC or PDF format, and should not include title page with author's name." Include SASE for results; mss will not be returned. **Entry fee:** $25. All entrants will receive a copy of the winning book. **Deadline:** submit September 1-November 30 (postmark). 2006 winner was Anne Caston (*Judah's Lion*). 2007 judge: Tony Hoagland.

$☐ CNW/FFWA FLORIDA STATE WRITING COMPETITION

Florida Freelance Writers Association, P.O. Box A, North Stratford NH 03590-0167. (603)922-8338. E-mail: contest@writers-editors.com. Web site: www.writers-editors.com. Established 1978. **Contact:** Dana K. Cassell, award director. Offers annual awards for nonfiction, fiction, children's literature, and poetry. Awards for each category are 1st Prize: $100 plus certificate; 2nd Prize: $75 plus certificate; 3rd Prize: $50 plus certificate; plus Honorable Mention certificates. Poetry submissions must be unpublished. Submit any number of poems on any subject in traditional forms, free verse, or children's. Entry form and guidelines available for SASE or on Web site. **Entry fee:** $3/poem (members), $5/poem (nonmembers). **Deadline:** March 15. Competition receives 350-400 entries/year. Competition is judged by writers, librarians, and teachers. Winners will be announced on May 31 by mail and on Web site.

$✎ COLORADO PRIZE FOR POETRY

Center for Literary Publishing, Dept. of English, Colorado State University, Fort Collins CO 80523. (970)491-5449. E-mail: creview@colostate.edu. Web site: http://coloradoreview.colostate.edu. Established 1967. **Contact:** Stephanie G'Schwind, editor. The annual Colorado Prize for Poetry awards an honorarium of $1,500 and publication of a book-length ms. Submission must be unpublished as a collection, but individual poems may have been published elsewhere. Submit approximately 40-100 pages of poetry (no set minimum or maximum) on any subject, in any form, double- or single-spaced. Include 2 titles pages: one with ms title only, the other with ms title and poet's name, address, and phone number. Enclosed SASP for notification of receipt and SASE for results; no mss will be returned. Guidelines available for SASE or by e-mail. **Entry fee:** $25; includes one-year subscription to *Colorado Review* (see separate listing in Magazines/Journals). **Deadline:** submission period was October 1-January 12 for 2007. Winner announced in May. 2006 winner was Jaswinder Bolina (*carrier wave*). 2007 judge: Paul Hoover.

$✎ CRAB ORCHARD SERIES IN POETRY FIRST BOOK AWARD

Dept. of English, Mail Code 4503, Faner Hall 2380, Southern Illinois University Carbondale, 1000 Faner Dr., Carbondale IL 62901. Web site: www.siu.edu/~crborchd. Established 1995. **Contact:**

John Tribble, series editor. The Crab Orchard Series in Poetry First Book Award offers $2,500 ($1,000 prize plus $1,500 honorarium for a reading at Southern Illinois University Carbondale) and publication. "Manuscripts should be 50-75 pages of original poetry, in English, by a U.S. citizen or permanent resident who has neither published, nor committed to publish, a volume of poetry 40 pages or more in length (individual poems may have been previously published). Current students and employees of Southern Illinois University and authors published by Southern Illinois University Press are not eligible." See guidelines for complete formatting instructions. Guidelines available for SASE or on Web site. **Entry fee:** $25/submission; includes subscription to *Crab Orchard Review* (see separate listing in Magazines/Journals). Make checks payable to Crab Orchard Series in Poetry. **Deadline:** see guidelines or check Web site. 2006 winner was Mary Jo Firth Gillet (*Soluble Fish*).

$⊠ CRAB ORCHARD SERIES IN POETRY OPEN COMPETITION AWARDS

Dept. of English, Mail Code 4503, Faner Hall 2380, Southern Illinois University Carbondale, 1000 Faner Dr., Carbondale IL 62901. Web site: www.siu.edu/~crborchd. Established 1995. **Contact:** Jon Tribble, series editor. The Crab Orchard Series in Poetry Open Competition Awards offer 1st Prize: $3,500 and publication of a book-length ms; and 2nd Prize: $1,500 and publication of a book-length ms. "Cash prize totals reflect a $1,500 honorarium for each winner for a reading at Southern Illinois University Carbondale. Publication contract is with Southern Illinois University Press. Entrants must be U.S. citizens or permanent residents." Submissions must be unpublished as a collection, but individual poems may have been previously published elsewhere. Accepts simultaneous submissions, but series editor must be informed immediately upon acceptance. Manuscripts should be typewritten or computer-generated (letter quality only, no dot matrix), single-spaced; clean photocopy is recommended as mss are not returned. See guidelines for complete formatting instructions. Guidelines available for SASE or on Web site. **Entry fee:** $25/submission; includes subscription to *Crab Orchard Review* (see separate listing in Magazines/Journals). Make checks payable to Crab Orchard Series in Poetry. **Deadline:** see guidelines or check Web site. 2006 winners were Moira Linehan (1st prize, *If No Moon*) and Fanonne Jeffers (2nd prize, *Red Clay Suite*).

$⊡ LOIS CRANSTON MEMORIAL POETRY PRIZE

Calyx, Inc., P.O. Box B, Corvallis OR 97339. E-mail: calyx@proaxis.com. Web site: www.calyxpress.org. Established 2002. *CALYX* (see separate listing in Magazines/Journals) offers the annual Lois Cranston Memorial Poetry Prize of $300, publication in *CALYX*, and a one-volume subscription. Finalists will be published on the *CALYX* Web site and receive a one-volume subscription. No previously published poems or simultaneous submissions. Submit up to 3 poems/entry (6 pages total maximum). Include separate cover letter with poet's name, address, phone number, e-mail address, and title(s) of poem(s). No names on poems. No mss will be returned. Guidelines available for SASE, by e-mail, or on Web site. **Entry fee:** $15 for up to 3 poems. Make checks payable to *CALYX*. **Deadline:** submit March 1-May 31 (inclusive postmark dates). Winners notified by October 30 and announced on *Calyx*'s Web site. 2006 winner was Gail Griffin ("War Stories"). 2007 judge: Paulann Peterson.

⊡ CREATIVITY UNLIMITED PRESS® ANNUAL POETRY COMPETITION

30819 Casilina Dr., Rancho Palos Verdes CA 90275. E-mail: ihf@cox.net. Established 1978. **Contact:** Shelley Stockwell-Nicholas, PhD, editor. Annual invitation to submit offers possible widespread publication, with full credit to the author—Creativity Unlimited Press® uses poetry submitted in published texts and newsletters. "We often use poems as chapter introductions in self-help books. Short, clever, quippy, humorous, and delightful language encouraged. No inaccessible, verbose, esoteric, obscure poetry." Enter no more than 2 pages/poem, double-spaced, one side of page. Submissions may be previously published "provided writer has maintained copyright and notifies us." Accepts e-mail submissions. **Deadline:** December 31.

$✉ DANA AWARD IN POETRY

200 Fosseway Dr., Greensboro NC 27455. (336)644-8028 (for emergency questions only). E-mail: danaawards@pipeline.com. Web site: www.danaawards.com. Established 1996. **Contact:** Mary Elizabeth Parker, award chair. Offers annual award of $1,000 for the best group of 5 poems. Submissions must be unpublished and not under promise of publication when submitted; may be simultaneously submitted elsewhere. Submit 5 poems on any subject, in any form; no light verse. Include separate cover sheet with name, address, phone, e-mail address, and titles of poems. Entries by regular mail only. Include SASE for winners list only; no mss will be returned. Guidelines available for SASE, by e-mail, or on Web site. **Entry fee:** $15/5 poems. **Deadline:** October 31 (postmark). Competition receives 400-500 poetry entries. Recent judges: Enid Shomer and Michael White. Winner will be announced in early spring by phone, letter, and e-mail.

$□ DANCING POETRY CONTEST

Artists Embassy International, 704 Brigham Ave., Santa Rosa CA 95404-5245. (707)528-0912. E-mail: jhcheung@aol.com. Web site: www.DANCINGPOETRY.com. Established 1993. **Contact:** Judy Cheung, contest chair. Annual contest offers 3 Grand Prizes of $100, five 1st Prizes of $50, ten 2nd Prizes of $25, and twenty 3rd Prizes of $10. The 3 Grand Prize-winning poems will be choreographed, costumed, premiered, and videotaped at the annual Dancing Poetry Festival at Palace of the Legion of Honor, San Francisco; Natica Angilly's Poetic Dance Theater Company will perform the 3 Grand Prize-winning poems. In addition, "all prizes include an invitation to read your prize poem at the festival, and a certificate suitable for framing." Submissions must be unpublished or poet must own rights. Submit 2 copies of any number of poems, 40 lines maximum (each), with name, address, phone number on one copy only. Foreign language poems must include English translations. Include SASE for winners list. Entry form available for SASE. No inquiries or entries by fax or e-mail. **Entry fee:** $5/poem or $10/3 poems. **Deadline:** May 15 annually. Competition receives about 500-800 entries. 2006 Grand Prize winners were Joyce P. Hardy, Gerard F. Keogh, Jr., and Sandra W. Soli. Judges for upcoming contest: members of Artists Embassy International. Winners will be announced by mail; Grand Prize winners will be contacted by phone. Ticket to festival will be given to all winners. Artist Embassy International has been a nonprofit educational arts organization since 1951, "Furthering intercultural understanding and peace through the universal language of the arts."

✪ $✉ DEHN POETRY COMPETITION FOR COLLEGE UNDERGRADUATES

Connecticut Poetry Society, P.O. Box 270554, West Hartford CT 06127-0554. E-mail: connpoetry@comcast.net. Web site: www.ct-poetry-society.org. **Contact:** Contest Coordinator. The Dehn Poetry Competition honors Adolf and Virginia Dehn, visual artists who supported creativity and excellence in all art forms. Offers prizes of $150, $100, and $50; prize poems will be published in *Long River Run II*. Submit up to 3 unpublished poems, any form, 40 line limit. Include 2 copies of each poem: one with complete contact information including college or university affiliation and one with NO contact information. Both copies must be marked: Dehn Poetry Competition. Include SASE for results only (no poems will be returned). Winning poems must be submitted by disc or e-mail following notification. **Entry fee:** $10 for up to 3 poems. Make checks payable to Connecticut Poetry Society. **Deadline:** submit December 1-March 15.

$☺ DEL SOL PRESS ANNUAL POETRY PRIZE

89 Elm Ridge Rd., Stow MA 01775. E-mail: editor@webdelsol.com. Web site: http://webdelsol.com/DelSolPress. Established 2003. **Contact:** Michael Neff, publisher. Offers annual award of a $1,200 honorarium, book publication, and 20 author copies. Submissions may include previously published poems and may be entered in other contests. "Poet should have some prior publication of individual poems." Submit 50-100 typed ms pages; start each poem on new page. Type or word-

process on standard white paper, one side of page only. Paginate consecutively with a table of contents. Bind with a binder clip (no paperclips). Include two cover pages: one with poet's contact information (phone, e-mail, address), one with the ms title only. Poet's name should not appear on the manuscript itself. Attach publications acknowledgments, if any. Include SASP for notification of receipt of ms; no mss will be returned. Guidelines available on Web site. **Entry fee:** $24 (includes copy of winning book if 8 × 10 SASE with sufficient postage is sent with entry). Make checks payable to Web del Sol. **Deadline:** mid-January; see Web site for current deadline. Most recent winner was David Ray Vance (*Vitreous*). 2006 judge: Thomas Lux. Winners will be announced on Web site. Copies of winning books available from Del Sol Press. "Web del Sol is the nation's largest online publisher of contemporary periodicals and hosts many poetry-related journals, including *Perihelion* (www.webdelsol.com/Perihelion), as well as columns and articles on poetry. It also hosts online publication-oriented poetry workshops (www.webdelsol.com/Algonkian/Poetry)." Advice: "Send only your best. Our standards are high. Check the poetry we publish on webdelsol.com."

$⬚ DIAGRAM/NEW MICHIGAN PRESS CHAPBOOK CONTEST

648 Crescent NE, Grand Rapids MI 49503. E-mail: nmp@thediagram.com. Web site: www.newmich iganpress.com/nmp. Established 2000. **Contact:** Ander Monson, editor. The annual *DIAGRAM/ New Michigan Press Chapbook Contest* offers $1,000 plus publication and author's copies, with discount on additional copies. Also publishes 2-4 finalist chapbooks each year. Submit 18-44 pages of poetry, fiction, mixed-genre, or genre-bending work. Include SASE. Guidelines available on Web site. **Entry fee:** $15. **Deadline:** April of each year.

$⬚ "DISCOVERY" POETRY CONTEST: The Joan Leiman Jacobson Poetry Prizes

Unterberg Poetry Center, 92nd Street Y, 1395 Lexington Ave., New York NY 10128. (212)415-5759 (voicemail). Web site: www.92y.org/poetry. **Contact:** Contest Coordinator. The "Discovery" Poetry Contest is designed to attract large audiences to poets who have not yet published a book. Awards a cash prize to 4 winners, plus a reading at The Unterberg Poetry Center and publication in a literary journal of national distribution, to be announced. New guidelines available on Web site. Endowed by Joan L. and Dr. Julius H. Jacobson, II.

$⬚ DREAM HORSE PRESS NATIONAL POETRY CHAPBOOK PRIZE

P.O. Box 2080, Aptos CA 95001-2080. E-mail: dreamhorsepress@yahoo.com. Web site: www.drea mhorsepress.com. Established 1999. **Contact:** J.P. Dancing Bear, editor/publisher. The Dream Horse Press National Poetry Chapbook Prize offers an annual cash prize and multiple copies of a handsomely printed chapbook (prize amounts change yearly, check Web site for current information; 2007 prize was $500 and 25 copies). All entries will be considered for publication. Submissions may be previously published in magazines/journals but not in books or chapbooks; may be entered in other contests with notification. "Submit 16-24 double-spaced pages of poetry in a readable font with acknowledgments, bio, e-mail address for results, and entry fee. Poet's name should not appear anywhere on the manuscript." Multiple submissions acceptable (with separate fee for each entry). Manuscripts will be recycled after judging. Guidelines available on Web site. **Entry fee:** changes annually; check Web site (2007 fee was $15). Make checks/money orders made payable to Dancing Bear. **Deadline:** check Web site (2007 deadline was May 31). 2006 winner was Cynthia Arrieu King (*The Small Anything City*). 2007 judge: C.J. Sage.

⬚ $⬚ ⬚ T.S. ELIOT PRIZE (Specialized: collections published in the UK & Ireland)

The Poetry Book Society, 4th Floor, 2 Tavistock Place, London WC1H 9RA England. (44)(207)833-9247. Fax: (44)(207)833-2990. E-mail: info@poetrybooks.co.uk. Web site: www.poetrybooks.co. uk. Established 1993. **Contact:** Chris Holifield, award director. Offers annual award for the best poetry collection published in the UK/Republic of Ireland each year. Prize: £10,000 (donated by

Mrs. Valerie Eliot). Submissions must be previously published and may be entered in other contests. Book/ms must be submitted by publisher and have been published (or scheduled to be published) the year of the contest. Entry form and guidelines available for SASE or by fax or e-mail. **Deadline:** early August. Competition receives 100 entries/year. 2006 winner was Seamus Heaney (*District and Circle*). Recent judges: Sean O'Brien, Sophie Hannah, and Gwyneth Lewis. Winner will be announced in January.

$⊘ T.S. ELIOT PRIZE FOR POETRY

Truman State University Press, 100 E. Normal, Kirksville MO 63501-4221. (660)785-7336. Fax: (660)785-4480. E-mail: tsup@truman.edu. Web site: http://tsup.truman.edu. Press established 1986. **Contact:** Nancy Rediger. Offers annual award of $2,000 and publication. "The manuscript may include individual poems previously published in journals or anthologies, but may not include a significant number of poems from a published chapbook or self-published book." Submit 60-100 pages. Include 2 title pages: one with poet's name, address, phone number, and ms title; the other with ms title only. Include SASE for acknowledgment of ms receipt only; mss will not be returned. Guidelines available for SASE or on Web site. **Entry fee:** $25. **Deadline:** October 31. Competition receives more than 500 entries/year. 2007 winner was Carol V. Davis (*Into the Arms of Pushkin: Poems of St. Petersburg*). 2007 judge: Alberto Rios.

$⊘ ◎ EMERGING VOICES (Specialized: writers from minority, immigrant, and underserved communities)

PEN USA, % Antioch University, 400 Corporate Pointe, Culver City CA 90230. (310)862-1555, ext. 358. Fax: (310)862-1556. E-mail: ev@penusa.org. Web site: www.penusa.org. **Contact:** Christine Lanoie-Newman, director. Annual program offering $1,000 stipend and 8-month fellowship to writers in the early stages of their literary careers. Program includes one-on-one sessions with mentors, seminars on topics such as editing or working with agents, courses in the Writers' Program at UCLA Extension, and literary readings. Participants selected according to potential, experience, and goals. No age restrictions; selection is not based solely on economic need. Participants need not be published, but "the program is directed toward poets and writers of fiction and creative nonfiction with clear ideas of what they hope to accomplish through their writing. Mentors are chosen from PEN's comprehensive membership of professional writers and beyond. Participants are paired with established writers sharing similar writing interests and often with those of the same ethnic and cultural backgrounds." Program gets underway in January. **Deadline:** September 7, 2007 (for 2008 cycle). "Materials must arrive in the PEN offices by the submission deadline—no exceptions." See Web site for brochure and complete guidelines.

$⊘ ERSKINE J. POETRY PRIZE

P.O. Box 22161, Baltimore MD 21203. E-mail: sreichert@smartishpace.com. Web site: www.smartishpace.com. Established 1999. **Contact:** Stephen Reichert, editor. The annual Erskine J. Poetry Prize offers 1st Prize: $200 and publication of the winning poem in *Smartish Pace* (see separate listing in Magazines/Journals); 2nd and 3rd Prizes: winning poems will be published in *Smartish Pace*. Winners also receive additional Internet and advertising exposure. All entries will be considered for publication in *Smartish Pace*. Submit 3 poems, with poet's name, address, e-mail, telephone number (preferred), and "Erskine J." at the top of each page of poetry submitted. Include bio. Entries may be submitted online or by e-mail (as attachment) or regular mail. Include SASE with postal entries. Guidelines available on Web site. **Entry fee:** $5/3 poems; additional poems may be submitted for $1/poem (limit of 12 poems). Make checks/money orders payable to *Smartish Pace*. **Deadline:** August 15. 2006 winners were Kevin McFadden, Amber L. Cohen, and Angie Mazakis. Judges: Stephen Reichert (editor) and Daniel J. Todd, (senior editor).

$☑ THE EVIL GENIUS CHAPBOOK CONTEST

Platonic 3Way Press, P.O. Box 844, Warsaw IN 46581. (317)457-3505. E-mail: evilgenius@platonic3 waypress.com. Web site: www.Platonic3WayPress.com. Established 2005. **Contact:** Oren Wagner, Steve Henn, and Don Winter, co-editors. The annual Evil Genius Chapbook Contest offers $50, publication, 50 author's copies, and "some publicity. We will submit the winning chap for review by various nationally recognized magazines and reviewers." Accepts simultaneous submissions "as long as you keep us informed of the status." Submit 16-23 poems. Include SASE for reply or return of ms. Guidelines available in *Fight These Bastards* (see separate listing in Magazines/Journals), published by Platonic 3Way Press (see separate listing in Book/Chapbook Publishers), or on Web site. **Entry fee:** $12; includes a copy of the winning chapbook. "All other proceeds go to the continuing publication of *Fight These Bastards*." Make checks, bank drafts, or money orders made payable to Platonic 3Way Press. **Deadline:** was July 1 for 2007; see Web site or Spring issue of *Fight These Bastards* for 2008. "Winners will be announced in fall issues of *Fight These Bastards*."

$☑ THE WILLIAM FAULKNER-WILLIAM WISDOM CREATIVE WRITING COMPETITION

The Pirate's Alley Faulkner Society, Inc., 624 Pirate's Alley, New Orleans LA 70116. (504)586-1609. Fax: (504)522-9725. E-mail: faulkhouse@aol.com. Web site: www.wordsandmusic.org. Established 1992. **Contact:** Rosemary James, award director. Offers annual publication in *The Double Dealer Redux*, cash prize of $750, gold medal, and trip to New Orleans from any continental U.S. city. "Foreign nationals are eligible, but the society pays transportation to awards ceremony from U.S. cities only. Winners must be present at annual meeting to receive award." Submissions must be previously unpublished. Submit one poem of no more than 750 words on any subject in any English-language form. Multiple entries permitted. Entry form (required) and guidelines available for SASE or on Web site. **Entry fee:** $25/entry. **Deadline:** submit January 15-April 1 (postmark). "No entries before January 15, please." Competition receives 1,600 (for 7 categories) entries/year. 2006 winner was Mary Ann O'Gorman. 2006 judge: Laura Mullen. Winners are announced on the society's Web site between January 1 and January 15. "Competition is keen. Send your best work."

$☑ THE FIELD POETRY PRIZE

Oberlin College Press, Oberlin College, 50 N. Professor St., Oberlin OH 44074. (440)775-8408. E-mail: oc.press@oberlin.edu. (inquiries only). Web site: www.oberlin.edu/ocpress. Established 1969. **Contact:** David Young. The annual *FIELD* Poetry Prize for a book-length collection of poems offers $1,000 and publication in the *FIELD* Poetry Series. Submit non-returnable ms of 50-80 pages. Guidelines available for SASE or on Web site. **Entry fee:** $22; includes one-year subscription to *FIELD* (see separate listing in Magazines/Journals). Make checks payable to Oberlin College Press. **Deadline:** submit during May only (postmark). 2006 winner was Mary Cornish (*Red Studio*).

$☑ THE ANNIE FINCH PRIZE FOR POETRY

The National Poetry Review, P.O. Box 2080, Aptos CA 95001-2080. E-mail: editor@nationalpoetry review.com. Web site: www.nationalpoetryreview.com. **Contact:** C.J. Sage, editor. The Annie Finch Prize for Poetry offers $300 plus publication in *The National Poetry Review*. All entries will be considered by the editor for publication. Submissions must be unpublished and uncommitted. Accepts simultaneous submissions, "but if the work is selected by *The National Poetry Review* for the prize or for publication, it must be withdrawn from elsewhere unless you have withdrawn it from us two weeks before our acceptance." Submit up to 3 poems/entry (10 pages maximum per group of 3). Include cover letter with bio and contact information, including e-mail address for results. Guidelines available on Web site. **Entry fee:** $15/entry; accepts multiple submissions with separate entry fee for each 3-poem group. "If you include a small book-sized SASE with $1.30 postage with your entry, we will provide you a copy of the winner's issue." Make checks payable to C.J. Sage only. **Deadline:** April 30 (postmark). 2006 final judge: Bob Hicok.

$☑ THE FINISHING LINE PRESS OPEN CHAPBOOK COMPETITION

Finishing Line Press, P.O. Box 1626, Georgetown KY 40324. (859)514-8966. E-mail: FinishingBooks @aol.com. Web site: www.finishinglinepress.com. Established 1998. **Contact:** Leah Maines, poetry editor. The Finishing Line Press Open Chapbook Competition offers a $1,000 cash award and publication. All entries will be considered for publication. Open to all poets regardless of past publications. Submit up to 26 pages of poetry. Include bio, acknowledgments, and cover letter. Guidelines available by e-mail or on Web site. **Entry fee:** $15. **Deadline:** June 30 (postmark) for 2006.

$☑ FLUME PRESS CHAPBOOK COMPETITION

California State University at Chico, 400 W. First St., Chico CA 95929-0830. (530)898-5983. E-mail: flumepress@csuchico.edu. Web site: www.csuchico.edu/engl/flumepress. Established 1984. **Contact:** Casey Huff, poetry editor. Flume Press selects chapbooks for publication through its biennial competition (alternates between poetry and fiction). Winner receives $500 and 25 author's copies. Submission must be unpublished as a collection, but individual poems may have been previously published. Considers simultaneous submissions if poet agrees to withdraw ms from other competitions if chosen as a winner by Flume. Submit 24-30 pages, including title, table of contents, and acknowledgments page. Include cover sheet with poet's name and address; poet's name should not appear on ms pages. Include SASE for return of ms and comments. Guidelines available on Web site. **Entry fee:** $20 (each entrant receives a copy of the winning chapbook). **Deadline:** December 1 (postmark); check Web site for appropriate year for poetry. Chapbooks available for $8 from Flume Press.

$☑ THE 49TH PARALLEL POETRY AWARD

Bellingham Review, Western Washington University, Mail Stop 9053, Bellingham WA 98225. (360)650-4863. E-mail: bhreview@cc.wwu.edu. Web site: www.wwu.edu/~bhreview. **Contact:** Contest Director. The annual 49th Parallel Poetry Award offers 1st Prize of $1,000, plus publication in and a year's subscription to *Bellingham Review* (see separate listing in Magazines/Journals). Runners-up and finalists may be considered for publication. Submissions must be unpublished and not accepted for publication elsewhere; work under consideration elsewhere must be withdrawn from the competition if accepted for publication. Submit up to 3 poems. "Poems within a series will each be treated as a separate entry." For each entry, include a 3×5 index card stating the title of the work, the category (poetry), the poet's name, phone number, address, and e-mail. "Make sure writing is legible on this card. Author's name must not appear anywhere on the manuscript." Include SASE for results only; mss will not be returned. Guidelines available for SASE or on Web site. **Entry fee:** $15 for first entry (up to 3 poems); $10 each additional poem. Make checks payable to *Bellingham Review*. "Everyone entering the competition will receive a complimentary two-issue subscription to *Bellingham Review*." **Deadline:** entries must be postmarked December 1-March 15. 2006 winner was Maya Pindyck ("So Much Went Into"). 2006 judge: Timothy Liu. Winners will be announced in summer.

◩ $☑ THE ROBERT FROST FOUNDATION ANNUAL POETRY AWARD (Specialized: poems written in the spirit of Robert Frost)

The Robert Frost Foundation, Lawrence Library, 51 Lawrence St., Lawrence MA 01841. (978)725-8828. E-mail: frostfoundation@comcast.net. Web site: www.frostfoundation.org. Established 1997. Offers annual award of $1,000. Submissions may be entered in other contests. Submit up to 3 poems of not more than 3 pages each (2 copies of each poem, one with name, address, and phone number), written in the spirit of Robert Frost. Guidelines available for SASE and on Web site. **Entry fee:** $10/poem. **Deadline:** September 5. Competition receives over 600 entries/year. 2006 winner was Rob Smith. Winners will be announced at the annual Frost Festival and by SASE following the Festival (late October). Winning poem can be viewed on Web site.

$⊘ ◎ KINERETH GENSLER AWARD (Specialized: New England, NY, NJ residents)

Alice James Books, 238 Main St., Farmington ME 04938. Phone/fax: (207)778-7071. E-mail: ajb@u mf.maine.ed. Web site: www.alicejamesbooks.org. Established 1973. **Contact:** Contest Coordinator. The Kinereth Gensler Award offers $2,000 and publication by Alice James Books (see separate listing in Book/Chapbook Publishers); winners become members of the Alice James Books cooperative, with a 3-year commitment to the editorial board. **Entrants must reside in New England, New York, or New Jersey.** Submissions must be unpublished as a collection, but individual poems may have been previously published elsewhere (in publications of less than 48 pages). Submit 2 copies of ms of 50-70 pages, typed single-spaced and paginated, with table of contents and acknowledgments page; bio is optional. Use binder clips; no staples, folders, or printer-bound copies. Title page of each ms copy must include poet's name, address, and phone number. Enclose SASP for acknowledgment of receipt of ms, #10 SASE for results; no mss will be returned. Guidelines available for SASE or on Web site. **Entry fee:** $25/ms. Make checks/money orders payable to Alice James Books. For a free book (does not apply to books not yet published), include an additional 6×9 envelope with $2 in postage attached; write title of selection on back of envelope. **Deadline:** was October 1 (postmark) for 2006. 2006 winners were Bill Rasmovicz (*The World in Place of Itself*), Ann Killough (*Dog in the Road*), and Peter Waldor (*The Warmth of The Ones I Love*). Judges: members of the Alice James Books Editorial Board. Winners announced in December. Copies of winning books available through Web site.

✖ $⊘ ◎ GERTRUDE PRESS POETRY CHAPBOOK CONTEST (Specialized: gay, lesbian, bisexual, transgendered, queer-identified & allied)

P.O. Box 83948, Portland OR 97283. E-mail: editor@gertrudepress.org. (inquiries only). Web site: www.gertrudepress.org. Established 1998. **Contact:** Eric Delehoy, founding editor. Gertrude Press (see separate listing in Books/Chapbooks) sponsors an annual chapbook competition. Offers $50, publication, and 50 author copies (out of a press run of 200) to the winning poet. Individual poems may have been previously published; unpublished poems are welcome. Submit 16-20 pages of poetry (postal submissions only). "Poetry may be of any subject matter, and writers from all backgrounds are encouraged to submit." Include list of acknowledgments and cover letter indicating how poet learned of the contest. Guidelines available in *Gertrude* (see separate listing in Magazines/Journals), for SASE, by e-mail, or on Web site. **Entry fee:** $12; includes one-year subscription to *Gertrude*. **Deadline:** submit September 1-January 15 (postmark) annually. 2006 winner was Kate Gray (*Bone Knowing*).

$⊘ ALLEN GINSBERG POETRY AWARDS

Poetry Center, Passaic County Community College, One College Blvd., Paterson NJ 07505-1179. (973)684-6555. E-mail: mgillan@pccc.edu. Web site: www.pccc.edu/poetry. Established 1979. **Contact:** Maria Mazziotti Gillan, editor/executive director. The Allen Ginsberg Poetry Awards offer annual prizes of 1st Prize: $1,000, 2nd Prize: $200, and 3rd Prize: $100. All winning poems, honorable mentions, and editor's choice poems will be published in *Paterson Literary Review* (see separate listing in Magazines/Journals). Winners will be asked to participate in a reading that will be held in the Paterson Historic District. Poems must be unpublished. Submit up to 5 poems (no poem more than 2 pages long). Send 4 copies of each poem entered. Include cover sheet with poet's name, address, phone number, and poem titles. Poet's name should not appear on poems. Include SASE for results only; poems will not be returned. Guidelines available for SASE or on Web site. **Entry fee:** $15 (includes subscription to *Paterson Literary Review*). Write "poetry contest" in memo section of check and make payable to PCCC. **Deadline:** April 1 (postmark). Winners will be announced the following summer by mail and in newspaper announcements. 2006 winners were Don Schofield (1st), Hal Sirowitz and Len Roberts (2nd), and Joe Aimone (3rd).

⚡ $⊚ GOVERNOR GENERAL'S LITERARY AWARDS (Specialized: Canadian citizens/permanent residents; English- and French-language works)

The Canada Council for the Arts, P.O. Box 1047, 350 Albert St., Ottawa ON K1P 5V8 Canada. (613)566-4414, ext. 5573. Fax: (613)566-4410. E-mail: christian.mondor@canadacouncil.ca. Web site: www.canadacouncil.ca/prizes/GGLA. Established 1957. **Contact:** Christian Mondor, administrative coordinator. Established by Parliament, the Canada Council for the Arts "provides a wide range of grants and services to professional Canadian artists and art organizations in dance, media arts, music, theater, writing, publishing, and the visual arts." The Governor General's Literary Awards, valued at $15,000 CAD each, are given annually for the best English-language and best French-language work in each of 7 categories, including poetry. Non-winning finalists each receive $1,000 CAD. Books must be first edition trade books written, translated, or illustrated by Canadian citizens or permanent residents of Canada and published in Canada or abroad during the previous year (September 1 through the following September 30). Collections of poetry must be at least 48 pages long, and at least half the book must contain work not published previously in book form. In the case of translation, the original work must also be a Canadian-authored title. Books must be submitted by publishers with a Publisher's Submission Form, which is available on request from the Writing and Publishing Section of the Canada Council for the Arts. Guidelines and current deadlines available by mail, telephone, fax, or e-mail.

$🖋 GRANDMOTHER EARTH NATIONAL AWARD

Grandmother Earth Creations, P.O. Box 2018, Cordova TN 38088. (901)309-3692 or (901)216-4496 (cell). E-mail: Gmoearth@aol.com. Web site: www.grandmotherearth.org. Established 1994. **Contact:** Frances Cowden, award director. Offers annual award of $1,250 with varying distributions each year; $1,250 minimum in awards for poetry and prose; $200 first, etc., plus publication in anthology; non-winning finalists considered for anthology if permission is given. Send published or unpublished work. Submissions may be entered in other contests. Submit at least 3 poems, any subject, in any form. Include SASE for winners list. Guidelines available for SASE or on Web site. **Entry fee:** $10/3 works, $2 each additional work. Entry fee includes a copy of the anthology. **Deadline:** July 15. 2006 winners were Florence Bruce, Timothy Russell, Carrille Colins Burk, and N. Colwell Snell. 2006 judge: Amy Jo Zook. Winners will be announced in October at the Mid-South Poetry Festival in Memphis. Copies of winning poems or books available from Grandmother Earth Creations.

$▢ THE GREAT BLUE BEACON POETRY CONTEST

1425 Patriot Dr., Melbourne FL 32940. (321)253-5869. E-mail: ajircc@juno.com. Established 1997. **Contact:** A.J. Byers, award director. Offers prizes approximately 3 times/year, as announced, of 1st Prize: $25; 2nd Prize: $15; 3rd Prize: $10. "Winning poem to be published in *The Great Blue Beacon*. Prize amounts will be increased if sufficient entries are received." Submissions must be unpublished and may be entered in other contests. Submit up to 3 poems maximum on any subject, in any form. Submit 3 typed copies of each entry, no more than 24 lines/poem. On one copy, put poet's name, address, and telephone number in the upper left-hand corner of the first page; no name or address on the second or third copies. "Contestants must send SASE or e-mail address with entry to receive notification of results. Follow guidelines, particularly line limits. Submit your best work." Guidelines available for SASE or by e-mail. **Entry fee:** $3/poem ($2 for subscribers to *The Great Blue Beacon*). Make checks payable to Andy Byers. **Deadline:** see guidelines. Competition receives 200-300 entries/year. Most recent winners were Anna Evans (NJ), 1st and 2nd places; and Barbara Anton (FL). Winners are announced approximately 2 months after deadline date. *The Great*

Blue Beacon is a quarterly newsletter for all writers. Sample copy: $1 and 60¢ postage (or IRC). Subscription: $10/year; students $8; $14 outside the U.S.

$⚫ GREAT LAKES COLLEGES ASSOCIATION NEW WRITERS AWARD

GLCA, 535 W. William, Ste. 301, Ann Arbor MI 48103. (734)661-2350. Fax: (734)661-2340. E-mail: shackelford@glca.org. Web site: www.glca.org. **Contact:** Deanna Shackelford, program coordinator. Director of Program Development: Gregory Wegner. Offers annual award to the best first book of poetry and the best first book of fiction among those submitted by publishers. The winning authors tour several of the 12 GLCA-member colleges (as invited) reading, lecturing, visiting classes, doing workshops, and publicizing their books. Each writer receives an honorarium of at least $300 from each college visited, as well as travel expenses, hotel accommodations, and hospitality. Usually, one winner (fiction) tours in the fall, and the other winner (poetry) tours in the spring, following the competition. Submissions must be previously published. Publishers should submit 4 copies of galleys or the printed book plus a statement of the author's agreement to commit to the college tour. Guidelines available for SASE, by e-mail, or on Web site. **Deadline:** February 28 (submit as early as possible after January 1). Competition receives about 50 entries for poetry, 35 for fiction/year. 2006 poetry winner was Anele Rubin (*Trying to Speak*); 1st runnerup was Tyechimba Jess (*leadbelly*). Winners will be announced in May.

$⚫ THE GREEN ROSE PRIZE IN POETRY

New Issues Poetry & Prose, Dept. of English, Western Michigan University, 1903 W. Michigan Ave., Kalamazoo MI 49008-5331. (269)387-8185. Fax: (269)387-2562. Web site: www.wmich.edu/newiss ues. Established 1996. The Green Rose Prize in Poetry offers $2,000 and publication of a book of poems by an established poet who has published one or more full-length collections of poetry. *New Issues* may publish as many as 3 additional mss from this competition. Accepts simultaneous submissions, but *New Issues* must be notified of acceptance elsewhere. Submit a ms of at least 48 pages, typed, single-spaced preferred. Clean photocopies acceptable. Do not bind; use manila folder or metal clasp. Include cover page with poet's name, address, phone number, and title of the ms. Also include brief bio, table of contents, and acknowledgments page. No e-mail or fax submissions. Include SASP for notification of receipt of ms and SASE for results only; no mss will be returned. Guidelines available for SASE, by fax, e-mail, or on Web site. **Entry fee:** $20. Make checks payable to *New Issues Poetry & Prose*. **Deadline:** submit May 1-September 30 (postmark). Winner is announced in January or February on Web site. 2006 winner was Noah Eli Gordon (*A Fiddle Pulled from the Throat of a Sparrow*). Judge: *New Issues* editors.

$⚫ THE DONALD HALL PRIZE IN POETRY

AWP Award Series in Poetry, The Association of Writers & Writing Programs, Carty House, Mail Stop 1E3, George Mason University, Fairfax VA 22030-4444. E-mail: chronicle@awpwriter.org. (inquiries only). Web site: www.awpwriter.org. Established 2003. The Association of Writers & Writing Programs (AWP) sponsors an annual competition for the publication of excellent new book-length works, the AWP Award Series, which includes The Donald Hall Prize in Poetry. Offers annual award of $4,000 and publication for the best book-length ms of poetry (book-length defined for poetry as 48 pages minimum of text). Open to published and unpublished poets alike. "Poems previously published in periodicals are eligible for inclusion in submissions, but manuscripts previously published in their entirety, including self-published, are not eligible. As the series is judged anonymously, no list of acknowledgments should accompany your manuscript. You may submit your manuscript to other publishers while it is under consideration by the Award Series, but you must notify AWP immediately in writing if your manuscript is accepted elsewhere. Your manuscript must be submitted in accordance with the eligibility requirements, format guidelines, and entry requirements or it will be disqualified." Complete guidelines, including important formatting information, eligibility requirements, and required entry form available on Web site. **Entry fee:** $10 (AWP members) or $25 (nonmembers). Make checks/money orders payable in U.S. dollars only to AWP. **Deadline:** mss accepted January 1-February 28. 2006 winner was Angela Ball (*Night Clerk at the Hotel of Both Worlds*). 2007 judge: Bob Hicok.

$☑ ◎ J.C. AND RUTH HALLS, AND DIANE MIDDLEBROOK FELLOWSHIPS IN POETRY (Specialized: MFA or PhD in creative writing required)

Wisconsin Institute for Creative Writing, English Dept., 600 North Park St., Madison WI 53706. Web site: http://creativewriting.wisc.edu. Established 1986. **Contact:** Jesse Lee Kercheval, director. Offers annual fellowships, will pay $25,000 for one academic year. Applicants will teach one creative writing class/semester at University of Wisconsin and give a public reading at the end of their stay. Submissions may be entered in other contests. Submit 10 poems maximum on any subject, in any form. Applicants must have a MFA or PhD in creative writing. Applicants cannot have published a book (chapbooks will not disqualify an applicant). Guidelines available on Web site. **Reading fee:** $20. **Deadline:** applications must be received in the month of February. Competitions receive 300 entries/year. Judges: faculty of the creative writing program. Results will be sent to applicants by May 1. "The fellowships are administered by the Program in Creative Writing at the University of Wisconsin-Madison. Funding is provided by the Jay C. and Ruth Halls Writing Fund and the Carl Djerassi and Diane Middlebrook Fund through the University of Wisconsin Foundation."

$ BEATRICE HAWLEY AWARD

Alice James Books, 238 Main St., Farmington ME 04938. Phone/fax: (207)778-7071. E-mail: ajb@umf.maine.ed. Web site: www.alicejamesbooks.org. Established 1973. **Contact:** Contest Coordinator. The Beatrice Hawley Award offers $2,000 and publication by Alice James Books (see separate listing in Book/Chapbook Publishers). Winners have no cooperative membership commitment. "In addition to the winning manuscript, one or more additional manuscripts may be chosen for publication." Entrants must reside in the U.S. Submissions must be unpublished as a collection, but individual poems may have been previously published elsewhere (in publications of less than 48 pages). Submit 2 copies of ms of 50-70 pages, typed single-spaced and paginated, with table of contents and acknowledgments page; bio is optional. Use binder clips; no staples, folders, or printer-bound copies. Title page of each ms copy must include poet's name, address, and phone number. Include SASP for acknowledgment of receipt of ms, #10 SASE for results only; no mss will be returned. Guidelines available for SASE or on Web site. **Entry fee:** $25/ms. Make checks/money orders payable to Alice James Books (write "Beatrice Hawley Award" on memo line). **Deadline:** was December 1 (postmark) for 2006. 2006 winner was Henrietta Goodman (*Take What You Want*). Judges: members of the Alice James Books Editorial Board. Winners announced in April. Copies of winning books available through Web site.

$☑ JAMES HEARST POETRY PRIZE

North American Review, University of Northern Iowa, 1222 West 27th St., Cedar Falls IA 50614-0516. (319)273-6455. Fax: (319)273-4326. E-mail: nar@uni.edu. Web site: http://webdelsol.com/NorthAmReview/NAR. **Contact:** Vince Gotera, poetry editor. The James Hearst Poetry Prize offers 1st Prize: $1,000; 2nd Prize: $100; and 3rd Prize: $50. All winners and finalists will be published in *North American Review* (see separate listing in Magazines/Journals). Submissions must be unpublished. No simultaneous submissions. Submit up to 5 poems, 2 copies each; **NO NAMES** on ms pages. Cover sheet is required (MS Word or PDF). Include SASP for acknowledgment of receipt of ms and #10 SASE for results (or provide e-mail address on cover sheet); mss will not be returned. Guidelines available for SASE, by fax, e-mail, or on Web site. **Entry fee:** $18 (includes one-year subscription). Make checks/money orders payable to *North American Review*. **Deadline:** October 31 (postmark).

⊛ $◎ FELICIA HEMANS PRIZE FOR LYRICAL POETRY (Specialized: University of Liverpool members & students)

The University of Liverpool, Foundation Building, Brownlow Hill, Liverpool L69 72X England. (44)(151)794-2458. E-mail: wilderc@liv.ac.uk. Established 1899. **Contact:** Chief Operating Officer, University of Liverpool. Offers annual award of £30. Submit one poem. Submissions may be entered in other contests. Open to past or present members and students of the University of Liverpool. Guidelines available for SASE only. **Deadline:** May 1. Competition receives 12-15 entries. Judges are the Professors of English Literature in the University. The winner and all other competitors will be notified by mail in June.

$◿ THE ALFRED HODDER FELLOWSHIP

Program in Creative Writing, 185 Nassau St., Princeton NJ 08542. (609)258-4096. Fax: (609)258-2230. E-mail: debbin@princeton.edu. Web site: www.princeton.edu/~humcounc. **Contact:** Debbi Nichols. "Stipends of $58,000 will be given to three writers of exceptional promise to pursue independent projects and teach one course in the humanities at Princeton University during the 2007-2008 academic year. Typically the fellows are poets, playwrights, novelists, creative nonfiction writers, and translators who have published one highly acclaimed work and are undertaking a significant new project that might not be possible without the 'studious leisure' afforded by the fellowship." Preference is given to applicants outside academia. Candidates for the Ph.D. are not eligible. Submit a résumé, sample of previous work (10 pages maximum, not returnable), a project proposal of 2-3 pages, and SASE. Guidelines available on Web site. **Deadline:** November 1 (postmark). Announcement of the Hodder Fellow is posted on the Web site in March.

$◿ TOM HOWARD/JOHN H. REID POETRY CONTEST

Tom Howard Books, ℅ Winning Writers, 351 Pleasant St., PMB 222, Northampton MA 01060-3961. (866)946-9748. Fax: (413)280-0539. E-mail: johnreid@mail.qango.com. Web site: www.winningwriters.com. Established 2003. **Contact:** John H. Reid, award director. Offers annual award of 1st Prize: $1,000; 2nd Prize: $400; 3rd Prize: $200; 7 High Distinction Awards of $100 each; 10 Highly Commended Awards of $70 each; and 10 Commended Awards of $50 each. The top 10 entries will be published on the Winning Writers Web site. Submissions may be published or unpublished, may have won prizes elsewhere, and may be entered in other contests. Submit poems in any form, style, or genre. "There is no limit on the number of lines or poems you may submit." No name on ms pages; type or computer-print on letter-size white paper, single-sided. Submit online or by regular mail. Guidelines available for SASE or on Web site. **Entry fee:** $6 USD for every 25 lines (exclude poem titles and any blank lines from line count). **Deadline:** December 15-September 30. Competition receives about 1,000 entries/year. 2006 winner was Debbie Camelin ("Intimidation"). 2006 judges: John H. Reid and Dee C. Konrad. Winners announced in February at WinningWriters.com. Entrants who provide valid e-mail addresses will also receive notification.

$◿ HENRY HOYNS & POE/FAULKNER FELLOWSHIPS (Specialized: MFA candidates in creative writing)

Creative Writing Program, 219 Bryan Hall, P.O. Box 400121, University of Virginia, Charlottesville VA 22904-4121. (434)924-6675. Fax: (434)924-1478. E-mail: SHB7F@virginia.ed. Web site: www.engl.virginia.edu/cwp. **Contact:** Sydney Blair, program director. Annual fellowships in poetry and fiction of varying amounts for candidates for the MFA in creative writing. Sample poems/prose required with application. **Deadline:** January 1. Competition receives 400-500 entries.

⬛ $◿ THE INTRO PRIZE IN POETRY

Four Way Books, Box 535, Village Station, New York NY 10014. (212)334-5430. Fax: (212)334-5435. E-mail: four_way_editors@yahoo.com. Web site: www.fourwaybooks.com. Established

1993. **Contact:** Martha Rhodes, director. The Intro Prize in Poetry, offered biennially in even-numbered years, awards book publication, honorarium ($1,000), and a reading at one or more participating series. Open to U.S. poets who have not yet published a book-length collection. "Submit one manuscript, 48-100 pages suggested. You may submit via e-mail or regular mail by the deadline. For complete information, you must refer to our guidelines on our Web site." **Entry fee:** $25. **Deadline:** March 31 (postmark). 2006 winner was Claire Kageyama (*Shadow Mountain*). Winner announced by mail and on Web site. Copies of winning books available through Four Way Books online and at bookstores (to the trade through University Press of New England).

$◩ THE IOWA POETRY PRIZES

The University of Iowa Press, 100 Kuhl House, 119 West Park Rd., Iowa City IA 52242-1000. (319)335-2000. E-mail: uipress@uiowa.edu. Web site: www.uiowapress.org. The University of Iowa Press offers the annual Iowa Poetry Prizes for book-length mss (50-150 pages) "written originally in English" by new or established poets. Winners will be published by the Press under a standard royalty contract. Poems from previously published books may be included only in mss of selected or collected poems, submissions of which are encouraged. Considers simultaneous submissions if Press is immediately notified if the book is accepted by another publisher. Guidelines available on Web site. **Entry fee:** $20. **Deadline:** postmarked during April only. 2006 winners were *American Spikenard* by Sarah Vap and *Sunday Houses the Sunday House* by Elizabeth Hughey.

$◎ JOSEPH HENRY JACKSON AWARD (Specialized: northern CA or NV residents ages 20-35)

% Intersection for the Arts, 446 Valencia St., San Francisco CA 94103. (415)626-2787. Fax: (415)626-1636. Web site: www.theintersection.org. Established 1955. **Contact:** Awards Coordinator. The Joseph Henry Jackson Award offers $2,000 to the author of an unpublished work-in-progress of fiction (novel or short stories), nonfictional prose, or poetry. Applicants must be residents of northern California or Nevada for 3 consecutive years immediately prior to the March 31 deadline and must be between the ages of 20 and 35 as of the deadline. Guidelines and entry form (required) available on Web site. **Entry fee:** none. **Deadline:** March 31. Competition receives 150-180 entries. 2006 winner was Karan Mahajan (fiction, "What's a Flyover to a Family?").

$◩ ◎ JAPANESE LITERARY TRANSLATION PRIZE (Specialized: Japanese into English)

Donald Keene Center of Japanese Culture, Columbia University, 507 Kent Hall, New York NY 10027. (212)854-5036. Fax: (212)854-4019. E-mail: donald-keene-center@columbia.edu. Web site: www.donaldkeenecenter.org. **Contact:** Miho Walsh, associate director. Established 1981. The Donald Keene Center of Japanese Culture at Columbia University annually awards $5,000 for the Japan-U.S. Friendship Commission Prize for the Translation of Japanese Literature. A prize is given for the best translation of a modern work of literature or for the best classical literary translation, or the prize is divided between a classical and a modern work. "Special attention is given to new or unpublished translators, and citizens of all nationalities are eligible." Submissions may be previously published and entered in other contests. Translated works submitted for consideration may include: a) unpublished mss; b) works in press; c) translations published after January 1, 2000. Submit 7 hard copies of book-length ms or published book. Entry form and guidelines available for SASE, by fax, e-mail, or on Web site. **Deadline:** was March 1 for 2007. Competition receives 20-25 entries/year. 2006 award winners were Joel Cohn for his translation of *Botchan: A Modern Classic* by Natsume Sôseki, and Edward Fowler for his translation of *A Man With No Talents* by Oyama Shiro. Winners are announced through press releases and on Web site.

$☐ ◎ HELEN VAUGHN JOHNSON MEMORIAL HAIKU AWARD (Specialized: traditional 5-7-5 haiku)

Women in the Arts, P.O. Box 2907, Decatur IL 62524. Established 2001. **Contact:** Linda Hutton, vice-president. The Helen Vaughn Johnson Memorial Haiku Award, presented annually for traditional haiku, offers 1st Prize: $25; 2nd Prize: $15; 3rd Prize: $10. Submissions may be previously published and may be entered in other contests. Submit unlimited number of poems of 5 lines each in traditional 5-7-5 haiku format about nature; must not refer to people; no title. Name, address, and phone number should appear in upper right-hand corner of each page. Guidelines available for SASE. **Entry fee:** $1/haiku. Make check payable to WITA. **Deadline:** January 17 (postmark) annually. Competition receives 100 entries. "Judge is a publishing, professional writer living outside the state of Illinois. New judge annually." Winners will be announced February 20 annually. "Study traditional haiku; we do not accept anything but 5-7-5."

$☑ JUNIPER PRIZE FOR POETRY

University of Massachusetts Press, Amherst MA 01003. (413)545-2217. Fax: (413)545-1226. E-mail: info@umpress.umass.edu. Web site: www.umass.edu/umpress. Established 1964. **Contact:** Carla Potts. The University of Massachusetts Press offers the annual Juniper Prize for Poetry, awarded in alternate years for first and subsequent books. Prize includes publication and $1,500 in addition to royalties. In even-numbered years (2008, 2010, etc.), only "subsequent" books will be considered: mss whose authors have had at least one full-length book or chapbook (of at least 30 pages) of poetry published or accepted for publication. Self-published work is not considered to lie within this "books and chapbooks" category. In odd-numbered years (2009, 2011, etc.), only "first books" will be considered: mss by writers whose poems may have appeared in literary journals and/or anthologies but have not been published, nor accepted for publication, in book form. Manuscripts may be submitted to other publishers, "but if accepted for publication elsewhere, please notify us immediately. Manuscripts by more than one author, entries of more than one manuscript simultaneously or within the same year, and translations are not eligible." Submit paginated ms of 50-70 pages of poetry, with paginated contents page, credits page, and information about previously published books. Include 2 cover sheets: one with contact information, one without. Manuscripts will not be returned. Guidelines available for SASE or on Web site. **Entry fee:** $20. **Deadline:** submit August 1-September 30 (postmark). 2006 winner was Michael Dumanis (*My Soviet Union*). Winners announced in April on Web site. Copies of winning books available through Web site.

$☑ ELLEN LAFORGE POETRY PRIZE (formerly Grolier Poetry Prize)

172 Auburn St., Unit 2, Cambridge MA 02139. Web site: www.ellenlaforge.org. Established 1983. The Ellen LaForge Poetry Prize is open to all poets who have not published a book of poetry, including vanity, small press, chapbook or trade book. The winner receives an honorarium of $1,000. Up to 6 poems by the winner and 4 by each of 3 runners-up are chosen for publication in the poetry prize annual. Submissions must be unpublished and not under consideration elsewhere. Submit up to 6 poems, no more than 12 double-spaced pages. Submit one ms in duplicate, without name of poet. On a separate sheet, provide contact information, including e-mail address and titles of poems. Guidelines available for SASE or on Web site. **Entry fee:** $10. **Deadline:** entries accepted February 1-June30 (postmark). Winner and runners-up are notified by October 1. Copies of the annual are available from the Foundation at the above address.

$☑ ◎ HAROLD MORTON LANDON TRANSLATION AWARD (Specialized: any language into English)

The Academy of American Poets, 584 Broadway, Suite 604, New York NY 10012-3210. (212)274-0343. Fax: (212)274-9427. E-mail: jkronovet@poets.org. Web site: www.poets.org. Award established 1976. **Contact:** Jennifer Kronovet, awards coordinator. Offers one $1,000 award each year to recognize a published translation of poetry from any language into English. Guidelines available for SASE or on Web site. **Deadline:** December 31 (postmark) of year in which book was published. 2006 winner was Richard Zenith for *Education by Stone: Selected Poems*. 2006 judge: Willis Barnstone.

$☑ THE JAMES LAUGHLIN AWARD

The Academy of American Poets, 584 Broadway, Suite 604, New York NY 10012. (212)274-0343. Fax: (212)274-9427. E-mail: jkronovet@poets.org. Web site: www.poets.org. Offered since 1954. **Contact:** Jennifer Kronovet, awards coordinator. Offers $5,000 prize to recognize and support a poet's second book (ms must be under contract to a publisher). Submissions must be made by a publisher in ms form. The Academy of American Poets purchases copies of the Laughlin Award-winning book for distribution to its members. Poets must be U.S. citizens. Entry form, signed by the publisher, required. Entry form and guidelines available for SASE (in January) or on Web site. **Deadline:** submissions accepted between January 1 and May 15. Winners announced in August. 2006 winner was Tracy K. Smith for *Duende*. 2006 judges: Elizabeth Alexander, Kimiko Hahn, and Terrance Hayes.

$☑ THE LAUREATE PRIZE FOR POETRY

The National Poetry Review, P.O. Box 2080, Aptos CA 95001-2080. E-mail: editor@natonalpoetryreview.com. Web site: www.nationalpoetryreview.com. **Contact:** C.J. Sage, editor. The Laureate Prize for Poetry, an annual award of $300 and publication in *The National Poetry Review* (see separate listing in Magazines Journals), "will honor one new poem that *TNPR* believes has the greatest chance of standing the test of time and becoming part of the literary canon." Submissions must be unpublished and uncommitted (not promised for first publication elsewhere). Accepts simultaneous submissions, "but if the work is selected by *TNPR* for the prize or for publication, it must be withdrawn from elsewhere unless you have withdrawn it from us two weeks before our acceptance." Submit up to 3 poems (10 page maximum per group of 3). Include a brief bio, contact information, and poet's e-mail address for results. **Entry fee:** $15/entry; accepts multiple submissions with separate entry fee for each 3-poem group. "If you include a small book-sized SASE with $1.30 postage with your entry, we will provide you a copy of the winner's issue." Make checks payable to C.J. Sage only. **Deadline:** August 31 (postmark).

⚡ $◎ THE STEPHEN LEACOCK MEMORIAL MEDAL FOR HUMOUR (Specialized: humor by Canadian citizens)

Stephen Leacock Associates, P.O. Box 854, Orillia ON L3V 3P4 Canada. (705)835-7061. Fax: (705)835-7062. E-mail: spruce@encode.com. Web site: www.leacock.ca. **Contact:** Marilyn Rumball, corresponding secretary. Award Chairman: Judith Rapson. Annual award of the Silver Leacock Medal for Humour and T.D. Canada Trust cash award of $10,000. Presented for a book of humor in prose, verse, drama, or any book form—by a Canadian citizen. "Book must have been published in the current year and no part of it may have been previously published in book form." Submit 10 copies of book, 8×10 b&w photo, bio, and entry fee. **Entry fee:** $100 CAD. **Deadline:** December 31. Competition receives 40-50 entries. 2006 winner was *Pitch Black* by Arthur Black. The committee also publishes *The Newspacket* 3 times/year.

$◻ THE LEAGUE OF MINNESOTA POETS CONTEST

Web site: www.mnpoets.org (see Web site for current contact information). **Contact:** Christina Flaugher, contest chair. Annual contest offers 18 different categories, with 3 prizes in each category ranging from $10-125. See guidelines for poem lengths, forms, and subjects. Guidelines available for #10 SASE, by e-mail, or on Web site. **Entry fee:** (nonmembers) $1/poem per category; $2/poem (limit 6) for Grand Prize category; (members) $5 for 17 categories; $1/poem (limit 6) for Grand Prize category. Make checks payable to LOMP Contest. **Deadline:** July 31. Nationally known, non-

Minnesota judges. Winners will be announced at the October LOMP Conference and by mail. Additional information regarding LOMP membership available on Web site.

⚡ $☑ THE LEVIS POETRY PRIZE

Four Way Books, Box 535, Village Station, New York NY 10014. (212)334-5430. Fax: (212)334-5435. E-mail: four_way_editors@yahoo.com. Web site: www.fourwaybooks.com. Established 1993. **Contact:** Martha Rhodes, director. The Levis Poetry Prize, offered biennially in odd-numbered years, offers book publication, honorarium ($1,000), and a reading at one or more participating series. Open to any U.S. poet. "Submit one manuscript, 48-100 pages suggested. More than one manuscript may be submitted, but each must be entered separately. Your name should appear on the entry form and the title page of the manuscript and nowhere else." Include SASE for results only. Entry form and guidelines available for SASE or on Web site. **Entry fee:** $25. **Deadline:** March 31 (postmark). Receives about 1,000 entries/competition. 2005 winner was John Gallaher (*The Little Book of Guesses*). 2007 judge: Tony Hoagland. Winner announced by mail and on Web site. Copies of winning books available through Four Way Books online and at bookstores (to the trade through University Press of New England).

$◻ ◎ LITTLE BITTY POETRY COMPETITION (Specialized: short poetry 3-12 lines)

Shadow Poetry, 1209 Milwaukee St., Excelsior Springs MO 64024. Fax: (208)977-9114. E-mail: shadowpoetry@shadowpoetry.com. Web site: www.shadowpoetry.com. Established 2000. **Contact:** James Summers, award director. Offers quarterly award of 1st Prize: $50; 2nd Prize: $25; 3rd Prize: $10; plus the top 3 winners also receive a certificate, printed copy of winning poem, and a ribbon. Submissions may be previously published. Submit unlimited number of poems of 3-12 lines on any subject, in any form. "Entry form must be present with mail-in entries. Submit entries in duplicate with name, address, phone number, e-mail address (when available) on upper left-hand corner of one sheet. Enclose #10 SASE for winners list. Include an additional SASE for entry receipt (optional). If no SASE is included for receipt, Shadow Poetry will e-mail an entry confirmation to the contestant, if applicable." Entry form and guidelines available for SASE or on Web site. **Entry fee:** $2/poem. Make checks/money orders payable to Shadow Poetry. **Deadline:** March 31, June 30, September 30, and December 31. Winners will be announced "30 days after each quarterly contest ends, by e-mail and to those who requested a winners list. Results will also be posted on the Shadow Poetry Web site."

$☑ ◎ NAOMI LONG MADGETT POETRY AWARD (Specialized: African American)

Lotus Press, P.O. Box 21607, Detroit MI 48221. (313)861-1280. Fax: (313)861-4740. E-mail: lotuspress@aol.com. Web site: www.lotuspress.org. Established 1973. **Contact:** Constance Withers. Offers annual award of $500 and publication by Lotus Press, Inc. for a book-length ms by an African American poet. Individual poems may be previously published, but "no poems published in a collection of your own work, self-published or not, should be included. Please do not submit a manuscript which you have submitted, or which you plan to submit during the period of consideration, to another publisher. However, you may enter another competition as long as you notify us that you have done or plan to do so. If you are notified that your manuscript has won another award or prize, you must inform us of this immediately." Submit 2 complete copies of 60-90 page ms, exclusive of table of contents or other optional introductory material. **See guidelines for special formatting instructions.** Enclose stamped, self-addressed postcard to confirm receipt of material; no SASE as mss will not be returned. Mail by First Class Priority; no Certified, Federal Express, or other mail requiring a signature. **Deadline:** entries must be received between January 2 and March 31. Guidelines available for SASE, by e-mail, or on Web site. Winner and judges announced no later than June 1. Copies of winning books available from Lotus Press at the address above. "If you have already had a book published by Lotus Press, you are ineligible. However, inclusion in a Lotus Press anthology does not disqualify you." Advice: "Read some of the books we have published, especially award winners. Read a lot of good contemporary poetry. Those who have worked over a period of years at developing their craft will have the best chance for consideration. The work of novices is not likely to be selected."

$☑ MAIN STREET RAG'S ANNUAL CHAPBOOK CONTEST

P.O. Box 690100, Charlotte NC 28227-7001. (704)573-2516. E-mail: editor@mainstreetrag.com. Web site: www.MainStreetRag.com. Established 1996. **Contact:** M. Scott Douglass, editor/publisher. Annual chapbook contest by *Main Street Rag* (see separate listing in Magazines/Journals) offers 1st Prize: $500 and 50 copies of chapbook. "As many as 19 runners-up have been published in previous contests, and every manuscript entered is considered for publication." All entrants receive a copy of the winning chapbook. Submit 24-32 pages of poetry, no more than one poem/page. Guidelines available for SASE, by e-mail, or on Web site. **Entry fee:** $15. **Deadline:** May 31. 2006 winner was Stacey Waite (*Love Poem to Androgyny*).

$☑ MAIN STREET RAG'S ANNUAL POETRY BOOK AWARD

P.O. Box 690100, Charlotte NC 28227-7001. (704)573-2516. E-mail: editor@mainstreetrag.com. Web site: www.MainStreetRag.com. Established 1996. **Contact:** M. Scott Douglass, editor/publisher. *Main Street Rag*'s Annual Poetry Book Award offers 1st Prize: $1,000 and 50 copies of book; runners-up may also be offered publication. Submit 48-80 pages of poetry, no more than one poem/page (individual poems may be longer than one page). Guidelines available for SASE, by e-mail, or on Web site. **Entry fee:** $20 (or $25 to include a copy of the winning book). **Deadline:** January 31. 2006 winner was Jennifer K. Sweeney (*Salt Memory Poems*).

Ⓝ $☑ MANY MOUNTAINS MOVING POETRY BOOK CONTEST

Many Mountains Moving Press, 549 Rider Ridge Dr., Longmont CO 80501. E-mail: info@mmminc.org. Web site: www.mmminc.org. The Many Mountains Moving Poetry Book Contest offers $500 and publication of a book-length poetry ms by Many Mountains Moving Press. Open to all poets writing in English. More than half of ms may not have been published as a collection, but individual poems and chapbook-length sections may have been previously published if publisher gives permission to reprint. Accepts simultaneous submissions "if the poet agrees to notify MMM Press of acceptance elsewhere." Submit 50-100 typed pages of poetry, single- or double-spaced. Include cover letter with ms title, brief bio, poet's name, address, phone number, and e-mail address(es). Poet's name must not appear anywhere on ms. Acknowledgments may be sent but are not required. Include SASE for results only; no mss will be returned. Guidelines available on Web site. **Entry fee:** $20; entitles entrant to free back issue of *Many Mountains Moving*, discount on subscription, and discount on any one of selected Many Mountains Moving Press books (use order form, available on Web site). Make checks/money orders payable to Many Mountains Moving Press. **Deadline:** submit December 1-May 1 (postmark). 2007 final judge: Yusef Komunyaaka.

$☑ MARSH HAWK PRESS POETRY PRIZE

P.O. Box 206, East Rockaway NY 11518-0206. E-mail: marshhawkpress1@aol.com. Web site: www.MarshHawkPress.org. Established 2001. **Contact:** Prize Director. The Marsh Hawk Press Poetry Prize offers $1,000 plus publication of a book-length ms. Submissions must be unpublished as a collection, but individual poems may have been previously published elsewhere. Submit 48-70 pages of original poetry in any style in English, typed single-spaced, paginated, and bound with a spring clip. Include 2 title pages: one with ms title, poet's name, and contact information only; one with ms title only (poet's name must not appear anywhere in the ms). Also include table of contents and acknowledgments page. Include SASE for results only; will not be returned. Guidelines available on Web site. **Entry fee:** $20. Make check/money order payable to Marsh Hawk Press. **Deadline:** see Web site. 2006 winner was Steve Fellner (*Blind Date with Cavafy*). 2007 judge: David Shapiro.

$☑ THE LENORE MARSHALL POETRY PRIZE
The Academy of American Poets, 584 Broadway, Suite 604, New York NY 10012. (212)274-0343. Fax: (212)274-9427. E-mail: jkronovet@poets.org. Web site: www.poets.org. Established 1975. **Contact:** Jennifer Kronovet, awards coordinator. Offers $25,000 for the most outstanding book of poems published in the U.S. in the previous year. Contest is open to books by living American poets published in a standard edition (40 pages or more in length with 500 or more copies printed). Self-published books are not eligible. Publishers may enter as many books as they wish (books must be submitted in the year after their publication). Four copies of each book must be submitted and none will be returned. Guidelines, required entry form available for SASE or on Web site. **Entry fee:** $25/title. **Deadline:** entries must be submitted between April 1 and June 15. Finalists announced in October; winner announced in November. 2006 winner was Eleanor Lerman for *Our Post-Soviet History Unfolds*. 2006 judges: Carl Dennis, Tony Hoagland, and Carol Muske-Dukes.

✖ $☐ MILFORD FINE ARTS COUNCIL NATIONAL POETRY CONTEST
Milford Fine Arts Council, 40 Railroad Ave., South, Milford CT 06460. Web site: www.milfordarts.org. Established 1976. **Contact:** Tom Bouton, Letters Committee chairperson. Offers annual award of 1st Prize: $100; 2nd Prize: $50; 3rd Prize: $25; plus winners will be published in MFAC's annual publication, *High Tide*. Submissions must be unpublished and not under consideration by any other publication or contest. Poems entered may not have won any other prizes or honorable mentions. Poets must be 18 years and older. "Poems must be typed single-spaced on white standard paper, 10-30 lines (including title), no more than 48 characters/line, on any subject, in any style, rhymed or unrhymed. Use standard font, clear and legible, one poem/page, no script or fax. NO foul language. No bio or date, only the words 'Unpublished Original' typed above the poem." Include poet's name, address, ZIP code, and phone number or e-mail address in the middle back of the submitted poem, no identifying information on the front of the page. Poems will be judged on form, clarity, originality, and universal appeal. "Entries may be considered for publication in *High Tide*. If you do not want your poems considered for publication, then you *must* print on the back of the poem (below your name, address, and ZIP code) 'For National Poetry Contest Only.'" Include SASE for results only, with NOTIFICATION printed on bottom left corner of envelope; no poems will be returned. Guidelines available for SASE or on Web site. **Entry fee:** $3 for one poem, $6 for 3 poems, $2 for each additional poem after 3. Contestants may enter an unlimited number of poems (will be judged individually, not as a group). Check or money order accepted, no cash. **Deadline:** February 28 for 2008.

$☑ EDNA ST. VINCENT MILLAY "BALLAD OF THE HARP WEAVER" AWARD (Specialized: narrative poems)
Verdure Publications, P.O. Box 640387, Beverly Hills FL 34464-0387. E-mail: verdure@tampabay.rr.com. Established 1989. **Contact:** Madelyn Eastlund, editor. The annual Edna St. Vincent Millay "Ballad of the Harp Weaver" Award offers $50 and publication in *Harp-Strings Poetry Journal* for a narrative poem, 40-100 lines. Guidelines available for SASE. **Entry fee:** $5 for 1-3 poems. Make checks payable to Madelyn Eastlund. **Deadline:** July 15.

$☑ MISSISSIPPI REVIEW PRIZE
118 College Dr. #5144, Hattiesburg MS 39406-0001. (601)266-4321. Fax: (601)266-5757. E-mail: rief@mississippireview.com. Web site: www.mississippireview.com. The *Mississippi Review* Prize offers an annual award of $1,000 each in poetry and fiction. Winners and finalists comprise one issue of *Mississippi Review*. Submissions must be unpublished. Submit up to 3 poems/entry (total-

ing 10 pages or less). No limit on number of entries. Put "*MR* Prize" plus poet's name, address, phone number, e-mail address, and title(s) on page one of entry. Manuscripts will not be returned. **Entry fee:** $15/entry. Make checks payable to *Mississippi Review*. Each entrant receives a copy of the prize issue. **Deadline:** submit April 1-October 1 (postmark). Winners announced in January.

$☐ MISSISSIPPI VALLEY POETRY CONTEST

Midwest Writing Center, P.O. Box 3188, Rock Island IL 61204. (563)359-1057. **Contact:** Max J. Molleston, chairman. Offers annual prizes of approximately $1,000 for unpublished poems in categories for students (elementary, junior, and senior high), adults, Mississippi Valley, senior citizens, jazz, religious, humorous, rhyming, haiku, ethnic, and history. Submissions must be unpublished. **Entry fee:** (adults) $10 for up to 5 poems, no limit to number of entries; (children) $5 for up to 5 poems. Send check or U.S. dollars. **Deadline:** April 1. Professional readers present winning poems to a reception at an award evening in May. Competition receives 700 entries.

$☑ JENNY MCKEAN MOORE WRITER IN WASHINGTON

Dept. of English, George Washington University, Washington DC 20052. (202)994-6515. Fax: (202)994-7915. E-mail: dmca@gwu.edu. Web site: www.gwu.edu/~english. Offers fellowship for a visiting lecturer in creative writing, about $50,000 for 2 semesters. Teaching duties involve 2 workshops per semester—one for undergraduate students, the other free to the community. Apply with résumé and writing sample of 25 pages or less. Books may be submitted but will not be returned without SASE. Awarded to writers in different genres each year, typically alternating between poets and fiction writers. Check Web site for specific genre each year. **Deadline:** November 15.

$☑ SAMUEL FRENCH MORSE POETRY PRIZE

Dept. of English, 406 Holmes, Northeastern University, Boston MA 02115. (617)373-4546. Fax: (617)373-2509. E-mail: g.rotella@neu.edu. Web site: www.english.neu.edu. **Contact:** Prof. Guy Rotella, editor. Offers annual prize of book publication (ms 50-70 pages) by NU/UPNE and $1,000. Open to U.S. poets who have published no more than one book of poetry. Entry must be unpublished in book form but may include poems published in journals and magazines. Manuscripts will not be returned. Guidelines available on Web site (under "Publications"). **Entry fee:** $20. **Deadline:** August 1 for inquiries; September 15 for single copy of ms. Competition receives approximately 400 entries/year. Recent winners include Jennifer Atkinson, Ted Genoways, and Dana Roeser. Previous judges: Marilyn Hacker, Rosanna Warren, Robert Cording, and Ellen Bryant Voigt.

$☑ THE KATHRYN A. MORTON PRIZE IN POETRY

Sarabande Books, Inc., P.O. Box 4456, Louisville KY 40204. E-mail: info@sarabandebooks.org. Web site: www.SarabandeBooks.org. Established 1994. **Contact:** Sarah Gorham, editor-in-chief. Member: CLMP. The Kathryn A. Morton Prize in Poetry is awarded annually to a book-length ms (at least 48 pages). Winner receives $2,000, publication, and a standard royalty contract. All finalists are considered for publication. Entry form and SASE are required. Guidelines available for SASE, by e-mail, or on Web site. **Entry fee:** $25. **Deadline:** submit January 1-February 15 (postmark) only. Competition receives 1,200 entries. 2006 winner was Gabriel Fried (*Making the Lamb Take*). 2007 judge: Jane Hirshfield. "To avoid conflict of interest, students in a degree-granting program or close friends of a judge are ineligible to enter the contest in the genre for which their friend or teacher is serving as judge. Sarabande, as a member of CLMP, complies with its Contest Code of Ethics."

$☑ NATIONAL BOOK AWARD

The National Book Foundation, 95 Madison Ave., Suite 709, New York NY 10016. (212)685-0261. E-mail: nationalbook@nationalbook.org. Web site: www.nationalbook.org. Presents $10,000 in each of 4 categories (fiction, nonfiction, poetry, and young people's literature), plus 16 short-list prizes of $1,000 each to Finalists. Submissions must be previously published and **must be entered by the publisher**. General guidelines available on Web site; interested publishers should phone or e-mail the Foundation. **Entry fee:** $125/title. **Deadline:** see Web site for current year's deadline. 2006 poetry winner was Nathaniel Mackey for *Splay Anthem*.

$☑ THE NATIONAL POET HUNT CONTEST

Schoolcraft College, 18600 Haggerty Rd., Livonia MI 48152-2696. (734)462-4400, ext. 5327. Fax: (734)462-4679. E-mail: macguffin@schoolcraft.edu. Web site: www.schoolcraft.edu/macguffin. Established 1996. **Contact:** Carol Was, poetry editor. The National Poet Hunt Contest offers 1st Prize: $500 and publication in a future issue of *The MacGuffin*; may also award 2 Honorable Mentions and publication. Open to all writers. Submissions must be unpublished and may be entered in other contests. Submit 5 typed poems on any subject, in any form. Put name and address on separate 3×5 index card only. Include SASE for winners' list only; entries will not be returned. Guidelines available for SASE, by fax, e-mail, or on Web site. **Entry fee:** $15/entry (5 poems). Make checks payable to Schoolcraft College. **Deadline:** check Web site for current deadline. 2007 judge: Thomas Lux.

N $☑ THE NATIONAL POETRY REVIEW BOOK PRIZE

E-mail: nationalpoetryreview@yahoo.com. Web site: www.nationalpoetryreview.com. *The National Poetry Review* Book Prize offers $500, publication of a book-length ms, and 20 author copies. All entries will be considered for publication. Submit 45-60 pages of poetry. Include cover letter with bio and acknowledgments page. **See Web site for entry address and details.** Include e-mail address for results (no SASEs; mss will not be returned). Guidelines available on Web site. **Fee:** $20. Make checks payable to CJ Sage only. **Deadline:** October 31 (postmark).

$◎ HOWARD NEMEROV SONNET AWARD

The Formalist, 320 Hunter Dr., Evansville IN 47711. Web site: www2.evansville.edu/theformalist. Established 1994. Although *The Formalist* has ceased publication, it continues to sponsor the annual Howard Nemerov Sonnet Award. Offers $1,000 prize; winner and 11 finalists will be published in *Measure: An Annual Review of Formal Poetry* (see separate listing in Magazines/Journals). Submit original, unpublished sonnets, no translations; sonnet sequences acceptable, but each sonnet will be considered individually. Poets may enter as many sonnets as they wish. Poet's name, address, and phone number should be listed on the **back** of each entry. Enclose SASE for contest results; entries cannot be returned. Guidelines available for SASE or on Web site. **Entry fee**: $3/sonnet. Make all checks payable to *The Formalist*. **Deadline:** November 15 (postmark). Past winners include Rhina P. Espaillat, Marion Shore, Deborah Warren, and A.M. Juster. 2007 judge: Frederick Turner.

$☑ THE PABLO NERUDA PRIZE FOR POETRY

Nimrod, Literary Contest—Poetry, The University of Tulsa, 600 S. College, Tulsa OK 74104. Web site: www.utulsa.edu/nimrod. **Contact:** Contest Coordinator. The annual *Nimrod*/Hardman Writing Awards include The Pablo Neruda Prize for Poetry, which offers 1st Prize: $2,000 and publication in *Nimrod: International Journal of Poetry and Prose* (see separate listing in Magazines/Journals); and 2nd Prize: $1,000 and publication. *Nimrod* retains the right to publish any submission. Submissions must be unpublished and not under consideration or accepted for publication elsewhere. Work must be in English or translated by original author. Submit 3-10 pages of poetry (one long poem or several short poems). Poet's name must not appear on ms. Include cover sheet with poem title(s), poet's name, address, phone and fax numbers, and e-mail address (poet must have a U.S. address by October of contest year to enter). Mark "Contest Entry" on submission envelope and cover sheet. Include SASE for results only; mss will not be returned. Guidelines available for #10 SASE or on Web site. **Entry fee:** $20; includes one-year subscription (2 issues) to *Nimrod*.

Make checks payable to *Nimrod*. **Deadline:** entries accepted January 1-April 30 (postmark). 2006 winners were John Surowiecki (1st Prize, "American Stroke") and Daniel Lusk (2nd Prize, "The Shower Scene from Hamlet"). Winners will be announced on *Nimrod's* Web site.

$⬙ NERVE COWBOY CHAPBOOK CONTEST

P.O. Box 4973, Austin TX 78765. Web site: www.jwhagins.com/ChapContest.html. Established 1995. **Contact:** Joseph Shields and Jerry Hagins, co-editors. The *Nerve Cowboy* Chapbook Contest offers 1st Prize: $100, publication, and 50 author's copies; 2nd Prize: $50, publication, and 30 author's copies; 3rd Prize: lifetime subscription to *Nerve Cowboy* (chapbook will not be published). Submit 24-40 pages of poetry and/or short fiction. Include SASE for return of ms. Guidelines available on Web site. **Entry fee:** $10 (all entrants receive a copy of the winning chapbook and a discount on the 2nd-Prize chapbook). Make checks payable to *Nerve Cowboy*. **Deadline:** January 31. 2006 winners included David J. Thompson (1st Prize, *Outliving Elvis*) and Joan Jobe Smith and Fred Voss (2nd Prize, *Teatime @ The Bouquet Morale*).

$⬜ ◉ NEW EDEN CHAPBOOK COMPETITION (Specialized: spiritual poetry)

Power of Poetry, 5890 Birch Ct., Oakland CA 94618-1627. Fax: (510)596-1860. E-mail: cjrenzop@yahoo.com. Web site: http://popruah.opwest.org. Established 1990. **Contact:** C.J. Renz, O.P., general editor. The New Eden Chapbook Competition offers $100, publication of the chapbook within a volume of the literary annual *Ruah* (see separate listing in Magazines/Journals), and 25 copies of that issue. "The New Eden Chapbook Competition is named in honor of Leo Thomas, O.P., founder of 'Healing Ministry,' a parish-based program which provides spiritual support for those in need of healing. The essence of Fr. Thomas' life and ministry recollects how Divine healing leads to a renewed experience of the Original Blessedness found in the garden of Eden. The Chapbook Contest recognizes that poetry, particularly spiritual poetry, leads us to this place of healing particularly when it helps us touch the Divine." Entries must be unpublished as a collection, but individual poems may have been previously published. Submit up to 24 pages of verse, any style. Include 2 title pages: one with name, address, and phone number, the other with title only. Provide table of contents and acknowledgments page. Include SASE for results. Guidelines available on Web site. **Entry fee:** $10 (includes the previous issue of *Ruah*). **Deadline:** December 31 postmark (submit September-December).

$⬙ THE NEW ISSUES POETRY PRIZE

New Issues Poetry & Prose, Dept. of English, Western Michigan University, 1903 W. Michigan Ave., Kalamazoo MI 49008-5331. (269)387-8185. Fax: (269)387-2562. Web site: www.wmich.edu/newissues. Established 1996. The New Issues Poetry Prize offers $2,000 plus publication of a book-length ms. Open to "poets writing in English who have not previously published a full-length collection of poems in an edition of 500 or more copies." Additional mss will be considered from those submitted to the competition for publication in the New Issues Press Poetry Series. Accepts simultaneous submissions, but New Issues must be notified of acceptance elsewhere. Submit ms of at least 48 pages, typed, single-spaced preferred. Clean photocopies acceptable. Do not bind; use manila folder or metal clasp. Include cover page with poet's name, address, phone number, and title of the ms. Also include brief bio and acknowledgments page. No e-mail or fax submissions. Include SASP for notification of receipt of ms and SASE for results only; no mss will be returned. Guidelines available for SASE, by fax, by e-mail, or on Web site. **Entry fee:** $15. Make checks payable to New Issues Poetry & Prose. **Deadline:** November 30 (postmark). Winner announced the following April. 2006 winner was Jason Bredle (*Standing in Line for the Beast*). "A national judge selects the prize winner and recommends other manuscripts. The editors decide on the other books considering the judge's recommendation, but are not bound by it." 2007 judge: Marie Howe.

$✍ NEW RIVER POETS TRIANNUAL POETRY AWARDS

New River Poets, 36929 Grace Ave., Zephyrhills FL 33542. Established 2000. **Contact:** Verna Thornton, awards coordinator. Offers 1st Prize: $75; 2nd Prize: $50; 3rd Prize: $40; plus 5 Honorable Mentions at $5 each. Submissions may be previously published, may be entered in other contests, and may have previously won prizes. Submit up to 4 poems of no more than 42 lines each. Subject and form are poet's choice; "please identify structured form." Send 2 copies of each poem on $8\frac{1}{2} \times 11$ white paper; list deadline in upper right-hand corner of both copies. On second copy only, in upper right-hand corner under deadline, list name and full address. Include #10 SASE with entry. **Entry fee:** up to 4 poems for $5; $1 each additional poem; no limit. Make checks payable to New River Poets and mail to Verna Thornton at the above address. **Deadline:** February 15, June 15, and October 15 (all postmark). "Winning entries will be selected by a highly qualified poet or a panel of established poets. New River Poets is a chartered chapter of the Flordia State Poets Association, Inc., and a member of the National Federation of State Poetry Societies (NFSPS). Its purpose is to acknowledge and reward outstanding poetic efforts."

$✍ ◎ NEW WOMEN'S VOICES CHAPBOOK COMPETITION

Finishing Line Press, P.O. Box 1626, Georgetown KY 40324. (859)514-8966. E-mail: FinishingBooks @aol.com. Web site: www.finishinglinepress.com. Established 1998. **Contact:** Leah Maines, poetry editor. The New Women's Voices Chapbook Competition offers $1,000 and publication for a chapbook-length ms by a woman poet who has not yet published a full-length collection (previous chapbook publication is okay). All entries will be considered for publication; up to 10 entries will be selected for the New Women's Voices series. Submit up to 26 pages of poetry. Include bio, acknowledgments, and SASE. Guidelines available on Web site. **Entry fee:** $15. **Deadline:** February 15 (postmark). Judge: Leah Maines.

$✍ NEWBURYPORT ART ASSOCIATION ANNUAL SPRING POETRY CONTEST

12 Charron Dr., Newburyport MA 01950. E-mail: rpespaillat@verizon.net. Web site: www.newbury portart.org. Established 1990. **Contact:** Rhina P. Espaillat, contest coordinator. Offers annual awards of 1st Prize: $200; 2nd Prize: $150; 3rd Prize: $100; plus a number of Honorable Mentions and certificates. All winners, including Honorable Mention poets, are invited to read their own entries at the Awards Day Reading in May. Open to anyone over 16 years old. Submissions must be previously unpublished; may be entered in other contests. Submit any number of poems, each no more than 3 pages in length. Submit 2 copies: one with poet's name, address, phone number, and e-mail address, the second without identifying information. Include SASE for results. Any number of poems accepted, but all must be mailed together in a single envelope with one check covering the total entry fee. Guidelines available for SASE, by e-mail, or on Web site. **Entry fee:** $3/poem. Make checks payable to NAA Contest (one check for all entries). **Deadline:** March 15 (postmark). 2006 winners were Daniel Waters, Colette Anderson Gill, and Len Krisak. 2006 judge: Erica Funkhouser. **Do not submit entries without first securing a copy of the guidelines, then follow them carefully.**

$□ ◎ NFSPS COLLEGE/UNIVERSITY LEVEL POETRY AWARDS (Specialized: student writing)

P.O. Box 520698, Salt Lake City UT 84152-0698. (801)484-3113. Fax: (801)606-3444. E-mail: SBSeni or@juno.com. Web site: www.nfsps.org. **Contact:** N. Colwell Snell, chairman. Offers 2 annual awards of $500 each; one as the Edna Meudt Memorial Award, the second as the Florence Kahn Memorial Award. Each prize includes publication of winning ms, with 75 copies awarded to the respective poet. Recipients will be invited to read at the annual NFSPS (National Federation of State Poetry Societies) convention; NFSPS will provide an additional travel stipend to be presented at the convention to recipients in attendance (winners are responsible for the balance of convention costs). Open to all freshmen, sophomores, juniors, and seniors of an accredited university or college. Submit a ms of 10 original poems, one poem to each page, single-spaced, each poem titled. Each poem must be no more than 46 lines (including spaces between stanzas) and have no more than 50 characters/line (including spaces between words and punctuation). Manuscript must be titled and must include cover page with name, address, phone number in upper left-hand corner; ms title centered on page. May include dedication page. No other identification on any page other than cover page. **NOTE:** A current, official NFSPS application, completed and duly notarized, must accompany ms at time of submission. No e-mail submissions or special deliveries; First Class Mail only. Entry form and guidelines available for SASE or on Web site. **Entry fee:** none. **Deadline:** notarized applications and mss received on or before February 1 (no entry mailed before January 1). Winners will be selected on or before March 31 and announced after April 15. Each recipient's state poetry society is also notified. Copies of winning books available on NFSPS Web site.

$⬜ NFSPS COMPETITIONS

Contact: Theda Bassett, Contest Chair, 30 West Lester Ave., D-27, Salt Lake City UT 84107. (801)281-5529. E-mail: theda_bassett2002@yahoo.com. Web site: www.nfsps.org. NFSPS sponsors a national contest with 50 different categories each year, including the NFSPS Founders Award of 1st Prize: $1,500; 2nd Prize: $500; 3rd Prize: $250. Rules for all contests are given in a brochure available from Madelyn Eastlund, editor of *Strophes* newsletter, at 310 South Adams St., Beverly Hills FL 34465 (e-mail: verdure@tampabay.rr.com); or from Theda Bassett at the address above; or on the NFSPS Web site. **Entry fee:** (for members) $1/poem or $8 total for 8 or more categories, plus $5/poem for NFSPS Founders Award (limit 4 entries in this category alone). All poems winning over $15 are published in the *ENCORE Prize Poem Anthology*. NFSPS also sponsors the annual Stevens Poetry Manuscript Competition and the NFSPS College/University Level Poetry Awards (see separate listings in this section).

$☑ JESSE BRYCE NILES MEMORIAL CHAPBOOK AWARD

4956 St. John Dr., Syracuse NY 13215. (315)488-8077. E-mail: poetry@comstockreview.org. Web site: www.comstockreview.org. The Jesse Bryce Niles Memorial Chapbook Award offers $1,000 plus publication and 50 author's copies; each entrant also receives a copy. Submissions must be unpublished as a collection, but individual poems may have been previously published in journals. Accepts simultaneous submissions "as long as the poet notifies us immediately upon acceptance elsewhere." Submit 25-34 pages of poetry, single-spaced (one page = 38 lines maximum, including spacing between lines; poems may run longer than one page). **Manuscripts either too short or too long will be disqualified.** "Do not count title page, acknowledgments, dedication, or bio in the page length. Do not send illustrations, photos, or any other graphics attached to the poems. You may submit a Table of Contents, which may list the manuscript name only, not the poet's name (not counted in page total for manuscript)." Manuscripts should be paginated and secured with a binder clip; no staples or plastic covers. Include 2 cover pages: one with ms title, poet's name, address, phone number, and e-mail address; second with ms title only. List acknowledgments on a separate, removable page with same identifying information. Poet's name should not appear on poems. Include SASE for results only; mss will not be returned. Guidelines available for SASE or on Web site. **Entry fee:** $15/chapbook. **Deadline:** submit August 1-September 30 (postmark). **Offered every other year.** 2005 winner was J.F. Connolly (*Among the Living*). 2007 judge: Kathleen Bryce Niles; all entries are screened by the editors of *The Comstock Review* (see separate listing in Magazines/Journals). Winner is notified in December. Copies of winning chapbooks are available for $10 saddle-stitched, $11.50 perfect-bound. E-mail for ordering details.

⊞ $◎ NSW PREMIER'S LITERARY AWARD "THE KENNETH SLESSOR PRIZE"
(Specialized: Australian citizens only)

Arts NSW, P.O. Box A226, Sydney South NSW 1235 Australia. E-mail: mail@arts.nsw.gov.au. Web site: www.arts.nsw.gov.au. Established 1980. Offers annual award of $15,000 AUD for a book of poetry (collection or long poem) published in the previous year. **Open to Australian citizens only.** Books may be nominated by poets or by their agents or publishers. Write for entry form and guidelines or check Web site. **Deadline:** November (check guidelines). Winners will be announced in May. "Obtain copy of guidelines before entering."

$◻ OHIO POETRY DAY CONTESTS

Ohio Poetry Day Association, Dept. of English, Heidelberg College, 310 East Market, Tiffin OH 44883. Web site: www.geocities.com/theohiopoetryassociation. Established 1937. **Contact:** Bill Reyer, contest chair. Offers annual slate of 30-40 contest categories. Prizes range from $75 down; all money-winning award poems are published in an annual anthology (runs over 100 pages). Submissions must be unpublished. Submit one poem/category on topic and in form specified. Some contests open to everyone, but others open only to Ohio poets. "Each contest has its own specifications. Entry must be for a specified category, so entrants need rules." Entry form and guidelines available for SASE. **Entry fee:** $10 inclusive, unlimited number of categories. **Deadline:** usually end of May; see guidelines for each year's deadline. Competition receives over 4,000 entries/year. Winners and judges for most recent contest listed in winners' anthology. Judges are never announced in advance. Winners list available in August for SASE (enclose with poem entries); prizes given in October. Copies of annual prize anthologies available from Amy Jo Zook, contest treasurer (3520 State Route 56, Mechanicsburg OH 43044) for $9 plus postage (prices can differ from year to year). "Ohio Poetry Day is the umbrella. Individual contests are sponsored by poetry organizations and/or individuals across the state. OPD sponsors one, plus Poet of the Year and Student Poet of the Year; have four memorial funds." Join mailing list at any time by sending contact information by postcard or letter. Advice: "Revise, follow rules, look at individual categories for a good match."

$◉ OHIOANA POETRY AWARD (Helen and Laura Krout Memorial) (Specialized: native & resident OH authors)

Ohioana Library Association, 274 E. First Ave., Suite 300, Columbus OH 43201. (614)466-3831. Fax: (614)728-6974. E-mail: ohioana@SLOMA.state.oh.us. Web site: www.ohioana.org. **Contact:** Linda Hengst, executive director. Offers annual Ohioana Book Awards. Up to 6 awards may be given for books (including books of poetry) by authors born in Ohio or who have lived in Ohio for at least 5 years. The Ohioana Poetry Award of $1,000 (with the same residence requirements), made possible by a bequest of Helen Krout, is given yearly "to an individual whose body of published work has made, and continues to make, a significant contribution to poetry, and through whose work as a writer, teacher, administrator, or in community service, interest in poetry has been developed." **Deadline:** nominations to be received by December 31. Competition receives several hundred entries. 2006 award winners were George Bilgere (poetry award) and Elton Glaser (book award/poetry). *Ohioana Quarterly* regularly reviews books by Ohio authors and is available through membership in Ohioana Library Association ($25/year).

$◪ THE ONTARIO PRIZE

Black Lawrence Press, P.O. Box 9, Watertown NY 13601. E-mail: info@blacklawrencepress.com. Web site: www.blacklawrencepress.com. Established 2003. **Contact:** Colleen Ryor, editor. The Ontario Prize is awarded annually for an unpublished collection of poetry or short stories. Winner receives $1,000, publication, 10 author copies, and an interview in *The Adirondack Review* (see separate listing in Magazines/Journals). Finalists and semifinalists will receive a copy of the winning book. All finalists will be considered for standard publication. Accepts simultaneous submissions, but notify immediately if ms is accepted elsewhere. Submit book-length ms, paginated, with cover letter with brief bio and contact information (including valid e-mail), table of contents, and an acknowledgments page (if applicable). "Finalists will be notified and asked to submit another copy of the manuscript for final judging." Include two cover pages: one with ms title, brief bio, and poet's contact information (including e-mail); the second with ms title only. Clip together the cover letter, cover pages, acknowledgments, and entry fee. No e-mail submissions. Include SASE or e-mail address for results only; mss will not be returned. Guidelines available on Web site. **Entry fee:** $25. Make checks/money orders payable to Black Lawrence Press. **Deadline:** February 28.

$☑ THE ORPHIC PRIZE FOR POETRY

Dream Horse Press, P.O. Box 2080, Aptos CA 95001-2080. E-mail: dreamhorsepress@yahoo.com. Web site: www.dreamhorsepress.com. Established 1999. **Contact:** J.P. Dancing Bear, editor/publisher. The Orphic Prize for Poetry offers an annual award of $1,000 and publication of a book-length ms by Dream Horse Press. All entries will be considered for publication. Both free and formal verse styles are welcome. Submissions may be entered in other contests, "but if your manuscript is accepted for publication elsewhere, you must notify Dream Horse Press immediately." Submit 48-80 pages of poetry, paginated, with table of contents, acknowledgments, and bio. Include separate cover letter with poet's name, biographical information, and e-mail address (when available). Poet's name should not appear anywhere on the ms. Manuscripts will be recycled after judging. Guidelines available on Web site. **Entry fee:** $25/ms entered. Entry fees are non-refundable. Make checks/money orders payable to Dancing Bear. **Deadline:** October 31 for 2007; check Web site for deadlines and details for subsequent years. 2006 winner was Gaylord Brewer (*The Martini Diet*). Judge: judging will be anonymous.

$☑ THE PATERSON POETRY PRIZE

Poetry Center, Passaic County Community College, One College Blvd., Paterson NJ 07505-1179. (973)684-6555. E-mail: mgillan@pccc.edu. Web site: www.pccc.edu/poetry. Established 1979. **Contact:** Maria Mazziotti Gillan, editor/executive director. The Paterson Poetry Prize offers an annual award of $1,000 for the strongest book of poems (48 or more pages) published in the previous year. The winner will be asked to participate in an awards ceremony and to give a reading at The Poetry Center. Minimum press run: 500 copies. Publishers may submit more than one title for prize consideration; 3 copies of each book must be submitted. Include SASE for results; books will not be returned (all entries will be donated to the Poetry Center Library). Guidelines and application form (required) available for SASE or on Web site. **Entry fee:** none. **Deadline:** February 1 (postmark). Winners will be announced in *Poets & Writers Magazine* and on Web site. 2006 winner was Luis J. Rodriguez (*My Nature is Hunger*).

$☑ PAVEMENT SAW PRESS CHAPBOOK AWARD

P.O. Box 6291, Columbus OH 43206-0291. E-mail: info@pavementsaw.org. Web site: www.pavementsaw.org. Established 1992. **Contact:** David Baratier, editor. Pavement Saw Press Chapbook Award offers $500, publication, and 50 author copies. Open to all poets regardless of previous publication history. Submit up to 32 pages of poetry. Include signed cover letter with poet's name, address, phone number, e-mail, publication credits, a brief biography, and ms title. Also include 2 cover sheets: one with poet's contact information and ms title, one with the ms title only. Do not put poet's name on mss pages except for first title page. No mss will be returned. Guidelines available for SASE or on Web site. **Entry fee:** $12. "Every entrant will receive the equivalent cost of the entry fee in Pavement Saw Press titles." Make checks payable to Pavement Saw Press. **Deadline:** December 30 (entries must be postmarked by this date to be eligible). 2006 winner was Joshua Corey (*Composition Marble*).

$☑ PEARL POETRY PRIZE

Pearl Editions, 3030 E. Second St., Long Beach CA 90803-5163. (562)434-4523 or (714)968-7530. E-mail pearlmag@aol.com. Web site: www.pearlmag.com. Established 1974. **Contact:** Joan Jobe

Smith, Marilyn Johnson, and Barbara Hauk, poetry editors. The annual Pearl Poetry Prize awards $1,000, publication, and 25 author's copies for a book-length ms. Guidelines available for SASE or on Web site. **Entry fee:** $20 (includes a copy of the winning book). **Deadline:** submit May 1-July 15 only. 2006 winner was Kevin Griffith (*Denmark, Kangaroo, Orange*). 2007 judge: David Hernandez.

$☐ ◎ JUDITH SIEGEL PEARSON AWARD (Specialized: subject concerning women)

Wayne State University/Family of Judith Siegel Pearson, 5057 Woodward Ave., Suite 9408, Detroit MI 48202. (313)577-2450. Fax: (313)577-8618. E-mail: rhonda@wayne.edu. **Contact:** Rhonda Agnew, competition coordinator. Offers an annual award of up to $250 for the best creative or scholarly work on a subject concerning women. The type of work accepted rotates each year: essays in 2006; fiction in 2007; drama and nonfictional prose in 2008; poetry in 2009; essays in 2010. Open to all interested writers and scholars. Submissions must be unpublished. Submit 4-10 poems (20 pages maximum). Guidelines available for SASE or by fax or e-mail. **Deadline:** March 1.

$◎ PEN CENTER USA LITERARY AWARD IN POETRY (Specialized: writers living west of the Mississippi)

PEN Center USA, % Antioch University Los Angeles, 400 Corporate Pointe, Culver City CA 90230. (310)862-1555, ext. 361. Fax: (310)862-1556. E-mail: awards@penusa.org. Web site: www.penusa. org. **Contact:** Awards Coordinator. Offers annual $1,000 cash award to a book of poetry professionally published during the previous calendar year. Open to writers living west of the Mississippi. Submit 4 copies of the entry. Entry form and guidelines available for SASE, by fax, e-mail, or on Web site. **Entry fee:** $35. **Deadline:** December 14. 2006 winner was Brian Turner for *Here, Bullet* (Alice James Books). 2006 judges: Terry Wolverton, Elena Karina Byrne, and Sholeh Wolpe. Winner will be announced in the summer and honored at a ceremony in Los Angeles in November.

$⟁ PENNSYLVANIA POETRY SOCIETY ANNUAL CONTEST

E-mail: pps_contest_chair@hotmail.com. Web site: www.geocities.com/paperlesspoets/contests.h tml. **Contact:** Steve Concert, Contest Chair, 6 Kitchen Ave., Harvey's Lake PA 18618. Offers annual contest with Grand Prize awards of $100, $50, and $25; other categories offer $25, $15, and $10. May enter 5 poems for Grand Prize at $2 each for members and nonmembers alike. Also offers prizes in other categories of $25, $15, and $10 (one entry/category); only one poem accepted in each of remaining categories. A total of 18 categories open to all, 4 categories for members only. Guidelines available for SASE or on Web site. **Entry fee:** for members entering categories 1-22, $5 inclusive; for nonmembers entering categories 2-18, $2 each. **Deadline:** January 15. Also offers: 1) *The Pegasus Contest* for PA students only, grades 5-12. Guidelines available for SASE (to Marilyn Downing, Pegasus Contest Chair, 137 Apple Lane, Hershey PA 17033) or on Web site. **Deadline:** February 1. 2) *Carlisle Poets Contest* open to all poets. Guidelines available for SASE (to Joy Campbell, Contest Chair 10 Polecat Rd., Landisburg PA 17040) or on Web site. **Deadline:** October 31. The Society publishes a quarterly newsletter, *Penns to Paper*, with member poetry and challenges, plus an annual soft-cover book of prize poems from the annual contest. Winning Pegasus Contest poems are published in a booklet sent to schools. PPS membership dues: $17/fiscal year. Make checks payable to PPS, Inc., mail to Steven Concert, Membership Liaison, 6 Kitchen Ave., Harvey's Lake PA 18618.

$⟁ ◎ PERUGIA PRESS PRIZE (Specialized: first or second poetry book by a woman)

P.O. Box 60364, Florence MA 01062. E-mail: info@perugiapress.com. Web site: www.perugiapress. com. Established 1997. **Contact:** Susan Kan, director. The Perugia Press Prize for a first or second poetry book by a woman offers $1,000 and publication. Poet must be a living U.S. resident with no more than one previously published book of poems (chapbooks don't count). Submissions must be unpublished as a collection, but individual poems may have been previously published in journals, chapbooks, and anthologies. Considers simultaneous submissions if notified of acceptance elsewhere. Submit 48-72 pages (white paper) "with legible typeface, pagination, and fastened with a removable clip. No more than one poem per page." Two cover pages required: one with ms title, poet's name, address, telephone number, and e-mail address; and one with ms title only. Include table of contents and acknowledgments page. No e-mail submissions. No translations or self-published books. Multiple submissions accepted if accompanied by separate entry fee for each. Include SASE for winner notification only; mss will be recycled. Guidelines available on Web site. **Entry fee:** $20. Make checks payable to Perugia Press. **Deadline:** submit August 1-November 15 (postmark). "Use USPS only, not FedEx or UPS." Winner announced by April 1 by e-mail or SASE (if included with entry). Judges: panel of Perugia authors, booksellers, scholars, etc.

$⊘ THE RICHARD PETERSON POETRY PRIZE

Dept. of English, Mail Code 4503, Faner Hall 2380, Southern Illinois University Carbondale, 1000 Faner Dr., Carbondale IL 62901. Web site: www.siu.edu/~crborchd. Established 1995. **Contact:** Jon Tribble, managing editor. The Richard Peterson Poetry Prize offers $1,500 plus publication in the Winter/Spring issue of *Crab Orchard Review* (see separate listing in Magazines/Journals). "Submissions must be unpublished original work not under consideration elsewhere, written in English by a U.S. citizen or permanent resident. Name, address, telephone number, and/or e-mail address should appear only on the title page of manuscript; author's name should not appear on any subsequent pages. Mark 'poetry' on outside of envelope. Include #10 SASE for notification of winners." See guidelines for complete formatting instructions. Guidelines available for SASE or on Web site. **Entry fee:** $15/entry (1-5 pages, no more than one poem per page; poet may submit up to 3 separate entries if not entering the fiction or nonfiction categories of the contest). Each fee entitles entrant to a one-year subscription, extension of current subscription, or gift subscription to *Crab Orchard Review*; indicate choice and include complete address. Make checks payable to *Crab Orchard Review*. **Deadline:** see guidelines or check Web site.

$⊘ ◎ JAMES D. PHELAN AWARD (Specialized: CA-born writers ages 20-35)

% Intersection for the Arts, 446 Valencia St., San Francisco CA 94103. (415)626-2787. Fax: (415)626-1636. Web site: www.theintersection.org. Established 1935. **Contact:** Awards Coordinator. The James D. Phelan Award offers $2,000 to the author of an unpublished work-in-progress of fiction (novel or short stories), nonfictional prose, poetry, or drama. Applicants must be California-born (although they may now reside outside of the state), and must be between the ages of 20 and 35 as of the March 31deadline. Guidelines and entry form (required) available on Web site. **Entry fee:** none. **Deadline:** March 31. Competition receives 150-180 entries. 2006 winner was Akemi Johnson (fiction, "Assigned to Okinawa").

$⊘ ◎ PINEWOOD HAIKU CONTEST

Wisteria, P.O. Box 150932, Lufkin TX 75915-0932. E-mail: wisteriajournal@gmail.com. (inquiries only). Web site: www.wistaria.blogspot.com. Established 2006. **Contact:** T.A. Thompson, founder. The annual Pinewood Haiku Contest offers 1st Prize: $100; 2nd Prize: $50; 3rd Prize: $25. Winners will be published in the April issue of *Wisteria: A Journal of Haiku, Senryu, and Tanka*. For contemporary English-language haiku; no rules as to syllable or line count. Submissions must be unpublished. Submit 2 copies of each haiku, typed, on a 3×5 index card. One card only should include the poet's name, address, and e-mail for contact purposes. Only one haiku/card. No e-mail submissions. Guidelines available for SASE or on Web site. **Entry fee:** $2/poem or 3 poems for $5; 3 poems maximum, cash or money order only, no checks. Make money orders payable to T.A. Thompson. **Deadline:** accepts entries November 1-February 14. Winners will be notified by e-mail and postal mail; no SASE required.

$✎ POETIC LICENSE CONTEST

Mkashef Enterprises, P.O. Box 688, Yucca Valley CA 92286-0688. E-mail: alayne@inetworld.net. Web site: www.asidozines.com. Established 1998. **Contact:** Alayne Gelfand, poetry editor. Offers biannual poetry contest with awards of 1st Prize: $500; 2nd Prize: $100; 3rd Prize: $40; plus publication in anthology and one copy. Five honorable mentions receive one copy; other poems of exceptional interest will also be included in the anthology. Themes and deadlines available for SASE. Submit any number of poems, any style, of up to 50 lines/poem (poems may have been previously published). Include name, address, and phone number on each poem. Enclose a SASE for notification of winners. Accepts e-mail (as attachment or pasted into body of message), disk, or postal mail submissions. "Judges prefer original, accessible, and unforced works." Guidelines available for SASE or by e-mail. **Entry fee:** $1/poem. **Deadline:** available for SASE or by e-mail. "We're looking for fresh word usage and surprising imagery. Please keep in mind that our judges prefer non-rhyming poetry. Each contest seeks to explode established definitions of the theme being spotlighted. Be sure to send SASE or e-mail for current theme and deadline."

$✎ POETRY 2008 INTERNATIONAL POETRY COMPETITION

Atlanta Review, P.O. Box 8248, Atlanta GA 31106. E-mail: dan@atlantareview.com. (inquiries only). Web site: www.atlantareview.com. Established 1994. **Contact:** Dan Veach, editor/publisher. *Atlanta Review* (see separate listing in Magazines/Journals) sponsors an annual international poetry competition, offering $2,008 Grand Prize, 20 International Publication Awards (winners will be published in *Atlanta Review*), and 30 International Merit Awards (includes certificate, Honorable Mention in *Atlanta Review*, and free issue). Poems must not have been published in a nationally distributed print publication. Put your name and address on each page (e-mail and phone optional). Include SASE for results only (outside of U.S., SAE only, no IRC required); no entries will be returned. Guidelines available on Web site. **Entry fee:** $5 for the first poem, $3 for each additional poem. Make checks payable to *Atlanta Review*. "Checks in your national currency are acceptable at the current exchange rate. We also accept uncancelled stamps from your country." **Deadline:** during May (check Web site for specific date). Winners will be announced in August; Contest Issue published in October. Contest Issue available for $4, or free with $10 subscription to *Atlanta Review*.

❖ $✎ THE POETRY CENTER BOOK AWARD

1600 Holloway Ave., San Francisco CA 94132. (415)338-2227. Fax: (415)338-0966. E-mail: poetry@sfsu.edu. Web site: www.sfsu.edu/~poetry. Established 1980. **Contact:** Elise Ficarra, business manager. Offers award to an outstanding book of poems published by an individual author in the current year. Awards one prize of $500 and an invitation to read at The Poetry Center. Books by a single author; no collaborative works, anthologies, or translations. Must be published and copyrighted during year of contest. Publisher, author, or reader may submit entries. **Entry fee:** $10. **Deadline:** July 1-January 31 annually (e.g., entries published during 2008 will be accepted up until January 31, 2009). Competition receives 200-250 entries annually. 2005 winner was Dara Wier (*Reverse Rapture*, Verse Press). Winner will be announced on Web site and through press release. "The Poetry Center and American Poetry Archives at San Francisco State University were established in 1954. Its archives include the largest circulating tape collection of writers reading their own work in the United States."

$✎ ◎ THE POETRY COUNCIL OF NORTH CAROLINA ANNUAL POETRY CONTEST
(Specialized: NC residents or anyone with NC connection)

Web site: www.ncneighbors.com. (choose Arts/Culture from directory, then Poetry Council of North Carolina). **Contact:** check Web site for current contact information. The Poetry Council of North Carolina is "an organization whose sole purpose is to sponsor annual adult and student poetry contests and to publish the winning poems in our book, *Bay Leaves*. There is no membership fee. All winners are invited to read their poems at Poetry Day in the fall of each year, either late September or early October." Open to residents and anyone with a "North Carolina connection" (persons born in NC, transients from other states who either attend school or work in NC, and NC residents temporarily out of state). Offers 4 adult and 2 student contests with prizes ranging from $10 to $25; all winning poems plus Honorable Mentions will be published in *Bay Leaves* (50 + pages, perfect-bound). Guidelines available for SASE or on Web site. **Entry fee:** $3/poem, one poem/contest. **Deadline:** see Web site. Competition receives 200 + entries/year. Winners list available for SASE, also appears in *Bay Leaves* and on Web site. Copies of *Bay Leaves* available from Poetry Council of North Carolina. "Please read the guidelines carefully. Send only your best work. You can enter only one poem in each contest."

⊠ $☐ POETRY IN PRINT CONTEST

P.O. Box 30981, Albuquerque NM 87190-0981. Phone/fax: (505)888-3937. Established 1991. **Contact:** Robert G. English, award director. Offers annual award of 1st Prize: $1,000; 2nd Prize: Poetry Portfolio; and 3rd Prize: First Draft Manuscript; 1st, 2nd, 3rd, and Honorable Mention receive award plaques. Submissions may be previously published and may be entered in other contests. Submit unlimited number of poems, on any topic, 60 lines total. Include name and telephone number on each page of submission. Include SASE for notification of winners. Guidelines available for SASE or by fax. **Entry fee:** $10. **Deadline:** August 1. Judge: Robert G. English. Winners announced September 1. "Think TRUTH. I like humanitarian, although I accept any subject."

$☑ POETRY SOCIETY OF AMERICA AWARDS

Poetry Society of America, 15 Gramercy Park, New York NY 10003. (212)254-9628. E-mail: psa@poetrysociety.org. Web site: www.poetrysociety.org. Offers the following awards **open to PSA members only**: *The Writer Magazine/Emily Dickinson Award* ($250, for a poem inspired by Dickinson though not necessarily in her style); *Cecil Hemley Memorial Award* ($500, for a lyric poem that addresses a philosophical or epistemological concern); *Lyric Poetry Award* ($500, for a lyric poem on any subject); *Lucille Medwick Memorial Award* ($500, for an original poem in any form on a humanitarian theme); *Alice Fay Di Castagnola Award* ($1,000 for a manuscript-in-progress of poetry or verse-drama). The following awards are **open to both PSA members and nonmembers**: *Louise Louis/Emily F. Bourne Student Poetry Award* ($250, for the best unpublished poem by a student in grades 9-12 from the U.S.); *George Bogin Memorial Award* ($500, for a selection of 4-5 poems that use language in an original way to reflect the encounter of the ordinary and the extraordinary and to take a stand against oppression in any of its forms); *Robert H. Winner Memorial Award* ($2,500, to acknowledge original work being done in mid-career by a poet who has not had substantial recognition, open to poets over 40 who have published no more than one book). Entries for the *Norma Farber First Book Award* ($500) and the *William Carlos Williams Award* (purchase prize between $500 and $1,000, for a book of poetry published by a small press, nonprofit, or university press) **must be submitted directly by publishers**. Complete submission guidelines for all awards are available on Web site. **Entry fee:** all of the above contests are free to PSA members; nonmembers pay $15 to enter any or all of contests 6-8; $5 for high school students to enter single entries in the student poetry competition; high school teachers/administrators may submit unlimited number of students' poems (one entry/student) to student poetry award for $20. **Deadline:** submissions accepted October 1-December 21 (postmark). Additional information available on Web site.

$☐ THE POETRY SOCIETY OF VIRGINIA ANNUAL ADULT AND STUDENT CONTESTS

PSV, P.O. Box 35685, Richmond VA 23235. E-mail: contest@poetrysocietyofvirginia.org. (for information only). Web site: www.PoetrySocietyOfVirginia.org. (for rules and guidelines). **Contact:** Contest Chair. Adult contest offers many categories for original, unpublished poems—both specified and unspecified forms and topics. Student contest is school grade-specific. Offers numerous cash prizes (varies by year). Guidelines available for SASE or on Web site (guidelines must be followed). **Entry fee:** $3/poem for adults; no fee for students and PSV members. ("Membership fee of $25 covers entries in all categories and can be sent with entry and membership form, available on Web site or for SASE.") Designate entries as "adult" or "student" and send to Contest Chair at the above address. **Deadline:** January 19 (postmark) annually (Edgar Allan Poe's birthday). Winning entries may be published in a booklet or on the PSV Web site unless author indicates otherwise on each poem entered. "Follow guidelines to ensure inclusion of poem in contest. Always include SASE for any return information."

$ ☑ ◎ THE POETS ON PARNASSUS PRIZE (Specialized: poetry on a medical subject)

The Foundation for Humanities in Medicine/*The Pharos Magazine*, 350 Parnassus Ave., Suite 900, San Francisco CA 94117. (415)759-2121. E-mail: hdwatts@earthlink.net. Web site: http://poetry-and-jazz.com. Established 2000. **Contact:** David Watts, MD; Joan Baranow, PhD, award directors. Offers annual award (although sometimes skips a year). 1st Prize: $500 and publication in *The Pharos*; 2-4 runners-up also published. Submissions must be unpublished; may be entered in other contests. Submit up to 5 pages of poetry on a medical subject, in any form. **Entry fee:** $7.50/entry. **Deadline:** May 15. Competition receives 120 submissions/contest. Recent judges: John Stone and Jack Coulehan. Winners announced in *The Pharos* ("we telephone the winners"). "Poets on Parnassus is a campus organization that brings readings, workshops, and special poetry events to a health sciences campus."

$ ◻ POETS' DINNER CONTEST

2214 Derby St., Berkeley CA 94705-1018. (510)841-1217. **Contact:** Dorothy V. Benson. Contestant must be present to win. Submit 3 anonymous typed copies of original, unpublished poems in not more than 3 of the 8 categories (Humor, Love, Nature, Beginnings & Endings, Spaces & Places, People, Theme (changed annually), and Poet's Choice). Winning poems (Grand Prize, 1st, 2nd, 3rd) are read at an awards banquet and Honorable Mentions are presented. Cash prizes awarded; Honorable Mention receives books. The event is nonprofit. "Since 1927 there has been an annual awards banquet sponsored by the ad hoc Poets' Dinner Committee, currently at Francesco's in Oakland." Guidelines available for SASE. **Entry fee:** none. **Deadline:** January 17. Competition receives about 300 entries. Recent contest winners include Gayle Eleanor (Grand Prize), Connie Post, Andrew MacRae, Ellaraine Lockie, Katie Weaver, Katy Brown, Amy Miller, Ruth Levitan, and David Alpaugh (1st Prizes). 2006 judges: Alan Birkelbach, David Hedges, Rose Ann Spaith, Sandra Lake Lassen, and Maureen Fry. *Remembering*, an anthology of winning poems from the Poet's Dinner over the last 25 years, is available by mail for $10.42 from Dorothy V. Benson at the contest address.

✪ $ ☑ FELIX POLLAK PRIZE IN POETRY

University of Wisconsin Press, Dept. of English, 600 N. Park St., University of Wisconsin, Madison WI 53706. E-mail: rwallace@wisc.edu. Web site: www.wisc.edu/wisconsinpress/index.html. Established 1994. **Contact:** Ronald Wallace, poetry series editor. The annual Felix Pollack Prize in Poetry is one of 2 prizes awarded by the University of Wisconsin Press (see separate listing for the Brittingham Prize in Poetry). Offers $1,000 plus publication, with an additional $1,500 honorarium to cover expenses of a reading in Madison. Submissions must be unpublished as a collection, but individual poems may have been published elsewhere (publication must be acknowledged). Considers simultaneous submissions if notified of selection elsewhere. Submit 50-80 unbound ms pages, typed single-spaced (with double spaces between stanzas) or double-spaced. Clean photocopies are acceptable. Include title page with poet's name, address, and telephone number. No translations. Include SASE for results only; mss will not be returned. Guidelines available for SASE or on Web site. **Entry fee:** $25. **NOTE:** $25 fee applies to consideration of same entry for the Brittingham Prize in Poetry—one fee for 2 contest awards. Make checks/money orders payable to University of Wisconsin Press. **Deadline:** submit September 1-30 (postmark). 2005 Pollak Prize winner was Jennifer Michael Hecht (*Funny*). Qualified readers will screen all mss. Judge: "a distinguished poet who will remain anonymous until the winners are announced in mid-February."

$☑ PORTLANDIA CHAPBOOK CONTEST

The Portlandia Group, PMB 225, 6663 SW Beaverton-Hillsdale Hwy., Portland OR 97225. E-mail: braucher@portlandia.com. Established 1999. **Contact:** Karen Braucher, award director. Offers biennial prize of $200, publication of chapbook, and 30 copies. Submissions must be unpublished as a collection, but individual poems may have been previously published in journals. Submissions may be entered in other contests. Submit 24 pages of poetry with table of contents, acknowledgments, and bio. Include 2 title pages: one with ms title and personal info, the other with ms title only. Include SASE for results only; no mss will be returned. "See guidelines for the year you are submitting." Guidelines available for SASE or by e-mail. **Entry fee:** $12/entry, includes copy of winning chapbook. **Deadline:** March 1 for 2008 (check biennial guidelines). Competition receives about 200 entries/year. Past winners include Judith Taylor, Kurt S. Olsson, Elisa A. Garza, John Surowiecki, Ron Drummond, and John Pursley III. Copies of winning chapbooks ($8, includes shipping) are available from The Portlandia Group.

$☺ A. POULIN, JR. POETRY PRIZE

BOA Editions, Ltd., 260 East Ave., Rochester NY 14604. (585)546-3410. Web site: www.boaeditions .org. Established 1976. **Contact:** Thom Ward, poetry editor. BOA Editions, Ltd. sponsors the annual A. Poulin, Jr. Poetry Prize for a poet's first book. Awards $1,500 and publication. Individual poems may have been previously published; collection may be simultaneously submitted elsewhere. Submit 48-100 pages of poetry. Ms must be paginated consecutively, typed or computer-generated in 11 pt. font; bind with spring clip (no paperclips). Include name, address, and telephone number on cover/title page; Table of Contents; list of acknowledgments; and entry form (available for download on Web site). Multiple entries accepted with separate entry fee for each. No e-mail submissions. Include SASP for notification of receipt and SASE for results. Mss will not be returned. Guidelines available on Web site in May. **Entry fee:** $25. **Deadline:** submit August 1-November 30 annually. 2007 judge: Edward Hirsch. Winner announced in March.

$☑ THE PRAIRIE SCHOONER BOOK PRIZE SERIES

University of Nebraska Press, 201 Andrews Hall, P.O. Box 880334, University of Nebraska, Lincoln NE 68588-0334. (402)472-0911. Fax: (402)472-9771. E-mail: psbookseries2@unl.edu. Web site: http://prairieschooner.unl.edu. Established 1926. **Contact:** Contest Director. The annual *Prairie Schooner* Book Prize Series offers $3,000 and publication of a book-length collection of poetry by the University of Nebraska Press; one runner-up receives $1,000. Individual poems may have been previously published elsewhere. Considers simultaneous submissions if notified immediately of acceptance elsewhere. Submit at least 50 pages of poetry with acknowledgments page (if applicable). Poet's name should not appear on ms pages. Xeroxed copies are acceptable. Bind with rubber band or binder clip only. Include 2 cover pages: one with poet's name, address, phone number, and e-mail address; the other with ms title only. Include SASP for acknowledgment of receipt of ms and #10 SASE for results only; mss will not be returned. Guidelines available for SASE, by e-mail, or on Web site. **Entry fee:** $25. Make checks payable to *Prairie Schooner*. **Deadline:** was January 15-March 15 for 2007. 2006 winner was Paul Guest (*Notes for My Body Double*). Winners announced on Web site by July 1, with results mailed shortly thereafter. (See separate listing for *Prairie Schooner* in Magazines/Journals.)

$☑ THE PSA NATIONAL CHAPBOOK FELLOWSHIPS

Poetry Society of America, 15 Gramercy Park, New York NY 10003. (212)254-9628. E-mail: psa@po etrysociety.org. Web site: www.poetrysociety.org. Established 2002. The PSA National Chapbook Fellowships offer 2 prizes of $1,000 and publication of winning chapbook mss, with distribution by the Poetry Society of America. Open to any U.S. resident who has not published a full-length poetry collection. **(Poets who apply to this contest may not apply to The PSA New York Chapbook Fellowships.)** Does not accept entries by fax or e-mail. Guidelines available for SASE or on Web site. **Entry fee:** $12 for both PSA members and nonmembers. Make checks/money orders payable to Poetry Society of America. **Deadline:** submit October 1-December 21 (postmarked). 2006 winners were Dan Chelotti (*The Eights*) and Maureen Thorson (*Mayport*). Most recent judges: Harryette Mullen and Mark Strand. Additional information available on Web site.

$☑ ◎ THE PSA NEW YORK CHAPBOOK FELLOWSHIPS (Specialized: open to NYC residents only)

Poetry Society of America, 15 Gramercy Park, New York NY 10003. (212)254-9628. E-mail: psa@po etrysociety.org. Web site: www.poetrysociety.org. Established 2002. The PSA New York Chapbook Fellowships offer 2 prizes of $1,000 and publication of each of winning chapbook mss, with distribution by the Poetry Society of America. Open to any New York City resident (in the 5 boroughs) who is 30 or under and has not published a full-length poetry collection. **(Poets who apply to this contest may not apply to The PSA National Chapbook Fellowships.)** Does not accept entries by fax or e-mail. Guidelines available for SASE or on Web site. **Entry fee:** $12 for both PSA members and nonmembers. Make checks/money orders payble to Poetry Society of America. **Deadline:** submit October 1-December 21 (postmarked). 2006 winners were Jessica Fjeld (*On animate life: its profligacy, organ meats, &c*) and Maya Pindyck (*Locket, Master*). Most recent judges: Rae Armantrout and Kevin Young. Additional information available on Web site.

$☑ THE PULITZER PRIZE IN LETTERS

The Pulitzer Prize Office, 709 Journalism, Columbia University, New York NY 10027. (212)854-3841. Fax: (212)854-3342. E-mail: pulitzer@www.pulitzer.org. Web site: www.pulitzer.org. **Contact:** the Pulitzer Prize Board. The Pulitzer Prize for Letters offers 5 prizes of $10,000 and certificate each year, including one for original verse by an American author. Books must have been published in the calendar year preceding the award. Anyone, including the author, may submit a book that's eligible. Submit 4 copies of published books (or galley proofs if book is being published after October 15), completed entry form, one photograph, and one biography. Entry form and guidelines available for SASE, by fax, or on Web site. **Entry fee:** $50. **Deadline:** October 15. Competition receives about 150 entries/year. 2007 poetry winner was Natasha Trethewey for *Native Guard* (Houghton Mifflin). 2007 judges: Cynthia Huntington, Rafael Campo, and Claudia Emerson.

▓ $◎ QWF A.M. KLEIN PRIZE FOR POETRY (Specialized: books by Quebec authors)

Quebec Writers' Federation, 1200 Atwater Ave., Montreal QC H3Z 1X4 Canada. Phone/fax: (514)933-0878. E-mail: admin@qwf.org. Web site: www.qwf.org. **Contact:** Lori Schubert, executive director. Offers annual awards of $2,000 CAD each for poetry, fiction, nonfiction, first book, and translation. Submissions must be previously published. Open to authors "who have lived in Quebec for at least three of the past five years." Submit 4 copies of a book of at least 48 pages. Write for entry form. **Entry fee:** $20 CAD/submission. **Deadline:** May 31 for books published between October 1 and May 15; August 1 for books published between May 15 and September 30 (bound proofs are acceptable; the finished book must be received by September 30). Poetry competition receives approximately 10 entries. 2006 winner was Susan Elmslie (*I, Nadja and Other Poems*). Winners announced in November. "QWF was formed in 1988 to honor and promote literature written in English by Quebec authors.'' QWF also publishes *QWRITE*, ''a newsletter offering information and articles of interest to membership and the broader community.''

$ ⬜ ◎ THE RAIZISS/DE PALCHI TRANSLATION AWARDS (Specialized: Italian poetry translated into English)

The Academy of American Poets, 584 Broadway, Suite 604, New York NY 10012. (212)274-0343. Fax: (212)274-9427. E-mail: jkronovet@poets.org. Web site: www.poets.org. Established 1934. **Contact:** Jennifer Kronovet, awards coordinator. Awarded for outstanding translations of modern Italian poetry into English. A $5,000 book prize and a $20,000 fellowship are awarded in alternate years. Guidelines and entry form available for SASE or on Web site. **Deadline:** see Web site for current deadlines for book and fellowship awards. 2005 book prize winner was John Du Val (*Tales of Trilussa* by Carlo Alberto Salustri). 2005 judges: Geoffrey Brock, Charles Martin, and Michael Palma. 2004 fellowship winner was Ann Snodgrass (*Selected Poems of Vittorio Sereni*). 2004 judges: Phillis Levin, Charles Martin, and Michael Palma. Winner announced in January.

Ⓝ $◪ RATTLE POETRY PRIZE

RATTLE, 12411 Ventura Blvd., Studio City CA 91604. (818) 505-6777. E-mail: timgreen@rattle.com. Web site: www.rattle.com. Established 2006. The *RATTLE* Poetry Prize awards 1st Prize of $5,000, plus ten $100 Honorable Mentions. Additional entries may be offered publication as well. Open to writers worldwide (see Web site for special international guidelines). Poems must be written in English (no translations). No previously published poems or works accepted for publication elsewhere. No simultaneous submissions. Submit no more than 5 poems/entry. Multiple entries by a single poet accepted; however, each 5-poem group must be treated as a separate entry with its own cover sheet and entry fee. Include cover sheet with poet's name, address, e-mail address, phone number, and poem titles. No contact information should appear on poems. Include SASE for results only; no poems will be returned. **Note:** Poems also may be entered through online submission on Web site. Guidelines available by e-mail or on Web site. **Entry fee:** $16; includes one-year subscription to *RATTLE* (see separate listing in Magazines/Journals). Make checks/money orders payable to *RATTLE* (for credit card entries, see Web site). **Deadline:** August 1 (postmark). 2006 winner was Sophia Rivkin (''Conspiracy''). Judge: editors of *RATTLE* in blind review. Winners announced in September.

$◎ MARGARET REID POETRY CONTEST FOR TRADITIONAL VERSE

Tom Howard Books, % Winning Writers, 351 Pleasant St., PMB 222, Northampton MA 01060-3961. (866)946-9748. Fax: (413)280-0539. E-mail: johnreid@mail.qango.com. Web site: www.winningwriters.com. Established 2004. **Contact:** John Reid, award director. Offers annual award of 1st Prize: $1,000; 2nd Prize: $400; 3rd Prize: $200; 7 High Distinction Awards of $100 each; 10 Highly Commended Awards of $70 each; and 30 Commended Awards of $50 each. The top 10 entries will be published on the Winning Writers Web site. Submissions may be published or unpublished, may have won prizes elsewhere, and may be entered in other contests. Submit poems in traditional verse forms, such as sonnets, ballads, odes, blank verse, and haiku. No limit on number of lines or number of poems submitted. No name on ms pages; type or computer-print on letter-size white paper, single-sided. Guidelines available for SASE or on Web site. Submit online or by mail. **Entry fee:** $6 USD for every 25 lines (exclude poem title and any blank lines from count). **Deadline:** November 15-June 30. 2006 winner was Susan Keith (''Remembrance''). 2006 judges: John H. Reid and Dee C. Konrad. Winners announced in September at WinningWriters.com; entrants who provide valid e-mail addresses also receive notification.

$⬜ ◎ RHYME TIME POETRY CONTEST (Specialized: rhymed poetry)

Shadow Poetry, 1209 Milwaukee St., Excelsior Springs MO 64024. Fax: (208)977-9114. E-mail: shadowpoetry@shadowpoetry.com. Web site: www.shadowpoetry.com. Established 2000. **Con-**

tact: James Summers, award director. Offers quarterly awards of 1st Prize: $50; 2nd Prize: $25; 3rd Prize: $10; plus top 3 winners also receive a certificate, printed copy of winning poem, and a ribbon. Submissions may be previously published. Submit unlimited number of poems of 4-28 lines each, on any subject. **All poems must rhyme.** "Entry form must be present with mail-in entries. Submit entries in duplicate with name, address, phone number, and e-mail address (when available) on upper left-hand corner of one sheet. Enclose #10 SASE for winner's list and an additional SASE for entry receipt (optional). If no SASE is included for receipt, Shadow Poetry will e-mail an entry confirmation to the contestant, if applicable." Entry form and guidelines available for SASE, by fax, or on Web site. **Entry fee:** $2/poem. Make checks/money orders payable to Shadow Poetry. **Deadline:** March 31, June 30, September 30, and December 31. Winners will be announced 30 days after each quarterly contest ends by e-mail and to those who requested a winner's list with SASE. Results also will be posted on the Shadow Poetry Web site.

$🖉 RIVERSTONE POETRY CHAPBOOK AWARD

Riverstone, A Press for Poetry, P.O. Box 1421, Carefree AZ 85377. Established 1992. Web site: www.riverstonepress.org. **Contact:** Margaret Holley, editor. The Riverstone Poetry Chapbook Award offers $100, publication, and 50 copies to the winner. Submissions may include previously published poems; consideres simultaneous submissions. Submit chapbook ms of 16-24 pages of poetry; include "poems in their proposed arrangement, title page, table of contents, and acknowledgments. All styles welcome." Accepts multiple entries with separate entry fees. Include SASE for contest results; no mss will be returned. Guidelines available for SASE or on Web site. **Entry fee:** $10. "All entrants will receive a copy of the most recent winning chapbook." **Deadline:** check Web site. Order sample chapbooks by sending $5 plus $1 shipping.

🔘 ROANOKE-CHOWAN POETRY AWARD (Specialized: NC resident authors)

The North Carolina Literary & Historical Association, 4610 Mail Service Center, Raleigh NC 27699-4610. (919)807-7290. Fax: (919)733-8807. E-mail: michael.hill@ncmail.net. Web site: www.ah.dcr.state.nc.us/affiliates/lit-hist/awards/awards.htm. **Contact:** Michael Hill, awards coordinator. Offers annual award for "an original volume of poetry published during the 12 months ending June 30 of the year for which the award is given." Open to "authors who have maintained legal or physical residence, or a combination of both, in North Carolina for the three years preceding the close of the contest period." Submit 3 copies of each entry. Guidelines available for SASE or by fax or e-mail. **Deadline:** July 15. Competition receives about 15 entries. 2006 winner was James Applewhite (*Selected Poems*). Winner announced by mail October 15.

$🖉 🔘 BEULLAH ROSE POETRY PRIZE (Specialized: poetry by women)

P.O. Box 22161, Baltimore MD 21203. E-mail: cbanks@smartishpace.com. Web site: www.smartishpace.com. Established 1999. **Contact:** Clare Banks, associate editor. The annual Beullah Rose Poetry Prize for exceptional poetry by women offers 1st Prize: $200 and publication of the winning poem in *Smartish Pace* (see separate listing in Magazines/Journals); 2nd and 3rd Prizes: winning poems will be published in *Smartish Pace*. Winners also receive additional Internet and advertising exposure. Submit 3 poems, with poet's name, address, e-mail, telephone number (preferred), and "Beulah Rose Poetry Prize" at the top of each page of poetry submitted. Include bio. Entries may be submitted online or by e-mail (as attachment) or regular mail. Include SASE with postal entries. Guidelines available on Web site. **Entry fee:** $5 for 3 poems; additional poems may be submitted for $1/poem (12 poem maximum). Make checks/money orders payable to *Smartish Pace*. **Deadline:** November 1. Judges: Clare Banks and Traci O'Dea, associate editors.

$🖰 ERNEST SANDEEN PRIZE IN POETRY

Dept. of English, University of Notre Dame, Notre Dame IN 46556-5639. (574)631-7526. Fax: (574)631-4795. E-mail: creativewriting@nd.edu. Web site: www.nd.edu/~ndr/sandeen.html. Established 1994. **Contact:** Director of Creative Writing. The Sandeen Prize in Poetry offers $1,000 (a $500 award and a $500 advance against royalties from the Notre Dame Press) and publication of a book-length ms. Open to poets who have published at least one volume of poetry. "Please include a photocopy of the copyright and the title page of your previous volume. Vanity press publications do not fulfill this requirement. We will pay special attention to second volumes. Please include a vita and/or a biographical statement that includes your publishing history. We will be glad to see a selection of reviews of the earlier collection." Submit 2 copies of ms (inform if ms is available on computer disk). Include SASE for acknowledgment of receipt of ms and SASE for return of ms. **Entry fee:** $15; includes one-year subscription to *Notre Dame Review* (see separate listing in Magazines/Journals). Make checks payable to University of Notre Dame. **Deadline:** submit May 1-September 1. 2007 winner was Jude Nutter (*The Curator of Silence*). Winners announced by the end of January.

$◙ SAWTOOTH POETRY PRIZE

Ahsahta Press, MS1525, 1910 University Dr., Boise State University, Boise ID 83725-1525. (208)426-2195. Fax: (208)426-4373. E-mail: ahsahta@boisestate.ed. Web site: http://ahsahtapress.boisestate .edu. The Sawtooth Poetry Prize, sponsored by Ahsahta Press (see separate listing in Books/Chapbooks), honors a book of original poetry in English by a single author. Offers a $1,500 honorarium upon publication and 25 author's copies. Translations are not eligible for this award. "Students and former students of Boise State University and of this year's judge may not enter; close friends of the judge are also not considered eligible." Accepts simultaneous submissions, "but entrants are asked to notify Ahsahta Press immediately if a manuscript becomes committed elsewhere." Submit 48-100 pages of poetry, single-spaced, printed on one side of $8\frac{1}{2} \times 11$ or A4 page only. Number pages consecutively. Include acknowledgments page and biographical note, which will be removed before judging. Include two title pages: one with poet's name, address, phone number, and e-mail address (if available); and one without. Poet's name should not appear anywhere else on ms; only the anonymous title page will be sent to the readers and judge. Contain pages in a plain manila folder or bind manuscript with a secure clip; do not bind ms in a notebook. Include SASP for notification of receipt of ms and SASE (#10 business) for results; mss will not be returned. Guidelines available on Web site. **Entry fee:** $25/ms. Make checks payable to Ahsahta Press. (See Web site for payment options outside the U.S.) "Entrants will receive a copy of the winning book when it is printed if they include a 7×10 self-addressed mailer with $3.95 postage. Our books measure 6×8 and will not fit in smaller-sized mailers." **Deadline:** submit January 1-March 1 (postmark). "In addition to announcements in national publications, the winning book and author will be featured on the Ahsahta Web site, as will lists of finalists and semi-finalists." 2006 winner was Paige Ackerson-Kiely (*In No One's Land*). 2008 judge: C.D. Wright. "Ahsahta Press, a member of the Council of Literary Magazines and Presses, conforms to the CLMP Code of Ethics and participated in its drafting."

$◙ ◎ HELEN SCHAIBLE SHAKESPEAREAN/PETRARCHAN SONNET CONTEST

Poets' Club of Chicago, 1212 S. Michigan Ave., Apt. 2702, Chicago IL 60605. **Contact:** Tom Roby, president and contest chair. The annual Helen Schaible Shakespearean/Petrarchan Sonnet Contest is open to anyone. **For sonnets only!** Offers 1st Prize: $50; 2nd Prize: $35; 3rd Prize: $15; plus 3 Honorable Mentions and 3 Special Recognitions (non-cash). Submit only one entry (2 copies) of either a Shakespearean or a Petrarchan sonnet, which must be original and unpublished. Entry must be typed on $8\frac{1}{2} \times 11$ paper, double-spaced. Name and address in the upper right-hand corner on only one copy. All necessary guidelines appear in this listing. Include SASE with entry to receive winners' list. **Entry fee:** none. **Deadline:** September 1 (postmark). Competition receives 150 entries/year. 2006 contest winners were Larry Turner, Greg Hagan, and Alice Rasmussen Nichols. Winners will be notified by mail by October 31. The Poets' Club of Chicago meets monthly at

Chicago's Chopin Theater to critique their original poetry, which the members read at various venues in the Chicago area and publish in diverse magazines and books. Members also conduct workshops at area schools and libraries by invitation. "Read the guidelines—one sonnet only!"

$□ ◎ MONA SCHREIBER PRIZE FOR HUMOROUS FICTION & NONFICTION

15442 Vista Haven Place, Sherman Oaks CA 91403. E-mail: brashcyber@pcmagic.net. Web site: www.brashcyber.com. Established 2000. **Contact:** Brad Schreiber. Offers annual awards of 1st Prize: $500; 2nd Prize: $250; 3rd Prize: $100. All winners are posted on Web site and receive a copy of *What Are You Laughing At?: How to Write Funny Screenplays, Stories & More* by Brad Schreiber. Submissions must be unpublished and may be entered in other contests. Submit any number of poems, 750 words maximum/poem. Include contact information on each poem submitted. Guidelines available on Web site. **Entry fee:** $5/poem. **Deadline:** December 1 annually. Competition receives 340-350 entries/year. Judge: Brad Schreiber. Winners announced December 24 by phone (if U.S. and Canada) or by e-mail. "Take risks in form, content, theme, and language."

$□ ◎ CLAUDIA ANN SEAMAN POETRY AWARD (Specialized: students grades 9-12)

The Community Foundation of Dutchess County, 80 Washington St., Suite 201, Poughkeepsie NY 12601. (845)452-3077. Fax: (845)452-3083. Web site: www.CFDCNY.org. **Contact:** Nevill Smythe, Vice President/Programs. Established 1983. Annual national contest offering award of $500 (1st Prize). Open to U.S. students grades 9-12. Submissions must be unpublished but may be entered in other contests. Submit 1-2 unpublished poems on any subject, in any form. "Entry must contain student and school names, addresses, and phone numbers and the name of the English or writing teacher." Entry guidelines available on Web site. **Entry fee:** none. **Deadline:** June 1. Winner contacted by phone or in writing. Copies of last year's winning poem may be obtained by contacting the Community Foundation by phone, in writing, or on Web site. "The Community Foundation is a nonprofit organization serving Dutchess and Ulster County, New York, and the surrounding area; it administers numerous grant programs, scholarship funds, and endowment funds for the benefit of the community. This is an excellent opportunity for young, previously unpublished poets to earn recognition for their work. Since there's no fee, there is little to lose; realize, however, that a national contest will have more entries than a regional competition."

$◎ SEASONAL POETRY COMPETITION (Specialized: 4 seasons, holidays)

1209 Milwaukee St., Excelsior Springs MO 64024. Fax: (208)977-9114. E-mail: shadowpoetry@shadowpoetry.com. Web site: www.shadowpoetry.com. Established 2000. **Contact:** James Summers, award director. Offers biannual award of 1st Prize: $100; 2nd prize: $50; 3rd Prize: $25; plus the top 3 winners also receive a certificate, printed copy of winning poem, and a ribbon. Submissions may be previously published. Submit maximum of 10 poems/poet, 30 line limit/poem, must be written on the topics of the 4 seasons (winter, spring, summer, and/or fall) or the holidays (Christmas, Valentine's Day, Easter, etc.), in any form. "Entry form must be present with mail-in entries. Submit entries in duplicate with name, address, phone number, and e-mail address (when available) on upper left-hand corner of one sheet. Enclose #10 SASE for winners list. Include an additional SASE for entry receipt (optional). If no SASE is included for receipt, Shadow Poetry will e-mail an entry confirmation to the contestant, if applicable." Entry form and guidelines available for SASE or on Web site. **Entry fee:** $3/poem. Make checks/money orders payable to Shadow Poetry. **Deadline:** June 30 and December 31. Winners will be announced "30 days after each contest ends, by e-mail and to those who requested a winners list. Results will also be posted on the Shadow Poetry Web site."

$□ SHADOW POETRY'S BIANNUAL CHAPBOOK COMPETITION

Shadows Ink Publications, 1209 Milwaukee St., Excelsior Springs MO 64024. Fax: (208)977-9114. E-mail: shadowpoetry@shadowpoetry.com. Web site: www.shadowpoetry.com. Established 2000.

Contact: James Summers, award director. Offers biannual award of $100, 50 copies of published chapbook, and 25% royalties paid on each copy sold through Shadow Poetry (retail only). Submissions must be unpublished as a whole (collection) and not under consideration elsewhere. (Winning poet retains copyrights and may publish individual poems elsewhere later.) Submit ms of 16-40 pages, acknowledgments, table of contents, poet bio, etc., in addition to the poetry. Poetry to be submitted on any subject, in any form, in good taste. "Cover letter required with name, address, phone, age, and e-mail address. Enclose cover letter, manuscript, and cover ideas/art, if applicable, in #90 (9×12) envelope. Include #10 SASE for winner notification and SASP for entry receipt (optional)." Guidelines available for SASE or on Web site. **Entry fee:** $15/ms. Make checks/money orders payable to Shadow Poetry. **Deadline:** June 30 and December 31. "Notification of winners no later than 30 days after deadline by SASE." Copies of winning or sample chapbooks available from Shadow Poetry for $6.25 (see Web site for titles).

$☐ SHADOWS INK POETRY CONTEST

Shadows Ink Publications, 1209 Milwaukee St., Excelsior Springs MO 64024. Fax: (208)977-9114. E-mail: shadowpoetry@shadowpoetry.com. Web site: www.shadowpoetry.com. Established 2000. **Contact:** James Summers, award director. Offers annual award of 1st Prize: $100 and publication in chapbook (plus 20 copies of published work); 2nd Prize: $75; 3rd Prize: $35; top 3 winners also receive a certificate, printed copy of winning poem, and a ribbon. The top 40 placing poems will be published in a *Shadows Ink Poetry Chapbook*, and all poets appearing in this publication will receive one free copy (additional copies available for $5 each plus shipping). Submissions must be unpublished and not under consideration elsewhere. (Winning poets retain copyrights and may publish poems elsewhere later.) Submit maximum of 10 poems, 24 line limit each, on any subject, in any form. "Entry form must be present with mail-in entries. Submit entries in duplicate with name, address, phone number, and e-mail address (when available) on upper left-hand corner of one sheet. Enclose #10 SASE for winners list. Include an additional SASE for entry receipt (optional). If no SASE is included for receipt, Shadow Poetry will e-mail an entry confirmation to the contestant, if applicable." Entry form and guidelines available for SASE or on Web site. **Entry fee:** $5/poem. Make checks/money orders payable to Shadow Poetry. **Deadline:** December 31. Competition receives 150 entries/year. "Winners will be announced February 1 by e-mail and to those who requested a winners list. Results will also be posted on the Shadow Poetry Web site."

$☑ SLAPERING HOL PRESS CHAPBOOK COMPETITION

300 Riverside Dr., Sleepy Hollow NY 10591-1414. (914)332-5953. Fax: (914)332-4825. E-mail: info@writerscenter.org. Web site: www.slaperingholpress.org. Established 1990. **Contact:** Margo Stever. The Slapering Hol Press Chapbook Competition offers an annual award of $1,000, publication, 10 author's copies, and a reading at The Hudson Valley Writers' Center (see separate listing in Organizations). Open only to poets who have not previously published a book or chapbook. Submit 16-20 pages of poetry (collection or one long poem), any form or style. Manuscript should be anonymous with separate cover sheet containing name, address, phone number, e-mail address, a bio, and acknowledgments. Include SASE for results only; manuscripts will not be returned. Guidelines available for SASE, by fax, e-mail, or on Web site. **Entry fee:** $15. Make checks payable to The Hudson Valley Writers' Center. **Deadline:** May 15. Winner will be announced in September. Competition receives more than 300 entries. 2006 winner was Mary Kaiser (*Falling Into Velázquez*). Winning chapbooks available through Web site andwww.amazon.com.

$☑ SLIPSTREAM POETRY CHAPBOOK CONTEST

Dept. W-1, P.O. Box 2071, Niagara Falls NY 14301-0071. (716)282-2616 (after 5 PM, EST). E-mail: editors@slipstreampress.org. Web site: www.slipstreampress.org. Established 1980. **Contact:** Contest Director. The annual Slipstream Poetry Chapbook Contest awards $1,000, publication of a chapbook ms, and 50 author's copies. All entrants receive copy of winning chapbook and an issue of *Slipstream* (see separate listing in Magazines/Journals). Considers simultaneous submissions if informed of status. Accepts previously published work with acknowledgments. Submit up to 40 pages of poetry, any style, format, or theme. Include SASE with correct postage for return of ms. **Entry fee:** $15. **Deadline:** December 1. Guidelines available for SASE or on Web site. 2006 winner was Terry Godbey (*Behind Every Door*). Winner announced late spring/early summer.

$◎ HELEN C. SMITH MEMORIAL AWARD FOR BEST BOOK OF POETRY (Specialized: TX-born/-resident poets)

Web site: www.smu.edu/english/creativewriting/the_texas_institute_of_letters.htm. Established 1936. The Texas Institute of Letters gives annual awards for books by Texas authors, including the Helen C. Smith Memorial Award for Best Book of Poetry, a $1,200 award. Books must have been first published in the year in question, and entries may be made by authors or by their publishers. Complete guidelines and award information available on Web site. **Deadline:** see Web site. Receives about 30 entries/year. 2006 winner was John Brieuth (*As Long As It's Big*).

$◻ KAY SNOW WRITING AWARDS

Willamette Writers, 9045 SW Barbur Blvd., Suite 5A, Portland OR 97219-4027. (503)452-1592. Fax: (503)452-0372. E-mail: wilwrite@willamettewriters.com. Web site: www.willamettewriters.com. Established 1986. **Contact:** Pat Macaodha, award director. Offers annual awards of 1st Prize: $300; 2nd Prize: $150; 3rd Prize: $50 in several genres, including poetry. Submissions must be unpublished. Submit up to 2 poems (one entry fee), maximum 5 pages total, on any subject, in any style or form, single-spaced, one side of paper only. Entry form and guidelines available for SASE or on Web site. **Entry fee:** $10 for members of Willamette Writers; $15 for nonmembers. **Deadline:** May 15. Competition receives 150 entries. 2006 poetry winners were Patricia Mees Armstrong, Amy Miller, and Amy Alterman. Winners will be announced July 31. "Write and send in your very best poem. Read it aloud. If it still sounds like the best poem you've ever heard, send it in."

⚡ $◻ THE RICHARD SNYDER MEMORIAL PUBLICATION PRIZE

Ashland Poetry Press, 401 College Ave., Ashland University, Ashland OH 44805. (419)289-5979 or (419)289-5110. Web site: www.ashland.edu/aupoetry. Established 1997. **Contact:** Stephen Haven, award director. Offers annual award of $1,000 plus book publication in a paper-only edition of 1,000 copies. Submissions must be unpublished in book form and may be entered in other contests. Submit 50-80 pages of poetry. **Entry fee:** $25. **Deadline:** May 15 annually. Competition receives 350 entries/year. 2004 winner was Christine Gelineau (*Remorseless Loyalty*). Annual judge: Robert Phillips. Winners will be announced in *Writer's Chronicle* and *Poets & Writers*. Copies of winning books available from Small Press Distribution and directly from the Ashland University Bookstore online. The Ashland Poetry Press publishes 2-4 books of poetry/year.

$◻ SOUL-MAKING LITERARY COMPETITION

National League of American Pen Women, Nob Hill, San Francisco Bay Area Branch, 1544 Sweetwood Dr., Colma CA 94015-2029. Phone/fax: (650)756-5279. E-mail: PenNobHill@aol.com. Web site: www.soulmakingcontest.us. Established 1993. **Contact:** Eileen Malone, award director. Annual open contest offers cash prizes in each of 9 literary categories, including poetry and prose poem. 1st Prize: $100; 2nd Prize: $50; 3rd Prize: $25. Submissions in some categories may be previously published. Submit 3 one-page poems on soul-making theme; any form for open poetry category. No names or other identifying information on mss; include 3×5 card with poet's name, address, phone, fax, e-mail, title(s) of work, and category entered. Include SASE for results only; mss will not be returned. Guidelines available on Web site. **Entry fee:** $5/entry. **Deadline:** November 30. Competition receives 300 entries/year. Names of winners and judges are posted on Web site. Winners announced in January by SASE and on Web site. Winners are invited to read at the Koret Auditorium, San Francisco. Event is televised. "National League of American Pen Women is a professional organization of writers, artists, and composers headquartered in Washington, D.C.; includes membership of 6,000. Pen Women are involved in a variety of community arts outreach programs. 'Some say the world is a vale of tears, I say it is a place of soul making.' Use this quote as inspiration."

$ ⬙ THE SOW'S EAR CHAPBOOK COMPETITION

355 Mount Lebanon Rd., Donalds SC 29638-9115. E-mail: errol@kitenet.net. Web site: www.sows-ear.kitenet.net. Established 1988. **Contact:** Errol Hess, managing editor. *The Sow's Ear Poetry Review* (see separate listing in Magazines/Journals) sponsors an annual chapbook competition. Offers $1,000, publication as the Spring issue of the magazine, and 25 author's copies. Open to adults. Accepts simultaneous submissions, "but if your chapbook is accepted elsewhere, you must withdraw promptly from our competition." Poems previously published individually are acceptable if poet holds publication rights. Include SASE or e-mail address for results only; entries will not be returned. Submit 22-26 pages of poetry; no length limit on poems, but no more than one poem on a page. Include title page and table of contents. Poet's name should not appear on poems, title page, or table of contents. Include separate sheet with chapbook title, poet's name, address, phone number, e-mail address (if available), and publication credits for submitted poems, if any. Guidelines available for SASE, by e-mail, or on Web site. **Entry fee:** $20; includes subscription. Make checks payable to *The Sow's Ear Poetry Review*. **Deadline:** May 1 (postmark).

$ ⬙ THE SOW'S EAR POETRY COMPETITION

355 Mount Lebanon Rd., Donalds SC 29638-9115. E-mail: errol@kitenet.net. Web site: www.sows-ear.kitenet.net. Established 1988. **Contact:** Errol Hess, managing editor. *The Sow's Ear Poetry Review* (see separate listing in Magazines/Journals) sponsors an annual contest for unpublished poems. Offers $1,000 and publication in *The Sow's Ear Poetry Review*; also offers the option of publication for top finalists. Submit up to 5 unpublished poems. Include separate sheet with poem titles, poet's name, address, phone number, and e-mail address (if available). "We will check with finalists before sending to final judge." Poet's name should not appear on poems. Include SASE for results only; entries will not be returned. Guidelines available for SASE, by e-mail, or on Web site. **Entry fee:** $20 for up to 5 poems. Contestants receive a year's subscription. Make checks payable to *The Sow's Ear Poetry Review*. **Deadline:** November 1 (postmark). Past judges include Gregory Orr and Elizabeth Spires. "Four criteria help us judge the quality of submissions: 1) Does the poem make the strange familiar or the familiar strange, or both? 2) Is the form of the poem vital to its meaning? 3) Do the sounds of the poem make sense in relation to the theme? 4) Does the little story of the poem open a window on the Big Story of the human situation?"

$ ◻ SPIRE PRESS POETRY CONTEST

532 LaGuardia Place, Suite 298, New York NY 10012. E-mail: editor@spirepress.org. Web site: www.spirepress.org. Established 2002. **Contact:** Shelly Reed, award director. Offers annual award of publication with royalty contract and promotion; sometimes cash prizes (see guidelines for each year). Submissions must be unpublished and may be entered in other contests as long as Spire Press is informed. Submit a chapbook ms of 18-40 pages of poetry in any form (shorter poems preferred). Include SASE. **Entry fee:** $12/ms. **Deadline:** May 1. Competition receives 300 entries/year. 2006 winner was Matthew Hittinger (*Pear Slip*). Winners will be announced on Web site after contest deadline. Copies of winning chapbooks available through Web site, Amazon, selected bookstores, and Spire Press.

$☑ THE ST. LAWRENCE BOOK AWARD

Black Lawrence Press, P.O. Box 9., Watertown NY 13601. E-mail: info@blacklawrencepress.com. Web site: www.blacklawrencepress.com. Established 2003. **Contact:** Colleen Ryor, editor. The St. Lawrence Book Award is presented annually for a first collection of poetry or short stories. Prize includes $1,000, publication, 10 author copies, and an interview with the winner in *The Adirondack Review* (see separate listing in Magazines/Journals). Prizes awarded on publication. Finalists and semifinalists will receive a copy of the winning book. All finalists will be considered for standard publication. "Entrants must not have had a full-length book published. Chapbooks do not count as full-length books." Considers simultaneous submissions, but notify immediately if ms is accepted elsewhere. Submit book-length ms, paginated, with cover letter with brief bio and contact information (including valid e-mail), table of contents, and an acknowledgments page (if applicable). "Finalists will be notified and asked to submit another copy of the manuscript for final judging." Include two cover pages: one with ms title, brief bio, and poet's contact information (including e-mail); the second with ms title only. Clip together the cover letter, cover pages, acknowledgments, and entry fee. No e-mail submissions. Include SASE or e-mail address for results only; mss will not be returned. Guidelines available on Web site. **Entry fee:** $25. Make checks/money orders payable to Black Lawrence Press. **Deadline:** August 31 annually. 2005 winner was Stefi Weisburd (*The Wind-Up Gods*).

$☑ THE WALLACE STEVENS AWARD

The Academy of American Poets, 584 Broadway, Suite 604, New York NY 10012-3210. (212)274-0343. Fax: (212)274-9427. Web site: www.poets.org. Award established 1994. Awards $100,000 annually to recognize outstanding and proven mastery in the art of poetry. **No applications are accepted.** 2006 winner was Michael Palmer. 2006 judges: Robert Hass, Fanny Howe, Susan Stewart, Arthur Sze, and Dean Young.

$☐ STEVENS POETRY MANUSCRIPT CONTEST

22614 N. Santiam Hwy., Lyons OR 97358. E-mail: eberry@wvi.com. Web site: www.nfsps.org. **Contact:** Eleanor Berry, contest chair. National Federation of State Poetry Societies (NFSPS) offers annual award of $1,000, publication of ms, and 50 author's copies. Individual poems may have been previously published in magazines, anthologies, or chapbooks, but not the entire ms as a collection; accepts simultaneous submissions. Submit 35-60 pages of poetry by a single author, typewritten, one poem or column of poetry to a page. Number pages, but no author identification throughout ms. Include 2 cover/title pages; one with no author identification, the other with name of poet, address, phone number, and state poetry society member affiliation, if applicable. No bulky folders or binders; plain manila folder and/or staples permitted. No illustrations. No disk submissions; no certified or registered mail. Include SASE for results only; mss will not be returned. Guidelines available for SASE or on Web site. **Entry fee:** $15 for NFSPS members; $20 for nonmembers. Make checks/money orders payable to NFSPS. **Deadline:** October 15 (postmark). Winners announced in January following deadline; entrants who include a SASE will be notified of winner. Winning ms will be sold at annual NFSPS convention and winning poet (if present) will read from the ms. Copies of winning mss available through NFSPS Web site.

$☑ THE RUTH STONE PRIZE IN POETRY

Vermont College, 36 College St., Montpelier VT 05602. (802)828-8633. Fax: (802)828-8649. E-mail: hungermtn@tui.edu. Web site: www.hungermtn.org. Established 2002. **Contact:** Caroline Mercurio, managing editor. The annual Ruth Stone Prize in Poetry offers $1,000 and publication in *Hunger Mountain: The Vermont College Journal of Arts & Letters* (see separate listing in Magazines/Journals); 2 Honorable Mentions also published. Submit up to 3 poems, not to exceed 6 pages. **Entry fee:** $15 (includes copy of prize issue). **Deadline:** December 10. Guidelines available in magazine, for SASE, by fax, e-mail, or on Web site. "Include SASE and index card with poem titles and address; do not put name on poems."

⬠ ⬡ $⬢ THE DAN SULLIVAN MEMORIAL POETRY CONTEST

The Writers' Circle of Durham Region, Bayly Postal Outlet, Health Rite Pharmacy, P.O. Box 14558, 75 Bayly St. W, Ajax ON L1S 7K7 Canada. (905)686-0211. E-mail: info@wcdr.org. Web site: www.w cdr.org. Established 1995. Sponsored by The Writers' Circle of Durham Region in memory of Dan Sullivan, member and poet who passed away in 1995. Offers annual award in 3 categories. Children: 1st Prize: $45; 2nd Prize: $35; 3rd Prize: $25. Youth: 1st Prize: $45; 2nd Prize: $35; 3rd Prize: $25. Adult: 1st Prize: $300; 2nd Prize: $200; 3rd Prize: $100. Winners published in *The Word Weaver* and on WCDR Web site. Contest open to **international submissions by e-mail only.** Submissions must be unpublished. "Poems may be of any subject matter, type, or style. Length of each entry must not exceed 30 written lines. This may be one poem, or up to 3 short poems whose cumulative total does not exceed 30 lines. There are no limits to the number of entries a person may submit, but each must be submitted separately with the appropriate entry fee." Bios will be solicited from the winners. No e-mail submissions. Entries will not be returned. Guidelines available on Web site. **Entry fee:** $5/entry for adults; free for youth and children. Send money orders to mailing address or pay by PayPal through Web site. **Deadline:** February 15. Competition receives about 200-250 entries/year. 2006 adult winners were Sheila Stewart, Dorothy Sjöholm, and Keith Garebian and Elise Kubsch (tie). Winners announced in June and winning entries posted on Web site. "The Writers' Circle of Durham Region is a nonprofit umbrella organization dedicated to encouraging and promoting the art and skill of writing, fostering literacy, and providing moral support to writers through education and networking, both independently and in cooperation with existing organizations." Advice: "Be original in your writing, but follow the rules when submitting."

$⬢ MAY SWENSON POETRY AWARD

Utah State University Press, Logan UT 84322-7800. (435)797-1362. Fax: (435)797-0313. E-mail: michael.spooner@usu.edu. Web site: www.usu.edu/usupress. Established 1996. **Contact:** Michael Spooner, poetry editor. Utah State University Press publishes poetry books through the annual May Swenson Poetry Award competition only. Has published *Dear Elizabeth* and *May Out West* by May Swenson, *Where She Always Was* by Frannie Lindsay, *The Beautiful Lesson of the I* by Frances Brent, and *Haywire* by George Bilgere. Guidelines available on Web site.

$⬢ LENA-MILES WEVER TODD POETRY SERIES BOOK COMPETITION

Pleiades Press, Dept. of English, Central Missouri State University, Warrensburg MO 64093. (660)543-8106. E-mail: kdp8106@cmsu2.cmsu.edu. Web site: www.cmsu.edu/englphil/pleiades. Established 1990. **Contact:** Kevin Prufer, editor. The annual Lena-Miles Wever Todd Poetry Series Book Competition offers $1,000 and publication of a book-length ms. Open to all American writers, regardless of previous publication. Submission must be unpublished as a collection, but individual poems may have been previously published elsewhere. Submit at least 48 pages of poetry (one copy). Include 2 cover sheets: one with ms title, poet's name, address, and phone number; the second with ms title only. Also include acknowledgments page for previously published poems. Enclose SASE for results; for an additional large SASE with $1.24 postage affixed, entrant will receive a copy of the winning book. Guidelines available for SASE or on Web site. **Entry fee:** $15. Make checks/money orders payable to Pleiades Press. **Deadline:** September 30 (postmark). 2006 winner was Julianna Baggott (*Compulsions of Silk Worms and Bees*). 2007 final judge: James Richardson.

⬠ $⬢ ◎ TOWSON UNIVERSITY PRIZE FOR LITERATURE (Specialized: book MD writer)

Towson University, College of Liberal Arts, Towson MD 21252. (410)704-2128. Fax: (410)704-6392. E-mail: eduncan@towson.edu. Web site: www.towson.edu. **Contact:** Chair of the English Dept.

Offers annual prize of $1,000 "for a single book or book-length manuscript of fiction, poetry, drama, or imaginative nonfiction by a Maryland writer. The prize is granted on the basis of literary and aesthetic excellence as determined by a panel of distinguished judges appointed by the university. The first award, made in the fall of 1980, went to novelist Anne Tyler." Work must have been published within the 3 years prior to the year of nomination or must be scheduled for publication within the year in which nominated. Submit 5 copies of work in bound form or in typewritten, double-spaced ms form. Entry form and guidelines available for SASE or on Web site (search "Towson Prize for Literature"). **Deadline:** June 15. Competition receives 8-10 entries. 2006 winner was Joelle Biele (*White Summer*, Southern Illinois Press).

$☑ TRANSCONTINENTAL POETRY AWARD

Pavement Saw Press, P.O. Box 6291, Columbus OH 43206-0291. E-mail: info@pavementsaw.org. Web site: www.pavementsaw.org. Established 1992. **Contact:** David Baratier, editor. The Transcontinental Poetry Award offers $1,000, publication, and a percentage of the print run for a first book. "Each year, Pavement Saw Press will seek to publish at least one book of poetry and/or prose poems from manuscripts received during this competition, which is open to anyone who has not previously published a volume of poetry or prose. Writers who have had volumes of poetry and/or prose under 40 pages printed, or printed in limited editions of no more than 500 copies, are eligible." Submit 48-70 pages of poetry (one poem/page), paginated and bound with a single clip. Include 2 cover sheets: one with ms title, poet's name, address, phone number, and e-mail, if available, the second with ms title only (this sheet should be clipped to ms). Also include one-page cover letter (a brief biography, ms title, poet's name, address, and telephone number, e-mail, and poet's signature) and acknowledgments page (journal, anthology, chapbook, etc., and poem published). Include SASP for acknowledgment of receipt. SASE unnecessary as result will be sent with free book and no mss will be returned. Guidelines available for SASE or on Web site. **Entry fee:** $18. "All U.S entrants will receive books, chapbooks, and journals equal to, or more than, the entry fee. Add $3 (USD) for other countries to cover the extra postal charge." Make checks payable to Pavement Saw Press. **Deadline:** reads submissions in June, July, and until August 15 (must have August 15 or earlier postmark).

$☑ ◎ TUFTS POETRY AWARDS (Specialized: for emerging poet & for first book)

The Center for the Arts and Humanities at Claremont Graduate University, 160 E. 10th St., Harper East B7, Claremont CA 91711-6165. (909)621-8974. Web site: www.cgu.edu/tufts. Established 1992. **Contact:** Patricia Easton, dean and program manager. The annual Kingsley Tufts Poetry Award offers $100,000 for a work by an emerging poet, "one who is past the very beginning but has not yet reached the acknowledged pinnacle of his/her career." The Kate Tufts Discovery Award ($10,000) is for a first book. Books considered for the 2008 awards must have been published between September 15, 2006 and September 15, 2007. Entry form and guidelines available for SASE or on Web site. **Deadline:** September 15 for 2007. 2007 winners are Rodney Jones (*Salvation Blues*) and Eric McHenry (*Potscrubber Lullabies*). Winners announced in February. Check Web site for updated deadlines and award information.

$☑ ◎ WAR POETRY CONTEST (Specialized: war-themed poetry)

Winning Writers, 351 Pleasant St., PMB 222, Northampton MA 01060-3961. (866)946-9748. Fax: (413)280-0539. E-mail: adam@winningwriters.com. Web site: www.winningwriters.com. Established 2002. **Contact:** Adam Cohen, award director. Offers annual award of 1st Prize: $2,000; 2nd Prize: $1,200; 3rd Prize: $600; 12 Honorable Mentions of $100 each. All prizewinners receive online publication at WinningWriters.com; selected finalists may also receive online publication. Submissions must be unpublished and may be entered in other contests. Submit 1-3 poems of up to 500 lines total on the theme of war, any form, style, or genre. No name on ms pages, typed or computer-printed on letter-size white paper, single-sided. Submit online or by regular mail. Guidelines available for SASE or on Web site. **Entry fee:** $15 for group of 1-3 poems. **Deadline:** November 15-May 31. Competition receives about 800 entries/year. 2006 winner was Ed Frankel for ''Instrumentum Vocale'' and ''Gladium Vocale.'' 2006 judge: Jendi Reiter. Winners announced on November 15 at WinningWriters.com and in free e-mail newsletter. Entrants who provided valid e-mail addresses will also receive notification. (See separate listing for the Wergle Flomp Humor Poetry Contest in this section and for Winning Writers in the Additional Resources section.)

$🖉 ◎ ROBERT PENN WARREN AWARDS (Specialized: free verse only)

P.O. Box 5, Windsor VT 05089. (802)674-2315. Fax: (802)674-5767. E-mail: newvtpoet@aol.com. Web site: www.newenglandwriters.org. Established 1986. **Contact:** Susan Anthony, contest coordinator. The Robert Penn Warren Awards are given annually for free verse poems. Offers 1st Prize: $300; 2nd Prize: $200; 3rd Prize: $100; 10 Honorable Mentions; 10 Commendables; 10 Editor's Choice; winning poems published in *The Anthology of New England Writers*. Submissions must be unpublished and not submitted elsewhere. Submit 3 poems of 10-30 lines each, each poem titled, no name/address on ms. Include 3×5 card with name, address, and titles of poems. Mss will not be returned. Guidelines available for SASE, by e-mail, or on Web site. **Entry fee:** $5 for 3 poems (unlimited entries). Make checks payable to New England Writers (see separate listing in Organizations). **Deadline:** submit January through June 15 (postmark) only. Winners announced at the New England Writers Conference in July; winners are notified and posted on Web site.

$🖉 WASHINGTON POETS ASSOCIATION ANNUAL POETRY CONTEST

Washington Poets Association, 2442 NW Market St., Seattle WA 98107. E-mail: treasurer@washingtonpoets.org. Web site: www.washingtonpoets.org. Established 1971. **Contact:** Jed Myers, contest chair (2007). Sponsored annually by the Washington Poets Association (see separate listing in Organizations), offers over $1,000 total in cash awards plus Honorable Mentions. Entries accepted in 4 categories: *William Stafford Award* (any form), *Carlin Aden Award* (traditional rhyme/meter), *Charlie Proctor Award* (humorous, any form), and *Francine Porad Award* (haiku). Poems must be unpublished and must not have won awards in other contests. Submit as many poems as you like up to 50 lines each, one poem to a page. Entry form required. See guidelines for complete instructions. Include SASE for notification; poems will not be returned. Entry form and guidelines available on Web site. **Entry fee:** $5 general fee, plus $1/poem entered. **Deadline:** was March 15 for 2007. Winners are notified by SASE after judges' decisions. ''Washington Poets Association reserves the right to publish winning poems in its newsletter and Web site and is granted permission to print Award and Honorable Mention poems in future anthologies.''

$🖉 THE WASHINGTON PRIZE

The Word Works, P.O. Box 42164, Washington DC 20015. E-mail: editor@wordworksdc.com. (inquiries only). Web site: www.wordworksdc.com. Established 1981. **Contact:** Miles Moore, prize administrator. The Washington Prize offers $1,500 and publication of a book-length ms of original poetry in English by a living American poet (U.S. or Canadian citizen or resident). Submit a ms of 48-64 pages. Include title page with poet's name, address, phone number, e-mail address, and signature. Poet's name and contact information should appear on the title page only. Also include table of contents (with ms title) and a cover letter containing acknowledgments and a brief bio. Ackowledgments and biographical material must not appear elsewhere in the ms. Use a binder clip to secure the ms. Indicate the information source where you learned about the Washington Prize (for example, AWP newsletter, *Poets & Writers Magazine*, the Word Works Web site). **SEND ENTRIES TO THIS ADDRESS ONLY** by First Class Mail: Steven B. Rogers, Washington Prize Director, Word Works Washington Prize, 3201 Taylor St., Mt. Rainier MD 20712. Enclose SASE for results only; no mss will be returned. **Entry fee:** $20 (includes copy of winning book). Make checks payable to The Word Works. **Deadline:** submit January 15-March 1 (postmark). Winners will be announced in July. 2006 winner was John Surowiecki (*The Hat City After Men Stopped Wearing Hats*).

$☑ ◎ WERGLE FLOMP HUMOR POETRY CONTEST (Specialized: parody of vanity contest entries)

Winning Writers, 351 Pleasant St., PMB 222, Northampton MA 01060-3961. (866)946-9748. Fax: (413)280-0539. E-mail: adam@winningwriters.com. Web site: www.winningwriters.com. Established 2002. **Contact:** Adam Cohen, award director. Offers annual award of 1st Prize: $1,359; 2nd Prize: $764; 3rd Prize: $338; plus 12 Honorable Mentions of $72.95 each. All prizewinners receive online publication at WinningWriters.com. Submissions may be previously published and may be entered in other contests. Submit one poem of any length, in any form, but must be "a humor poem that has been submitted to a 'vanity poetry contest' as a joke. See Web site for examples." Entries accepted only through Web site; no entries by regular mail. Guidelines available on Web site. **Entry fee:** none. **Deadline:** August 15-April 1. Competition receives about 1,000 entries/year. 2006 winner was Nicholas Moore for "How to Write a Poem." 2006 judge: Jendi Reiter. Winners announced on August 15 at WinningWriters.com and in free e-mail newsletter. "Please read the past winning entries and the judge's comments published at WinningWriters.com. Guidelines are a little unusual—please follow them closely."

⊕ $◎ WESTERN AUSTRALIAN PREMIER'S BOOK AWARDS (Specialized: native & resident poets of Western Australia)

State Library of Western Australia, Alexander Library Bldg., Perth Cultural Centre, Perth WA 6000 Australia. (61)(8)9427-3330. Fax: (61)(8)9427-3336. E-mail: doug.george@slwa.wa.gov.au. Web site: www.slwa.wa.gov.au/pba.html. Established 1982. **Contact:** Doug George, award director. Offers annual poetry prize of $7,500 AUD for a published book of poetry. Winner also eligible for Premier's Prize of $20,000 AUD. Submissions must be previously published. Open to poets born in Western Australia, current residents of Western Australia, or poets who have resided in Western Australia for at least 10 years at some stage. Entry form and guidelines available for SASE or on Web site. **Entry fee:** none. **Deadline:** was January 5 for 2007. Competition receives about 10-15 entries in poetry category per year (130 overall). 2005 poetry winner was *The Paradoxes of Water: Selected and New Poems, 1970-2005* by Rod Moran. Judges: Mr. Andrew Taylor, Ms. Chloe Mauger, Prof. Ed Jaggard, and Ms. Lucille Fisher. Winners announced in June each year (i.e., June 2008 for 2007 awards) at a presentation dinner given by the Premier of Western Australia. "The contest is organized by the State Library of Western Australia, with money provided by the Western Australian State Government to support literature."

$◎ WHITE LOTUS HAIKU COMPETITION (formerly Zen Garden Haiku Contest)

Shadow Poetry, 1209 Milwaukee St., Excelsior Springs MO 64024. Fax: (208)977-9114. E-mail: shadowpoetry@shadowpoetry.com. Web site: www.shadowpoetry.com. Established 2000. **Contact:** James Summers, award director. Offers annual award of 1st Prize: $100; 2nd Prize: $50; 3rd Prize: $25, plus the top 3 winners also receive a certificate, a printed copy of winning haiku, and a ribbon. The top 10 placing haiku will be published in the Spring/Summer issue of *White Lotus Magazine* (see separate listing in Magazines/Journals). Submissions must be previously unpublished, not under consideration elsewhere, free form or 5/7/5, and written in the traditional 3-line format. "Haiku entries are accepted on 8½ × 11 paper or on 3 × 5 index cards, submitted in duplicate, neatly handwritten or typed. The poet's name, address, phone number, and e-mail address (if applicable) should appear in the upper left-hand corner of one sheet or on the back of one index card. Repeat this method for multiple submissions." Enclose #10 SASE for winners list. Include SASE for entry receipt (optional). "If no SASE is included for receipt, Shadow Poetry will e-mail an entry confirmation to the contestant, if applicable." Entry form and guidelines available for

SASE or on Web site. **Entry fee:** $5 for 3 haiku or $2 per each individual haiku (entries are unlimited). Make checks/money orders payable to Shadow Poetry. **Deadline:** December 31. Winners announced February 1 each year "by e-mail and to those who requested a winners list with SASE. Results will also be posted on the Shadow Poetry Web site and printed in *White Lotus*."

$⬚ THE WHITE PINE PRESS POETRY PRIZE

White Pine Press, P.O. Box 236, Buffalo NY 14201. E-mail: wpine@whitepine.org. Web site: www.whitepine.org. Established 1973. **Contact:** Dennis Maloney, editor. The White Pine Press Poetry Prize offers $1,000 plus publication for a book-length collection of poems by a U.S. author. Submissions must be unpublished as a collection, but individual poems may have been previously published elsewhere. Submit 60-80 pages of poetry, typed, with table of contents. Include cover sheet with poet's name, address, e-mail address, and phone number. No e-mail submissions. Include SASP for notification of receipt of ms and SASE for results only; mss will not be returned. Guidelines available for SASE or on Web site. **Entry fee:** $20. Make checks payable to White Pine Press. **Deadline:** submit July 1-November 30 (postmark). 2006 winner was Jennifer Kwon Dobbs (*Paper Pavilion*). Judge: poet of national reputation. Winning books available from local booksellers and White Pine Press.

$⬚ THE WALT WHITMAN AWARD

The Academy of American Poets, 584 Broadway, Suite 604, New York NY 10012. (212)274-0343. Fax: (212)274-9427. E-mail: jkronovet@poets.org. Web site: www.poets.org. Award established 1975. **Contact:** Jennifer Kronovet, awards coordinator. Offers $5,000, publication of a poet's first book by Louisiana State University Press, and a one-month residency at the Vermont Studio Center. The Academy of American Poets purchases copies of the Whitman Award-winning book for distribution to its members. Submit mss of 50-100 pages. Poets must be American citizens. Entry form required; entry form and guidelines available for SASE (in August) or on Web site. **Entry fee:** $25. **Deadline:** submit between September 15 and November 15. 2006 winner was Anne Pierson Wiese (*Floating City*). 2007 judge: August Kleinzahler. Winner announced in May.

$⬚ STAN AND TOM WICK POETRY PRIZE

Wick Poetry Center, 301 Satterfield Hall, Kent State University, P.O. Box 5190, Kent OH 44242-0001. (330)672-2067. Fax: (330)672-3333. E-mail: wickpoet@kent.edu. Web site: http://dept.kent.edu/wick. Established 1994. **Contact:** Maggie Anderson, director. Offers annual award of $2,000 and publication by Kent State University Press. Open to poets writing in English who have not yet published a full-length collection. Submissions must be unpublished as a collection, but individual poems may have been previously published elsewhere. Accepts simultaneous submissions as long as the Wick Poetry Center receives notice upon acceptance elsewhere. Submit 50-70 pages of poetry. Include cover sheet with poet's name, address, telephone number, e-mail address, and title of ms. Guidelines available for SASE or on Web site. **Entry fee:** $20. **Deadline:** submit February 1-May 1. Competition receives 700-800 entries.

$⬚ THE RICHARD WILBUR AWARD (Specialized: American poets only)

Dept. of English, University of Evansville, 1800 Lincoln Ave., Evansville IN 47722. (812)488-2963. Web site: http://english.evansville.edu/english/WilburAwardGuidelines.htm. **Contact:** William Baer, series director. Offers a biennial award (even-numbered years) of $1,000 and book publication to "recognize a quality book-length manuscript of poetry." Submissions must be unpublished original poetry collections ("although individual poems may have had previous journal publications") and "public domain or permission-secured translations may comprise up to one-third of the manuscript." Submit ms of 50-100 typed pages, unbound, bound, or clipped. Open to all American poets. Manuscripts should be accompanied by 2 title pages: one with collection's title, author's name, address, and phone number; one with only the title. Include SASE for contest results. Submissions may be entered in other contests. Manuscripts are not returned. Guidelines available for SASE or on Web site. **Entry fee:** $25/ms. **Deadline:** December 1. Competition receives 300-500 entries. Winning ms is published and copyrighted by the University of Evansville Press.

$☑ MARJORIE J. WILSON AWARD FOR BEST POEM CONTEST

MARGIE/The American Journal of Poetry, P.O. Box 250, Chesterfield MO 63006-0250. E-mail: margie review@aol.com. Web site: www.margiereview.com. The Marjorie J. Wilson Award for Best Poem Contest offers $2,500 and publication in *MARGIE* (see separate listing in Magazines/Journals). All entries will be considered for publication. Entries must be unpublished; may be under consideration elsewhere. Submit 3 poems, 60-line limit/poem. Include single cover sheet with poet's name, address, phone number, e-mail (if available), and poem titles. No names should appear on the poems themselves; do not send originals. Include SASE for results only; no poems will be returned. Guidelines available for SASE or on Web site. **Entry fee:** $15/3 poems; $5 for each additional poem. Make checks payable to MARGIE, Inc. **Deadline:** March 31 (postmark). 2006 winner was Jill Drumm (''Just Like You Had Flown Away''). 2007 judge: David Wagoner.

✪ $☑ WALLACE W. WINCHELL POETRY CONTEST

Connecticut Poetry Society, P.O. Box 270554, West Hartford CT 06127-0554. E-mail: connpoetry@co mcast.net. Web site: www.ct-poetry-society.org. **Contact:** Contest Coordinator. The Wallace W. Winchell Poetry Contest, sponsored by the Connecticut Poetry Society, is open to all poets. Offers prizes of $150, $100, and $50; prize poems will be published in *Connecticut River Review*. Send up to 3 unpublished poems, any form, 40 line limit. Include 2 copies of each poem: one with complete contact information and one with NO contact information. Both copies must be marked: Winchell Contest. Include SASE for results only (no poems will be returned). Winning poems must be submitted by disc or e-mail following notification. **Entry fee:** $10 for up to 3 poems. Make checks payable to Connecticut Poetry Society. **Deadline:** submit October 1-December 31. 2006 judge: John Surowiecki.

$☑ ◎ WORKING PEOPLE'S POETRY COMPETITION

Blue Collar Review, P.O. Box 11417, Norfolk VA 23517. E-mail: red-ink@earthlink.net. (inquiries only). Web site: www.partisanpress.org. The Working People's Poetry Competition offers $100 and a one-year subscription to *Blue Collar Review* (see separate listing in Magazines/Journals). ''Poetry should be typed as you would like to see it published, with your name and address on each page. Include cover letter with entry.'' Guidelines available on Web site. **Entry fee:** $15. Make checks payable to Partisan Press. **Deadline:** May 1. 2006 winner was Bobbi Dykema Katsanis.

$☑ THE W.B. YEATS SOCIETY ANNUAL POETRY COMPETITION

W.B. Yeats Society of New York, National Arts Club, 15 Gramercy Park S, New York NY 10003. (212)780-0605. Web site: www.YeatsSociety.org. Established 1990. **Contact:** Andrew McGowan, president. Offers annual $250 cash prize for 1st Place, $100 cash prize for 2nd Place, and optional Honorable Mentions. Open to beginner as well as established poets. Winners are invited to read their poems at an awards event held each spring in New York; also inducted as Honorary Members of the W.B. Yeats Society, a 501(c)(3) charitable organization (see separate listing in Organizations). Submissions must be unpublished and may be entered in other contests. Submit any number of unpublished poems in any style or form, up to 60 lines each, typed on letter-size paper without poet's name. Guidelines available for SASE or on Web site; no entry form required. **Entry fee:** $8 for first poem, $7 for each additional poem. Attach a 3×5 card to each entry containing the poem's title along with the poet's name, address, and phone/fax/e-mail. **Deadline:** February 15 annually. Receives 200-300 entries/year. 2006 winners were Mary Legato Brownell, Mike Hammer, Nan Becker, M. Schoofs, and Dolores Hayden. 2006 judge: Marie Ponsot. Winners selected by March

31 and announced in April. Winning entries and judge's report are posted on the Society's Web site. Printed report available for SASE.

ℕ $⊘ THE YELLOWWOOD POETRY AWARD

Yalobusha Review, Dept. of English, University of Mississippi, P.O. Box 1848, University MS 38677-1848. Established 2007. Web site: www.olemiss.edu/Yalobusha. The annual Yellowwood Poetry Award offers $250, publication in *Yalobusha Review* (see separate listing in Magazines/Journals), exclusive publication on Web site, and 2 contributor's copies to winner. Submit 3-5 poems. Include cover leter with poet's contact information and poem titles. Poet's name should not appear on poems. Include SASE for results only. **Entry fee:** $10. Make checks/money orders payable to *Yalobusha Review*. **Deadline:** was July 15-October 1 (postmark) for 2007. Judge: all submissions will be ranked by *Yalobusha Review* editors; final judge is Beth Ann Fennelly. Winner notified in December.

ADDITIONAL CONTESTS & AWARDS

The following listings also contain information about contests and awards. Turn to the page numbers indicated for details about their offerings.

NOTES

Grants

State & Provincial

Arts councils in the United States and Canada provide assistance to artists (including poets) in the form of fellowships or grants. These grants can be substantial and confer prestige upon recipients; however, **only state or province residents are eligible**. Because deadlines and available support vary annually, query first (with a SASE) or check Web sites for guidelines.

UNITED STATES ARTS AGENCIES

Alabama State Council on the Arts, 201 Monroe St., Montgomery AL 36130-1800. (334)242-4076. E-mail: staff@arts.alabama.gov. Web site: www.arts.state.al.us.

Alaska State Council on the Arts, 411 W. Fourth Ave., Suite 1-E, Anchorage AK 99501-2343. (907)269-6610 or (888)278-7424. E-mail: aksca_info@eed.state.ak.us. Web site: www.eed. state.ak.us/aksca.

Arizona Commission on the Arts, 417 W. Roosevelt St., Phoenix AZ 85003-1326. (602)771-6501. E-mail: info@azarts.gov. Web site: www.azarts.gov.

Arkansas Arts Council, 1500 Tower Bldg., 323 Center St., Little Rock AR 72201. (501)324-9766. E-mail: info@arkansasarts.com. Web site: www.arkansasarts.com.

California Arts Council, 1300 I St., Suite 930, Sacramento CA 95814. (916)322-6555. E-mail: info@caartscouncil.com. Web site: www.cac.ca.gov.

Colorado Council on the Arts, 1625 Broadway, Suite 2700, Denver CO 80202. (303)892-3802. E-mail: online form. Web site: www.coloarts.state.co.us.

Connecticut Commission on Culture & Tourism, Arts Division, One Financial Plaza, 755 Main St., Hartford CT 06103. (860)256-2800. Web site: www.cultureandtourism.org.

Delaware Division of the Arts, Carvel State Office Bldg., 4th Floor, 820 N. French St., Wilmington DE 19801. (302)577-8278 (New Castle Co.) or (302)739-5304 (Kent or Sussex Counties). E-mail: delarts@state.de.us. Web site: www.artsdel.org.

District of Columbia Commission on the Arts & Humanities, 410 Eighth St. NW, 5th Floor, Washington DC 20004. (202)724-5613. E-mail: cah@dc.gov. Web site: http://dcarts .dc.gov.

Florida Arts Council, Division of Cultural Affairs, R.A. Gray Building, Third Floor, 500 S. Bronough St., Tallahassee FL 32399-0250. (850)245-6470. E-mail: info@florida-arts.org. Web site: www.florida-arts.org.

Georgia Council for the Arts, 260 14th St., Suite 401, Atlanta GA 30318. (404)685-2787. E-mail: gaarts@gaarts.org. Web site: www.gaarts.org.

Guam Council on the Arts & Humanities Agency, P.O. Box 2950, Hagatna GU 96932. (671)646-2781. Web site: www.guam.net.

Hawaii State Foundation on Culture & the Arts, 2500 S. Hotel St., 2nd Floor, Honolulu HI 96813. (808)586-0300. E-mail: ken.hamilton@hawaii.gov. Web site: www.state.hi.us/sfca.

Idaho Commission on the Arts, 2410 N. Old Penitentiary Rd., Boise ID 83712. (208)334-2119 or (800)278-3863. E-mail: info@arts.idaho.gov. Web site: www.arts.idaho.gov.

Illinois Arts Council, James R. Thompson Center, 100 W. Randolph, Suite 10-500, Chicago IL 60601. (312)814-6750. E-mail: iac.info@illinois.gov. Web site: www.state.il.us/agency/iac.

Indiana Arts Commission, 150 W. Market St., Suite 618, Indianapolis IN 46204. (317)232-1268. E-mail: IndianaArtsCommission@iac.in.gov. Web site: www.in.gov/arts.

Iowa Arts Council, 600 E. Locust, Des Moines IA 50319-0290. (515)281-6412. Web site: www.iowaartscouncil.org.

Kansas Arts Commission, 700 SW Jackson, Suite 1004, Topeka KS 66603-3761. (785)296-3335. E-mail: KAC@arts.state.ks.us. Web site: http://arts.state.ks.us.

Kentucky Arts Council, 21st Floor, Capital Plaza Tower, 500 Mero St., Frankfort KY 40601-1987. (502)564-3757 or (888)833-2787. E-mail: kyarts@ky.gov. Web site: http://artscouncil.ky.gov.

Louisiana Division of the Arts, Capitol Annex Bldg., 1051 N. 3rd St., 4th Floor, Room #420, Baton Rouge LA 70804. (225)342-8180. Web site: www.crt.state.la.us/arts.

Maine Arts Commission, 193 State St., 25 State House Station, Augusta ME 04333-0025. (207)287-2724. E-mail: MaineArts.info@maine.gov. Web site: www.mainearts.com.

Maryland State Arts Council, 175 W. Ostend St., Suite E, Baltimore MD 21230. (410)767-6555. E-mail: msac@msac.org. Web site: www.msac.org.

Massachusetts Cultural Council, 10 St. James Ave., 3rd Floor, Boston MA 02116-3803. (617)727-3668. E-mail: mcc@art.state.ma.us. Web site: www.massculturalcouncil.org.

Michigan Council for Arts & Cultural Affairs, 702 W. Kalamazoo St., P.O. Box 30705, Lansing MI 48909-8205. (517)241-4011. E-mail: artsinfo@michigan.gov. Web site: www.michigan.gov/hal/0,1607,7-160-17445_19272---,00.html.

Minnesota State Arts Board, Park Square Court, 400 Sibley St., Suite 200, St. Paul MN 55101-1928. (651)215-1600 or (800)866-2787. E-mail: msab@arts.state.mn.us. Web site: www.arts.state.mn.us.

Mississippi Arts Commission, 501 N. West St., Suite 701B, Woolfolk Bldg., Jackson MS 39201. (601)359-6030. Web site: www.arts.state.ms.us.

Missouri Arts Council, 815 Olive St., Suite 16, St. Louis MO 63101-1503. (314)340-6845 or (866)407-4752. E-mail: moarts@ded.mo.gov. Web site: www.missouriartscouncil.org.

Montana Arts Council, 316 N. Park Ave., Suite 252, Helena MT 59620-2201. (406)444-6430. E-mail: mac@mt.gov. Web site: www.art.state.mt.us.

National Assembly of State Arts Agencies, 1029 Vermont Ave. NW, 2nd Floor, Washington DC 20005. (202)347-6352. E-mail: nasaa@nasaa-arts.org. Web site: www.nasaa-arts.org.

Nebraska Arts Council, 1004 Farnam St., Plaza Level, Omaha NE 68102. (402)595-2122 or (800)341-4067. Web site: www.nebraskaartscouncil.org.

Nevada Arts Council, 716 N. Carson St., Suite A, Carson City NV 89701. (775)687-6680. E-mail: online form. Web site: http://dmla.clan.lib.nv.us/docs/arts.

New Hampshire State Council on the Arts, 2½ Beacon St., 2nd Floor, Concord NH 03301-4974. (603)271-2789. Web site: www.nh.gov/nharts.

New Jersey State Council on the Arts, 225 W. State St., P.O. Box 306, Trenton NJ 08625. (609)292-6130. Web site: www.njartscouncil.org.

New Mexico Arts, Dept. of Cultural Affairs, P.O. Box 1450, Santa Fe NM 87504-1450. (505)827-6490 or (800)879-4278. Web site: www.nmarts.org.

New York State Council on the Arts, 175 Varick St., New York NY 10014. (212)627-4455. Web site: www.nysca.org.

North Carolina Arts Council, 109 East Jones St., Cultural Resources Building, Raleigh NC 27601. (919)807-6500. E-mail: ncarts@ncmail.net. Web site: www.ncarts.org.

North Dakota Council on the Arts, 1600 E. Century Ave., Suite 6, Bismarck ND 58503. (701)328-7590. E-mail: comserv@state.nd.us. Web site: www.state.nd.us/arts.

Commonwealth Council for Arts and Culture (Northern Mariana Islands), P.O. Box 5553, CHRB, Saipan MP 96950. (670)322-9982 or (670)322-9983. E-mail: galaidi@vzpacifica.net. Web site: www.geocities.com/ccacarts/ccacwebsite.html.

Ohio Arts Council, 727 E. Main St., Columbus OH 43205-1796. (614)466-2613. Web site: www.oac.state.oh.us.

Oklahoma Arts Council, Jim Thorpe Building, 2101 N. Lincoln Blvd., Suite 640, Oklahoma City OK 73105. (405)521-2931. E-mail: okarts@arts.ok.gov. Web site: www.arts.state.ok.us.

Oregon Arts Commission, 775 Summer St. NE, Suite 200, Salem OR 97301-1280. (503)986-0082. E-mail: oregon.artscomm@state.or.us. Web site: www.oregonartscommission.org.

Pennsylvania Council on the Arts, 216 Finance Bldg., Harrisburg PA 17120. (717)787-6883. Web site: www.pacouncilonthearts.org.

Institute of Puerto Rican Culture, P.O. Box 9024184, San Juan PR 00902-4184. (787)724-0700. E-mail: www@icp.gobierno.pr. Web site: www.icp.gobierno.pr.

Rhode Island State Council on the Arts, One Capitol Hill, Third Floor, Providence RI 02908. (401)222-3880. E-mail: info@arts.ri.gov. Web site: www.arts.ri.gov.

American Samoa Council on Culture, Arts and Humanities, P.O. Box 1540, Office of the Governor, Pago Pago AS 96799. (684)633-4347. Web site: www.prel.org/programs/pcahe/PTG/terr-asamoa1.html.

South Carolina Arts Commission, 1800 Gervais St., Columbia SC 29201. (803)734-8696. E-mail: info@arts.state.sc.us. Web site: www.southcarolinaarts.com.

South Dakota Arts Council, 711 E. Wells Ave., Pierre SD 57501-3369. (605)773-3301. E-mail: sdac@state.sd.us. Web site: www.artscouncil.sd.gov.

Tennessee Arts Commission, 401 Charlotte Ave., Nashville TN 37243-0780. (615)741-1701. Web site: www.arts.state.tn.us.

Texas Commission on the Arts, E.O. Thompson Office Building, 920 Colorado, Suite 501, Austin TX 78701. (512)463-5535. E-mail: front.desk@arts.state.tx.us. Web site: www.arts. state.tx.us.

Utah Arts Council, 617 E. South Temple, Salt Lake City UT 84102-1177. (801)236-7555. Web site: http://arts.utah.gov.

Vermont Arts Council, 136 State St., Drawer 33, Montpelier VT 05633-6001. (802)828-3291. E-mail: online form. Web site: www.vermontartscouncil.org.

Virgin Islands Council on the Arts, 5070 Norre Gade, St. Thomas VI 00802-6872. (340)774-5984. Web site: http://vicouncilonarts.org.

Virginia Commission for the Arts, Lewis House, 223 Governor St., 2nd Floor, Richmond VA 23219. (804)225-3132. E-mail: arts@arts.virginia.gov. Web site: www.arts.state.va.us.

Washington State Arts Commission, 711 Capitol Way S., Suite 600, P.O. Box 42675, Olympia WA 98504-2675. (360)753-3860. E-mail: info@arts.wa.gov. Web site: www.arts.wa.gov.

West Virginia Commission on the Arts, The Cultural Center, Capitol Complex, 1900 Kanawha Blvd. E., Charleston WV 25305-0300. (304)558-0220. Web site: www.wvculture. org/arts.

Wisconsin Arts Board, 101 E. Wilson St., 1st Floor, Madison WI 53702. (608)266-0190. E-mail: artsboard@arts.state.wi.us. Web site: www.arts.state.wi.us.

Wyoming Arts Council, 2320 Capitol Ave., Cheyenne WY 82002. (307)777-7742. E-mail: ebratt@state.wy.us. Web site: http://wyoarts.state.wy.us.

CANADIAN PROVINCES ARTS AGENCIES

Alberta Foundation for the Arts, 10708 - 105 Ave., Edmonton AB T5H 0A1. (780)427-9968. Web site: www.cd.gov.ab.ca/all_about_us/commissions/arts.

British Columbia Arts Council, P.O. Box 9819, Stn. Prov. Govt., Victoria BC V8W 9W3. (250)356-1718. E-mail: BCArtsCouncil@gov.bc.ca. Web site: www.bcartscouncil.ca.

The Canada Council for the Arts, 350 Albert St., P.O. Box 1047, Ottawa ON K1P 5V8. (613)566-4414 or (800)263-5588 (within Canada). Web site: www.canadacouncil.ca.

Manitoba Arts Council, 525-93 Lombard Ave., Winnipeg MB R3B 3B1. (204)945-2237 or (866)994-2787 (in Manitoba). E-mail: info@artscouncil.mb.ca. Web site: www.artscouncil.mb.ca.

New Brunswick Arts Board (NBAB), 634 Queen St., Suite 300, Fredericton NB E3B 1C2. (506)444-4444 or (866)460-2787. Web site: www.artsnb.ca.

Newfoundland & Labrador Arts Council, P.O. Box 98, St. John's NL A1C 5H5. (709)726-2212 or (866)726-2212. E-mail: nlacmail@nfld.net. Web site: www.nlac.nf.ca.

Nova Scotia Department of Tourism, Culture, and Heritage, Culture Division, 1800 Argyle St., Suite 601, P.O. Box 456, Halifax NS B3J 2R5. (902)424-4510. E-mail: cultaffs@gov.ns.ca. Web site: www.gov.ns.ca/dtc/culture.

Ontario Arts Council, 151 Bloor St. W., 5th Floor, Toronto ON M5S 1T6. (416)961-1660 or (800)387-0058 (in Ontario). E-mail: info@arts.on.ca. Web site: www.arts.on.ca.

Prince Edward Island Council of the Arts, 115 Richmond St., Charlottetown PE C1A 1H7. (902)368-4410 or (888)734-2784. E-mail: info@peiartscouncil.com. Web site: www.peiart scouncil.com.

Québec Council for Arts & Literature, 79 boul. René-Lévesque Est, 3e étage, Québec QC G1R 5N5. (418)643-1707 or (800)897-1707. E-mail: info@calq.gouv.qc.ca. Web site: www.calq. gouv.qc.ca.

The Saskatchewan Arts Board, 2135 Broad St., Regina SK S4P 1Y6. (306)787-4056 or (800)667-7526 (Saskatchewan only). E-mail: sab@artsboard.sk.ca. Web site: www.artsbo ard.sk.ca.

Yukon Arts Section, Cultural Services Branch, Dept. of Tourism & Culture, Government of Yukon, Box 2703 (L-3), Whitehorse YT Y1A 2C6. (867)667-8589 or (800)661-0408 (in Yukon). E-mail: arts@gov.yk.ca. Web site: www.btc.gov.yk.ca/cultural/arts.

Conferences, Workshops & Festivals

There are times when we want to immerse ourselves in learning. Or perhaps we crave a change of scenery, the creative stimulation of being around other artists, or the uninterrupted productivity of time alone to work.

That's what this section of *Poet's Market* is all about, providing a selection of writing conferences and workshops, artist colonies and retreats, poetry festivals, and even a few opportunities to go travelling with your muse. These listings give the basics: contact information, a brief description of the event, lists of past presenters, and offerings of special interest to poets. Contact an event that interests you for additional information, including up-to-date costs and housing details. **(Please note that most directors had not finalized their 2008 plans when we contacted them for this edition of *Poet's Market*. However, where possible, they provided us with their 2007 dates, costs, faculty names or themes to give you a better idea of what each event has to offer.)**

Before you seriously consider a conference, workshop or other event, determine what you hope to get out of the experience. Would a general conference with one or two poetry workshops among many other types of sessions be acceptable? Or are you looking for something exclusively focused on poetry? Do you want to hear poets speak about poetry writing, or are you looking for a more participatory experience, such as a one-on-one critiquing session or a group workshop? Do you mind being one of hundreds of attendees, or do you prefer a more intimate setting? Are you willing to invest in the expense of travelling to a conference, or would something local better suit your budget? Keep these questions and others in mind as you read these listings, view Web sites and study conference brochures.

Some listings are coded with symbols to provide certain "information at a glance." The (**N**) symbol indicates a recently established conference/workshop; the (◩) symbol indicates this conference/workshop did not appear in the 2007 edition; the (◪) symbol denotes a Canadian event and the (⊕) symbol one located outside the U.S. and Canada.

The Additional Conferences & Workshops list at the end of this section cross-references conference, workshop and festival information in other sections of this book. To find out more, go to the page number indicated for each listing.

🌐 ANAM CARA WRITER'S AND ARTIST'S RETREAT

Eyeries, Beara, Co. Cork, Ireland. (353)(027)74441. Fax: (353)(027)74448. E-mail: anamcararetreat @eircom.net. Web site: www.anamcararetreat.com. **Contact:** Sue Booth-Forbes, director. Offers up to one-month individual retreats as well as workshops for writers and artists. Length of workshops varies with subject and leader/facilitator. Location: "Beara is a rural and hauntingly beautiful part of Ireland that is kept temperate by the Gulf Stream. The retreat sits on a hill overlooking Coulagh Bay, the mountains of the Ring of Kerry, and the Slieve Mishkish Mountains of Beara. The village of Eyeries is a short walk away." Average attendance: 5 residents at the retreat when working individually; 12-18 workshop participants.

Purpose/Features "Anam Cara is open to novice as well as professional writers and artists. Applicants are asked to provide a written description on the focus of their work while on retreat. Residencies are on a first-come, first-deposit-in basis." 2007 workshops included sessions on poetry, painting, haiku, creative nonfiction, and fiction.

Costs/Accommodations 2007 cost: residency fee ranges from €600-700/week for individual retreats, depending on room, and includes full room and board; editorial consulting; laundry; sauna; hot tub overlooking Coulagh Bay; 5 acres of gardens, meadows, riverbank and cascades, river island, swimming hole, and several unique working spots, such as the ruin of a stone mill and a sod-roofed beehive hut. Overflow from workshops stay in nearby B&Bs, a 10-minute walk or 2-minute drive away. Transportation provided if needed. Details regarding transporation to Anam Cara available on Web site.

Additional Information Requests for specific information about rates and availability can be made through the Web site; also available by fax or e-mail. Brochure available on request.

🌐 ART WORKSHOPS IN GUATEMALA

4758 Lyndale Ave. S., Minneapolis MN 55419-5403. (612)825-0747. E-mail: info@artguat.org. Web site: www.artguat.org. Established 1995. **Contact:** Liza Fourre, director. Annual 10-day creative writing courses, held in February, March, July, and October. Location: workshops held in Antigua, the old colonial capital of Guatemala. Average attendance: limit 10 students.

Purpose/Features Art Workshops in Guatemala provides "the perfect getaway for creative writers of all skill levels looking for a memorable and inspiring writing/travel experience." For 2007, offered poets "Journey of the Soul" (with Sharon Doubiago, July 21-30) and "Snapshots in Words" (with Roseann Lloyd).

Costs/Accommodations 2007 cost: $1,625. Includes "tuition, lodging in a beautiful old colonial home, a hearty breakfast, ground transportation, and some pretty interesting cultural field trips."

Additional Information Individual poetry critiques included. Call, write, e-mail, or check Web site.

ASPEN SUMMER WORDS WRITING RETREAT & LITERARY FESTIVAL

110 E. Hallam St., Suite 116, Aspen CO 81611. (970)925-3122. Fax: (970)920-5700. E-mail: info@asp enwriters.org. Web site: www.aspenwriters.org. Established 1976. Annual 5-day writing retreat and concurrent 5-day literary festival. 2007 dates: June 24-28. Location: The Gant resort in Aspen (retreat site); Belly Up Aspen (festival site). Average attendance: 120 for the retreat, 300 for the festival.

Purpose/Features Offers a celebration of words and ideas featuring 30 top authors, agents, and editors in up to 5 daily literary events for readers and writers. Offers poetry workshops, readings, publishing panels, interviews, Q&As, and agent/editor meetings. 2007 poetry faculty included Dorianne Laux.

Costs/Accommodations 2007 cost: $475 for 4-day workshop and a $25 reading fee for juried workshops; $250 for 2-day symposium; $175 for 2-day reader's retreat; $200 for literary festival (5-day pass). Offers $50 discount for workshop participants and Aspen Writers' Foundation members.

Participants responsible for dinner only; lunch and a continental breakfast are included in the tuition. "We offer two wine and hors d'oeuvres receptions for ASW registrants." Information on overnight accommodations available on Web site.

Additional Information Deadline for admission is April 1; deadline for discount housing is May 9. Writing sample required for some courses. A limited number of partial-tuition scholarships available. Brochure and application available by phone, fax, e-mail (include regular mailing address with all e-mail inquiries), or can be downloaded from Web site.

AUSTIN INTERNATIONAL POETRY FESTIVAL

P.O. Box 41224, Austin TX 78704. E-mail: aipfinfo@aipf.org. Web site: www.aipf.org. Established 1993. Annual 4-day event. 2007 dates: April 12-15. Location: Austin, TX. Average attendance: 250.
Purpose/Features Open to all poets. Offers poets workshops, faculty readings, participant readings, and slams. 2007 featured poets included Ekiwah Adler-Belendez (Mexico), Felix Cheong (Singapore), Jill Alexnader Essbaum (Switzerland), Agnes Meadows (England), and Bob Mudd (Australia), plus many U.S. and Austin area poets.
Costs/Accommodations 2007 cost: $30-50, depending on level of registration. Participants responsible for all meals. Accommodations available at area hotels. Information on overnight accommodations available on Web site.
Additional Information Offers poetry contest as part of festival. Guidelines available on Web site. Registration form available on Web site. "Largest nonjuried poetry festival in the U.S.!"

BREAD LOAF WRITERS' CONFERENCE

Middlebury College, Middlebury VT 05753. (802)443-5286. Fax: (802)443-2087. Email: blwc@middlebury.edu. Web site: www.middlebury.edu/~blwc. **Contact:** Noreen Cargill, administrative manager. Director: Michael Collier. Established 1926. Annual 11-day event. 2007 dates: August 15-26. Location: mountain campus of Middlebury College. Average attendance: 200+.
Purpose/Features Conference is designed to promote dialogue among writers and provide professional critiques for students. Offers poets workshops, lectures, faculty readings, and ms critiques. 2007 poetry presenters include Eavan Boland, Michael Collier, Brigit Pegeen Kelly, James Longenbach, Steve Orlen, Arthur Sze, and Natasha Trethewey.
Costs/Accommodations 2007 cost: $2,260 (general applicant) or $2,160 (auditor), including tuition, room, and board. Conference fellowships and scholarships available. See Web site for eligibility guidelines, application deadlines, and other important information.
Additional Information Sponsors the Bakeless Literary Publication Prizes, an annual book series competition for new authors of literary works in poetry, fiction, and creative nonfiction (see separate listing in Contests & Awards).

BURNING WORD

Washington Poets Association, 2442 NW Market St., Seattle WA 98107. E-mail: treasurer@washingtonpoets.org. Web site: www.washingtonpoets.org. Established 2004. **Contact:** Victory Schouten, Burning Word committee chair. Annual daylong event held the last Saturday in April. Location: Greenbank Farm, Whidbey Island, WA. Average attendance: 400.
Purpose/Features Celebration of poetry, music, and performance open to all poets. Offers poets workshops; participant readings; nonstop poetry reading on the main stage; an open mic stage; a workshop tent; and small press fair. Past headliners include Carolyn Kizer, Tess Gallagher; Sam Hamill, Tim McNulty, Naomi Shihab Nye, and George Bowering.
Costs/Accommodations 2007 cost: $15 for all readings and workshops. Participants responsible for all meals. Accommodations available at area hotels.
Additional Information Registration form available on Web site.

CATSKILL POETRY WORKSHOP

Hartwick College, Oneonta NY 13820. (607)431-4448. Fax: (607)431-4457. E-mail: frostc@hartwick .edu. Web site: http://info.hartwick.edu/library/catskill/poetry.htm. **Contact:** Carol Frost, director. Annual weeklong event. 2007 dates: July 9-15. Location: Pine Lake campus of Hartwick College, a small, private college in the Catskill Mountain area (includes private chef and rustic cottages). Average attendance: 20-25.

Purpose/Features Open to "talented adult writers" of poetry. Offerings cover "traditional meters, free verse lineation, and uses of metaphor; individual instruction." 2007 poetry instructors included Stephen Dunn, Carol Frost, Lynn Emanuel, Jay Hopler, Tom Sleigh, Chase Twichell, and Michael Waters.

Costs/Accommodations 2007 cost: $1,250, including tuition, room and board; $900 for commuters, tuition and lunch included. Accommodations available on site.

Additional Information Direct contact with 4 faculty poets, including one individual conference scheduled for each participant. Registration forms available for SASE and on Web site.

◎ CAVE CANEM (Specialized: African American poets)

584 Broadway, Suite 508, New York NY 10012. (212)941-5720. E-mail: ccpoets@verizon.net. Web site: www.cavecanempoets.org. Established 1996. **Contact:** Alison Myers, foundation director. Annual weeklong workshop for African American poets. Usually held last week in June. Location: University of Pittsburgh at Greensburg, PA. Average attendance: 50.

Purpose/Features Open to African American poets. Participants selected based on a sample of 6-8 poems. Offerings include workshops by fellows and faculty, evening readings. Participants are assigned to groups of about 9 and remain together throughout session, with different faculty leading each workshop. 2007 faculty included Toi Derricotte, Cornelius Eady, Cyrus Cassells, Yusef Komunyakaa, Erica Hunt, and Patricia Smith. Guest poet: Carl Phillips.

Costs/Accommodations 2007 cost: $495. Meals and other services included. For complete information, contact Cave Canem.

Additional Information Poets should submit 6-8 poems with cover letter. 2007 postmark deadline: March 15, with accepted poets notified by April 30. Cave Canem Foundation also sponsors the Cave Canem Poetry Prize (see separate listing in Contests & Awards section). Brochure and registration information available for SASE and on Web site.

CHAUTAUQUA WRITERS' CENTER

Box 1377, Chautauqua NY 14722. (216)295-1824. E-mail: pataverbach@hotmail.com. Web site: http://writers.ciweb.org. Established 1988. **Contact:** Patricia Averbach, director. Annual season of 9 separate weeklong workshops held late June to late August. Participants may attend one week or more. Location: Victorian lakeside village in western New York; most Writers' Center programs offered in the CLSC Alumni Hall. Average attendance: no more than 12 workshop particpants and 5 nonparticipaing auditors may enroll in each workshop to assure individual attention.

Purpose/Features Provides "a lively community of writers at all levels of development who cultivate the courage, craft, and vision necessary to grow as artists" under the tutelage of nationally recognized poets-in-residence. Poetry workshops meet 2 hours daily, 8:30-10:30 a.m. 2007 poetry faculty includes Robert Cording, Kevin Young, William Heyen, Mark DeFoe, Aimee Nezhukumatathil, Rick Hilles, and John Hoppenthaler. Other features include prose workshops, free Sunday afternoon readings by writers-in-residence, Creative Writing Symposiums on Wednesday evenings, Brown Bag lunches and lectures every Friday at noon, and open mic events every Sunday.

Costs/Accommodations 2007 cost: $95/weeklong workshop. Participants responsible for gate fees ($245/week), housing, and meals. See Web site for accommodations options, which range from the Atheneum Hotel to local rooming houses and condos.

Additional Information Most workshop leaders offer private half hour conferences. Fee: $25, payable directly to leader. Additional information available by phone, e-mail, or on Web site. Also sponsors The Chautauqua Writers' Festival (2007 dates: June 14-17). Publishes *Chautauqua Literary Journal* (see separate listing in Magazines/Journals).

THE COLRAIN POETRY MANUSCRIPT CONFERENCE

Concord Poetry Center, 40 Stow. St., Concord MA 01742. (978)897-0054. E-mail: cpc@concordpoetry.org. Web site: www.concordpoetry.org/Colrain. Established 2004. **Contact:** Joan Houlihan, director. Usually held 4-5 times/year in 3-day, weekend sessions starting in March. Location: The Round House, Colrain, MA, and Crossways Lodge, Harvard, MA. Average attendance: 20 poets.

Purpose/Features "The first poetry conference realistically designed to set poets who have a completed manuscript or a manuscript-in-progress on a path toward book publication. Three-day intensive conference includes a manuscript preparation workshop and in-depth meetings with poetry press editors." Also offers evening poetry readings, an editorial panel Q&A, and an after-conference strategy session. 2007 faculty include Joan Houlihan, Frederick Marchant, Jeffrey Levine (Tupelo Press), Martha Rhodes (Four Way Books), Jeffrey Shotts (Graywolf Press), Michael Simms (Autumn House), and others.

Costs/Accommodations 2007 cost: $795, includes lodging, meals, and tuition.

Additional Information Details, application, and registration form available on Web site.

◎ THE CONFERENCE ON POETRY AND TEACHING (Specialized: for high school and middle school teachers)

The Frost Place, P.O. Box 74, Franconia NH 03580. (603)823-5510. E-mail: rfrost@ncia.net. Web site: www.frostplace.org. **Contact:** Jim Schley and Baron Wormser, co-directors. Annual event. 2007 dates: June 25-29.

Purpose/Features Designed for high school and middle school classroom teachers. Brings together poets and teachers to address how poetry can be taught most effectively. Offers first-hand experience about how poems are created and how poets view their art. 2007 guest poetry faculty included Patricia Fargnoli, Renée Olander, Dzvinia Orlowsky, Tim Seibles, and BJ Ward.

Costs/Accommodations 2007 cost: $500 ($400 NH teachers), plus $80 for daily lunch and 2 dinners. Additional cost of $375 for 3 graduate credits through the University System of New Hampshire. Overnight accommodations available locally.

Additional Information To apply, send letter describing current teaching situation and literary interests. Additional information available on Web site.

GERALDINE R. DODGE POETRY FESTIVAL

Geraldine R. Dodge Poetry Program, P.O. Box 1239, Morristown NJ 07962-1239. (973)540-8442 ext. 5. Web site: www.dodgepoetryfestival.org. Established 1986. Biennial 4-day event usually held in early fall. 2006 dates: September 28-October 1; check Web site for 2008 dates. Location: Waterloo Village in Stanhope, NJ. Average attendance: nearly 17,000 in 2006.

Purpose/Features Biennial celebration of poetry for poets, students, teachers, and the general public. Presents panels, talks, and workshops covering a range of topics and issues related to poetry; offers an ambitious schedule of poetry readings featuring the cream of contemporary poets. 2006 featured poets included Billy Collins, Taha Muhammad Ali, Kurtis Lamkin, Sekou Sundiata, Linda Pastan, Lucille Clifton, Andrew Motion, and many more.

Costs/Accommodations Fee charged; check Web site for latest information. Passes can be purchased for multiple days. Participants responsible for own lodging and meals. Information on overnight accommodations in area hotels available on Web site.

Additional Information Brochure and registration form available on Web site; sign up online for mailing list for future brochures and announcements.

⚑ ⚑ ◎ FESTIVAL INTERNATIONAL DE LA POÉSIE (Specialized: poetry readings in French)

Maison de la Poésie, 1497 Laviolette, C.P. 335, Trois-Rivières QC G9A 5G4 Canada. (819)379-9813. Fax: (819)376-0774. E-mail: info@fiptr.com. Web site: www.fiptr.com. Established 1985. President/Founder: Gaston Bellemare. Annual 10-day poetry festival. 2007 dates: September 28-October 7. Location: Trois Rivières, Quebec, Canada. Average attendance: 35,000-40,000.

Purpose/Features The International Poetry Festival/Festival international de la poésie has become "a veritable literary Happening." Showcases 150 poets from 30 countries spanning 5 continents. Poets participate in over 450 events in more than 80 different venues, including cafes, bars, restaurants, art galleries, theatres, and museums. Readings are all in French. Program and list of participating poets available on Web site.

Costs/Accommodations Dinner and lunch reservations recommended at restaurants where poetry readings take place. Accommodations available at local inns, pensions, motels, and hotels. Information on travel and overnight accommodations available from the Tourism Bureau (Office de Tourisme et des Congrès de Trois-Rivières) at www.tourismetroisrivieres.com.

Additional Information Offers several festival prizes for published and unpublished poets. Guidelines available on Web site.

FINE ARTS WORK CENTER

24 Pearl St., Provincetown MA 02657. (508)487-9960, ext. 103. Fax: (508)487-8873. E-mail: workshops@fawc.org. Web site: www.fawc.org. Established 1968. **Contact:** Dorothy Antczak, summer program director. Offers 80 weekend and weeklong workshops in poetry, fiction, and creative nonfiction. Location: The Fine Arts Work Center in Provincetown.

Purpose/Features The Fine Arts Work Center in Provincetown is "a nonprofit organization dedicated to providing emerging writers and visual artists with time and space in which to pursue independent work in a community of peers." Seven-month fellowships are awarded to poets and fiction writers in the emerging stages of their careers; professional juries make admissions decisions.

Costs/Accommodations 2007 cost: Summer Workshop Program fees range $600-725 for weeklong workshops and $295-325 for weekend workshops. Accommodations available at the Work Center for $625 for 6 nights (not available for weekends). Additional accommodations available locally.

Additional Information See Web site for details and an application form.

⚑ FISHTRAP

P.O. Box 38, Enterprise OR 97828. (541)426-3623. E-mail: rich@fishtrap.org. Web site: www.fishtrap.org. **Contact:** Rich Wandschneider, director. Established 1988. Holds annual summer workshops. 2007 dates: July 8-13. Location: "the old Methodist Camp at the edge of the Eagle Cap Wilderness." Average attendance: 12/workshop; 8 workshops offered, not all in poetry.

Purpose/Features Open to anyone. "Fishtrap's goal is to promote good writing and clear thinking in and about the West. Also to encourage and promote new writers." Offers poets workshops. 2007 poetry workshop instructor: Peter Sears.

Costs/Accommodations 2007 cost: $350 for 5-day workshop; $75-150/person for cabin lodging; $40-150 for meal tickets. Other accommodations available locally. Information on overnight accommodations available on Web site.

Additional Information Awards up to 5 fellowships. Covers room and board and workshop registration. Additional information available on Web site.

FROST PLACE ANNUAL FESTIVAL OF POETRY

The Frost Place, P.O. Box 74, Franconia NH 03580. (603)823-5510. E-mail: rfrost@ncia.net. Web site: www.frostplace.org. Established 1978. Executive Director: Jim Schley. Annual weeklong conference. 2007 dates: July 29-August 4. Location: Robert Frost's historic house and barn, now a center for poetry and the arts. Average attendance: 50-55.

Purpose/Features Open to poets only. Offers daily craft talk, reading, and organized critique of participant work. 2007 guest faculty: Martha Collins, Martín Espada, Edward Hirsch, Ellen Bryant Voigt, and Eleanor Wilner; Faculty Fellows Kazim Ali, Ellen Dudley, Fred Marchant, and Barbara Ras; and Jody Gladding, Resident Poet.

Costs/Accommodations 2007 cost: $900, participant; reduced fee for auditors. Room and board available locally; information sent upon acceptance to program.

Additional Information For participants, application should be accompanied by 3 pages of your own poetry and $25 reading fee. Auditors apply by brief letter describing literary interests, accompanied by $15 reading fee. Additional information available on Web site.

THE FROST PLACE SEMINAR

The Frost Place, P.O. Box 74, Franconia NH 03580. (603)823-5510. E-mail: rfrost@ncia.net. Web site: www.frostplace.org. **Contact:** Jeanne Marie Beaumont, seminar director. Held annually in early August following the Frost Place Annual Festival of Poetry. 2007 dates: August 5-10. Average attendance: limited to 16 participants.

Purpose/Features Priority given to those who have participated in the Festival of Poetry at least once before. Offers daily lecture on poetry of the past, workshop focusing on participant poems, and evening reading. 2007 poetry staff: Jeanne Marie Beaumont, Suzanne Cleary, David Graham, and Baron Wormser.

Costs/Accommodations 2007 cost: $725 tuition; $150 (separate check) for meals.

Additional Information Admission competitive. To apply, send cover letter outlining goals for your participation and 3 pages of your own poetry as well as $25 reading fee. Additional information available on Web site.

GREEN LAKE WRITERS CONFERENCE

Green Lake Conference Center, W2511 State Highway 23, Green Lake WI 54941-9599. (800)558-8898. E-mail: program@glcc.org. Web site: www.glcc.org. Established 1948. **Contact:** Pat Zimmer. Annual weeklong event. 2007 dates: August 12-17. Location: Green Lake, WI. Average attendance: 40-60.

Purpose/Features "Our only requirement is a desire to learn and grow in your craft." Offers poets workshop with discussions and assignments. 2007 poetry presenter was Barbara Smith.

Costs/Accommodations For costs and accommodations, see information on Web site.

Additional Information Offers poetry contest as part of conference. Guidelines available for SASE, by e-mail, or on Web site. Scholarships available. Brochure available on Web site.

HIGHLAND SUMMER WORKSHOP

Appalachian Regional Studies Center, P.O. Box 7014, Radford University, Radford VA 24142. (540)831-5366. Fax: (540)831-5951. E-mail: jasbury@radford.edu. Web site: www.radford.edu/~arsc. Established 1977. **Contact:** Dr. Grace Toney Edwards, director. Annual 2-week event. Dates: first 2 weeks in June. Location: Radford University campus. Average attendance: 20-25.

Purpose/Features Open to everyone. "The conference, a lecture/seminar/workshop combination, is conducted by well-known guest writers and offers the opportunity to study and practice creative and expository writing within the context of regional culture." Poetry, fiction, and essays (prose) are generally covered each year, as are various topics. The last workshop was led by Robert Morgan, Richard Hague, Kathryn Stripling Byers, and Sharyn McCrumb.

Costs/Accommodations 2007 cost: $544-1,426; meal plan is $18.56/day. Individual meals may also be purchased. On-site housing costs range from $24-34/night. On-site accommodations available at Ingles Hall. Accommodations also available at local motels.

Additional Information Brochure and registration form available for SASE.

⚒ HOFSTRA UNIVERSITY SUMMER WRITING WORKSHOPS

University College for Continuing Education, 250 Hofstra University, Hempstead NY 11549. (516)463-7600. E-mail: uccelibarts@hofstra.edu. Web site: www.hofstra.edu/UCCE/summerwriting. **Contact:** Richard Pioreck and Judith Reed, co-directors. Established 1972. Annual 2-week event. 2007 dates: July 9-20. Location: Hofstra University. Average attendance: 60-70.

Purpose/Features Open to all writers. "Each workshop includes both group and individual sessions and totals more than 35 contact hours in a genuine workshop environment." 2007 poetry presenter was Julie Sheehan.

Costs/Accommodations 2007 cost: $429 residence fee and $490 tuition (non-credit); banquet included for workshop registrants. "Lodging in residence halls can be arranged for participants 19 years of age or older."

Additional Information Undergraduate and graduate credit (3 s.h.) available at current Hofstra University tuition rates. Additional information available by phone, e-mail, or on Web site.

INDIANA UNIVERSITY WRITERS' CONFERENCE

464 Ballantine Hall, Indiana University, Bloomington IN 47405. (812)855-1877. Fax: (812)855-9535. E-mail: writecon@indiana.edu. Web site: www.indiana.edu/~writecon. Established 1940. **Contact:** Bob Bledsoe, director. Annual weeklong event. 2007 dates: June 10-15. Location: Bloomington campus of Indiana University. Average attendance: 100.

Purpose/Features Open to all. Offers poets workshops, classes, readings, and ms critiques. 2007 poetry presenters included Heather McHugh, Khaled Mattawa, Catherine Bowman, and Crystal Wilkenson.

Costs/Accommodations 2007 cost: $500 for workshop (including all classes); $300 for classes only. $50 application fee. Accommodations available on site. Information on overnight accommodations available on Web site.

Additional Information Poetry workshop applicants must submit up to 10 pages of poetry with application. Brochure and registration form available for SASE, by e-mail, or on Web site.

IOWA SUMMER WRITING FESTIVAL

C215 Seashore Hall, University of Iowa, Iowa City IA 52242. (319)335-4160. Fax: (319)335-4039. E-mail: iswfestival@uiowa.edu. Web site: www.uiowa.edu/~iswfest. Established 1987. **Contact:** Amy Margolis, director. Annual 6-week event. 2007 dates: June 10-July 27. Includes one-week and weekend workshops at the University of Iowa campus. Average attendance: 150/week.

Purpose/Features "Open to all adults 21 and over who have a desire to write." Offers poets workshops, lectures, discussions, and participant readings in either weeklong or weekend formats. Participants in weeklong workshops have private conference/critique with workshop leader. 2007 poetry staff included Jane Mead, Christine Hemp, Bruce Bond, Jim Heynen, Michael Morse, Michael Dennis Browne, Katie Ford, and Vince Gotera.

Costs/Accommodations 2007 cost: $250 for a weekend course and $500-525 for a one-week course. Participants responsible for most meals. Accommodations available at area hotels. Information on overnight accommodations available by phone or on Web site.

Additional Information Brochure and registration form available for SASE or on Web site.

◎ THE IWWG SUMMER CONFERENCE

The International Women's Writing Guild, P.O. Box 810, Gracie Station, New York NY 10028. (212)737-7536. Fax: (212)737-9469. E-mail: iwwg@iwwg.org. Web site: www.iwwg.org. Established 1978. **Contact:** Hannelore Hahn, executive director. 2007 dates: June 15-22. Location: Skidmore College in Saratoga Springs, NY. Average attendance: 500 maximum.

Purpose/Features Open to all women. Around 65 workshops offered each day. 2007 poetry staff included Barbara Garro, Marj Hahne, D.H. Melhem, Myra Shapiro, and Susan Baugh.

Costs/Accommodations 2006 cost: $1,004 (single), $869 (double) for IWWG members; $1,034 (single), $899 (double) for nonmembers. Includes program and room and board for 7 nights, 21 meals at Skidmore College. Shorter conference stays available, such as 5 days or weekend. Commuters welcome.

Additional Information Post-conference retreat weekend also available. Additional information available for SASE, by e-mail, or on Web site.

JENTEL ARTIST RESIDENCY PROGRAM

Jentel Foundation, 130 Lower Piney Creek Rd., Banner WY 82832. (307)737-2311. Fax: (307)737-2305. E-mail: jentel@jentelarts.org. Web site: www.jentelarts.org. Established 2000. One-month residencies throughout the year, scheduled the 15th of one month through the 13th of the following month. Application deadlines are September 15 and January 15 annually. Location: Banner, WY. Average attendance: 2 writers in any genre (also 4 visual artists in any media).

Purpose/Features Residency program for writers and visual artists who are U.S. citizens or from the international community currently residing in the U.S., are 25 years and older, and are not matriculated students. "Set in a rural ranch setting in the foothills of the Big Horn Mountains of North Central Wyoming, Jentel offers unfettered time and space to focus on the creative process, experience of Wyoming landscape, and interact as desired with a small community of writers and artists." Special features include Jentel Presents, a monthly evening of slide presentations and readings by residents in one of the surrounding communities.

Costs/Accommodations Residents are responsible for travel expenses and personal items. "Jentel provides a private accommodation in a shared living space, a comfortable private studio, and a stipend to help defray the cost of food and personal expenses. Staff takes residents grocery shopping weekly after the stipend is distributed. Staff will pick up and drop off residents at the airport and bus station in Sheridan, 20 miles from the ranch setting of Jentel." Accommodation provided in a large house with common living and dining areas; fully equipped kitchen; library with computer, printer, and Internet access; media room with television, video player, and CD player; spacious private bedroom; and separate private studio.

Additional Information Brochure and application form available for self-addressed mailing label and 58 cents postage, or on Web site.

◎ LIFE PRESS CHRISTIAN WRITERS' CONFERENCE

P.O. Box 2018, Cordova TN 38088. (901)309-3692. E-mail: gmoearth@aol.com. Web site: www.grandmotherearth.org. Established 1998. **Contact:** Frances Cowden. Annual one-day event. 2007 date: August 4. Location: Cordova, TN. Average attendance: 45.

Purpose/Features Open to all writers. Offers poets workshops, lectures, readings, and ms critiques. 2007 staff included Robert Hall, Florence Bruce, Cindy Beebe, and Sarah Hull Gurley.

Costs/Accommodations 2007 cost: $35 registration fee (includes one contest entry, critique of all entries, continental breakfast and lunch); $30 (includes registration with entries plus food, but no critique); or $25 (includes food, no entries); $20 fee for spouses. Information on overnight accommodations available in brochure.

Additional Information Individual poetry critiques available. Poets should submit a limit of 6 works/category and $10 fee. "One payment for all entries—send with entries." Sponsors contest for "poetry and prose in general, open to all writers. Other contests require attendance." National Awards for poetry (open to everyone, 50-line limit) are $50, $25, $15, and $10. Conference Awards for poetry (open to those who register for the conference, 30-line limit) are $50, $15, and $10.

Entry fee: "$5 entitles you to one entry; $2 for each additional entry." **Deadline:** July 6 for 2007. Critique from the judges is available for $10 for all entries. Guidelines available for SASE.

LIGONIER VALLEY WRITERS CONFERENCE

P.O. Box B, Ligonier PA 15658. (724)593-7294. E-mail: jgallagher@LHTC.net. Web site: www.ligonervalleywriters.org. Established 1986. **Contact:** Judith Gallagher. Annual 2-day event. 2007 dates: July 27 and 28. Location: Ramada Inn in Ligonier, PA. Average attendance: 40-50.

Purpose/Features Open to anyone interested in writing. Past poetry faculty have included P.J. Corso, Lynn Emmanuel, Jim Daniels, Julia Kasdorf, and Jeffrey Thomson.

Costs/Accommodations 2006 cost: $70-175 for members, $80-190 for nonmembers, depending on number of days attending and early registration discounts. Tuition includes Saturday dinner and lecture, and publishing roundtable. Friday picnic and Saturday lunch available for additional fee. Overnight accommodations available on site. Information on overnight accommodations available on Web site.

Additional Information Registration form and additional information available on Web site. "Ligonier Valley Writers also publishes *The Loyalhanna Review*, a literary journal, which is open to participants."

◎ MONTEREY COWBOY POETRY & MUSIC FESTIVAL

1120 Forest Ave., #319, Pacific Grove CA 93950. (800)722-9652. E-mail: info@montereycowboy.com. Web site: www.montereycowboy.com. Established 1998. **Contact:** J.P. "Mick" Vernon, president. Annual 2-day, 3-night event. 2007 dates: December 7, 8, and 9. Location: Monterey Conference Center. Average attendance: 2,000.

Purpose/Features Open to the general public. Celebrates cowboy poetry and music. Offerings include 9 separate shows of varying theme, most featuring 2 poets and 2 musicians; a few feature strictly poets. Other special features include an open mic at noon on Saturday and Sunday, and a Western art and gear show.

Costs/Accommodations 2007 cost: admission either $15 or $35; an All-Event Pass, $190. Covers admission costs only; participants responsible for own housing and meals. Information on overnight accommodations available. Accommodations include special rates at area hotels.

Additional Information Brochure available on Web site.

✪ MONTEVALLO LITERARY FESTIVAL

Sta. 6420, University of Montevallo, Montevallo AL 35115. (205)665-6420. Fax: (205)665-6422. E-mail: murphyj@montevallo.edu. Web site: www.montevallo.edu/english. Established 2003. **Contact:** Dr. Jim Murphy, director. Annual 2-day event. 2007 dates: April 13-14. Location: several sites on the bucolic University of Montevallo campus. Average attendance: 60-100.

Purpose/Features Presents "a unique opportunity for participants to interact with some of the top writers in the country. Participants attend workshops in poetry, prose, or drama, working closely on their own writing with some of the country's most distinguished poets, fiction writers, playwrights, and writers of nonfiction." Offers poets readings, panels, workshops, and ms critiques. 2007 poetry workshop leader: Catherine Bowman. Prior poetry workshop leaders have included Angela Ball, Don Bogen, Andrew Hudgins, Rodney Jones, Jeff Thomson, Natasha Trethewey, and Frank X Walker.

Costs/Accommodations 2007 cost: $45 for festival, including meals; $95 for festival, including meals and workshop. Offers overnight accommodations at Ramsay Conference Center on campus; rooms $40/night. Call (205)665-6280 for reservations. Free on-campus parking. Additional information available at www.montevallo.edu/cont_ed/ramsay.shtm.

Additional Information Poetry workshop participants submit up to 5 pages of poetry; e-mail as

Word doc to Jim Murphy (murphyj@montevallo.edu) at least 2 weeks prior to festival. Brochure available on Web site. Information on upcoming festival available in February.

NAPA VALLEY WRITERS' CONFERENCE

Napa Valley College, 1088 College Ave., St. Helena CA 94574. (707)967-2900. E-mail: writecon@napavalley.edu. Web site: www.napawritersconf.org. **Contact:** Anne Evans, managing director; or Nan Cohen, poetry director. Established 1981. Annual weeklong event. 2007 dates: July 29-August 3. Location: Upper Valley Campus in the historic town of St. Helena, 25 miles north of Napa in the heart of the valley's wine growing community. Average attendance: 48 in poetry and 48 in fiction.

Purpose/Features "Serious writers of all backgrounds and experience are welcome to apply." Offers poets workshops, lectures, faculty readings, ms critiques, and meetings with editors. "Poetry session provides the opportunity to work both on generating new poems and on revising previously written ones." 2007 poetry faculty included Jane Hirshfield, Elizabeth Alexander, Stephen Dunn, and David St. John.

Costs/Accommodations 2007 cost: $700, including breakfast, lunch, 2 dinners, and attendance at all conference events. Scholarships are available. Information on overnight accommodations available. Limited accommodations in local homes available on a first-come, first-served basis; $30 one-time placement fee.

Additional Information All applicants are asked to submit a qualifying ms with their registration (no more than 5 poems) as well as a brief description of their writing background. Include $10 reading fee and $75 tuition deposit with application. 2007 application deadline: May 16. Brochure and registration form available for SASE or on Web site.

S.O.M.O.S., SOCIETY OF THE MUSE OF THE SOUTHWEST

P.O. Box 3225, Taos NM 87571. (505)758-0081. Fax: (505)758-4802. E-mail: somos@laplaza.com. Web site: www.somostaos.org. Established 1983. **Contact:** Dori Vinella, executive director. "We offer readings, special events, and workshops at different times during the year." Length of workshops varies. Location: various sites in Taos. Average attendance: 10-50.

Purpose/Features Open to anyone. "We offer workshops in various genres—fiction, poetry, nature writing, etc." Past workshop presenters have included Denise Chavez, Marjorie Agosin, Judyth Hill, Robin Becker, Sawnie Morris, and Lise Goett. Other special features include the 2-day Annual Taos Storytelling Festival in October, a Winter Writers Series (January-February), and Summer Writer's Series (July-August).

Costs/Accommodations See Web site for current information.

Additional Information Additional information available by fax, e-mail, or on Web site. "Taos has a wonderful community of dedicated and talented writers who make S.O.M.O.S. workshops rigorous, supportive, and exciting." Also publishes *Chokecherries*, an annual anthology.

◪ SAGE HILL SUMMER WRITING EXPERIENCE

P.O. Box 1731, Saskatoon SK S7K 3S1 Canada. Phone/fax: (306)652-7395. E-mail: sage.hill@sasktel.net. Web site: www.sagehillwriting.ca. Established 1990. **Contact:** Steven Ross Smith, executive director. Annual 10-day adult summer program. 2007 dates: July 23-August 2. Location: St. Michael's Retreat, Lumsden, Saskatchewan. Average attendance: varies according to specific workshop (usually 5-11 participants).

Purpose/Features Open to writers, 19 years of age and older, who are working in English. No geographic restrictions. Offers poets workshops, labs, colloquia, and readings. 2007 poetry staff included Jeanette Lynes, John Steffler, and Nicole Brossard.

Costs/Accommodations 2007 cost: $1,095 CAD, including instruction, accommodations, meals, and all facilities. Accommodations available on site.

Additional Information Writing sample and $50 CAD deposit required with application. Additional information available for SASE, by phone, e-mail, or on Web site.

THE SANDHILLS WRITERS CONFERENCE

Augusta State University, Augusta GA 30904. (706)729-2417. Fax: (706)729-2247. E-mail: akellman @aug.edu. Web site: www.sandhills.aug.edu. Established 1975. **Contact:** Anthony Kellman, conference director. Annual 3-day event usually held the third weekend in March. 2007 dates: March 22-24. Location: campus of Augusta State University. Facilities are handicapped accessible. Average attendance: 100.

Purpose/Features Designed to "hone the creative writing skills of participants and provide networking opportunities." Open to all aspiring writers. Offers poets craft lectures, ms evaluations, and readings. 2007 poetry presenters included Stephen Dunn.

Costs/Accommodations 2007 cost: $156 full conference registration; $110 conference-only registration (no ms critique); $76 full conference student registration. All registrations include 2 lunches. Accommodations available at area hotels. Information on overnight accommodations available on Web site.

Additional Information Offers poetry contest as part of conference; also offers scholarships to college students. Guidelines available by e-mail or on Web site. Brochure and registration form available for SASE or on Web site.

SANTA BARBARA WRITERS CONFERENCE

P.O. Box 6627, Santa Barbara CA 93160. (805)964-0367. E-mail: info@sbwritersconference.com. Web site: www.sbwritersconference.com. Established 1973. **Contact:** Marcia Meier, executive director. Annual event. 2008 dates: June 20-27. Location: Fess Parker's Doubletree Resort in Santa Barbara. Average attendance: 450.

Purpose/Features Open to everyone. Covers all genres of writing. Offers poets workshops, lectures, faculty readings, participant readings, ms critiques, master classes, young writers program, and meetings with agents and editors. 2007 poetry presenters included Christopher Buckley and Perie J. Longo.

Costs/Accommodations 2007 cost: $625 before March 1, $825 after (including all workshops and lectures, closing dinner, and final awards breakfast). Accommodations available on site or nearby. Information on overnight accommodations available by e-mail or on Web site.

Additional Information Offers poetry contest as part of conference. Guidelines available on Web site. Brochure and registration form available on Web site.

◨ SASKATCHEWAN FESTIVAL OF WORDS

Moose Jaw Cultural Centre, 217 Main St. N., Moose Jaw SK S6H 0W1. (306)691-0557. Fax: (306)693-2994. E-mail: word.festival@sasktel.net. Web site: www.festivalofwords.com. Established 1997. **Contact:** Gary Hyland, artistic director; Christie Saas, manager of operations. Annual 4-day event. 2007 dates: July 19-22. Location: Moose Jaw Library/Art Museum complex in Crescent Park. Average attendance: about 4,000 admissions.

Purpose/Features "The Saskatchewan Festival of Words celebrates the imaginative uses of language, and features fiction and nonfiction writers, screenwriters, poets, children's authors, songwriters, dramatists, and film makers. Our festival is an ideal place for people who love words to mingle, promote their books, get acquainted, share ideas, conduct impromptu readings, and meet their fans." Offers poets workshops, readings, and open mics. 2006 poetry program presenters included Daniel Scott Tysdal, Karen Solie, David Seymour, and Jeanette Lynes.

Costs/Accommodations 2007 cost: $8 CAD for adults; some adult events with front-line entertainment and meals cost $15-20 CAD. "Patrons can save up to 50% by purchasing a festival pass, especially before the end of June." Accommodations available at local inns, campgrounds, and bed & breakfast establishments. Information on overnight accommodations available for SASE or by phone or e-mail.

Additional Information Complete information about festival presenters, events, costs, and schedule available on Web site. Festival presented by Living Skies Festival of Words, Inc.

SEWANEE WRITERS' CONFERENCE

735 University Ave., Sewanee TN 37383-1000. (931)598-1141. E-mail: cpeters@sewanee.edu. Web site: www.sewaneewriters.org. Established 1990. **Contact:** Cheri B. Peters, creative writing programs manager. Annual 12-day event held the last 2 weeks in July. Location: the University of the South ("dormitories for housing, Women's Center for public events, classrooms for workshops, Sewanee Inn for dining, etc."). Attendance: about 120.

Purpose/Features Open to poets, fiction writers, and playwrights who submit their work for review in a competitive admissions process. "Participants belong to a workshop devoted to constructive critique of members' manuscripts; in addition, each participant has an individual, private manuscript conference with a faculty member. Readings, craft lectures, panels, and Q&A sessions round out the formal offerings; numerous social functions offer opportunities for informal exchange and networking. Workshops are genre-based rather than theme-based." 2007 poetry presenters featured Brad Leithauser, Charles Martin, Mary Jo Salter, Alan Shapiro, Mark Strand, and Greg Williamson. Guest poets Daniel Anderson, Andrew Hudgins, and Mark Jarman will give readings, as will conference director Wayatt Prunty.

Costs/Accommodations 2007 cost: $1,600, including shared-occupancy room; single rooms are available for a modest additional fee. Each year scholarships and fellowships based on merit are available on a competitive basis.

Additional Information A ms should be sent in advance after admission to the conference. Write for brochure and application forms; no SASE necessary. Additional information available on Web site.

⊠ SOUTHAMPTON WRITERS CONFERENCE

Stony Brook Southampton, 239 Montauk Hwy., Southampton NY 11968. (631)632-5030. E-mail: southamptonwriters@notes.cc.sunysb.edu. Web site: www.stonybrook.edu/writers. **Contact:** Adrienne Unger, coordinator. Established 1976. Annual 11-day event. 2007 dates: July 18-29. Location: Stony Brook Southampton's seaside campus "in the heart of the Hamptons." Average attendance: 12/workshop.

Purpose/Features Open to new and established writers, graduate students, and upper-level undergraduate students. Offers poetry workshops and readings. 2007 poetry staff included Billy Collins and Carol Muske-Dukes.

Costs/Accommodations 2007 cost: $25 application fee; $2,050 for workshop, room and board; $1,450 workshop only (includes breakfast and lunch). Accommodations available on site.

Additional Information "Evening events will feature regular faculty and award-winning visiting authors. Participants will also enjoy a rich schedule of formal and informal social gatherings—author receptions, open mic nights, and special literary events. Early application is encouraged." Brochure and registration form available by e-mail or on Web site.

SPLIT ROCK ARTS PROGRAM

University of Minnesota, 360 Coffey Hall, 1420 Eckles Ave., St. Paul MN 55108-6084. (612)625-8100. Fax: (612)624-6210. E-mail: srap@cce.umn.edu. Web site: www.cce.umn.edu/splitrockarts. Established 1983. **Contact:** Anastasia Faunce, program director. Summer series of weeklong and 3-day workshops in creative writing, visual art, and design. 2008 dates: June 15-August 1. Location: University's Twin Cities campus Cloquet Forestry Center in Northern MN. Average attendance: 550.

Purpose/Features Open to anyone over 18 years old interested in literary and visual arts and design. Offers writers a variety of intensive workshops with renowned faculty. 2008 faculty to be determined. 2007 writing faculty included Wesley Brown, W.S. Di Piero, Carolyn Forché, Robin Hemley, Susan Hubbard, Tyehimba Jess, Susan Shreve, Frank X Walker, and more.

Costs/Accommodations 2007 cost: $550 tuition (noncredit); undergraduate/graduate credit available for additional fee. Scholarships available. Participants responsible for most meals. Accommodations available on site or at area hotels.

Additional Information Print catalogs available in February. Registration opens in late February. Additional information available on Web site.

SQUAW VALLEY COMMUNITY OF WRITERS POETRY WORKSHOP

P.O. Box 1416, Nevada City CA 95959. (530)470-8440. E-mail: info@squawvalleywriters.org. Web site: www.squawvalleywriters.org. Established 1969. **Contact:** Brett Hall Jones, executive director. Annual 7-day event. 2007 dates: July 21-28. Location: The Squaw Valley USA's Lodge in the Sierras near Lake Tahoe. Average attendance: 60 for poetry.

Purpose/Features Open to talented writers of diverse ethnic backgrounds and a wide range of ages. "The Poetry Program differs in concept from other workshops in poetry. Our project's purpose is to help participants break through old habits and write something daring and difficult. Workshops are intended to provide a supportive atmosphere in which no one will be embarrassed, and at the same time to challenge the participants to go beyond what they have done before. Admissions are based on quality of the submitted manuscripts." Offers poets regular morning workshops, craft lectures, and staff readings. "Participants gather in daily workshops to discuss the work they wrote in the previous 24 hours." 2007 poetry presenters included Robert Hass, Sharon Olds, Jimmy Santiago Baca, Brenda Hillman, and Claudia Rankine.

Costs/Accommodations 2007 cost: $750 for poetry tuition (includes 6 evening meals), $25 reading/application fee. Accommodations extra. "We arrange housing for participants in local houses and condominiums at a variety of rates." Information on overnight accommodations available on Web site.

Additional Information Brochure available by e-mail (include mailing address for response) or on Web site. Also publishes the annual *Squaw Valley Community of Writers Omnium Gatherum and Newsletter* containing "news and profiles on our past participants and staff, craft articles, and book advertising."

STEAMBOAT SPRINGS WRITERS CONFERENCE

P.O. Box 774284, Steamboat Springs CO 80477. (970)879-8079. E-mail: sswriters@cs.com. Web site: www.steamboatwriters.com. Established 1982. **Contact:** Harriet Freiberger, director. Annual one-day event usually held in mid-July. Location: a "renovated train station, the Depot is home of the Steamboat Springs Arts Council—friendly, relaxed atmosphere." Average attendance: 35-40 (registration limited).

Purpose/Features Open to anyone. Conference is "designed for writers who have limited time. Instructors vary from year to year, offering maximum instruction during a weekend at a nominal cost." Previous poetry instructors include David Mason, Renate Wood, Jim Tipton, and Donald Revell.

Costs/Accommodations 2006 cost: $25 members, $35 nonmembers before May 19; then $35 and $45 respectively. Includes seminar and catered luncheon. "A variety of lodgings available."

Additional Information Brochure and registration form available for SASE, by e-mail, or on Web site. Optional: Friday evening dinner (cost not included in registration fee); readings by participants (no cost).

TAOS SUMMER WRITERS' CONFERENCE

University of New Mexico, Dept. of English Language and Literature, MSC03 2170, 1 University of New Mexico, Albuquerque NM 87131-0001. (505)277-5572. Fax: (505)277-2950. E-mail: taosconf@unm.edu. Web site: www.unm.edu/~taosconf. Established 1999. **Contact:** Sharon Oard Warner, director. Annual 5-day (weeklong) and 2-day (weekend) workshops usually held mid-July. Location: Sagebrush Inn in Taos. Average attendance: 180 total; 100 places available in weekend, 180 places available in weeklong workshops. Class size limited to 12/class, usually smaller.

Purpose/Features Open to everyone, beginners to experienced. Minimum age is 18. Friendly, relaxed atmosphere with supportive staff and instructors. Offers both weekend and weeklong workshops in such areas as fiction, poetry, memoir, publishing, screenwriting, and craft, with master classes in novel, poetry, and memoir. One-on-one consultations with agents and editors available. Workshop presenters have included Pam Houston, Antonya Nelson, Hilda Raz, Demetria Martinez, and John Dufresne. Special features include evening readings and panels, open mic sessions, and tours of the D.H. Lawrence Ranch.

Costs/Accommodations 2007 cost: $300 for weekend, $600 for weeklong sessions, $825 combo, including workshop registration and special events. Nearest airport is Albuquerque International Sunport. Taos is about 170 miles north of Albuquerque. Information on overnight accommodations available. Sagebrush Inn and Comfort Suites offer special rates.

Additional Information Brochure and registration form available by e-mail or on Web site. "Taos is a unique experience of a lifetime. The setting and scenery are spectacular; historical and natural beauty abound. Our previous attendees say they have been inspired by the place and by the friendly, personal attention of our instructors."

⊕ TY NEWYDD WRITERS' CENTRE

Llanystumdwy, Criccieth, Gwynedd LL52 0LW Wales. (44)(1766)522 811. Fax: (44)(1766)523095. E-mail: post@tynewydd.org. Web site: www.tynewydd.org. Established 1990. **Contact:** Director. Holds 4½-day courses throughout the year, as well as writers' retreats. Location: Ty Newydd, The National Writers' Centre for Wales. Average attendance: 16/course maximum.

Purpose/Features Open to anyone over 16 years of age. Courses are designed to "promote the writing and understanding of literature by providing creative writing courses at all levels for all ages. Courses at Ty Newydd provide the opportunity of working intimately and informally with two professional writers." Courses specifically for poets of all levels of experience and ability are offered throughout the year.

Costs/Accommodations 2008 cost: check Web site. 2007 cost for a 4½-day course was £460 (private room) and £410 (shared room). Information about accommodations available on Web site.

Additional Information Brochure and registration form available for SASE, or request by e-mail. Also offers the Gwyl Ty Newydd Festival in June; see Web site for details.

⊡ VICTORIA SCHOOL OF WRITING

Suite 306-620 View St., Victoria BC V8W 1J6 Canada. (250)595-3000. E-mail: info@victoriaschoolof writing.org. Web site: www.victoriaschoolofwriting.org. Established 1995. **Contact:** Jill Margo, executive director. Annual 5-day event. 2007 dates: July 15-20. Location: "Residential school in natural, park-like setting. Easy parking, access to university, downtown." Average attendance: 100.

Purpose/Features "A three- to ten-page manuscript is required as part of the registration process, which is open to all. The general purpose of the workshop is to give hands-on assistance with better writing, working closely with established author-instructors." Offers poets intensive 5-day workshops (15 hours of instruction and one-on-one consultation). 2007 poetry presenters included Di Brandt and Tom Wayman.

Costs/Accommodations 2007 cost: $610 CAD, including 5 lunches and final barbeque. Various meal/accommodation packages available; see Web site.

Additional Information Brochure and registration form available through online request form.

WESLEYAN WRITERS CONFERENCE

Wesleyan University, Middletown CT 06457. (860)685-3604. Fax: (860)685-2441. E-mail: agreene@wesleyan.edu. Web site: www.wesleyan.edu/writers. Established 1956. **Contact:** Anne Greene, director. Annual 5-day event. 2007 dates: June 17-22. Location: the campus of Wesleyan University "in the hills overlooking the Connecticut River, a brief drive from the Connecticut shore. Wesleyan's outstanding library, poetry reading room, and other university facilities are open to participants." Average attendance: 100.

Purpose/Features "The conference welcomes everyone interested in the writer's craft. Participants are a diverse, international group. Both new and experienced writers are welcome. You may attend all of the seminars, including poetry, the novel, short story, fiction techniques, literary journalism, and memoir." Offers poets workshops, lectures, readings, ms critiques, meetings with editors and agents, and special panel presentations. 2007 poetry presenters included Honor Moore, Sherwin Bitsui, and Laura Cronk.

Costs/Accommodations 2007 cost: $830 day student rate (includes tuition only); $1,050 day student rate, full program (includes tuition and meals); $1,250 boarding student rate (includes tuition, meals, room for 5 nights). Accommodations available on site or at area hotels. Information on overnight accommodations available on Web site.

Additional Information Registration for critiques must be made before the conference. Additional information available by phone, fax, or on Web site.

WHIDBEY ISLAND WRITERS' CONFERENCES

The Whidbey Island Writers' Association, P.O. Box 1289, Langley WA 98260. (360)331-6714. E-mail: writers@writeonwhidbey.org. Web site: www.writeonwhidbey.org. Established 1997. Annual event. 2008 dates: February 29-March 2. Location: South Whidbey High School and various sites in the Whidbey Island area. Average attendance: 250.

Purpose/Features Open to writers of every genre and skill level. Offers poets workshops, lectures, readings, author critiques, and "Author Fireside Chats." 2007 poetry presenters included Michael Dylan Welch, Thomas Hubbard, Gloria Burgess, and Dick Warwick.

Costs/Accommodations 2008 cost: $375 WIWA members, $395 nonmembers. Participants responsible for most meals. Accommodations available at area hotels. Information on overnight accommodations available on Web site.

Additional Information Offers Benefactor's Award Writing Contest as part of conference. Open to conference attendeees only. Guidelines available on Web site. Program and registration form available on Web site. Brochure available by calling (360)331-6714.

WINTER POETRY & PROSE GETAWAY IN CAPE MAY

18 North Richards Ave., Ventnor NJ 08406. (609)823-5076. E-mail: info@wintergetaway.com. Web site: www.wintergetaway.com. Established 1994. **Contact:** Peter E. Murphy, founder/director. Annual 4-day event. 2008 dates: January 18-21. Location: The Grand Hotel on the Oceanfront in Historic Cape May, NJ. Average attendance: 200 (10 or fewer participants in each poetry workshop).

Purpose/Features Open to all writers, beginners and experienced, over the age of 18. "The poetry workshop meets for an hour or so each morning before sending you off with an assignment that will encourage and inspire you to produce exciting new work. After lunch, we gather together to read new drafts in feedback sessions led by experienced poet-teachers who help identify the poem's virtues and offer suggestions to strengthen its weaknesses. The groups are small, and you receive positive attention to help your poem mature. In late afternoon, you can continue writing or schedule a free, personal tutorial session with one of the poets on staff." 2007 poetry presenters included Stephen Dunn, Kurt Brown, Catherine Doty, Douglas Goetsch, James Richardson, and many more.

Costs/Accommodations 2007 cost: $350 registration, including lunch and receptions, 3 days of workshops, and a 20-minute tutorial with one of the poets on staff. Accommodations, including breakfast, cost an additional $215 for a double room or $350 for a single. A $25 Early Bard Discount is available if paid in full by November 15.

Additional Information Brochure and registration form available by mail or on Web site. "The Winter Getaway is known for its challenging and supportive atmosphere that encourages imaginative risk-taking and promotes freedom and transformation in the participants' writing."

THE WRITERS WORKSHOP

Kenyon College, Gambier OH 43022. (740)427-5207. E-mail: reacha@kenyon.edu. Web site: www.kenyonreview.org/workshops. **Contact:** Anna Duke Reach, Director of Summer Programs and Special Events. Annual 8-day event. 2007 dates: June 16-23. Location: the Kenyon College campus. Average attendance: 10/class.

Purpose/Features Offers the time, setting, and community for writers to practice and develop their art. Focuses on the generation and revision of new work, although participants may bring works-in-progress. Offers poets one-on-one meetings with instructors, exercises and discussions, and public readings by distinguished visiting writers and workshop participants. 2007 poetry instructors were David Baker and Rosanna Warren.

Costs/Accommodations 2007 cost: $1,995 (includes tuition, room, and meals). A $200 discount is offered to returning participants. Participants are housed in modern campus apartments with computer access.

Additional Information College and nondegree graduate credit available. Online application form and writing sample submission available on Web site. Early application is encouraged as space is limited.

WRITERS@WORK

Conference Registration, P.O. Box 540370, North Salt Lake UT 84054-0370. (801)292-9285. E-mail: contact@writersatwork.org. Web site: www.writersatwork.org. Established 1985. **Contact**: Lisa Peterson, administrative assistant. Annual event. 2007 dates: June 18-22. Location: Westminster College campus in Salt Lake City. Average attendance: limited to 15/workshop.

Purpose/Features Open to writers of all levels. Offers poets workshops, panel discussions, ms critiques, and readings. 2007 faculty: Olena Kalytiak Davis.

Costs/Accommodations 2007 cost: $495, including workshop, afternoon sessions, and 30-minute ms consultation. Limited number of suites available on site for $175.

Additional Information Schedule and registration information available on Web site.

◎ THE YOUNG POETS CONFERENCE (formerly The Frost Place Young Poets Conference)

The Frost Place, P.O. Box 74, Franconia NH 03580. (603)823-5510. E-mail: rfrost@ncia.net. Web site: www.frostplace.org. **Contact:** Jim Schley, executive director. Annual event. 2007 dates: April 27-29.

Purpose/Features Designed for high school students along with high school and middle school classroom teachers. "An intensive poetry experience in a historic New England inn, with time for writing, revision, workshops, readings, and games; and with a field trip to the nearby Frost Place, Robert Frost's former home." 2007 faculty poets included Eloise Bruce, Geof Hewitt, and Elizabeth Powell.

Costs/Accommodations 2007 costs: $275. Includes local housing and meals.

Additional Information To apply, send a brief letter describing interests in poetry and noting current year in school, mailing address, phone number, and e-mail address. Also enclose 3 original poems and a letter of recommendation from a teacher. Additional information available on Web site.

ADDITIONAL CONFERENCES, WORKSHOPS & FESTIVALS

The following cross-references listings in other sections of this book that include information about conferences, workshops, conventions and festivals. Among these are state and local poetry groups that may offer a variety of workshop opportunities for their members.

Resources

Resources

Organizations

There are many organizations of value to poets. These groups may sponsor workshops and contests, stage readings, publish anthologies and chapbooks or spread the word about publishing opportunities. A few provide economic assistance or legal advice. The best thing organizations offer, though, is a support system to which poets can turn for a pep talk, a hard-nosed (but sympathetic) critique of a manuscript or simply the comfort of talking and sharing with others who understand the challenges, and joys, of writing poetry.

Whether national, regional or as local as your library or community center, each organization has something special to offer. The listings in this section reflect the membership opportunities available to poets with a variety of organizations. Some groups provide certain services to both members and nonmembers.

These symbols may appear at the beginning of some listings: The (**N**) symbol indicates a recently established organization new to *Poet's Market*; the (**↗**) symbol indicates this organization did not appear in the 2007 edition; the (**✦**) symbol denotes a Canadian organization and the (**⊕**) symbol one headquartered outside the U.S. and Canada.

Since some organizations are included in listings in the other sections of this book, we've cross-referenced these listings under Additional Organizations at the end of this section. For further details about an organization associated with a market in this list, go to that market's page number.

To find out more about groups in your area (including those that may not be listed in *Poet's Market*), contact your YMCA, community center, local colleges and universities, public library and bookstores (and don't forget newspapers and the Internet). If you can't find a group that suits your needs, consider starting one yourself. You might be surprised to discover there are others in your locality who would welcome the encouragement, feedback and moral support of a writer's group.

⊕ ACADEMI—YR ACADEMI GYMREIG/THE WELSH ACADEMY

Mount Stuart House, 3rd Floor, Cardiff CF10 5FQ Wales. (44)(29)2047-2266. Fax: (44)(29)2049-2930. E-mail: post@academi.org. Web site: www.academi.org. Established 1959. **Contact:** Peter Finch, chief executive. Literary center "promotes literature in Wales and assists in the maintaining of its standard." The Welsh National Literature Promotion Agency and Society of Writers is open to "the population of Wales and those outside Wales with an interest in Welsh writing." Currently has 2,000 members. Levels of membership/dues: associate, full, and fellow; £15/year (waged) or £7.50/year (unwaged). Offerings include promotion of readings, events, conferences, exchanges, tours; employment of literature-development workers; publication of a bimonthly events magazine; publication of a literary magazine in Welsh (*Taliesin*) and another (*NWR*) in English. Sponsors conferences/workshops and contests/awards. Publishes *A470: What's On In Literary Wales*, a magazine appearing 5 times/year containing information on Welsh literary events. Available to nonmembers for £15 (annual subscription). Additional information available for SASE (or SAE and IRC), by fax, e-mail, or on Web site.

THE ACADEMY OF AMERICAN POETS

584 Broadway, Suite 604, New York NY 10012-5243. (212)274-0343. Fax: (212)274-9427. E-mail: academy@poets.org. Web site: www.poets.org. Executive Director: Tree Swenson. Established 1934. The Academy of American Poets was founded to support the nation's poets at all stages of their careers and to foster the appreciation of contemporary poetry. Levels of membership/dues: begin at $35/year (contributing member). Administers The Walt Whitman Award; The James Laughlin Award; The Harold Morton Landon Translation Award; The Lenore Marshall Poetry Prize; The Raiziss/de Palchi Translation Award; and The Wallace Stevens Award. (For further details, see individual listings in the Contests & Awards section.) Also awards The Fellowship of the Academy of American Poets ($25,000 to honor distinguished poetic achievement, no applications accepted) and The University & College Poetry Prizes. Publishes *American Poet*, an informative biannual journal sent to all Academy members. The Academy's other programs include National Poetry Month (April), the largest literary celebration in the world; the Poetry Audio Archive, a 700-volume audio library capturing the voices of contemporary American poets for generations to come; an annual series of poetry readings and special events; and Poets.org, which includes thousands of poems, hundreds of essays and interviews, lesson plans for teachers, a National Poetry Almanac, a national Calendar of Events, and the National Poetry Map.

THE AMERICAN POETS' CORNER

The Cathedral Church of St. John the Divine, 1047 Amsterdam Ave., New York NY 10025. (212)316-7540. Web site: www.stjohndivine.org. Initiated in 1984 with memorials for Emily Dickinson, Walt Whitman, and Washington Irving. Similar in concept to the British Poets' Corner in Westminster Abbey, was established and dedicated to memorialize this country's greatest writers. A board of electors chooses one deceased author each year for inclusion in The American Poets' Corner. The Cathedral is also home to the Muriel Rukeyser Poetry Wall, a public space for posting poems, which was dedicated in 1976 by Ms. Rukeyser and the Cathedral's Dean. Send poems for the Poetry Wall to the above address. Designated a National Poetry Landmark by the Academy of American Poets.

ARIZONA AUTHORS ASSOCIATION

P.O. Box 87857, Phoenix AZ 85080-7857. (623)847-9343. E-mail: info@azauthors.com. Web site: www.azauthors.com. Established 1978. **Contact:** Toby Heathcotte, president. Provides education and referral for writers and others in publishing. Statewide organization. Currently has 150 members. Levels of membership/dues: Published, Unpublished (seeking publication), Professional (printers, agents, and publishers), and Student; $45/year for authors, $30/year students, $60/year professionals. Sponsors conferences, workshops, contests, awards. Sponsors annual literary contest in poetry, short story, essay, unpublished novels, and published books (fiction, children's, and nonfiction). Publishes *Arizona Literary Magazine* and *Arizona Authors Newsletter*. Members meet monthly. Additional information available on Web site.

THE ASSOCIATION OF WRITERS AND WRITING PROGRAMS (AWP)

Mail Stop 1E3, George Mason University, Fairfax VA 22030-4444. (703)993-4301. E-mail: services@awpwriter.org (membership contact). Web site: www.awpwriter.org. Established 1967. Offers a variety of services for writers, teachers, and writing programs, including networking and resources, job placement assistance (helps writers find jobs in teaching, editing, and other related fields), writing contests, literary arts advocacy, and forums. Levels of membership/dues: annual individual membership is $65/year; $110 for 2 years; students who provide photocopy of valid student ID pay $37/year (all prices apply to U.S. residents only). Membership includes 6 issues of *The Writer's Chronicle* (containing information about grants and awards, publishing opportunities, fellowships, and writing programs); access to the online *AWP Job List* (employment opportunity listings for writers); access to AWP eLink, a members-only Web site; a 50% discount on AWP Award Series entry fees; 18% discount on registration for annual conference; and more. *The Writer's Chronicle* is available by subscription only for $20/year (6 issues). The AWP Award Series for novel, poetry, fiction, and creative nonfiction includes the Donald Hall Prize for Poetry (see separate listing in Contests & Awards). Additional information available on Web site.

THE BEATLICKS

940½ W. Van Patten, Las Cruces NM 88005. E-mail: beatlickjoe@yahoo.com. Web site: www.beatlick.com. Established 1988. **Contact:** Joe Speer, editor. International organization open to "anyone interested in literature." Currently has 200 members. "There is no official distinction between members, but there is a core group that does the work, writes reviews, organizes readings, etc." Offerings include publication of work (have published poets from Australia, Egypt, India, and Holland) and reviews of books and venues. Publishes *Beatlick News* 4 times/year, a networking tool designed to inform poets of local events and to bring awareness of the national scene. "We include poems, short fiction, art, photos, and articles about poets and venues." Submit short pieces, no vulgar language. "We try to elevate the creative spirit. We publish new voices plus well-established talents." Subscription: $15/year. Additional information available for SASE or by e-mail. "We promote all the arts."

BRIGHT HILL LITERARY CENTER

P.O. Box 193, 94 Church St., Treadwell NY 13846-0193. (607)829-5055. Fax: (607)829-5054. E-mail: wordthur@stny.rr.com. Web site: www.brighthillpress.org. Established 1992. **Contact:** Bertha Rogers, founding director. Bright Hill Literary Center serves residents in the Catskill Mountain region, greater New York, and throughout the U.S. Includes the Bright Hill Library & Internet Center, with "thousands of volumes of literary journals, literary prose and poetry, literary criticism and biography, theater, reference, art, and children's books available for reading and research (noncirculating, for the time being). Wireless Internet access is available." Sponsors workshops for children and adults. Sponsors contests/awards (Bright Hill Press book and chapbook competitions; see separate listings in Contests & Awards). Publishes 5-7 books of poetry each year.

🔲 BURNABY WRITERS' SOCIETY

6584 Deer Lake Ave., Burnaby BC V5G 3T7 Canada. E-mail: info@bws.bc.ca. Web site: www.bws.bc.ca. Established 1967. **Contact:** Eileen Kernaghan. Corresponding membership in the society, including a newsletter subscription, is open to anyone, anywhere. Currently has 100 members. Levels of membership/dues: regular ($30 CAD); students/seniors ($20 CAD/year). Sample newsletter in return for SASE with Canadian stamp. Holds monthly meetings at The Burnaby Arts Centre (located at 6450 Deer Lake Ave.), with a business meeting at 7:30 followed by a writing workshop or speaker. Members of the society stage regular public readings of their own work. Sponsors open mic readings for the public. Sponsors a poetry contest open to British Columbia residents. Competition receives about 100-200 entries/year. Past contest winners include Mildred Tremblay, Irene Livingston, and Kate Braid. Additional information available on Web site.

CALIFORNIA STATE POETRY SOCIETY

CSPS/CQ, P.O. Box 7126, Orange CA 92683. Web site: www.californiaquarterly.blogspot.com. **Contact:** Membership Chair. The California State Poetry Society "is dedicated to the adventure of poetry and its dissemination. Although located in California, its members are from all over the U.S. and abroad." Levels of membership/dues: $25/year. Benefits include membership in the National Federation of State Poetry Societies (NFSPS); 4 issues of *California Quarterly* (see separate listing in Magazines/Journals), *Newsbriefs*, and *The Poetry Letter*. Sponsors monthly and annual contests. Additional information available for SASE or on Web site.

⬛ CANADIAN POETRY ASSOCIATION

331 Elmwood Dr., Suite 4-212, Moncton NB E1A 1X6 Canada. Phone/fax: (506)386-2862. E-mail: info@canadianpoetryassoc.com. Web site: www.canadianpoetryassoc.com. Established 1985. "We promote all aspects of the reading, writing, publishing, purchasing, and preservation of poetry in Canada. The CPA promotes the creation of local chapters to organize readings, workshops, publishing projects, and other poetry-related events in their area." Membership is open to anyone with an interest in poetry, including publishers, schools, libraries, booksellers, and other literary organizations. Levels of membership/dues: $30 CAD/year; seniors, students, and fixed income, $20 CAD; International, $40 USD. Publishes a magazine, *Poemata*, featuring news articles, chapter reports, poetry by new members, book reviews, markets information, announcements, and more. Membership form available for SASE or on Web site. Also sponsors The CPA Annual Poetry Contest, with 3 cash prizes plus up to 5 Honorable Mentions. **Open to CPA members only.** Winning poems published in *Poemata* and on CPA Web site. **Deadline:** December 31 (postmark) annually. Guidelines available for SASE or on Web site.

COLUMBINE POETS OF COLORADO (formerly Columbine State Poetry Society)

P.O. Box 6245, Westminster CO 80021. (303)431-6774. E-mail: anitajg5@aol.com. Web site: www.Nazcaresources.com/columbine. Established 1978. **Contact:** Anita Jepson-Gilbert, secretary/treasurer. Statewide organization open to anyone interested in poetry. Currently has 100 members. An affiliate of the National Federation of State Poetry Societies (NFSPS). Levels of membership/dues: Members at Large, who do not participate in the local chapters but who belong to the National Federation of State Poetry Societies and to the Colorado Society; and local members, who belong to the national, state, and local chapters in Denver or Salida, Colorado ($15 state and national; $35 local, state, and national). Offerings for the Denver Chapter include weekly workshops and monthly critiques. Sponsors contests, awards for students and adults. Sponsors the Annual Poets Fest, where members and nationally known writers give readings and workshops that are open to the public. Members meet weekly. Additional information available for SASE, by phone, e-mail, or on Web site.

COUNCIL OF LITERARY MAGAZINES AND PRESSES (CLMP)

154 Christopher St., Suite 3C, New York NY 10014. (212)741-9110. E-mail: info@clmp.org. Web site: www.clmp.org. Established 1967. Dedicated "to supporting and actively promoting the field of independent literary publishing." Open to publishers who are primarily literary in nature, have published at least one issue/title prior to applying for membership, publish at least one issue/title annually on an ongoing basis, have a minimum print run of 500 per issue or title, do not charge

authors a fee, are not primarily self-publishing, and do not primarily publish children's/students' work. Currently has 347 members. Levels of membership/dues: based on publishing organization's annual budget. See Web site for complete member application process. Benefits include free and discounted monographs, subscription to *CLMP Newswire*, annual copy of *The Literary Press and Magazine Directory*, plus many valuable services. Additional information available by e-mail or on Web site.

◎ FURIOUS FLOWER POETRY CENTER (Specialized: African American poetry)

MSC 3802, James Madison University, Harrisonburg VA 22807. (540)568-8883. Fax: (540)568-8888. E-mail: caranjg@jmu.edu. Web site: www.jmu.edu/furiousflower. Established 1999. **Contact:** Julie Caran, editorial assistant. Executive Director: Dr. Joanne Gabbin. A non-membership-based organization. "The mission of the Furious Flower Poetry Center is to advance the genre of African American poetry by providing opportunities for education, research, and publication." Sponsors workshops and conferences related to African American poetry, including an annual poetry camp for children of the community. Sponsored national conferences in 1994 and 2004. Nationally known writers give readings that are open to the public. Sponsors open mic readings for the public; also sponsors the Central Shenandoah Valley Slam Team. Additional information available by e-mail or on Web site.

GREATER CINCINNATI WRITERS' LEAGUE

Web site: www.cincinnatiwritersleague.org. Established 1930. **Contact:** GCWL President (see Web site for current contact information). Purpose is to "support those who write poetry in the Cincinnati area and to promote excellence in poetry writing. We believe in creative freedom, with open, constructive critique as a learning tool." Currently has 30 members and participants ("many are published poets"). Levels of membership/dues: $25/year. Offerings include monthly meetings with critique or a workshop on a subject of interest to poets. Poems submitted by members are critiqued by guest critics (published poets who are also teachers or professors of poetry and/or creative writing) who also lead a group discussion of the critiqued poems. Sponsors fall poetry contest with cash prizes; also sponsors a category of the annual Ohio Poetry Day contest with cash prizes. Occasionally publishes an anthology. Members occasionally give readings that are open to the public (see Web site for meeting time and place). Additional information available on Web site.

◎ HAIKU SOCIETY OF AMERICA

578 3rd Ave., San Francisco CA 94118-3903. E-mail: lstparker@cs.com. Web site: www.hsa-haiku.org. Established 1968. **Contact:** Lane Parker, secretary. The Haiku Society of America is composed of haiku poets, editors, critics, publishers, and enthusiasts dedicated to "promoting the creation and appreciation of haiku and related forms (haibun, haiga, renku, senryu, sequences, and tanka) among its members and the public." Currently has over 800 members. Levels of membership/dues: $33 U.S.; $30 seniors or full-time students (in North America); $35 USD in Canada and Mexico; $45 USD for all other areas. Membership benefits include a year's subscription (3 issues in 2007) to the Society's journal, *Frogpond* (see separate listing in Magazines/Journals), and to the quarterly *HSA Newsletter*; the annual information sheet; an annual address/e-mail list of HSA members; and eligibility to submit work to the members' anthology. Administers the following annual awards: The Harold G. Henderson Awards for haiku, The Gerald Brady Awards for senryu, The Bernard Lionel Einbond Awards for renku, The Merit Book Awards, and The Nicholas Virgilio Haiku Awards for youth. Guidelines available in the newsletter or on Web site. Meets quarterly at various locations throughout the U.S. Additional information available for SASE or on Web site.

THE HUDSON VALLEY WRITERS' CENTER

300 Riverside Dr., Sleepy Hollow NY 10591. (914)332-5953. Fax: (914)332-4825. E-mail: info@write rscenter.org. Web site: www.writerscenter.org. Established 1988. **Contact:** Jerri Lynn Fields, execu-

Resources

Resources

tive director. "The Hudson Valley Writers' Center is a nonprofit organization devoted to furthering the literary arts in our region. Its mission is to promote the appreciation of literary excellence, to stimulate and nurture the creation of literary works in all sectors of the population, and to bring the diverse works of gifted poets and prose artists to the attention of the public." Open to all. Currently has 350 members. Levels of membership/dues: individual ($35/year), family ($50/year), senior/student ($25/year), and friend ($100/year and up). Offerings include public readings by established and emerging poets/writers, workshops and classes, monthly open mic nights, paid and volunteer outreach opportunities, and an annual chapbook competition with Slapering Hol Press (see separate listing in Contests & Awards). Additional information available for SASE, by fax, e-mail, or on Web site.

◎ INTERNATIONAL WOMEN'S WRITING GUILD

P.O. Box 810, Gracie Station, New York NY 10028. (212)737-7536. Fax: (212)737-9469. E-mail: iwwg@iwwg.org. Web site: www.iwwg.org. Established 1976. **Contact:** Hannelore Hahn, founder/executive editor. A network for the personal and professional empowerment of women through writing. Levels of membership/dues: $45/year (domestic and overseas). The Guild publishes a bimonthly 32-page journal, *Network,* which includes members' achievements, contests, calendar, and extensive publishing opportunities. Other benefits include regional/local writing groups and kitchen tables, agent list, and dental and vision insurance. "We offer a minimum of eight writing workshops throughout the U.S., including the weeklong summer conference held at Skidmore College in Saratoga Springs, New York. Poetry workshops are interspersed in the conference programs." Additional information available by fax, e-mail, or on Web site.

◎ IOWA POETRY ASSOCIATION (Specialized: IA residents only)

2325 61st St., Des Moines IA 50322. (515)279-1106. Web site: www.iowapoetry.com. Established 1945. **Contact:** Lucille Morgan Wilson, editor. Statewide organization open to "anyone interested in poetry, with a residence or valid address in the state of Iowa." Currently has about 425 members. Levels of membership/dues: Regular ($8/year) and Patron ($15 or more/year; "same services, but patron members contribute to cost of running the association"). Offerings include "semiannual workshops to which a poem may be sent in advance for critique; annual contest—also open to nonmembers—with no entry fee; *IPA Newsletter,* published five or six times/year, including a quarterly national publication listing of contest opportunities; and an annual poetry anthology, *Lyrical Iowa,* containing prize-winning and high-ranking poems from contest entries, available for $10 postpaid. No requirement for purchase to ensure publication." Semiannual workshops "are the only 'meetings' of the association." Additional information available for SASE or on Web site.

THE KENTUCKY STATE POETRY SOCIETY

E-mail: SAdkins932@aol.com. Web site: www.kystatepoetrysociety.org. Established 1966. **Contact:** Sally Adkins, president. Regional organization open to all. Member of The National Federation of State Poetry Societies (NFSPS). Currently has about 230 members. Levels of membership/dues: students ($5); adults ($20); senior adults ($15); other categories: Life; Patron; Benefactor. Offerings include association with other poets; information on contests and poetry happenings across the state and nation; annual state and national contests; national and state annual conventions with workshops, selected speakers, and open poetry readings. Sponsors workshops, contests, awards. Membership includes the quarterly *KSPS Newsletter.* Also includes a quarterly newsletter, *Strophes,* of the NFSPS; and the KSPS journal, *Pegasus,* published 3 times/year: a Spring/ Summer and Fall/ Winter issue which solicits good poetry for publication (need not be a member to submit), and a Prize Poems issue of 1st Place contest winners in over 30 categories. Members or nationally known writers give readings that are open to the public. Members meet annually. Membership information available by e-mail or on Web site.

◩ THE LEAGUE OF CANADIAN POETS

92 Yonge St., Suite 608, Toronto ON M4W 3C7 Canada. (416)504-1657. E-mail: readings@poets.ca. Web site: www.poets.ca Established 1966. **Contact:** Ingrel Madrus, Readings/Membership Coordinator. A nonprofit national association of professional publishing and performing poets in Canada. Its purpose is "to enhance the status of poets and nurture a professional poetic community to facilitate the teaching of Canadian poetry at all levels of education and to develop the audience for poetry by encouraging publication, performance, and recognition of Canadian poetry nationally and internationally. As well as providing members and the public with many benefits and services, the League speaks for poets on many issues such as freedom of expression, Public Lending Right, CanCopy, contract advice, and grievance." Open to all Canadian citizens and landed immigrants; applications are assessed by a membership committee. Currently has 600 members. Levels of membership/dues: Full ($175 CAD); Associate ($60 CAD); Student ($20 CAD); and Supporting ($100 CAD). Membership benefits include a one-year subscription to monthly e-newsletter, discount on Gift Shop purchases, listing in online members' catalog, and more (benefits increase with membership level). Sponsors The Pat Lowther Memorial Award (for a book of poetry by a Canadian woman published in the preceding year; $1,000 CAD prize) and The Gerald Lampert Memorial Award (recognizes the best first book of poetry published by a Canadian in the preceding year; $1,000 CAD). Additional information available on Web site.

THE LOFT LITERARY CENTER

Suite 200, Open Book, 1011 Washington Ave. S, Minneapolis MN 55414. (612)215-2575. E-mail: loft@loft.org. Web site: www.loft.org. Established 1974. The largest and most comprehensive literary center in the country, serving both writers and readers with a variety of educational programs, contests and grants, and literary facilites. Levels of membership/dues: Individual ($60/year); Household ($75/year); Low Income/Full-Time Student ($25/year); Donor ($125/year). Membership benefits include discounted tuition, admission charges, and contest fees; check-out privileges at The Loft's Rachel Anne Gaschott Resource Library; rental access to the Book Club Meeting Room and writers' studios; a year's subscription to *A View from the Loft*; and more. Sponsors classes/workshops, contests, and grants (information available on Web site). Sponsors readings by local and national writers. Additional information about The Loft and associated services and programs available on Web site.

◩ MAINE POETS SOCIETY

P.O. Box 316, Madison ME 04950. E-mail: rmerrill44@hotmail.com. Web site: www.robinmerrill.com. Established 1936. **Contact:** Robin Merrill, president. Maine Poets Society is an organization "committed to fostering poetry in Maine and beyond. Membership open to all poets who reside at least part-time in Maine." Levels of membership/dues: $15. Make checks payable to Anne Hammond, Treasurer, and send to above address. Membership benefits include access to writing groups and round robins as well as a subscription to *Stanza*, a newsletter published 3 times/year containing contest-winning poems. Sponsors 3 contests/year with cash prizes for 1st, 2nd, and 3rd Prize; open to members only. Meets third Saturday of February, May, and September. "Our locations change to allow Mainers from across the state to easily join us." Additional information available by e-mail or on Web site.

MASSACHUSETTS STATE POETRY SOCIETY , INC.

64 Harrison Ave., Lynn MA 01905. E-mail: msps.jcmaes@comcast.net. Web site: http://mastatepoetrysociety.tripod.com/. Established 1959. **Contact:** Jeanette C. Maes, president. Dedicated to the writing and appreciation of poetry and promoting the art form. Statewide organization open to anyone with an interest in poetry. Currently has 200 members. Levels of membership/dues: $15/year. Member benefits include subscription to *Bay State Echo*, published 5 times/year with mem-

bers' news and announcements; members-only contests; round-robin critique groups; members-only annual anthology; workshops at society meetings; and automatic membership in National Federation of State Poetry Societies (NFSPS). Sponsors contests open to all poets. Guidelines available for SASE or on Web site. Members or nationally known writers give readings that are open to the public. Sponsors open mic readings for members and the public for National Poetry Day. Members meet 5 times/year. Additional information available for SASE or on Web site.

⊞ MOUNTAIN WRITERS SERIES

Mountain Writers Center, 2804 S.E. 27th Ave., #2, Portland OR 97202. (503)232-4517. E-mail: pdxmws@mountainwriters.org. Web site: www.mountainwriters.org. **Contact:** Bob Kreider, program associate. Established 1973. ''Mountain Writers Series is an independent nonprofit organization dedicated to supporting writers, audiences, and other sponsors by promoting literature and literacy through artistic and educational literary arts events in the Pacific Northwest.'' Currently has about 150 members. Levels of membership/dues: Basic ($50); Student/Retired ($25); Family ($75); Contributing ($100); Supporting ($500); and Patron ($1,000). ''Members have access to our extensive poetry library, resource center, and space, as well as discounts to most events. Members receive a triannual newsletter. Mountain Writers Series offers intensive one-day and 2-day workshops, weekend master classes, 5-week, 8-week, and 10-week courses about writing.'' Authors who have participated recently include David James Duncan, Linda Gregg, C.K. Williams, Li-Young Lee, Kim Addonizio, and David St. John. Publishes the *Mountain Writers Center Newsletter*. Available to nonmembers for $12/year. Sponsors readings that are open to the public. Nationally and internationally known writers are sponsored by the Mountain Writers Series Northwest Regional Residencies Program (reading tours) and the campus readings program (Pulitzer Prize winners, Nobel Prize winners, MacArthur Fellows, etc.). Additional information available for SASE, by fax, e-mail, or on Web site.

NATIONAL FEDERATION OF STATE POETRY SOCIETIES, INC. (NFSPS)

Web site: www.nfsps.org. Established 1959. ''NFSPS is a nonprofit organization exclusively educational and literary. Its purpose is to recognize the importance of poetry with respect to national cultural heritage. It is dedicated solely to the furtherance of poetry on the national level and serves to unite poets in the bonds of fellowship and understanding.'' Currently has 7,000 members. Any poetry group located in a state not already affiliated, but interested in affiliating, with NFSPS may contact the membership chairman (see Web site). In a state where no valid group exists, help may also be obtained by individuals interested in organizing a poetry group for affiliation. Most reputable state poetry societies are members of the National Federation and advertise their various poetry contests through the NFSPS quarterly newsletter *Strophes* (sample copy available for SASE and $1), edited by Madelyn Eastlund, 310 South Adams St., Beverly Hills FL 34465 (e-mail: verdure@tampab ay.rr.com). **Beware of organizations calling themselves state poetry societies (however named) that are not members of NFSPS, as such labels are sometimes used by vanity schemes trying to sound respectable.** NFSPS holds an annual 3-day convention in a different state each year with workshops, an awards banquet, and addresses by nationally known poets. Sponsors an annual 50-category national contest (see separate listing for NFSPS Competitions in Contests & Awards). Additional information available by e-mail or on Web site.

NATIONAL WRITERS ASSOCIATION

10940 S. Parker Rd., #508, Parker CO 80134. (303)841-0246. Fax: (303)841-2607. Web site: www.na tionalwriters.com. Established 1937. **Contact:** Sandy Whelchel, executive director. National organization with regional affiliations open to writers. Currently has 3,000 members. Levels of membership/dues: Professional ($85); Regular and Student ($65). Hosts an annual Summer Conference where workshops, panels, etc., are available to all attendees, including poets. Also offers a yearly poetry writing contest with cash awards of $100, $50, and $25. **Entry fee:** $10/poem. **Deadline:** October 1. Send SASE for judging sheet copies. Publishes *Authorship*, an annual magazine. Sample copy available for 9×12 envelope with $1.21 postage. Available to nonmembers for $20. Members meet monthly. Additional information available for SASE, by fax, e-mail, or on Web site.

NEVADA POETRY SOCIETY

P.O. Box 7014, Reno NV 89510. (775)322-3619. Established 1976. **Contact:** Sam Wood, president. Statewide organization. Currently has 30 members. Levels of membership/dues: Active and Emeritus ($10). Offerings include membership in the National Federation of State Poetry Societies (NFSPS), which includes a subscription to their publication, *Strophes*; monthly challenges followed by critiquing of all new poems; lessons on types of poetry. Members of the society are occasionally called upon to read to organizations or in public meetings. Members meet monthly. Additional information available for SASE. "We advise poets to enter their poems in contests before thinking about publication."

NEW ENGLAND WRITERS

P.O. Box 5, Windsor VT 05089. (802)674-2315. Fax: (802)674-5767. E-mail: newvtpoet@aol.com. Web site: www.newenglandwriters.org. Established 1986. **Contact:** Susan Anthony, director. New England Writers was founded "to encourage precision and ingenuity in the practice of writing and speaking, whatever the form and style." Currently has 500 members. Levels of membership/dues: $10/year (regular); $7/year (senior citizens and students). Publishes the biannual newsletter, *New-Script*. Sponsors the New England Writers Conference. Additional information available for SASE, by e-mail, or on Web site.

NEW HAMPSHIRE WRITERS' PROJECT

2500 North River Rd., Manchester NH 03106. (603)314-7980. Fax: (603)314-7981. E-mail: info@nh writersproject.org. Web site: www.nhwritersproject.org. Established 1988. **Contact:** Barbara Yoder, executive director. Statewide organization open to writers at all levels in all genres. Currently has 700+ members. Levels of membership/dues: $45/year; $25/year for seniors and students. Offerings include workshops, seminars, an annual conference, and a literary calendar. Sponsors daylong workshops and 4- to 6-week intensive courses. Also sponsors the biennial New Hampshire Literary Awards for outstanding literary achievement (including The Jane Kenyon Award for Outstanding Book of Poetry). Publishes *NH Writer*, a bimonthly newsletter for and about New Hampshire writers. Members and nationally known writers give readings that are open to the public. Additional information available for SASE, by fax, e-mail, or on Web site.

✪ ◎ NEWTOWN WRITERS (Specialized: gay/lesbian/bisexual/transgendered)

E-mail: frauman8@aol.com. Web site: www.newtownwriters.org. Established 1980. **Contact:** Director. NewTown Writers, a gay and lesbian writers' salon based in Chicago, IL, is dedicated to advancing gay literary expression. "NewTown Writers' mission is to foster and give voice to literature—plays, novels, poetry, short stories, essays—which springs from our experiences." Open to anyone. Sponsors weekly workshop-style meetings, a performance series, and publishes *Off the Rocks* (anthology) and *Swell* (see separate listing in Magazines/Journals). Additional information available by e-mail or on Web site.

◎ THE NORTH CAROLINA POETRY SOCIETY (Specialized: NC poets)

Officers change annually; please contact through Web site at www.ncpoetrysociety.org. Established 1932. Purpose is "to foster the writing of poetry; to bring together in meetings of mutual interest and fellowship the poets of North Carolina; to encourage the study, writing, and publication of poetry; and to develop a public taste for the reading and appreciation of poetry." Statewide and out-of-state organization open to "all interested persons." Currently has about 320 members. Levels of membership/dues: Adult ($25/year) and Student ($10/year). NCPS conducts 6 general meetings and numerous statewide workshops each year; sponsors annual poetry contests with categories for adults and students (open to anyone, with small fee for nonmembers; December/January deadline; cash prizes); publishes the contest-winning poems in the annual anthology *Pinesong*; publishes a newsletter; and supports other poetry activities. Also sponsors the annual Brockman/Campbell Book Award for a book of poetry (over 20 pages) by a North Carolina poet (native-born or current resident for 3 years). Prize: $200. **Entry fee:** $10 for nonmembers. **Deadline:** May 1. Competitions receive 300 entries/year. Nationally known writers give readings that are open to the public. Sponsors open mic readings that are open to the public. Additional information available on Web site.

OHIO POETRY ASSOCIATION

Web site: www.geocities.com/theohiopoetryassociation. Established in 1929 as Verse Writers' Guild of Ohio. **Contact:** Bob Casey, president, 129 Columbus Rd., Fredericktown OH 43019. (740)694-5013. E-mail: bob@poeticaljourneys.com. Promotes the art of poetry, and furthers the support of poets and others who support poetry. Statewide membership with additional members in several other states, Japan, and England. Affiliated with the National Federation of State Poetry Societies (NFSPS). Open to poets and writers of all ages and ability, as well as to nonwriting lovers of poetry. Currently has about 215 members. Levels of membership/dues: Regular ($15); Student (including college undergrads, $5); Associate ($5); Senior ($12); Life; and Honorary. Member benefits include regular contests; meeting/workshop participation; assistance with writing projects; networking; twice-yearly magazine, *Common Threads* (see separate listing in Magazines/Journals), publishing only poems by members; quarterly *Ohio Poetry Association Newsletter*; quarterly NFSPS newsletters (*Strophes*); automatic NFSPS membership; and contest information and lower entry fees for NFSPS contests. Members are automatically on the mailing list for Ohio Poetry Day contest guidelines (OPA financially supports Ohio Poetry Day; see separate listing in Contests & Awards). Individual chapters regularly host workshops and seminars. Members and nationally known writers give readings that are open to the public (at quarterly meetings; public is invited). Sponsors open mic readings for members and the public. Past readers have included Lisa Martinovic, David Shevin, Michael Bugeja, David Citino, and Danika Dinsmore. Members meet quarterly (September, December, March, May). Additional information available by e-mail or on Web site. "In short, OPA provides poets with opportunities to share info, critique, publish, sponsor contests, and just socialize."

PEN AMERICAN CENTER

588 Broadway, Suite 303, New York NY 10012. (212)334-1660. E-mail: pen@pen.org. Web site: www.pen.org. Established 1922. PEN American Center "is the largest of the 141 centers of International PEN, the world's oldest human rights organization and the oldest international literary association. PEN American Center works to advance literature, to defend free expression, and to foster international literary fellowship." The 2,900 members of the PEN American Center include poets, playwrights, essayists, editors, novelists (for the original letters in the acronym PEN), as well as translators and those editors and agents who have made a substantial contribution to the literary community. Levels of membership/dues: $75 Member (must meet standard qualifications to become a Member; see Web site); $40 Associate Member and $20 Student (both open to everyone). Membership benefits include subscription to *PEN America Journal*, discounts on admission to public programs, discounted access to *Grants and Awards Available to American Writers* (an online database), access to online bulletin board, and more (additional benefits at Member level, including reciprocal privileges in PEN American Center branches and in foreign centers for those traveling abroad). Sponsors public literary programs, forums on current issues, visits by prominent authors to inner-city schools, the promotion of international literature to U.S. readers, and grants and loans to writers with emergency financial need. Publishes *PEN America Journal* (available through Web site and selected bookstores, or by subscription at $18/year); and *Grants and Awards Available to*

American Writers online (access available through membership or nonmember subscription of $12/year). Administers the PEN/Joyce Osterwell Award for Poetry for a new and emerging American poet of literary character ($5,000), and the PEN Award for Poetry in Translation ($3,000) for book-length translations of poetry into English from any language. Also sponsors the annual PEN World Voices: The New York Festival of International Literature. Additional information on membership and all programs and activities available on Web site.

✪ PITTSBURGH POETRY EXCHANGE

P.O. Box 4279, Pittsburgh PA 15203. (412)481-POEM. Web site: http://pghpoetryexchange.pghfree. net. **Contact:** Michael Wurster, coordinator. Established 1974. A community-based volunteer organization for local poets, it functions as a service organization and information exchange, conducting ongoing workshops, readings, forums, and other special events to promote poets and poetry. No dues or fees. "Any monetary contributions are voluntary, often from outside sources. We've managed not to let our reach exceed our grasp." Currently has about 30 members (with a mailing list of 300). Reading programs are primarily committed to local and area poets, with honorariums of $25-85. Sponsors a minimum of 3 major events each year in addition to a monthly workshop (first Monday, 8 p.m., City Books); these include reading programs in conjunction with community arts festivals, such as South Side Poetry in October—a series of readings throughout the evening at various shops, galleries, and bookstores. Poets from out of town may contact the Exchange for assistance in setting up readings at bookstores to help sell their books. "We have been partnering with Autumn House Press in co-sponsoring events and bringing some of its authors to town." Members meet on an ongoing basis, at least twice monthly. Additional information available for SASE or on Web site. "Pittsburgh is a very exciting literary town."

🌐 POETRY BOOK SOCIETY

4th Floor, 2 Tavistock Place, London WC1H 9RA England. (44)(207)833-9247. E-mail: info@poetry books.co.uk. Web site: www.poetrybooks.co.uk; www.childrenspoetrybookshelf.co.uk; www.poet rybookshoponline.com. Established 1953. A book club that promotes "the best newly published contemporary poetry to as wide an audience as possible." Levels of membership/dues: £40/year Full Member; £12/year Associate Member; £50/year Full International Member. All members receive a subscription to the quarterly *PBS Bulletin*, 25% discount on almost all poetry books published in the UK, and advance notice of poetry events; Full Members also receive 4 PBS Choice selections free. New members receive a welcome gift. The PBS selectors also recommend other books of special merit each quarter. Sponsors The Children's Poetry Bookshelf (a poetry book club for children ages 7-11) and Poetry Bookshop Online, selling all poetry in print in the UK and Ireland. The Poetry Book Society is subsidized by the Arts Council of England. Additional information available by e-mail or on Web site.

THE POETRY FOUNDATION

444 N. Michigan Ave., Suite 1850, Chicago IL 60611-4034. (312)787-7070. Fax: (312)787-6650. E-mail: mail@poetryfoundation.org. Web site: http://poetryfoundation.org. Established 2003. President: John Barr. The Poetry Foundation is "an independent literary organization committed to a vigorous presence for poetry in our culture. It exists to discover and celebrate the best poetry and to place it before the largest possible audience." Initiatives include publishing *Poetry* magazine (see separate listing); funding and promoting Ted Kooser's American Life in Poetry newspaper project (in partnership with the Library of Congress); funding and promotion of Poetry Out Loud: National Recitation Contest (in partnership with the National Endowment for the Arts and state arts associations); and commissioning "Poetry in America: A Research Study," the first scientific study of American attitudes toward poetry (available for download from Web site). The Poetry Foundation also added to its existing awards (the Ruth Lilly Poetry Prize, an annual award of $100,000, and

the Ruth Lilly Poetry Fellowship, 2 annual awards of $15,000 to young poets to support their further studies in poetry) by establishing a family of prizes called the Pegasus Awards to honor under-recognized poets and types of poetry (The Neglected Masters Award, The Emily Dickinson First Book Award, The Mark Twain Poetry Award, The Randall Jarrell Award in Criticism, The Children's Poet Laureate, and The Verse Drama Award). In addition, The Poetry Foundation established and maintains a major Web site for English-language poetry, which includes access to a major archive of poems, poetry-related articles and essays, a news blog, and other features. Additional information available on Web site.

⬛ ⊕ THE POETRY SOCIETY
22 Betterton St., London WC2H 9BX United Kingdom. (44)(207)420-9880. Fax: (44)(207)240-4818. E-mail: info@poetrysociety.org.uk. Web site: www.poetrysociety.org.uk. Established 1909. One of Britain's most dynamic arts organizations, with membership open to all. "The Poetry Society exists to help poets and poetry thrive in Britain today. Our members come from all over the world, and their support enables us to promote poetry on a global scale." Publishes *Poetry Review*, Britain's most prominent poetry magazine, and *Poetry News*, the Society's newsletter, as well as books and posters to support poetry in the classroom. Runs the National Poetry Competition and The Foyle Young Poets of the Year Award (for poets ages 11-17), as well as many other competitions, services, and education projects for readers and writers of poetry. "Visit the Web site for a full idea of the range of activities The Poetry Society is engaged with."

POETRY SOCIETY OF AMERICA
15 Gramercy Park, New York NY 10003. (212)254-9628. Web site: www.poetrysociety.org. Established 1910. Executive Director: Alice Quinn. The Poetry Society of America is a national nonprofit organization for poets and lovers of poetry. Levels of membership/dues: Student ($25); Member ($45); Supporter ($65); Sustainer ($100); Patron ($250); Benefactor ($500); and Angel ($1,000). All paid members receive *Crossroads: The Journal of the Poetry Society of America*; additional benefits available as membership levels increase. Sponsors readings and lectures as well as the Poetry in Motion program. Provides free-to-join PSA electronic mailing list for news of upcoming events. PSA also sponsors a number of competitions for members and nonmembers.

POETRY SOCIETY OF NEW HAMPSHIRE
31 Reservoir, Farmington NH 03835. (603)332-0732. E-mail: frisella@worldpath.net. Established 1964. **Contact:** Patricia L. Frisella, president. A statewide organization for anyone interested in poetry. Member of the National Federation of State Poetry Societies (NFSPS). Currently has 200 members. Levels of membership/dues: Junior ($10); Regular ($20). Offerings include annual subscription to quarterly magazine, *The Poet's Touchstone*; membership in NFSPS; critiques, contests, and workshops; public readings; and quarterly meetings with featured poets. *The Poet's Touchstone* is available to nonmembers for $4.50 (single issue). Members and nationally known writers give readings that are open to the public. Sponsors open mic readings for members and the public. Additional information available for SASE or by e-mail. "We do sponsor a national contest four times a year with $100, $50, and $25 prizes paid out in each one. People from all over the country enter and win."

⬛ THE POETRY SOCIETY OF SOUTH CAROLINA (PSSC)
P.O. Box 1090, Charleston SC 29402. E-mail: poetrysocietysc@aol.com. Web site: www.poetrysocietysc.org. Established 1920. **Contact:** Susan Meyers, president. The Poetry Society of South Carolina supports "the reading, writing, study, and enjoyment of poetry." Statewide organization open to anyone interested in poetry. Offers programs in Charleston that are free and open to the public September-May (except for members-only holiday party in December). Currently has 150 members.

Levels of membership/dues: $15 student, $25 individual, $35 family, $50 patron, and $100 business or sponsor. Membership year runs July 1-June 30. Membership benefits include discounts to PSSC-sponsored seminars and workshops held in various SC locations; a copy of the annual *Yearbook* of contest-winning poems; eligibility to read at the open mic and to enter contests without a fee; and an invitation to the annual holiday party. Sponsors a monthly Writers' Group, a January open mic reading featuring PSSC members, a Charleston Poetry Walk during Piccolo Spoleto in June, and a May Forum leading to an audience-selected poetry prize. Sponsors two yearly contests, totaling 20-25 contest categories, some with themes; some are open to all poets, others open only to SC residents or PSSC members. Guidelines available on Web site. **Deadline:** November 15 (Fall round) and February 15 (Spring round). Also offers the Skylark Prize, a competition for SC high school students. Sometimes offers a chapbook competition. Members and nationally known writers give readings that are open to the public. Poets have included Billy Collins, Henry Taylor, Cathy Smith Bowers, and Richard Garcia, as well as emerging poets from the region. Additional information available by e-mail or on Web site.

POETRY SOCIETY OF TENNESSEE

18 S. Rembert St., Memphis TN 38104. E-mail: RSTRpoet@cs.com. Web site: www.tpstn.org. Established in 1953. **Contact:** Russell H. Strauss, president. Purpose is "to promote the creative poetry of its members, poetry in the community, improving poetry writing skills, and creative poetry among young people." Statewide "but we have some associate members out of state." Affiliated with the National Federation of State Poetry Societies (NFSPS). Organization open to anyone interested in poetry. Currently has 115 members. Levels of membership/dues: $20/year for adults; $5 for students. Offerings include monthly speakers, contests, and poetry readings; an annual poetry festival; and 2 student poetry contests each year. Sponsors conferences/workshops. "We publish a yearly anthology of poems, *Tennessee Voices*, that has won in various festival, monthly, and special contests." Also publishes a newsletter called *Tennessee Voices* 4-6 times/year as needed; contains information on meetings and speakers, contests and winners, various activities, etc. Not available to nonmembers. "We have readings four times a year at various bookstores and restaurants in Memphis. Nonmembers are invited to participate also." Additional information available for SASE, by e-mail, or on Web site. "Our meetings are held at 2 p.m. on the first Saturday of each month from September through May at the Evergreen Presbyterian Church across from the campus of Rhodes College in Memphis." Contest brochure available after June 1 for SASE or on Web site.

THE POETRY SOCIETY OF TEXAS

7231 Alto Caro Dr., Dallas TX 75248. (972)490-4605. E-mail: dallasstacy@sbcglobal.net. Web site: www.poetrysocietyoftexas.org. **Contact:** Marilyn Stacy. Established 1921. "The purpose of the society shall be to secure fuller public recognition of the art of poetry, to encourage the writing of poetry by Texans, and to kindle a finer and more intelligent appreciation of poetry, especially the work of living poets who interpret the spirit and heritage of Texas." Poetry Society of Texas is a member of the National Federation of State Poetry Societies (NFSPS). Has 25 chapters in cities throughout the state. Currently has 300 members. Levels of membership/dues: Active ($25) for native Texans, Citizens of Texas, or former Citizens of Texas who were active members; Associate ($25) for all who desire to affiliate; also Student ($12.50); Sustaining; Benefactors; and Patrons of the Poets. Offerings include annual contests with prizes in excess of $5,000 as well as monthly contests (general and humorous); 8 monthly meetings; annual awards banquet; annual summer conference in a different location each year; round-robin critiquing opportunities sponsored at the state level; and Poetry in Schools with contests at state and local chapter levels. "Our monthly state meetings are held at the Preston Royal Branch of the Dallas Public Library. Our annual awards banquet is held at the Crown Plaza Suites in Dallas. Our summer conference is held at a site chosen by the hosting chapter. Chapters determine their meeting sites." Publishes *A Book of the Year*, which presents annual and monthly award-winning poems, coming contest descriptions, minutes of meetings, by-laws of the society, history, and information. Also publishes the *Poetry Society of Texas Bulletin*, a monthly newsletter that features statewide news documenting contest winners, state meeting information, chapter and individual information, news from the NFSPS, and announcements of coming activities and offerings for poets. "*A Book of the Year* is available to nonmembers for $8." Members and nationally known writers give readings. "All of our meetings are open to the public." Members meet monthly. Additional information available for SASE, by e-mail, or on Web site.

POETS & WRITERS, INC.

72 Spring St., Suite 301, New York NY 10012. (212)226-3586. Web site: www.pw.org. Established 1970. Poets & Writers' mission is "to foster the professional development of poets and writers, to promote communication throughout the U.S. literary community, and to help create an environment in which literature can be appreciated by the widest possible public." The largest nonprofit literary organization in the nation, P&W offers information, support, resources, and exposure to poets, fiction writers, and nonfiction writers at all stages in their careers. Sponsors the Readings/Workshops Program, through which P&W sponsors more than 1,700 literary events in New York, California, and other cities in the U.S. Publishes the online *Directory of American Poets and Writers* with a searchable database of over 7,000 writers; *Poets & Writers Magazine* (print); and *Poets & Writers Online*, which offers topical information, the Speakeasy Message Forum (a central meeting place for writers), and links to over 1,500 Web sites of interest to writers. Sponsors the Writers Exchange Contest (emerging poets and fiction writers are introduced to literary communities outside their home states); the Jacobson Poetry Prize ($50,000 award for an early to mid-career poet; no nominations accepted); the Barnes & Noble Writers for Writers Award; and the Amy Award (see separate listing in Contests & Awards).

POETS' AND WRITERS' LEAGUE OF GREATER CLEVELAND

12200 Fairhill Rd., Townhouse 3-A, Cleveland OH 44120. (216)421-0403. E-mail: pwlgc@yahoo.com. Web site: www.pwlgc.com. Established 1974. **Contact:** Darlene Montonaro, executive director. Founded "to foster a supportive community for poets and writers throughout Northern Ohio and to expand the audience for creative writing among the general public." Currently has 300 members. Levels of membership/dues: $25/year. Membership benefits include subscription to *Ohio Writer Magazine* and discounts on services and facilities at the Literary Center. The Literary Center offers classes, meeting space, and a retreat center for writers. PWLGC conducts a monthly workshop where poets can bring their work for discussion. Publishes a monthly calendar of literary events in NE Ohio; a bimonthly magazine, *Ohio Writer*, which includes articles on the writing life, news, markets, and an annual writing contest in all genres; and 2 chapbooks/year featuring an anthology of work by area poets. "The PWLGC also sponsors a dramatic reading series, 'Poetry: Mirror of the Arts,' which unites poetry and other art forms performed in cultural settings; and 'Writers & Their Friends,' a biennial literary showcase of new writing (all genres), performed dramatically by area actors, media personalities, and performance poets." Additional information available for SASE, by e-mail, or on Web site.

POETS HOUSE

72 Spring St., New York NY 10012. (212)431-7920. Fax: (212)431-8131. E-mail: info@poetshouse.org. Web site: www.poetshouse.org. **Note: Poets House will relocate to a new space in 2008; see Web site for details.** Established 1985. Poets House, a literary center and poetry archive, is a "home for all who read and write poetry." Levels of membership/dues: begin at $40/year; along with other graduated benefits, each new or renewing member receives free admission to all regularly scheduled programs. Resources include the 45,000-volume poetry collection, conference room, exhibition space,

and a Children's Room. Over 60 annual public programs include panel discussions and lectures, readings, seminars and workshops, and The People's Poetry Gathering. In addition, Poets House continues its collaboration with public library systems, Poetry in The Branches, a multi-faceted program model to help libraries nationwide create a complete environment for poetry locally (see Web site for information). Finally, each April Poets House hosts the Poets House Showcase, a comprehensive exhibit of the year's new poetry releases from commercial, university, and independent presses across the country. (**Note: Poets House is not a publisher.**) Copies of new titles become part of the library collection, and comprehensive listings for each of the books are added to *Directory of American Poetry Books*, a free, searchable online database featuring over 20,000 poetry titles published 1996-2007. "Poets House depends, in part, on tax-deductible contributions of its nationwide members." Additional information available by fax, e-mail, or on Web site.

QUINCY WRITERS GUILD

P.O. Box 433, Quincy IL 62306. (217)885-3327. E-mail: chillebr@adams.net. Established 1989. **Contact:** Carol Hillebrenner, treasurer. Purpose is "to encourage writers to write and, if they wish, get published." Regional organization open to all those who love to write and want mutual support in their passion. Currently has 18 members. Levels of membership/dues: $15/year. Offers "support, encouragement, whatever information we can gather for each other, and an occasional newsletter and special speakers on the writing craft." Meets at the local public library the first Monday of most months. Sponsors conferences/workshops. Publishes a newsletter about upcoming meetings and "anything the editor thinks might interest others." Newsletter is free for one year. Members meet monthly. Additional information available by e-mail.

SCIENCE FICTION POETRY ASSOCIATION (Specialized: science fiction, fantasy, horror)

1225 West Freeman St., Apt. 12, Carbondale, IL 62901. E-mail: SFPATreasurer@gmail.com. Web site: www.sfpoetry.com. Established 1978. **Contact:** Helena Bell, treasurer. The Science Fiction Poetry Association was founded "to bring together poets and readers interested in science fiction poetry (poetry with some element of speculation, usually science fiction, fantasy, or horror)." Levels of membership/dues: $21 USD (U.S., Canada, Mexico) for one-year memberships/renewals; $25 USD for overseas. Membership benefits include 6 issues/year of *Star*Line* (see separate listing in Magazines/Journals), a journal filled with poetry, reviews, articles, and more; one issue of the annual *Rhysling Anthology* of the best science fiction poetry of the previous year; opportunity to nominate one short poem and one long poem to be printed in the anthology, and to vote for which poems should receive that year's Rhysling award; half-priced advertising on the SFPA Web site, with greater subject matter leeway than non-members; eligibility to vote for SFPA officers (or run for officer); mailings with the latest news. Additional information available on Web site.

SCOTTISH POETRY LIBRARY

5 Crichton's Close, Edinburgh EH8 8DT Scotland. (44)(131)557-2876. Fax: (44)(131)557-8393. E-mail: inquiries@spl.org.uk. Web site: www.spl.org.uk. **Contact:** Julie Johnstone, librarian. Director: Robyn Marsack. A reference information source and free lending library, also lends by post and from its 13 outreach collections. Arranges poetry-writing workshops throughout Scotland, mainly for young people. The library has a Web-based catalogue available at www.spl.org.uk, which allows searches of all the library's resources, including books, magazines, and audio material—over 10,000 items of Scottish and international poetry. Need not be a member to borrow material; memberships available strictly to support the library's work. Levels of membership/dues: £20 individual; £10 concessionary; £30 organizational. Benefits include biannual newsletter, annual report, new publications listing, book offers, special events, and use of members' room at the library. The School of Poets is open to anyone; "at meetings, members divide into small groups in

which each participant reads a poem, which is then analyzed and discussed.'' Meetings normally take place at 7:30 p.m. on the second Tuesday of each month at the library. Also offers a Critical Service in which groups of up to 6 poems, not exceeding 200 lines in all, are given critical comment by members of the School: £15 for each critique (with SAE). Publishes the *Scottish Poetry Index*, a multi-volume indexing series, photocopied, spiral-bound, that indexes poetry and poetry-related material in selected Scottish literary magazines from 1952 to present; an audio CD of contemporary Scottish poems, *The Jewel Box* (January 2000); and various anthologies available from www.spl.org.uk. A wide range of poetry events takes place throughout the year. Additional information available by e-mail or on Web site.

SMALL PRESS CENTER FOR INDEPENDENT PUBLISHING

The General Society of Mechanics & Tradesmen, 20 W. 44th, New York NY 10036. (212)764-7021. Fax: (212)840-2046. E-mail: info@smallpress.org. Web site: www.smallpress.org. Established 1984. ''The Small Press Center is a nonprofit educational program and resource center for independent publishing, as well as a membership organization of independent and small press publishers and their enthusiasts.'' National organization open to ''any person, company, or organization that supports the small press.'' Levels of membership/dues: Friends Membership ($50 Individual, $75 Dual/Family, $100 Contributing Friends, $250 Literary Benefactors, $300 Corporate Sponsors, $500 Patrons); Publisher Membership ($75 for one year; $100 for 2 years). Membership benefits include the quarterly *Small Press Center Newsletter*; discounts on workshops, lectures, and audiotapes; invitations to readings and special events; and discount on *Books on Writing & Publishing: A Bibliography in Progress*, with 1,700 listings (additional or unique benefits available according to membership type and level). Sponsors the Small Press Book Fair in March and the New York Round Table Writers' Conference (www.writersconferencenyc.org) in April. Offers ''a place in which the public may examine and order the books of independent publishers, free from commercial pressures. The Center is open five days a week.'' Additional information available for SASE, by fax, e-mail, or on Web site.

SOUTH DAKOTA STATE POETRY SOCIETY

Box 398, Lennox SD 57039. (605)647-2447. Web site: www.sdstatepoetrysociety.com. Established 1926. **Contact:** Verlyss V. Jacobson, membership chair/editor. Regional organization open to anyone. Currently has 150-175 members. Levels of membership/dues: Regular ($20); Patron ($30); Student ($5); and Foreign ($35). Sponsors conferences/workshops. Sponsors 2 annual contests, one for adults and one for students, with 12 categories. **Deadline:** August 1 for adults, February 1 for students. Competition receives 300-500 entries/year for both contests. Publishes the magazine *Pasque Petals* 4 times/year. Members meet biannually. Additional information available for SASE.

◎ TANKA SOCIETY OF AMERICA

1636 Edward's Dr., Point Roberts WA 98281. E-mail: macrury@whidbey.com. Web site: www.tanksocietyofamerica.com. Established 2000. **Contact:** Carole MacRury, secretary. The Tanka Society of America, a nonprofit volunteer organization, aims to further the writing, reading, study, and appreciation of tanka poetry in English. Open to anyone interested in tanka. Levels of membership/dues: $25 USD/year U.S., $30 USD/year Canada, $35 USD/year rest of world. Membership offerings include the quarterly *Ribbons: Tanka Society of America Journal* (see separate listing in Magazines/Journals) and eligibility to submit poems to annual members' anthology. Sponsors annual contest. Additional information available by e-mail or on Web site.

THE UNTERBERG POETRY CENTER OF THE 92ND STREET Y

1395 Lexington Ave., New York NY 10128. (212)415-5759. E-mail: unterberg@92y.org. Web site: www.92y.org/poetry. Established 1939. The Unterberg Poetry Center offers ''students of all ages the opportunity to hone their skills as writers and deepen their appreciation as readers." Offers annual series of readings by major literary figures (weekly readings late September through May), writing workshops, master classes in fiction and poetry, and lectures and literary seminars. Also co-sponsors the "Discovery" Poetry Contest (see separate listing in Contests & Awards).

VIRGINIA WRITERS CLUB

P.O. Box 29363, Richmond VA 23242. (434)842-6203. E-mail: VWCMail@aol.com. Web site: www. virginiawritersclub.org. Established 1918. **Contact:** Linda Layne, editor/executive director. Promotes the art and craft of writing and serves writers and writing in Virginia. Statewide organization with 8 regional chapters open to "any and all writers." Currently has over 200 members. Levels of membership/dues: $30/year. Offerings include networking with other poets and writers, discussions on getting published, workshops, an annual conference and symposium, and a newsletter, *The Virginia Writer*, published 4 times/year. Nationally known writers give readings that are open to the public. Members meet 4 times/year as well as at workshops, conferences, and monthly chapter meetings. Additional information available for SASE, by fax, e-mail, or on Web site.

WASHINGTON POETS ASSOCIATION

Web site: www.washingtonpoets.org. Established 1971. **Contact:** Victory Lee Schouten, president. The Washington Poets Association seeks to "serve and inspire individuals and communities across the state by supporting the creation, presentation, and appreciation of poetry through events, publications, recognition, and education." Regional organization open to poets and fans of poetry. Currently has 275 members. Levels of membership/dues: $15/year. Membership benefits include e-newsletter; discounted admission to Burning Word Festival and other events; ability to submit to WPA anthology (plus one free copy and discounts on the purchase of additional copies); and advance notification of contests, events, readings, and publishing opportunities. Sponsors conferences/workshops, including the annual Burning Word Festival (see separate listing in Conferences, Workshops & Festivals). Also sponsors On the Road poetry workshops for underserved areas in Washington state. Sponsors the Washington Poets Association Annual Poetry Contest (see separate listing in Contests & Awards). Publishes quarterly newsletter, *Word!*; available to nonmembers free on Web site. Members and nationally known writers give readings that are open to the public. Sponsors open mic readings for the public "scheduled weekly, monthly, and quarterly at venues across the state." Additional information available on Web site.

THE WRITER'S CENTER

4508 Walsh St., Bethesda MD 20815. (301)654-8664. Fax: (801)730-6233. E-mail: postmaster@writer.org. Web site: www.writer.org. Established 1976. **Contact:** Gregory Robison, executive director. Voluntary, membership organization open to all skill levels. "The Writer's Center is a nonprofit community of writers supporting each other in the creation and marketing of literary texts." Levels of membership/dues: $40/year individual; $25/year full-time student; $50/year family. Annually conducts hundreds of workshops; hosts literary events, readings, and conferences; publishes *Writer's Carousel*, a quarterly magazine of articles and writing news for members. Also publishes *Poet Lore*, America's oldest poetry journal (see separate listing in Magazines/Journals). Additional information available by e-mail or on Web site.

◼ WRITERS' FEDERATION OF NOVA SCOTIA

1113 Marginal Rd., Halifax NS B3H 4P7 Canada. (902)423-8116. Fax: (902)422-0881. E-mail: talk@writers.ns.ca. Web site: www.writers.ns.ca. Established 1975. **Contact:** Jane Buss, executive director. Pupose is "to foster creative writing and the profession of writing in Nova Scotia; to provide advice and assistance to writers at all stages of their careers; and to encourage greater public recognition of Nova Scotian writers and their achievements." Regional organization open to anybody who writes. Currently has 650 members. Levels of membership/dues: $40 CAD annually ($20 CAD students). Offerings include resource library with over 2,500 titles, promotional services, workshop series, annual festivals, manuscript reading service, and contract advice. Sponsors the Atlantic Writing Competition for unpublished works by beginning writers, and the annual Atlantic Poetry Prize for the best book of poetry by an Atlantic Canadian. Publishes *Eastword*, a bimonthly newsletter containing "a plethora of information on who's doing what; markets and contests; and current writing events and issues." Members and nationally known writers give readings that are open to the public. Additional information available on Web site.

✪ ◎ WRITERS INFORMATION NETWORK (Specialized: Christian)

The Professional Association for Christian Writers, P.O. Box 11337, Bainbridge Island WA 98110. (206)842-9103. Fax: (206)842-0536. E-mail: WritersInfoNetwork@juno.com. Web site: www.christ ianwritersinfo.net. **Contact:** Elaine Wright Colvin, director. Established 1983. Founded "to provide a much needed link between writers and editors/publishers of the religious publishing industry, to further professional development in writing and marketing skills of Christian writers, and to provide a meeting ground of encouragement and fellowship for persons engaged in writing and speaking." International organization open to anyone. Currently has 1,000 members. Levels of membership/dues: (all membership dues include subscription to *The Winn-Informer*) $49.95 USD/ one year, $90 USD/2 years; $60 USD/year for Canada and foreign, $110 USD/2 years. Offerings include market news, networking, editorial referrals, critiquing, and marketing/publishing assistance. Sponsors conferences and workshops around the country. Publishes a 24- to 36-page bimonthly magazine, *The Win-Informer*, containing industry news and trends, writing advice, announcements, and book reviews. The magazine will also consider "writing-related poetry, up to 24 lines, with inspirational/Christian thought or encouragement. We accept first rights only." Sample copy: $10. Additional information available for SASE, by e-mail, or on Web site.

THE WRITERS ROOM

740 Broadway, 12th Floor, New York NY 10003. (212)254-6995. Fax: (212)533-6059. E-mail: writers room@writersroom.org. Web site: www.writersroom.org. Established 1978. Provides a "home away from home" for any writer who needs space to work. Open 24 hours a day, 7 days a week, **for members only**. Currently has about 350 members. Emerging and established writers may apply. Levels of membership/dues: vary from $400 to $600/half year, plus one-time initiation fee of $75. Large loft provides desk space, Internet access, storage, and more. Call for application or download from Web site.

◎ W.B. YEATS SOCIETY OF NEW YORK

National Arts Club, 15 Gramercy Park S, New York NY 10003. Web site: www.YeatsSociety.org. Established 1990. **Contact:** Andrew McGowan, president. Founded "to promote the legacy of Irish poet and Nobel Laureate William Butler Yeats through an annual program of lectures, readings, poetry competition, and special events." National organization open to anyone. Currently has 450 members. Levels of membership/dues: $25/year; $15/year students. Sponsors The W.B. Yeats Society Annual Poetry Competition (see separate listing in Contests & Awards) and *Poet Pass By!*, an annual "slam" of readings, songs, and music by poets, writers, entertainers. Also sponsors conferences/ workshops. Each April, presents an all-day Saturday program, "A Taste of Yeats Summer School in Ireland." Nationally known writers give readings that are open to the public. Members meet approximately monthly, September to June. Additional information available on Web site.

ADDITIONAL ORGANIZATIONS

The following listings also contain information about organizations. Turn to the page numbers indicated for details about their offerings.

Additional Resources

This section lists publications and Web sites that focus on information about writing and publishing poetry. While few provide markets for your work, some of these resources do identify promising leads for your submission efforts. You'll also find advice on craft, poet interviews, reviews of books and chapbooks, events calendars and other valuable material. For print publications, we provide contact information; however, you may also find these publications in your library or bookstore or be able to order them through your favorite online booksellers.

These symbols may appear at the beginning of some listings: The (![N]) symbol indicates a recently established resource new to *Poet's Market*; the (![star]) symbol indicates this resource did not appear in the 2007 edition; the (![maple leaf]) symbol denotes a Canadian resource and the (![globe]) symbol one headquartered outside the U.S. and Canada.

Internet resources for poetry continue to grow, and there are far too many to list here. However, among the following listings you'll find those key sites every poet should bookmark. Although we confirmed every address at press time, URLs can become outdated quickly; if a site comes up "not found," enter the name of the site in a search engine to check for a new address.

Some listings in the other sections of this book include references to informative print publications (such as handbooks and newsletters) and online resources. We've cross-referenced these markets in the Additional Resources of Interest list at the end of this section. To find out more about a resource associated with one of these markets, go to that market's page number.

Resources

THE ACADEMY OF AMERICAN POETS

Web site: www.poets.org. One of the most comprehensive poetry Web sites on the Internet.

ALIEN FLOWER

Web site: www.alienflower.org. An interactive medium for poets to share ideas about poetry and its place in society; includes advice, articles, exercises, and offers a free e-mail newsletter, *The Mothership*.

AMERICAN LIFE IN POETRY

Web site: www.americanlifeinpoetry.org. A project initiated by Ted Kooser, former U.S. Poet Laureate, to provide newspapers and online publications with a free weekly column featuring a brief poem by a contemporary American poet, with introductory commentary by Kooser. Funded and supported by The Poetry Foundation (publisher of *Poetry* magazine) in partnership with the Library of Congress. Current and archived columns are available on the Web site or by weekly e-mail (free registration available online).

ASK.COM (formerly ASK JEEVES)

Web site: www.ask.com. Internet search engine.

ASSOCIATION OF WRITERS AND WRITING PROGRAMS (AWP)

Web site: www.awpwriter.org. Home site for AWP; offers membership information, AWP contest guidelines, articles and advice, and career links for writing and publishing. Also links to the Writers' Conferences & Centers (WC&C) online resource. AWP publishes *The Writer's Chronicle*. (See separate listing for Association of Writers and Writing Programs in the Organizations section.)

◪ CANADA POST

Web site: www.canadapost.ca. Provides all necessary information about postal mail to, from, and within Canada. Includes *Canada Postal Guide* online (several chapters printable as PDF).

◪ CANADIAN POETRY: STUDIES, DOCUMENTS, REVIEW

Dept. of English, University of Western Ontario, London ON N6A 3K7 Canada. E-mail: canadianpoetry@uwo.ca. Web site: www.canadianpoetry.ca. **Contact:** Prof. D.M.R. Bentley, general editor; R.J. Shroyer, associate editor. Established 1977. A refereed journal devoted to the study of poetry from all periods in Canada, published biannually (Spring/Summer and Fall/Winter). Subscription: $15 CAD. **Publishes no poetry except as quotations in articles.** Also offers Canadian Poetry Press Scholarly Editions. Details available for SASE or on Web site.

CAVE CANEM

Web site: www.cavecanempoets.org. Site for the Cave Canem group offers ''A Home for Black Poetry'' on the Internet. Includes information about Cave Canem programs, publications, and calendar; an online newsletter and forum; and extensive links. (See separate listings in the Contests & Awards and Conferences & Workshops sections.)

◪ ⊕ COMPETITIONS BULLETIN

17 Greenhow Ave., West Kirby, Wirral CH48 5EL England. E-mail: carolebaldock@hotmail.com. Established 2000. **Contact:** Carole Baldock, editor. Publishes information about contests, anthology collections, etc., as well as details of magazines (particularly new ones), requests for submissions, and publication opportunities. ''Details of well over £100,000 in prize money each issue, 50-plus competitions for poetry, around 40 for short stories. Plus collections, anthologies, playwriting,

nonfiction, books, etc.'' *Competitions Bulletin* is 28 pages, digest-sized, professionally printed. For convenience, can be e-mailed overseas as a PDF file. Single copy: £2.50 UK; Overseas, €5, $7; subscription: 6 issues pa, £15 UK; Overseas, £20, €30, $38 USD.

⌦ COUNCIL OF LITERARY MAGAZINES & PRESSES (CLMP)

154 Christopher St., Suite 3C, New York NY 10014. (212)741-9110. E-mail: info@clmp.org. Web site: www.clmp.org. Established 1967. Dedicated ''to supporting and actively promoting the field of independent literary publishing.'' Online resources for nonmembers include a thorough Frequently Asked Questions (FAQ) section covering CLMP, writing, and publishing; a Literary Landscape section offering information about independent publishing and an index to member journals and publishers; a comprehensive links page; and information about joining CLMP. (See separate listing in Organizations section.)

DOGPILE

Web site: www.dogpile.com. Uses metasearch technology to ''search the search engines'' and return results from Google, Yahoo! Search, MSN, Ask.com, About, MIVA, LookSmart, and more.

DUSTBOOKS

P.O. Box 100, Paradise CA 95967. (800)477-6110. Fax: (530)877-0222. E-mail: publisher@dustbook s.com. Web site: www.dustbooks.com. Dustbooks publishes a number of books useful to writers. Send SASE for catalog or check Web site. Regular publications include *The International Directory of Little Magazines & Small Presses*, published annually with 900 pages of magazine and book publisher listings, plus subject and regional indexes. *Directory of Poetry Publishers* has similar information for over 2,000 poetry markets. *Small Press Review* is a bimonthly magazine carrying updates of listings in *The International Directory*, small press needs, news, announcements, and reviews.

ELECTRONIC POETRY CENTER

Web site: http://epc.buffalo.edu. Online resource offering links to magazines, presses, blogs, and other sites of interest on the Internet; includes an international digital poetry festival.

FAVORITE POEM PROJECT

Web site: www.favoritepoem.org. Site for the project founded by former U.S. Poet Laureate Robert Pinsky to celebrate, document, and promote poetry's role in American lives.

GOOGLE

Web site: www.google.com. Internet search engine; includes hundreds of user groups for/about poets and poetry.

HAIKU SOCIETY OF AMERICA

Web site: www.hsa-haiku.org. Includes membership and organization information, submission guidelines for *Frogpond* (HSA's quarterly magazine), contest guidelines, announcements, haiku and senryu archives, links, and more.

INDEPENDENT PUBLISHER ONLINE

Jenkins Group Inc., 1129 Woodmere, Traverse City MI 49686. (800)706-4636 or (231)933-0445 (main). E-mail: online form. Web site: www.independentpublisher.com. **Contact:** Jim Barnes, managing editor. For 25 years, the mission at *Independent Publisher* has been to recognize and encourage the work of publishers who exhibit the courage and creativity necessary to take chances, break new ground, and bring about change in the world of publishing. The Independent Publisher Book

Awards, conducted annually to honor the year's best independently published titles (including poetry), accept entries from independent publishers worldwide who publish for the North American market, ranging from self-publishers to major university presses. The "IPPY" Awards were launched in 1996 to bring increased recognition to unsung titles published by independent authors and publishers.

INTERNAL REVENUE SERVICE
Web site: www.irs.ustreas.gov. Includes U.S. federal tax information, resources, publications, and forms for individuals and businesses.

⚅ ⚅ THE LEAGUE OF CANADIAN POETS
Web site: www.poets.ca. Web site includes membership information, details of League programs and projects, an online members' catalog, guidelines to League-sponsored contests, bookstore and gift shop, links, and much more. (See separate listing in Organizations.)

THE LIBRARY OF CONGRESS
Web site: www.loc.gov/poetry. The poetry pages on the Web site of The Poetry & Literature Center of the Library of Congress feature links to information about U.S. Poet Laureates past and present; a list of readings, news, and events related to poetry; an online search for recorded poetry archives at the Library of Congress; Webcasts of 2 series, *Poet Vision* and *The Poet and the Poem*; links to the Poetry 180 Project (promoting poetry to high school students) and The Learning Page (with extensive resources, Internet links, and lesson plans to help educators explore literature and poetry with their students); and much more.

⚅ LIGHT'S LIST OF LITERARY MAGAZINES
Web site: www.bluechrome.co.uk (for orders). Established 1986. *Light's List* is an annual publication that lists 1,500 small press magazines publishing creative writing in English and artwork. Listings consist of names, addresses, prices, page counts, frequency, and brief notes of interest for magazines published in the United Kingdom, Europe, United States, Canada, Australia, Africa, and Asia. The 22nd edition (2007) is the first to be published by bluechrome. Single copy: £7.99. Editor John Light can be reached at Photon Press, 37 The Meadows, Berwick-Upon-Tweed, Northumberland TD15 1NY England; (44)(1289)306523; photon.press@virgin.net; www.photonpress.co.uk **(information only, no orders)**.

⚅ MILLENNIUM ARTS MAGAZINE
P.O. Box 71, Prestatyn LL19 7WU North Wales. Phone/fax: (44)(1745)856064. E-mail: mamuk@webspawner.com. Web site: www.webspawner.com/users/mamuk/index.html. Established 1995. Primarily an art-associated News-'n'-Information Web site (Fine Arts, Performing Arts, Literary Arts) covering UK North West and North Wales; includes Opportunities Section and a Literary Arts section with competition news and other information.

NATIONAL FEDERATION OF STATE POETRY SOCIETIES (NFSPS)
Web site: www.nfsps.org. Site for this national umbrella organization includes NFSPS contest information, contact information and links to affiliated state poetry societies, and an online version of the quarterly newsletter *Strophes*.

PARNASSUS: POETRY IN REVIEW
205 W. 89th St., #8F, New York NY 10024-1835. (212)362-3492. Fax: (212)875-0148. Web site: www.parnassuspoetry.com. Established 1972. **Contact:** Herbert Leibowitz, publisher/editor. *Parnassus: Poetry in Review* provides "comprehensive and in-depth coverage of new books of poetry,

including translations from foreign poetry.'' Subscription: $24/year for individuals, $46/year for libraries. Back issues available; see Web site. Make checks payable to Poetry in Review Foundation. **Not open to unsolicited poetry.**

🌐 POETRY BOOK SOCIETY

E-mail: info@poetrybooks.co.uk. Web site: www.poetrybooks.co.uk. The Web site for the Poetry Book Society (see separate listing in Organizations) provides membership information, poetry resources and links, quarterly poetry book recommendations from the Society's selectors, news, PBS bestsellers' list, and more. Links to The Children's Poetry Bookshelf (www.childrenspoetrybookshelf.co.uk), a poetry book club for children ages 7-11; and Poetry Bookshop Online (www.poetrybookshoponline.com), which offers for sale all poetry in print in the UK and Ireland.

POETRY DAILY

Web site: www.poems.com. A new poem every day, plus news and archived reviews and special features. Register online for free weekly e-mail newsletter.

⭐ THE POETRY FOUNDATION

444 North Michigan Ave., Suite 1850, Chicago IL 60611-4034. (312)787-7070. Fax: (312)787-6650. E-mail: mail@poetryfoundation.org. Web site: http://poetryfoundation.org. Established 2003. John Barr, president. Initiatives of The Poetry Foundation include publishing *Poetry* magazine; funding and promoting Ted Kooser's American Life in Poetry newspaper project (in partnership with the Library of Congress); funding and promotion of Poetry Out Loud: National Recitation Contest (in partnership with the National Endowment for the Arts and state arts associations); and commissioning ''Poetry in America: A Research Study,'' the first scientific study of American attitudes toward poetry (available for download from Web site). Maintains a major Web site for English-language poetry, which includes access to a major archive of poems, poetry-related articles and essays, a news blog, and other features.

POETRY SOCIETY OF AMERICA

Web site: www.poetrysociety.org. Includes membership and award information, poet resources, and more. (See separate listing in Organizations.)

⭐ 🌐 THE POETRY SOCIETY

22 Betterton St., London WC2H 9BX United Kingdom. (44)(207)420-9880. Fax: (44)(207)240-4818. E-mail: info@poetrysociety.org.uk. Web site: www.poetrysociety.org.uk. Established 1909. One of Britain's most dynamic arts organizations. Web site offers membership information, events calendar, links, news, Society contest guidelines, the ''Poetry Landmarks of Britain'' interactive map, and much more. (See separate listing in Organizations.)

📧 POETS & WRITERS ONLINE

Web site: www.pw.org. Includes searchable *Directory of American Poets and Writers*, excerpts from *Poets & Writers Magazine*, informational resources, and more. (See separate listing for Poets & Writers, Inc. in Organizations.)

THE POET'S CORNER

Web site: www.theotherpages.org/poems. Text site that includes 6,725 works by 780 poets, plus poet bios and photos, indexes, and The Daily Poetry Break.

PUSHCART PRESS

P.O. Box 380, Wainscott NY 11975. (631)324-9300. **Contact:** Bill Henderson, editor. The Pushcart Press, an affiliate publisher of W.W. Norton & Co., publishes the acclaimed *The Pushcart Prize* annual anthology, the winner of the Pushcart Editor's Book Award, and other quality literature, both fiction and nonfiction. "*The Pushcart Prize* was named among the most influential projects in the history of American publishing by *Publishers Weekly*." The most recent edition of *The Pushcart Prize* is available for $35 (hardcover) or $16.95 (paperback).

RAIN TAXI REVIEW OF BOOKS

P.O. Box 3840, Minneapolis MN 55403. E-mail: info@raintaxi.com. Web site: www.raintaxi.com. Established 1996. *Rain Taxi Review of Books* is a quarterly publication produced in both print and online versions (the latter with completely different material). The print version is available by subscription and for free in bookstores nationwide. "We publish reviews of books that are overlooked by mainstream media, and each issue includes several pages of poetry reviews, as well as author interviews and original essays." Poets and publishers may send books for review consideration. Subscription: $12 domestic, $25 international. Sample: $4. "We DO NOT publish original poetry. **Please don't send poems.**"

SMALL PRESS CENTER FOR INDEPENDENT PUBLISHING

20 West 44th St., New York NY 10036. (212)764-7021. E-mail: info@smallpress.org. Web site: www.smallpress.org. Provides information to and about independent and small publishers. "The Small Press Center provides access to education and expertise in the field of independent publishing, encouraging excellence and free expression in publishing through workshops, lectures, book fairs, exhibits, and a reference collection. The Center is committed to preserving the craft and art of publishing through a library dedicated to its history." Web site includes resources, publisher news, and member directory. (See separate listing in Organizations.)

◎ SPECULATIVE LITERATURE FOUNDATION

P.O. Box 1693, Dubuque IA 52004-1693. Web site: http://speculativeliterature.org. Established 2004. A nonprofit organization dedicated to promoting literary quality in speculative fiction. "Speculative literature is a catch-all term meant to inclusively span the breadth of fantastic literature, encompassing literature ranging from hard science fiction to epic fantasy to ghost stories to horror to folk and fairy tales to slipstream to magical realism to modern myth-making—and more." Includes resources and information of value to writers of specualtive poetry.

◎ TANKA SOCIETY OF AMERICA

Web site: www.tankasocietyofamerica.com. Offers membership information, contest guidelines and winning poems, and definitions and discussion of tanka.

U.S. COPYRIGHT OFFICE

Web site: www.copyright.gov. Offers copyright basics and FAQ, step-by-step directions for registering work for copyright, full schedule of related fees, records search, and other information.

U.S. POSTAL SERVICE

Web site: www.usps.com. Extensive site includes postage rates, mail preparation and mailing directions, online postage and label printing, domestic and foreign shipping options, and much more.

WEB DEL SOL

Web site: http://webdelsol.com. Must-see site for anyone interested in contemporary literary arts. Web del Sol "is a collaboration on the part of scores of dedicated, volunteer editors, writers, poets, artists, and staff whose job it is to acquire and frame the finest contemporary literary art and culture available in America, and abroad, and to array it in such a manner that it speaks for itself . . . at

WDS we employ the traditional and electronic means necessary to bring a whole new readership to the contemporary literary arts."

WINNING WRITERS.COM

Web site: www.winningwriters.com. Quality resources for poets and writers, including *Poetry Contest Insider* (quarterly, published online, subscription required), a variety of links, manuscript tips, "bad contest" warning signs, Winning Writers contests, and more. Register online for free e-mail newsletter. (See separate listing for Wergle Flomp Humor Poetry Contest and War Poetry Contest in Contests & Awards.)

WRITER BEWARE

Web site: www.sfwa.org/beware. Science Fiction and Fantasy Writers of America, Inc. offers this resource on their Web site devoted to scam alerts, common publishing practices that take advantage of writers, case studies, "thumbs down" lists of publishers and agents, and the Writer Beware blog.

WRITER'S DIGEST BOOKS

4700 East Galbraith Rd., Cincinnati OH 45236. (800)448-0915. Web site: www.wdeditors.com; www.writersdigest.com; www.fwbookstore.com. Writer's Digest Books publishes an array of books useful to all types of writers. In addition to *Poet's Market*, books for poets include *The Rhythm Method, Razzmatazz and Memory: How to Make Your Poetry Swing* by Keith Flynn; *Writing Metrical Poetry* by William Baer; *Creating Poetry* and *The Poetry Dictionary* by John Drury, and *The Art and Craft of Poetry* by Michael J. Bugeja. Also of interest to poets are *The Portable MFA* and *The Writer's Digest Writing Clinic* (both of which include sections on poetry), and *The Pocket Muse* by Monica Wood (stimulating inspiration for all writers, including poets). Call or write for a complete catalog or log on to www.fwbookstore.com. **PLEASE NOTE:** *Writer's Digest Books* **does not publish poetry.**

YAHOO!

Web site: www.yahoo.com. Internet search engine; site includes thousands of Yahoo! Groups for poets and poetry, many genre- or culture-specific.

⊠ ⊡ YOUNG POETS

E-mail: ypeditor@gmail.com. Web site: www.youngpoets.ca. Established 2001. **Contact:** Shannon Cowan, editorial coordinator. A project of The League of Canadian Poets, the Young Poets site provides separate sections and content for Youth and Teachers. The Youth section includes resources, online forum, games and activities, collaborative poetry, and *Re:verse*, a zine for young poets. The "Teacher's Staff Lounge" includes workshop ideas, poetry teaching links, information on Poets in the Schools, a digital history of Canadian poetry, a "poem in progress" feature with commentary from the poet, and a Listserv for teachers.

Resources

Resources

Poets in Education

Whether known as PITS (Poets in the Schools), WITS (Writers in the Schools), or similar names, programs exist nationwide that coordinate residencies, classroom visits and other opportunities for experienced poets to share their craft with students. Many state arts agencies include such "arts in education" programs in their activities (see Grants on page 419 for contact information). Another good source is the National Assembly of State Arts Agencies (see below), which offers an online directory of contact names and addresses for arts education programs state-by-state. The following list is a mere sampling of programs and organizations that link poets with schools. Contact them for information about their requirements (some may insist poets have a strong publication history, others may prefer classroom experience) or check their Web sites where available.

The Academy of American Poets, 584 Broadway, Suite 604, New York NY 10012-5243. (212)274-0343. E-mail: academy@poets.org. Web site: www.poets.org (includes links to state arts in education programs).

Arkansas Writers in the Schools, WITS Director, 333 Kimpel Hall, University of Arkansas, Fayetteville AR 72701. (479)575-5991. E-mail: wits@cavern.uark.edu. Web site: www.uar k.edu/ ~ wits.

California Poets in the Schools, 1333 Balboa St. #3, San Francisco CA 94118. (415)221-4201. E-mail: info@cpits.org. Web site: www.cpits.org.

e-poets.network, a collective online cultural center that promotes education through video-conferencing (i.e., "distance learning"); also includes the *Voces y Lugares* project. Web site: http://learning.e-poets.net (includes online contact form).

Idaho Writers in the Schools, Log Cabin Literary Center, 801 S. Capitol Blvd., Boise ID 83702. (208)331-8000. E-mail: info@thecabinidaho.org. Web site: www.thecabinidaho.org.

Indiana Writers in the Schools, University of Evansville, Dept. of English, 1800 Lincoln Ave., Evansville IN 47722. (812)488-2962. E-mail: rg37@evansville.edu. Web site: http:// english.evansville.edu/WritersintheSchools.htm.

Michigan Creative Writers in the Schools, ArtServe Michigan, 17515 W. Nine Mile Rd., Suite 1025, Southfield MI 48075. (248)557-8288 **OR** 1310 Turner St., Suite B, Lansing MI 48906. (517)371-1720 (toll free at (800)203-9633). E-mail: online form. Web site: www.art servemichigan.org.

National Assembly of State Arts Agencies, 1029 Vermont Ave. NW, 2nd Floor, Washington DC 20005. (202)347-6352. E-mail: nasaa@nasaa-arts.org. Web site: www.nasaa-arts.org.

National Association of Writers in Education (NAWE), P.O. Box 1, Sheriff Hutton, York YO60 7YU England. (44)(1653)618429. Web site: www.nawe.co.uk.

Oregon Writers in the Schools, Literary Arts, 224 NW 13th Ave., Suite 306, Portland OR 97209. (503)227-2583. E-mail: john@literary-arts.org. Web site: www.literary-arts.org/wits.

PEN in the Classroom (PITC), Pen Center USA, % Antioch University, 400 Corporate Pointe, Culver City CA 90230. (310)862-1555. E-mail: pitc@penusa.org. Web site: www.penusa.org/go/classroom.

"Pick-a-Poet," The Humanities Project, Arlington Public Schools, 1439 N. Quincy St., Arlington VA 22207. (703)228-6299. E-mail: online form. Web site: www.humanitiesproject.org.

Potato Hill Poetry, 6 Pleasant St., Suite 2, South Natick MA 01760. (888)5-POETRY. E-mail: info@potatohill.com. Web site: www.potatohill.com (includes online contact form).

Seattle Writers in the Schools (WITS), Seattle Arts & Lectures, 105 S. Main St., Suite 201, Seattle WA 98104. (206)621-2230. Web site: www.lectures.org/wits.html.

Teachers & Writers Collaborative, 520 Eighth Ave., Suite 2020, New York NY 10018. (212)691-6590 or (888)BOOKS-TW (book orders). E-mail: info@twc.org. Web site: www.twc.org. A catalog of T&W books is available online, or call toll-free to request a print copy.

Texas Writers in the Schools, 1523 W. Main, Houston TX 77006. (713)523-3877. E-mail: mail@witshouston.org. Web site: www.writersintheschools.org.

Writers & Artists in the Schools (WAITS), COMPAS, Landmark Center, Suite 304, 75 Fifth St. West, St. Paul MN 55102-1496. (651)292-3254. E-mail: daniel@compas.org. Web site: www.compas.org.

Youth Voices in Ink, Badgerdog Literary Publishing, Inc., P.O. Box 301209, Austin TX 78703-0021. (512)538-1305. E-mail: info@badgerdog.org. Web site: www.badgerdog.org.

Resources

Glossary of Listing Terms

A3, A4, A5. Metric equivalents of $11^{3}/_{4} \times 16^{1}/_{2}$, $8^{1}/_{4} \times 11^{3}/_{4}$, and $5^{7}/_{8} \times 8^{1}/_{4}$ respectively.

Acknowledgments page. A page in a poetry book or chapbook that lists the publications where the poems in the collection were originally published; may be presented as part of the copyright page or as a separate page on its own.

Anthology. A collection of selected writings by various authors.

Attachment. A computer file electronically "attached" to an e-mail message.

AUD. Abbreviation for Australian Dollar.

b&w. Black & white (photo or illustration).

Bio. A short biographical statement often requested with a submission.

CAD. Abbreviation for Canadian Dollar.

Camera-ready. Poems ready for copy camera platemaking; camera-ready poems usually appear in print exactly as submitted.

Chapbook. A small book of about 24-50 pages.

Circulation. The number of subscribers to a magazine/journal.

CLMP. Council of Literary Magazines and Presses; service organization for independent publishers of fiction, poetry, and prose.

Contributor's copy. Copy of book or magazine containing a poet's work, sometimes given as payment.

Cover letter. Brief introductory letter accompanying a poetry submission.

Coverstock. Heavier paper used as the cover for a publication.

Digest-sized. About $5^{1}/_{2} \times 8^{1}/_{2}$, the size of a folded sheet of conventional printer paper.

Download. To "copy" a file, such as a registration form, from a Web site.

Electronic magazine. See *online magazine.*

E-mail. Mail sent electronically using computer and modem or similar means.

Euro. Currency unit for the 27 member countries of the European Union; designated by EUR or the € symbol.

FAQ. Frequently Asked Questions.

Font. The style/design of type used in a publication; typeface.

Galleys. First typeset version of a poem, magazine, or book/chapbook.

GLBT. Gay/lesbian/bisexual/transgender (as in "GLBT themes").

Honorarium. A token payment for published work.

Internet. A worldwide network of computers offering access to a variety of electronic resources.

IRC. International Reply Coupon; a publisher can exchange IRCs for postage to return a manuscript to another country.

JPEG. Short for *Joint Photographic Experts Group*; an image compression format that allows digital images to be stored in relatively small files for electronic mailing and viewing on the Internet.

Magazine-sized. About $8^{1}/_{2} \times 11$, the size of an unfolded sheet of conventional printer paper.

ms. Manuscript.

mss. Manuscripts.

Multi-book review. Several books by the same author or by several authors reviewed in one piece.

Offset-printed. Printing method in which ink is transferred from an image-bearing plate to a "blanket" and then from blanket to paper.

Online magazine. Publication circulated through the Internet or e-mail.

p&h. Postage & handling.

p&p. Postage & packing.

"Pays in copies." See *contributor's copy*.

PDF. Short for *Portable Document Format*, developed by Adobe Systems, that captures all elements of a printed document as an electronic image, allowing it to be sent by e-mail, viewed online, and printed in its original format.

Perfect-bound. Publication with glued, flat spine; also called "flat-spined."

POD. See *print-on-demand*.

Press run. The total number of copies of a publication printed at one time.

Previously published. Work that has appeared before in print, in any form, for public consumption.

Print-on-demand. Publishing method that allows copies of books to be published as they're requested, rather than all at once in a single press run.

Publishing credits. A poet's magazine publications and book/chapbook titles.

Query letter. Letter written to an editor to raise interest in a proposed project.

Reading fee. A monetary amount charged by an editor or publisher to consider a poetry submission without any obligation to accept the work.

Rich Text Format. Carries the .rtf filename extension. A file format that allows an exchange of text files between different word processor operating systems with most of the formatting preserved.

Rights. A poet's legal property interest in his/her literary work; an editor or publisher may acquire certain rights from the poet to reproduce that work.

ROW. "Rest of world."

Royalties. A percentage of the retail price paid to the author for each copy of a book sold.

Saddle-stapled. A publication folded, then stapled along that fold; also called "saddle-stitched."

SAE. Self-addressed envelope.

SASE. Self-addressed, stamped envelope.

SASP. Self-addressed, stamped postcard.

Simultaneous submission. Submission of the same manuscript to more than one publisher at the same time.

Subsidy press. Publisher who requires the poet to pay all costs, including typesetting, production, and printing; sometimes called a "vanity publisher."

Tabloid-sized. 11×15 or larger, the size of an ordinary newspaper folded and turned sideways.

Text file. A file containing only textual characters (i.e., no graphics or special formats).

Unsolicited manuscript. A manuscript an editor did not ask specifically to receive.

URL. Stands for "Uniform Resource Locator," the address of an Internet resource (i.e., file).

USD. Abbreviation for United States Dollar.

Web site. A specific address on the Internet that provides access to a set of documents (or "pages").

Resources

Glossary of Poetry Terms

This glossary is provided as a quick-reference only, briefly covering poetic styles and terms that may turn up in articles and listings in *Poet's Market*. For a full understanding of the terms, forms, and styles listed here, as well as common literary terms not included, consult a solid textbook or handbook, such as John Drury's *The Poetry Dictionary* (Writer's Digest Books). (Ask your librarian or bookseller for recommendations).

Abstract poem: conveys emotion through sound, textures, and rhythm and rhyme rather than through the meanings of words.

Acrostic: initial letters of each line, read downward, form a word, phrase, or sentence.

Alliteration: close repetition of consonant sounds, especially initial consonant sounds. (Also known as *consonance*.)

Alphabet poem: arranges lines alphabetically according to initial letter.

American cinquain: derived from Japanese haiku and tanka by Adelaide Crapsey; counted syllabic poem of 5 lines of 2-4-6-8-2 syllables, frequently in iambic feet.

Anapest: foot consisting of 2 unstressed syllables followed by a stress (- - ').

Assonance: close repetition of vowel sounds.

Avant-garde: work at the forefront—cutting edge, unconventional, risk-taking.

Ballad: narrative poem often in ballad stanza (4-line stanza with 4 stresses in lines 1 and 3, 3 stresses in lines 2 and 4, which also rhyme).

Ballade: 3 stanzas rhymed *ababbcbC* (*C* indicates a refrain) with envoi rhymed *bcbC*.

Beat poetry: anti-academic school of poetry born in '50s San Francisco; fast-paced free verse resembling jazz.

Blank verse: unrhymed iambic pentameter.

Caesura: a deliberate rhetorical, grammatical, or rhythmic pause, break, cut, turn, division, or pivot in poetry.

Chant: poem in which one or more lines are repeated over and over.

Cinquain: any 5-line poem or stanza; also called "quintain" or "quintet." (See also *American cinquain*.)

Concrete poetry: see *emblematic poem*.

Confessional poetry: work that uses personal and private details from the poet's own life.

Consonance: see *alliteration*.

Couplet: stanza of 2 lines; pair of rhymed lines.

Dactyl: foot consisting of a stress followed by 2 unstressed syllables (' - -).

Didactic poetry: poetry written with the intention to instruct.

Eclectic: open to a variety of poetic styles (as in "eclectic taste").

Ekphrastic poem: verbally presents something originally represented in visual art, though more than mere description.

Elegy: lament in verse for someone who has died, or a reflection on the tragic nature of life.

Emblematic poem: words or letters arranged to imitate a shape, often the subject of the poem.

Enjambment: continuation of sense and rhythmic movement from one line to the next; also called a "run-on" line.

Envoi: a brief ending (usually to a ballade or sestina) no more than 4 lines long; summary.

Epic poetry: long narrative poem telling a story central to a society, culture, or nation.

Epigram: short, witty, satirical poem or saying written to be remembered easily, like a punchline.

Epigraph: a short verse, note, or quotation that appears at the beginning of a poem or section; usually presents an idea or theme on which the poem elaborates, or contributes background information not reflected in the poem itself.

Epitaph: brief verse commemorating a person/group of people who died.

Experimental poetry: work that challenges conventional ideas of poetry by exploring new techniques, form, language, and visual presentation.

Fibs: short form based on the mathematical progression known as tje Fibonacci sequence; syllable counts for each line are 1/1/2/3/5/8/13 (count for each line is derived by adding the counts for the previous two lines).

Flarf: a malleable term that may refer to 1) poetic and creative text pieces by the Flarflist Collective; any poetry created from search engine (such as Google) results; any intentionally bad, zany, or trivial poetry.

Foot: unit of measure in a metrical line of poetry.

Found poem: text lifted from a non-poetic source such as an ad and presented as a poem.

Free verse: unmetrical verse (lines not counted for accents, syllables, etc.).

Ghazal: Persian poetic form of 5-15 unconnected, independent couplets; associative jumps may be made from couplet to couplet.

Greeting card poetry: resembles verses in greeting cards; sing-song meter and rhyme.

Haibun: originally, a Japanese form in which elliptical, often autobiographical prose is interspersed with haiku.

Haikai no renga: see *renku*.

Hay(na)ky: a 3-line form, with 1 word in line 1, 2 words in line 2, and 3 words in line 3.

Haiku: originally, a Japanese form of a single vertical line with 17 sound symbols in a 5-7-5 pattern. In English, typically a 3-line poem with fewer than 17 syllables in no set pattern, but exhibiting a 2-part juxtapositional structure, seasonal reference, imagistic immediacy, and a moment of keen perception of nature or human nature. The term is both singular and plural.

Hokku: the starting verse of a renga or renku, in 5, 7, and then 5 sound symbols in Japanese; or in three lines, usually totaling fewer than 17 syllables, in English; the precursor for what is now called haiku. (See also *haiku*).

Iamb: foot consisting of an unstressed syllable followed by a stress (- ').

Iambic pentameter: consists of 5 iambic feet per line.

Imagist poetry: short, free verse lines that present images without comment or explanation; strongly influenced by haiku and other Oriental forms.

Kyrielle: French form; 4-line stanza with 8-syllable lines, the final line a refrain.

Language poetry: attempts to detach words from traditional meanings to produce something new and unprecedented.

Limerick: 5-line stanza rhyming *aabba*; pattern of stresses/line is traditionally 3-3-2-2-3; often bawdy or scatalogical.

Line: basic compositional unit of a poem; measured in feet if metrical.

Linked poetry: written through the collaboration of 2 or more poets creating a single poetic work.

Long poem: exceeds length and scope of short lyric or narrative poem; defined arbitrarily, often as more than 2 pages or 100 lines.

Lyric poetry: expresses personal emotion; music predominates over narrative or drama.

Metaphor: 2 different things are likened by identifying one as the other (A = B).

Meter: the rhythmic measure of a line.

Minute: a 12-line poem consisting of 60 syllables, with a syllabic line count of 8,4,4,4,8,4,4,4, 8,4,4,4; often consists of rhyming couplets.

Modernist poetry: work of the early 20th century literary movement that sought to break with the past, rejecting outmoded literary traditions, diction, and form while encouraging innovation and reinvention.

Narrative poetry: poem that tells a story.

New Formalism: contemporary literary movement to revive formal verse.

Nonsense verse: playful, with language and/or logic that defies ordinary understanding.

Octave: stanza of 8 lines.

Ode: a songlike, or lyric, poem; can be passionate, rhapsodic, and mystical, or a formal address to a person on a public or state occasion.

Pantoum: Malayan poetic form of any length; consists of 4-line stanzas, with lines 2 and 4 of one quatrain repeated as lines 1 and 3 of the next; final stanza reverses lines 1 and 3 of the previous quatrain and uses them as lines 2 and 4; traditionally each stanza rhymes *abab*.

Petrarchan sonnet: octave rhymes *abbaabba*; sestet may rhyme *cdcdcd, cdedce, ccdccd, cddcdd, edecde,* or *cddcee.*

Prose poem: brief prose work with intensity, condensed language, poetic devices, and other poetic elements.

Quatrain: stanza of 4 lines.

Refrain: a repeated line within a poem, similar to the chorus of a song.

Regional poetry: work set in a particular locale, imbued with the look, feel, and culture of that place.

Renga: originally, a Japanese collaborative form in which 2 or more poets alternate writing 3 lines, then 2 lines for a set number of verses (such as 12, 18, 36, 100, and 1,000). There are specific rules for seasonal progression, placement of moon and flower verses, and other requirements. (See also *linked poetry.*)

Rengay: an American collaborative 6-verse, thematic linked poetry form, with 3-line and 2-line verses in the following set pattern for 2 or 3 writers (letters represent poets, numbers indicate the lines in each verse): A3-B2-A3-B3-A2-B3 or A3-B2-C3-A2-B3-C2. All verses, unlike renga or renku, must develop at least one common theme.

Renku: the modern term for renga, and a more popular version of the traditionally more aristocratic renga. (See also *linked poetry.*)

Rhyme: words that sound alike, especially words that end in the same sound.

Rhythm: the beat and movement of language (rise and fall, repetition and variation, change of pitch, mix of syllables, melody of words).

Rondeau: French form of usually 15 lines in 3 parts, rhyming *aabba aabR aabbaR* (*R* indicates a refrain repeating the first word or phrase of the opening line).

Senryu: originally, a Japanese form, like haiku in form, but chiefly humorous, satirical, or ironic, and typically aimed at human foibles. (See also *haiku* and *zappai.*)

Sequence: a group or progression of poems, often numbered as a series.

Sestet: stanza of 6 lines.

Sestina: fixed form of 39 lines (6 unrhymed stanzas of 6 lines each, then an ending 3-line stanza), each stanza repeating the same 6 non-rhyming end-words in a different order; all 6 end-words appear in the final 3-line stanza.

Shakespearean sonnet: rhymes *abab cdcd efef gg.*

Sijo: originally a Korean narrative or thematic lyric form. The first line introduces a situation or problem that is countered or developed in line 2, and concluded with a twist in line 3. Lines average 14-16 syllables in length.

Simile: comparison that uses a linking word (*like, as, such as, how*) to clarify the similarities.

Sonnet: 14-line poem (traditionally an octave and sestet) rhymed in iambic pentameter; often presents an argument but may also present a description, story, or meditation.

Spondee: foot consisting of 2 stressed syllables (' ').

Stanza: group of lines making up a single unit; like a paragraph in prose.

Strophe: often used to mean "stanza"; also a stanza of irregular line lengths.

Surrealistic poetry: of the artistic movement stressing the importance of dreams and the subconscious, nonrational thought, free associations, and startling imagery/juxtapositions.

Tanka: originally, a Japanese form in one or 2 vertical lines with 31 sound symbols in a 5-7-5-7-7 pattern. In English, typically a 5-line lyrical poem with fewer than 31 syllables in no set syllable pattern, but exhibiting a caesura, turn, or pivot, and often more emotional and conversational than haiku.

Tercet: stanza or poem of 3 lines.

Terza rima: series of 3-line stanzas with interwoven rhyme scheme (*aba, bcb, cdc . . .*).

Trochee: foot consisting of a stress followed by an unstressed syllable (' -).

Villanelle: French form of 19 lines (5 tercets and a quatrain); line 1 serves as one refrain (repeated in lines 6, 12, 18), line 3 as a second refrain (repeated in lines 9, 15, 19); traditionally, refrains rhyme with each other and with the opening line of each stanza.

Visual poem: see *emblematic poem.*

Waka: literally, "Japanese poem," the precursor for what is now called tanka. (See also *tanka.*)

War poetry: poems written about warfare and military life; often written by past and current soldiers; may glorify war, recount exploits, or demonstrate the horrors of war.

Zappai: originally Japanese; an unliterary, often superficial witticism masquerading as haiku or senryu; formal term for joke haiku or other pseudo-haiko.

Zeugma: a figure of speech in which a single word (or, occasionally, a phrase) is related in one way to words that precede it, and in another way to words that follow it.

Resources

Chapbook Publishers

A poetry chapbook is a slim volume of 24-50 pages (although chapbook lengths can vary; some are even published as inserts in magazines). Many publishers and journals solicit chapbook manuscripts through competitions. Read listings carefully, check Web sites where available, and request guidelines before submitting. See Frequently Asked Questions on page 9 for further information about chapbooks and submission formats.

Book Publishers Index

The following are magazines and publishers that consider full-length book manuscripts (over 50 pages, often much longer). See Frequently Asked Questions on page 9 for further information about book manuscript submission.

Openness to Submissions

In this section, all magazines, publishers, and contests/awards with primary listings in *Poet's Market* are categorized according to their openness to submissions (as indicated by the symbols that appear at the beginning of each listing). Note that some markets are listed in more than one category.

◯ WELCOMES SUBMISSIONS FROM BEGINNING POETS

✪ PREFERS SUBMISSIONS FROM EXPERIENCED POETS, WILL CONSIDER WORK FROM BEGINNING POETS

◗ PREFERS SUBMISSIONS FROM SKILLED, EXPERIENCED POETS, FEW BEGINNERS

◎ MARKET WITH A SPECIALIZED FOCUS

Special Indexes

Geographical Index

This section offers a breakdown of U.S. publishers and conferences/workshops arranged alphabetically by state or territory, followed by listings for Canada, Australia, France, Ireland, Japan, the United Kingdom, and other countries—a real help when trying to locate publishers in your region as well as conferences and workshops convenient to your area.

Book/Chapbook Publishers

Conferences, Workshops & Festivals

COLORADO
Magazines/Journals

Book/Chapbook Publishers

Spring: The Journal of the E.E.
Cummings Society 278
Struggle: A Magazine of Proletarian
Revolutionary Literature 282
Third Coast 296

Book/Chapbook Publishers
DIAGRAM/New Michigan Press
Chapbook Contest 371
Green Rose Prize in Poetry, The 377
Madgett Poetry Award, Naomi Long
383
Minas Tirith Evening-Star: Journal of
the American Tolkien Society 191
New Issues Poetry Prize, The 388

MINNESOTA
Magazines/Journals
Spout Magazine 278
Studio One 283
Writers' Journal 319

Book/Chapbook Publishers
Coffee House Press 330
Graywolf Press 334
Loonfeather Press 339
Meadowbrook Press 341
Midwest Villages & Voices 341
Milkweed Editions 342

**Conferences, Workshops &
Festivals**
Split Rock Arts Program 436

MISSISSIPPI
Magazines/Journals
Bell's Letters Poet 75
VOX 309
Yalobusha Review 320

MISSOURI
Magazines/Journals
Funny Paper, The 136
Green Hills Literary Lantern 142

Inverted-A Horn 158
MARGIE/The American Journal of
Poetry 186
Mid-America Poetry Review, The 190
New Letters 201
Pleiades 225
SP Quill Quarterly Magazine 274
White Lotus: A Journal of Haiku &
Senryu Poetry 312

Book/Chapbook Publishers
Eliot Prize for Poetry, T.S. 372
Inverted-A Horn 158
Mid-America Poetry Review, The 190
Shadow Poetry's Biannual Chapbook
Competition 403
Todd Poetry Series Book Competition,
Lena-Miles Wever 408

MONTANA
Magazines/Journals
Blind Man's Rainbow, The 81
Rocky Mountain Rider Magazine 258
Superior Christian News 285

NEBRASKA
Magazines/Journals
Plainsongs 224
Prairie Schooner 244

Book/Chapbook Publishers
Backwaters Press, The 325
Lone Willow Press 339
Prairie Schooner Book Prize Series,
The 398

NEVADA
Magazines/Journals
Pegasus 221
Rainbow Curve 249
Red Rock Review 252
Sierra Nevada College Review 265

Book/Chapbook Publishers

Book/Chapbook Publishers

Blue Collar Review 81
Bogg: A Journal of Contemporary
    Writing 82
Hall Prize in Poetry, The Donald 377
Plan B Press 345
Red Dragon Press 349
Red Moon Press 349

**Conferences, Workshops &
Festivals**

Highland Summer Workshop 430

WASHINGTON

Magazines/Journals

Aim Magazine 47
Arch and Quiver 55
Babel: The multilingual, multicultural
    online journal and community of
    arts and ideas 68
Barnwood 71
Bellingham Review 74
Edgz 118
Image: Art, Faith, Mystery 157
Tundra: The Journal of the Short
    Poem 303

Book/Chapbook Publishers

Barnwood Press 326
Floating Bridge Press 333
Press Here 346
Rose Alley Press 350

**Conferences, Workshops &
Festivals**

Burning Word 426
Whidbey Island Writers' Conferences
    439

WEST VIRGINIA

Magazines/Journals

Art With Words Poetry Quarterly 58
Bibliophilos 78
Laurels 172

WISCONSIN

Magazines/Journals

Cream City Review, The 110
Deronda Review, The 113
Magazine of Speculative Poetry, The
    183
Porcupine Literary Arts Magazine 241
SEEMS 262
Straylight 281

Book/Chapbook Publishers

Brittingham Prize in Poetry 366
Pollak Prize in Poetry, Felix 397
Seaweed Sideshow Circus 350

**Conferences, Workshops &
Festivals**

Green Lake Writers Conference 430

WYOMING

Magazines/Journals

Voicings from the High Country 309

Book/Chapbook Publishers

High Plains Press 335

**Conferences, Workshops &
Festivals**

Jentel Artist Residency Program 432

AUSTRALIA

Magazines/Journals

Idiom 23 155
SpeedPoets Zine 275
Studio, A Journal of Christians
    Writing 282

Book/Chapbook Publishers

Ginninderra Press 333

CANADA

Magazines/Journals

Apple Valley Review: A Journal of
    Contemporary Literature 54

OTHER COUNTRIES

Special Indexes

Subject Index

This index focuses on markets indicating a specialized area of interest, whether regional, poetic style, or specific topic (these markets show a ◙ symbol at the beginning of their listings). It also includes markets we felt offered special opportunities in certain subject areas. Subject categories are listed alphabetically, with additional subcategories indicated under the "Specialized" heading (in parentheses behind the market's name). **Please note:** 1) This index only partially reflects the total markets in this book; many do not identify themselves as having specialized interests and so are not included here. 2) Many specialized markets have more than one area of interest and will be found under multiple categories. 3) When a market appears under a heading in this index, it does not necessarily mean it considers *only* poetry associated with that subject, poetry *only* from that region, etc. It's still best to read all listings carefully as part of a thorough marketing plan.

Bilingual/Foreign Language

Buddhism

Catholic

Form/Style

Form/Style (Asian)

Special Indexes

Poetry by Children (considers submissions)

Poetry by Teens (considers submissions)

Poetry for Children

Poetry for Teens

Political

West End Press 353

Working People's Poetry Competition 413

Regional

Academi—Yr Academi Gymreig/The Welsh Academy (Wales) 444

Amy Award for Poetry, The (women age 30 & under living in NYC metropolitan area & Long Island) 359

Arc Publications (UK writers) 325

Arkansas Literary Forum (AR resident writers) 56

Arkansas Review: A Journal of Delta Studies (7-state Mississippi River Delta) 56

Artist Trust (WA residents) 360

Aurorean, The (reflective of the Northeast) 65

Beltway Poetry Quarterly (D.C.-area poets) 76

Best of Ohio Writers Writing Contest (OH resident writers) 363

Bottom Dog Press, Inc. (writing from the Midwest) 328

Briar Cliff Review, The (Siouxland writers & subjects) 84

CAA Poetry Award (Canadian poets) 367

Cleveland State University Poetry Center (book contest for OH poets) 330

Coteau Books (Canadian writers) 331

Cottonwood (Midwest emphasis) 108

Eliot Prize, T.S. (collections published in the UK, Ireland) 371

epitome (NE OH women) 121

Floating Bridge Press (WA poets) 333

Gensler Award, Kinereth (New England, NY, NJ residents only) 375

Goose Lane Editions (Canadian poets) 334

Governor General's Literary Awards (Canadian citizens/permanent residents) 376

Heartlands: A Magazine of Midwest Life & Art 149

High Plains Press (WY, the American West) 335

Idiom 23 (central Queensland region of Australia) 155

Iowa Poetry Association (IA resident poets) 448

Jackson Award, Joseph Henry (northern CA & NV residents ages 20-35) 380

Journal of New Jersey Poets (of/by/ for NJ poets) 163

Kaimana: Literary Arts Hawai'i 165

Kelsey Review (Mercer Co., NJ writers only) 167

Landfall: New Zealand Arts and Letters (by/about NZ writers) 171

Leacock Memorial Medal for Humour, The Stephen (Canadian citizens) 382

Link & Visitor, The (Canadian writers only) 174

Long Island Quarterly (Long Island NY writers) 177

Loonfeather Press (for MN-area writers) 339

Louisiana Literature (strives to showcase LA writers) 177

Louisiana Review, The (LA poets, LA-related poetry) 178

Maine Poets Society 449

Mānoa (Asian/Pacific) 185

Mid-America Poetry Review, The (poets living in MO, IL, AR, OK, KS, NE, IA) 190

Midwest Villages & Voices 341

North Carolina Literary Review (NC topics; work by NC authors) 207

North Carolina Poetry Society, The (NC poets) 451

Religions (various)

Religious Poetry

Spirituality/Inspirational

Sports/Recreation

Students

Themes

Translations

Women (various)

Working Class Issues

Writing

General Index

Markets that appeared in the 2007 *Poet's Market* but are not included in this edition are identified by two-letter codes explaining their absence. These codes are: *(DS) discontinued; (ED) editorial decision; (HA) on hiatus; (NP) no longer publishing poetry; (NR) no (or late) response to requested verification of information; (OB) out of business* (or, in the case of contests or conferences, canceled); *(OS) overstocked; (RR) removed by request of the market* (no reason given); *(UF) uncertain future; (UC) unable to contact;* and *(RP) restructuring/purchased.*

General Index

Special Indexes

Special Indexes

General Index

X